Contract Law in Hong Kong

Contract Law in Hong Kong

Michael J. Fisher and Desmond G. Greenwood

Fourth Edition by Michael J. Fisher

HKU
PRESS
香港大學出版社

Hong Kong University Press
The University of Hong Kong
Pok Fu Lam Road
Hong Kong
https://hkupress.hku.hk

ISBN 978-988-8842-81-0 (*Hardback*)
ISBN 978-988-8842-78-0 (*Paperback*)

British Library Cataloguing-in-Publication Data
A catalogue record for this book is available from the British Library.

Digitally printed

Contents

Preface

When Desmond Greenwood and I produced the first edition of this book, in 2007, we noted that it was the first comprehensive student text on this subject for over 10 years. Fifteen years later, with the publication of this fourth edition, it remains one of very few textbooks focused on Hong Kong contract law at the undergraduate or graduate level.

Much has changed in the Hong Kong legal arena since 2007. Many of those changes directly affect contract law; others do so more tangentially. Hong Kong's first post-1997 Chief Justice, Andrew Li, who did so much to maintain Hong Kong's judicial independence and autonomy, has gone but his legacy is an important one. By making consistent use of the facility, provided for in the Basic Law, to invite overseas judges to sit in the Court of Final Appeal (CFA), Chief Justice Li helped to ensure that Hong Kong's appellate judges are constantly exposed to influences from elsewhere in the common law world. Nor is "traffic" all one way, as Hong Kong is gradually being recognised as a "source" of common law wisdom, as well as its recipient. This is vital for the development of Hong Kong's jurisprudence and will, over time, ensure that Hong Kong's law (including its contract law) will develop a flavour of its own. Exposure to external common law sources is crucial at a time of increasing "localisation" of the judiciary and the increasing use of Cantonese in the courts. While there is much to welcome in this development, it poses the risk of insularity, as Chief Justice Li so wisely observed. It is to be further welcomed that under Andrew Li's successor, Geoffrey Ma CJ, exposure to "external" common law judicial influence has continued, despite some hostility from the so-called "loyalist" camp for whom judicial autonomy is an anathema. Time will tell whether Ma CJ's successor, Andrew Cheung, will continue to encourage the crucial exposure to "external" common law sources. It is a matter of regret that this exposure to other common law experience is now under threat, with the resignation of some overseas CFA judges and the prospect of more.

Not all changes, to put it mildly, have been for the better and, while the use of Chinese suggests increased "access" to law for Hong Kong's citizens, this is significantly countered by increased legal costs which put litigation out of the reach of many. Promises to increase legal aid spending have been implemented, but access to justice remains out of reach for many in the "sandwich class". Increased support for mediation and assistance for the unrepresented litigant are a poor substitute for the provision of adequate legal aid. This affects the nature of contract cases contested at the highest level, where property (land) issues dominate, and partly accounts for the observation that there have been few landmark contract cases in Hong Kong in the past few years. That said, there has been significant development and refinement of existing principles and the Court of Final Appeal, far more active than its Privy Council predecessor, has led the way.

This fourth, considerably expanded edition seeks to deal with the major Hong Kong contract case law (and, to a limited extent, statutory law) since it last went to press in 2011. Additionally, I have sought to "fill in gaps" which our prior commitment to conciseness may have engendered. Of course, more recent decisions from elsewhere in the common law world have also been included and I make no apology for the fact that these are predominantly English decisions, given Hong Kong law's long-standing and continuing links to the English common law. Nevertheless, as we said in introducing the first edition, "'1997' has presented Hong Kong with the opportunity to develop a unique jurisprudence, influenced by a combination of sources—from the former colonial power, from China mainland and, most important, from within Hong Kong itself".

Given the developments in contract law since 2017, I feel that a revised, expanded and readable text, suitable for law students, is long overdue. I stress "readability" since, except for the largely descriptive first two chapters, this text places particular focus on the "stories", the cases which form the foundation of Hong Kong contract law. As a "common law"-based jurisdiction, Hong Kong's law derives primarily from the decided cases and this is particularly true in the areas of contract and tort law. While legislative rules are an increasingly important source of Hong Kong contract law, especially in the area of consumer protection and, lately, privity, the role of legislation remains to "fill the gaps" rather than, as in civil law jurisdictions, to provide a complete, codified legal framework. I believe, therefore, in conveying contract law through the careful examination and explanation of case illustrations. This has the further advantage that the study of cases is far more reader-friendly than a focus on dense, legalistic text, especially given that many readers will be studying law in their second language.

As already implied, this book is written principally for the law student, though it should be of interest to students of other disciplines who need an understanding of contract law. I am also gratified to know that many members of the legal profession here have expressed interest in, and support for, this text.

Finally, I wish briefly to explain two issues of style. The first relates to the use of terms such as "plaintiff", "defendant", etc. In England, though not in Hong Kong, the terminology has changed over the last few years such that the former "plaintiff" has now become the "claimant". What I have endeavoured to do throughout is to use the terminology prevalent at the time a particular case was reported. The second explanation relates to the use of the expression "he" to include both the masculine and the feminine. This "Interpretation Act" approach avoids the use of the clumsy s/he pronoun or the grammatically incorrect use of "they" and "their" to indicate a gender-neutral singular. I am, of course, fully aware that women make contracts and have full contractual capacity in Hong Kong.

I have endeavoured to state the law accurately as of 25 February 2023.

MJF

Table of Cases

Table of Legislation

1

The Nature of Contract Law in Hong Kong

OVERVIEW

Contracts may take a huge variety of forms; from the simplest, small "one-off" transaction like buying a newspaper, to a complicated commercial contract, written in technical language and intended to be of lengthy duration. Nevertheless, the same basic rules as to formation, performance and enforcement apply to all contracts.

The purpose of this chapter is to ask what contract law is, what it does and what, if anything, is unique or special about Hong Kong contract law. In keeping with the largely non-theoretical nature of this book and the constraints of space, the answers to the above questions will be based on traditional notions of contract and more radical formulations will be merely alluded to. This should not be taken as a rejection of more radical views but an assertion that the objective is to reflect how contract law is generally viewed, by traditional judges, lawyers and legal writers.

In asking what contract law is, we may begin with the statement that contracts are *legally enforceable agreements*. In defining contract, these two elements: an agreement between the parties, and some form of enforcement thereof, are crucial. We might, perhaps, wish to add another requirement; the agreement should not have been procured by improper means such as threats or dishonesty. We would also wish to qualify the first basic element, since agreement, especially where the parties are of unequal bargaining power, is often more theoretical than real. I may make a contractual "agreement" to travel on a bus every morning but if I dislike the "infotainment" provided or the sub-zero air conditioning I am in a "take it or leave it" situation, unable to vary the conditions of travel or to negotiate a reduced fare for travelling in discomfort. My alternative is to walk or take a taxi!

The notion of "agreement" must also be qualified by saying that whether parties have agreed is usually judged "objectively" rather than "subjectively". This means that what is actually in a party's mind is usually irrelevant; what matters is that a "reasonable person", assessing the party's words and deeds, should conclude that he has "agreed".

Moreover, agreement, while a necessary requirement of contract, is not a sufficient one; many agreements may lack contractual force because of other deficiencies. A particular feature of contract in common law systems, such as Hong Kong and England, is the requirement of "consideration" which means, essentially, that no one may enforce an agreement unless he has given something of value to the other party to the agreement, either in the form of a "benefit" to that other party or a "detriment" to himself. Further, an agreement may be non-contractual where it is viewed by the courts as a purely social arrangement, never intended to be legally binding. Additionally, a party to an agreement may be found to lack contractual "capacity" because of his youth or other disability; some agreements, such as those concerning the transfer of land, may lack the necessary written formality; and the threats or dishonesty mentioned above may constitute "vitiating" elements sufficient to invalidate the agreement. Nevertheless, despite these additional requirements, *agreement* remains the fundamental basis for contractual liability. Legal obligations may exist in the absence of agreement but they will not be contractual ones.

The element of "enforceability" in contract law also requires qualification in so far as it implies that parties may be required to honour their promises. In fact, actual "enforcement", by an order known as "specific performance", is exceptional and the normal result of the breach of a contractual undertaking by one party is that he is required to pay monetary compensation (damages) to the "innocent" party.

Nonetheless, enforcement, in the sense of being entitled to seek legal redress for breach, is what distinguishes contracts from other, non-binding types of agreement. While parties may seek to avoid litigation, especially where they have dealt with one another over a long period, the importance of the right to seek compensation for breach "as a last resort" is fundamental.

Having outlined what contract is, we next need to ask what it "does". In traditional terms, the law of contract, put most simply, allows people to make their own contracts with minimal interference and then insists on performance. In theoretical language, these are known as the principles of *freedom* and *sanctity* of contract. "Freedom of contract" denotes that it is for the parties to make their own contracts without the intervention of government, legislation or the courts. "Sanctity of contract" upholds the principle that once agreements are made they should be honoured. Where a contracting party does not honour the agreement, the other party will be entitled to a legal remedy.

Freedom of contract has never been total, either in Hong Kong or England; it has always been recognised, for example, that a contract to do something criminal would be unenforceable. Legislative restrictions on contractual freedom in most common law jurisdictions have, indeed, now become so numerous that many writers regard freedom of contract as of only historical importance. Such restrictions have been engendered primarily by a recognition that the main beneficiaries of complete contractual freedom are the rich and powerful. Legislation has gone some way to redressing the balance, particularly in the areas of consumer protection and employees' rights. Hong Kong governments, however, have had, since colonial times, a barely-concealed "close relationship" with big business, such that legislative intervention into the so-called "free market" has been avoided, where politically possible, and otherwise delayed. This reluctance to act is exemplified by Hong Kong's inadequate employment protection laws, limited control of anti-competitive practices, and relatively undeveloped consumer protection legislation.

Sanctity of contract, unlike freedom of contract, has remained largely intact in the common law world. It remains the case that, unless the performance of a contract becomes illegal or impossible, full performance, or at least compensation for failure to perform, is required.

1.1 What Contract Is

A contract may be described as a "legally enforceable agreement". That simple statement summarises the rules on contract to be found in the decided cases and the relevant legislation.[1] The element of *agreement* is of crucial importance since, while not all agreements are contracts, all contracts require at least an apparent agreement. Moreover, it is the element of agreement that distinguishes contracts from other forms of obligation, notably tortious ones.

The need for "agreement", however, must be qualified. First, it is clear that in many cases agreement is more apparent than real. The idealised view of agreement involving intense haggling, give and take and ultimate consensus is replaced, in many cases, by something more akin to "take it or leave it". The consumer who buys a new car, signs a contract for electricity supply, or purchases private schooling, is unlikely to have any say in the "form" of the contract. Even the argument that he can go elsewhere if he does not like the terms imposed loses much of its force in those situations where, as in the case of new car sales, "standard" terms are likely to apply wherever the car is purchased. It is in such cases of inequality of bargaining power that legislative and judicial "interference" with the contract is more likely.

It should also be pointed out that "agreement" is judged objectively, thus:

> If, whatever a man's real intention may be, he so conducts himself that a reasonable
> man would believe that he was assenting to the terms proposed by the other party,
> and that other party upon that belief enters into the contract with him, the man thus
> conducting himself would be equally bound as if he had intended to agree to the
> other party's terms.[2]

So, if A genuinely and reasonably believes that B agrees to his terms, the necessary "agreement" exists, irrespective of B's subjective belief. Suppose, for example,

---

1. For more on the sources of Hong Kong contract law, see chapter 2.
2. Per Blackburn J in *Smith v Hughes* (1871) LR 6 QB 597.

that A advertises an item on the internet and seeks bids. B offers to buy for $10,000 and A immediately accepts. There is the objective appearance of agreement and a court would generally ignore a subsequent claim by B that he was "mistaken" and meant to offer only $1,000. A reasonable person looking at the agreement would say it was a contract to sell for $10,000 and this would be the legal position. A similar situation arose in *Centrovincial Estates plc v Merchant Investors Insurance Co Ltd*.[3] Here the plaintiffs, in renegotiating a lease, "offered" a rental of £65,000 per year, which the defendants accepted. The plaintiffs pleaded that there was no contract as they had been "mistaken". The previous price was over £68,000 per year in a rising market and the plaintiffs said that they "meant" to state a price of £126,000 per year. The court upheld the figure of £65,000 since it had been clearly expressed in writing and accepted by the other party.

It would have been different if it could have been clearly shown that, in the circumstances of the case, the defendants must have known that the plaintiffs were making a mistake and took advantage of the situation.[4] In the absence of conclusive evidence of such bad faith, however, there was, "objectively", an offer to let at £65,000 per year and an acceptance thereof.[5]

Agreement is generally viewed as comprising two elements: an offer by one party and an acceptance of that offer by the other.[6] There are exceptional cases where contracts have been upheld although agreement, at least in terms of offer and acceptance between the so-called "parties", is difficult to discern. In *Clarke v Dunraven*,[7] the respondent's boat was sunk by the appellant's boat, during a sailing race, as a result of the appellant's breach of the race rules. All parties in the race had agreed with the organisers to abide by the rules and, in the event of non-compliance, to pay compensation for any resulting damage. The House of Lords, in upholding the respondent's claim, found that there was a contract between appellant and respondent though neither had made an agreement with the other. Given the absence of a developed tort of negligence at the time this case was decided, the only potential remedy available to the respondent lay in contract[8] and the decision may be viewed as one in which the court did justice by means of extreme "creativity".[9] Certainly the parties were happy to agree to the terms of the race, but it was surely artificial to imply that the plaintiff and defendant had made an "agreement" with each other. Without disapproving this decision, the highest courts have upheld the principle, in

---

3.   [1983] Com LR 158. See also *Tamplin v James* discussed at 10.4.
4.   As in *Roberts & Co Ltd v Leicestershire CC* discussed at 10.6.
5.   The decision has been criticised: see P. S. Atiyah, "The Hannah Blumenthal & Classical Contract Law", (1986) 102 LQR 363.
6.   There must, it is said, be a meeting of minds or *consensus ad idem*.
7.   [1897] AC 59.
8.   The respondent was entitled to statutory compensation but this was very limited.
9.   See 1.2.2.

contemporary cases, that there should invariably be offer and acceptance as between the parties.[10]

Nor is it always sufficient to focus on the *existence* of an agreement, since the *time* at which the agreement is formed may also be highly significant. Discussion of this question usually focuses on narrow issues of when (or where) a contract made by telephone, email or fax is concluded. While there may be significant jurisdictional implications in such cases, the "time of formation" involves far wider issues, since so many of the courts' deliberations are required to focus on the time at which the contract is made. If, for example, one party wishes to rely on an exemption clause[11] in the contract, its existence must have been made known to the other party before the contract was concluded. Moreover, where the "reasonableness" of the exemption is significant, this must be judged as at the time the contract was made. Where a party wishes to escape liability to pay damages for misrepresentation,[12] he must prove a genuine and reasonable belief in the truth of his false statement up to the time when the contract was made. It is not enough that his belief was genuine at the time his statement was made. In those rare cases where common mistake[13] is operative this will require a mistake as to a fundamental state of affairs already existing at the time the contract was made. If a subsequent event fundamentally alters the agreement, it cannot constitute mistake (though it could amount to a "frustration"). The doctrine of frustration itself,[14] which arises where an event occurs after a contract is formed (but before the time for performance) which makes performance impossible, may not be successfully invoked by a party who should have foreseen, at the time the contract was made, the subsequent serious event. In the case of damages,[15] too, the time when the contract was made may be crucial, since the "reasonableness", and hence enforceability, of the pre-estimate of loss in a so-called "liquidated damages" clause is judged as at the time the contract was made, not in light of what actually happened as the result of one party's breach.[16] Moreover, a party in breach will only be liable in damages for consequences which should have been foreseen as likely to result from the breach at the time the contract was made.

In summary, the circumstances existing when the parties *agree* a contract may have profound consequences for the contract later.

While agreement is always necessary, it is not sufficient, in itself, to prove the existence of a contract. Given a clear agreement between the parties, other requirements remain to be fulfilled.

---

10. See, for example, *Gibson v Manchester CC* discussed at 3.2.
11. See 8.6.
12. See chapter 9.
13. See 10.3.2.
14. See 14.4.
15. See 15.1.
16. The civil law approach is different and it appears that English law may be changing in this area (see chapter 15).

For hundreds of years in England, and throughout Hong Kong's common law history, the further requirement of "consideration"[17] is demanded in all cases of contracts made other than under seal.[18] Thus,

> the growth of the doctrine of consideration as a limitation on what promises will be enforced seems to have been prompted by the adoption in the sixteenth century of a new form of action, the action of assumpsit, to enforce promises. Before that, promises were actionable in the royal courts only if they were part of one of a recognised type of exchange such as a sale, or were made (under seal)[19]

The consideration requirement has proved an extremely elastic one and most of the "rules" of consideration are subject to exception, as we shall see in chapter 4. Where the courts have wanted to enforce an agreement they have normally been able to discover consideration. In short, the requirement of consideration remains but is capable of considerable "adaptation" by the courts where appropriate.

It is also now generally accepted that a contract requires an intention[20] to be bound by both parties. While this proposition is a relatively new one and is not without its critics (notably Professor Williston),[21] the cases indicate that intention must be viewed as a separate, essential element for the formation of a contract, albeit that intention, like agreement, must be judged "objectively".[22]

The agreement on which a contract is based is also subject to the rules of contractual capacity[23] and, exceptionally, to any special requirements as to form.[24] Further, even where a contractual agreement contains all the necessary requirements for its formation there may be some "vitiating" element, such as misrepresentation or mistake, which precludes, in whole or in part, the enforcement of the agreement.[25]

It is "enforceability" which distinguishes contracts from other forms of agreement. Enforceability does not mean that a party in breach can be required to perform his contractual undertaking; such a requirement ("specific performance") by the courts is the exception rather than the rule. What an "innocent" party may always do, however, is obtain compensation for the consequences of the other's breach. Where such breach has caused no loss, the court will award nominal damages in recognition of the breach. Traditionally, via the principle of "sanctity", courts have always enforced contracts whatever the circumstances of the failure to perform. The

---

17. See chapter 4.
18. This was once a cumbersome procedure involving waxed seals but is now very simple. Indeed, many businesses conclude their agreements under seal to avoid the consideration requirement.
19. Beale, Bishop and Furmston, *Contract Cases and Materials* (Oxford: Oxford University Press, 5th edn, 2007), p 8.
20. See chapter 5.
21. See chapter 5.
22. See, for example, *Jones v Padavatton* [1969] 1 WLR 328, [1969] 2 All ER 616.
23. See chapter 6.
24. See chapter 7.
25. See chapters 9–12.

word "sanctity" implies a moral element, that parties ought to keep their side of the bargain because they have formally promised to do so. Such a moral aspect is now generally rejected in favour of more pragmatic approaches. It would now be more common to view the enforcement of agreements as producing certainty in the market place, or preventing parties taking the law into their own hands. Economic approaches talk in terms of whether it is more "efficient" to perform rather than pay compensation for non-performance and the moral aspect of keeping a promise is rarely expressed. Nevertheless, even with the innovation of "frustration", a limited exception to sanctity introduced in the nineteenth century, courts remain reluctant to excuse non-performance. A finding of frustration is exceptional[26] and a party who fails fully to complete his side of the contract is almost invariably liable for breach.

1.1.1 The Boundaries of Contract Law

Before considering the function or purpose of contract law, we will first try to outline what areas a typical contract law text, such as this, will deal with. It might be thought that "contract law" would include study of all types of contract, but this is not the case. Some areas, especially those which are highly specialised or statute-based, are dealt with as separate subjects in their own right. Contracts of employment, for example, are treated, generally, as falling within the scope of "employment law". This has much to do with the fact that legislative rules are far more important in this area than common law[27] contractual principles. When considering the employee's contract of employment, for example, we say that the contract may improve the employee's guaranteed statutory rights but cannot diminish them, irrespective of its express terms. Such a limitation on the parties' "freedom" applies in both England and Hong Kong, though it should be appreciated that the protection of employees' "rights" is far less developed in Hong Kong. Likewise, specialised treatment of "sale of goods" contracts tends to be dealt with in "commercial law", again because the subject is highly statute-based. As a final example, detailed treatment of the sale of land is more likely to occur in the context of "land law" or "real property law"; once again the relevant rules are primarily statutory rather than "common law".

The huge diversity of contract types has led some commentators to say we should talk of a law of "contracts" rather than contract, just as, in respect of non-contractual obligations, we talk of a law of "torts" rather than tort, on the basis that there are few principles common to all torts. The analogy is questionable, however, because, while we can see that there is little similarity between, for example, the torts of negligence and defamation, there are rules common to all contracts. Sale

---

26. See, for example, *Davis Contractors Ltd v Fareham UDC* [1956] AC 696, [1956] 3 WLR 37, [1956] 2 All ER 145.
27. While "common law" has various meanings (see chapter 2), in this context it refers to those rules deriving from cases rather than legislation.

of goods, for example, may be a specialised area, but the more specific rules will not begin to operate unless the basic contractual elements (agreement, consideration and so on) exist. The concept that there are basic rules applicable to all contractual situations was emphasised in the case of *Cehave v Bremer (The Hansa Nord)*[28] where Roskill LJ responded to the argument that there should be a different classification of terms in sale of goods contracts by stating:

> Sale of goods is but one branch of the general law of contract. It is desirable that the same legal principles should apply to the law of contract as a whole and that different legal principles should not apply to different branches of that law.[29]

This view lends support to the view that judges should recognise some generally applicable contractual principles. These may be amended, or dispensed with, by legislation but, absent legislation, these general contractual principles will apply.

In short, the focus of this book will be on the general principles applicable in the law of contract. The order of substantive topics will be:

- the necessary elements for the formation of a contract (chapters 3–7);
- the contents, or terms, of a contract (chapter 8);
- "vitiating" elements which make the agreement defective in some way (chapters 9–13);
- how contracts come to an end (termination) (chapter 14); and
- remedies for breach of contract (chapter 15).

The final chapter (chapter 16) is about "privity" of contract, the basis of which is that only parties to the contractual agreement have rights and obligations under it. Since "agreement" is our starting point, privity can be seen as completing the circle.

It may seem odd that, although we will not consider all types of contract in depth, we do find time to consider some overlapping areas of tort law which deal with obligations arising other than through agreement. However, tort is relevant to the study of misrepresentation, for example, since, while misrepresentations "induce" the making of a contract, damages for misrepresentation are tortious. Consideration of these remedies is within the scope of this book since to deal with the meaning of misrepresentation but not its consequences would be artificial. Similar overlaps will be apparent when we deal with attempts to exclude liability in contract and tort and when we look at the difference between the "remoteness" rules in contract and tort. No detailed tort knowledge will be required, however, to understand this text.

The contract law we will examine in this book is built, primarily, on two foundations: the cases, or "precedents", which form its overall framework, and the legislation which has supplemented this case law, or "common law" as it is also known. Since Hong Kong law, post-1997, comprises a unique blend of English common

---

28. [1976] QB 44, [1975] 3 WLR 447, [1975] 3 All ER 739.
29. [1975] 3 All ER 739 at 756.

law and legislation, Hong Kong common law and legislation and, to lesser extents, Chinese customary law and legislation, chapter 2 is devoted to the sometimes complex issue of the "sources" of Hong Kong contract law.

1.2 The Function of Contract Law

Some writers draw a distinction between the role of the contract and the role of contract law. The former may often be expressed in quite limited terms, such as "informing" the parties of their respective rights and obligations and assisting their "planning". The focus here will be on the function of contract law; asking what it does and, by implication what would happen if we had no law of contract.

Until comparatively recently the predominant theory of contract could be described as the "will theory"—that the role of the courts was to identify and enforce the contractual will of the parties and to intervene as little as possible in respect of bargains freely made by competent adults. The emphasis has been on contractual "freedom". Freedom of contract remains a dominant principle in the United States where state intervention in the free market is strongly resisted.

More recently, in England and, to a lesser extent, Hong Kong, it has been possible to identify a more "interventionist" approach by legislation and the courts. Such intervention has been broadly "protectionist"—seeking to support the weaker contracting party from the "dominance" of the other, stronger party. This approach can be discerned, legislatively, in the area of employees' rights, consumer protection and anti-discrimination laws. Judicial intervention can be seen in the increasingly restrictive approach to exemption clauses[30] and the expansion of the doctrines of "duress" and "undue influence".[31] Interventionism is based on the premise that complete freedom of contract tends to favour those who have more negotiating power because of their greater resources, contractual experience, access to legal advice and so on.

It is the "balance" between freedom of contract approaches and intervention to assist the weaker party with which we will be chiefly concerned in this chapter.[32]

1.2.1 The Will Theory of Contract

In classical contract theory the role of the courts is to permit, even encourage, free bargaining by competent adults. The function of the court, if called upon, is to discover the true nature of the parties' agreement and, in the case of breach of

---

30. See 8.6.
31. See chapter 11.
32. There are, of course, far more radical approaches to contract law, some of which see law in general and contract law in particular in a far less favourable light. Such theoretical approaches are outside the scope of a book of this nature.

such agreement, to compensate the innocent party. This theory reached its high point in the highly industrialised, economically dominant England of the nineteenth century. The theory was underpinned by the twin ideals of "freedom of contract" and "sanctity of contract". The notion of freedom of contract is not merely that an agreement is required but that such agreement represents the entire contract; provided the agreement was made freely, the courts and legislature should not intervene. Only in the event of a breach of the agreement should the courts be concerned. A classic definition of the freedom (and sanctity) of contract approach is provided by Jessell MR:

> (if) there is one thing which more than another public policy requires it is that men of full age and competent understanding shall have the utmost liberty of contracting, and that their contracts . . . entered into freely and voluntarily shall be held sacred.[33]

There have always been exceptions or qualifications to this theory in its pure form. Courts have always asserted the right to "police" the bargain and a freely-made contract will be invalidated if it is shown to be illegal or induced by one party's fraud. Since the agreement must be a genuine one, the common law has long recognised the vitiating element of duress (the use or threat of physical force) as invalidating a contract if the "victim" so wishes. Given the narrow constraints of traditional duress, equity developed a doctrine of undue influence where

> one party had induced the other to enter into the transaction by actual pressure which equity regarded as improper but which was formerly not thought to amount to duress at common law because no element of violence to the person was involved.[34]

Duress itself has been considerably expanded by a recognition by the courts that it can apply to "economic" as well as physical pressure. Even in the absence of wrongdoing by either party, mistakes of a fundamental nature may render a contract void, though this occurs rarely in practice.

Since it is also implicit that agreements will be enforced only against competent parties, rules on capacity restrict the scope of minors, drunkards and the mentally ill to make enforceable agreements. Further, since corporations can impose their own restraints on their contractual capacity via their memorandum and articles of association, the courts have the power to declare a company's contracts *ultra vires*. However, given that Hong Kong law no longer requires a memorandum of association, this is unlikely to be a problem in practice.

Long before the development of consideration, intention and the various vitiating elements, English law restricted the making of informal contracts by the requirement that certain contracts had to be made under seal, in writing, or via written evidence. The Statute of Frauds, 1677, initially required that various categories of contract had to be evidenced in writing. Most of these formal requirements have

---

33. Cited in Beale, Bishop, and Furmston (n 18 above), p 47.
34. E. Peel, *Treitel: The Law of Contract* (London: Sweet & Maxwell, 14th edn, 2015), pp 506–507.

now been abolished. However, one important category remains of great significance in Hong Kong: contracts for the sale or other disposition of land, which must be evidenced in writing or supported by an unequivocal act of part performance.[35]

The most significant interference with contractual "freedom", however, arises via the intervention of "implied" terms. Implied terms are regarded as part of the contract even though not expressed by the parties. Such terms may arise through the custom of a particular trade or market, to give "business efficacy" to a contract, or where the term is seen as omitted only because it is so obvious it "goes without saying". In all these cases the implied term may be viewed as part of the parties' "real" intention; something they meant to include but did not or, at the very least, something they would have included if they had considered the matter more carefully.

However, the traditional view, that implied terms do not undermine contractual freedom but are merely an expression of the parties' true intention, can no longer be viewed as absolute. Many statutory implied terms are now non-excludable even by the clearest exemption clauses, even if such exemptions have been read, understood and signed by the party seeking to escape the exemption. Such statutory implied terms are legislative consumer protection which owes nothing to the expressed "will" of the parties. While such consumer protection legislation is more widespread in England, the (previously) most important restriction on exemption clauses, the Unfair Contract Terms Act 1977 (now largely superseded by the Consumer Rights Act 2015) has been reproduced with little amendment in Hong Kong via the Control of Exemption Clauses Ordinance (CECO). There are also terms implied "in law" which cannot be said to be based on the parties' presumed intention but are simply required to be present in contracts of a certain type.[36]

It is more common, therefore, to regard "freedom of contract" as a concept steeped in the ideology of nineteenth century "laissez-faire" industrial England and long abandoned in favour of more "protectionist" judicial and statutory intervention. Increased intervention, in England, would be seen as a natural consequence of a move from a free market economy to a more welfare-based society.[37] The interventionist trend appears to have continued despite over 20 years of Conservative and "new right" Labour government. Freedom of contract still has its adherents, however, especially in the still-significant economy of the United States. The American view remains that intervention into the contractual agreements of individual, cognisant adults should be exceptional and restricted. It might be assumed that Hong Kong's less welfare-oriented political system would be reflected in a free-market, non-interventionist approach to contract but this is not entirely the case.

---

35. In England these formal requirements have become more restrictive since the contract must now be written as opposed to evidenced in writing and the (equitable) part-performance doctrine has been abolished.
36. See *Liverpool City Council v Irwin* [1977] AC 239 and 8.4.
37. See, for example, P.S. Atiyah, *The Rise and Fall of Freedom of Contract* (Oxford: Clarendon Press, 1979).

A more recent articulation of freedom of contract is the ideal of "party autonomy". This is, again, predicated on the fundamental principle that the parties to a contract should be free to make their own agreement, without court interference (at least provided that both parties have negotiated from a position of equal bargaining power). The reader may wish to consider whether party autonomy is undermined by "the penalty rule" (chapter 15) and whether, for example, courts should refuse to enforce "onerous or oppressive" contractual terms to which both parties have freely agreed (chapter 8).

1.2.1.1 Legislative Restraints on Freedom of Contract in Hong Kong

Despite the growth of "welfarism" in England, it might be assumed such judicial and, more importantly, legislative restraints on contractual freedom have never been in vogue in Hong Kong, reputedly one of the world's "freest" economies. Hong Kong has certainly proved less interventionist than England in this regard. This reflects Hong Kong's avowed free market approach and its freedom from EU law encroachment, the largest factor in the growth of consumer protection legislation in England. Yet, even in Hong Kong, legislation and judicial intervention have put limits on unfettered market freedom. There may be a free market in *goods*, yet legislation restricts the "market" in *money* in that there is a limit on the interest rates which moneylenders (though not banks) are permitted to charge. If "market competition" worked perfectly there would be no need for such restrictions. Employment legislation imposes regulations as to working conditions, rest days and the Mandatory Provident Fund. It now also imposes a general minimum wage. Legislation also exists in relation to various forms of discrimination in employment practices. All of these changes to the law relating to the contract of employment can be seen as restricting the "freedom" of the employer and employee to negotiate their own contract free from outside interference. Implicitly, however, they recognise that total freedom of contract would allow the more powerful employer to dictate terms to the weaker employee.

Interventionist, welfare-based approaches are criticised by "free-marketeers" on the basis that they not only restrict freedom but also fail to have their desired effect of improving the lot of the poor and disadvantaged. It has been argued, by its opponents, that the introduction of a general minimum wage in Hong Kong will increase unemployment as firms "outsource" more jobs or relocate to areas where unskilled labour is cheaper. It could also be argued that more foreign domestic helpers would be employed in Hong Kong were the minimum wage (long-established in respect of domestic helpers) to be abolished. Proponents of the free market would assert that the protectionism involved in the setting of a minimum wage merely restricts the right of employers to make free bargains, on lesser terms, which many overseas domestic helpers would be more than willing to accept. Legislation here, therefore, involves a delicate balance between total freedom and the prevention of exploitation.

Probably the most conspicuous legislative restraints on the parties' ability to contract "freely" in Hong Kong are in the area of consumer protection. The Control of Exemption Clauses Ordinance (CECO), dealt with in chapter 8, and the Unconscionable Contracts Ordinance (UCO), dealt with in chapter 12, are important examples of such statutory intervention.

1.2.1.2 Judicial Restraints on Freedom of Contract

It has been said that "English judges have always been stronger in doing justice in a pragmatic fashion"[38] since English legal education and training tend to be practical rather than theoretical. Given their similar educational and training background, the same "pragmatic" approach can be seen amongst the Hong Kong judiciary. The approach of the judges may be seen in terms of enforcing freely-made agreements in so far as to do so does not produce an "unjust" or unfair result. Where, however, freedom of contract has resulted in the imposition of terms by a dominant party on a weaker one, the courts are likely to intervene.

The search for a "fair" solution appears to contradict the view that contract law is not concerned with fairness; that if one party has freely made a bad bargain he should be expected to keep to it. Indeed, it has been said that:

> In commercial transactions one party may take advantage of his greatly superior bargaining power to drive a very hard bargain . . . A party may also take advantage of his superior knowledge.[39]

In the case of *Turner v Green*,[40] the plaintiff solicitor took advantage of his knowledge of the outcome of a case to make a favourable contract with the defendant who, the plaintiff knew, was unaware of the result of the case. The court held that this was a "shabby trick" but that the contract was nonetheless valid. More recently, in *Walford v Miles*,[41] the House of Lords underlined the "adversarial" nature of bargaining. Lord Ackner said:

> Each party to the negotiations is entitled to pursue his (or her) own interest, so long as he avoids making misrepresentations.[42]

The role for the court, according to common law principles, is to uphold hard bargaining but to determine when the line has been crossed such that the agreement infringes specific common law or statutory rules.

---

38. Atiyah (ibid), p 405.
39. R. Brownsword (ed), *Smith & Thomas: A Casebook on Contract* (London: Sweet & Maxwell, 13th edn, 2015), p 33.
40. [1895] 2 Ch 205, referred to in *Smith & Thomas* (ibid), p 29.
41. [1992] 1 All ER 453, discussed at 3.8.5.
42. Ibid at 460.

Certainly the law on consideration supports the "freedom of contract" rule, since the rule is that "consideration need not be adequate"; that what one party gives need not be equal to the other party's contribution to the contract. In practice, however, the fairness, or unfairness, of a bargain is likely to be significant in a number of ways; "mere" unfairness will not invalidate a contract but the unfair nature of a contract may encourage the courts to look for other "vitiating" factors. So, for example, a written agreement to sell a valuable car for $100 might be acceptable from a consideration point of view. In such circumstances, however, the courts are more likely to believe the "victim's" assertion that he was tricked or threatened and invalidate the agreement accordingly.

An obvious illustration of the relevance of fairness in contract is provided by the example of equity, which is specifically preserved, by the Basic Law, as a source of law in Hong Kong post-1997.[43] Equity was founded on principles of morality and its main court, Chancery, was a "court of conscience". While the courts of common law and equity were fused well over one hundred years ago in England, the role of equity as a "court of conscience" remains. The maxims of equity still direct the courts in the exercise of their discretion whether or not to grant equitable relief. The principle that "he who comes to equity must come with clean hands" means that equitable remedies, or "relief", will only be granted to those who have acted fairly in respect of the contract.[44] The principle that "he who seeks equity must do equity" means that equitable relief will be granted only where the claimant is prepared to comply with the requirements of the court to do justice to the other party.[45]

As a further example, it is now generally recognised that the rationale for finding that an agreement is "frustrated",[46] by a post-contractual event which makes performance impossible, is that it would be unfair to demand contractual performance in such cases.

"Fairness" is also relevant to the question of non-statutory "unconscionability", as well as the statutory form mentioned above.[47] Hong Kong courts have overturned agreements on the basis of unconscionability where one party has taken advantage of a superior bargaining position to produce an unfair agreement. In *Lo Wo and Others v Cheung Chan Ka Joseph and Another*,[48] a Hong Kong court overturned, for unconscionability, the sale of a half share of property in Hong Kong by elderly mainland women. The main justification for the court's action was that the buyers had failed to mention that they had paid far more for the other half share and had not advised the sellers to take independent advice.

---

43. See 2.2.
44. See *D&C Builders v Rees* [1966] 2 QB 617, [1966] WLR 288, [1965] 3 All ER 837 discussed at 4.7.3.3.
45. See *Cheese v Thomas* [1994] 1 WLR 129, [1994] 1 All ER 35 discussed at 11.2.4.
46. See 14.4.
47. See 1.2.1.1 and chapter 12.
48. [2001] 3 HKC 70, discussed at 12.2.

While the above examples may be seen as limited exceptions to the principle of contractual freedom, it has been argued that there has been a more general shift by the courts away from freedom of contract towards an interventionist approach seeking to protect the weaker party from the stronger in an attempt to produce a "fair" result.

Reiter states:

the courts have overridden 'contract principles' and have established limits on the exercise of contract power . . . Through a great variety of techniques, the courts have paid lip service to contract law in theory, and have ignored it in practice.[49]

Reiter's view is that judges have intervened consistently in order to achieve a "fair" result at the expense of the principle of contractual "freedom". A clear example would be the judicial refusal to uphold contractual "penalties" even where they have been freely agreed by the parties. While this may be true of English judges, it is questionable how relevant it is to the Hong Kong scenario where the tradition has been, at least until recently, to apply the approaches of the English courts rather than to adapt precedents to perceived Hong Kong needs. Even here, however, there appears to be a gradual change. The *Lo Wo* case, considered above, is a clear example, since the court could have held that the buyers had merely exercised their right to strike a hard bargain and that the elderly sellers had acted imprudently.

1.2.2 Judicial Creativity in Contract Law

What the "fairness" discussion indicates is that judges actually have far more flexibility than is generally believed by the layman. Many Hong Kong students commence their studies believing that the "answer" to a legal problem should always be discoverable by an application of the relevant statutory and "common law"[50] rules to the facts of a case. Statutory rules must be followed by the courts and past judicial "precedents" from the higher courts must be adhered to. This should produce predictability and certainty in the law; a potential claimant, or his legal adviser, should be able to predict the outcome of proposed litigation and respond accordingly. Indeed, in a truly "certain" system cases should only come to court on novel points of law not previously covered by legislation or judicial decision. Such a "rational"[51] system would leave no creative role for the judge; his role would be merely to "find and apply" the relevant rules. In practice, this narrow view of the judicial function is generally seen as unrealistic, especially in common law systems[52] where most of the rules are to be found in previous decided cases rather than legislative rules or written

---

49. B. Reiter, "The Control of Contract Power", (1981) 1 Oxford Journal of Legal Studies 347 at 360.
50. Considered in more detail in chapter 2.
51. See M. Weber, *On Law in Economy and Society* (Cambridge, MA: Harvard University Press, 1954).
52. In this context, "common law" refers to those legal systems which derive from the English rather than the Continental European system.

codes. In determining any case, a judge has to decide which *facts* are "relevant". Even more importantly, the judge has to determine which *rules* are relevant. Those precedents which would produce an unwelcome decision may be found to be irrelevant or inapplicable in the present case. Even legislative rules do not produce the certainty the layman tends to assume, since laws must be first "interpreted" before they can be applied, and that interpretation has to be made by the judge (or judges).

Further scope for judicial flexibility is provided by the emphasis, in common law systems, on the concept of "reasonableness". Agreement is judged, as we have already seen, primarily on the basis of whether a "reasonable man" would assume agreement in the circumstances; the validity of an exemption clause may depend on its "reasonableness", and an innocent party must take all "reasonable" steps to keep loss resulting from the other's breach to a minimum (to "mitigate"). In all such cases, of course, the ultimate decision on reasonableness is a matter for the judge.

In short, therefore, the common law system is far more flexible than it first appears and judges often "create" law rather than simply finding and applying it. The very fact that senior judges, in a particular case, may disagree strongly as to its outcome illustrates the lack of certainty in the law. Throughout this book you will see examples of judges reaching very different conclusions as to the proper outcome of a case or, even where they agree as to the outcome, differing as to the reasons for it. Schur writes:

> Judicial precedent and legal doctrine can be found or developed to support almost any outcome. The real decision is made first—on the basis of the judge's conceptions of justice—and then it is 'rationalized' in the written opinion.[53]

To Schur, then, the decision comes first and the explanation follows. A less extreme view is expressed by Lord Radcliffe, a former House of Lords judge, as follows:

> there was never a more sterile controversy than whether a judge makes law. Of course he does. How can he help it? The legislature and the judicial process respectively are two complementary sources of law making.[54]

There may be scope for disagreement as to the scope for creativity. Paterson[55] found that some law lords dealing with final appeals thought there would rarely be a "right" answer; others felt that in many cases the decision inevitably went one way.[56] What we can say with some assurance is that the student coming to contract for the

---

53. E.M. Schur, *Law and Society* (New York: Random House, 1968), p 43.
54. Lord Radcliffe, *Not in Feather Beds* (London: Hamish Hamilton, 1968), p 215.
55. A. Paterson, *The Law Lords* (London: Palgrave-MacMillan, 1982), pp 190–193.
56. The legal "formalist", Ronald Dworkin, believes that, invariably, there is a "right" answer but that judges frequently fail to find it.

first time is likely to be surprised by the relative lack of certainty in the law and the scope for judicial disagreement.[57]

Judicial creativity, while generally seen as an attempt to do justice in a particular case, is not without its problems. The first is that it erodes the principle of treating like cases alike and the accompanying certainty in the law. If judges can ignore or overrule existing precedents at will, contracting parties will not know where they stand. Commercial contracts may be drawn up, after legal advice, on the basis of the law as it stands. Some would argue that it is more "just" to uphold the existing law, even if it is "defective", than to change the law and cause resentment and confusion as a result.

It is also the case that seeking a "just" solution depends on the judge's perception of what is just in a particular case. This, as the so-called "realists" argue, depends on his social and political view of the world. While we have so far attributed a benign role to judicial creativity, others would see it in less positive terms, ranging from deliberate political or "class" bias to an unconscious lack of sympathy for those of a different background. Scrutton LJ has said:

> The habits you are trained in, the people with whom you mix, lead to your having a certain class of ideas of such a nature that, when you have to deal with other ideas, you do not give as sound and accurate judgments as you would wish . . . It is very difficult sometimes to be sure that you have put yourself into a thoroughly impartial position between two disputants, one of your own class and one not of your own class.[58]

How applicable is this to Hong Kong judges? There has been remarkably little research in this area, in part, perhaps, because colonial judges were seen largely as applying English law, subject to exceptions, and not to be cultivating a distinct Hong Kong jurisprudence. In short, Hong Kong judges have not been seen as a suitable topic of research in their own right.[59] However, much of what has been said about the background of the English judiciary would be echoed in Hong Kong, at least until recently. Most Hong Kong judges were from the more wealthy sections of society. They were either expatriates (usually British) or local judges trained at the English Bar. They would tend to have the same "conservative" (with a small "c") outlook and would prescribe to the view that individual effort rather than collective strength is the ideal. Of course, post-1997, the official political allegiance of Hong Kong judges has changed, and judicial demography is changing too, as colonial-era judges retire and are replaced by local judges. This change is particularly noticeable at the lower

---

57. See, for example, the *Schuler v Wickman* case discussed at 8.5.2.
58. Quoted in J.A.G. Griffith, *The Politics of the Judiciary* (Glasgow: Fontana, 1977), p 173.
59. A notable exception exists in the work of the University of Hong Kong Professor Simon Young who has extensively researched the work of the Court of Final Appeal. See S.N.M. Young and Y. Ghai (eds), *Hong Kong's Court of Final Appeal* (Cambridge: Cambridge University Press, 2013), chapters 6 and 10.

levels of judicial office. One clear reflection of the change is the increased proportion of cases heard entirely in Chinese. Nonetheless, at the highest level of the judiciary, the stereotypical judge will have been educated for some years in England, have studied for the English Bar and be from a relatively privileged background.[60]

As to the extent that the judicial background described affects decisions, it is difficult to draw conclusions, except to the effect that Hong Kong judges continue to be heavily influenced (some might say "over-influenced") by English decisions, even those made post-1997 and therefore not binding in Hong Kong. This is a theme to which we will return in chapter 2.

1.2.3 Contract Law as Dynamic

We can see, then, that judges have the capacity to adopt a creative role in order to achieve what they perceive as a "just" solution. Where such creativity follows a pattern, contract law will be seen to be evolving. In fact, such evolution is inevitable since the "stories" (cases) change significantly over time and the stories inevitably help shape the law. Nineteenth century contract law is dominated by tales of smoke balls, letters lost in the post and the sale of oats and horses. Today contracts are made on the internet, few know what oats are, and horses are seen, in Hong Kong, only in Shatin or Happy Valley. We should not be surprised that different rules are required when disputes are more likely to concern construction, employment contracts and cancelled flights.

But is contract law sufficiently adaptable to changing social conditions? One dilemma for the courts is the extent to which they should reflect current commercial practice. It has been argued that, unless courts do this, contracting parties will not use the courts and will seek alternative methods to resolve disputes. Scrutton LJ has stated:

> I regret that in many commercial matters the English law and the practice of com-
> mercial men are getting wider apart, with the result that commercial business is
> leaving the courts and is being decided by commercial arbitrators with infrequent
> reference to the courts.[61]

Already, in Hong Kong, we see an increase in the use of alternative dispute resolution (ADR) despite the fact that the costs of such alternatives are rarely less than those involved in litigation. ADR is used particularly widely in specialised areas such as construction law.[62] The English case of *Williams v Roffey*,[63] and its Hong Kong counterpart *UBC (Construction) Ltd v Sung Foo Kee Ltd*,[64] can be seen as

---

60. See 2.4.
61. *Hillas & Co Ltd v Arcos Ltd* (1932) 147 LT 503 at 506.
62. Taking the forms of arbitration, mediation and, imminently, statutory adjudication.
63. *Williams v Roffey Bros & Nicholls (Contractors) Ltd* [1990] 1 All ER 512, and see 4.5.
64. [1993] 2 HKLR 207, and see 4.5.2.

examples of the courts trying to make decisions in line with existing practice—what "everyone does" in building and construction—at the expense of long-established rules of consideration in contract. The counter-argument is that law should not be merely "reflective" but should retain a role as "educator"; to make pronouncements on what business practices should be, rather than merely reflecting, uncritically, what they are.

Lord Devlin[65] recognised that judicial creativity could take two forms: "activist" and "dynamic". The former, which he supports, involves judges reaching a decision "creatively" so as to bring the law in line with the common consensus. The latter involves judges being creative so as to change the existing consensus and point the way to reform; this he disapproves of, regarding such change as a task for the elected legislature. It is clear that analogies with Hong Kong are difficult; consensus may be hard to identify in a democracy but in a non-democratic entity like Hong Kong it is far more so. Arguments that dynamism should be left to elected representatives are also inapplicable to a largely (non-elected) executive-led entity. Whatever the merits of Devlin's view, we will see clearly in the following chapters that there have been dynamic contract law changes in the twentieth century, in relation to the phenomena of agreement, consideration, the effect of undue influence on third parties, remedies for non-financial loss, and the effect of mistake, all of which are the results of judicial creativity rather than legislative intervention.

There are, however, limits on judicial creativity and dynamism. In particular, "bad" or outdated rules need to be considered by a higher court before they can be overturned. Where this higher court is the House of Lords (or its successor the Supreme Court) or Hong Kong's Court of Final Appeal, access is an important issue. In practice, poor decisions may never be appealed (or poor principles may never be questioned) because the costs involved in any potential appeal to the highest court outweigh the potential benefits (especially since risk is always involved). In England, for example, appellate courts have "raised judicial eyebrows" at the so-called "fiction of fraud" applied in the Court of Appeal case of *Royscot Trust Ltd v Rogerson*[66] but, absent a direct challenge in the Supreme Court, the fiction must continue to represent the law. Similarly, lawyers representing the losing party in *Collier v Wright*[67] were astonished by an adverse Court of Appeal decision, which appeared to fly in the face of established principles, but felt unjustified in appealing given the relatively small sums involved. Creativity in Hong Kong has been further restrained, at least until 1997, by the dominant position of the English common law, such that departure from its established principles was only possible in cases where Hong Kong legislation had amended the common law or where there was clear evidence that the English common law was inconsistent with local conditions.

---

65. See P. Devlin, *The Judge* (Oxford: Oxford University Press, 1979), pp 5–17.
66. [1991] 3 All ER 294.
67. [2007] EWCA Civ 1329, discussed at 4.7.3.5.

Development of the law, where judges have proved unwilling or unable to respond to changing social needs or conditions, requires legislation. This has been enacted in Hong Kong, especially in the field of consumer protection; in relation to the control of exemption clauses and restrictions on "unconscionable" contracts for example. However, legislative action has generally been tardy[68] and often inadequate. One problem has been that Hong Kong legislation tended to mirror that in England, irrespective of local conditions and despite criticisms of the legislation in England.[69]

Such legislative reform as has been enacted in Hong Kong has generally followed reports and recommendations by the Law Reform Commission of Hong Kong (LRCHK) and it is a matter of some concern that a significant number of recommendations, made in LRCHK Reports some time ago, have not been adopted legislatively. The post-1997 record of legislative follow-up to LRCHK recommendations has been lamentable. It is to be welcomed that, following criticism of this situation,[70] legislative reform (in the contract law-related area) has finally been enacted in relation to privity of contracts.[71]

1.2.4 Enforceability

What all approaches to contract law agree on is the significance of enforcement. If freedom of contract has been eroded, the principle of "sanctity" remains firmly established. Sanctity of contract[72] requires that once contractual promises are made the law will enforce them, irrespective of factors which may make performance difficult or impossible. However, "enforcement" does not, generally, mean that a contracting party is compelled by the courts to perform as promised since, as American jurist, Oliver Wendell Holmes, has stated:

> The duty to keep a contract at common law means a prediction that you must pay damages if you do not keep it and nothing else.[73]

It is on this basis that "legal economists" talk of "efficient breach", whereby a party may "efficiently" break his contract where the other party's recoverable loss would be less than the profit it obtained via the breach. Recognition and approval of

---

68. The Control of Exemption Clauses Ordinance (Cap 71), for example, was enacted 12 years after its English forerunner, the Unfair Contract Terms Act 1977.
69. The Misrepresentation Ordinance (Cap 284), for example, did nothing to deal with the major ambiguities and uncertainties of the English Misrepresentation Act 1967.
70. The *South China Morning Post* reported in December 2010 that, of 27 post-1997 Law Reform Commission Reports, 22 had not been implemented by legislation: see "Series of Law Reform ideas left to gather dust", 20 December 2010.
71. In force (in diluted form) some 12 years after the Commission's recommendations for change! See chapter 16.
72. Corresponding, broadly, with the civil law "pacta sunt servanda" (agreements *must* be kept).
73. O.W. Holmes, "The Path of the Law", (1897) 10 Harvard Law Review 457 at p 462.

"efficient breach" distinguish contract from tort; where the potential exists to award (punitive) "exemplary" damages to show a tortfeasor that "tort does not pay". Breach of contract can, and frequently does, pay.

Contractual duties are applying the principle of "sanctity", regarded as "absolute". The best-known statement as to the absolute nature of obligations is to be found in the old case of *Paradine v Jane*,[74] where it was stated:

> but when the party by his own contract creates a duty or charge upon himself, he is bound to make it good, if he may, notwithstanding any accident by inevitable necessity, because he might have provided against it by his contract.[75]

The context of the words makes clear that the "may", which appears to allow some excuse for non-performance, is restricted to performance which would be illegal. The more recent doctrine of frustration has provided some alleviation of the sanctity principle, but is only rarely applied. Non-performance may be allowed in cases other than supervening illegality but only in extreme situations, where performance has become impossible or where the supervening event has destroyed the whole underlying basis of the contract.[76]

Outside the doctrine of frustration there is little judicial support for the relaxation of the principle of the "absolute" nature of contractual obligations. There is some tension, however, between the absolute theory and the recognition that, in contracts of a continuing nature especially, "things change" and parties expect to be able to renegotiate in situations where new circumstances have arisen falling short of frustration. This sort of situation is encompassed in the so-called "relational" theory of contract, which recognises, for example, that continuing relations over a period of time, as opposed to "one-off" contracts, require that the parties allow for a measure of adaptation over time.[77] This may be done expressly within the contract by such devices as price variation clauses. In reality, however, changes are more likely to be based on implied assumptions by the parties that terms will not remain inflexible indefinitely.

Enforceability, in common law systems, also connotes more than the mere existence of possible redress for breach. It involves also the nature of the procedures for redress. Hong Kong is frequently said to have a "competitive advantage" over the PRC because of its "rule of law". Yet, if we look at the recently drafted contract law "code" in the PRC we can see that its rules are very similar to those in Hong Kong. Wherein, then, lies Hong Kong's advantage? The answer lies in the difference between "form" and "substance" or what some writers call "law in books" as

---

74. (1647) Aleyn 26.
75. Ibid at 27.
76. See 14.4.
77. See, for example, D. Campbell (ed), *The Relational Theory of Contract: Selected Works of Ian Macneil* (London: Sweet & Maxwell, 2001).

opposed to "law in action". Hong Kong's system may be far from perfect: the rich get better access to justice than the middle class, for example. Nonetheless, those who come to court with a contract dispute in Hong Kong, unlike litigants in the PRC, can expect an impartial decision based on the evidence, by a skilled judge who will give his decision free from state interference and without fear of the consequences. The "loser" may dislike the decision but he will have been fairly heard. Hong Kong courts have shown themselves prepared to find against the Hong Kong government (though it has not always accepted the decision!)[78] and to make judgments critical of the most powerful companies. For an excellent example of a judgment highly critical of one of Hong Kong's most important institutions see Waung J's judgment in *Esquire Electronics Ltd v Hong Kong and Shanghai Banking Corporation Ltd* discussed in chapter 11. While the judgment itself, including the tone of the trial judge's remarks, was the subject of severe criticism in the Hong Kong Court of Appeal, this was based on perceived errors of law and procedure, including excessive judicial delay, which rendered the judge's remarks unjustified.

A number of writers have suggested that enforcement is not the prime consideration of contracting parties. They indicate that parties tend to think more in terms of the contractual terms "defining" their contractual obligations and providing guidelines. No doubt, given the time and expense involved, parties will generally wish to avoid litigation, especially when the parties have dealt with one another over a considerable period. It may also be the case that, for many parties, loss of reputation would be a greater consideration than the amount of damages involved.[79] However, as a "last resort", the existence of contractual remedies available via a competent and trusted legal system is a key factor influencing the initial creation of a contract. This is especially true for contracts which are likely to involve heavy cost and a lengthy performance time.

One key feature of litigation in common law systems is that the result is likely to be a "win/lose" situation, with the court finding for one party or the other. Some flexibility exists in that the court may not find for the claimant on all counts and may not always award full costs against the loser. There is also some scope for flexibility where an "equitable" remedy is sought, since the court may insist that the "winner" makes some allowance to the loser. Essentially, however, where the plaintiff wins, the defendant loses and it might be thought that this runs counter to traditional "Confucian" principles of compromise. Discussion of compromise raises the issue of

---

78. In his research in this area, Professor Simon Young of the University of Hong Kong found that Hong Kong's Court of Final Appeal had found against the government in around 50% of cases (see Young and Ghai (eds), n 57 above, at p 163). This compares with Macau's one adverse government decision in its first 11 years! Cf J. Godinho and P. Cardinal, *Macau's Court of Final Appeal* in Young and Ghai (eds), chapter 23.

79. This may well have been the case in respect of HSBC's appeal in the *Esquire* case (above) where its good name had been seriously called into question at first instance.

alternative dispute resolution (ADR), especially in the form of mediation. Mediation is a growth area in Hong Kong, encouraged by the former and current Secretaries for Justice and both post-1997 Chief Justices.[80] Mediation is seen by its supporters as a beneficial means of resolving disputes, intended to avoid or reduce conflict and especially valuable where, as in matrimonial disputes, the parties will need to continue interaction. Critics of mediation, both in Hong Kong and Britain, see it as a cost-cutting measure frequently denying to deserving claimants the benefits of genuine litigation.[81]

Arbitration has a special significance for post-1997 Hong Kong, given the rapid increase in cross-border (strictly "cross-boundary") integration and the "joint venture" agreement. Enforcement of cross-boundary contracts is crucial if confidence is to be maintained in the integration process and, while mutual enforcement of civil judgments has been agreed in respect of cross-boundary contracts, the practical reality is that Hong Kong businessmen prefer to effect enforcement via the mutual recognition of arbitral awards.[82] Hong Kong has great aspirations for its arbitration system and intends to become a major world forum for arbitration, given its unique position as a (common law) gateway to the PRC contractual market.

The "win/lose" consideration raises the more profound question of whether Hong Kong's esteemed "rule of law" in general, and contract law in particular, should be seen as a "colonial" relic unsuited to an increasingly Chinese society. Pragmatically, whether or not this is so, what we shall see in chapter 2 is that the English rules of contract continue to exert huge influence on Hong Kong's own contract law. This is so both because of guarantees for the continuation of the common law, post-1997, and because, over the years of British rule in Hong Kong, common law concepts have become instilled in what is now the Hong Kong SAR, not least amongst the lawyers and judges who make the system work. Moreover, in form, at least, mainland China's own contract law is becoming increasingly aligned to common law principles rather than its previous socialist foundations. This leads us to ask what, if anything, is "special" about Hong Kong's law in general and contract law in particular.

---

80. At the 2008 Opening of the Legal Year, for example, then Chief Justice Andrew Li stated that: "The benefits of mediation have been increasingly recognised in Hong Kong. The governing bodies of both branches of the legal profession fully understand its importance and are committed to its development. The promotion of mediation is now a matter of government policy."

81. See, notably, H. Genn, *Judging Civil Justice* (Cambridge/New York: Cambridge University Press, 2009).

82. Essentially there is much greater confidence in the PRC arbitration system than in its courts.

1.3 Is Hong Kong's Contract Law "Special"?

Any discussion of the special nature of Hong Kong law must start with its unique constitutional experiment, Deng Xiaoping's "one country, two systems", enshrined in Hong Kong's post-1997 constitution, the Basic Law. While the Basic Law is of chief concern to public/constitutional lawyers it is central to an understanding of every branch of the law in Hong Kong today. Crucially, the Basic Law guarantees the continuance of the common law and Hong Kong's capitalist[83] way of life (for at least 50 years) while confirming Hong Kong's status as part of the People's Republic of China (PRC). Hong Kong constitutes, therefore, a small common law island in the midst of a vast civil/socialist law sea.

In comparing Hong Kong with the rest of the common law world, therefore, it can be seen as untypically undemocratic[84] and with limited power over its legal and political affairs. This limitation, however, has had little effect, in practice, on Hong Kong's legal development.

Much more significant has been the continuance of the colonial government's close (some would say sycophantic) relationship with big business. As many common law jurisdictions have evolved from "freedom of contract" models towards consumer-welfarism, Hong Kong has remained dedicated to the interests of big business at the expense of the consumer/employee. While a minimum wage was finally introduced in 2011,[85] employment protection is very poorly developed and those found to have been unfairly dismissed receive inadequate levels of compensation.[86]

Further examples of the pro-business approach (in the contract area) can be seen in the lack of legislative control of misleading developers/estate agents' claims as to new housing developments,[87] a constant source of consumer complaint. Proposed legislation to increase consumers' welfare is constantly halted or slowed by vested interests.[88] On the same day as the announcement that legislation would (finally) be introduced in relation to privity of contract and the supply of goods,[89] the government also announced the shelving of legislation in respect

---

83. Given developments in the rest of China, capitalism is not under threat. Hong Kong's richest businessman, the recently retired Li Ka-shing, has been feted by the PRC.
84. The Basic Law permits an "orderly" transition towards democracy but, between 1997 and 2017, there has been almost no progress in that direction.
85. At HK$28 per hour.
86. The "activist" Cathay Pacific pilots found to have been unfairly dismissed for their union activities received moderate levels of compensation only because the judge was able to invoke the law of defamation (though the defamation compensation was significantly reduced on appeal: *Campbell Richard Blakeney-Williams & Others v Cathay Pacific Airways & Others* (2012) 15 HKCFAR 261).
87. "Bel Air on The Peak", for example, is not on The Peak. The *South China Morning Post* reports that the Law Reform Commission had recommended reforms in this area 15 years ago: "Series of law reform ideas left to gather dust", 20 December 2010.
88. The Chief Executive's "cabinet" (ExCo) is dominated by businessmen.
89. In the latter case, a mere nine years after the LRCHK's Report.

of unsafe products.[90] Some would see the lack of legislative intervention in the market place as evidence of sensible "non-intervention" in the free market.[91] Hong Kong is (or was) lauded as one of the freest economies in the world by those with only scant knowledge of the political reality.[92] Genuinely free economies encourage competition (the United States, for example, has rigorous anti-trust laws) yet Hong Kong has only recently implemented competition legislation first recommended (by the Consumer Council) in 1996.[93] The effects of non-intervention are not difficult to identify. Land sales, for example, on which the Hong Kong government has been able to base its low taxation system, are effected in a cosy relationship between the government and bidders whose practices bear little resemblance to genuine auctions. The vast majority of supermarket retailing is in the hands of a duopoly which eschews genuine competition. Long queues, for example, wait at understaffed checkouts despite climbing Hong Kong unemployment; the unhappy consumer has no better, available source.

In respect of the Hong Kong SAR, comparison (and interface) with the rest of China, the contrast is one of *practice* rather than *form*, at least as far as contract law is concerned. Students of the common law coming to the PRC Code on Contract would find little that is unfamiliar to them. What is *fundamentally* different is how such law is developed and applied. Hong Kong teachers of contract law report that one of the most difficult concepts to convey to PRC students is that the law is generally to be found by reading cases rather by scrutinising the words of a code or statute. This has enormous significance for legal development, since common law principles support the view that an interpretation by a senior court will be adopted in later analogous cases rather than being determined *ab initio* by a subsequent court adopting its own interpretation.

A key distinction, which is reflected, again, in practice rather than form, is that of the independence and professionalisation of judges. Judicial independence is a fundamental principle of the common law and is expressly preserved in Hong Kong's Basic Law. Conversely, the PRC judiciary is constitutionally subservient to the socialist "state".[94] There is also a huge difference in judicial *quality* between Hong Kong and the rest of China. Hong Kong's judges are selected from the best of practitioners from the Bar. Moreover, judicial training is an area which has been prioritised and developed. In the PRC, on the other hand, judicial expertise lags far behind. This is scarcely surprising given that the judicial class was all but eliminated

---

90. On the basis that the "community" [*sic*] is unlikely to reach consensus.
91. Such had been the justification for the delay of legislation on a minimum wage.
92. See, for example, the seminal *Free to Choose* by Milton and Rose Friedmann.
93. A *South China Morning Post* editorial on 25 February 2011 noted that Chief Executive, Donald Tsang, had pledged to begin legislative work "within 2007"!
94. Article 9 of the Law on Judges (2000) dictates that judges must "support the Constitution of the PRC" which includes reference to the primacy of the Communist Party of China. Moreover, judges are appointed by (and more importantly removable by) People's Congresses (national or local).

in the Mao Zedong era and it is to the PRC's credit that a lot of improvement has subsequently been effected in a short time.[95]

In identifying what is special about Hong Kong's contract law it would be gratifying to say that, post-1997, Hong Kong has gone its own way and begun developing a genuinely local contract jurisprudence. Alas, there is little evidence of this and, even in respect of novel points of law, Hong Kong has tended to follow legislative and judicial practice from England. However, given the psychological boost of a robust 2008 clarification of Hong Kong's precedent position, post-1997, by the then Chief Justice,[96] there are signs that Hong Kong judges are gradually taking the opportunity to look elsewhere in the common law world for inspiration, where appropriate.

---

95. Professor Albert Chen has described how law "neither existed as an academic discipline nor as a rational mechanism of social control" after the Cultural Revolution and how re-establishment did not begin until 1972: A. Chen, *An Introduction to the Legal System of the PRC* (Hong Kong: LexisNexis, 3rd edn, 2004).
96. See *A Solicitor v Law Society of Hong Kong* [2008] 2 HKC 1.

2

Sources of Hong Kong Contract Law

OVERVIEW

Hong Kong contract law, like Hong Kong law in general, has been dominated, for 150 years, by the common law of England. Hong Kong's post-colonial "constitution", the Basic Law, guarantees that the common law will continue in force for 50 years from the transfer of sovereignty of Hong Kong in 1997, but it is to be expected that, by a process of divergence, the common law of Hong Kong will become increasingly distinct from the common law of England.

The Basic Law, the constitutional basis for the Hong Kong Special Administrative Region (HKSAR), states that:[1]

> The laws previously in force in Hong Kong, that is, the common law, rules of equity, ordinances, subordinate legislation and customary law shall be maintained, except for any that contravene this Law, and subject to any amendment by the legislature of the Hong Kong Special Administrative Region.

The intention of this section is that the general principles of the common law will continue in force and that the specific rules existing before 1997[2] will also do so unless they are amended or found to be contrary to the Basic Law. While this appears to be a simple proposition, the operational realities are somewhat more complex and need to be examined in detail.

It is also clear that, while Hong Kong's judicial system now enjoys the right of "final adjudication",[3] Hong Kong may continue to be guided by the courts of other common law jurisdictions since the Basic Law expressly permits reference to such precedents.[4]

---

1. Article 8.
2. Although the transfer of sovereignty took place at midnight on 30 June 1997, we will refer to "pre-1997" and "post-1997".
3. Subject to exception relating to such matters as national security and foreign affairs.
4. Article 84.

The intention, then, is that rules of English common law formulated post-1997 will be of no binding effect but merely available for guidance in the same way as the rules of any other common law jurisdiction. While this may be the theoretical position, in practice there is little doubt that post-1997 English court decisions weigh far more heavily with the Hong Kong judiciary than those of other common law jurisdictions, at least as far as the law of contract is concerned.

2.1 Hong Kong Contract Law before 1997

Following the Treaty of Nanking signed by China and Britain in 1842, Hong Kong became a legal possession of Britain. Later treaties, the Conventions of Peking of 1860 and 1898, ceded further territory to Britain, though under differing terms. After the Treaty of Nanking was ratified by Britain, a constitution for the new territory was established by two documents. The first, known as the Letters Patent, outlined the constitutional structure and conferred powers upon the governor while making provision for the assistance of an Executive Council and Legislative Council. The second constitutional document, the Royal Instructions, set out the rules relating to the composition of the Executive and Legislative Councils and detailed the procedures to be observed in the passing of laws.

After 1843, this constitutional framework allowed laws to be created in Hong Kong. One such example was the Supreme Court Ordinance (SCO), 1844,[5] which is significant in that it incorporated the laws of England, existing in 1843, into Hong Kong law. English laws were to have effect in the colony except as they might be inapplicable to local circumstances or inhabitants, and subject to any modification by the local legislative structure. The SCO also established the court system of Hong Kong.

In 1966 the Application of English Law Ordinance[6] (AELO) was passed. Section 3 provided that:

(1) the common law and the rules of equity shall be in force in Hong Kong:
   (a) so far as they are applicable to the circumstances of Hong Kong or its inhabitants;
   (b) subject to any modifications as such circumstances may require;
   (c) subject to any amendment thereof (whenever made) by
      (i)   any Order in Council which applies to Hong Kong;
      (ii) any Act which applies to Hong Kong;
      (iii) any Ordinance.

On 1 July 1997, AELO was "not adopted" as a law of the HKSAR via the procedure whereby the Standing Committee of the National People's Congress (NPCSC)

---

5.   No 15 of 1844.
6.   Cap 88.

is authorised to determine which of the laws previously in force are inconsistent with the Basic Law. This non-adoption confirms that Britain may no longer legislate for Hong Kong. AELO remains significant, however, in identifying which were the laws previously in force as of 1 July 1997. Such laws will, subject to repeal (or inconsistency with the Basic Law), continue in force post-1997.[7]

Thus, prior to the transfer of sovereignty of Hong Kong in 1997, its contract law was dominated by the English rules of contract. These rules were largely "common law", in the sense of being derived from cases rather than legislation. Nonetheless, while there is no overall written "code" for English contract law, legislation does exist in many specific areas, notably in the area of consumer protection. Throughout the examination of the influence of English rules pre-1997, the underlying theme is the concept of binding precedent; that "decisions" of higher courts in England are binding on lower courts in England (and generally in Hong Kong). While it is a necessary shorthand to talk about the binding nature of "decisions" it is, strictly, only the legal reason for the decision, the *ratio decidendi*, which is binding and there are many occasions when this is difficult to ascertain. An in-depth study of precedent is not possible in a work on contract and can be better gleaned from works on "legal system"[8] or "legal method". However, a working knowledge of the precedent system is essential for a proper understanding of the influence of English law on that of Hong Kong, both before and after 1997.

2.1.1 The Significance of English Statutory Rules Pre-1997

The status of English statutes, pre-1997, was that they were not automatically in force in Hong Kong. Statutes could be stated to apply to Hong Kong and would then have this effect. Otherwise they could be adopted by Hong Kong legislation. The tendency was for most English contract law statutes to be adopted in Hong Kong, though, in some instances, much later than in England.[9] A residual list of statutes was listed in the schedule to AELO.[10] These statutes were to remain in force until removed by the Legislative Council. The list was abolished after 1997 and, in any event, few of the rules in the schedule are significant to the study of Hong Kong contract law.

One consequence of Hong Kong's former colonial status was a tendency to copy English legislation even where this had proved controversial or unsatisfactory. The English Misrepresentation Act 1967, for example, is badly drafted and, in part, difficult to construe. Further, the legislators did not take the opportunity to

---

7. Article 8, Basic Law.
8. See, for example, M. J. Fisher, *Text, Cases & Commentary on the Hong Kong Legal System* (Hong Kong: Hong Kong University Press, 2019).
9. The English Unfair Contract Terms Act 1977 was not enacted in Hong Kong, as the Control of Exemption Clauses Ordinance (Cap 71), until 1989.
10. Cap 88.

define the term "misrepresentation" which remains a matter of some difficulty. Hong Kong, however, adopted the Act, via the Misrepresentation Ordinance,[11] without amendment.

Even before 1997, however, there were some signs of an increasing independence in the area of legislation. To take two examples relevant to contract: the English Law of Property (Miscellaneous Provisions) Act 1989, which requires that contracts for the sale or other disposition of land must be in writing, was not adopted in Hong Kong. Conversely, the Unconscionable Contracts Ordinance,[12] enacted in Hong Kong pre-1997, owes nothing to English influence and is, in fact, modelled on Australian legislation.

2.1.2 The Influence of the English Common Law Pre-1997

While the expression "common law" has differing meanings according to the context in which it is used, in the present context we are referring to the rules developed by the English courts via their judgments, as opposed to the legislative rules described above.

Prior to the transfer of sovereignty in 1997, Hong Kong was bound automatically by the rules of the English common law and equity in so far as they were "applicable to the circumstances of Hong Kong or its inhabitants".[13] Where common law rules were inapplicable to local conditions, Chinese customary law should apply. A rare, but clear, example of this principle is to be found in *Yau Yeong Wood and Another v The Standard Oil Co of New York*[14] where the Hong Kong Chief Justice stated:

> I think it cannot fail to have struck even the learned Counsel who relied on these (English) cases how very inapplicable many of them seemed to be on the face of them to Chinese contractors . . . English law is only in force here under the Charter in so far as it may be applicable, and when I come to a series of decisions, the key-note to which is the custom or practice of a certain class of people who enter into contracts in England, I hesitate to apply them as of necessity to the people in Hong Kong.[15]

Given the dominance of the English common law rules, the two key courts were the English Judicial Committee of the House of Lords (House of Lords) and the Judicial Committee of the Privy Council (Privy Council). The former court, as the highest appeal court in England, represented the ultimate articulation of the state of the English law and, since that English law was, generally, binding in Hong Kong,

---

11. Cap 284.
12. Cap 458.
13. AELO s 3.
14. [1907] HKLR 55.
15. Ibid at 59.

the House of Lords pronouncements would constitute the law in Hong Kong, unless found to be inapplicable to Hong Kong circumstances.

The Privy Council was, pre-1997, the final court of appeal for Hong Kong. Technically, the Privy Council's judgments on appeal from Hong Kong, expressed as "advice to the sovereign", were only "persuasive" in England and elsewhere in the common law world (where laws might differ from those of Hong Kong), but they were binding on Hong Kong courts.

With the transfer of sovereignty in 1997, the binding nature of House of Lords and Privy Council judgments ceased, in respect of decisions delivered post-1997 (although an "academic" argument can be made for their continuing dominance).[16] As regards pre-1997 decisions, the position has been carefully explained in the Court of Final Appeal's landmark decision in *A Solicitor v Law Society of Hong Kong*.[17] Andrew Li CJ, delivering the leading judgment, explained that pre-1997 decisions of the Privy Council involving appeals from Hong Kong[18] would continue to be binding on Hong Kong courts *except* the Court of Final Appeal (CFA). The CFA would treat such Privy Council decisions with respect but would be free to depart from them. Pre-1997 House of Lords decisions would not *directly* bind Hong Kong courts but would, again be treated with the greatest respect. Post-1997 decisions of the Privy Council, the House of Lords (and its successor the Supreme Court) would have no binding force but would, again, be treated with respect, mindful of the English common law heritage in Hong Kong.

Although the continuation of the common law post-1997 is enshrined in the Basic Law, there was already some slight indication of Hong Kong developing a common law "flavour" of its own, even before 1997. In particular, there was a willingness among some judges to consider non-English common law decisions; a practice now specifically provided for in the Basic Law.[19] This was, in part, the result of the influence of non-English personnel practising in Hong Kong in the legal professions and on the bench.

This divergence from the English common law will inevitably increase in the post-1997 era. Indeed, at first sight it might be thought that such a process would be speedy, given that the new Hong Kong Court of Final Appeal (Hong Kong's highest court), which deals with far more cases than its predecessor, the Privy Council, is dominated by Hong Kong judges. The Basic Law provides that the Court of Final Appeal may appoint "judges" from other common law jurisdictions to sit as judges of the court where appropriate. It has, however, been decided "extra-judicially" that only one such judge may be appointed at any time. The consequence is that four of

---

16. See 2.3.1 below.
17. [2008] 2 HKC 1.
18. Chief Justice Andrew Li confirmed that Privy Council decisions other than on appeal from Hong Kong have never been binding here.
19. Article 84.

the five judges normally sitting will be Hong Kong judges. In practice, however, such judges are predominantly English-trained and steeped in the ways of the English common law, such that increasing divergence is likely to be a slow process.[20]

Ironically, however, the English courts themselves are moving away from the traditions of the common law as a result of the increasing influence of the rules of what was previously known as the European Economic Community and is now called the "European Union". This influence has extended to the English law of contract, especially in areas involving consumer protection. Many European Union rules were directly applicable in England and others have been adopted via domestic legislation. The Unfair Terms in Consumer Contracts Regulations, 1994, for example, were a response to a European Union Directive. While Britain has decided to leave the European Union, its influence will not disappear overnight.

Having no legal requirement to adopt European legislation, Hong Kong will doubtless eschew such rules, which largely overlap with existing legislation[21] and serve merely to introduce confusion.

English judges, too, are becoming increasingly influenced by "European" considerations. Lord Steyn in the House of Lords, for example, was particularly well-versed in the European civil-law tradition and, although he was the only Law Lord not to take up a place in the Supreme Court which replaced the House of Lords, such influences are likely to grow as the English legal professions have continued to insist on coverage of European Community law within legal training and as law schools embrace the "European dimension" as a fertile growth area for research.[22]

None of this "Europeanisation" is likely to impact on Hong Kong, since it has nothing to do with the Hong Kong experience, nor with the common law. Indeed, while English contract rules and factual scenarios become increasingly intertwined with those of Europe, the standard Hong Kong experience is likely to revolve around China and the "joint venture" agreement. While the development of the common law is said to depend upon principles rather than factual scenarios, the facts of cases inevitably affect the principles to be applied, and in this respect Hong Kong will gradually develop a "common law" of its own.

2.2 The Effect of the "Handover" and the Basic Law: Hong Kong's Present System

On 30 June 1997 the transfer of sovereignty over Hong Kong from the United Kingdom to China marked a significant change in the status of Hong Kong. From

---

20. See 2.4 below.
21. Most of the Regulations, updated in 1999, dealt with areas already covered by the Unfair Contract Terms Act 1977, and its Hong Kong equivalent, the Control of Exemption Clauses Ordinance (Cap 71). The Regulations have now been superseded by the Consumer Rights Act, 2015.
22. The impact of "Brexit" (assuming it proceeds) on the "EU Law industry" remains to be seen.

its position as a colony of the United Kingdom it has now become a Special Administrative Region (SAR) of the People's Republic of China (PRC).

The Joint Declaration on the Question of Hong Kong contains the agreement reached between the PRC and the United Kingdom concerning Hong Kong's future. The Joint Declaration, which was ratified by the respective governments in 1985, provided that, from 1 July 1997, Hong Kong was to be restored to Chinese sovereignty. Essentially, the Joint Declaration provides that Hong Kong is to be largely self-governing and that the laws previously in force are to remain unchanged unless they are in conflict with the Basic Law, or unless amended by the HKSAR legislature. This is in accordance with the so-called "one country, two systems" principle. The principles of the Joint Declaration are enshrined in the Basic Law, Hong Kong's post-1997 "mini-constitution". The main features, as regards the post-1997 law in Hong Kong, are as follows.

Article 5 of the Basic Law provides that socialist systems and policies shall not be practised in the HKSAR and that the previous capitalist system and way of life shall remain unchanged for 50 years. The common law legal system governing Hong Kong will therefore remain fundamentally unchanged well into the twenty-first century.

Article 18 of the Basic Law states that:

> The laws in force in the Hong Kong Special Administrative Region shall be this Law, the laws previously in force in Hong Kong as provided for in Article 8 of this Law, and the laws enacted by the legislature of the Region.

Article 8 of the Basic Law states that:

> The laws previously in force in Hong Kong, that is, the common law, rules of equity, ordinances, subordinate legislation and customary law shall be maintained, except for any that contravene this Law, and subject to any amendment by the legislature of the Hong Kong Special Administrative Region.

Article 160 of the Basic Law provides:

> Upon the establishment of the Hong Kong Special Administrative Region, the laws previously in force in Hong Kong shall be adopted as laws of the Region except for those which the Standing Committee of the National People's Congress declares to be in contravention of this Law. If any laws are later discovered to be in contravention of this Law, they shall be amended or cease to have force in accordance with the procedure as prescribed by this Law.

The main sources of Hong Kong contract law today, therefore, are:

1. the Basic Law;
2. local (Hong Kong) legislation;
3. laws passed by the National People's Congress of China on HKSAR matters;

4. common law and equity; and
5. Chinese customary law.

One might also add Hong Kong's Bill of Rights Ordinance (BORO) as a source of law in so far as it lays down requirements which should be met by legislation in Hong Kong.[23] However, few of BORO's sections have relevance to the study of contract with the possible exception of Article 1, which deals with the existence of rights without discrimination, and Article 7, which forbids imprisonment for breach of contract.

The main features of the Basic Law have already been outlined and laws of the PRC to be applied in Hong Kong have little relevance to the study of contract, dealing, as they do, with issues relating to defence, foreign affairs and the national flag and emblems. The major focus, therefore, will be on Hong Kong legislation, common law and equity.

2.2.1 *Hong Kong Legislation*

The HKSAR has the power to make new laws through the legislature.[24] Such laws need to be reported to the Standing Committee of the National People's Congress in order for accurate records to be kept. The law-making body in the SAR is the Legislative Council, which has wide law-making powers except in the areas of defence, foreign affairs and other matters as specified.

The Letters Patent and Royal Instructions ceased to have effect on 30 June 1997. Since that date the United Kingdom can no longer make legislation applying to Hong Kong. Existing Hong Kong legislation based on English provisions continues to be valid subject to amendment or cancellation by the SAR legislature.

Where Hong Kong has passed legislation which is substantially the same as its counterpart in England, amendments to the English legislation will be important, but will only become law if the Legislative Council incorporates the changes into new local legislation or the Hong Kong courts choose to incorporate them as elements of the Hong Kong common law.

Legislation in the area of contract law remains unusual and students will generally discover the relevant contractual rules via the study of decided cases. Indeed, there is some concern that recommendations for legislation made by the Law Reform Commission of Hong Kong, especially in respect of consumer protection, have been ignored.

---

23. BORO's initial requirement that prior inconsistent laws would be implicitly repealed was overturned, post-1997, by the Standing Committee of the National People's Congress on the grounds of incompatibility with the Basic Law.
24. Article 17, Basic Law.

2.2.2 *The Common Law*

It has already been observed that, under Article 8 of the Basic Law, the common law and rules of equity previously in force in Hong Kong before 1997 will continue to apply unless amended by legislation. The Hong Kong Reunification Ordinance[25] reaffirms Article 8. The case of *HKSAR v Ma Wai Kwan David and Others*[26] also confirms that the laws previously in force (including the common law) were adopted as part of the laws of the HKSAR on 1 July 1997. Since these rules of common law and equity were based originally on English law, the historical context needs to be examined if the concept of the common law is to be understood.

The term "common law" has several meanings and the term can mean different things depending on context. For example:

1. common law can be compared with *equity*: here common law means the law originating from cases developed by the English common law courts as contrasted with principles of equity developed originally by the Courts of Chancery;

2. common law can be compared with *legislation* (statutes or Ordinances): here common law means case law and custom as contrasted with law made by legislation;

3. common law can be compared with *civil law*: this refers to a style or type of legal system in which law derives primarily through judicial precedent, expanded by legislation where appropriate. Common law systems include England and Wales, Hong Kong, Malaysia, Singapore, Australia, New Zealand and the United States. In contrast, civil law legal systems are based on written documents such as constitutions, codes, statutes and regulations. Many continental European countries, Middle Eastern states and countries of South America have civil law legal systems in which, for example, the whole law of contract would be based on a single written code;

4. common law can be compared with *local law*: common law in this context refers to the law which is common to the whole of a country, as contrasted with laws that apply only in particular localities or areas.

In the context of that which is to be preserved, post-1997, it is item 3 above which is relevant. The common law system is one based primarily on principles derived from cases as opposed to the civil system based primarily on written codes.

All common law legal systems developed originally from the English legal system. Consequently, it is important to understand some of the history of the English legal system. The English legal system is a common law legal system comprising ancient customs, judicial precedents and enacted laws. It is so called because

---

25. Cap 2601.
26. [1997] 2 HKC 315.

it was made common to the whole of England and Wales after the Norman Conquest in 1066.

As far back as the thirteenth century, an action at common law was commenced by issuing a writ. The writ contained a specific complaint (and these covered limited types of complaint). The person making the complaint was called the plaintiff and the other party, the defendant. Certain procedural rules had to be followed and if, for example, the plaintiff's complaint fell outside the standard wording, no action could begin. This system was used for actions in contract and tort primarily for the purposes of claiming damages. While there have been considerable legal refinements regarding this process, it still forms the basis of a civil (non-criminal) action today.

The most important feature of common law systems is their adherence to a principle of "judicial precedent" by which the "decisions" of the higher courts in previous cases are followed in later cases. Crucially, it is not, strictly, the "decision" which is subsequently followed but the legal reason for that decision, the so-called *ratio decidendi*. The study of any case-law subject, such as contract, requires an understanding on the part of the reader of the terms *ratio decidendi* (the reason for the decision) and *obiter dicta* (things said by the way). Such an understanding is assumed in this book and constant reference is made to *ratio* and *obiter*.[27]

Since July 1997, the principles of common law and equity have continued to apply. As yet there are no examples of major departures from the principles of common law and equity that existed prior to the handover but it is envisaged that Hong Kong will develop more localised versions of some of these principles over time. Local legislation will amend some English-based principles; the Court of Final Appeal will overturn some previously binding English precedents; and English law will develop via cases which may not be followed in Hong Kong. This and increased reference to common law jurisdictions other than those of England and Wales will, over time, produce a Hong Kong common law increasingly divergent from that of England. The indications are, however, that this will not happen quickly.[28]

2.2.3 *Equity as a Source of Law*

The early common law was extremely restrictive and inflexible. The insistence of the common law on the right form of action or no remedy, the sole limited remedy of damages available at common law, and the fact that important parties could defy the common law meant that many people were unable to pursue a legal remedy. In time, people became dissatisfied and turned to the King, who was regarded as the "fountain of justice". The King, unable to deal with all issues personally, delegated this responsibility to his Chancellor. The Lord Chancellor in turn established his own

---

27. For useful explanations of these concepts see P. Wesley-Smith, *An Introduction to the Hong Kong Legal System* (Hong Kong: Oxford University Press, 3rd edn, 1998).
28. See 2.4 below.

court: the Court of Chancery. One of the Chancellor's chief duties was to supervise the issue of all writs, and eventually this task passed to the Chancery Courts and not the common law courts. Over time, these new courts provided different forms of remedy for people seeking solutions to their disputes.

The type of justice achieved by these courts became known as equity. Equity, unlike common law, had no binding rules and each Chancellor was able to give judgment in an issue in a way that satisfied his own conscience. Over a period of time, equity built up its own series of rules and precedents, creating, for example, the law of trusts and the special remedies of injunction and specific performance. As the courts of equity increasingly followed their previous decisions, the procedures of equity became at least as rigid and time-consuming as those of the common law.[29]

2.2.3.1 Common Law and Equity Compared

Traditionally, equity was viewed not as a separate, entire, system of its own but as a means of supplementing the common law, of "filling in the gaps" where the common law was unable or unwilling to provide a remedy.[30] The principle of equity was that where there was a wrong, there should be a remedy. This idea of equity merely "supplementing" the common law can be seen in the principle (in relation to remedies) that equity would not intervene where the common law remedy (damages) is adequate.[31] This limited view of equity's role is now difficult to support, given the recognition of conflict between the systems and the rule that in the case of such conflict the rule of equity shall prevail.[32] This rule implies two separate systems since "this conflict could never occur if substantive fusion had occurred".[33] Recent cases have shown the English courts' readiness to apply principles of equity even where they fly in the face of long-established rules of the common law.[34]

Both systems are similar in that they rely on the doctrine of precedent,[35] and both have been, on occasion, incorporated in statute. For example, common law rules appear in the English Sale of Goods Act 1979, and equitable principles are embodied in the Trustee Act 1925. The Hong Kong equivalents of these two Acts are the Sale of Goods Ordinance (SOGO)[36] and the Trustee Ordinance.[37]

---

29. Charles Dickens, in *Bleak House*, described a (fictitious) interminable Chancery case, *Jarndyce v Jarndyce*. The lengthy procedures of equity came to be described as "Bleak House Chancery".
30. Initially via applications to the Chancellor, the increase in which necessitated a separate Chancellor's Court (Chancery).
31. For fuller discussion, see chapter 15 at 15.2.
32. The *Earl of Oxford's Case* (1615) 1 Ch Rep 1. Statutorily recognised by the Judicature Acts 1873–1875. This is reflected in Hong Kong by s 16(2) of the High Court Ordinance (Cap 4).
33. L. Ma and M. Lower, *Principles of Equity & Trusts in Hong Kong* (Hong Kong: LexisNexis, 2009).
34. See, for example, *Collier v Wright*; discussed in chapter 4 at 4.7.3.5.
35. See 2.2.2.
36. Cap 26.
37. Cap 29.

Perhaps one of the most important differences is that, at common law, the court must grant a remedy to a plaintiff who can prove he has a right, whereas a plaintiff seeking an equitable remedy cannot be sure that it will be granted even if there appears to be a good case. This is because equitable remedies are merely discretionary, the court deciding whether or not to award a remedy.

In exercising this discretion, the court will take into account several rules or maxims. For instance, the previous behaviour of the plaintiff will be significant, so the court will apply the maxim "He who comes to equity must come with clean hands". If you are not acting with a clear conscience when you seek the help of equity, you will not be granted the remedy you seek. Another maxim, "He who seeks Equity must do Equity", means, in simple terms, that a claimant seeking an equitable remedy must be prepared to comply with conditions imposed by the court.[38]

The principles of equity remain important today since, while all courts may now dispense common law and equitable remedies, those of equity remain "discretionary". Equitable remedies such as specific performance and injunction may be important where financial compensation is inappropriate or inadequate, but the remedies are available only at the discretion of the court. The most important creation of equity is the trust, a very important area of legal study in its own right.

The availability of common law and equitable remedies in all courts is a consequence of the Judicature Acts, 1873–1875, by which the two separate court structures were merged. Any claimant may now, for example, seek the equitable remedy of specific performance and/or common law damages as appropriate. Given the differing approaches of the previously separate courts, possible conflicts were resolved by the rule that, in cases of conflict, the rule of equity must prevail.

2.2.4 *Judgments from Other Common Law Jurisdictions*

The Basic Law states that Hong Kong courts may refer to precedents of other common law jurisdictions,[39] though these will not, of course, be binding. We might expect that, given this Basic Law provision, there would be an increase in the number of references to Australian, Canadian and other common law cases, at the expense of English precedents. In practice there is little evidence of such a move and English precedents still form the most significant body of law to which Hong Kong judges refer. This no doubt owes much to the background and training of many of Hong Kong's existing judiciary.[40]

---

38. See also 11.2.4.
39. Article 84.
40. See 2.4.

2.2.5 Chinese Customary Law

Up to 1997 AELO[41] provided that English law would not apply in Hong Kong where it would result in injustice or oppression. In situations where English law was inapplicable and there was no local legislation covering the issue, Chinese law and custom applied, namely the Codes of the Qing dynasty and the customary rules accompanying the Codes which prevailed on 5 April 1843. Although undeniably a source of Hong Kong law, Chinese law and custom is today of very limited application, as local legislation and the rules of common law and equity accommodate most situations. However, the impact of the Codes is still evident in relation to land-holding in the New Territories. At one time it was also significant in aspects of family law and, in particular, marriage, divorce and succession to property. In these areas, common law was originally felt to be inappropriate for local circumstances. As an example, the customary practice of concubinage, though contrary to common law, was recognised as part of Hong Kong law. Nevertheless, reform of the law has eliminated many laws covering such customary practices.

Preservation of the remnants of Chinese customary law as applied in Hong Kong is provided for under Article 8 of the Basic Law. Analogously, "lawful, traditional" rights and interests of the "indigenous" New Territories inhabitants are also preserved under the Basic Law (Article 40). Our Court of Final Appeal, in upholding the iniquitous, discriminatory, and much-abused "small house policy", has decided that "traditional" rights are those dating all the way back . . . to 1990!

2.2.6 Academic (Secondary) Sources

The English common law tradition has always been to treat secondary sources, such as learned text books or practitioners' guides, with great caution. Indeed, it used to be said that a text could never constitute a "source" until its author was dead![42] Hong Kong courts, at least at the lower level, pay much greater heed to secondary sources. It is not uncommon to find a judgment where no cases appear to have been raised in argument or considered by the judge, and where the sole source has been a practitioner's text. A casual reader might believe, for example, "Chitty on Contract" to be a binding Court of Final Appeal contract case! There is considerable danger in this approach, since judicial precedents may be overruled by higher courts or "distinguished" by lower courts which perceive them as unattractive or out of date. Those dissatisfied with the law as reflected in a precedent may appeal in hopes of it being overturned by a higher court; the opinion of a text book writer, which is legally only an opinion, is difficult to appeal against. Given the wealth of judicial authorities

---

41. Cap 88.
42. On the basis that the author might later change his mind.

from the common law world which the Hong Kong courts are free to consider, it is to be hoped that greater use will be made of primary sources in future.

2.3 The Declaratory Theory of Judicial Precedent

The declaratory theory of common law is that judges do not make law; they merely find and apply it. When they state the law, they are declaring not merely what it is but what it always has been. According to the theory, even when a court overrules a long-standing precedent, it is not making new law but stating what it always has been; the previous court merely failed to explain the law correctly. It naturally follows from this that, unlike statutory law, case judgments can operate retrospectively. Even where, for example, a company has made commercial decisions based on an (English) Supreme Court precedent, such company may be adversely affected by a subsequent overruling by a subsequent Supreme Court since, in theory, the company has been acting on the basis of an incorrect assumption as to what the law always has been.

It is clear that the declaratory theory is a "fiction", even if the fiction has been useful in some respects. Most judges today accept that they do, on occasion, change the law or create new law.[43]

The myth of the declaratory theory was officially recognised by the House of Lords in *Kleinwort Benson Ltd v Lincoln City Council*[44] where the court overturned a 200-year-old rule that money paid under a mistake of law was irrecoverable. The court expressed the view that courts do indeed change the law on occasion. Nonetheless, the retrospective nature of their judgments[45] was maintained and indeed emphasised by the majority of the court.

2.3.1 The Declaratory Theory and Hong Kong

Were the declaratory theory still to be recognised in Hong Kong, it would have considerable theoretical, if not practical, significance. The law in force in Hong Kong, post-1997, should be, with some exceptions, that which existed on 30 June 1997. It could therefore be argued "declaratory-wise", that any judicial overruling by the English courts, post-1997, would still be effective in Hong Kong since it would merely "declare" the pre-handover law, albeit retrospectively. While it is true, of course, that *Kleinwort Benson* abandoned the declaratory theory, it is also true that it is a post-handover case. We are thus faced with a conundrum: if post-handover

---

43. See 1.2.2.
44. [1998] 4 All ER 513.
45. The changes are "retrospective" in the sense that they can impact upon, for example, contracts formed on the basis of the law as understood at the time but now changed. Parties to a concluded previous *decision* are unaffected by the change, however, via the principle of *res judicata*.

English judgments have no effect in Hong Kong, *Kleinwort Benson* need not be followed and a declaratory view may be taken, whereby English judgments would still be binding in Hong Kong as a reflection of the true state of the pre-handover law. However, if such a declaratory view is embraced, it should follow that *Kleinwort Benson's* abolition of the declaratory view represents what the law has always been. Declaratory theorists, therefore, should accept that the declaratory view was never part of the English common law!

A further problem is that the Basic Law states that the laws in force on 30 June 1997, will remain in force unless contrary to the Basic Law itself, or overturned by Hong Kong "legislation". There is, therefore, no express provision for the Hong Kong courts to amend the pre-handover laws. This is certainly not the intention of the Basic Law, which establishes a Court of Final Appeal in Hong Kong and declares the right of final adjudication (subject to minor limitations). Nor is it in accord with the general sentiment of the Basic Law that Hong Kong courts may, but need not, refer to judgments of other common law countries. The problem remains, however, that the Basic Law does not expressly authorise the Hong Kong *courts* to amend the laws in force on 30 June 1997. Of course, via a liberal application of the declaratory principle, post-1997 Hong Kong court decisions could be held to reflect the state of Hong Kong law, retrospectively, as at the date of the handover. However, as indicated above, it appears a declaratory approach can no longer be justified. Moreover, even if an argument could be made for preserving the declaratory theory in Hong Kong, post-1997, we would again face the problem that post-1997 English judgments would hold sway since they would more accurately reflect the English pre-handover law which, in general was binding in Hong Kong up to 30 June 1997, and the continuation of which is guaranteed by the Basic Law.

In practice, however, we must recognise that no amount of theorising will affect the political reality—that post-1997 English court judgments will have no binding effect in Hong Kong. A basic tenet of the Basic Law is that Hong Kong courts will generally have the right of final adjudication and that such right can be limited only by the medium of the PRC and not by judicial pronouncements in the former colonial power. There would, indeed, be little point in establishing the Hong Kong Court of Final Appeal to replace the Privy Council as the final court of appeal for Hong Kong were English courts still able to make pronouncements binding in Hong Kong. It is clear that in the pivotal case of *A Solicitor v Law Society of Hong Kong*[46] Hong Kong's Court of Final Appeal had no doubt as to its ability to overturn English precedents, nor of the merely "persuasive" (non-binding) status of post-1997 English decisions.

---

46. [2008] 2 HKC 1.

2.4 The Continuing Influence of English Law in Practice

While the principle that Hong Kong courts are not bound by post-1997 judgments of the English courts is established by the Basic Law, albeit not unproblematically, in practice the views of the English courts still hold great sway in Hong Kong. This is particularly true in the area of contract law where most rules remain grounded in case law rather than statute, and where the pre-handover Hong Kong law showed only minor areas of divergence from that of England. Indeed, were an alien, unfamiliar with Hong Kong's post-1997 legal and constitutional development, to read a typical post-1997 Hong Kong case, he would be hard-pressed to appreciate that things had, supposedly, changed!

Quite simply, Hong Kong judges are referred to, and apply, post-1997 English precedents as a matter of course and the issue of whether such precedents need to be followed is rarely raised. A typical example can be seen in *Bank of China (Hong Kong) Ltd v Wong King Sing & Others*,[47] heard in the Court of First Instance before Recorder Geoffrey Ma SC (as he then was). The case involves the area of undue influence and the situation in which a bank, or other lender, should be put on notice as to the possible undue influence of a husband over his wife. The leading case in England is *Royal Bank of Scotland v Etridge (No 2)*[48] which goes on to explain the steps which a bank should take when placed "on notice", including whether to advise the wife to take independent advice in a private meeting in the absence of her spouse. In the Hong Kong case, Recorder Ma showed exemplary understanding of the complex, and then recent, *Etridge* case, produced an excellent summary thereof, and applied its principles precisely to the case at hand. Nowhere, however, is there any reference to the status of *Etridge*, a post-1997 decision; that the decision should be followed is viewed as unproblematic.

The above example is an entirely typical one. It could be said that, in terms of Hong Kong contract law, it is almost as if 1997 never happened as far as the Hong Kong courts are concerned. Since 1998 the cases "referred to" in Hong Kong contract cases have been overwhelmingly from England, as opposed to elsewhere in the common law world. Moreover, in the secondary sources referred to, text and practitioner books are predominantly English. Where primary and secondary sources are not from England they are generally from Hong Kong relating to areas covered by statutory rules specific to Hong Kong. There is a marked shortage of precedents cited from other common law jurisdictions, despite the apparent aim of the Basic Law to reduce the influence of English precedents *vis-a-vis* those of other common law jurisdictions. This pattern does not appear to have changed significantly in later years, nor is the ratio noticeably different in respect of post-1997 cases "referred to".

---

47. [2002] 1 HKC 83.
48. [2001] 4 All ER 449 and see 11.2.3.

Of course, given that pre-1997 English precedents are usually binding in Hong Kong unless overruled, emphasis on such precedents is unsurprising. What does need explanation is the continued (over-)emphasis on post-1997 English precedents. One explanation is a "realist" one.[49] Hong Kong's judiciary remains dominated by English or English-trained judges, especially at the senior level. Cases cited to the courts by counsel will still reflect the current background of the Hong Kong Bar whose senior members reflect a similar demography. Even junior members of the Bar will have been taught, primarily at the University of Hong Kong, in an institution heavily influenced by English teachers and, more importantly, by English jurisprudence.[50] On this analysis, as Hong Kong's law schools become less "British", and a greater proportion of its fledgling lawyers are trained entirely in Hong Kong, we would expect to see an erosion of English law influence.

An alternative explanation for the continued influence of English precedents is simply the fact that the pre-1997 contract law in Hong Kong was, predominantly English, and that developments in Hong Kong contract law will inevitably draw disproportionately on English jurisprudence, especially at its highest level. In *A Solicitor v Law Society of Hong Kong*,[51] Chief Justice Li stated:

> Bearing in mind that, historically, Hong Kong's legal system originated from the British legal system, decisions of the Privy Council and the House of Lords should of course be treated with great respect. Their persuasive effect would depend on all relevant circumstances, including, in particular, the nature of the issue and the similarity of any statutory or constitutional provision.[52]

On this explanation, it may be some time before Hong Kong is able to develop a truly independent jurisprudence, especially in largely non-statutory areas of law, such as contract.[53]

---

49. That is, put simply, that judicial backgrounds and attitudes affect outcomes (see 1.2.2).
50. Reading lists for many "core" legal subjects in Hong Kong universities remain dominated by English texts; even in areas such as criminal law where the law of the two jurisdictions differ markedly.
51. [2008] 2 HKC 1.
52. Ibid at para 17.
53. Things are slowly changing, however, and in the area of "unconscionability" Hong Kong has been more influenced by Australian jurisprudence than that of England (see chapter 12).

3

Agreement

Overview

As was stated in chapter 1, a contract may be described as a voluntary agreement that the law will enforce.[1] The parties are generally free to negotiate the terms of the contract and, in the absence of a recognised vitiating factor such as misrepresentation or mistake, the courts will not intervene or seek to "rewrite" the agreement.[2]

In order to establish the existence of a contractual agreement, a claimant can adduce oral and/or written evidence and may also be able to rely on the conduct of the parties. While the law requires the element of writing only in exceptional cases,[3] from the perspective of proof it is always advisable to reduce the agreement to writing.

While agreement is a necessary element it is not in itself sufficient; a claimant will also have to show consideration[4] and intention to create legal relations.[5] Where appropriate the claimant must also show that the other party had the legal capacity to make a contract.[6]

Agreement is invariably considered by the courts in terms of a clear offer and an unqualified acceptance thereof. This is taken to be the clearest indication of a meeting of minds or "*consensus ad idem*". Consensus also implies that the "offeror's" intention to be bound should remain unchanged up the time of the "offeree's" acceptance. This, at least, is the traditional and generally accepted view. Lord Denning, a previous Master of the Rolls in England, tended to adopt a more "flexible" approach to the issue of agreement. He expressed the view that courts should look at the overall situation: if the parties have reached agreement on the material terms, a contract

---

1. But see chapter 1 as to qualifications in respect of the words "agreement" and "enforce".
2. See chapters 9–12.
3. See chapter 7.
4. See chapter 4.
5. See chapter 5.
6. See chapter 6.

should be found irrespective of whether "offer and acceptance", in the strict sense, exist. The English House of Lords[7] favoured the traditional approach and it will be an exceptional case in which a contractual agreement is held to exist in the absence of a clear offer and acceptance.

It should be noted that this chapter is concerned with the question of whether a contractual agreement has been reached (that question is, generally, answered by applying an "objective" approach to determine the parties' agreement). The "meaning" of the contract (how it is "construed") will be dealt with in chapter 8.

3.1 The Significance of Agreement

The phenomenon of agreement is significant in that it provides an initial requirement for the very existence of a contract. It is also, as noted, in chapter 1, what distinguishes contractual obligations from tortious ones. Agreement also has the significance of regulating in advance many subsequent developments. The "reasonableness" of an exemption clause, for example, is to be judged, statutorily,[8] as at the time the contract is made. Frustration depends on what circumstances a party should have foreseen at the time the contract was made. A party in breach is liable for those consequences of his breach which should have been seen as likely at the time the contract was made. The question of whether a clause should be viewed as "liquidated damages" depends on the parties' expectations of possible damage at the time the contract was made. In all these cases the key point in time is the time when the agreement was made and the courts should not make determinations based on the advantages of hindsight.[9]

3.2 The Requirement of Offer and Acceptance

A valid contract requires agreement. This is usually defined in terms of a clearly defined "offer" being unambiguously "accepted". Exceptionally, it may be difficult to identify the elements of *offer* and *acceptance*. In *Clarke v Dunraven*,[10] the House of Lords found that there was a valid contract when an entrant in a yacht race collided with another causing the latter's boat to sink. Each entrant in the yacht race had signed an undertaking to abide by the rules of the yacht club but there was no direct contact between the plaintiff and defendant and it was therefore impossible to discern an offer and acceptance between them.

There may be other exceptional cases where it is difficult to identify a strict "offer" and "acceptance". For example, two people may have simultaneously signed a written contract that was prepared for them by a third person. Clearly there would

---

7. Now replaced by the Supreme Court.
8. See Control of Exemption Clauses Ordinance (Cap 71).
9. But see discussion of the *Golden Straits* case in chapters 14 and 15.
10. [1897] AC 59 and see chapter 1.

be an intention to agree shown on both sides but neither party has, strictly, made an "acceptance" of an "offer". In such cases, however, a court would almost certainly uphold the existence of a contract; the written and signed "evidence" of a common intention would suffice. Another example occurs where a person becomes a member of a company by subscribing for shares from the company or acquiring them from an existing shareholder. Here the subscriber becomes bound by contract with all the other members of the company and with the company itself.[11]

In *Gibson v Manchester City Council*[12] Lord Denning MR went as far as to suggest that the requirement of offer and acceptance is not an absolute one. However, Lord Denning's Court of Appeal was overruled on this point by the House of Lords in the same case. Lord Diplock stated that only in "exceptional" circumstances, such as in *Clarke v Dunraven*, should the "conventional" requirement of offer and acceptance be abandoned.

Hong Kong courts have tended to follow the traditional approach. In *Calimpex International v ENZ*[13] the Court of Appeal rejected the plaintiff's submission that a more liberal approach should be adopted in order to find a contract. Godfrey JA said:

> the case for the plaintiff comes down to this: that the court should look at the documents as a whole and the conduct of the parties and see therefrom whether the parties have come to an agreement on everything that was material . . . in my judgment it is still necessary to analyse cases of this commonplace sort by reference to the familiar concepts of offer and acceptance.

However, some support for Lord Denning's more flexible view is to be found in the later English Court of Appeal case of *G Percy Trentham v Archital Luxifer*[14] where Steyn LJ, delivering the leading judgment, stated that a formal offer and acceptance may not be required where a contract has come into being during, and as a result of, performance. A similar approach was taken in the case of *RTS Flexible Systems Ltd v Molkerei Alois Muller GmbH & Co KG (UK Production)*[15] discussed below.[16]

Given, then, that "offer" and "acceptance" are invariably required, how are the two concepts to be identified? Although not statutorily defined, an offer can be described as "an indication of a willingness to be bound on certain terms made with the intention to be bound as soon as the offer is accepted."[17] The intention can be actually expressed or inferred "objectively" by the way in which the "offeror" has spoken or acted. This is determined by asking whether or not a reasonable person

---

11. See s 86 of the Companies Ordinance (Cap 622).
12. [1979] 1 WLR 294.
13. [1994] 1 HKC 191.
14. [1993] 1 LLR 25.
15. [2010] UKSC 14.
16. See 3.4.1.
17. Edwin Peel, *Treitel: The Law of Contract* (London: Sweet & Maxwell, 14th edn, 2015), p 10.

would assume an offer has been made from the words and actions of the "offeror". A simple example is provided in the Privy Council (on appeal from Canada) decision in *Montreal Gas Co v Vasey*[18] where an assertion that, on completion of a five-year contract, "favourable consideration" would be given to an extension, was held *not* to amount to a binding offer to extend. The objective test would prevent a party who has made a clear offer avoiding his contractual obligations by asserting that he did not intend to be bound. Thus, if X offers a car to Y for $100,000 and Y accepts the offer, X cannot escape liability merely by asserting that his actual intention was to offer the car for $200,000.[19] The objective test may, however, be tempered by some element of subjectivity. For example, if there is evidence to show that the offeree knew that the offeror did not intend to be bound, there will be no contract.[20]

The offeror (the person making the offer) is said to be the master of the offer in that he can specify the method by which the offer is to be accepted. For example, the offeror might state that the offer can only be accepted in writing, in which case an oral acceptance would not be effective. The offeror can also withdraw the offer at any time before acceptance unless the offeree has provided some *consideration*[21] to keep the offer open.[22]

3.3 Offer Distinguished from Invitation to Treat

The law draws a distinction between those unequivocal statements of an intention to contract on stated terms (offers) and steps in preliminary negotiations which may encourage the other party to make a definite offer but do not constitute offers in their own right (invitations to treat).

3.3.1 The Importance of the Distinction

Once an offer is accepted a contract exists. It is therefore crucial to distinguish an offer, which is capable of producing a contract, from a mere indication that a party may, perhaps, consider forming a contract but is not yet fully committed. Consider the following examples:

1. I am thinking of selling my car. Would you be interested in buying it?
2. I offer to sell you my (only) car for $50,000.
3. I would be prepared to sell my car for $50,000.

---

18. [1900] AC 595.
19. For a case on similar facts see *Centrovincial Estates plc v Merchant Investors Insurance Co Ltd* [1983] Com LR 158.
20. This is the clear conclusion to be drawn from the *Smith v Hughes* quotation cited in chapter 1 at 1.1. It is supported in the Hong Kong case of *Etacol (Hong Kong) Ltd v Sinomast Ltd (No 2)* [2007] 2 HKC 73.
21. See chapter 4.
22. See *Dickinson v Dodds* (1876) 2 Ch D 463.

The first example is clearly not an offer. The second one is definitely an offer. The third is uncertain: "would be prepared" is rather vague wording and it is not clear to whom the statement is directed.

Contract law, then, separates clear "offers" from preliminary negotiating steps which are not binding. The distinction between the two, though crucial, is not always easy to make as illustrated in *Harvey v Facey*,[23] eventually decided in the Privy Council.

Harvey v Facey

Harvey sent a telegram to Facey asking: "Will you sell us Bumper Hall Pen [a piece of real estate in Jamaica]? Telegraph lowest cash price." Facey replied: "Lowest price for Bumper Hall Pen £900". Harvey then replied by telegram: "We agree to buy Bumper Hall Pen for the sum of £900 asked by you." Facey refused to sell and the Privy Council held that he was not bound. No valid contract had been formed. The first telegram from Harvey had asked two questions and Facey had answered only the second one. He had made no promise—express or implied—to sell. In other words, his reply was an invitation to treat and not an offer.

The court dismissed the suggestion that Facey had made a clear promise of his willingness to sell. Lord Morris said:

> Their Lordships are of the opinion that the mere statement of the lowest price at which the vendor would sell contains no implied contract to sell at that price to the person making the inquiry.

The court was also perhaps influenced by the fact that this case concerned the sale of real property and, therefore, were reluctant to find a binding contract without strong cogent evidence to that effect.[24]

Another instructive example is *Gibson v Manchester City Council*,[25] a case with a strong political element.

Gibson v Manchester City Council

The Conservative ruling party of Manchester City Council had a policy of selling council houses to existing tenants. The Labour party then gained control of the Council after elections and repealed the selling policy. However, it agreed to honour all previously completed agreements. Mr Gibson, like a number of other tenants, appeared to be still in the negotiating stage. He had been given a letter from the treasurer of the Council stating that the Council "may be prepared to sell at a price

---

23. [1893] AC 552.
24. At that time a contract for the sale of land could be effected by an exchange of correspondence. The situation is unchanged in Hong Kong today (see s 3 of the Conveyancing and Property Ordinance (Cap 219)). In England, however, a written contract is now required.
25. [1979] 1 WLR 294.

of £2,725 less 20% freehold" and that the letter was "not a firm offer of a mortgage". Mr Gibson was invited to make a formal application to purchase the house and to fill in a form to do so. He completed and returned the form but left the price blank because repairs needed to be done on the house. The Council said they had taken the state of repairs into account when fixing the price. Mr Gibson then asked them to process his application.

Lord Denning MR's Court of Appeal held there was a binding contract with Gibson which must be honoured. Lord Denning thought that the traditional approach should not be applied too rigidly but, that one ought to look at the conduct of the parties and see whether the parties have come to an agreement on everything that was material. Using his approach, he concluded that there was a binding contract between the parties. This was rejected, on appeal, by the House of Lords which preferred the traditional approach.

Lord Diplock conceded that there were

certain types of contract, though I think they are exceptional, which do not fit easily into the normal analysis of a contract as being constituted by offer and acceptance but a contract alleged to have been made by an exchange of correspondence is not one of these.

The key finding of the House of Lords was that the words "may be prepared to sell" did not constitute an offer from the Council and so no binding contract had yet been formed. *Gibson* illustrates the difficulty of determining when preliminary negotiations have ended and a definite offer has been made. A case to contrast with *Gibson* is *Storer v Manchester City Council*[26] where the court held that a contract had been concluded as negotiations had proceeded beyond the stage reached in *Gibson* although an exchange of contracts had not yet occurred.

In distinguishing between an offer and an invitation to treat much will depend on the intention of the offeror in the individual case but the courts have reached decisions in some areas which have attained the status of binding rules.

3.3.2 Display of Goods in a Shop Window

The courts have held that a shop display, even with a price ticket attached to the goods, is only an invitation to treat. *Pharmaceutical Society of Great Britain v Boots Cash Chemists (Southern) Limited*[27] concerned the plaintiff's assertion that the defendants were operating illegally what was then a novel self-service store. The factual scenario was that the customer was allowed to select goods from the shelves and take them to the cash desk. By the desk was a registered pharmacist who could prevent the removal of certain drugs from the store. The defendants were alleged to

---

26. [1974] 1 WLR 1403.
27. [1953] 2 WLR 427.

be in breach of an English statute[28] which said there must be a registered pharmacist to "supervise sale". The main issue in the case was whether the display of goods on the shelves of the self-service store was an offer or an invitation to treat. If the display was an offer, then the taking of the goods from the shelf by the customer and putting them in his basket would, it was alleged, constitute an acceptance. The sale would, therefore, take place without the requisite supervision and so an offence would be committed under the statute. The court held that the display amounted only to an invitation to treat.

The court reasoned that if the plaintiff was correct the customer, once he had placed the goods in his basket, could not then change his mind and substitute the goods for other goods without being liable to pay for the goods originally chosen. This would be commercially disastrous for self-service stores as customers would be too afraid to patronise them. However, this part of the court's reasoning is questionable. It would be possible to hold that a self-service shop is making an offer but to assert that the customer only accepts same at check-out by, for example, proffering cash or credit card. This, indeed, was the finding in the later English case of *Debenhams Retail Plc v Commissioners of Customs and Excise*[29] where it was held that a customer in a supermarket completed acceptance by clicking the "accept" button at check-out. The court emphasised, however, that the precise point at which acceptance takes place depends on the individual circumstances of the case.

A further explanation of the "invitation only" finding was that the shopkeeper should have the right to refuse to sell the goods to a customer since shops are, theoretically, places to bargain, although Somervell LJ conceded:

> The assistant in 999 times out of 1,000 says: 'That is all right.' and the money passes and the transaction is completed.

In other words, the law does not conform to commercial reality! A similar issue arose in *Fisher v Bell*,[30] where it was held that a display of a flick-knife in a shop window was an invitation to treat and, therefore, did not amount to an "offer to sell" such a knife. If the display had been construed as an offer the shopkeeper would have guilty of an offence.[31] The main rationale for the "only an invitation" approach by the English courts, then, is the outdated notion that shops are places to "haggle" over price, a notion more suited to market trading than to modern, supermarket practices. The notion that the checkout operative at "ParknShop" may be prepared to reduce the price of goods in response to the customer's entreaties is, of course, risible (as Somervell LJ conceded in the English context). An attempt by Magistrate Kevin

---

28. Section 18 of the Pharmacy and Poisons Act 1933.
29. [2004] EWHC 1540.
30. [1961] 1 QB 394.
31. Under the Restriction of Offensive Weapons Act 1959.

Browne[32] to bring this area of Hong Kong law into the 21st century was defeated in the following case.

HKSAR v Wan Hon Sik[33]

The defendant shopkeeper, by his own admission, was in possession of pirated VCDs and was "introducing" them to Japanese tourists. He was charged with one count of offering them for sale. The prosecution was successful in the Magistrate's Court, where Magistrate Browne determined that there was no Hong Kong jurisprudence on *Fisher v Bell* lines and that the English contract law principles were inapplicable in the context of Hong Kong criminal law. The conviction was overturned on appeal to the Court of First Instance, where Deputy Judge Longley preferred to follow the English approach on the basis that, since the relevant legislation referred elsewhere to "exposing" discs for sale, it must have been intended that mere display would not constitute an "offer for sale". Deputy Judge Longley concluded:

> The learned Magistrate could not therefore, simply on the basis that they were on display, find that the appellant was offering the infringing discs for sale.

The case highlights the reluctance of Hong Kong courts to seek to develop a "local" jurisprudence, and the continued dominance of English decisions, even post-1997. It should be pointed out, however, that both in England and Hong Kong circumstances may defeat the "shop-haggling" argument. Were a store, for example, to promise to sell a single, identified item at a specific (low) price to the first person entering the store on Monday morning, it would be difficult to argue that this was merely an invitation to treat.

The justification of the "only an invitation" approach on the basis of shops as places to bargain implies that different rules could apply to modern, internet "shopping". Since the computer cannot "haggle" it might be assumed that when the customer clicks the "I accept" button he is, indeed, accepting an internet "offer" and thereby concluding a contract. This view was endorsed some time ago by Lord Denning in respect of ticket machines. Since the machine cannot bargain, Lord Denning held, a contract is concluded when the customer puts his money into the machine in response to its "offer".[34] An analogous "machine" situation may arise in the case of petrol retailing. English authorities support the view that where the customer's car is filled by a petrol station employee, the customer offers to buy; such offer being accepted when the petrol is inserted.[35] Conversely, in self-service stations, the machine apparently makes the offer which the customer accepts by

---

32. Subsequently District Court Judge.
33. [2001] 3 HKLRD 283.
34. See *Thornton v Shoe Lane Parking* discussed at 8.6.1.2.
35. See *Re Charge Card Services* [1989] Ch 497.

taking the petrol.[36] Hong Kong current practice is still generally of the "employee serves" variety. However, one important distinction between the physical shop and the internet is the "finite supply" principle. An internet advertiser might have only a limited supply and should not be regarded as making an offer to all with the potential for multiple breaches. This approach appears to have been favoured (at the High Court stage) in the persuasive (non-binding) but significant Singapore case of *Chwee Kin Keong v Digilandmall.com Pte Ltd*[37] discussed below.[38] Conversely, and perhaps compellingly, internet advertisers frequently encourage the notion of their "offer" being accepted by the customer's pressing of the "agree" button. Moreover, since such "click" acceptance can only be effected while the "offer" remains displayed, the efficient advertiser has the option of removing the advertisement as soon as stocks are exhausted. This is different from the "limited stock" argument applied to newspaper or journal advertisements discussed below.[39] Indeed, this distinction was recognised in the electronic offer and acceptance case of *Pereira Fernandes SA v Mehta*.[40] By this logic, an internet advertisement should be viewed, in appropriate circumstances, as an offer capable of acceptance except in clear cases of the "offeree" taking advantage of a clear mistake by the advertiser (as in *Chwee Kin Keong*).

While section 37 of the Electronic Transactions Ordinance[41] deals with "formation" and the validity of electronic agreements, it sheds no light on the extent to which an electronic advertisement may be viewed as a binding offer. Finally, it should be noted that the "right" of a seller to refuse to sell to a customer (one explanation for the "only an invitation" approach), is no longer an absolute one as a result of legislative change. In Hong Kong, for example, the Sex Discrimination Ordinance,[42] Disability Discrimination Ordinance[43] and Race Discrimination Ordinance[44] prevent a shopkeeper from refusing to sell goods or services to a person because of that person's gender, disability or race.

3.3.3 Auctions

The advertisement of an auction, or the display of lots at an auction, is an invitation to treat. It is the bidder who makes the offer, which the auctioneer can accept

---

36. On the *Thornton* principle.
37. [2004] 2 SLR 594.
38. See 10.5.1 where the case is considered in the context of mistake.
39. See *Partridge v Crittenden* discussed at 3.3.4 below.
40. [2006] 2 All ER 891. The agreement failed on the ground of lack of necessary "formality" (cf chapter 7).
41. Cap 553.
42. Cap 480.
43. Cap 487.
44. Cap 602.

or reject: *Payne v Cave*.[45] Acceptance would occur on the fall of the hammer. This common law rule is incorporated in section 60(2) of the Sale of Goods Ordinance (SOGO)[46] which states:

> A sale by auction is complete when the auctioneer announces its completion by the fall of the hammer, or in other customary manner; and until the announcement is made any bidder may retract his bid.

Since the contract of sale is not concluded until the bidder's offer is accepted, difficulties arise with auctions advertised as "without reserve". In *Warlow v Harrison*,[47] the defendant, an auctioneer, advertised horses for sale without reserve. The plaintiff was the highest bona fide bidder for a horse but the owner unfairly made a higher bid. The plaintiff tendered his bid to the auctioneer and claimed the horse. The auctioneer refused and the plaintiff sued. He lost on a technicality but the court said, *obiter*, that if he had so claimed he could have received damages for breach of an implied promise to sell to the highest bidder.

In other words, the contract of sale is not complete before the fall of the hammer *but* the highest bidder whose bid is refused may, in "without reserve" cases, sue the auctioneer on his separate implied promise to sell to the highest bidder. This *obiter* view in *Warlow* has subsequently been approved by the English Court of Appeal in *Barry v Heathcote Ball & Co (Commercial Auctions) Ltd*.[48]

Where an auctioneer wrongly describes an auction as "without reserve", or otherwise accepts a highest bid which does not meet the owner's reserve, there would be no sale because there is no authority to sell *but* the auctioneer would be liable to pay damages to the disappointed bidder.[49] This principle has been emphatically confirmed in the case of *Hoie Sook Fong & Another v Ismail Halima & Another*[50] where Sakhrani J stated:

> An agent, including an auctioneer, who sells property without or in excess of authority will be liable to the purchaser in damages for breach of the implied warranty (of authority) . . .
>
> . . . if the authority of the auctioneer to sell a property has in fact been revoked by the vendor before the auction, the auctioneer can give the highest bidder no right to the property, even though the bidder is unaware of the revocation.
>
> . . . where a reserve price has been fixed by the vendor and the sale is expressed to be subject to a reserve, the auctioneer has no authority to sell below it.[51]

---

45. (1789) 100 ER 502, [1775-1802] All ER Rep 492.
46. Cap 26.
47. (1859) 1 LT 211, [1843-60] All ER Rep 620.
48. [2001] 1 All ER 944.
49. See *Kwok Lai Ting v Hughes & Hough* (1922) 17 HKLR 51.
50. [2009] 1 HKC 326.
51. At paras 21–23.

Hong Kong also has legislation covering sale of land by auctions[52] and prohibiting various fraudulent practices relating to auction sales.[53]

3.3.4 Advertisements: Bilateral and Unilateral Contracts

Contracts can "bilateral" or "unilateral" in nature. The distinction is important in the offer and acceptance context since the courts approach each differently.

A "bilateral" (two-sided) contract is a promise in exchange for another promise such that both parties have contractual obligations. Common examples include contracts for the sale of goods and services. One party, the seller, promises to provide the goods or services while the other the party promises to pay for such goods or services. As will be explained in chapter 4, the consideration for such a contract is termed "executory" meaning that binding promises have been exchanged but the parties have yet to execute consideration.

A "unilateral" (one-sided) contract occurs when one party makes a promise of "reward" on performance of some action. The offer is accepted by the performance of the requested action. The contract is one-sided because the offeror is required to pay the reward if the act is performed *but* no one is legally obliged to perform, or even attempt, the act. If I promise to pay $10,000 to any person who swims across Hong Kong Harbour, no one is obliged to complete, or even attempt, the swim. However, any person who knows about this offer may complete the act and claim the reward. There is no "acceptance" until the act is complete and consideration is "executed".[54]

Advertisements of a bilateral nature are generally only invitations to treat; advertisements of a unilateral nature are more likely to be regarded as offers. The distinction is well illustrated by considering the two cases of *Carlill v Carbolic Smoke Ball Company*[55] (perhaps the most famous of all English contract cases) and *Partridge v Crittenden*.[56]

Carlill v Carbolic Smoke Ball Company

The defendants advertised their product, the carbolic smoke ball, a supposed preventative and cure for influenza. The defendants promised that any person who used their product as directed for two weeks and still caught influenza would be paid £100 in compensation. The advertisement stated: "£1,000 is deposited with the Alliance Bank, Regent Street, showing our sincerity in the matter." Mrs Carlill, on the faith of the advertisement, bought one of the balls, used it as directed and then contracted

---

52. Sale of Land by Auction Ordinance (Cap 27).
53. Mock Auctions Ordinance (Cap 255).
54. See 4.1.3.
55. [1893] 1 QB 256.
56. [1968] 1 WLR 1204.

influenza. She sued for the promised compensation when the defendants refused to pay. The action was successful.

The crucial question before the court was whether the advertisement was an offer or an invitation to treat. The defendants mounted a number of arguments including that, as there was no time limit fixed for the catching of the influenza, the terms were too vague to be treated as a definite offer. The court did not accept this argument and said that the time could be fixed as being either during the use of the ball or during the prevalence of the influenza epidemic or a reasonable time after using the ball. The defendants also contended that the advertisement was in the nature of a "puff" or a proclamation[57] rather than a promise or offer intended to mature into a contract when accepted. Bowen LJ said:

> It seems to me that in order to arrive at a right conclusion we must read this adver-tisement in its plain meaning, as the public would understand it. It was intended to be issued to the public and to be read by the public. How would an ordinary person reading this document construe it? . . . Was it intended that the £100 should, if the conditions were fulfilled, be paid? The advertisement says that £1,000 is lodged at the bank for the purpose. Therefore, it cannot be said that the statement that £100 would be paid was intended to be a mere puff. I think it was intended to be under-stood by the public as an offer which was to be acted upon.

So, in *Carlill*, the court held that the advertisement was an offer, giving rise to a unilateral contract. A similar unilateral contract was found in *Bowerman v Association of British Travel Agents (ABTA)*[58] where a promise by the defendants to reimburse any customer booking a holiday with an ABTA member which failed financially, before the holiday, was held to be binding.[59] "Bilateral" advertisements are far more likely to be viewed as merely invitations to treat.

Partridge v Crittenden

The appellant inserted a notice in a periodical which read: "Bramblefinch cocks and hens, 25s each." If this was construed as an offer the seller would be liable to be charged with an offence under the Protection of Birds Act 1954. The court held that there had been no offer for sale.

In explaining the decision Lord Parker said:

> I think that when one is dealing with advertisements and circulars, unless they indeed come from manufacturers, there is business sense in their being construed as invitations to treat and not offers for sale.

---

57. This defence was accepted, albeit *obiter*, in the case of *Koo Ming Kown (or Kwon) v Next Media & Others* [2009] 2 HKC 214.

58. [1995] NLJ 1815.

59. An apparent "offer to the world" was not upheld in the Hong Kong case *Koo Ming Kown* (n 57 above) on the basis that it was insufficiently certain.

The "business sense" referred to by Lord Parker is that the suppliers only have a limited amount of stock and if the advertisement were an offer then the number of potential offerees might make it impossible for the seller to satisfy the demand. The supplier would then be in breach of contract if he could not supply the goods. A similar decision was reached in *Grainger v Gough*[60] where the court held that the circulation of a price list did not amount to an offer. These cases lend support to the view that internet "offers" only constitute invitations to treat.[61]

So, in the unilateral *Carlill* case, the advertisement constituted an offer (to the world at large) while in *Partridge* and *Grainger*, bilateral situations, the court found the advertisement to constitute only an invitation to treat.

3.3.5 Requests for Tenders

A request for businesses to submit tenders—the price at which, for example, they are prepared to provide services or to pay for shares—is only an invitation to treat *unless* it is coupled with a promise to accept the lowest, or the highest, tender. The reason for this is that, while the price is an important term of any contract, the choice of a supplier or purchaser may depend on many other considerations. In *Spencer v Harding*[62] the defendant sent a circular which said "we are instructed to offer to the wholesale trade for sale by tender" certain stock-in-trade. The plaintiff made the highest offer, which the defendants rejected. The plaintiffs then sued for breach of contract. The court held that the circular was only an invitation to treat.

A more recent tender illustration is provided by *Harvela Investments Ltd v Royal Trust Co of Canada Ltd.*[63] Here, the first defendants agreed to sell shares to the highest bidder, thus constituting an offer. The bidding was to be in secret. The plaintiffs bid $2,175,000. The second defendants bid $2,100,000 or $100,000 in excess of any other offer (a "referential" bid as it was by reference to another bid). The first defendants felt obliged to take the second defendants' bid as it was higher. The plaintiffs contended that their "non-referential" bid should have been accepted. The House of Lords upheld the plaintiffs' contention. Curiously, therefore, the question was not whether there was an offer but which of the parties had legally accepted the offer.

Lord Templeman gave a number of reasons in support of the court's decision. One was that allowing referential bids could result in the sale being aborted as all the bidders may have made such a type of bid. A second reason was that, if referential bids were permissible, there was a possibility, which in fact occurred, that one bidder would never have an opportunity to buy.

---

60. [1896] AC 325.
61. See 3.3.2 above.
62. (1870) LR 5 CP 561.
63. [1985] 3 WLR 276.

In *Lobley Co Ltd & Another v Tsang Yuk Kiu*,[64] the Privy Council, on appeal from Hong Kong, applied the *Harvela* principles to determine that a party who had clearly indicated that the highest tender would be accepted was in breach of contract in not accepting such highest tender.

Although, in the absence of a promise to the contrary, there is no requirement to accept the best tender, where clear instructions are given as to the form and submission date of tenders, there may be an obligation to give "due consideration" to those tenders conforming with instructions. This was the decision of the English Court of Appeal in the following case.

Blackpool and Fylde Aeroclub Ltd v Blackpool Borough Council[65]

The defendants wrote to the plaintiffs and six others inviting tenders, specifying procedures for submitting tenders and fixing a clear deadline of 12 noon on 17 March 1983, after which no tenders would be accepted. The plaintiffs submitted their tender to the defendants' letter box at 11 am on the deadline date. However, the letter box was not cleared by council staff at 12 noon as it should have been. The club's tender was recorded as having been received late and was not considered. The club sued for breach of an alleged collateral contract that a tender received by the deadline would be considered. The action succeeded in the English Court of Appeal.

Bingham LJ was sympathetic to the invitee, who is often put to much trouble and expense in preparing a tender, but acknowledged that the tendering procedure is heavily weighted in favour of the invitor and that the invitor need not give reasons to justify his acceptance or rejection of any tender received. However, he said:

> the invitee is in my judgment protected at least to this extent: if he submits a conforming tender before the deadline he is entitled, not as a matter of mere expectation but of contractual right, to be sure that his tender will after the deadline be opened and considered in conjunction with all other conforming tenders or at least that his tender will be considered if others are.

He went on to conclude that, to the limited extent set out above, the council's invitation to tender was an offer, and the club's submission of a timely and conforming tender an acceptance. So, even though the council had not promised to accept the highest tender, it was implied that they would at least consider all tenders which conformed with the requirements.

The same "due consideration" approach was upheld by the Hong Kong courts in *City University of Hong Kong v Blue Cross (Asia-Pacific) Insurance Ltd*,[66] in which

---

64. [1997] 2 HKC 442.
65. [1990] 1 WLR 1195.
66. [2001] 1 HKC 463.

it was held that the plaintiffs had an implied duty to give due consideration to the defendants' timely tender.[67]

3.4 The Nature of Acceptance

Acceptance may be defined as a final and unqualified assent to the terms of an offer.[68] The key requirements are that the acceptance must "match" the offer fully and that no conditions or qualifications be attached. As with "offer", the courts adopt an "objective" approach. For example, the auctioneer who intentionally brings down the hammer will not be permitted to argue that he did not intend to accept the bidder's offer.

3.4.1 Acceptances Made "Subject to Contract"

On the basis of the above definition, an acceptance made "subject to contract" is nearly always insufficient to conclude a contract as it is not unqualified and is still subject to a further condition being met.

Attorney General and Another v Humphreys Estate (Queen's Garden) Ltd[69]

The Hong Kong government and a local property company entered into an agreement in principle to enter into a land exchange under which the company would obtain a grant of land in exchange for a number of apartments in a company development. The apartments were to be used as government accommodation. The agreement was expressed to be "subject to contract". The court noted that the government was fully aware and intended that either party could at any time and without any reason withdraw from the agreement in principle. The government acted to their detriment by taking possession of the flats, fitting them out and demolishing the former government quarters. When the company refused to transfer the apartments, the government sued. The action failed in the Privy Council.

In expressing the view of the court, Lord Templeman said:[70]

> In the present case the government acted in the hope that a voluntary agreement in principle expressly made "subject to contract" and therefore not binding would eventually be followed by the achievement of legal relationships in the form of grants and transfers of property. It is possible but unlikely that in circumstances at

---

67. In this case due consideration was given and the defendant's lowest tender "accepted". They were able to escape the consequences of their ultra-low tender, however, since the contract required City University to contact any party which may have made a mistake and confirm its willingness to proceed.
68. Treitel (n 17 above) at p 19.
69. [1987] HKLR 427.
70. Ibid at 435.

present unforeseeable a party to negotiations set out in a document expressed to be "subject to contract" would be able to satisfy the court that the parties had subsequently agreed to convert the document into a contract or that some form of estoppel had arisen to prevent both parties from refusing to proceed with the transaction envisaged by the document. But in the present case the government chose to begin and elected to continue on terms that either party might suffer a change of mind and withdraw.

A similar result occurred in relation to a lease of property in *Darton Ltd v Hong Kong Island Development Ltd*.[71] The issue here was that while the letter sent by the defendant offering to let the property to the plaintiff, was made "subject to contract", it *also* contained a clause under which the plaintiff was required to pay a deposit which was non-refundable if the plaintiff did not proceed to execute the formal tenancy agreement. This clause was "expressly *not* subject to contract". The plaintiff signed the letter and paid the deposit but failed to enter into a formal agreement. The defendant retained the deposit and the plaintiff brought proceedings seeking its return. At issue on appeal was whether the deposit was recoverable. The defendant argued that a term was necessarily implied[72] in the letter that the defendant forbear from leasing the premises to other prospective tenants, and this, coupled with its actual forbearance, constituted sufficient consideration[73] for the deposit. The Hong Kong Court of Appeal held that the deposit was recoverable. The fact that the agreement referred to an offer being made on a "subject to contract" basis was a clear indication that the parties meant the agreement to be subject to, and dependent on, a formal contract being prepared; it was not a binding agreement. The addition of the "non-refundable deposit" clause made no difference: a provision as to the disposition of the deposit, if contractual, had to be supported by consideration and no consideration had been provided by the defendant. Furthermore, the court held that there was no implied term that the defendant forbear.

However, the presumption that an agreement "subject to contract" is never binding since it remains conditional is not an irrebuttable one. In *Alpenstow Ltd & Another v Regalian Properties Plc*,[74] where a "subject to contract" agreement was held binding, Nourse J stated:

the words "subject to contract" have a clear prima facie meaning, being in themselves merely conditional. But there might be a very strong and exceptional context which would induce the court not to give them that meaning in a particular case.

Such an exceptional case might arise where the parties have acted upon the assumption that a binding agreement is in place. Thus, in *RTS Flexible Systems Ltd*

---

71. [2001] 3 HKLRD 479 (leave to appeal to the CFA denied: [2002] 1 HKLRD 145).
72. See 8.4.
73. See chapter 4.
74. [1985] 2 All ER 545.

v Molkerei Alois Muller Gmbh & Co KG the English Supreme Court, reversing the Court of Appeal's decision, upheld a contract, made "subject to contract", where all important terms had been agreed, performance had occurred and partial payment had been made.[75] More recently, the English courts have endorsed the notion that "subject to contract" will have its normal "still conditional" meaning *unless* it is clear that *both* parties have expressly or implicitly agreed that such meaning shall be "expunged".[76] The Hong Kong courts have, likewise, found (rare) exceptions to the proposition that a "subject to contract" agreement is always conditional and non-binding.[77]

3.4.2 Conditional and Provisional Agreements

In practice, the word "conditional" means there is no final acceptance while the word "provisional" means there will be a contract until such time as the parties replace it with a more formal one.

This issue often occurs in Hong Kong with the sale and purchase of land. In most cases the parties enter into a provisional sale and purchase agreement which is then replaced by a formal agreement for sale and purchase. In *Yiu Yau Ping v Fong Yee Lan*,[78] the Hong Kong Court of Appeal upheld a provisional agreement for the sale and purchase of a flat rejecting the argument that there had been no formal agreement. Nazareth JA said:[79]

> That a provisional agreement calls for a formal agreement that will supersede it, is not inconsistent with the former being a binding agreement.

The same issue came before the same judge in *Au Wing Cheung v Roseric Ltd*.[80] Here Nazareth JA confirmed that a provisional agreement was a binding contract. He went further and commented on negotiations made between the time the provisional agreement was signed and when the formal agreement was executed by saying that there would be good reason for the plaintiff to ensure that changes or additions put forward for consideration were not taken as agreed or as altering the provisional agreement except in the formal context of the final (formal) contract.

---

75. [2010] 3 All ER 1.
76. See *Astra Asset Management UK Ltd v The Co-operative Bank plc* [2019] EWHC 897 (Comm); *Joanne Properties Ltd v Moneything Capital Ltd & Another* [2020] EWCA Civ 1541.
77. Cf *Wong Lai Ha v Chung Sau Wah & Others* [1994] 2 HKC 646.
78. [1992] 2 HKLR 167.
79. Ibid at 174.
80. [1992] 1 HKC 149.

3.4.3 Acceptance and Counter-Offer

A purported acceptance which does not precisely correspond with the offer is not an acceptance as it would not amount to an "unqualified assent to the terms of the offer". The introduction of new terms by the offeree will amount to a "counter-offer" which the original offeror may accept or reject. In common parlance the counter-offer "kills the offer" and effectively becomes the offer "on the table".[81] The contrasting English cases of *Hyde v Wrench*[82] and *Stevenson v McLean*[83] illustrate the difference between an acceptance and a counter-offer. In *Hyde*, the defendant offered to sell land to the plaintiff for £1,000. The plaintiff offered £950, which the defendant refused. The plaintiff then said he would pay £1,000 and claimed the estate. However, it was held that there was no binding contract as the plaintiff had rejected the offer previously made by the defendant. There would have needed to be acceptance of the counter-offer of £950 before there would be a binding contract between the parties. The *Hyde v Wrench* approach was adopted in the Hong Kong case of *Capacious Investments Ltd v Secretary of Justice*,[84] where a purported "acceptance" of a Hong Kong government offer of compensation for the acquisition of the plaintiffs' land was coupled with additional demands. It was held that these amounted to a counter-offer which brought the original offer to an end. Conversely, in *Stevenson*, the defendant offered to sell warrants for iron for forward delivery at 40s net cash. The plaintiff then replied: "Please wire whether you would accept forty for delivery over two months, or if not, longest limit you would give." The court held that the plaintiff's reply was only a mere enquiry which did not terminate the offer.

The difference between the two cases is that, in the view of the courts, the *Hyde* plaintiff was initially rejecting the original offer, by substituting alternative terms, while in *Stevenson* he was saying "I accept; I'd prefer time to pay but, if this is not acceptable, I'll comply fully with your offer." In practice the distinction is likely to be a fine one in many cases. A similarly fine distinction may be drawn between the imposition of "conditions" on acceptance (which would render an "acceptance" ineffective) and a requirement that the offeror comply with normal legal requirements. Thus, in *Yau Fook Hong Company Ltd v Attorney General (Hong Kong)*[85] the UK Privy Council (on appeal from Hong Kong) upheld a contract in which the Hong Kong government accepted the appellant's offer to give up properties to offset debts of its parent company (Chinachem). The government required that the appellants must show relevant proof of title of these properties; but such a requirement was not seen as a "conditional" or "counter" offer.

---

81. See *Lee Siu Fong Mary v Ngai Yee Chai* [2006] 1 HKC 157.
82. (1840) 3 Beav 334.
83. (1880) 5 QBD 346.
84. [2001] 1 HKC 219. And see *Combi (Singapore) Pte Ltd v Winston Camera & Radio Co Ltd* [1988] HKC 151; *Shun Ho Energy Development Co Ltd v Golden Crown Industries Ltd* [2015] HKCU 1484.
85. [1987] UKPC 41.

It appears in this context that the courts will not countenance a "partial" acceptance. In *Cathay Pacific Airways Ltd v Hong Kong Air Cargo Terminals Ltd*,[86] the parties attempted to conclude a formal contract. The defendants drafted a proposal with an arbitration clause and the plaintiffs responded with a differently worded proposal which also had an arbitration clause. No formal offer and acceptance was ever concluded but the parties "performed" despite this. On a subsequent dispute the defendants argued that each party had agreed to arbitration. The court's view was that there was no such agreement since each party had submitted its arbitration proposal as part of proposals which had never been finally agreed, despite the fact that both parties had suggested arbitration to settle disputes.

3.4.4 The Battle of the Forms

Where an acceptance is said to be "on our usual terms" which do not correspond with the offer, this will, again be a counter-offer. Such a position may give rise to what has been called a "battle of the forms". This phrase refers to situations in which two parties keep exchanging counter-offers with each party trying to impose its own standard terms or standard form contract. There would appear to be no contract formed as no valid acceptance is made. However, what may happen in practice is that there is some "performance", such as the supply of goods, even though there does not yet appear to be a binding contract. If a dispute arises between the parties over the terms at some later date the court may have to determine what the terms of the transaction are. One way of resolving such disputes is the "last shot" rule which provides that whichever form was sent last is the final counter-offer which was then impliedly accepted when the goods were supplied in response.

Sometimes a party will attempt to avoid the "last shot" rule by inserting a clause in its standard form to the effect that its terms shall prevail over any other party's standard form. However, this will not always be successful as shown in the following.

Butler Machine Tool Ltd v Ex-Cell-O-Corp (England) Ltd[87]

The sellers offered to sell a machine tool to the buyers for £75,535 with delivery in ten months. This offer included a price variation clause. The buyers replied "accepting" the offer but on their own standard form which made no provision for a price variation. The buyers' standard form had a tear off strip which the sellers returned and which contained the wording "we accept your order on the terms and conditions thereon". When the sellers returned the slip they also enclosed a letter stating that the buyer's order was entered into in accordance with the original offer. The sellers eventually delivered the machine but claimed an extra £2,892 under the price variation clause. The buyers refused to pay. The English Court of Appeal held that the

---

86. [2002] 2 HKC 193.
87. [1979] 1 All ER 965.

contract had been concluded on the buyer's terms and conditions and so the sellers were not entitled to the extra payment. The return of the acknowledgement slip amounted to an acceptance of the buyer's counter-offer and the attempt to resurrect the sellers' standard form terms was ineffective.

While the sending of the tear-off slip in *Butler* provided the basis for a relatively straightforward analysis of the situation using the traditional approach of offer and acceptance, this will not always be the case and Lord Denning took the opportunity to press for other, more radical, methods of solving the "battle of the forms" problem, such as leaving it to the courts to imply the terms where the terms asserted by the two parties are in conflict. Such a suggestion, involving the "rewriting" of the contract by the courts, has not received judicial support.[88]

What *Butler* does support, uncontentiously, is the notion that a court is far more likely to find a contract where significant performance has taken place. This is consistent, of course, with Lord Steyn's view (in the *Archital Luxifer* case) that a contract may come into existence, without offer and acceptance, "during, and as a result of, performance".[89]

A further English "battle of the forms" occurs in the case of *Balmoral Group Ltd v Borealis*[90] where it was held in the High Court that a supplier's terms would be the operative ones because although they had been initially superseded by the buyer's conditions, the latter had been merely referred to and this "in poor typescript". It was felt that the supplier was justified in assuming that its terms had been accepted since the buyer had accepted goods over a number of years without ever voicing objections. More recently, as part of a "preliminary issue" in *Transformers & Rectifiers Ltd v Needs Ltd*,[91] Edwards-Stuart J found that *neither* side's standard terms applied since neither had been clearly accepted nor had there been consistent dealings based on one or the other.[92]

The Hong Kong courts dealt, tangentially, with a battle of forms situation in *Manohar Chugh T/A Electric & Electronic Industries v OKA Electronics Ltd*.[93] In this case, each party asserted that a contract had been concluded on its own (differing) terms. The plaintiff's employee had deleted the words "clean mate's receipt" before faxing back a copy of agreement. The Court of Appeal upheld a request for a new trial on the basis of insufficient investigation by the trial judge of the issue of whether the plaintiff's (revised) terms had been rejected by the defendant or accepted by conduct.

---

88. The "traditional offer and acceptance analysis" was endorsed by the English Court of Appeal in *Tekdata Interconventions Ltd v Amphand Ltd* [2009] EWCA Civ 1209.
89. See 3.2 above; see also *Circle Freight International Ltd v Medeast Gulf Exports* [1988] 2 Lloyd's Rep 427.
90. [2006] CLC 220.
91. [2015] EWHC 269.
92. *Circle Freight* distinguished on this point.
93. [1991] 2 HKC 1.

3.4.5 Acceptance Where More Than One Offer Exists

The scenario of the offeror making more than one offer (not all the same) is an unusual one but came before the English Court of Appeal in the following case.

Pickfords Ltd v Celestica Ltd[94]

The claimant was a well-known removal company which was approached by the defendant to relocate its office and equipment. The claimant sent a fax dated 13 September (the First Document) to the defendant containing an estimate of the cost of such an exercise. On 27 September a second, far more detailed document entitled "Proposal to Undertake to Move Managed Relocation" (the Second Document) was sent by the claimant to the defendant. The essential difference between the two documents was that the second was a fixed price quotation and the first was not. On 15 October the defendant sent a fax to the claimant and asserted that this was an acceptance of the First Document. The claimant argued that it was an acceptance of the Second Document and that the first had been implicitly revoked by the second.

The issues before the court were whether or not the offer contained in the Second Document revoked the offer contained in the First Document and, if not, which one of the two offers was accepted by the fax of 15 October. The court found that the second offer did revoke the first offer and that, on its proper construction, the claimant's fax of 15 October was an acceptance of the offer in the First Document. Since the "acceptance" was of an offer no longer in existence, it represented a new offer based on the terms of the First Document. By carrying out the work the claimant had implicitly accepted this new offer!

In explaining the decision Dyson LJ said:

> It is as if the facts of this case have been devised for an examination question on the law of contract for first year law students . . .
>
>   What is the position where A makes an offer to B and then makes a later offer to B? By making the later offer, does A withdraw the earlier one? . . . No authority has been cited to us in which this question has been considered. In my judgment it must depend on the nature of the two offers and the circumstances in which they are made.[95]

3.5 Communication of Acceptance

Since acceptance is a *response* to an offer it naturally follows that acceptance will not normally be regarded as effective unless and until such response is communicated to the offeror.

---

94. [2003] EWCA Civ 1741.
95. Ibid, paras 2 and 17.

3.5.1 The General Rule

The general rule, that acceptance must be brought to the notice of the offeror, is illustrated in *Powell v Lee*[96] where the plaintiff applied for the post of headmaster at a school. The managers of the school voted to appoint the plaintiff but no directions were given as to communicating the results of the voting to the plaintiff. One manager, without authority, wrote to the plaintiff and told him he had been appointed. A subsequent resolution rescinded the previous resolution and appointed someone else as headmaster. The plaintiff was then informed about the appointment of the other person and sued, alleging breach of contract and claiming damages. The court held there was no contract as there had been no *authorised* communication of intention to contract on the part of the school body to the selected candidate. While it can strongly be argued that even an authorised communication to Powell would have only constituted an offer of appointment (still to be accepted by him) the court appears to have proceeded on the basis that such a communication would have brought a contract into being.[97]

One reason for the rule that acceptance must be communicated is the difficulty of proving an uncommunicated decision to accept.[98] However, the main reason is that hardship could be caused to the offeror if he were bound without having knowledge of the acceptance. Lord Denning, in *Entores v Miles Far East Corporation*,[99] expressed the point graphically:

> Suppose, for instance, that I shout an offer to a man across a river or courtyard but I do not hear his reply because it is drowned by an aircraft flying overhead. There is no contract at that moment. If he wishes to make a contract, he must wait till the aircraft is gone and then shout back his acceptance so that I can hear what he says. Not until I have his answer am I bound.

More recently, in *Apple Corps Ltd v Apple Computer Inc*,[100] the trial judge expressed the view that, in principle, a contract could be concluded simultaneously in two jurisdictions. This would be so, for example, where an acceptance was sent from a jurisdiction that held agreement to be concluded when/where acceptance is sent, to a jurisdiction which recognised completion on *receipt* of acceptance.

---

96. (1908) 99 LT 284.
97. The school was described as the "offeree" so the court seems to have regarded Powell as making an offer to provide his services. Modern employment practice would be that the potential employer would write offering employment and asking the employee to confirm his acceptance.
98. See Treitel (n 17 above) at p 26.
99. [1955] 2 QB 327.
100. [2004] EWHC 768.

3.5.2 *Silence Is Not Sufficient*

As acceptance must be communicated to the offeror, silence is not normally sufficient to amount to acceptance. The following case provides the classic illustration of this principle.

Felthouse v Bindley[101]

An uncle wrote to his nephew offering to buy his horse and added: "If I hear no more about him, I consider the horse is mine at £30 and 15s." No reply was sent to this letter, nor was any money paid and the horse remained in the nephew's possession. However, the nephew evidenced his intention to agree to his uncle's terms by asking the auctioneer about to sell the horse not to do so. The auctioneer then sold the horse contrary to the instruction and the uncle attempted to sue him. The dispute centred on whether the uncle (as opposed to the nephew) had any right to bring an action. It was held that he did not since the horse had not become his; his nephew's agreement to sell had never been communicated to his uncle.

Willes J noted that the nephew had intended his uncle to have the horse at the price above:

> but he had not communicated such intention to his uncle, or done anything to bind himself. Nothing, therefore, had been done to vest the property in the horse to the plaintiff.

The principle that "acceptance by silence" cannot be imposed is a sound one and has been recognised statutorily in England, though not in Hong Kong.[102] The rule prohibits, for example, "inertia selling" whereby businesses may deliver unsolicited goods and then demand payment on the basis that the "customer" has accepted the goods by not expressly rejecting them. The law is clear that silence in the face of an offer should be viewed as a *rejection* not an acceptance. The rule is harder to justify where, as in *Felthouse*, the silent offeree clearly did wish to accept.[103]

The need for communication of the acceptance to the offeror may be "waived" by the offeror, at least in unilateral cases.[104] In *Carlill v Carbolic Smoke Ball Co*[105] the defendants contended that, even if the advertisement of the smoke ball was an offer, it had not been accepted as there had been no notification of such to the advertiser. Bowen LJ dismissed this argument. He said:

---

101. (1862) 11 CBNS 869.
102. See Unsolicited Goods and Services Act 1971.
103. The *Felthouse* case has been explained on the basis of a failure to comply with the formal requirements of the Statute of Frauds, 1677, but this explanation is unconvincing.
104. See 3.3.4.
105. [1893] 1 QB 256.

One cannot doubt that, as an ordinary rule of law, an acceptance of an offer made ought to be notified to the person who makes the offer, in order that the two minds may come together . . . But there is this clear gloss to be made upon that doctrine, that as notification of acceptance is required for the benefit of the person who makes the offer, the person who makes the offer may dispense with notice to himself if he thinks it desirable to do so, and I suppose there can be no doubt that where a person in an offer made by him to another person, expressly or impliedly intimates a particular mode of acceptance as sufficient to make the bargain binding, it is only necessary for the other person to whom such offer is made to follow the indicated method of acceptance; and if the person making the offer, expressly or impliedly intimates in his offer that it will be sufficient to act on the proposal without communicating acceptance if it to himself, performance of the condition is a sufficient acceptance without notification.

It could, of course, be argued that *Felthouse* is a case in which the offeror "waived" the need for communication of acceptance.

There may be exceptional cases where silence may be viewed as assent to offered terms. Such a situation arose in *Rust v Abbey Life Insurance Co Ltd*[106] where a plaintiff expressing the wish to be insured with the defendants was held to have accepted their proposed policy by simply failing to reject the proposal for seven months. In the circumstances, this "assent by silence" is clearly distinguishable from an "unsolicited services" situation.

3.5.3 Method of Communication of Acceptance

The method of acceptance must be a suitable one. The rules on method of communication of acceptance are outlined in *Yates Building Co Ltd v Pulleyn & Sons (York) Ltd*.[107] Here, the offeror asked for acceptance by registered or recorded post. The offeree sent a letter of acceptance by ordinary mail which arrived just as fast. The offeror then argued that there was no contract formed as the method of acceptance actually used was not one specified in the offer. The court held that there was a valid contract formed as the method used was just as good for the offeror as the method specified in the offer.

The court stated the following principles:

1. If the offeror *insists* on a particular method of communication of acceptance, then the offeree must comply.
2. If the offeror only *recommends* a method then any method no less favourable to the offeror will suffice. If there is no recommendation/instruction as to method of communication, acceptance must be communicated by a "reasonable" method.

---

106. [1979] 2 Lloyds Rep 334.
107. (1975) 119 SJ 370.

The court added that there would be a presumption that the offeror was recommending rather than insisting.

Similar views had been expressed in *Manchester Diocesan Council for Education v Commercial and General Investments Ltd*[108] where Buckley J said:

> It may be that the offeror, who by the terms of his offer insists upon acceptance in a particular manner, is entitled to insist that he is not bound unless acceptance is effected or communicated in that precise way, although it seems probable that, even so, if the other party communicates his acceptance in some other way, the offeror may by conduct or otherwise waive his right to insist upon the prescribed method of acceptance. Where, however, the offeror has prescribed a particular method of acceptance, but not in terms insisting that only acceptance in that mode shall be binding, I am of the opinion that acceptance communicated to the offeror by any other mode which is *no less advantageous* to him will conclude the contract.[109]

In *Tinn v Hoffman*[110] acceptance was requested "by return of post". The court held that this did not exclusively require a reply by letter or return of post; it merely indicated the need for a quick reply. A reply by telegram or by verbal message or by any other means "equally expeditious" as a letter written by return of post would also be effective acceptance.

3.5.4 When Acceptance Takes Effect

The "general rule" is that acceptance takes effect when (and where) notice is received by the offeror. To this rule there is a major exception in respect of letters sent through the post. Difficulties may also arise in those situations where "notice" of acceptance has been received rather than actual knowledge.

3.5.4.1 The General Rule

The leading authority for the proposition that acceptance takes effect when notice is received is *Entores Ltd v Miles Far East Corporation*.[111] In *Entores*, the plaintiffs in London made an offer by telex to the defendants in the Netherlands which the defendants accepted by telex sent from the Netherlands and received in England. The plaintiffs then sued the defendants for breach of contract. The defendants claimed that the English courts had no jurisdiction in the matter as the contract had been completed in the Netherlands. The English Court of Appeal unanimously held that the contract was completed in England as acceptance was not final until actually received by the plaintiffs in England.

---

108. [1970] 1 WLR 241.
109. Ibid at 246. Emphasis added.
110. (1873) 29 LT 271.
111. [1955] 2 QB 327.

In his judgment Lord Denning cited a number of hypothetical examples in support of the "acceptance on receipt of notice" principle. One example was of the offeree attempting to accept by telephone and the offeror not hearing what the offeree is saying. If the offeree is asked to repeat his statement, it is only when this is repeated *and* heard/understood by the offeror that acceptance is complete. In *Entores*, the crucial question was "where" rather than "when" the acceptance was complete, but the answer to the former question is dependent on the latter.[112]

A similar result to *Entores* was reached in Hong Kong in *Susanto Wing Sun Co Ltd v Yung Chi Hardware Machinery Co Ltd*,[113] where the parties concluded a contract via exchange of faxes. The plaintiff's acceptance was faxed from Hong Kong to Taiwan. The Hong Kong High Court concluded that the contract had been concluded in Taiwan.

In *Brinkibon Ltd v Stahag Stahl*,[114] the House of Lords approved and followed *Entores*. Lord Wilberforce said, that in the area of "instantaneous communications":

> No universal rule can cover all such cases; they must be resolved by reference to the intentions of the parties, by sound business practice and in some cases by a judgment where the risks should lie.

This passage suggests that notice may be crucial, rather than knowledge. Thus if an offeree sends an acceptance by instantaneous communication and reasonably believes that his message has been received *and* the offeror is at fault in not actually receiving it, the offeror will be estopped from denying receipt. Support for this can be found in *The Brimnes*,[115] where the English Court of Appeal found that a message sent during ordinary business hours withdrawing a ship from service was "deemed" to have been received by the close of business hours on that day. Presumably the same result would occur if the message was one purporting to accept an offer. By extension to the above analysis, a message sent after business hours would not be effective until the next working day. Clear support for this view is provided by the English case of *Mondial Shipping & Chartering BV v Astarte Shipping Ltd*.[116]

Hong Kong legislation on electronic contracts supports the existing principles in stating that, in the absence of other agreement, receipt will take place when and where received. The assumption will be that such receipt is at the place of business of the addressee.[117]

---

112. In *Apple Corps Ltd v Apple Computer, Inc* [2004] EWHC, a contract was completed by telephone between a party in England and a party in the United States. Mann J held that in principle a contract could be formed simultaneously in two places.
113. [1989] 2 HKC 504.
114. [1982] 1 All ER 293.
115. *Tenax SS Co Ltd v Reinante Transoceania Navegacion SA (The Brimnes)* [1974] 3 All ER 88, [1974] 3WLR 613.
116. [1995] CLC 1011.
117. Section 19 of the Electronic Transactions Ordinance (Cap 553).

3.5.4.2 Email and Telephone Answering Machines

Email may be thought of as being an instantaneous communication. However, this is not strictly the case, as a message will have to pass through at least one server to reach its target destination. The sender knows that the recipient will only check his mail inbox from time to time. This means there will usually be a delay before it is read. Similarly, with telephone answering machines, the sender knows that the message has not been instantaneously received by the offeror. It could, therefore, be argued, on the basis of "business efficacy", that the so-called "postal rule"[118] should apply and these methods of communication should be treated as analogous to letters. Were this argument to be adopted, e-mail acceptances, for example, would take effect as soon as sent. However, given that the courts have shown a reluctance to extend the postal rule to other areas, it is far more likely that e-mails and similar will be viewed as subject to the normal rules, acceptance taking effect when and where notice of acceptance is received. In the absence of direct Hong Kong authority, regard should be had to the Singapore decision in *Chwee Kin Keong v Digilandmall.com. Pte Ltd*[119] which supports the view that email acceptance takes effect on receipt.[120]

3.5.4.3 The Postal Rule

Where post is an acceptable method of communication of acceptance, acceptance takes place when the acceptance letter is validly posted,[121] *even if it never arrives*. The so-called "postal rule", therefore, operates as an exception to the general rule that acceptance must be communicated to the offeror. At one time, given the importance of the postal service to the formation of contracts, this exception was as important as the rule itself. With the decreasing use of "snail mail" and the increase in other methods of communication, the significance of the postal rule has diminished and courts have been unwilling to extend its principles outside the area of letters and (almost obsolete) telegrams. The origin of the rule lies in the case of *Adams v Lindsell*[122] where the court held that acceptance by post is effective as soon as the letter is put in the control of the post office. This usually means when the letter is placed in the post box but it could also mean handing the letter to a postman authorised to receive it. The rationale for the rule is sometimes said to be business certainty or efficacy but such a view is hard to justify. The major justification is that the rule only applies where the offeror has indicated his willingness to use the post to make

---

118. See 3.5.4.3 below.
119. [2004] 2 SLR 594.
120. In the English case of *Thomas & Another v BPE Solicitors (A Firm)* [2010] EWHC 306 the court accepted that e-mail acceptance takes effect on "receipt" but left open the question of whether such receipt requires "subjective" knowledge or merely "objective" notice.
121. A "misdirected" letter of acceptance takes effect at the least favourable time for the offeree: *Korbetis v Transgrain Shipping BV* [2005] EWHC 1345 (QB).
122. (1818) 1 B&A 681.

the contract; he is deemed to be taking the attendant risk of, for example, letters going astray. The alternative, of acceptance taking effect only when the acceptance letter arrives, is viewed as unfair to the offeree who will then be uncertain as to whether or not a contract has been concluded. The likelihood is that the court in *Adams* were influenced by the fact that the offeror had carelessly directed the offer letter, such that the letter of acceptance should have been received some days earlier than it was. Nonetheless the case has been followed in numerous subsequent cases including *Household Fire Insurance Co v Grant*[123] where Thesiger LJ added further justification for the rule by saying that one could treat the post office as the agent of both parties.

The postal rule is restricted in that it applies only to letters and telegrams (and presumably to telemessages). It is unlikely to apply to e-mail acceptances nor to be applied outside its current limited scope.[124] There are further limitations on the rule, in that it applies only where post is an acceptable method of communication;[125] only in respect of *acceptances;* and only in the absence of a clear stipulation to the contrary by the offeror.

In *Byrne v Van Tienhoven*,[126] the defendants posted an offer to sell to the plaintiffs on 1 October. The defendants then changed their minds and posted a revocation of the offer on 8 October. The plaintiffs received the offer on 11 October and telephoned their acceptance to the defendants. They also sent a letter of acceptance on 15 October. The revocation was received by the plaintiffs on 20 October. The court held that a contract had been formed at the latest on 15 October as, although the letter of *acceptance* was effective on posting, the letter of *revocation* was not effective until it had been actually received by the plaintiffs.

The rule will be displaced where receipt of notification of acceptance is requested by the offeror. The request may be express or implicit. In *Holwell Securities v Hughes*,[127] the defendant granted the plaintiff an option to purchase certain freehold property. The agreement provided: "The said option shall be exercisable by notice in writing to [the defendant] at any time within six months from the date hereof." The court held that this wording was sufficient to exclude the postal rule and require actual notification of acceptance to the offeror. The court expressed the view that the postal rule was based on convenience rather than sound theory. It is capable of producing a contract even though there was never a time when both parties were *ad idem* (willing to contract on the same terms) as, indeed, was the case in the *Van Tienhoven* case. This runs counter to the principle that contract should require "agreement".

---

123. (1879) 4 ExD 216.
124. See 3.5.4.2 above.
125. See 3.5.3 above.
126. (1880) 5 CPD 344.
127. [1974] 1 All ER 161.

3.5.5 Acceptance by Conduct

While acceptance normally requires a positive agreement to the terms offered by the other party, in exceptional cases it may be constituted by conduct. The leading case is *Brogden v Metropolitan Railway Co*, ultimately decided in the House Lords.[128] Here, the appellant had supplied coal to the respondents for some time. The parties decided to create a more formal agreement. The respondents drafted a proposal and the appellant amended it (a counter-offer) and returned it to the respondents. The latter did not communicate acceptance, retained the document and supplied in accordance with the appellant's counter-offer. Following a later dispute and litigation, the court determined that there was acceptance of the appellant's counter-offer via the respondents' conduct. Since recognition of such acceptance is exceptional, it depends on "unequivocal" evidence that the offeree's conduct must have been in response to the offeror's offer and that there is *no other explanation.*[129] In *Shanghai Tongji Science & Industrial Co Ltd*[130] the Court of Final Appeal rejected an assertion of acceptance by conduct because although the conduct was "consistent" with the alleged acceptance, it was not "unequivocal".[131]

3.6 Acceptance in Ignorance of the Offer

Logic demands that, since we cannot "accept" that of which we are unaware, there can be no acceptance (and therefore no contract) where the offeree is unaware of the existence of the offer.[132] The cases support this proposition, though they have not always been properly understood.

3.6.1 Ignorance and the Reward Cases

The leading English case on "acceptance in ignorance" is *Williams v Carwardine.*[133] Here the defendant offered a reward to anyone giving information leading to the discovery of the identity of a particular murderer. The plaintiff was subsequently attacked and beaten up by Mr Williams. Believing she was going to die, and to ease her conscience, she gave the required information which led to Williams's conviction for murder. The plaintiff later recovered and claimed the reward. The court held

---

128. (1877) 2 App Cas 666.
129. Confirmed in *Jayaar Impex Ltd v Toaken Group Ltd* [1996] 2 Lloyd's Rep 437. Cf *Northern Foods Ltd v Focal Foods Ltd* [2001] EWCA Civ 1262.
130. [2004] 2 HKLRD 548.
131. In other words, there were other possible explanations for the conduct. The requirement that the conduct must be "unequivocally referable" to the offer alleged to have been accepted mirrors the strict test for "part performance" in relation to the equitable enforcement of contracts for the disposition of land (see 7.3.2.1.2).
132. See also 4.1.1 for an alternative explanation of this principle in the context of consideration.
133. (1833) 5 C&P 566.

that she was entitled to the reward and that her motive in giving the information was irrelevant.

The point was emphasised by Littledale J who said:

> If the person knows of the handbill [containing the information about the reward] and does the thing, that is quite enough.

Patteson J added:

> The plaintiff being within the terms, her motive is not material.

The *Carwardine* case remains the leading English authority on acceptance in ignorance but a possibly different approach was adopted by the High Court of Australia in *R v Clarke*,[134] where a reward was offered "for such information as shall lead to the arrest and conviction of the murderers of two police officers". The notice added that if the information was given by an accomplice who was not himself the murderer he would receive a free pardon. Clarke saw the offer, provided the required information and claimed the reward. Unfortunately for him he was honest enough to say that he had acted solely to clear his own name in the matter and that at the time he gave the information the reward was not on his mind. The High Court of Australia held that his claim must fail as he should be regarded in the same way as if he had never heard of the reward.

It is unclear from the judgments whether Clarke's "motive" was crucial to the decision but the correct view is probably that he was treated as having accepted in ignorance since, in the words of Higgins J:

> Clarke had seen the offer, indeed; but . . . he had forgotten it . . . There cannot be assent without knowledge of the offer; and ignorance of the offer is the same thing whether it is due to never hearing of it or forgetting it after hearing.

On this basis the case accords with *Carwardine*. However, if *Clarke* is taken to require both knowledge of the reward *and* the appropriate motivation, it is in conflict with *Carwardine* and the other cases in this area. It has also been pointed out that it would conflict with *Carlill*[135] where the claimant's motivation was the avoidance of influenza rather than the receipt of a reward.[136] *Clarke* has been criticised by commentators, not least on the basis that, other than in the clearest "ignorance" cases, an offeror who has obtained a desired benefit should be required to make the promised payment therefor.[137]

The English case of *Gibbons v Proctor*[138] is sometimes regarded as an exception to the rule that acceptance in ignorance of the offer is not permitted, though

---

134. (1927) 40 CLR 227.
135. [1893] 1 QB 256.
136. See Treitel (n 17 above) at p 41.
137. See, for example, Hudson, "Gibbons v Proctor (Revisited)", (1968) 84 LQR 503.
138. (1891) 64 LT 594.

such an interpretation is probably erroneous. In *Gibbons*, a reward was offered to anyone giving certain information, leading to a conviction, to a police officer, Superintendent Penn. Information about the reward was printed on handbills and the plaintiff, a policeman, was not aware of the handbills when he sent in the required information to a superior. He was, nonetheless, held entitled to the reward. While the case is sometimes taken as permitting an "acceptance in ignorance", the fullest report of the case[139] suggests that by the time the information reached Superintendent Penn (the time when acceptance became complete) the plaintiff *did* have the requisite knowledge.[140]

In conclusion, the consensus from both the English and Australian precedents is that acceptance in ignorance is not permitted. That proposition is also endorsed elsewhere in the common law world[141] and supported, albeit *obiter*, in the Hong Kong case of *Koo Ming Kown (or Kwon) v Next Media & Others*.[142]

3.6.2 Cross-offers

Cross-offers are two identical offers that happen to cross in the mail. These apparently do not result in a binding contract because neither communication can be viewed as an "acceptance". Each communication purports to be merely an offer and, even if the courts were prepared to treat either as an attempt to "accept", such acceptance would be in ignorance of the other's offer.[143] This problem was discussed, *obiter*, in *Tinn v Hoffman*,[144] where a majority of the court came to a "no contract" conclusion. Blackburn J expressed the majority viewpoint that grave inconvenience could arise in mercantile contracts if such instances gave rise to valid contracts, since doubts would then arise about the validity of acceptances made in ignorance of the offer.

3.7 Termination of Offer

Offers do not last indefinitely. They may be expressed to remain open for a specific period. In such cases they come to an end at the expiry of the period. In other cases, offers come to an end via rejection, revocation, lapse of time and, perhaps, as a result of the death of the offeror or offeree prior to acceptance.

---

139. Under the name *Gibson v Proctor* 55 JP 616.
140. Higgins J in *R v Clarke* wrongly states that the claimant in *Proctor* was still unaware when the information reached Penn. On this erroneous basis, he opines that the case is wrongly decided.
141. See the American case of *Fitch v Snedaker* 38 NY 248 (1868).
142. [2009] 2 HKC 214.
143. See 3.6 above.
144. (1873) 29 LT 271.

3.7.1 Rejection by the Offeree

An offer will come to an end if it is rejected by the offeree. Once rejected, an offer cannot be revived without the consent of the offeror. In *Lee Siu Fong Mary v Ngai Yee Chai*,[145] the plaintiff rejected the defendant's offer to partially repay disputed loans. Suing on the loans much later, the plaintiff sought to rely on the defendant's offer to circumvent the limitation period. The Hong Kong Court of Appeal rejected her claim on the basis that she had previously rejected the defendant's offer and could not now resurrect it. In this context a counter-offer has the same effect as a rejection as in *Hyde v Wrench, Capacious Investments* etc.[146]

3.7.2 Revocation by the Offeror

Revocation is possible and effective at any time before acceptance: *Payne v Cave*.[147] If the offer does set a deadline for acceptance the offeror can still revoke the offer before this deadline unless the offeree provides consideration to keep the offer open: *Routledge v Grant*.[148] If such consideration is paid then a separate and binding "option" contract is created which prevents the offeror from legally revoking the offer before the deadline.

While revocation of an offer is possible at any time before acceptance is complete, it takes effect only when communicated. Accordingly revocation by post (as opposed to acceptance by post), only takes effect when notice is received by the other party: *Byrne & Co v Van Tienhoven*.[149] This can produce the anomaly that an offeree can accept an offer even if, at the time of acceptance, the offeror has already decided he no longer wishes to contract with the offeree.[150]

However, while notification of revocation is required, it need not be communicated personally by the offeror as the following famous case makes clear.

Dickinson v Dodds[151]

The defendant gave a written offer to the plaintiff to sell a house. The offer was made on 10 June and was "to be left open until 12th". On 11 June the defendant sold the house to a third party. The same evening a Mr Berry, a fourth party acting for the plaintiff, told the plaintiff of the sale. On the morning of 12 June the plaintiff handed the defendant a formal letter of acceptance. The plaintiff then claimed specific performance of the agreement.

---

145. [2006] 1 HKC 157.
146. See 3.4.3 above.
147. (1789) 100 ER 502, [1775–1802] All ER Rep 492 and see 3.3.3.
148. (1828) 4 Bing 653.
149. (1880) 5 CPD 344.
150. See 3.5.4.3.
151. (1876) 2 Ch D 463.

The court held that the offer had been revoked as the plaintiff had been notified of the sale through Berry and, therefore, knew of the defendant's change of intention to sell the property to him. The offer had been validly withdrawn and the claimant could not accept it on 12 June.

The court repeated the *Routledge* principle; that the promise to keep the offer open until 12 June was a *nudum pactum* (without consideration) and could be withdrawn at any time by the offeror before this deadline. Some emphasis was placed on the fact that Berry was a reliable source and that the result may have been different if the plaintiff had only heard a rumour.

In "consensus" terms the decision is a sound one; Dickinson should not be able to accept an offer which he knows is no longer "on the table". The result, however, is that an offeror's liability may depend on the whim of a third party whether or not to pass on news. No doubt the revocation will only be effective in cases like *Dickinson* where the informant is known to be well-informed and reliable.

Where an offer is made to the whole world, as in the *Carlill* case, it seems that a revocation notice will be effective provided it has the same notoriety as the original. There are no binding English or Hong Kong cases on this point but the American Supreme case of *Shuey v US*[152] establishes the "equal notoriety" proposition which most writers assume would be followed by English and Hong Kong courts.[153] In *Shuey*, rewards were offered for information by proclamation of the Secretary of War. There was no time limit but some months later the President ordered the offer to be terminated. Subsequently the claimant gave information and claimed the reward. The court found against him on the basis that the President's order, having the same notoriety as the original offer, constituted a revocation.

It could be, of course, that in such cases the offeree knew of the reward but not the revocation; there would be "notice" rather than "knowledge".[154]

A matter of considerable academic debate is whether a unilateral offer of a reward in return for an act done can be revoked once the offeree begins the act but before he completes it. Under the *Routledge v Grant*[155] principle, revocation should be possible at any time before acceptance is completed. This seems particularly harsh where acceptance involves an act of a continuing nature. Should the offeror who promises a large sum to anyone swimming across Hong Kong harbour in January be able to inform a "complying" swimmer, metres short of his destination, that the offer is revoked? Should the Carbolic Smoke Ball Co have been allowed to cancel their offer after Mrs Carlill started sniffling but before influenza began?[156] The generally accepted position is that the offeror cannot withdraw the offer once the offeree has

---

152. (1875) 92 US 73.
153. See, for example, C. P. Chui, *Law of Contract in Hong Kong* (Hong Kong: Hong Kong University Press, 1988), p 16.
154. See discussion of "*The Brimnes*" above at 3.5.4.1.
155. (1828) 4 Bing 653.
156. [1893] 1 QB 256.

started to perform the required act. This was the view of the English Court of Appeal in *Errington v Errington & Woods*.[157] Here, a father bought a house for his son and daughter-in-law to live in. The father paid the deposit on the house and borrowed the balance of the purchase price. He told the daughter-in-law that the deposit was a present to them but that they had to repay the loan instalments themselves. He told her that the house would be theirs once the loan had been repaid and that when he retired he would transfer it into their names. The father died before the loan had been repaid and the personal representatives of the father's estate sought to revoke the arrangement. The court held that the father's promise was a unilateral offer which could not be revoked once the couple had embarked on performance provided they did not leave performance "incomplete and unperformed".

The contract here was "unilateral" in that the "children" had no more obligation to pay the mortgage than Mrs Carlill had to use the smoke ball as directed. Once the act was complete, however, an obligation to transfer the property would have arisen. While the "acceptance" by the children was not complete at the time of the father's death, it was held that his estate could not revoke his promise since acceptance had begun. The children had to have the opportunity to complete acceptance and only in the event of their default could the offer be revoked.

The result in *Errington* was supported by the English Court of Appeal, albeit *obiter*, in *Daulia Ltd v Four Millbank Nominees Ltd*.[158] An opposing view is to be found, however, in *Luxor (Eastbourne) Ltd v Cooper*[159] where an owner of land promised to pay an estate agent a commission if he brokered the sale of land. Before any sale was effected the offer was revoked. The House of Lords held that the owner could revoke his offer at any time before completion of the sale. The court refused to find that there was an implied term that the owner could not so revoke his offer.

The distinction between the *Errington* and *Luxor* approaches may be that the former involves acts of a continuing nature while the latter involves a "one off" act.[160] More compelling, though, is the fact that the agent in *Luxor* stood to gain a significant fee over a short period of time and should be made to bear the commercial risk of the deal not going through. In such circumstances the court saw no need to find an implied term that the offer would not be revoked once performance had begun; the court decided otherwise in the different circumstances of *Errington*. The *Errington* approach has been subsequently endorsed by the English Court of Appeal in *Soulsbury v Soulsbury*[161] where Lord Justice Longmore stated:

---

157. [1952] 1 All ER 149.
158. [1978] Ch 231, [1978] 2 All ER 557 (the court decided that the offerees had completed acceptance before the attempted revocation).
159. [1941] AC 108.
160. It is hard to reconcile this explanation with views expressed in the *Daulia* case.
161. [2007] EWCA Civ 969.

This is a classic unilateral contract of the *Carlill . . .* or the "walk to York" kind. Once the promise acts on the promise by inhaling the smoke ball, by starting the walk to York . . . the promisor cannot revoke or withdraw his offer. But there is no obligation on the promisee to continue to inhale, (or) to walk the whole way to York . . . It is just that if she inhales no more (or) gives up the walk to York . . . she is not entitled to claim the promised sum.

3.7.3 *Lapse of Time*

Where an offer is stipulated to last for a fixed time, it comes to an end when that time expires. If an offer does not set a deadline for acceptance, it will remain open only for a reasonable time: *Ramsgate Victoria Hotel Co v Montefiore.*[162] What is reasonable depends on the facts of each case; an offer to sell a stable, durable commodity will last longer than an offer to sell perishable goods, such as fresh fruit, or volatile ones, such as shares.

3.7.4 *Death*

The effect of the death of the offeror on the offer raises issues which are more appropriately handled in a course on probate law. It is clear, though, that if the offeree knows of the offeror's death he cannot accept the offer: *Re Whelan.*[163] In the absence of such knowledge, the offer will normally remain open. Thus, if the offeree performs an act of acceptance in ignorance of the offeror's death, *Bradbury v Morgan*[164] suggests that the offer may still be accepted.[165] This case involved a guarantee and the offer consisted of a promise that was independent of the offeror's personality and could be satisfied out of the deceased's estate. However, where some "personal element" of the offeror is involved his death would terminate negotiations.

There is little authority on the effect of the offeree's death on an offer, but such as there is suggests that the offeree's death brings an offer to an end such that the deceased's estate cannot accept for him.[166]

3.8 Certainty of Agreement

Attempts to reach agreement will not amount to contracts if there is uncertainty as to whether the parties have reached a final agreement or as to the precise nature of its terms. Where courts are convinced that the parties intended a binding contract they will do their best to find one, even if this involves some "creativity".

---

162. (1866) LR 1 Ex 109.
163. [1897] 1 IR 575.
164. (1862) 1 H & C 249.
165. A contrary view was later expressed *obiter* by Mellish LJ in *Dickinson v Dodds* (1876) 2 Ch D 463.
166. See *Reynolds v Atherton* (1921) 125 LT 690 and the Canadian case of *Re Irvine* [1928] 3 DLR 268.

3.8.1 Vagueness and Uncertainty

Where the parties have omitted, or have vaguely expressed, key terms, the courts will have no alternative but to hold the agreement void for uncertainty. In *Kwan Siu Man v Yaacov Ozer*[167] the Hong Kong Court of Final Appeal held that the date of completion is an essential term in contracts for the sale and purchase of land. Litton PJ[168] said:

> as is common knowledge in Hong Kong, the property market is highly volatile. Whatever might have been the position in England in the last century—when the concept of an 'open contract' was first developed in a climate of a stable pound sterling and no inflation—in the Hong Kong of today, the date of completion is an essential term of any contract for the sale and purchase of land.

In the absence of a clear agreement on the completion date the court was forced to decide that there was no concluded, binding contract.

The issue of uncertainty has been considered, not always consistently, in a number of English cases. In *Hillas & Co Ltd v Arcos Ltd*,[169] the appellants agreed to buy from the respondents "22,000 standards of softwood of fair specification over the season 1930." There was an option to purchase a further 100,000 in 1931 but no reference to the type of wood or its quality. The appellants wished to exercise this option but the respondents repudiated and sold to a third party. The appellants finally succeeded in the House of Lords where it was held that by reference to previous dealings and trade practice it was possible to find a contract. By implication the option was for softwood of fair specification.

The *Hillas* case adopts the line that the courts will find a binding contract exists where possible so that parties may not escape from their obligations. The court expressed the view that:

> the parties, being business men, ought to be left to decide what degree of precision it is essential to express in their contracts, if no legal principle is violated.[170]

The alternative, that contracts will be disallowed wherever there is the slightest hint of uncertainty, would make it practically very difficult for businesses to make large forward contracts because of the difficulty, if not impossibility, of specifying in advance all the details of performance required by the parties. In theoretical terms, the "relational" theory of contract addresses this issue in terms of the need for more flexible approaches to contract where agreements are to be long-standing and require

---

167. [1999] 1 HKC 150.
168. Ibid at 159.
169. [1932] All ER Rep 494.
170. See also *Pagnan SpA v Feed Products* [1987] 2 Lloyd's Rep 601 where the court upheld an agreement where there had been agreement on the "essential terms".

a measure of flexibility, co-operation and mutual "understanding".[171] A similar result was reached in *Foley v Classique Coaches Ltd*[172] where the parties made two linked agreements. Under the first, the plaintiff agreed to sell some land to the defendants and under the second, described as "supplemental" to the first, the defendants agreed to buy petrol exclusively from the plaintiff at a price "to be agreed by the parties in writing and from time to time". A dispute arose, the defendants arguing that there was no binding contract as no price had been set. At trial the plaintiff was granted damages and an injunction to prevent the defendants from buying petrol elsewhere. The Court of Appeal, relying implicitly on section 8 of the Sale of Goods Act 1893,[173] rejected the defendants' appeal.

The *Foley* decision is difficult to reconcile with that in *May & Butcher Ltd v R*,[174] decided very soon afterwards. In *May*, the parties made an agreement for the supply of the whole stock of the defendant's material (tentage) with prices and dates of payment to be "agreed from time to time". The contract provided for any disputes "with reference to and arising out of" the agreement to go to arbitration. The petition of the "suppliants", May and Butcher, that there was a binding contract, was finally rejected by the House of Lords on the basis that the terms as to prices and dates of payment were too vague. Section 8 of the Sale of Goods Act was felt to be inapplicable.

A factor explaining the different approaches in *May & Butcher* and *Foley* may have been the fact that the parties in *Foley* had operated on the basis that a contract existed for three years. Scrutton LJ, who was on the bench for both cases in the English Court of Appeal, thought there was a contract in each case. He criticised the decision in *May & Butcher* as being out of touch with commercial reality, adding that such an approach explained why businessmen were leaving the courts in favour of arbitration. Commenting on these cases, Cheshire, Fifoot and Furmston[175] write:

> The . . . decision of the House of Lords in *May & Butcher v R* . . . presents some difficulties of reconciliation. But it would appear from the judgments of the Court of Appeal in *Foley v Classique Coaches Ltd* . . . that the view expressed by the House of Lords in *Hillas v Arcos* offers the better guide in what must always be the difficult task of discovering the intention of the parties.[176]

A strict approach was also adopted by the English House of Lords in *Scammell v Ouston*,[177] though with obvious justification. In *Scammell*, the appellants were

---

171. See, for example, D. Campbell (ed), *The Relational Theory of Contract: Selected Works of Ian Macneil* (London: Sweet & Maxwell, 2001).
172. [1934] 2 KB 1.
173. See further discussion at 3.8.3.
174. [1934] 2 KB 17.
175. M. Furmston, *Cheshire, Fifoot & Furmston's Law of Contract* (Oxford/New York: Oxford University Press, 17th edn, 2017).
176. Ibid at p 56.
177. [1941] 1 All ER 14.

willing to sell to the respondents a motor van. The respondents stipulated that the order was given on the understanding that the balance of the purchase price could be had on hire-purchase terms over a period of two years. The House of Lords held that there never was any contract between the parties as the agreement was too vague. This was because the reference to "hire-purchase terms" was not precise enough as there were so many types of hire-purchase agreements. The result may have been different if there were any well-known "usual terms" in such a contract but at that time there were not.

The case is clearly distinguishable from *Hillas* and *Foley* since they both involve agreements in which the courts were convinced that the parties had reached final agreement. Although there was some uncertainty as to precise terms, these could be supplied via the surrounding circumstances.[178] In *Scammell*, the court felt there was simply no way to determine the precise meaning of "hire-purchase terms".

A more recent example of an insufficiently certain agreement (although not decided at the highest level) is provided by *Blue v Ashley*;[179] the facts of which are quite simple. In a pub (a bar) a businessman, Mike Ashley (A)*, told a financier, Mr Blue (the claimant), that if Blue (B) would use his expertise to get shares in A's company to £8, A would give B £15 million. Blue did his best and, indeed, the shares did later reach the figure, so Blue claimed his money and sued when Ashley refused to pay. The action failed, inter alia, because of a lack of contractual certainty. Ashley may have "offered" to pay on the share price reaching £8 *but* no time limit was placed on this event occurring, so was insufficiently certain.[180]

3.8.2 Meaningless Wording

Where vague or meaningless words can simply be omitted without affecting the sense of the agreement the courts will "sever" the words and uphold the contract. In *Nicolene Ltd v Simmonds*[181] a contract for the sale of goods contained the words, "We are in agreement that the usual conditions of acceptance apply." No such conditions existed and so these words were meaningless. The contract was upheld and the Court of Appeal merely ignored the meaningless wording. Denning LJ (as he then was) said:

> a distinction must be drawn between a clause which is meaningless and a clause which is yet to be agreed. (This) clause was so vague and uncertain as to be inca-pable of any precise meaning. It is clearly severable from the rest of the contract. It can be rejected without impairing the sense or reasonableness of the contract as a

---

178. What courts now tend to describe as the "factual matrix".
179. [2017] EWHC 1928 (Comm).
180. The case also features discussion of consideration and intention and will be dealt with later in these contexts.
181. [1953] 1 QB 543.

whole, and it should be so rejected. The contract should be held good and the clause ignored.[182]

The alternative to deleting meaningless words would be, as Denning LJ pointed out, that:

> You would find defaulters all scanning their contracts to find some meaningless clause on which to ride free.

The same approach was taken by the Hong Kong Court of Appeal in *Sun Wah Oil & Cereals Ltd v Gee Tai Trading Co Ltd*[183] where a meaningless force majeure/ arbitration clause was severed from a contract for the sale and purchase of goods.

The applicability of severance in this context depends on the contract being entire without the severed words; in *Scammell* the court found that the phrase about hire-purchase terms was integral to the contract and could not be struck out.

3.8.3 Reference to Price

It might be thought that, given its importance, omitting the price from an agreement would automatically defeat a contract for uncertainty. However, even here, the parties' presumed intention is crucial, though it will be difficult to convince a court that a binding contract has been formed if such an important element remains unstated.

It is quite common, though, for parties to commercial contracts to agree to settle the price by future agreement. It is wise to provide machinery or a formula to deal with a situation where the parties are unable to agree on future prices. Courts will hold agreements to be ineffective if there are defects in such machinery, but the House of Lords in *Sudbrook Trading Estate Ltd v Eggleton*[184] showed that the courts will take a liberal view in considering such cases. In *Sudbrook*, a series of leases granted the lessee (the plaintiff) an option to purchase property. The price was to be fixed by two valuers. One valuer was to be nominated by each party. If the two valuers disagreed, they would appoint a third party "umpire" to decide the price. The defendant refused to nominate a valuer and argued there was, therefore, no contract. The House of Lords, by a four to one majority (Lord Russell dissenting), held there was a contract. The majority held that that the provision for fixing the price by valuers was a decisive indication that the price was to be a reasonable price since such valuers were professionals who were obliged to apply professional and therefore reasonable standards. The agreement was valid but had defective machinery. Treitel[185] suggests that the option could be construed as an agreement to sell at

---

182. Ibid at 551.
183. [1993] 1 HKC 132.
184. [1982] 1 AC 444, [1983] 3 All ER 315.
185. Note 17 above.

a *reasonable* price to be determined by valuers. The nomination of a valuer by each party was a subsidiary and inessential part of the price-fixing machinery. The court could intervene if necessary to provide its own machinery, such as by appointing a valuer itself.

A court will not supply a missing term if the facts show that the parties intended to leave open the possibility of backing out if they did not agree on that term or if there is no mechanism for completing the terms. This is especially so with regard to price clauses. An example is provided by *Hong Kong Advanced Knitwear Company v Chan Chak-man*,[186] where the Hong Kong High Court interpreted the wording of a letter from the plaintiff to the defendant to conclude that the parties had deliberately "left the door open" so that either party could back out of the agreement.

More recently, the Hong Kong Court of Appeal in *Chu Yu Tin & Others v Lo Kwok Hung*[187] found that leaving the amount of a "premium payment" unspecified, and without any machinery whereby the amount could be ascertained, led to the conclusion that the parties had not concluded a sufficiently certain, legally-binding agreement.

However, the inclination of the courts is to try to save commercial agreements so far as they can do so without straining legal principles. This is particularly so when the contract has already been performed. The courts will construe terms by reference to past transactions between the parties, industry customs, legislation[188] or an arbitration clause. By doing so the courts often tread a fine line between construing a contract and making a contract. The difference between the two is really one of degree and the cases before the courts show a tension between them.

Statutory assistance can be found in Hong Kong in section 10 of the Sale of Goods Ordinance (SOGO)[189] which is headed "Ascertainment of price" and states:

(1) The price in a contract of sale may be fixed by the contract, or may be left to be fixed in manner thereby agreed, or may be determined by the course of dealing between the parties.

(2) Where the price is not determined in accordance with foregoing provisions, the buyer must pay a reasonable price. What is a reasonable price is a question of fact dependent on the circumstances of each particular case.

The above section was relied on, in *Goodman Corporation v Mataichi Kabushiki Kaisha*,[190] by Mills-Owens J who said:

---

186. [1965] HKLR 355.
187. [1995] 2 HKC 213.
188. For example, in *Anstalt Nybro v Hong Kong Resort Co Ltd* [1980] UKPC 4 (a case involving development at Discovery Bay) the Privy Council (on appeal from Hong Kong) was able to import then relevant Hong Kong company law legislation to provide a "model" set of Articles of Association in the absence of agreed ones.
189. Cap 26 (cf s 8, Sale of Goods Act 1979).
190. [1959] HKLR 421.

The main objection to be taken is that the prices at which the plaintiffs were to sell to the defendants were left to be determined in future. But is that a real objection; is there anything fundamentally wrong in parties concluding a legal relationship between themselves in two stages if at each stage there is consideration and an intention to create a legal relationship between themselves. The inclination of the courts must be to give legal efficacy to such commercial agreements so far as they can do so without straining legal principles, and if necessary I would be prepared to holds that section 10 of the Sale of Goods Ordinance could be relied upon to fill in the gap left by clause 4 of the agreement, namely to provide that the prices at which the defendants were to sell to the plaintiffs would, in the absence of mutual agreement, be reasonable prices dependent upon the dates and circumstances in which sales took place.[191]

The Supply of Services (Implied Terms) Ordinance[192] contains a similar provision with regard to contracts for the supply of services. Section 7 is headed "Implied term as to consideration." It reads:

(1) Where, under a contract for the supply of services, the consideration for the service is not determined by the contract, is not left to be determined in a manner agreed by the contract or is not determined by the course of dealing between the parties, there is an implied term that the party contracting with the supplier will pay a reasonable charge.
(2) What is a reasonable charge is a question of fact.

3.8.4 A Presumption of Certainty?

Hong Kong courts have shown a reluctance to find a contract void for uncertainty. In *China Great Wall Finance Co v Wonderyouth Industries Ltd*,[193] for example, Yuen JA said:

It is well established law that the court should be reluctant to find an agreement void for uncertainty.

Ma CJHC, sitting in the Court of Appeal, expressed similar sentiments in *The World Food Fair Limited and Another v Hong Kong Island Development Ltd*,[194] stating:

Of course, once essential terms have been agreed, there will not be any lack of certainty. And where there has been part performance, the court "will strain to the utmost to supply the want of certainty even to the extent of providing substitute

---

191. Ibid at 431–432.
192. Cap 457 (cf Supply of Goods and Services Act 1982).
193. [2004] 4 HKC 517.
194. [2005] 1 HKC 594.

machinery" . . . Thus, the court may imply terms, adopt usual covenants or even determine terms by reference to concepts of reasonableness.[195]

In the *World Food Fair* case, the Court of Appeal unanimously found on the facts that there was sufficient certainty of contract concerning the grant of a tenancy in the defendant's shopping mall. The defendant appealed to the Court of Final Appeal (CFA).[196] The higher court, while agreeing with the above passage, unanimously allowed the appeal. All the CFA judges agreed with the leading judgment of Ribeiro PJ which criticised the Court of Appeal's approach to the facts. The CFA found that the facts that a deposit had been paid and the proposed tenant had been allowed into possession of the premises were, at best, equivocal. They cited as authority the case of *Attorney-General and Another v Humphreys Estate (Queen's Garden) Ltd*[197] in which the handing over of possession of, and the effecting of works on, a site pursuant to an agreement "subject to contract" produced no concluded contract. The CFA further found that there was no concluded agreement on another essential term, the provision of a rent-free period.

Uncertainty was a key issue in the following unusual Hong Kong case.

Koo Ming Kown (or Kwon) v Next Media & Others[198]

The second defendant, well-known media magnate, Jimmy Lai, wishing to accelerate the pace of democratic reform in Hong Kong, had published an "offer" to pay half the advertising expenses of anyone prepared to "roar for democracy". The plaintiff, a businessman opposed to the "democratic camp",[199] had published a number of advertisements supporting the Hong Kong government's "go-slow" policy on electoral reform . . . and then claimed the 50% reimbursement! The plaintiff's action failed largely on the basis that the advertisement was insufficiently certain to amount to an offer and was merely an advertising ploy or "puff". The trial judge, Lok J, further indicated that even if the advertisement did constitute an offer to pay expenses, it could only be accepted by those generally supportive of the offeror's aims (which clearly did not apply here).[200]

---

195. Ibid at 604. Similar sentiments had been expressed by Lord Denning MR in *Sykes v Fine Fare* [1967] 1 Lloyds Rep 53 where he said that courts *"will do their best not to destroy the bargain."*
196. [2007] 1 HKLRD 498.
197. [1987] AC 114.
198. [2009] 2 HKC 214.
199. The third defendant, James To, was a leading Democratic Party member.
200. The plaintiff claimed not to understand the offer (which was the reason he sought reimbursement for all advertisements despite the "offer" only extending to Apple Daily ones). This the plaintiff blamed on misleading comments by the third defendant whom he sued in negligence. The trial judge took the view that this action was prompted by political motives.

3.8.4.1 A Different Approach

Professor McKendrick identifies a different approach to certainty exhibited in the UK Supreme Court decision in *Wells v Devani*,[201] where the emphasis is on an objective intention to be bound. Where the courts discern such intention, Mckendrick infers, sufficient certainty is "much more likely" to be found.[202]

3.8.5 *Contracts to Make a Contract or to Negotiate in Good Faith*

Hong Kong law has followed the English principle of not recognising "a contract to make a contract"[203] on the basis that the concept is too uncertain and would be impossible to police. English courts have also rejected the concept of a duty to negotiate "in good faith" for similar reasons. These issues came before the House of Lords in *Walford and Others v Miles and Another*[204] where Lord Ackner, delivering the leading judgment, endorsed the words of Lord Denning MR in *Courtney & Fairburn Ltd v Tolaini Bros (Hotels) Ltd*[205] where he said:

> It seems to me that a contract to negotiate, like a contract to enter into a contract, is not a contract known to law . . . I think we must apply the general principle that when there is a fundamental matter left undecided and to be the subject of negotiation, there is no contract.[206]

The Ackner view is open to criticism and has not been universally employed in the common law world.[207] A number of Australian and United States courts, for example, have adopted a different approach.[208] The Ackner view is based primarily on two propositions: that an "agreement to negotiate in good faith" is too vague; and that negotiating parties are in an adversarial position, each seeking to maximise its position at the expense of the other. Decisions in Australia, the United States, and elsewhere have recognised a duty to negotiate in good faith (even where this, ultimately, does not result in agreement). Moreover, numerous academics (and some judges) have pointed out that negotiating parties are often in a "relational" rather

---

201. [2019] UKSC 4.
202. Ewan McKendrick, *Contract Law: Text, Cases & Materials* (Oxford/New York: Oxford University Press, 9th edn, 2020) at p 128.
203. See *New World Development Co Ltd v Sun Hung Kai Securities Ltd* [2006] 3 HKLRD 345.
204. [1992] 1 ALL ER 453.
205. [1975] 1 All ER 716.
206. Quoted at [1992] 1 ALL ER 453 at 459.
207. Its "absolutist" nature has even been questioned in the English courts (see *Petromec v Petroleo Brasileiro* [2005] EWCA Civ 891).
208. See, for example, *United Group Rail Services Ltd v Rail Corporation of New South Wales* [2009] NSWCA 177 (Australia); *Copeland v Baskin Robbins USA et al* CA (Cal) B149851 (2002) (California, USA).

than an adversarial position.[209] In the New Zealand case of *Bobux Marketing Ltd v Raynor Marketing Ltd*[210] Thomas J emphatically stated:

> The fundamental flaw of the classical conception of contract law was its empirical premise that most contracts are discrete. That premise is false. Most commercial contracts are in fact relational contracts.

In *Hyundai Engineering and Construction Co Ltd v Vigour Ltd*,[211] Reyes J, having exhaustively reviewed the common law precedents on the issue, stated that:

> My survey of cases suggests that . . . there is no hard and fast rule that agreements to negotiate or mediate in good faith are *per se* unenforceable. The court must instead look at each situation and ask whether it is possible to frame objective criteria against which a party's reasonable compliance or non-compliance with a particular obligation can be assessed . . . If it is not possible, then the contract cannot be enforced. Otherwise, the agreement should be sustained and as much as possible the parties required to adhere to their bargain.[212]

The Reyes J reservations as to the English approach appear to have been abandoned by the Court of Appeal in the same case, where Rogers VP appears, uncritically, to have accepted Lord Ackner's depiction of adversarial negotiating parties in stating:

> In some cases part of a negotiating tactic may be to call off the negotiations hoping that better terms would be offered.

Currently, therefore, it appears that the Hong Kong courts agree with the English approach that there is no duty to negotiate in good faith.[213] It should be stressed, however, that while the House of Lords, in *Walford*, rejected the idea that a party could be "locked-in" to a promise to bargain with only one other party "in good faith", a "lock-out" agreement, whereby a party promises not to negotiate with anyone else, is enforceable in England provided that it is for a limited period and consideration is given in return.[214] The following case provides a clear illustration.

Pitt v PHH Asset Management[215]

The defendant proposed to sell property and the plaintiff wished to buy it but had a rival. Both parties tried to outbid each other. The plaintiff's bid was £200,000. The

---

209. See 1.2.4.
210. [2002] 1 NZLR 506.
211. [2004] 2 HKC 505.
212. At para 98.
213. Though in *World Sport Group Pte Ltd v Asian Tour International Ltd* (unrep, HCA 2779/2008, 18 February 2009) Deputy Judge Carlson indicated that a duty to negotiate in good faith was worthy of consideration in appropriate cases.
214. See chapter 4.
215. [1993] 4 All ER 961.

defendant then orally agreed not to deal with anyone else for a period of two weeks in return for the plaintiff being ready to exchange contracts within that period. If the plaintiff was not ready at that time the defendant was free to consider other offers. The next day the defendant stated that it would accept the rival's bid of £210,000 and did so. The plaintiff sued for damages and the action succeeded.

The English Court of Appeal held that:

1. There was a binding "lock-out" and that the plaintiff had a "clear run".
2. This agreement did not impose an obligation on the defendant to deal with the plaintiff but rather an obligation not to deal with anyone else.
3. There was consideration[216] for the promise in the plaintiff's promise to complete quickly.
4. Although the agreement to sell to the plaintiff was "subject to contract" and therefore unenforceable, the lock-out agreement was a separate, certain and binding contract.[217]
5. The plaintiff was entitled to damages for breach of the lock-out agreement.

Although *Pitt* is an English case, lock-out agreements have been adopted and found to be very useful in Hong Kong given the volatile property market.

In the complex case of *Hong Jing Co Ltd v Zhuhai Kwok Yuen Investment Co Ltd*[218] the Hong Kong Court of Appeal upheld the distinction between binding "lock-outs" and the non-binding "duty" to act in good faith. As to the latter, however, the court felt that where a "fiduciary" duty to negotiate (with the other party or a third party) exists, there *is* a contractual duty to make reasonable efforts to do so "in good faith".[219]

3.9 The "Objective" Test of Agreement

It should be remembered that the ultimate test of whether agreement has been reached is, generally, an "objective" one, to be determined by reference to the standard of the reasonable contracting party armed with the parties' knowledge of the surrounding circumstances.

In *Destiny 1 Ltd v Lloyds TSB Bank plc*[220] the English Court of Appeal was called upon to determine whether a contractual agreement had been finally concluded after a lengthy period of negotiations between the parties. It determined that it had not (despite the claimant's view to the contrary) since an important issue had been

---

216. See chapter 4.
217. Which, unlike the main contract to sell land, did not have to be in writing (see 7.3.2.1).
218. [2013] 1 HKLRD 441.
219. Ibid per Cheung JA at para 23.
220. [2011] EWCA Civ 831. See also *Inland Revenue Commissioners v Fry* [2001] All ER (D) 434 (Nov).

left unresolved. Moore-Bick LJ's leading judgment emphasised that the question of whether the parties have reached agreement is an objective one. He added:

> The difficulty for Destiny . . . is that the evidence does not support the conclusion that an agreement of that kind (asserted) was ever contemplated or entered into.

The most famous iteration of the "objective" principle is to be found in the words of Blackburn J in *Smith v Hughes*, quoted in the chapter 1 overview, which tells us that a man's "assent" should be judged according to the understanding of the "reasonable man", where the other party enters into an agreement "on that belief". This second requirement (that the other party must share "the man's" understanding) is often overlooked. It means that where party B *knows that* party A's assent is mistaken, the objective test of A's agreement is disavowed.[221]

This exception to the objective test of agreement is dealt with, inter alia, in the complex case of *Shanghai Tongji Science & Technology Industrial Co Ltd v Casil Clearing Ltd*[222] where Ribeiro PJ (quoting Chitty on Contracts) stated:

> the party who did not intend to be bound would not be bound if his state of mind was actually known to the other party.

Once a contractual *agreement* has been found, a further objective test will be applied to ascertain its *terms*. This latter determination will be dealt with in chapter 8.

---

221. For this reason, such cases are often dealt with under the topic of "mistake". Indeed, the *Digilandmall* case dealt with at 10.5.1 (Mistake) could equally be viewed as an application of the "subjective" test where a mistake is clearly known to the other party.
222. [2004] 2 HKLRD 548; (2004) 7 HKCFAR 79.

4

Consideration

OVERVIEW

Consideration is a requirement, in English and Hong Kong law, for all "simple" contracts (ie contracts not made under seal). Stated in its simplest terms, consideration means the giving of something of value to the other contracting party. Consideration is essentially a creation of the common law system and is not generally required in civil law systems such as those found in most of Western Europe. That being so, it is useful to ask why we have a doctrine of consideration; what is its purpose?

What consideration does *not* do is to prove that an agreement is fair. The rule is that consideration must be "sufficient" (of some value) but need not be "adequate" (of equal value to the other party's consideration). There is nothing wrong, in consideration terms, with an agreement to buy a valuable painting for $10, (although it might indicate that the agreement has been produced by fraud or threat, either of which would invalidate the agreement).

Consideration is, essentially, a token of a party's intention to make a legally binding contract, as opposed, for example, to a non-binding social arrangement. That token takes the form of the giving of something valuable in the eyes of the law. Consideration may not prove that a bargain is fair or equal but it *is* evidence of a legally enforceable contract, as opposed to a mere friendly arrangement never intended to be contractual.

In practical terms, while it is said that each party must provide consideration, it is for the party wishing to enforce an agreement to show that he has provided consideration. This is the usual meaning given to the requirement that "consideration must move from the promisee". Any legal pleading based on breach of a simple contract must describe the plaintiff's consideration. So, for example, the buyer who wishes to enforce a sale must show that he has given something of value to the seller. This may be the fact that he has already paid the price for the goods *or* that he has made a binding promise to do so (which he has not broken). In the former case, the buyer's consideration is said to be "executed"; in the latter it is "executory". Both forms of consideration are recognised by the courts.

The doctrine of consideration has been criticised as artificial and unnecessary. It is said that, where courts wish to uphold an agreement, they are prepared to "invent" consideration. Further, it is said, since the function of consideration is to provide evidence of an intention to make some contractual "bargain", rather than a merely social arrangement, a preferable approach would be to adopt the civil law emphasis on "intention", with the existence of consideration merely being a factor in determining the parties' intention. To take a simple example, if A promises B $500 if he will complete 50 "push-ups", B's completion of the act could clearly be seen as "executed" consideration. It might be, however, that in such a case a court would find that the parties never "intended" that such a trivial arrangement would constitute a binding contract.[1]

Despite the criticism of consideration from some judges and academics, the doctrine has remained largely intact and consideration remains a requirement for the formation of a contract and any "variation" thereof. The best-known definitions of consideration speak of the need for the party seeking to enforce the contract to show either that he has conferred some benefit on the other party or that he has incurred some detriment to himself. In many cases there will be both benefit and detriment. The buyer of goods will give the benefit of the price to the seller and incur the detriment of payment himself. It is not, however, necessary to show both elements. If a person swims across Hong Kong harbour in response to a promise of $5,000 reward to anyone who does so, he will incur a detriment but show no obvious benefit to the promisor.

In addition to the benefit/detriment requirement, it must also be shown that what the party seeking to enforce the contract has done, or promised, is in response to the other party's promise; it must be "the price of the promise". So, if our swimmer swam across the harbour the day *before* the promise of $500 reward was made, he could not claim the reward; he would not have done the act in response to the promise of reward. In legal terms, the swimmer's consideration is said to be "past" and the rule is that "past consideration is no consideration". Similarly, if the swimmer swam the harbour unaware of the offered reward of $500 he would not be entitled to it since his act would not in response to the promise of reward; his swim would not be "the price of the other party's promise".

Since the need for consideration is firmly established, most legal and academic debate is focused on the requirement that consideration must be of some value in the eyes of the law and the meaning to be given to "value", which normally requires that the party seeking to enforce the agreement, the "promisee", must have given some benefit to the other party or incurred some detriment to himself. The words "benefit"

---

1. See chapter 5.

and "detriment" have a somewhat different meaning to the contract lawyer than to the lay person.

Is it "beneficial" to one party, for example, that the other promises not to bring a legal action which has no chance of success? The promisor, in one sense, is not giving anything of value but the other party is getting the benefit of not having the trouble and expense of a legal action.

To take another example, is it "beneficial" to the other party not to break an enforceable contractual promise? Will a builder who promises not to "down tools" (stop work) be giving consideration for a promise by the other party to pay more?

The courts have recently expressed the view that such matters should be judged in terms of a "practical" rather than a legalistic approach. It might be thought improper that a party should be viewed as having given a benefit merely by promising not to break his contract; yet in practical terms the alternative would be for the other party to bring expensive legal proceedings which might produce inadequate compensation, many years later, against an opponent unable to pay. So, if A promises B *extra* remuneration if B will continue performance of the contract rather than break it, the attitude of the courts today is to accept the practical benefit in terms of consideration but to ensure that agreement was not produced by unfair pressure, known as "duress".[2]

In practice, given the lengthy duration of many modern commercial agreements, problems of consideration normally arise over the *variation* rather than initial *creation* of a contract. Prudent businessmen will often insert a "price variation" clause to protect themselves against serious market changes (such as cost of supplies or currency fluctuations) which would otherwise "ruin" their bargains. Where this does not happen, the party unaffected by the changes may well be prepared to pay more under the contract rather than lose the goodwill of the other contractual party or even put him out of business. It makes no commercial sense to insist on strict legal rights if the effect is to give you a right of action against someone who will never be able to pay. Again, the modern focus of the courts is on a practical rather than a legalistic approach.

As regards detriment, should it be regarded as "detrimental" that a party promises to forego a course of action that he had no intention to pursue? The apparent answer is that there is no detriment, since the "promisor" has really given up nothing. It could be argued, on the other hand, that he has given up his "legal right" to change his mind and pursue the action. Some authorities emphasise that the mere giving up of a "legal right" can constitute consideration. In practice, however, courts have refused to find consideration in such a case.

To take a second example, is there "detriment" if A promises to give up a course of conduct which he was legally entitled to pursue but which was physically harmful

---

2.   See 11.1.

such as smoking cigarettes? Here we can see the clear distinction between "legal" detriment and "actual" detriment. The smoker has promised to give up his "legal right" to continue smoking; a "legal" detriment though a physical benefit. Presented with such a case, courts would probably accept the consideration but refuse to enforce the agreement on the grounds that there was no "intention" to make a contract as opposed to a merely social arrangement.

A specific example of the difference between legal and practical benefits can be seen in relation to the rules on part-payment of a debt. A rigid adherence to consideration would dictate that part-payment could not discharge a debt since nothing would have been given in return for the release from part of the debt. Practically, however, the creditor may well have obtained a benefit since some payment would be preferable to none and an insistence on full legal rights might result in the creditor ultimately receiving nothing from a bankrupt debtor. So far, the law has not been relaxed in this area[3] and part-payment continues to be insufficient to discharge the whole debt. However, the courts have mitigated the harshness of this approach to some extent via the doctrine of promissory estoppel, a form of "waiver", under which the creditor who has clearly agreed to accept part-payment, in full satisfaction of a debt, may be prevented, at least temporarily, from enforcing the debt contrary to his promise. Were the courts to adopt a more flexible attitude towards consideration in this area, and to consider the "practical" benefit of receiving part-payment, the need for equitable intervention would no doubt be reduced.[4]

4.1 The Nature of Consideration

The basic requirement of consideration is that each party must give something of value, in the eyes of the law, in return for the other party's promise. The presence of consideration does not prove that a "fair" bargain has been made but it does prove the existence of a bargain, which the law will enforce, as opposed to a gratuitous promise which is not enforceable.

Consideration is frequently described in terms of "benefit" and "detriment": the promisee must show either that he has provided a benefit to the other party or suffered a detriment himself. Thus:

> A valuable consideration, in the sense of the law, may consist either in some right, interest, profit or benefit accruing to the one party or some forbearance, detriment, loss or responsibility, given, suffered or undertaken by the other.[5]

It is important to note that it is not required to show detriment to oneself as well as benefit to the other party in order to enforce an agreement. Earlier cases may

---

3. But cf 4.6 and 4.7 below.
4. Ibid.
5. *Currie v Misa* (1875) LR 10 Ex 153 at 162.

have suggested that *both* benefit and detriment are necessary.[6] However, it is clear that *either* will suffice. The person who walks from London to York in return for the promise of reward will be entitled to sue for that reward, on the basis of the detriment to himself, without showing that the walk provided any benefit to the promisor.

While the benefit/detriment analysis provides a useful starting point, it must be remembered that the benefit or detriment must be "in return" for the other party's promise; the "price" of the promise as it is sometimes described. Hence,

> An act or forbearance of one party, or the promise thereof, is the price for which the promise of the other is bought, and the promise thus given for value is enforceable.[7]

Curiously, perhaps, the English courts have found that while consideration must be "the price of the other party's promise", the promisee need not be aware that he has provided anything in return for the other party's promise. In *(Anthony) Pitts & Others v Andrew Jones*,[8] the plaintiffs ceded rights to compensation in return for the defendant's oral guarantee to reimburse them should the purchaser of the company in which they had shares default. They were unaware that they had incurred any "detriment" but were regarded *obiter* as having provided consideration. Their action still failed as an oral guarantee is unenforceable in England (though not in Hong Kong).[9]

4.1.1 Consideration and Conditional Gifts

While the benefit/detriment model will normally provide an adequate basis for deter-mining the existence of consideration, the "price of the promise" approach will better explain why a "conditional gift" does not constitute a binding promise. Suppose that A offers B, who lives on Hong Kong Island, a gift of $10,000 to be collected at A's office in Kowloon. On B's arrival, A changes his mind. B may argue that he has undertaken the journey to Kowloon and thereby contributed "detriment" considera-tion. The reality, however, is that the journey is not the price of A's promise; it has not been made "in exchange for" the promised money, it is merely a condition of receiv-ing the gift. The dividing line is a very narrow one, however. If, in this example, A had said, "I always love to see you; come to my office in Kowloon tomorrow and keep me company for an hour and I'll give you $10,000", the promise would clearly be enforceable; the visit would be the price of the promise.[10]

In *Shadwell v Shadwell*,[11] it appears that the majority of the court overlooked the price of the promise requirement in finding that a nephew had provided consideration

---

6. See, for example, the judgment of Byles J in *Shadwell v Shadwell* (1860) 9 CB (NS) 159.
7. P. H. Winfield, *Pollock's Principles of Contract* (London: Stevens & Sons, 13th edn, 1950), p 133.
8. [2007] EWCA Civ 1301.
9. See chapter 7 at 7.3.
10. See *Gilbert v Ruddeard* (1608) 3 Dy 272b.
11. See n 6 above.

for his uncle's promise of an allowance, on his starting out in marriage, by going through with the marriage to his fiancée. Erle CJ stated:

> the plaintiff, relying on this promise without any revocation on the part of the uncle, did marry Ellen Nicholl . . .
>
> Now, do these facts shew [*sic*] that the promise was in consideration either of a loss to be sustained by the plaintiff or a benefit to be derived from the plaintiff to the uncle, at his, the uncle's, request? My answer is in the affirmative.

While this was the view of the majority, the dissenting view of Byles J, that this was no more than a "letter of kindness", is to be preferred. Indeed, the case appears to involve no more than a promise to make a wedding gift. Such gifts will not be effected unless the parties go through with the marriage, but those promising wedding gifts would surely be surprised were it to be found that they could be sued for non-delivery! The wedding is, then, a condition of receiving the gift; it is not the "price of a promise".

The "price of the promise" definition also provides an alternative explanation of the "acceptance in ignorance cases".[12] While these cases tend to be decided on the basis that an offer cannot, logically, be "accepted" by one who is unaware of it, it can also be said that the act performed was not in response to the offer of reward so that the act was not the price of the offeror's promise. There was, in short, no "exchange" of promise/act. The non-validity of past consideration, too, can be easily understood from the "price of the promise" perspective.[13]

4.1.2 Benefits and Detriments: Legal and Factual

It must also be remembered that there is a difference between an actual detriment and a legal one. If X promises to give Y $1,000 if the latter refrains from smoking for six months, it is clear that the act of restraint, once concluded, will entitle Y to the money even though he will not have suffered a detriment in fact. He will have suffered a detriment in the eyes of the law since he will have given up the exercise of a legal right in return for X's promise. This point was, correctly, recognised by Erle J in *Shadwell*[14] when he stated that:

> I am aware that a man's marriage with the woman of his choice is in one sense a boon, and in that sense the reverse of a loss: yet, as between the plaintiff and the party promising to supply an income to support the marriage, it may well be also a loss.[15]

---

12. See 3.6.
13. See 4.2 below.
14. (1860) 9 CB (NS) 159.
15. Ibid at 164.

The point is very well illustrated in the United States case of *Hamer v Sidway*,[16] which, of course, is not a binding precedent in Hong Kong. In *Hamer*, an uncle promised his nephew US$5,000 if the latter would refrain from smoking, drinking, swearing and other bad habits until he reached the age of 21. The New York Court of Appeals subsequently upheld the nephew's claim for the promised sum and rejected the argument that he was, in fact, benefited by his abstinence. Parker J stated:

> It is sufficient that (the nephew) restricted his lawful freedom of action within certain prescribed limits upon the faith of his uncle's agreement . . . it is of no moment whether such performance actually proved a benefit to the promisor.

While the distinction drawn between factual and legal detriment is a sound one, the decision may be unsound in the Hong Kong/English law context in that the nephew's consideration had no obvious economic value.[17]

It has also been held, traditionally, that there is a difference between legal and "practical" benefits for the purposes of determining consideration. A creditor, for example, may agree to release a debtor from part of his debt, fearing that otherwise the debtor will go into liquidation and leave him with nothing. This practical benefit is not recognised as consideration for the debtor's partial release, however, since there is no "legal" benefit to the promisor; the debtor is doing only what he is already bound to do and gives nothing in return for the release. The traditional distinction between legal and practical benefits has been considerably eroded by more recent decisions.[18]

4.1.3 Executed and Executory Consideration

It is generally the case that "executory" consideration is just as valuable as "executed" consideration: ie the promise of an act is as effective as the act itself. For example, if a seller of goods fails to deliver them on time, the buyer has a right to sue even though the goods have not yet been paid for. Executory consideration exists in the buyer's promise to pay for the goods when required to do so. Provided that the buyer has not indicated that he is no longer willing or able to proceed; he is entitled to sue the seller for the latter's non-delivery. In cases of "unilateral" contracts, where only one party has undertaken obligations, the promisee's consideration can only exist in an act rather than a promise, since he gives no promise. Mrs Carlill,[19] for example, did not make any promises to the Carbolic Smoke Ball Co. Her consideration existed in the *act* of using the ball as directed; it was, in other words, executed rather than executory.

---

16. (1891) 27 NE 256.
17. See 4.4.2 below.
18. See 4.5.
19. *Carlill v Carbolic Smoke Ball Co* [1893] 1 QB 256 (see 3.3.4).

4.2 Past Consideration

While consideration may be executory or executed, it must not be "past". Past consideration exists when the apparent act, or promise, of consideration occurred *before* the promisor's promise. A simple illustration would be provided by the case of a drowning man, D, who cries for help. X generously rescues D who promises X a reward in gratitude. Since X's act of rescue occurred *before* D's promise, it is past consideration and the rule is that "past consideration is no consideration". The concept of past consideration is easy to understand if one bears in mind the requirement that consideration must be the "price" of the other party's promise: the act of rescue may well be a detriment to the rescuer but it cannot be the price of the rescued person's promise since that promise has not yet been made.

Re McArdle[20]

A father left his house to his children, provided that his wife could live there until her death. While the widow was living in the house, one of the children and his wife also lived there. The son's wife made improvements to the house and, on the mother's death, when the house passed to all the children, they promised to pay £488 to the wife in gratitude. When she later sued, on the children's refusal to pay, her action failed in the Court of Appeal, since her consideration was "past".

In summing up the view of the court, Jenkins LJ stated:

> The true position . . . was that, as the work had all been done and nothing remained to be done by Mrs McArdle at all, the consideration was wholly past, and, therefore, the beneficiaries' agreement for the repayment to her of the £488 out of the estate was *nudum pactum*—a promise with no consideration to support it.

There are, strictly, no exceptions to the rule that past consideration is not good consideration. However, the courts may enforce a promise of reward made after the claimant's action where the action was requested by the promisor[21] and it was implied that the action would be rewarded; the subsequent promise is treated as merely "quantifying" the implicitly promised reward. The most important statement on this point is that of Lord Scarman in the Privy Council case (on appeal from Hong Kong) of *Pao On v Lau Yiu Long*.[22] He stated:

> An act done before the giving of a promise to make a payment or to confer some other benefit can sometimes be consideration for the promise. The act must have been done at the promisor's request: the parties must have understood that the act

---

20. [1951] Ch 669, [1951] 1 All ER 905.
21. See the old case of *Lampleigh v Braithwait* (1615) Hob 105 (Common Bench).
22. [1980] AC 614, [1979] 3 WLR 435, [1979] 3 All ER 65.

was to be remunerated . . . and payment, or the conferment of a benefit, must have been legally enforceable had it been promised in advance.[23]

4.3 Consideration Must Move from the Promisee

Consideration, it is said, must move from the "promisee", the person who has received a promise. Yet, in the case of the typical contract formed by an exchange of promises, each party has given and received a promise. The rule that "consideration must move from the promisee" is generally taken to mean, in practical terms, that the party wishing to enforce the other party's promise must prove that he has personally provided something of value in return.[24] The leading case is *Tweddle v Atkinson*.[25] Here, John Tweddle and William Guy each agreed to pay a sum of money to the plaintiff (Tweddle's son) in consideration of his marrying Guy's daughter. Guy failed to pay and the plaintiff sued the estate of the now deceased Guy. His action failed on the basis that consideration had not come from the son (the plaintiff) but from his father.

This proposition is closely connected to the first branch of the rule of *privity* of contract;[26] namely that only parties to a contract may receive benefits under it. In *Tweddle*, the case could equally have been decided on the basis of privity. So, if A and B make an agreement that A will pay C $1,000 if B does so, B, having paid the money, will have the right to sue A if the latter defaults. C, however, will have no such right even though the contract is clearly intended to be for his benefit. The reason that C cannot sue may be stated as, "he has provided no consideration" or "he is not privy to the contract". The relationship between consideration and privity will be considered in more depth in chapter 16 (where it will be noted that the traditional view that a third party cannot enforce a contract, even if it is intended to benefit him, has been fundamentally altered).[27] Suffice to note, at this stage, that the generally accepted meaning of the principle "consideration must move from the promisee", adopted in this text, is not universally accepted.[28]

It should also be noted that while consideration must move *from* the promisee, it need not move *to* the promisor.[29] Y, for example, may give consideration to X (of the "detriment" type) by providing services to Z. So, in the scenario where Alan says to Brian, "if you give Colin $100 I will do the same", Alan's promise is binding. Having handed over the money, Brian has a right of action against Alan should he

---

23. See, also, *In re Casey's Patents* [1892] 1 Ch 104.
24. This is the meaning we have adopted, though it has been differently interpreted.
25. (1861) B & S 393.
26. See chapter 16.
27. See 16.4.
28. See, for example, the dispute as to whether judges properly applied the rule in *Roffey's* case (4.5 below).
29. See *Kao, Lee & Yip v Euro Treasure Ltd* [1985] 1 HKC 46 at 49 per Roberts CJ.

renege.[30] In benefit/detriment terms, Brian may have given Alan no benefit but he has himself incurred a detriment and this is enough.

4.4 Sufficiency of Consideration

The common law takes the view that consideration "must be sufficient but need not be adequate". What this means is that it must be of *some* value in the eyes of the law but need not be of *equivalent* value to the other party's consideration. In *Kao, Lee & Yip v Euro Treasure Ltd*[31] Roberts CJ stated:

> The authorities are clear that so long as consideration has some value, its worth is immaterial.

The fact that consideration need not be adequate is quite straightforward; the fact that one party gets the better of the bargain is no concern of the law, provided that this is not the result of misrepresentation, duress, undue influence or other "vitiating" factor.

The requirement of sufficiency is, however, much more difficult since there is much confusion as to what constitutes "value" in the eyes of the law. Many of the precedents in this area appear contradictory and few propositions as to "value" are without some exception.

4.4.1 Natural Love and Affection

It has been held that "natural love and affection" do not constitute consideration. In *Thomas v Thomas*,[32] a promise by executors to make a payment out of respect for the deceased's wishes, expressed during his life but *not* in his will, was held to be insufficient.[33] Patteson J described the executors' promise as merely "a pious respect for the wishes of the testator".

However, consideration has been found in an "object of interest to a near relative", which arose solely from family affection. In *Shadwell v Shadwell*,[34] for example, consideration was found via the act of marrying a fiancée of whom the promisor clearly approved.[35] Erle CJ stated:

> The marriage primarily affects the parties thereto; but in a secondary degree it may be an object of interest to a near relative, and in that sense a benefit to him.

---

30. Whether his claim is limited to "nominal" damages will be considered at 16.2.4.
31. [1985] 1 HKC 46.
32. (1842) 2 QB 851.
33. Though consideration was found on another ground.
34. (1860) 9 CBNS 159.
35. While this could have been construed as a legal detriment, the decision appears to have been based also on benefit to the promisor.

It is difficult to see how this statement can be reconciled with the general "natural love and affection" principle. An "only in Hong Kong" illustration of the insufficiency of "natural love and affection"[36] is provided by the case of *Chan Man Tin v Cheng Leeky*,[37] where the court refused to enforce an agreement involving a promise to be a "female intimate companion" in return for a promise to "cohabit with (the promisee) and live happily together". Not surprisingly, this agreement was felt to lack consideration as well as certainty.[38]

4.4.2 Need Consideration Be of Economic Value?

It has frequently been held that consideration must be of some "economic" value, albeit "inadequate",[39] yet it has been held to exist in valueless chocolate bar wrappers which the recipient merely threw away.

Chappell & Co Ltd v Nestle Co Ltd[40]

The plaintiffs owned the copyright in a song, "Rockin' Shoes". The Hardy company made records of the song which they sold to the defendants for 4d each. The defendants advertised them to the public for 1/6d each plus 3 wrappers from their 6d bars of chocolate. The plaintiffs sued for breach of copyright but the defendants claimed that they were operating within the 1956 Copyright Act which permitted sale provided that 6.25% of the "ordinary retail selling price" was offered to the copyright owner. The defendants had offered 6.25% of the 1/6d but the plaintiffs argued that this was not sufficient since there was no "ordinary retail selling price" (as this was not a simple sale for money). A majority of the House of Lords agreed with the plaintiffs that the worthless wrappers were part of the consideration so that there was no ordinary retail price.

The court was far from unanimous; three judges favouring the view that the wrappers were part of the consideration. The "dissenters" adopted the view that the records were sold for money *only* and that the provision of wrappers merely qualified the customer to be eligible for purchasing at the reduced price. In that case, of course, the legislation would have been complied with. The approach of the minority appears preferable. The customer would have to do a number of things to acquire the record: send a postal order for 1/6d, send three wrappers, buy a stamp, write and post a letter, etc. It is submitted that only the first of these constitutes consideration; the rest are merely qualifying conditions and not the price of the promise. A well-known analogy in Hong Kong is the offer of specified holidays only to those who

---

36. Though perhaps "natural" is inappropriate in this context!
37. [2008] 3 HKLRD 593.
38. It is likely that it would also have failed on grounds of its "immorality" (see chapter 13).
39. For example, *Thomas v Thomas* (n 32 above).
40. [1960] AC 87, [1959] 3 WLR 168, [1959] 2 All ER 701.

have acquired a particular credit card. The offer of the holiday is open only to those who qualify but the consideration for the holiday is solely the payment of money. In *Esso Petroleum Co Ltd v Customs & Excise Commissioners*,[41] Esso promised to give, to customers who bought four gallons of petrol, free "World Cup" coins, each of which bore the head of one of the 30 England World Cup Tournament players of 1970. It was argued that they must pay purchase tax on the coins since they were "produced in quantity for general sale". Clearly the coins were produced in quantity but a majority of the House of Lords agreed with Esso's contention that the coins were not "sold" but given away. The customer, it was held, did not buy four gallons plus a coin but only four gallons: the coin was merely a gift, and not part of the consideration. So, no purchase tax was payable; the only significance of the purchase of four gallons was that it was a "condition of receiving" the free gift.

Despite these reservations, the legal position in England remains, until overruled by the House of Lords, that the worthless wrappers, in a *Nestle* scenario, amount to part of the consideration.[42] Clearly, if they are capable of being part of the consideration, they could, equally, be the whole consideration. The proposition that consideration must always be of some economic value must, then, be viewed as doubtful. As Lord Somervell said in the *Nestle* case:

> A contracting party can stipulate for what consideration he chooses. A peppercorn does not cease to be good consideration if it is established that the promisee does not like pepper and will throw away the corn.[43]

Since *Nestle* is a decision of the House of Lords, it also represents the law in Hong Kong, in the absence of contrary local authority, legislative or judicial, post-1997.

Economic value is also hard to discern in a number of the "unilateral" contract cases, involving the promise of reward for an act. Mrs Carlill[44] may have bought the smoke ball but the offer of £100 was made to anyone who used the ball as directed (and still caught influenza). It is difficult to see any economic value in such an act.

4.4.3 Illusory and "Invented" Consideration

The confusion and contradictions outlined above have led critics to argue that the doctrine of consideration is a pretence; that where courts wish to uphold an agreement they will find, or "invent", consideration. Invented consideration certainly appears to be the explanation for the decision in *De La Bere v Pearson*[45] where the

---

41. [1976] 1 WLR 1, [1976] 1 All ER 117.
42. See also *Haigh v Brooks* (1839) 10 Ad & El 309, where the return of a worthless guarantee was held to be good consideration for the promise of payment.
43. [1959] 2 All ER 701 at 712.
44. See 3.3.4.
45. [1908] 1 KB 280.

defendants, who were newspaper owners, advertised to readers that they would provide an address to which they could write for financial advice. The plaintiff wrote and asked for the name of a "good stockbroker". The defendants negligently supplied the name of an undischarged bankrupt who defrauded the plaintiff. The plaintiff's action against the defendants succeeded despite the lack of obvious consideration provided by the plaintiff to the defendants.[46]

Given the absence, at that time, of an action in tort, a sympathetic court had to find a contract if the plaintiff was to be compensated. In so doing the court "invented" the possible benefit of a notional increase in newspaper sales because of the existence of the financial advice column.

Perhaps the best example of invented consideration occurs in *Shadwell v Shadwell*[47] where Erle CJ, in discovering "detriment" to the promisee in marrying his fiancée, stated:

> The plaintiff *may* have made a most material change in his position, and induced the object of his affection to do the same, and *may* have incurred pecuniary liabilities resulting in embarrassments which would be in every sense a loss if the income which had been promised should be withheld.[48]

Consideration is said to be "illusory" where it involves a promise to do something entirely at the discretion of the promisor. Treitel cites the example of a promise to do something "unless I change my mind".[49] It is also said that "it is no consideration to refrain from a course of conduct which it was never intended to pursue",[50] which sits uneasily with the finding of consideration in a promise to refrain from a course of conduct which the law does not permit.[51] Both situations involve the promisee forbearing to do something. In the first case he refrains from doing something unlikely; in the latter from doing something unlawful. This supports, again, the view that courts will be "creative" in discovering consideration where it produces the intended judicial outcome. This is said to be particularly the case where there is a commercial relationship between the parties.[52] In *Chong Cheng Lin Courtney v Cathay Pacific Airways Ltd*,[53] for example, the Hong Kong Court of Appeal held that a promise to give an airline employee an improved remuneration package was supported by the consideration of the employee continuing to work for the airline *even though*, of course, she may have done so anyway. The practical alternative to

---

46. It is generally accepted that such a case would now be decided on a tortious basis.
47. Cited above at 4.4.1.
48. Emphasis added. See also discussion of *Pitt v PHH* at 4.5.1 below.
49. Treitel, n 17 above, at p 84.
50. *Arrale v Costain Civil Engineering Ltd* [1976] 1 Lloyd's Rep 98.
51. Per Denning LJ in *Williams v Williams* (see 4.5).
52. Rhind J described "a trend towards a pragmatic appraisal of consideration in commercial relationships": *City Polytechnic of Hong Kong v Blue Cross (Asia Pacific) Insurance Ltd* [1995] 2 HKLR 103 at 109.
53. [2011] 1 HKLRD 10.

this finding would be that most promises by an employer of improved terms would lack consideration. Andrew Cheung J stated:

> The law must not depart from the reality of everyday life for no good reason . . . it would take very compelling reasons for the Court to hold that what were regarded as contractual by the parties actually had no contractual force in law for want of consideration . . . the necessary consideration for the variation was supplied by the employee not leaving Cathay.[54]

The court, in reaching this very sensible "policy" decision, referred to the authority of *Roffey* and the nebulous "practical benefit" requirement. In the absence of any indication that the claimant was contemplating a career move, such a "benefit" appears illusory.[55]

Ironically, however, it is the earlier lack of invention and creativity in respect of other areas of consideration[56] which has necessitated the intervention of equity in the form of promissory estoppel.[57]

It should be noted that while courts may be "creative" in finding consideration, the *legal requirement* of consideration remains firmly established. Failure to plead adequately the required consideration resulted in the Hong Kong Court of Appeal upholding an appeal in *Huen Wai Kei v Choy Kwong Wa Christopher (No 2)*.[58] In judgment Kwan JA stated:

> Consideration for the Security and Set-off Agreement is a material fact and should have been pleaded by the plaintiffs. This was not done . . .
>
> . . . Not only that, it is apparent on the evidence that there was no consideration for the Security and Set-Off Agreement.

4.4.4 Forbearance to Sue

A particular aspect of the adequacy/sufficiency rule relates to a promise not to pursue a legal action; a so-called "forbearance to sue". The question is whether there is consideration only in giving up a case likely to succeed or whether any forbearance is sufficient. On practical grounds, it seems that the latter approach is preferable since, otherwise, the strength of the original action would need to be tested by a court in order to determine whether sufficient consideration had been given. On theoretical grounds, too, this should be the case since giving up one's right to "a day in court" is a legal detriment even where the case is unlikely to succeed. Conversely,

---

54. Ibid at paras 51–52.
55. Nonetheless the same reasoning was later applied by the Hong Kong Court of Appeal in *Wu Kit Man v Dragonway* [2018] 2 HKLRD 117.
56. Notably part-payment of a debt (see 4.6).
57. See 4.7.
58. [2014] 4 HKLRD 782.

consideration must be of some "value" and it may be argued that a hopeless case has none. The matter was considered by the English courts in the following case.

Horton v Horton (No. 2)[59]

The defendant made an agreement under seal to pay the plaintiff, his wife, maintenance but the amount provided was lower than he intended because he had not taken taxation into account. The defendant then made a new, improved, agreement unsealed. After paying on the basis of the new agreement for some time he later ceased payment and argued that his wife could only claim under the old agreement since there was no consideration for the new one. The plaintiff's action to enforce the new agreement succeeded in the Court of Appeal which held there was consideration in the giving up of the right to claim rectification of the original contract.

Upjohn LJ endorsed a "sufficient not adequate" approach in stating:

> the wife would have been entitled to take rectification proceedings. Whether or not they would have succeeded does not matter but, on the evidence, she had some prospect of success.

The requirement, then, is that the party giving up the right of action must genuinely, rather than reasonably, believe in its chances of success. This approach has been endorsed by the Hong Kong courts.

Cosmo Sea Freight (HK) Ltd. v Gold King Consolidator Ltd.[60]

A dispute had arisen about the payment of compensation, under a compromise arrangement, for goods damaged during shipping. The defendants argued, amongst other things, that they should not have to pay the compensation since the plaintiffs' original claim against them had not been a good one.

Kaplan J, holding for the plaintiffs, stated that it was clear law that:

> the compromise of a disputed claim which is honestly made, whether legal proceedings have been instituted or not, constitutes valuable consideration, even if the claim ultimately turns out to be unfounded. It is not necessary that the question in dispute should be really doubtful, it is sufficient if the parties in good faith believe it to be so, even if such belief is founded on a misapprehension of a clear rule of law.

In *Fine Master Ltd v Nippon Circuits Ltd*[61] the Court of First Instance held that a forbearance in respect of a guarantee *even of an existing debt* could amount to a valid forbearance (and not infringe the past consideration rules). Deputy Judge Woo said:

> A guarantee even of a past debt or transaction will be valid if the creditor promises to forbear from suing or to give time to, the principal debtor, or if he actually does

---

59. [1961] 1 QB 215, [1960] 3 WLR 914, [1960] 3 All ER 649.
60. (unrep, HCA A8254/1992, 24 January 1994).
61. (unrep, HCA 919/2010 & 919A/2010, 12 March 2013).

so at the request of the surety. The mere fact of forbearance, however, is not enough: there must be an actual promise to do so, or the forbearance must be at the request . . . of the surety.[62]

4.5 Performance of Existing Duty

This topic is really an aspect of sufficiency, but is dealt with separately because of its complexity and topicality. Put simply, the general proposition was, until quite recently, that performance of an existing duty could not amount to consideration for the promise of additional "reward". The promisee, in such situations, has suffered no detriment since he has done only what he was already obliged to do; the promisor gets no legal benefit from the performance to which he was already entitled. Similarly, of course, the *promise* to do merely what one was already bound to do could not provide sufficient consideration in return for the promise of additional reward.

In fact, the common law recognised three separate duty situations: "public", or legal, duty; contractual duty owed to the promisor; and contractual duty owed to a third party. In the first two situations, the mere performance of an existing duty was traditionally held to be no consideration; in the last situation, the courts have long recognised that mere performance of an existing duty owed to a third party can be good consideration for the promisor's promise of "reward".

4.5.1 Public Duty

The traditional view is illustrated by the English case of *Collins v Godefroy*,[63] where the defendant promised to pay the plaintiff six guineas for his trouble in giving evidence in a case in which the defendant was involved. It was held that there was no consideration for this promise since the plaintiff was a subpoenaed witness and, therefore, legally obliged to give evidence. The plaintiff had done no more than his legal duty.

The principle that mere performance of an existing public duty cannot be good consideration for a promise was accepted in a number of English cases,[64] though whenever the court was well-disposed towards the claimant it tended to be "creative" in finding that he had done more than his duty. The principle itself was, however, doubted by Denning LJ, notably in the cases of *Ward v Byham*[65] and *Williams v*

---

62. Ibid at para 23.
63. (1831) 1 B & Ad 950.
64. For example, *Glasbrook Bros Ltd v Glamorgan County Council* [1925] AC 270; *Harris v Sheffield United Football Club Ltd* [1988] QB 77. Contrast *Leeds United FC Ltd v Chief Constable of West Yorkshire Police* [2012] EWHC 2113.
65. [1956] 1 WLR 496. Consideration was said to exist in a promise to look after a child and keep her happy: "invented" consideration?

Williams.[66] In the latter case, the parties were married. The wife deserted the husband and subsequently they made an agreement for him to pay her 1.5 pounds per month maintenance as long as: she lived a chaste life; she maintained herself and did not pledge his credit; she took no further action in the courts for maintenance provided that he paid maintenance punctually. The wife sued to enforce the maintenance agreement on the husband's default and her action succeeded in the Court of Appeal.

In support of the wife's claim, Denning LJ stated:

> Now I agree that, in promising to maintain herself whilst she was in desertion, the wife was only promising to do that which she was already bound to do. Nevertheless, a promise to perform an existing duty is, I think, sufficient consideration to support a promise, so long as there is nothing in the transaction which is contrary to the public interest. Suppose that this agreement had never been made, and the wife had made no promise to maintain herself and did not do so. She might then have sought and received public assistance or have pledged her husband's credit with tradesmen; in which case the National Assistance Board might have summoned him before the magistrates, or the tradesmen might have sued him in the county court. It is true that he would have an answer to those claims because she was in desertion, but nevertheless he would be put to all the trouble, worry and expense of defending himself against them. By paying her 30s. a week and taking this promise from her that she will maintain herself and will not pledge his credit, he has an added safeguard to protect himself from all this worry, trouble and expense. That is a benefit to him which is good consideration for his promise to pay maintenance.[67]

There are two significant points raised by Denning LJ: first, that mere performance of an existing public duty should be good consideration unless there is anything in the agreement which offends public policy; and second, that merely avoiding the trouble and expense of litigation may be viewed as sufficient benefit to constitute consideration. The first point was not agreed by his fellow Court of Appeal judges and, cognisant of the fact that his fellow judges would be reluctant to find consideration in the mere performance of a public duty, Denning LJ was able to find that Mrs Williams had, in fact, done more than the law required of her. It was this view that found favour with Hodson LJ and Morris LJ in upholding Mrs Williams's claim. Yet none of the "additional benefits" are convincing. Not pledging her husband's credit was seen as conferring on him a benefit, yet, as a wife in desertion, Mrs Williams had no legal right to pledge his credit. The notion that refraining from unlawful activity should be viewed as valuable consideration is a highly dubious one. Again, the argument that Mr Williams would be spared the "trouble, worry and expense" of (successfully) defending himself from tradesmen's legal actions posits a dangerous precedent. Were this to be accepted, the long-established rule as to part-payment of a debt would logically be extinguished, since acceptance of part-payment would

---

66. [1957] 1 All ER 305.
67. [1957] 1 All ER 305 at 307.

avoid the inconvenience of suing for the balance.[68] Nevertheless, some support for Denning LJ's view that avoiding "trouble, worry and expense" is good consideration can be found in *Pitt v PHH Asset Management Ltd*[69] where Peter Gibson LJ stated:

> I accept that that the threat of an injunction only had a nuisance value in that I cannot see how the plaintiff could have succeeded in any claim. Nevertheless, that nuisance was something which the defendant was freed from by the plaintiff agreeing to the lock out agreement. Further, the threat of causing trouble . . . was again a matter which could have been a nuisance to the defendant and again removal of that threat provided some consideration.[70]

While Denning LJ's views on the mere performance of existing public duty were not shared by his fellow Court of Appeal judges, they have subsequently been endorsed in the landmark case of *Williams v Roffey Brothers and Nicholls (Contractors) Ltd*[71] which will be discussed at length. While *Roffey* was concerned with the performance of contractual duty, the Court of Appeal established a general proposition that the mere performance of an existing duty would be recognised as good consideration provided that it conferred a "practical benefit" on the other party and was not tainted by "duress".[72] The *Roffey* approach has been adopted in its entirety by the Hong Kong courts.[73] Moreover, in *City Polytechnic of Hong Kong v Blue Cross (Asia-Pacific) Insurance Ltd*,[74] previously considered in relation to tenders,[75] the Hong Kong High Court appears to have accepted that the performance of a public duty can be good consideration. In the *Blue Cross* case, the plaintiffs had invited tenders. The defendants had submitted, and then withdrawn, a tender before acceptance. The court held that the plaintiffs had an obligation to consider all timely tenders since "a public body in Hong Kong, such as City Poly, formally inviting tenders, is certain to treat each and every applicant with scrupulous fairness as almost a reflex action conditioned by the Hong Kong Government's long-standing campaign against corruption."[76] The implied undertaking to consider all timely tenders "scrupulously"[77] was held to amount to consideration sufficient to enforce the defendants' implied promise not to withdraw their submitted tender before a decision on it had been made.

---

68. See 4.6 below.
69. [1993] 4 All ER 961, [1994] 1 WLR 327.
70. [1993] 4 All ER 961 at 966. Few of these examples are convincing.
71. [1991] 1 QB 1.
72. See below at 4.5.2.
73. See *UBC* case discussed below at 4.5.2.
74. [1994] 3 HKC 423.
75. See 3.3.5.
76. *Blue Cross* case at 428.
77. Does this imply a duty to negotiate in good faith? Cf 3.8.5.

4.5.2 *Contractual Duty Owed to Promisor*

As regards contractual duty owed to the other contracting party, the law had always been clear; the "mere" performance of existing duty was not sufficient consideration for a promise of extra reward or remuneration. The proposition was a simple one; if A has contracted to do a job for B for $1,000, B's subsequent promise to pay $2,000 is not binding *unless* A does something additional in return. The proposition was supported by two nineteenth century English cases; *Stilk v Myrick*[78] and *Hartley v Ponsonby*.[79] In *Stilk*, the defendants promised some sailors, including the plaintiff, extra wages for helping to sail their ship home short-handed after the crew numbers had been reduced. When the plaintiff subsequently sued on this promise his action failed as, it was held, he was already contractually bound to sail the ship for his originally promised wage and had, therefore, given no consideration for the additional sum.[80]

Lord Ellenborough, in reviewing the authorities,[81] considered, also, whether the sailors had exerted pressure. He stated:

> I think *Harris v. Watson* was rightly decided; but I doubt whether the ground of public policy, upon which Lord Kenyon is stated to have proceeded, be the true principle on which the decision is to be supported. Here, I say, the agreement is void for want of consideration. There was no consideration for the ulterior pay promised to the mariners who remained with the ship. Before they sailed from London they had undertaken to do all that they could under all the emergencies of the voyage. They had sold all their services till the voyage should be completed. If they had been at liberty to quit the vessel at Cronstadt, the case would have been quite different; or if the captain had capriciously discharged the two men who were wanting, the others might not have been compellable to take the whole duty upon themselves, and their agreeing to do so might have been a sufficient consideration for the promise of an advance of wages. But the desertion of a part of the crew is to be considered an emergency of the voyage as much as their death; and those who remain are bound by the terms of their original contract to exert themselves to the utmost to bring the ship in safety to her destined port. Therefore, without looking to the policy of this agreement, I think it is void for want of consideration, and that the plaintiff can only recover at the rate of £5 a month.

Lord Ellenborough's view, as elicited from this extracted "Campbell" report, appears unequivocal; the claim for additional promised sums must fail and the failure is due to lack of consideration. However, in the alternative "Espinasse" report, the emphasis is on public policy (as it had been in *Harris v Watson*); that to allow the

---

78. (1809) 2 Camp 317, 6 esp 129.
79. (1857) 7 E & B 872.
80. In the similar *Hartley* case the court found for the sailors since, in a situation of much increased danger, they were seen to have done more than their duty.
81. Including *Harris v Watson* (1791) Peake 102.

sailors extra pay would have encouraged them to exert pressure on their employers. The difference between the two approaches helps to explain how, in *Roffey*, the English Court of Appeal was able to undermine the previously accepted principle of *Stilk* while claiming to approve it!

Williams v Roffey Bros & Nicholls (Contractors) Ltd[82]

The defendants were building contractors who had a contract with a housing association to refurbish 27 flats. They were subject to a "penalty" clause if they finished late. They employed the plaintiff to do carpentry work for a total price of £20,000. By April 1986 the plaintiff had received £16,000 but had only completed carpentry in nine of the 27 flats. The plaintiff was in financial difficulty partly because the agreed price was too low. The defendants feared that the plaintiff would be late and they would have to pay penalties. They offered the plaintiff an extra £10,300 (£575 per completed flat). The plaintiff finished eight further flats but received only £1,500 extra. He abandoned the work and sued for damages. The plaintiff's action succeeded in the Court of Appeal where he was held entitled to payment for the 8 flats plus part of the balance of £4,000 on the basis that consideration had been given. There was a *practical* benefit to the defendants in the revised agreement and, since the initiative to pay the bonus came from the defendants and not the plaintiffs, there was no element of "economic duress".[83]

Given the novelty of the decision it has, not surprisingly, elicited mixed views. The basis for the decision is not entirely clear from the individual Court of Appeal judgments. Glidewell LJ took the view that the revised agreement gave a practical benefit to the defendant. The original price was too low and not in the interests of the defendant since "He will never get the job finished without paying more money". The plaintiff's completion of the carpentry work would avoid the defendant paying penalties or engaging others. To the argument that receiving what one is already owed is no "legal" benefit on the basis of *Stilk*, Glidewell LJ stated:

> It is not in my view surprising that a principle enunciated in relation to the rigours of seafaring life during the Napoleonic wars should be subjected during the succeeding 180 years to a process of refinement and limitation in its application in the present day.[84]

He preferred to endorse the view of Denning LJ in *Williams*, even though that was a case of public rather than contractual duty, and even though it is doubtful that Denning LJ would have extended his "duty as consideration" thesis to contractual duties. The Glidewell view was that the emerging doctrine of "economic duress"

---

82. [1991] 1 QB 1, [1990] 1 All ER 512.
83. See 11.1.3.
84. [1990] 1 All ER 512 at 522.

could adequately cover *Stilk*-type cases;[85] if a contractor has used unfair pressure to extract the promise of additional payment, his claim should be rejected. If not, he should be entitled to the "bonus" wherever a practical benefit has been conferred. Glidewell LJ further relied on dicta in the case of *Pao On v Lau Yiu Long*[86] despite the fact that this case involved the performance of a duty owed to a third party rather than the promisor, a situation which had long been regarded as legally distinct.[87]

Glidewell LJ summed up the present state of the law as follows:

(i)   if A has entered into a contract with B to do work for, or to supply goods or services to, B in return for payment by B, and

(ii) at some stage before A has completely performed his obligations under the contract B has reason to doubt whether A will, or will be able to, complete his side of the bargain; and

(iii) B thereupon promises A an additional payment in return for A's promise to perform his contractual obligations on time; and

(iv) as a result of giving his promise, B obtains in practice a benefit, or obviates a disbenefit; and

(v)   B's promise is not given as the result of economic duress or fraud on the part of A; then

(vi) the benefit to B is capable of being consideration for B's promise, so that the promise will be legally binding.[88]

Russell LJ largely concurred and added that:

In the late twentieth century I do not believe that the rigid approach to the concept of consideration to be found in *Stilk v Myrick* is either necessary or desirable . . . The defendants, through their [surveyor], recognised the price that had been agreed originally with the plaintiff was less than what [the surveyor] himself regarded as a reasonable price. There was a desire on [the surveyor's] part to retain the services of the plaintiff so that the work could be completed without the need to employ another subcontractor. There was further a need to replace what had hitherto been a haphazard method of payment by a more formalised scheme involving the payment of a specified sum on the completion of each flat. These were all advantages accruing to the defendants which can fairly be said to have been in consideration of their undertaking to pay the additional £10,300. True it was that the plaintiff did not undertake to do any work additional to that which he had originally undertaken to do but the terms upon which he was to carry out the work were varied and, in my judgment, that variation was supported by consideration which a pragmatic approach to the true relation between the parties readily demonstrates.[89]

---

85. Economic duress was described as a "more refined control mechanism" in *Opel & Renault v Mitras Automotive (UK) Ltd* [2008] EWHC 3205 (QB).
86. [1980] AC 614.
87. See discussion of *South Caribbean* case below.
88. [1990] 1 All ER 512 at 521–522.
89. Ibid at 524.

Purchas LJ also concurred and added:

> This arrangement was beneficial to both sides. By completing one flat at a time
> rather than half completing all the flats the plaintiff was able to receive moneys on
> account and the defendants were able to direct their other trades to do work in the
> completed flats which otherwise would have been held up until the plaintiff had
> completed his work . . .
>
> Prima facie this would appear to be a classic *Stilk v Myrick* case. It was,
> however, open to the plaintiff to be in deliberate breach of the contract in order to
> "cut his losses" commercially. In normal circumstances the suggestion that a con-
> tracting party can rely upon his own breach to establish consideration is distinctly
> unattractive. In many cases it obviously would be and if there was any element of
> duress brought upon the other contracting party under the modern development of
> this branch of the law the proposed breaker of the contract would not benefit.[90]

The case raises considerable problems. All three judges claim not to be overturning the *Stilk* principle and state that there is no consideration in mere performance of a duty which provides no "benefit". What remains unclear is what the
benefit (practical or otherwise) is in *Roffey*. Glidewell LJ's leading judgment focuses
on the "promise to finish on time", yet that promise had already been given under the
original contract. Glidewell LJ seems to suggest that avoiding the so-called "penalty
clause" is a benefit though, legally, such sums would be "legally" (though probably
not practically) recoverable from the plaintiff as a consequence of his breach were
he not to complete the work.[91] Russell LJ suggests that a less haphazard system
resulted from the new agreement, and Purchas LJ endorses the view that completion
of work on one flat at a time was beneficial to both parties. If the different method of
performance is viewed as crucial, it could be argued that *Roffey* does not change the
law and that something more than performance of contractual duty is still required.
This does not seem to be the overriding sentiment of the court, however, and it is
difficult to escape the conclusion that the court saw "practical" benefit in the avoidance of troublesome litigation, involving, no doubt, an impecunious carpenter. The
Hong Kong courts have certainly interpreted *Roffey* as finding consideration/practi-
cal benefit in the mere performance of duty and have followed the same line.

UBC (Construction) Ltd v Sung Foo Kee Ltd[92]

The plaintiff subcontractors claimed sums allegedly due to them by the defendant
main contractors arising out of a plastering subcontract concerning the construction of public housing blocks and related commercial centres. The dispute arose in
respect of 26 variation orders. The defendants raised various arguments as to why
they should not be liable.

---

90. Ibid at 525–527.
91. See discussion of the rule in *Hadley v Baxendale* at 15.1.2.
92. [1993] 2 HKLR 207, [1993] 2 HKC 458.

The plaintiffs' evidence in relation to the disputed variation orders was that they were asked by the defendants to quote for the work, did quote, their quote was agreed and they carried out the work. The defendants argued, amongst other things, that any agreement on their part to pay the plaintiffs for these works was void for want of consideration since the work was required to be done by the subcontract and was within the contract sum. In finding substantially for the plaintiffs, the Hong Kong High Court considered the question of consideration. Kaplan J found that the facts were similar to those in *Roffey*, the approach of which should be followed.

The main authority cited was a secondary one, *Keating on Building Contracts*, but the crucial reference in that text is to the *Roffey* case and reads as follows:

> An agreement to pay an additional sum for no extra work may not always fail for consideration. When a sub-contract carpenter was in financial difficulties and the agreed price for his work was too low, it was held that there was consideration for the main contractor's promise to pay an additional amount for the same work in that the main contractor thereby secured benefits or obviated disbenefits from the continuing relationship with the sub-contractor. The benefits were:
> (1) seeking to ensure that the sub-contractor did not stop work in breach of contract;
> (2) avoiding the penalty for delay; and
> (3) avoiding the trouble and expense of engaging others to complete the work.

Kaplan J added:

> UBC had in fact threatened to stop work and it was clearly to SFK's benefit to prevent this happening. They succeeded . . . I too would find it unconscionable on the facts of this case to hold that these freely entered into agreements were void for want of consideration. Such a finding would fly in the face of commercial reality and would bring the law into disrepute.[93]

There are three difficulties which arise from this exposition of the Hong Kong law. The first is that if UBC had "threatened to stop work", as Kaplan J found, this was analogous to the mutinying sailors and arguably "economic duress". A similar threat was found in *Atlas Express v Kafco (Importers and Distributors) Ltd*[94] where the plaintiffs were a large haulage firm and the defendants a small business. The plaintiffs agreed to carry the defendants' cartons at £1.10 per carton on the assumption that they would carry 400–600 cartons per load. In fact there were only 200 cartons on the first trip and the plaintiffs said they would only continue if the defendants guaranteed £440 payment per load. The defendants reluctantly agreed as they needed the business and could not find anyone else to carry their goods at short notice. The defendants later refused to pay the excess amount and the plaintiffs sued. The plaintiffs' action failed on the basis of their "economic duress" and lack of consideration.

---

93. [1993] 2 HKC 458 at 469.
94. [1989] 1 All ER 641.

While the concept was still a novel one, the trial judge, Tucker J, accepted that economic duress could invalidate an agreement. He also found that there was no consideration for the promise to pay extra since the plaintiffs were merely doing their contractual duty. This latter ground appears incompatible with *Roffey*, decided only one year later. The economic duress ground, however, remains good law and was clearly supported in *Roffey*. There is obviously a narrow dividing line between a revised agreement providing a "practical benefit" and a revised agreement produced by duress. What is supposed to justify the different approach in *Roffey* is that the promisor acted on his own initiative without any threat from the promisee. It can be strongly argued that *UBC* is closer on its facts to *Atlas* than *Roffey*.

The second difficulty with the *UBC* analysis is the emphasis on "commercial reality". The premise seems to be that, since this is how businesses act in practice, the law should reflect this. Law, in other words, should follow not lead. This raises philosophical arguments as to the proper role of law in society; whether it should merely reflect existing practices, good or bad, or whether it should take a role in advocating how people (and businesses) *should* act. It may be no coincidence that in the years following *Roffey* and *UBC* there has been a huge increase, in Hong Kong, in the practice of completing contracts for the Hong Kong government tardily. Contractors now wait for further "incentives" to speed up the work rather than the former practice of completing ahead of schedule and being paid a bonus accordingly.[95]

A further "commercial reality" is that it is no longer sensible to tender realistically. Suppose that HKG asks for tenders for a renewal project. X and Y respond. X submits a realistic tender of $10,000,000 after careful consideration of the requirements. Y submits an "optimistic" tender of $8,000,000 and is awarded the contract. Y is soon in difficulties but is allowed to raise the price in return for his undertaking to do that which he is already legally bound to do. The courts endorse the new agreement, applying Glidewell LJ's "practical benefit" approach. The careful businessman, X, loses out but the unrealistic businessman, Y, is rewarded.

The third problem is that, in addition to academic reservations, *Roffey* has now, in England, been the subject of judicial criticism.[96] In *South Caribbean Trading*

---

95. Contractors were, largely, kept to time for the massive airport project and surrounding infrastructure, completed in 1998. Conversely, the MTR Corporation has gone grossly over time and budget in its high speed rail project to (near) Guangzhou and was routinely rewarded with extra funds from the public purse. The Corporation later announced a healthy annual profit which accrued to shareholders rather than the taxpayers who have footed the increased bill.

96. Veiled criticism is apparent in the words of Deputy High Court Judge Donaldson (QC) who said in *Opel & Renault v Mitras Automotive (UK) Ltd* [2008] EWHC 3205 (QB) at para 42: "*Willams v Roffey* would seem to permit any variation of a contract, even if the benefits and burdens of the variation move solely in one direction, and I am bound to apply the decision accordingly whatever view I may take of its logical coherence". The judge felt reluctantly constrained to follow *Roffey*. Cf also *obiter* of Kwan DHCJ in *Re Tse Sheung Yan* (unrep, HCB 62/2000 & 484/2000, 7 July 2000) discussed at n 118 below.

Ltd v Trafigura Beeher BV,[97] Colman J criticised *Roffey* on the basis that it upholds an agreement where consideration did not "move from the promisee" and that it is based on decisions, such as *Pao On*, which are not analogous since they are tripartite rather than bipartite agreements.[98] There is some irony with the first criticism since the court in *Roffey* considered the "from the promisee" rule at great length and concluded that it had been complied with. This certainly seems to be the case as far as the rule is generally understood. The problem in *Roffey* is not that the consideration is not provided by the promisee but that there is really no consideration at all. The second criticism is, however, a valid one; since the tripartite cases deal with promises or acts which could not be enforced by the promisor and which therefore provide him with an additional benefit. The criticism is equally applicable to the *UBC* decision since Kaplan J made the same assumption as Glidewell LJ in *Roffey* that, if performance of a duty owed to a third party is good consideration, the same should apply to the performance of a duty owed to the promisor. With respect, this is unsound, since in the first situation the promisor obtains a benefit to which he has no legal entitlement and which he could not otherwise enforce; while in the second he obtains only that to which he is already entitled. It must be said that, taken literally, the words of Cons J in *Fong Huen v Anthony Wong*[99] appear to "anticipate" the *Roffey* and *UBC* developments by some years. Cons J stated:

> It is usual . . . to distinguish between a promise to perform a public duty imposed by law and a private duty imposed by contract. The former is generally not accepted as sufficient consideration . . . On the other hand the latter is.

However, in the context of the case Cons J was *probably* referring to a contractual duty owed to a third party.[100] The duty in question was the plaintiff's duty to hand over title deeds to a property at the request of the defendant promisor's *wife*. It was held that the delivery of the deeds to the *promisor* amounted to good consideration. Prior to *Roffey*, the distinction between these two types of contractual duty (one owed by the promisee to the promisor and not constituting consideration, the other owed by the promisee to a third party and binding on the promisor) had long been recognised, as the next section makes clear.

---

97. [2004] EWHC 2676. *Roffey* (performance of duty as consideration) was later followed, however, in *Opel & Renault v Mitras Automotive* (ibid), albeit reluctantly.
98. The same mistaken elision of different forms of duty can be seen in the judgment of Arden LJ in *MWB Business Exchange Centres Ltd v Rock Advertising* [2016] EWCA Civ 553 at paras 79–80.
99. [1974] HKCFI 2.
100. The judge referred to an article by Professor A. G. Davis, "Promise to Perform an Existing Duty", (1937) 6 Camb LJ 203 which dealt with the third party duty situation.

4.5.3 Performance of a Duty Owed to a Third Party

The courts have long accepted that the mere performance of a duty owed to a third party may be good consideration for a separate promisor's promise. In this situation, therefore, *Roffey* has done no more than uphold the already existing law. The situation was considered in several nineteenth-century English cases,[101] one of which was *Shadwell v Shadwell*.[102] In that case the plaintiff was engaged to marry Ellen Nicholl. His uncle wrote to him saying he was happy to hear of the engagement and promising to pay him "to assist you at starting" 150 pounds per year for the rest of his life until the plaintiff's earnings at the Bar reached 630 pounds per year. The payments were not all made and, after the uncle's death, the plaintiff brought an action against the estate for the arrears. The defendants argued that the plaintiff had provided no consideration for his uncle's promise, but the plaintiff's action succeeded in the High Court. This was despite the fact that the promisee was contractually bound to marry Ellen Nicholl and could have been sued by her for breach of promise of marriage had he not done so.[103]

The decision is open to criticism in that it treats as consideration that which is only the condition of receipt of a gift;[104] that a benefit was discovered in "an object of interest to a near relative" contrary to the "natural love and affection rule";[105] and that a detriment was found in the nephew's "possibly" taking on extra responsibility in return for the gift, surely a case of "invented" consideration.[106] The case also appears to ignore the presumption that family arrangements are not intended to be binding.[107] However, the determination that the performance of a duty owed to X is good consideration for a promise from Y is uncontentious and has been accepted since in a number of cases.[108]

There is no doubt that the "duty to third party consideration" rule is also applicable in Hong Kong since it was supported at the highest level in the Privy Council on appeal from Hong Kong in *Pao On v Lau Yiu Long*.[109] In this case (involving also the issue of "past" consideration) Lord Scarman stated that the performance of a contractual duty owed to a third party (as well as the promise of same) is good consideration for the promisor contracting party's promise.

101. See also *Chichester v Cobb* (1866) 14 LT 433; *Scotson v Pegg* (1861) 6 H & N 295.
102. (1860) 9 CBNS 159.
103. The action for breach of promise was abolished in England by the Law Reform (Miscellaneous Provisions) Act 1970 s 1 and in Hong Kong by the Law Amendment and Reform (Consolidation) Ordinance (Cap 23) s 23.
104. See 4.1.1 above.
105. See 4.4.1.
106. See 4.4.3 above.
107. See chapter 5.
108. See, notably, *New Zealand Shipping Co Ltd v AM Satterthwaite & Co Ltd (The Eurymedon)* (1975) AC 154.
109. [1980] AC 614, [1979] 3 ALL ER 65.

4.6 Part-payment of a Debt

The rules on part-payment of a debt are of great antiquity, having been founded in *Pinnel's Case*[110] at the beginning of the seventeenth century. The basic rule is that part-payment cannot fully discharge a debt since the debtor has given nothing in return for his release from part of the debt. In short, the debtor's consideration is insufficient.

Of course, there may be situations where the creditor gets a benefit from the part-payment, for example, if payment of the lower sum is made ahead of the date for repayment so that the creditor receives his money early. The rule in *Pinnel's* case recognises this possibility by holding that where payment, at the creditor's request, is made by goods instead of money, or is made at a different time, or place, from that originally required, the part-payment may fully discharge the debt. So, for example, the creditor may be happy to receive a lesser sum ahead of the date for payment where he has liquidity problems. In such a situation the agreement to accept a lesser sum will be binding since consideration is present; the creditor has received a "benefit" in exchange for the partial release. The question of payment "in a different form" was considered by the English Court of appeal in *D&C Builders v Rees*[111] the facts of which are considered more fully below.[112] One argument raised in the case was whether part payment by a cheque could constitute a different form of payment so as to satisfy this recognised exception to the *Pinnel* rule. Denning LJ stated:

> This case is of some consequence: for it is a daily occurrence that a merchant or tradesman, who is owed a sum of money, is asked to take less. The debtor says he is in difficulties. He offers a lesser sum in settlement, cash down. He says he cannot pay more. The creditor is considerate. He accepts the proffered sum and forgives him the rest of the debt. The question arises: is the settlement binding on the creditor? The answer is that, in point of law, the creditor is not bound by the settlement. He can the next day sue the debtor for the balance, and get judgment. The law was so stated in 1602 by Lord Coke in *Pinnel's Case*—and accepted by the House of Lords in *Foakes v Beer*.
>
> . . . No sensible distinction can be taken between payment of a lesser sum by cash and payment of it by cheque.[113]

Although of great longevity, the rule in *Pinnel's* case has been upheld on several occasions since. The House of Lords appeared to accept the principle in the following case.

---

110. (1602) 5 Co Rep 117a.
111. [1966] 2 QB 617, [1965] 3 All ER 837.
112. See 4.7.3.3.
113. [1965] 3 All ER 837 at 839–840.

Foakes v Beer[114]

Mrs Beer obtained a judgment debt against Dr Foakes. They agreed that if he paid part of the debt immediately and the rest by instalments she would take no further action. Interest is normally payable on judgment debts and when he had paid all the debt she decided to sue for interest. Her action succeeded, ultimately in the House of Lords, since, it was held, even if there was an implied promise on her part not to sue for interest, no consideration had been given in return.

The Earl of Selborne LC confirmed the rule in *Pinnel*'s case, stating:

> The (Pinnel) doctrine itself, as laid down by Sir Edward Coke, may have been criticised, as questionable in principle, by some persons whose opinions are entitled to respect, but it has never been judicially overruled; on the contrary I think it has always, since the sixteenth century, been accepted as law. If so, I cannot think that your Lordships would do right, if you were now to reverse, as erroneous, a judgment of the Court of Appeal, proceeding upon a doctrine which has been accepted as part of the law of England for 280 years.

Some doubts as to the status of *Foakes* were raised, implicitly, by Denning J's suggestion, in the *High Trees* case,[115] that the House of Lords in *Foakes* had overlooked a previous contrary precedent in that same court in *Thomas Hughes v Metropolitan Railway Company*.[116] Denning J implied that the former case had been decided on equitable principles and the latter on the basis of common law despite the fusion of the two systems some nine years earlier.[117] Those doubts have not been shared by others and it is generally accepted that the cases are distinguishable.[118]

The efficacy of the part-payment rule was again subject to scrutiny following the English Court of Appeal's landmark ruling in *Roffey*.[119] It was argued by academics that if a promise of additional reward is binding where a "practical" benefit is conferred on the promisor in return, then, logically, a promise to release part of a debt should also be binding where a practical benefit is received in return.[120] Just as in *Roffey*, the benefit might be no more than avoiding the cost and inconvenience of enforcing the right to the balance of the debt, or getting something rather than nothing from a debtor who might otherwise declare bankruptcy. Irrespective of the logic of the academic arguments, the English courts have since made clear that

---

114. (1884) 9 App Cas 605.
115. See 4.7 below.
116. (1877) 2 App Cas 439.
117. In which case the equitable rule should have prevailed; see 2.2.3.1.
118. Not least because *Hughes* involves only a "suspensory" promise (see 4.7.3.5). But now cf *Collier v Wright* discussed at length at 4.7 below.
119. See discussion at 4.5.2 above.
120. See Adams and Brownsword, "Contract, Consideration and the Critical Path", (1990) 53 MLR 536. This logic was noted (implicitly and *obiter*) in *Re Tse Sheung Yan* (unrep, HCB 62/2000 & 484/2000, 7 July 2000) at para 23 where Kwan DHCJ said he would prefer to follow *Selectmove* and *not* follow *Roffey*.

Foakes remains good law and that the "practical benefit" argument is not applicable to the rule on part payment of a debt, not least because *Foakes* is a decision of the House of Lords and can be overruled only by that court.

Re Selectmove[121]

A company (Selectmove) owed tax money to the Inland Revenue. They offered to pay by instalments and the Inland Revenue representative dealing with their case said he would come back to them if this was unsatisfactory. Selectmove paid some instalments but were then threatened with winding up if they did not pay arrears. The company argued they had provided consideration by conferring a "practical benefit" on the claimants in paying part of the debt, when otherwise they may have gone into liquidation and the Inland Revenue would have got nothing. The company's defence failed in the Court of Appeal.

Peter Gibson LJ referred to the statement of Lord Blackburn in *Foakes v Beer* that:

> all men of business, whether merchants or tradesmen, do every day recognise and act on the ground that prompt payment of a part of their demand may be more beneficial to them than it would be to insist on their rights and enforce payment of the whole.

However, he added:

> Yet it is clear that the House of Lords decided that a practical benefit of that nature is not good consideration in law. When a creditor and a debtor who are at arm's length reach agreement on the payment of the debt by instalments to accommodate the debtor, the creditor will no doubt always see a practical benefit to himself in so doing. In the absence of authority there would be much to be said for the enforce-ability of such a contract. But that was a matter expressly considered in *Foakes v Beer* yet held not to constitute good consideration in law.[122]

Of course, a court will find consideration if the debtor gives additional benefit over and above the part-payment. Such additional benefit may be tenuous. In *MWB Business Exchange Centres Ltd v Rock Advertising Ltd*,[123] the English Court of Appeal found consideration for a varied ("re-structured") tenancy debt in that:

> Rock would remain a licensee and continue to occupy the Property with the result that it would not be left standing empty for some time at further loss to MWB.

---

121. [1995] 2 All ER 531.
122. [1995] 2 All ER 531 at 537.
123. [2016] EWCA Civ 553; [2018] UKSC 24.

The part-payment rules were not subjected to the expected analysis on appeal to the UK Supreme Court, since its decision was based on the narrow ground that the re-structuring was precluded by a prior "non-variation" clause.

The part-payment rules have not been seriously questioned in Hong Kong, post-1997, and *Foakes* and *Selectmove*[124] appear to represent the law here. *Selectmove* has been followed in several cases including *Bank of China (Hong Kong) Ltd v Cosan Ltd*[125] and *Tam Moon Tong v Lucky Dragon Restaurant Ltd.*[126] In the latter case in the District Court, Deputy District Judge Anthony Chow chose to follow *Selectmove* and had to "distinguish" an apparently conflicting Hong Kong Court of First Instance (CFI) case, *Chiu Wing Hang v BG Lighting Co Ltd*,[127] which he felt was binding on him. In precedent terms there is some doubt as to whether the District Court is so bound.[128] Moreover, while *Selectmove* itself is a non-binding post-1997 English precedent, it applies a pre-1997 House of Lords precedent (*Foakes*) such that departure by a single CFI judge is highly unusual.[129] In any event post-*Chiu Wing Hang* acceptance of *Selectmove* by the CFI in the *Bank of China* case should be regarded as definitive.[130] The traditional approach to part-payment was upheld in *Vinson Engineering Ltd v Kin Shing Engineering (HK) Co Ltd*[131] where it was held that a promise by a creditor to accept full payment *by instalments* was not binding since the debtor had given nothing in return for the promise not to require timely payment in full. The present state of the law, then, is that a curious distinction is drawn between contracts for the provision of goods or services, where the "practical benefit" test applies, and contracts for the making of a payment, where it does not.

There are some other, limited, exceptions to the rule that part-payment cannot discharge the whole of a debt, notably involving "composition" agreements and part-payment by a third party. In the former, creditors agree amongst themselves that they will each take only a proportion of the debt owed to them, given the debtor's inability to pay them all in full; such an agreement is binding (and relieves the debtor

---

124. See also *Ferguson v Davies* [1997] 1 All ER 315. The *Foakes/Selectmove* approach to part-payment appears to have been only reluctantly accepted by the English Court of Appeal in the strange case of *Collier v Wright* [2007] EWCA Civ 1329 discussed at 4.7 below.

125. (unrep, HCA 1600/2004, 18 August 2006).

126. (unrep, DCCJ 1706/2001, 15 August 2001).

127. Labour Tribunal Appeal No 67 of 1999. The cases are indeed distinguishable since in *Lucky Dragon* the claimant agreed to take less than his rightful severance pay and got nothing in return while in *Chiu Wing Hang* workers collectively agreed to defer wage payments to help keep their struggling employer afloat and avoid losing their jobs.

128. Cf M.J. Fisher, *Text, Cases and Commentary on the Hong Kong Legal System* (Hong Kong: Hong Kong University Press, 2019) at pp 122–123.

129. Such House of Lords decisions should be accorded "the utmost respect" (per Li CJ *A Solicitor v Law Society of Hong Kong* [2008] 2 HKC 1).

130. Stephen Hall suggests that if the task of overturning *Foakes* is to be undertaken in Hong Kong it should be by the Court of Final Appeal "or perhaps the Court of Appeal": S. Hall, *Law of Contract in Hong Kong: Cases and Commentary* (Hong Kong: LexisNexis, 2nd edn, 2009), p 193.

131. [2007] 5 HKC 268.

of part of his total debt).[132] There is an obvious benefit to the creditors, here, in that all "get something" whereas, were some creditors to "beat others to the punch" and obtain payment in full, such others might receive nothing. However, such benefit has been conferred by the *fellow creditors* rather than the debtor. His right to avoid full liability based on the composition, appears, therefore, to run counter to the rule that "consideration must move from the promisee". In *Chiu Wing Hang & Others v BG Lighting Co Ltd*, Deputy Judge To, indeed, stated that:

> [a] more satisfactory explanation is simply to acknowledge that composition agreements are an exception to the rule that consideration must move from the promisee.

An alternative theory is that it would be a "fraud" on the fellow creditors for an individual creditor to break his promise to them and seek full payment from the debtor.

Similarly, it has been held that a promise not to sue the debtor for the balance, having accepted part-payment from a third party in full satisfaction, is binding on the creditor.

In *Hirachand Punamchand v Temple*,[133] the defendant owed money to the plaintiffs, who were moneylenders. The defendant's father offered the plaintiffs a lesser sum on condition that they took this in full settlement. The plaintiffs accepted this but then changed their minds and sued the defendant for the balance. The action failed.

Fletcher Moulton LJ, emphasising the special nature of third party part-payment, stated:

> whichever way it is put, it comes to the same thing, namely that, after acceptance by
> the creditor of a sum offered by a third party in settlement of the claim against the
> debtor, the creditor cannot maintain an action for the balance.

The principle that part-payment by a third party, accepted in full satisfaction by the creditor, does discharge the debtor's debt is a sound one. The third party has no obligation to pay anything, and if the creditor chooses to take his money in return for a promise not to proceed against the debtor, this should be viewed as a binding contract with consideration from the third party. However, as in the *Temple* case, we can see, once again, that consideration has not moved "from the promisee". As with compositions, it has been argued that it would be "a fraud" on the third party to break the promise and seek to claim the balance from the debtor.

Given the reform of the "privity" rules (both in England and, more recently, in Hong Kong)[134] an alternative explanation for compositions *and* the third party

---

132. See *Chiu Wing Hang & Others v BG Lighting Co Ltd* (2000) Labour Tribunal Appeal No 67 of 1999.
133. [1911] 2 KB 330.
134. See chapter 16.

"*Temple*" rule is that they involve agreements between contracting parties intended to benefit a third party (the debtor) and thus enforceable by him.[135]

4.7 Promissory Estoppel

Promissory estoppel, sometimes also referred to as "equitable" or "quasi" estoppel, represents most law students' least favourite contract subject! It involves a proposition which is relatively easy to remember but proves difficult to apply in a practical situation. The proposition is that:

> where one party has, by his words or conduct, made to the other a promise or assurance which was intended to affect the legal relations between them and to be acted on accordingly, then, once the other party has taken him at his word and acted on it, the one who gave the promise or assurance cannot afterwards be allowed to revert to the previous legal relations as if no such assurance had been made by him, but he must accept their legal relations subject to the qualification which he himself has so introduced, even though it is not supported in point of law by any consideration but only by his word.[136]

The development of the doctrine began with the following case.

Central London Property Trust Ltd v High Trees House Ltd[137]

The plaintiffs leased flats to the defendant at 2,500 pounds per year. Because of war conditions the defendants could not fully sublet so, in 1940, the plaintiffs agreed to accept half rent. The plaintiffs later went bankrupt and, after the war ceased, the plaintiffs' receiver tried to recover full rent for the last six months of 1945 (after the war was over and flats were fully sublet). The action was brought to test the legal position and it was assumed that if the plaintiffs were successful they would claim full rent for the period 1940–1945. Denning J, as he then was, found for the plaintiffs on the basis of their limited claim but went on to consider the hypothetical position were the plaintiffs to sue for full arrears.

Denning J stated that were the plaintiffs to sue for full arrears for the war year period, they would be precluded by equitable principles. The main authority relied upon was *Thomas Hughes v Metropolitan Railway Company*,[138] a case decided by the House of Lords. Denning J's rationale was a type of "estoppel", based on equitable principles, which had, somehow, to be reconcilable with the principle of common

---

135. This poses again the question of whether the rule that consideration must move from the promisee can be separated from the privity rule.
136. Per Denning LJ in *Combe v Combe* [1951] 2 KB 215, [1951] 1 All ER767.
137. [1947] KB 130.
138. (1877) 2 App Cas 439.

law that part-payment of a debt cannot discharge the whole debt, even if accepted in full settlement.[139]

4.7.1 Why "Estoppel"?

Estoppel takes various forms, many of which are outside the scope of a contract text. Estoppel as a principle of evidence operates to prevent a person who has held out one state of facts to be true from later denying the truth of the earlier statement. So, for example, if X claims to be acting on his own initiative, he cannot later claim to have been acting as the agent of Y *even if*, in fact, X always was Y's agent. X is prevented, or "estopped" from denying the truth of his earlier statement of fact. Similarly, with estoppel by convention, parties who have acted on a common underlying assumption may later be prevented from questioning that assumption. Promissory estoppel is analogous to these types of estoppel in that it prevents a person going back on a *promise*, express or implied, previously made. This promise does *not* have to be a statement of fact.

4.7.2 How Is "Promissory" Estoppel Different?

Genuine estoppel, as Denning J pointed out, is limited to promises as to existing fact and does not extend to promises as to future action.[140] "Promissory" estoppel, however, deriving from the *Hughes* case, can extend to promises as to the future. *Hughes*, itself, was a case involving an implicit promise not to enforce a forfeiture pending the outcome of negotiations between landlord and tenant for the tenant to buy up the lease. Although the landlord had previously given the tenant six months to repair or forfeit, it was held that there was an implied promise not to enforce the forfeiture while negotiations continued. Once these broke down, it was held, the notice period should begin to run again. Lord Cairns LC stated:

> it is the first principle upon which all Courts of Equity proceed, that if parties who have entered into definite and distinct terms—certain penalties or legal forfeiture— afterwards by their own act or with their own consent enter upon a course of negotiation which has the effect of leading one of the parties to suppose that the strict legal rights will not be enforced . . . the person who otherwise might have enforced those rights will not be allowed to enforce them where it would be inequitable having regard to the dealings which have thus taken place between the parties.

The case may have remained one of limited application, applied only to cases of forfeiture, but for the emphasis placed upon it by Denning J in *High Trees*. It is for this reason that promissory estoppel is often referred to as the *High Trees*

---

139. See 4.6 above.
140. See *Jordan v Money* (1854) 5 HL Cas 185.

doctrine, even though *Hughes* itself is a House of Lords decision. *Hughes* was not even referred to in *Foakes v Beer*[141] only seven years later, a fact which Denning J attributed to the then-recent fusion of common law and equity. In his view *Hughes* was decided on equitable lines and *Foakes* on a common law basis. Denning J said:

> There has been a series of decisions over the last fifty years which, although they are said to be cases of estoppel, are not really such. They are cases in which a promise was made which was intended to create legal relations and which, to the knowledge of the person making the promise, was going to be acted on by the person to whom it was made, and which was in fact so acted on. In such cases the courts have said that the promise must be honoured . . . In my opinion, the time has now come for the validity of such a promise to be recognised. The logical consequence, no doubt is that a promise to accept a smaller sum in discharge of a larger sum, if acted upon, is binding notwithstanding the absence of consideration: and if the fusion of law and equity leads to this result, so much the better. That aspect was not considered in *Foakes v Beer*. At this time of day, however, when law and equity have been joined together for over seventy years, principles must be reconsidered in the light of their combined effect.[142]

4.7.3 The Scope and Significance of the Doctrine

Promissory estoppel can apply wherever a party promises to give up a legal right and the doctrine is not limited to part-payment of a debt. Nonetheless, since a promise not to claim the balance of a debt is clearly within the scope of the doctrine, promissory estoppel is usually dealt with as a possible mitigation of the rule in *Foakes v Beer*.

It is clear that, despite indications to the contrary in *High Trees*, the promissory estoppel doctrine does not render enforceable promises made without consideration. The doctrine operates to prevent the promisor reneging on his promise and enforcing his strict legal rights where the other party has acted on the promise and where it would be inequitable to allow the promisor to enforce the legal rights. The requirements of the doctrine have been outlined by the Hong Kong Court of Appeal in *Dixie Engineering Company Ltd v Vernaltex Company Ltd (t/a Wing Wo Engineering Company)*[143] by Ma JA who said:

> Broken down into its component parts, the doctrine of equitable or promissory estoppel, insofar as it applies in contractual situations, consists of:–
> (1) A clear and unequivocal representation by A to B that he will not rely on his strict contractual rights. The representation may be by words or by conduct.

---

141. (1884) 9 App Cas 605.
142. [1947] KB 130 at 134.
143. (unrep, CACV 343/2002, 11 February 2003).

(2) The representation by A must be made with the intention by him "or at least the knowledge" that B will act on it.

(3) B must in fact have acted in reliance on the representation.

4.7.3.1 A Clear and Unequivocal Promise

It has been said that the doctrine only applies where there is a clear and unequivocal promise. The lack of a sufficiently precise promise prevented the doctrine from operating in *Woodhouse AC Israel Cocoa Ltd SA v Nigerian Produce Marketing Co Ltd*.[144] Delivering the leading judgment, Lord Hailsham LC stated that in the absence of a clear and unambiguous statement, the doctrine could not arise, even if the representee had acted upon it mistakenly. Nevertheless, this "clear" promise may be implied, as was the case in *Hughes* itself. The *Woodhouse* requirement of a lack of equivocation has been endorsed in two relatively recent English cases: *Kim and Kim v Chasewood Park Residents Ltd*[145] and *Closegate Hotel Development (Durham) Ltd & Another v McLean & Others*.[146] In the former (Court of Appeal) case, the strictness of the requirement is illustrated. The case involved "encouragement" by a residents' committee representing leaseholders for leaseholders to contribute to buying out the freehold; a "potential benefit" of which would be the avoidance of ground rent. The committee added that those not joining the freehold purchase would continue to pay ground rent. The appellants joined the scheme and subsequently refused to pay the ground rent still demanded. In defence to an action for arrears the appellants unsuccessfully pleaded promissory estoppel. The Court of Appeal view was that the "no ground rent" statement was not an unequivocal promise to halt such in the event of a successful buy-out.

4.7.3.2 "Shield Not a Sword"

The general requirement of consideration is preserved by the principle that consideration is needed to *enforce* an agreement but not to *escape* enforcement. It is said that the doctrine can operate as a "shield not a sword".

Combe v Combe[147]

The parties, a husband and wife, had a separation agreement under which the husband promised to pay maintenance. The wife, the plaintiff, relied on this promise and sought no maintenance in the courts. The husband then refused to pay the promised

---

144. [1972] AC 741.

145. [2013] EWCA Civ 239.

146. [2013] EWHC 3237.

147. [1951] 2 KB 215, [1951] 1 All ER 767. Approved in *Baird Textile Holdings Ltd v Marks & Spencer plc* [2001] EWCA Civ 274.

maintenance and the plaintiff sued. Her action succeeded at first instance on the basis of estoppel but this judgment was overturned by a unanimous Court of Appeal.

Denning LJ, now a Court of Appeal judge, stated:

> Much as I am inclined to favour the principle of the *High Trees* case, it is important that it should not be stretched too far lest it should be endangered. It does not create new causes of action where none existed before. It only prevents a party from insisting on his strict legal rights when it would be unjust to allow him to do so, having regard to the dealings which have taken place between the parties.
>
> Seeing that the principle never stands alone as giving a cause of action in itself, it can never do away with the necessity of consideration when that is an essential part of the cause of action. The doctrine of consideration is too firmly fixed to be overthrown by a side-wind. Its ill effects have been largely mitigated of late, but it still remains a cardinal necessity of the formation of a contract, although not of its modification or discharge. I fear that it was my failure to make this clear in *Central London Property Trust, Ltd v High Trees House, Ltd* which misled Byrne J, in the present case.[148]

This statement represents something of a retreat from the more emphatic "logical conclusion" proposition enunciated in *High Trees*. Mrs Combe may have acted in reliance on her husband's promise but this was not enough to found an action to *enforce* an agreement lacking in consideration.

The "shield not sword" expression can be misleading since it is often taken, erroneously, to mean that only a defendant may use the doctrine. In fact, while a claimant may not *base* an action on promissory estoppel, he may use the doctrine to refute a possible defence of the defendant. This point has been accepted by the Hong Kong courts.

Bestkey Development Ltd v The Incorporated Owners of Fine Mansion[149]

The parties' dispute involved a room "The Room") in the Fine Mansion Building, which had been used for 20 years as a management office. The Room had originally been specifically designated for the exclusive use of the developer but, on a subsequent assignment, had been omitted. It was held that, via promissory estoppel, The Room could not be removed from the list of facilities available to tenants who had taken with the honest belief that The Room was included.

Liu JA made clear that there is a difference between promissory and other types of estoppel (such as proprietary estoppel). He stated:

> [K]eeping these two varieties discrete in concept would be helpful. Indeed, there still exists the significant difference between a proprietary estoppel which entitles

---

148. [1951] 1 All ER 767 at 770.
149. [1999] 3 HKC 275.

the representee to attack and a promissory estoppel which would not, barring the attempt of a skilful pleader who may dexterously turn a shield into a sword.[150]

4.7.3.3 The Doctrine Does Not Apply Where It Would Operate Unfairly

As a creation of equity, promissory estoppel will not, of course, apply where the party seeking to rely on the doctrine has himself not acted "equitably".

D&C Builders Ltd v Rees[151]

The plaintiffs were a small building firm. They did a job for the defendant and submitted a bill for balance of payment. The defendant's wife, acting on his behalf, refused to pay the full amount (about £480) and offered a reduced figure of £300, saying "take it or leave it". The plaintiffs were in a bad financial position, about which Mrs Rees apparently knew, and reluctantly accepted. They agreed in writing to accept "a cheque for £300 in completion of account". Later they claimed the balance and their action succeeded before a unanimous Court of Appeal.

Lord Denning MR emphasised the "equitable" basis of promissory estoppel, stating:

> In applying this (promissory estoppel) principle, however, we must note the qualification. The creditor is barred from his legal rights only when it would be inequitable for him to insist on them. Where there has been a true accord, under which the creditor voluntarily agrees to accept a lesser sum in satisfaction, and the debtor acts on that accord by paying the lesser sum and the creditor accepts it, then it is inequitable for the creditor afterwards to insist on the balance. But he is not bound unless there has been truly an accord between them.[152]
>
> In the present case, on the facts as found by the judge, it seems to me that there was no true accord. The debtor's wife held the creditor to ransom.

Danckwerts LJ was equally emphatic, adding:

> Mr. and Mrs. Rees really behaved very badly. They knew of the plaintiffs' financial difficulties and used their awkward situation to intimidate them . . . I cannot see any ground in this case for treating the payment as a satisfaction on equitable principles.[153]

---

150. Ibid at 281.
151. [1966] 2 QB 617, [1966] WLR 288, [1965] 3 All ER 837.
152. [1965] 3 All ER 837 at 841.
153. Ibid at 842.

A similar approach was adopted in *Re Selectmove*[154] to justify not employing promissory estoppel. Peter Gibson LJ having found no consideration for the release from part of a tax debt added:

> nor, in the light of the further late payments of the October and November PAYE and NIC and of various of the monthly instalments of £1,000, was it unfair or inequitable to serve a statutory demand and present a winding-up petition to enforce the debt.[155]

The fairness principle is clearly established in the Hong Kong courts where, in the *Dixie* case,[156] Ma JA stated:

> It is, however, crucial to bear in mind that whether or not the doctrine applies so as to estop the representor . . . will depend upon the equity or fairness of the situation confronting the court. In short: would it be inequitable or unfair to allow the representor to go back on his promise or representation?

In *Collier v Wright*, discussed at some length below,[157] Lady Justice Arden implied that the "unfairness" test is not an onerous one for the promisee since, once a promise is given voluntarily by the promisor: "For him to resile will of itself be inequitable."

4.7.3.4 Acting on the Promise

It is a requirement of promissory estoppel that the promisee must act in reliance on the promise. Much debate has centred on whether the act must be to the promisee's detriment. Lord Denning MR stated on a number of occasions that the act need not be to the promisee's detriment.[158] That proposition was entirely supported in the Hong Kong Court of Appeal case of *Dixie Engineering Company Ltd v Vernaltex Company Ltd (t/a Wing Wo Engineering Company)*.[159] A major part of the case involved an additional management fee (raised from 38% to 42%) charged by the plaintiffs. The defendants argued that, despite any agreement to the increase, it was unsupported by consideration. The court held that promissory estoppel could operate since the plaintiffs had proceeded on the basis of receiving the additional sums, which they had spent on their business. Woo JA stated emphatically that:

> It is not necessary for the promisee or representee to prove detriment; his acting on the promise or representation is sufficient to found estoppel or waiver.

---

154. [1995] 2 All ER 531 and see 4.6 above.
155. [1995] 2 All ER 531 at 539.
156. See 4.7.3 above.
157. See 4.7.3.5.
158. See, for example, *Alan & Co Ltd v El Nasr Export and Import Co* [1972] 2 QB 189.
159. (unrep, CACV 343/2002, 11 February 2003) and see 4.7.3 above.

Indeed, were detriment to be required, the promisee would surely have provided consideration for the promisor's promise, such that equitable intervention would be unnecessary. Clearly, even those maintaining that "detriment" is required must mean this is in a sense other than the generally accepted one. The promisee in *High Trees* itself had merely paid less rent, which is scarcely a detriment. Only in the sense that *were* the promisor to be allowed to enforce his strict legal rights the promisee would be even worse off than before, is there a "detriment".[160]

4.7.3.5 Suspension and Abrogation

The doctrine does not abolish the rule that part payment of a debt cannot extinguish the whole debt. That rule, first enunciated in *Pinnel*'s case and reinforced in *Foakes*, has continued to be applied. Denning J's suggestion, that the House of Lords in *Foakes* "overlooked" *Hughes* because of the only recent fusion of common law and equity, has not found favour. Were this the case, the principle of equity should have prevailed. In fact, the courts have managed to rationalise *Hughes* and *Foakes*, on the basis that the doctrine can operate so as to suspend the exercise of legal rights but not to abrogate them totally. Such rights could be resumed where, as in *High Trees*, the reason for their suspension has ceased or where, as in *Hughes*, the suspension is intended to run only for a specified time. Further, where no such automatic resumption applies, rights can be resumed after "reasonable notice" has been served.

Tool Metal Manufacturing Co Ltd v Tungsten Electric Co Ltd[161]

The appellants granted to the respondents a 10-year licence to deal with metal alloys. It was envisaged that the respondents would use material supplied by the appellants. The respondents agreed that they would pay "compensation" if they used material not supplied by the appellants and if they used more than a fixed monthly quota. During the war the appellants "waived" compensation since production was in the national interest. In 1945 the appellants claimed compensation for "over-production" as from the end of the war. Their first action failed, on the basis of promissory estoppel, but they made a second claim, arguing that their first action constituted notice of their intention to resume their right to compensation. The House of Lords upheld the second claim.

Lord Tucker expressed the view of their Lordships in stating:

> It is, of course, clear . . . that there are some cases where the period of suspension clearly terminates on the happening of a certain event, or the cessation of a previously existing state of affairs, or on the lapse of a reasonable period thereafter.

---

160. This appears to be the sense in which detriment was understood by the Hong Kong Court of appeal in *Bestkey Development Ltd v The Incorporated Owners of Fine Mansion*, discussed at 4.7.3.2 above.

161. [1955] 1 WLR 761, [1955] 2 All ER 657.

In such cases, no intimation or notice of any kind may be necessary. But in other cases, where there is nothing to fix the end of the period which may be dependent on the will of the person who has given or made the concession, equity will, no doubt, require some notice or intimation together with a reasonable period for re-adjustment before the grantor is allowed to enforce his strict rights.[162]

Of course, by this reasoning, promissory estoppel would not arise where, as in *Foakes*, the implied promise concerned the complete abrogation of the right to sue for the balance of a debt. Accordingly, the *Hughes* rationale was not appropriate to the *Foakes* scenario and was rightly ignored.

Denning LJ, in *D&C Builders Ltd v Rees*,[163] appeared to question the "suspension only" approach by stating:

> It is worth noticing that the principle may be applied, not only so as to suspend strict legal rights, but also so as to preclude the enforcement of them.[164]

This proposition seems hard to reconcile with the leading precedents of *Foakes* and *Tool Metal* and it has been suggested that it is meant to apply only to the non-recoverability of periodic payments made before the original rights resumed, as in the *High Trees* and *Tool Metal* cases.[165] So, for example, the right to full rent resumed after the war years in *High Trees* but could not extend to recovery of reduced rent paid *during* the suspensory period.

This reconciliation of the (*Foakes/Selectmove*) part-payment rules and the doctrine of promissory estoppel has been thrown into doubt, in England, by the strange Court of Appeal decision (and in particular the leading judgment of Lady Justice Arden) in the following case.

Collier v P & MJ Wright (Holdings) Ltd[166]

Collier was a joint debtor owing money to Wright. As such, his creditor (Wright) was entitled to seek full payment of the debt from him. It was contended, however, that Wright had agreed that, if Collier would encourage his co-debtors to pay "their share" and pay one-third of the debt himself, Wright would seek the balance only from Collier's co-debtors. When these debtors went into bankruptcy, Wright issued a statutory demand for the full amount to Collier which the latter contested on the grounds that the "one-third only" agreement was binding or, alternatively, that Wright was precluded by promissory estoppel from seeking the full amount from Collier.

---

162. [1955] 2 All ER 657 at 675.
163. [1966] 2 QB 617, [1966] WLR 288, [1965] 3 All ER 837.
164. [1965] 3 All ER 837 at 840.
165. See J. Poole, *Casebook on Contract Law* (Oxford/New York: Oxford University Press, 13th edn, 2016), p 152.
166. [2007] EWCA Civ 1329.

The Court of Appeal upheld Collier's contention that there was an arguable case justifying the setting aside of the statutory demand. Lady Justice Arden, delivering the leading judgment, expressed reservations about the ancient rule in *Pinnel's* case[167] (that part-payment of a debt cannot fully discharge same) but felt obliged to uphold it in light of its endorsement by the House of Lords in *Foakes v Beer*[168] and, later, by the Court of Appeal in *Re Selectmove*.[169] She was able to circumvent the rule, however, by stating that there appeared here to be the basis of an assertion of promissory estoppel (in equity) such as to *extinguish* Wright's claim. Lady Justice Arden stated:

> if (1) a debtor offers to pay part only of the amount he owes; (2) the creditor voluntarily accepts that offer, and (3) in reliance on the creditor's acceptance the debtor pays that part of the amount he owes in full, the creditor will, by virtue of the doctrine of promissory estoppel, be bound to accept that sum in full and final satisfaction of the whole debt. For him to resile will of itself be inequitable. In addition, in these circumstances, the promissory estoppel has the effect of *extinguishing* the creditor's right to the balance of the debt. This part of our law originated in the brilliant *obiter dictum* of Denning J, as he then was, in the *High Trees* case.[170]

There are some problems with the Arden analysis. First, it treats as unproblematic the proposition that promissory estoppel may serve to extinguish rather than merely suspend the exercise of legal rights, a view not widely accepted by academics and the courts.[171] Second, it founds its outcome on the "brilliant" *obiter* statement of a, then, single High Court judge[172] though this statement results in the total undermining, in the instant case, of part-payment principles enunciated in the *rationes* of higher courts.[173] More fundamentally, it is questionable whether it is the role of equity to overturn common law principles established by the highest court. The part-payment rule may have been criticised by the Law Revision Committee (as long ago as 1937) but, absent legislation or Supreme Court intervention, it should not be called into question by the English Court of Appeal.[174]

It is to be hoped that, in the cause of certainty in the law, Hong Kong courts will ignore *Collier*, as of course they are fully entitled to do. There seems little point

---

167. Discussed at 4.6.
168. Ibid.
169. Ibid.
170. Emphasis added.
171. Cf, for example, E. Peel, *Treitel: The Law of Contract* (London: Sweet & Maxwell, 14th edn, 2015), pp 142–143. In *Collier*, Longmore LJ seems to have been doubtful on this point.
172. The "brilliant" *obiter* was largely recanted by the same Denning (as Denning LJ) in *Combe v Combe* [1951] 2 KB 215 only four years later.
173. Ibid.
174. *Collier* was endorsed (*obiter*) in the Court of Appeal in *MWB Business Exchange Centres Ltd v Rock Advertising Ltd* [2016] EWCA Civ 553 (in which Arden LJ also sat) but the case was decided on common law consideration principles.

in having a rule which says that part-payment of a debt cannot discharge the full amount if the rule can be avoided merely because the creditor has promised to accept less and the debtor has acted upon the promise by paying less![175] Certainly, there are indications of an English "rethink" with Patten LJ in *Kim and Kim v Chasewood Park Residents Ltd*[176] stating:

> The generally accepted view is that promissory estoppel is usually only suspensory and that the representor may resile from his promise on reasonable notice unless it would be unconscionable for him to do so.[177]

4.8 The Need for the Promissory Estoppel Doctrine

It could be argued that promissory estoppel would have been unnecessary had the courts been sufficiently flexible in applying consideration principles. Given the examples of "invented" consideration previously considered,[178] it is clear that the courts have not been consistently creative. In a *High Trees* scenario, for example, consideration could be found via the later "practical benefit" test. The adoption of this approach in respect of the payment of money has, however, been rejected.[179]

Despite the argument that consideration could have been more creatively applied,[180] it is undeniable that promissory estoppel is now firmly established and, although its precise scope remains uncertain, as does its relationship with other forms of estoppel, the doctrine will remain as a significant equitable amelioration of the consideration rules.

The promissory estoppel doctrine was enthusiastically applied by the Hong Kong Court of Final Appeal in *Luo Xing Juan Angela v The Estate of Hui Shui See, Willy & Others*[181] where a "common law wife", orally promised a 35% share of her "husband's" property (where they had lived together) on his death was able to set up the promise against the "husband's" family on his death. Ribeiro PJ stated:

> A promissory estoppel may be said to arise where (i) the parties are in a relationship involving enforceable or exercisable rights, duties or powers; (ii) one party ("the promisor"), by words or conduct, conveys . . . a clear and unequivocal promise or assurance to the other ("the promisee") that the promisor will not enforce or exercise some of those rights, duties or powers; and (iii) the promisee reasonably relies upon that promise and is induced to alter his or her position on the faith of it,

---

175. See a critique of *Collier* in R. Austen-Baker, "A Strange Sort of Survival for *Pinnel's* Case: *Collier v P & MJ Wright (Holdings) Ltd*", (2008) 71 MLR 611.
176. [2013] EWCA Civ 239.
177. Ibid at para 41.
178. See 4.4.3 above.
179. See *Re Selectmove* discussed at 4.6. But now cf discussion of *Collier v Wright* at 4.6 and 4.7.
180. Or that *Jorden v Money* was too restrictively interpreted: see P. Atiyah, *Essays on Contract* (Oxford: Clarendon Press, 1988) pp 231–239.
181. (2009) 12 HKCFAR 1.

so that it would be inequitable or unconscionable for the promisor to act inconsistently with the promise.[182]

With such a clear endorsement from Hong Kong's highest court, it is clear that the doctrine is secure.

4.9 Do We Still Need Consideration?

To end almost where we began, we may ask whether consideration still serves any useful function. Procedurally, it is true, we need to plead consideration in any breach of contract action; and failure to do so will defeat a plaintiff's claim. However, the weakening of the doctrine by the intervention of equity and, for example, statutory changes to the traditional privity rules, suggest that the significance of consideration is more apparent than real. Consider how easily traditional principles of consideration were abandoned in *Williams v Roffey* to bring the law in line with commercial practice.

Judicial hostility may be seen in the words of Lord Goff in White v Jones (ultimately resolved in tort) who opined:

Our law of contract is widely seen as deficient in the sense that it is perceived to be hampered by the presence of an unnecessary doctrine of consideration.[183]

On a more practical level, in *Blue v Ashley*, discussed above, Leggatt J (as he then was) disposing of a "no consideration" argument stated:

The requirement of consideration therefore does not (here) cause a problem. It would be unusual if it did, as I am not aware of any case in the twenty-first century in which a claim founded on an agreement has failed for want of consideration.[184]

It may be added that the preponderance of academic thought is critical of consideration (though it retains its supporters).[185] However, we may conclude, as does Professor Ewan McKendrick, that:

the fact is that English law has not been given, and may never be given, the opportunity to start afresh. This being the case, it is unlikely that the courts will . . . abandon the doctrine.[186]

---

182. Ibid at para 55.
183. [1995] 2 AC 207 at 262.
184. [2017] EWHC 1928 (Comm) at para 58.
185. Notably Professor Chen-Wishart. See, in particular *In Defence of Consideration* (2013) *Oxford Commonwealth Law Journal* 209.
186. Ewan McKendrick, *Contract Law: Text, Cases & Materials* (Oxford/New York: Oxford University Press, 9th edn, 2020).

5

Intention to Create Legal Relations

OVERVIEW

While it is well established that agreement (offer and acceptance) and consideration are essential to the formation of a contract, the requirement of an intention to create legal relations is more problematic, with a minority of academics arguing that intention is not, or should not be, a necessary contractual element. The basis of the minority view is that, since consideration is a token of the intention to be bound, to require a separate element of intention is unnecessary. Similarly, it can be argued that the requirement of offer and acceptance (agreement) obviates the need for a separate requirement of intention. This is particularly the case when one remembers that offer and acceptance must be sufficiently "certain". On many occasions, courts have inferred a lack of contractual intention from a lack of contractual certainty.

Given the considerable overlap with agreement and consideration, there is some merit in the argument that intention should not be a separate requirement. However, the clear pronouncements of the courts in a number of cases leads inevitably to the conclusion that the denial of the need for intention cannot be supported except to the extent that intention must be judged objectively, rather than subjectively.

The major argument produced by the courts for the separate requirement of intention is that, without it, the courts would be faced with a deluge of cases involving petty agreements which, though probably supported by consideration in the technical sense, were never intended to be anything other than friendly, or domestic, arrangements.

Given the requirement of intention, it is normal to divide agreements into those of a domestic or family nature and those which are "commercial". In the case of the former category, the courts normally adopt the presumption that there is no intention to create legal relations. However, this presumption is rebuttable if there is clear evidence to the contrary.

In the area of commercial arrangements, the opposite applies: there is a presumption of an intention to create legal relations. Again, this presumption is rebuttable but the cases strongly emphasise that this will be a heavy burden to discharge.

It has also been recognised, in Hong Kong, that there are exceptional cases where the agreement in question fits into neither the "social" nor "commercial" category.

5.1 Is Intention Necessary?

It is generally stated that, in addition to the need for agreement and consideration, the common law also requires proof of intention to create legal relations. The element of intention is far less often crucial than agreement or consideration. The main reason for this is that, since the major function of consideration is to show evidence of the parties' intention to make a binding agreement, where consideration is present intention will invariably follow. Indeed, some writers, notably Professor Williston,[1] have argued that common law systems should not require both consideration *and* intention. Williston states:

> there is no apparent reason why mere social promises should not create a contract if the requisites for the formation of a contract . . . exist . . . Naturally, the very existence of a social relationship might be a persuasive indicium that one or more of the elements ordinarily found in a contract are absent.

However, Williston appears to have gone further in stating that the common law simply does not demand a separate requirement of intention: if all the other elements are present, he says, a contract is formed even in social situations. He writes:[2]

> The common law does not require any positive intention to create a legal obligation as an element of contract.

The argument that intention *should* be unnecessary, given the function of consideration, has much to commend it. Indeed, most of the cases apparently decided on the basis of lack of intention could equally well have been decided on the basis of absence of consideration.[3] The major justification for the additional requirement of intention, however, is that, without it, the floodgates would be opened to many domestic and social arrangements where consideration can be identified. Thus:

> the small courts of this country would have to be multiplied one hundredfold if these arrangements were held to result in fact in legal obligations. They are not sued upon, and the reason they are not sued upon is not because the parties are reluctant

---

1. See R. A. Lord, *A Treatise on the Law of Contract by Samuel Williston* (Rochester, New York: Lawyers Cooperative Publishing, 4th edn, 2018).
2. Ibid, s 3.5, pp 228–229.
3. See, for example, *Balfour v Balfour* [1919] 2 KB 571.

to enforce their legal rights when the agreement is broken, bur because the parties, in the inception of the arrangement, never intended that they should be sued upon.[4]

Williston's proposition that an intention to create legal relations is not essential is difficult to sustain except in the narrow, literal sense that intention is judged objectively rather than subjectively. There are cases, admittedly rare, where consideration and all the other elements appear to be present but where there has been held to be no contract because of a lack of intention.

Jones v Padavatton[5]

A daughter, who had a good job in Washington, USA, was offered by her mother, who lived in Trinidad, an allowance of $200 a month if she would go to England to study for the Bar, with a view to practising in Trinidad. Although she did not want to leave Washington, the daughter agreed. She accepted payment of 200 West Indian dollars per month, even though she had expected 200 US dollars, which were worth considerably more. No written contract was made, nor was there any agreement as to the duration of the arrangement. The daughter came to England in 1962. In 1964, by a second agreement, it was arranged that the mother would buy a house in London for the daughter to live in. She was to rent out some of the rooms and use the income to maintain herself in place of the $200 per month. In 1967 the mother claimed possession of the house; the daughter had not yet passed the Bar examinations. The majority of the English Court of Appeal felt that the mother-daughter relationship was not contractual because of a lack of intention.

On the basis purely of consideration, it appears that the agreement would have been enforceable. Fenton Atkinson LJ stated that (the daughter)

> had never for a moment contemplated the possibility of the mother or herself going to court to enforce legal obligations, and that she felt it quite intolerable that a purely family arrangement should become the subject of proceedings in a court of law.

Danckwerts LJ agreed with the view that there had been no intention to create legal relations.

Salmon LJ dissented on the issue of whether or not there was intention. He found that there was such intention. He said that there was a binding agreement which was intended to last for a "reasonable time". As five years had passed, this time had lapsed and the agreement was unenforceable.

What is important to note is that, in the view of all three Court of Appeal judges, the intention of the parties was crucial.

We may, therefore, with some confidence, conclude that intention to create legal relations is a requisite element, though one less likely to be crucial than the

---

4. Ibid per Atkin LJ at 576.
5. [1969] 1 WLR 328, [1969] 2 All ER 616.

requirements of offer and acceptance and consideration. Unless a separate requirement of intention is demanded it is difficult to explain why a promise by a husband
to buy his wife a present in return for her cooking him a meal would not be binding,
given an unequivocal promise and clear consideration given in return. Yet to intervene in such matters would surely place the courts under impossible stress.

Cases such as *Jones v Padavatton* support Davies's[6] criticism of Williston that:

> the cases do not support [Williston's] argument and, since the cases are the law, the
> argument must be wrong.[7]

Only in the sense that intention must be viewed "objectively" can Williston's
denial of the need for intention be supported, and there are extracts from Williston's
work which support this more limited approach. Thus, he writes:

> Parties to an informal transaction frequently are not thinking of legal obligations.
> They may in fact intend an exchange; by contrast, they may intend a gift; or, they
> may intend merely to induce action by each other when they make their promises.
> To make the obligation of such promises dependent upon the mere fortuity of the
> promisor's subjective belief as to his legal situation would be inappropriate. Thus,
> when courts speak of an intention to create a legal relation as the test of the creation
> of a contract, they are actually fictitiously assuming that intent from the objective
> words and acts of the promisor. A deliberate promise, seriously made, is quite likely
> to be enforced irrespective of the promisor's views regarding his legal liability.[8]

The objective nature of intention is echoed by Lord Denning MR in *Merritt v
Merritt*[9] where he states:

> in all these cases the court does not try to discover the intention by looking into the
> minds of the parties. It looks at the situation in which they were placed and asks
> itself: would reasonable people regard this agreement as intended to be binding?

In Hong Kong, a similar approach is evident in the case of *Hong Kong Aircrew
Officers Association v Cathay Pacific Airways Ltd*[10] where Jerome Chan J stated
that the subjective intention of either of the parties should not be considered as it is
"self-serving".

Even more fundamentally, we might ask why "intention" is required, separately,
when the element of agreement already implies intention to be bound. The usual

---

6. Robert Upex, *Davies on Contract* (6th edn, 1991). Later versions of this book do not contain this
    quotation.
7. Ibid at p 46.
8. Note 1 above, s 3.5 at pp 218–221.
9. [1970] 1 WLR 1211 at 1213.
10. See 5.3.3 below.

rejoinder is that offer and acceptance prove an agreement between the parties but not a binding one. Thus, Hall[11] writes:

> Not all agreements are enforceable. Even when an offer has been accepted, the terms are certain, and the promises are supported by consideration, the agreement will not be an enforceable contract if the parties lacked an intention to be legally bound.

While this does, as Davies has noted (above), appear to reflect the judicial view, it is not in accord with the accepted definition of offer as "an expression of willingness to contract on specified terms, *made with the intention that it is to become binding* as soon as it is accepted by the person to whom it has been addressed".[12]

When added to the definition of acceptance as "a final and unqualified expression of assent to the terms of the offer",[13] such definitions lead to the conclusion that once there is offer and acceptance, intention to be bound is inevitable. Again, however, we must accept that there are cases (in England and Hong Kong) in which the court's decision as to the existence, or otherwise, of a contract depends on a finding as to the parties' "intention".[14]

5.2 Domestic and Social Arrangements

If an agreement is a "domestic" one, there is a presumption that there is no intention to create legal relations. However, the presumption is weakened where the relationship is less strong or where the nature of the agreement is more "business-like".

5.2.1 Spouses Living Together in Harmony

Where spouses are living "in amity" the presumption against intention is a strong one, as illustrated by the following case.

Balfour v Balfour[15]

A wife sought to enforce a promise made by her husband that he would pay her a certain sum of money per month while he worked abroad. The English Court of Appeal held that the wife's action must fail as she had not provided any consideration[16]

---

11. S. Hall, *Law of Contract in Hong Kong: Cases and Commentary* (Hong Kong: LexisNexis, 3rd edn, 2017), p 203.
12. E. Peel, *Treitel: The Law of Contract* (London: Sweet & Maxwell, 14th edn, 2015), p 10. Emphasis added.
13. Ibid at p 18.
14. As already noted, such intention is judged "objectively", as is the question of whether there is agreement.
15. [1919] 2 KB 571.
16. See chapter 4.

for the promise of her husband and because it was not intended that their agreement was to have legal consequences. In an oft-cited passage Atkin LJ said:[17]

> It is quite common . . . that the two spouses should make arrangements between themselves . . . To my mind those agreements, or many of them, do not result in contracts at all, and they do not result in contracts even though there may be what as between other parties would constitute consideration for the agreement . . . Nevertheless they are not contracts, and they are not contracts because the parties did not intend that they should be attended by legal consequences.[18]

Indeed, in *Balfour* the court said that family arrangements are outside the realm of contracts altogether. The courts are not keen on opening the floodgates to a torrent of cases dealing with disputes over the validity of domestic contracts and wish to stay "out of the bedroom". However, this stance can be criticised because of the increasing role of contract in family law. Commentators[19] have noted that, while *Balfour* remains a leading case in this area of law, modern family law is much more reliant on contract law than when *Balfour* was decided in the early part of the twentieth century.

5.2.2 Separated Spouses

The above presumption is rebuttable and the courts are more willing to infer the requisite intention to create legal relations where the parties are no longer on friendly terms. In fact, the courts have noted that the parties are likely to bargain very keenly indeed in such circumstances. They often do not trust each other and render their agreements formally and in writing so as to reduce any uncertainty as to what might have been agreed. This was shown in *Merritt v Merritt*[20] involving an agreement between a husband and wife who had separated. The English Court of Appeal had no difficulty in finding that the agreement was intended to be legally binding. Lord Denning MR said that *Balfour* did not apply to such situations. Indeed, he went so far as to suggest that the normal presumption against intention is "reversed" in such cases. An analogous situation arose in the Hong Kong case of *Ho Lai King v Kwok Fung Ying*.[21] Here, the Court of Appeal rejected the trial judge's finding of "no intention", despite the fact that the parties to the dispute were mother, daughter, and son-in-law. The appeal court was influenced by the fact that the parties' relationship had become "distant" and that the claimant had clearly expended considerable time and energy on the services for which payment was claimed. Moreover, the Court

---

17. At 578–579.
18. Cited with approval in the Hong Kong case of *Sun Er Jo v Lo Ching & Others* [1996] 1 HKC 1.
19. See, for example, Professor Michael Freeman, "Contracting in the Haven: *Balfour v Balfour* Revisited", in R. Halson (ed), *Exploring the Boundaries of Contract* (Aldershot: Dartmouth, 1996).
20. [1970] 1 WLR 1211.
21. [2020] HKEC 2224; [2020] HKCA 657.

of Appeal affirmed that the presumption is "only" a factual one and should not be treated as a presumption of law.

5.2.3 Other Relationships

A number of domestic agreements have been held to be enforceable, especially where the social or domestic nexus between the parties is not strong. In *Simpkins v Pays*,[22] in the English High Court, the parties were two members of a family living together and a paying boarder. They all regularly entered into a competition run by a newspaper. Each one contributed to each entry. This was done by each filling in one line on the entry form. However, the entry form was submitted in the householder's name only. Subsequently, when the "joint submission" won and the householder refused to pay the boarder any prize money, the boarder sued and the court held she was entitled to a third of the prize money; the parties had intended the agreement to be binding. Sellers J found that there was sufficient mutuality in the arrangements between the parties for there to be an agreement that, whichever line in the entry form won, all would share equally in the prize money.

A similar approach was taken by the Hong Kong courts in *Wu Chiu-kuen v Chu Shui-ching*,[23] where an agreement for the joint purchase of "Mark Six" tickets was held to be binding despite its apparently "social" nature. Deputy Judge P. Chan said:

> Arrangements of this sort are very often informal and even loose at times. What is important is that the persons involved have acted on the informal arrangements and conducted themselves in such a way that it is clear from all the circumstances that they have agreed and intended to buy the tickets together and share the winnings, if any, together.[24]

In *Parker v Clark*,[25] Devlin J held that an arrangement between relatives to share a house was binding in view of the fact that Parker had to take the drastic step of disposing of his own residence in order to join the arrangement. Such a step was clear evidence sufficient to rebut the presumption against an intention to create legal relations.

By contrast, the English Court of Appeal held that there was no intention to create legal relations between a mother and daughter in *Jones v Padavatton*[26] the facts of which are set out above.[27] This decision seems harsh on the daughter as

---

22. [1955] 1 WLR 975
23. (unrep, A4081/1991, 28 February 1992).
24. No such clarity existed in *Wilson v Burnett* [2007] EWCA Civ 1170, such that the "winner" of a giant lottery prize was not required to share with the claimants. Disputes as to the evidence led the Court of Appeal to determine that a certain agreement to share winnings could not be ascertained.
25. [1960] 1 WLR 286.
26. [1969] 1 WLR 328, [1969] 2 All ER 616.
27. See 5.1.

it could be argued that she had taken a step—giving up a good job and moving to England—just as drastic as that taken by the plaintiff in *Parker*.[28] The case of *Coward v Motor Insurers' Bureau*[29] involved the common practice of a worker providing fellow workmen with transport to and from work in return for a contribution towards travelling expenses. The plaintiff was killed in an accident while on the way to work and his widow sued for damages. The English Court of Appeal held there was no intention to create legal relations with regard to journeys to be undertaken *in the future*. They pointed out that the uncertainties of everyday life such as illness, holidays, change of shift times and suchlike coupled with the fact that the plaintiff had alternative means of transport open to him made it improbable that either party intended there to be any intention to be legally bound. This was despite the plaintiff's contribution to expenses. However, it does seem that such agreements do create an intention to create legal relations concerning journeys that have already been undertaken.[30] The main reason for so finding is that the parties have acted in reliance on the agreement and should be prevented from going back on their agreement. The *Coward* approach was disapproved by the House of Lords in *Albert v Motor Insurers' Bureau*, especially by Lord Cross who felt that the court in *Coward* had focused on the subjective intention of the parties themselves rather than adopting an objective test of whether a third party would believe there to be a contract in such circumstances.[31]

5.2.4 Rebutting the Presumption

While, in a social context, the onus is on the party denying intention, the courts have pointed out that the presumption against intention is "only" a factual one, and *not*, they assert, "a strong one". This is even more the case where the parties' relationship is not a close one, or is largely "historical". Evidence that siblings were "no longer close" was key to rebutting the presumption in *Ho Lai King v Kwok Fung Ying & Another*,[32] where the Hong Kong Court of Appeal overturned the trial judge's finding of "uncertainty" and lack of intention in an agreement between estranged family members.

---

28. However, even if the majority in the *Padavatton* case had found intention, it would not have been, as Salmon LJ indicated, of unlimited duration.
29. [1962] 1 All ER 531.
30. [1972] AC 301.
31. See discussion in 5.1 above.
32. [2020] 5 HKC 271.

5.3 Commercial Arrangements

If the contract is "commercial" in nature, then there is a presumption that it is intended to be legally binding.[33] This presumption can be rebutted but the "onus" (burden) of proof is on the party seeking rebut the presumption. The following cases show that this burden is a heavy one.

5.3.1 The Presumption

Edwards v Skyways Ltd[34]

The plaintiff was employed by the defendants as an airline pilot. The defendant informed him that they were making him redundant and gave him three months' notice. An agreement was reached between the parties concerning pension payments whereby the defendants would make, inter alia, an "*ex gratia*" payment to the claimant. The defendants then refused to make this payment saying that the words "*ex gratia*" showed they had no intention to create legal relations. The plaintiff successfully sued for breach of contract. The court interpreted the words "*ex gratia*" as meaning that the defendants did not admit to any pre-existing legal liability on their part. The wording itself was, at best, ambiguous. The defendants bore the burden of rebutting the presumption that there was an intention to create legal relations in commercial arrangements and they had failed to rebut this presumption. Similar reasoning was applied in *Lo Yuk Sui v Fubon Bank (HK) Ltd* where Ng J, in the Hong Kong Court of First Instance, held a commercial arrangement to be intended as a binding contract, notwithstanding that certain additional terms remained unresolved.

5.3.2 Rebutting the Presumption

In *Bowerman v Association of British Travel Agents Ltd*,[35] the English Court of Appeal emphasised the difficulty of rebutting the presumption of intention in the case of commercial agreements. The majority judgments stressed the need to exclude *expressly* any intention to be legally bound if intention is to be negatived. Such an express exclusion is to be found in the older cases of *Appleson v H Littlewood Ltd*[36] and *Jones v Vernon's Pools Ltd*.[37] Both cases involved football pools and the courts in both found the words "binding in honour only" sufficient to rebut the presumption such that the plaintiffs' claims failed.

---

33. See *Ma Ip (or Yip) Hung v Lai Chuen* [1957] HKLR 32; *Everlong Securities Co Ltd v Wong Sio Po* [2004] 1 HKC 702; *Lo Yuk Sui v Fubon Bank (HK) Ltd* [2016] 1 HKC 462.
34. [1964] 1 WLR 349.
35. [1996] CLC 451.
36. [1939] 1 All ER 464.
37. [1938] 2 All ER 626.

The following is the most emphatic case of a clause expressly excluding intention.

Rose and Frank Co v JR Crompton & Brothers Ltd[38]

The plaintiffs were a New York firm dealing in tissues for carbonising paper. The defendants manufactured such tissues in England. In 1913 the parties made a written agreement (the "Agreement") whereby the plaintiffs were given certain selling rights for a fixed period of time with an option to extend this time. The Agreement contained a clause described as "the Honourable Pledge Clause". It read:

> This arrangement is not entered into, nor is this memorandum written, as a formal or legal agreement, and shall not be subject to legal jurisdiction in the law courts either of the United States or England, but it is only a definite expression and record of the purpose and intention of the three parties concerned, to which they each honourably pledge themselves.

The Agreement was later extended to 1920. However, in 1919 the defendants terminated it without giving the requisite notice set out in the Agreement. They further refused to execute orders which had been received and accepted by them before termination of the Agreement. The plaintiffs sued for damages for breach of the Agreement and for non-delivery of goods related to these orders. The English Court of Appeal held that there was no binding agreement since the necessary intention was lacking. On appeal, the House of Lords held that the original "overall" three-year agreement was not enforceable because the parties had clearly expressed an intention not to be legally bound by it. However, each order already given and accepted constituted a separate contract which the defendants were bound to perform.

5.3.3 Exceptional Agreements

The issue of intention to create legal relations in a context seen as neither domestic nor social came before the Hong Kong Court of First Instance in *Cable & Wireless (Hong Kong) Ltd Staff Association v Hong Kong Telecom International Ltd*.[39] The court was asked to rule on the validity of an agreement between the plaintiff, the trade union of employees of the defendant, and the defendant concerning possible staff redundancies. Deputy Judge Muttrie noted that, although these so called collective agreements were not domestic agreements, they were generally considered unenforceable and that they were only intended to agree a framework for dealing with business relationships between the members of the trade union and the defendant. He relied on *Rose and Frank v Crompton* and distinguished *Edwards v Skyways Ltd*. There was nothing in the agreement itself indicating the requisite intention and

---

38. [1925] AC 445.
39. [2001] 2 HKC 233.

the surrounding circumstances led the deputy judge to conclude that this was a "gentlemen's agreement binding in honour only".[40]

Deputy Judge Muttrie's judgment is worthy of note in that he, untypically, deals with the relationship between Hong Kong and English courts decisions. He, first, makes clear that, *prima facie*, Hong Kong courts are bound by the English pre-1997 common law and refers specifically to Article 8 of the Basic Law. He points out that, under the English common law, "collective bargaining" agreements are presumed not to be binding. *However*, he goes on to show that one must look at the *local* circumstances prevailing in Hong Kong.[41] The key consideration appears to have been that "the climate of expert opinion in Hong Kong" is that collective agreements are not intended to be legally binding.

A similar approach had been taken in *Hong Kong Aircrew Officers Association v Cathay Pacific Airways Ltd*.[42] Here the parties had spent three years negotiating a new "basings" agreement whereby Cathay officers would be based throughout the world. One effect would be to severely reduce benefits to expatriate officers. Eventually a new basings contract was drawn up and new terms were introduced for new officers. The defendants then sought a declaration that the new terms were legally binding. The plaintiffs, representing most of the officers, resisted the declaration. Judge Jerome Chan, in the Hong Kong High Court, rejected the declaration.

The judge's view was that such collective agreements are neither social nor commercial.[43] The court should not take into account the parties "subjective" intent, since this was "self-serving".

The "objective" intent should be determined according to the surrounding circumstances. The judge held that this agreement was "binding in honour only". "Collective bargaining", industrial, disputes should be solved around the table and courts should be reluctant to interfere.

5.3.4 *"Mere Puffs"*

An exception to the presumption in favour of an intention to create legal relations in a commercial context arises in respect of "mere puffs". These occur in the case of obviously wild or exaggerated claims, usually in the form of advertisements, which no reasonable person would expect to be taken literally. These claims are called "puffs" in that they inflate the positive aspects of the product or service. An ancient case which illustrates the point is *Weeks v Tybald*,[44] where a father (the defendant)

---

40. Ibid at 254.
41. The English common law rules do not (and did not) apply in Hong Kong if inapplicable to local circumstances.
42. [1994] 2 HKLR 367.
43. The English courts, similarly, found a contractual situation neither "social" nor "commercial" in *Sadler v Reynolds* [2005] EWHC 309, involving an agreement to "ghost write" a book.
44. (1605) Noy 11.

affirmed and published that he would give £100 to him that should marry his daughter with his consent.

The plaintiff married the defendant's daughter and claimed the (monetary!) reward. His action failed since, in the view of the court, it would not be reasonable to bind the defendant by "general words spoken to excite suitors."

A far more recent, Hong Kong, example is provided in *Chan Yeuk Yu v Church Body of the Hong Kong Sheng Kung Hui*,[45] where the expression, "regal surroundings for the select few" in a property advertisement was held to be a mere puff which no reasonable person in Hong Kong would take literally. There is, perhaps, some irony in the fact that Hong Kong estate agents' advertisements are now so widely accepted as being exaggerated that no reasonable person would take them seriously.

The "mere puff" defence was also raised in the famous *Carlill*[46] case but failed because the defendants' deposit of money to meet claims was a clear refutation of their argument that they had not intended their promise to be taken seriously.

"Mere puff" was accepted (albeit implicitly) in the case of *Blue v Ashley*, discussed at some length in chapter 3.[47] While Mr Ashley's promise to pay a "reward" for successful efforts to raise the value of shares in his company had the outward appearance of a "commercial" venture, "setting" was all-important. Leggatt J, as he then was, stated:

> In the course of a jocular conversation with three investment bankers in a pub . . . Mr Ashley said that he would pay Mr Blue £15 million if Mr Blue could get the price of Sports Direct shares . . . to £8. Mr Blue expressed his agreement to that proposal & everyone laughed . . . no reasonable person present in the (pub) . . . would have thought that the offer to pay Mr Blue £15 million was serious and was intended to create a contract.[48]

While the court accepted that there was often alcohol in Mr Ashley's *business* meetings, there was a formal agenda at such meetings . . . and no contracts were concluded![49]

---

45. [2001] 1 HKC 621.
46. See 3.3.4.
47. See 3.8.1.
48. [2017] EWHC 1928 (Comm). Cited, though distinguished, in *Ho Lai King v Kwok Fung Ying*, discussed above.
49. Though *Blue v Ashley* is only a first instance case, it has been discussed and approved in several subsequent Hong Kong cases, including *Yu Ma Fung Alice v Chiau Sing Chi Stephen* [2020] HKCFI 2923; *Lok Wai Yee v Man Koon Hung* [2020] HKCFI 2549; *Ho Lai King v Kwok Fung Ying & Another* [2020] 5 HKC 271 (discussed above).

5.3.5 Letters of Comfort/Letters of Intent

These documents are often sent from one party to a contract to another party. They are usually not meant to have legal effect but merely to act as some sort of reassurance to the other party. The terms "letter of comfort" and "letter of intent" are not legally defined and are sometimes difficult to distinguish from guarantees or indemnities. In *Chemco Leasing v Rediffusion*,[50] the English Court of Appeal held that a "letter of comfort" in which the parent company undertook certain responsibilities should new shareholders not be acceptable to a lender was, in fact, an offer of a guarantee. Had it been accepted in time, it would have been binding. In the area of "letters of comfort/intent", there is an overlap between the question of intention to create legal relations and that of offer and acceptance. In many scenarios the defendant may be arguing that the parties never reached a "sufficiently certain"[51] concluded agreement, *or* that if they had, it was not intended to be legally binding. Both lines of defence were attempted (unsuccessfully) in the Hong Kong case of *New World Development Co Ltd v Sun Hung Kai Securities Ltd*[52] where the Court of Final Appeal rejected the defendants' argument that they were merely discussing "possible" future business. Moreover, as a commercial agreement between two major concerns, there was clearly a strong presumption of intention to create legal relations which had not been rebutted.

The court will view the letter objectively to decide if it is legally binding or not. The wording of the letter is critical as is any reliance placed on the letter by the recipient. A case which contrasts with *Chemco Leasing* is *Kleinwort Benson Ltd v Malaysian Mining Corp Bhd*[53] where a letter of comfort was sent by a company concerning a loan to a subsidiary company. The letter stated that the subsidiary "is at all times in a position to meet its liabilities in respect of the loan". This was held to be simply a statement of the head company's existing policy and did not amount to a contractual undertaking as to the future; the wording of the letter did not amount to a contractual promise.[54]

---

50. [1987] 1 FTLR 201.
51. A plea of "uncertainty" is often linked to a plea of lack of intention but, while there is some overlap, the concepts are theoretically separate.
52. [2006] 3 HKLRD 345.
53. [1989] 1 All ER 785.
54. A similar result occurred in *Hellmuth Obata & Kassabaum Inc v King* [2000] EWHC Technology 64.

6

Contractual Capacity

Overview

The general rule is that any person has the capacity to make a contract. Exceptions exist in relation to mental patients, drunkards, corporations, and minors. Of these, only the last two are significant and the rules on corporations are more suitably dealt with in the context of company law.

The law on minors, previously referred to as infants, is now similar in England and Hong Kong, having once been rather different. The Infants Relief Act 1874, which incorporated rules not enacted in Hong Kong, has now been abolished and similar common law and statutory rules are now found in both jurisdictions.

Three categories of contracts made with minors are recognised: enforceable contracts, voidable contracts and "other contracts". Before proceeding, it should be stressed that all three categories are enforceable *by* the minor;[1] the common law and statutory rules exist to protect the minor, *not* the adult who contracts with him.

"Enforceable"[2] contracts comprise contracts for necessary goods and services, and beneficial contracts of employment or service. When dealing with "necessaries" it should be remembered that this includes far more than the basic necessities of life. Any item necessary to maintain a particular minor in the "station of life in which he moves"[3] is within the definition. Thus, although courts might identify some items as "mere luxuries", incapable of being necessary, the usual question will be one of fact; is this item necessary for this particular minor? Those dealing with minors will, therefore, be at a disadvantage since no general definition exists; what may be necessary for a rich undergraduate may not be necessary for a poor, unemployed minor.

---

1. Though a minor cannot be granted specific performance, under the principle of "mutuality", since it cannot be awarded against him; see final paragraph of 6.3.1.2.
2. Although these contracts are described as "enforceable", the minor can only be required to pay a reasonable price for necessaries rather than the contract price. Specific performance can never be awarded against a minor.
3. Per Baron Parke in *Peters v Fleming* (1840) 6 M&W 42 at 46–47.

Further, even the rich minor will not be liable where he is already well supplied with goods of the type for which he has contracted.

The minor's liability to pay for necessaries may be seen as being not strictly contractual at all, but "quasi-contractual", since liability is not to pay the agreed contract price but to pay a "reasonable" price. Further, it appears that the minor has to pay not because he has promised to do so but because he has received a benefit. Thus the minor is not liable to pay for necessary goods which he has ordered but delivery of which he has refused to accept. There is some authority for the proposition that necessary services must be paid for, having been requested, even though the minor subsequently refuses the services.

Contracts of service or employment are enforceable against a minor if they are substantially for his benefit. Of course, contracts may contain a mixture of terms, some favouring the minor and others not. The test is whether the contract is beneficial overall.

Voidable contracts comprise a variety of agreements which have little in common except that they confer a permanent, or at least long-standing, interest. Thus, contracts for the purchase of shares, partnership contracts and contracts for a lease are all voidable. The effect of voidability is that the minor may cancel, or repudiate, these agreements at any time during his minority or within a reasonable time after attaining majority. When the minor has repudiated he has no further liabilities under the contract. However, obligations which accrued before repudiation may have to be honoured.[4]

All "other contracts" are unenforceable against the minor though, again, the minor may enforce them. Within this category are minors' trading contracts and loans to minors. Both English and Hong Kong law now permit the possibility of the minor acknowledging or "ratifying" such contracts after reaching majority. Where ratification occurs the contract becomes enforceable against the minor.

The minor's immunity from liability for most types of contract does not extend to tort, where minors are generally liable. This might, potentially, provide an alternative form of action for the adult dealing with a minor. However, the courts have made clear that a tort action will not be permitted against a minor which would, in effect, amount to enforcing an otherwise unenforceable contract; the minor's tort liability will, therefore, only arise when he does an act outside the contemplation of the contract.[5]

The above rules indicate that the adult dealing with the minor is often in a disadvantageous position. Equity gave some relief to the adult by permitting the "restitution" of property obtained by the minor by fraud (for example, falsely purporting to be an adult, acquiring non-necessary goods and refusing subsequently to pay for

---

4. There is considerable uncertainty here since the decided cases are not consistent on whether the minor's repudiation affects prior obligations.
5. See *Ballett v Mingay* [1943] KB 281.

them). The equitable remedy was limited, however, since it required evidence of wrongdoing by the minor and probably did not apply where the precise goods or money obtained could not be identified. Legislation has improved the adult's position considerably since proof of fraud is no longer required and courts now have a much wider discretion as to what may be "restored".[6]

The prudent adult may also protect himself by requiring that the minor's liability be "guaranteed"[7] by an adult at the time of making the contract. Hong Kong law has always recognised the enforceability of such guarantees and English law has adopted the same position via legislation.[8]

6.1 Drunkenness and Mental Incapacity

Generally, the law gives some protection to those who make contracts while drunk (or drugged) or suffering from such mental incapacity that they do not understand what they are doing. The contract is "voidable" so that the affected party may rescind the contract *provided that* it can be proved that the other party was aware of the affected party's incapacity. This "awareness" requirement is implicit in the alleged undue influence case involving Lei Shing Hong credit, discussed in chapter 12.[9] More emphatically, in cases where an order under the Mental Health Ordinance[10] has been made, the affected party's contractual capacity is formally ended and undertaken by others acting on his behalf.

Even where a contract is rescinded by the affected party on the grounds of the incapacity described there is a requirement to pay a "reasonable" amount for any "necessary" goods or services supplied under the contract. This is the same principle as that which applies to minors and the definition of "necessaries" and its significance will be dealt with below.[11]

6.2 Corporations

A corporation is a legal "person", capable, in law, of making contracts in the same way as an individual, subject to minor limitation. A corporation may be a

---

6. Minors' Contracts Act 1987 s 3, enacted in Hong Kong by the Age of Majority (Related Provisions) Ordinance (Cap 410) s 4.
7. Since a guarantee is an undertaking of secondary liability, it is arguable that, in the case of "absolutely void" agreements under the old Infants' Relief Act 1874, the adult was not a "guarantor" but an "indemnifier". The distinction is only important (in England) in terms of "formality" because guarantees must be evidenced in writing. This formal requirement no longer applies in Hong Kong (see chapter 7).
8. Minors' Contracts Act 1987 s 2.
9. See *Lei Shing Hong Credit Ltd v San Tong Lee Co Ltd & Others* [2021] 2 HKC 572 discussed at 11.2.3.1.
10. Cap 136, ss 11–13.
11. See 6.3.

corporation "sole" or corporation "aggregate". The former consists of one person only at any time, maintaining the same corporate identity where that person is succeeded by another as a result, for example, of resignation or death. The Archbishop of Canterbury would be a corporation sole.

A corporation aggregate consists of many individuals at any one time but has a single, separate, corporate identity. While the individuals in the corporation may change, its corporate identity remains the same.

Corporations may take various forms but by far the most common is the registered company. Companies are relevant to the issue of contractual capacity because, traditionally, they were required to have a Memorandum and Articles of Association, the former setting out the "objects" of the company. A company may engage in contractual activities only if they fall with its "objects clause". Attempts to engage in other activities may be challenged on the basis that they are *ultra vires* and exceed the company's legal capacity to contract. In theory, at least, this seems to represent a considerable restriction on a company's contractual capacity. In practice, companies tend to draw up rather vague objects clauses or, alternatively, very lengthy, all-embracing clauses, such that the *ultra vires* doctrine is less significant than might first appear. Under the new Companies Ordinance,[12] indeed, companies are no longer required to state their "objects".[13] If they do so state, however, a shareholder is entitled to restrain *ultra vires* activities via an injunction. However, any other party dealing with the *ultra vires* company in good faith (which is presumed) is entitled to enforce the *ultra vires* contract.

A detailed study of this area is not appropriate in a work on contract law and those wishing to look at this topic in more depth should consult a work on Hong Kong company law or business associations.[14]

6.3 Minors (Infants)

The most important area to consider in relation to contractual capacity is that concerning what used to be called "infants" but are now more often described as "minors". Minors are those who are under 18 years of age.[15] The law seeks to protect them from the consequences of making imprudent contracts as a result of their immaturity. As a result, the law recognises that some contracts, for "necessaries", should be enforceable against the minor, while others will be valid unless and until rescinded by the minor. A final category of contracts cannot be enforced against the minor unless he "ratifies" them on reaching the age of majority. This considerable

---

12. Cap 622. In force 3 March 2014.
13. Section 67 entirely abolishes the requirement of a memorandum of association.
14. See, for example, V. Stott, *Hong Kong Company Law* (Hong Kong: Pearson, 14th edn, 2015); S Lo & C Qu, *Law of Companies in Hong Kong* (Hong Kong: Sweet & Maxwell, 2nd edn, 2013).
15. Age of Majority (Related Provisions) Ordinance (Cap 410) s 2 (Hong Kong); Family Law Reform Act 1969 s 1 (England).

protection of the minor is subject only to limited amelioration for the adult via the doctrine of restitution, initially introduced by equity but subsequently put on a statutory footing.

Since the law on this subject is intended to protect only the minor, contracts are always enforceable *against* the adult who deals with a minor.[16]

6.3.1 *"Enforceable" Contracts*

The law recognises two categories of contracts enforceable against a minor: contracts for necessary goods or services, and beneficial contracts of service or employment. While these contracts are described as "enforceable" against the minor, this is only in the sense that the adult has a right to compensation should the minor default; the minor can never be compelled by the court to complete his side of the bargain.[17]

6.3.1.1 Contracts for Necessaries

In order to protect minors from the consequences of their inexperience, the common law held that they were liable to pay for necessary goods[18] and services but not for luxuries. Traditionally the question of whether an item was necessary was a question for judge and jury. A judge could decide that an item was a "mere luxury" and this determined the point. If the item was not so classified, it was for a jury to decide whether the item was necessary for the particular minor involved. This depended on his individual circumstances: his resources, his job requirements etc.

It has been suggested that a jury would be more likely than a judge to find an item "necessary".[19] It also depended on whether the minor was already sufficiently supplied with the item in question.[20] The common law rules for determining necessaries still remain, although the involvement of juries in such civil matters has long been abolished.

The minor is liable to pay only a "reasonable price" for necessaries. This supports the view that his liability is not contractual but "quasi-contractual". The concept of quasi-contract is rather complex and elusive but, in this context, refers to the proposition that a minor's liability, unlike that of an adult, is based not on his promise to pay but on an obligation to pay a reasonable amount in return for a

---

16. Even under the Infants' Relief Act 1874, which described certain contracts as "absolutely void", courts took the view that the minor could enforce the contract.
17. That is, specific performance (see 15.2) is never available *against* a minor.
18. A statutory definition of necessary goods was introduced, in England, by the Sale of Goods Act 1893 s 2 and, in Hong Kong, by the Sale of Goods Ordinance (Cap 26) s 4(2).
19. "Much difficulty was caused in the nineteenth century by the tendency of juries (consisting of 12 shopkeepers) to stretch the definition of necessaries beyond its legitimate limits." Treitel (op cit) at p 639.
20. Cf *Nash v Inman* [1908] 2 KB 1 discussed below.

benefit received.[21] This proposition is supported by the statutory rule that the minor is required to pay only a reasonable price and only for goods necessary at the time of sale *and delivery*. Section 4 of Hong Kong's Sale of Goods Ordinance[22] states that:

> where necessaries are sold and delivered to an infant or minor . . . he must pay a reasonable price therefor.
>
> In this section, "necessaries" means goods suitable to the condition in life of such infant or minor . . . and to his actual requirements at the time of the sale and delivery.

If this proposition is correct it means that a minor is not liable to pay for necessaries which he has ordered but of which he refuses to take delivery.

The wording of section 4 follows section 3 of the (English) Sale of Goods Act 1979, which itself repeats section 2 of the Sale of Goods Act 1893. The definition was applied in the following well-known case.

Nash v Inman[23]

The plaintiff was a tailor, the defendant a wealthy undergraduate minor. The plaintiff sold and delivered to the defendant a quantity of clothes including 11 fancy waistcoats. The defendant refused to pay for the goods, pleading "infancy". On receiving proof of the defendant's age and evidence that he was already well supplied with clothes, the judge held there was no issue to go to a jury and that the defendant was clearly not liable to pay. The plaintiff's appeal to the Court of appeal was unanimously rejected.

Cozens-Hardy MR, delivering the leading judgment, stated:

> The defendant pleads infancy at the date of the sale, and his plea is proved. What is the consequence of that? The consequence of that is that the Infants' Relief Act, 1874, becomes applicable . . . It is not sufficient, in my view, for (the plaintiff) to say, "I have discharged the onus which rests upon me if I simply shew [*sic*] that the goods supplied were suitable to the condition in life of the infant at the time". There is another branch of the definition which cannot be disregarded. Having shewn that the goods were suitable to the condition in life of the infant, he must then go on to shew that they were suitable to his actual requirements at the time of the sale *and* delivery.[24]

Following the *Nash* approach, the adult supplier of goods to a minor appears to be at a considerable disadvantage. If he makes a contract to deliver goods to a minor he may find that, at the time for delivery, the minor refuses to accept them, or is already well supplied, and is not obliged to pay. However, if the adult, on discovering

---

21. Such liability is described as "*re*" rather than "*consensu*".
22. Cap 26.
23. [1908] 2 KB 1.
24. Emphasis added.

the incapacity of the minor, decides against delivery, he may be sued for breach of contract since the incapacity rules protect the minor but not the adult! It will be difficult for the adult to know if the minor is already well supplied unless he has had previous dealings with him. Indeed, where the adult is unaware of the minor's minority he will not even have cause to enquire whether he is already well-supplied.

In reality, the position of the adult is less hazardous than it appears, since, following the reduction of the age of majority, in England and Hong Kong, from 21 to 18,[25] few adults deliver goods on credit to minors and, once the minor has paid, he generally has no right to recover his payment. The adult may also protect himself by requiring that an adult guarantee the minor's payment. Such a guarantee is enforceable both in English and Hong Kong law.[26]

The view expressed in the *Nash* case that a minor has only to pay for a benefit actually received is supported by the fact that there is no case in which a minor has been held liable on an "executory" promise to pay for goods, "necessary" or otherwise. There is, however, some authority that a minor may be liable on an executory promise for necessary *services*.

Roberts v Gray[27]

The plaintiff was a leading billiards player. The defendant, a minor, made a contract with the plaintiff by which he was to accompany him on an 18 months' world tour for which the plaintiff was to pay but be reimbursed from the tour profits. Following a dispute about the balls to be used, the defendant repudiated the contract before the tour commenced. The plaintiff claimed damages for loss of expenses already incurred. His action succeeded before a unanimous Court of Appeal.

Cozens-Hardy MR seemed content to treat this executory promise as different from one to pay for goods and concluded:

> If, therefore, this is a contract falling within a class to which the doctrine of necessaries applies, and if, taken as a whole, it is for the infant's benefit, I see no foundation whatever for the argument that the infant is not liable for damages in the event of his repudiating or declining to perform the contract entered into.

To treat a promise to pay for necessary services differently from one to pay for necessary goods is difficult to justify and it is perhaps significant that Cozens-Hardy MR and his fellow judges, while referring to "necessaries", based their decision largely on a case involving beneficial contracts of service,[28] the second category of contracts enforceable against minors.

---

25. In England by the Family Law Reform Act 1969 s 1; in Hong Kong by the Age of Majority (Related Provisions) Ordinance (Cap 410) s 2.
26. In England by the Minors' Contracts Act 1987 s 2; in Hong Kong by the Age of Majority (Related Provisions) Ordinance (Cap 410) s 3.
27. [1913] 1 KB 520.
28. Notably *Clements v London & North Western Railway Co* [1894] 2 QB 482.

6.3.1.2 Beneficial Contracts of Service or Employment

The common law took the view that contracts of employment or service could be enforced against a minor provided they were substantially for his benefit. It would be in the interest of minors to encourage adults to make such contracts by upholding them. "Trading" contracts, on the other hand, would not be upheld since these were potentially dangerous for minors. When the age of majority was 21, there were many situations in which minors made, often lengthy, contracts of apprenticeship. Even today there are numerous examples of young performers who make contracts involving large financial sums and then regret them if a better offer later arises. The enforceability of such agreements depends, as it always has, on whether the agreement is, *overall*, for the minor's benefit. An emphatically non-beneficial contract is illustrated by the case of *De Francesco v Barnum*,[29] where the plaintiff had engaged a minor as an apprentice dancer under very restrictive conditions. The minor was to be entirely at the disposal of the plaintiff; she was to receive poor payment; she would receive no pay unless employed by the plaintiff who had no obligation to employ her; she could be dismissed at the will of the plaintiff and could accept no alternative employment without his consent. The defendant wished to engage the minor and the plaintiff sued him for inducing breach of contract. The action failed since it was held that the apprenticeship was clearly not beneficial to the minor and was therefore unenforceable against her. On this basis, it was determined that the defendant could not be liable for inducing the minor to break a contract which she was legally entitled to break. Perhaps curiously this proposition was challenged in the much later case of *Proform Sports Management Ltd v Proactive Sports Management Ltd and Another*,[30] involving the footballer, Wayne Rooney. Rooney had signed a contract with the claimants when only 15 and without legal advice. The court felt no need to determine whether the contract was substantially beneficial to Rooney since the trial judge, Judge Hodge QC, felt the case was not analogous to a contract of employment or apprenticeship and was therefore automatically voidable at Rooney's option. The judge distinguished cases of employment or apprenticeship where the contract gave the minor the opportunity to work. In Rooney's case, the minor was *already* working (as an Everton footballer) when making his contract with the claimants. Essentially, their input was to attend to Rooney's image and marketability. Having decided that the Rooney-Proform contract was voidable, the judge went on to confirm the *De Francesco* view that there can be no liability for inducing the breach of a voidable contract.

Given the oppressive nature of the contract in the *De Francesco* case, it was not difficult for the court to determine that the minor was not bound by it and that the defendant was entitled to offer the minor an alternative arrangement without

---

29. (1890) 45 Ch D 430.
30. [2006] EWHC 2812.

being penalised. Other cases are less clear cut and involve the court weighing the beneficial and detrimental aspects of the agreement to determine whether, overall, it was in the minor's interest when the contract was made. In *Clements v London and North Western Railway*[31] the plaintiff, a minor, was employed by the defendants as a railway porter and joined their insurance scheme. Under this scheme, the plaintiff would be paid compensation for injury at work arising in various ways but agreed to give up rights under the Employers' Liability Act 1880. The statute provided for higher amounts of compensation but they were payable in a smaller variety of situations than the insurance scheme. The plaintiff was injured at work and made a claim under statute, arguing that he was not bound by the scheme since it was not for his benefit. The Court of Appeal unanimously rejected the plaintiff's claim, holding that the insurance scheme was substantially for his benefit.

In summing up the view of the court, Kay LJ stated:

> I agree with the Divisional Court that, on examination of the whole contract, it is for the benefit of the infant, although it contains terms that, standing alone, would not be for his advantage. There is, therefore, no right on the part of the infant to repudiate the contract.

A more complex discussion of the meaning of "beneficial" emerges from the following case.

Chaplin v Leslie Frewin (Publishers) Ltd[32]

The plaintiff, while a minor, made a contract with the defendants to write a book about his life. The defendants were attracted by the fact that, although the plaintiff was the son of a very rich and world-famous actor, he lived a "Bohemian" lifestyle and was unemployed. The plaintiff subsequently regretted the decision to write for the defendants and attempted to repudiate the contract after the book was largely prepared. The Court of Appeal, by a two to one majority, refused his claim to repudiate; holding that the agreement was, when made, substantially for the plaintiff's benefit.

The majority view was that, when made, the agreement was beneficial to the minor since it allowed him to be paid for a work that was "worthless from a literary point of view" and "vulgar trash".[33] Lord Denning MR, dissenting, adopted a broader approach to the concept of "benefit". He said:

> I cannot think that a contract is for the benefit of a young man if it is to be a means of purveying scandalous information ... It is not for his good that he should exploit his discreditable conduct for money, no matter how much he is paid for it.[34]

---

31. [1894] 2 QB 482.
32. [1966] 1 Ch 71, [1966] 2 WLR 40.
33. Per Danckwerts LJ.
34. [1966] 2 WLR 40 at 50.

Lord Denning did, however, add that the disclosures involved could result in a libel action, which would of course be disadvantageous, and Danckwerts LJ himself expressed the view that parts of the book contained blasphemies which could, theoretically, have led to criminal prosecution.

Finally, it should be remembered that whether or not the contract of service or employment is regarded as "enforceable", the only remedy for breach remains damages; specific performance is never awarded against a minor.[35] Applying the equitable principle of mutuality,[36] the minor is, correspondingly, not eligible for an award of specific performance.

6.3.2 Voidable Contracts

The category of "voidable" contracts comprises four types of contract: contracts concerning land; contracts of partnership; contracts to buy shares and marriage settlement contracts.

The effect of voidability is that the contract is binding upon the minor unless and until he repudiates it. Repudiation must be during minority or within a reasonable period after reaching majority. Once a minor repudiates he can incur no future liabilities under the contract. However, any money already paid by the minor is irrecoverable. The law is uncertain as to whether those liabilities already incurred before repudiation but not yet discharged must be met by the minor.

The following is the leading case on voidable contracts.

Steinberg v Scala (Leeds) Ltd[37]

The plaintiff, while still a minor, applied for shares in the defendants' company. The shares were allotted to her and she paid the first instalment. Eighteen months later, she repudiated the contract and claimed back the money she had paid. Her action for repayment failed in the Court of Appeal since, although she had received no dividends, the shares had been of value and recovery of money paid was only possible in the case of a total failure of consideration.

Younger LJ stated:

> the authorities appear to me to establish that where something has been made available for the infant under the contract in the period during which she has not sought to avoid it moneys paid cannot be recovered back, although on the subsequent repudiation of the contract by the infant all liability in respect of further payments disappears.[38]

---

35. Specific performance of a personal service contract is, in any event, almost unknown (see 15.2).
36. "Mutuality" means that specific performance will not be awarded *to* a party if it cannot be awarded *against* him.
37. [1923] 2 Ch 452.
38. Ibid at 463.

The category of voidable contracts is a strange one since there seems to be no obvious justification for treating these contracts differently from other contracts unenforceable against the minor. The usual justification, that these contracts confer a permanent or long-standing interest, is not entirely convincing. Treitel[39] states:

> There seems to be no satisfactory explanation for the existence of this separate class of voidable contracts. It provides perhaps the clearest illustration of the dilemma in which the law sometimes finds itself when it tries at the same time to protect minors and not to cause undue hardship to adults who deal with them. But this dilemma exists in all cases of contracts with minors and scarcely justifies special treatment of the four voidable contracts. Perhaps this is based on social and economic factors which have long since passed away.

6.3.3 *"Other Contracts"*

All contracts which are neither "enforceable" nor "voidable" are unenforceable against the minor although, again, the minor may enforce them against the adult. Within the "other contracts" category are included minors' trading contracts and loans to a minor. Where the loan is for the purpose of buying necessaries, and the money is actually so spent, the lender has the same rights as the unpaid seller of necessaries (that is, to the reasonable price of the necessaries bought) under the equitable doctrine of "subrogation". In the case of this category of contracts the minor may "ratify" them on reaching majority,[40] in which case they become enforceable against him.

It should be noted that these contracts are merely unenforceable against the minor, rather than "void". Hence, where the minor has performed the contract he will be unable to recover back money paid or goods transferred under it since the contract under which performance was rendered was a valid one.

6.3.4 *Minors' Liability in Tort*

Although minors are generally not liable for breach of contract, there is no such immunity in tort. The potential would exist, therefore, to circumvent a minor's immunity in contract by suing him in tort over what is really a contractual issue. To prevent this, the courts have held that a minor cannot be sued in tort if the true effect of the action would be to enforce an otherwise unenforceable contract. If the minor is to be sued in tort he must have done something outside the contemplation

---

39. Treitel (op cit) at p 648.
40. English law first permitted, then abolished ratification. The statute which abolished ratification, the Infants' Relief Act 1874, has itself been abolished and the possibility of ratification is, therefore, restored. Hong Kong never introduced the Infants' Relief Act, so ratification has always been possible.

of the contract so that any action would be genuinely tortious. So, for example, it has been held that a minor who hired a non-necessary horse and rode it too hard could not be liable in tort since, in reality, the minor had merely broken an unenforceable contract.[41] Conversely, in *Ballett v Mingay*,[42] the defendant, a minor, paid to hire valuable electrical equipment from the plaintiff. Subsequently the plaintiff asked for the return of the equipment but the defendant was unable to comply since he had lent it to a third party. The plaintiff's action, in the tort of detinue,[43] succeeded before a unanimous Court of Appeal.

Lord Greene MR made clear that the contract of hire contemplated that the minor would not part with the goods. He said:

> From the evidence it seems that, properly construed, the terms of the bailment of these articles to the defendant did not permit him to part with their possession at all . . . On that basis, there is a remedy against the defendant in tort, because the circumstances in which the goods passed from his possession and ultimately disappeared were outside the purview of the contract of bailment altogether.

The dividing line between a tort action which is regarded as properly contractual and one which is genuinely tortious is a narrow one. In *Ballett v Mingay* the deciding factor was probably the valuable nature of the property hired; it might be expected that one would lend out a bicycle to a friend but not expensive electrical equipment.

Under the principle that a tort action may not be used to enforce an otherwise unenforceable contract against a minor, it is not permitted to sue, in the tort of deceit, a minor who induces an unenforceable contract by pretending to be an adult.[44]

6.3.5 Restitution in Equity

In order to give some relief to the adult who dealt with a dishonest minor, equity permitted the remedy of restitution of property obtained by fraud. This had two important limitations: that it only applied where the minor had acted fraudulently, and that it perhaps only applied where the precise goods obtained could be identified. Thus, if fraudulently obtained goods were sold, the adult might be unable to recover the money paid for them. Similarly, where money was obtained by fraud, it might be impossible to obtain restitution unless the precise coins or notes could be identified. The position can be better understood by comparing the cases of *Stocks v Wilson*[45]

---

41. *Jennings v Rundall* (1799) 8 TR 335. However, a minor was held liable in tort in *Burnard v Haggis* (1863) 14 CB (NS) 45, where he hired a horse for riding and, contrary to the express terms of the contract, took it jumping.
42. [1943] KB 281.
43. This action, now abolished in England, was available where a party was *unable* to return the goods of another but did not question his title to them.
44. *R Leslie Ltd v Sheill* [1914] 3 KB 607.
45. [1913] 2 KB 235.

and *R Leslie v Sheill*.[46] In *Stocks*, a minor obtained goods by fraudulently pretending to be an adult. He was ordered to restore the value of the goods thus obtained. In the *Leslie* case, a minor obtained £400 in cash from the plaintiff moneylenders by, again, falsely purporting to be an adult. The plaintiffs' subsequent action to recover the money failed. The cases are hard to reconcile, though Goff and Jones[47] attempt to do so. They write:

> *Stocks* . . . is reconcilable with *R Leslie v Sheill*. The basis of the latter decision is, we suggest, the rule of policy that personal remedies in restitution are not to be employed indirectly to enforce contracts which are at law not binding on the minor. This rule of policy overrides the equity whereby a minor would otherwise have to pay for goods obtained by fraud or to repay money obtained fraudulently under a contract of loan. Where a minor has obtained property under a contract (other than a contract for the loan of money) induced by his fraud, he will be compelled in equity to restore (it or) . . . refund the proceeds. Here the rule of policy does not bar recovery. But the minor is under no liability to pay the contract price for the property . . . because to do so would indirectly enforce the contract. Similarly if he has obtained the money under a contract of loan, he will not be liable to repay it.[48]

The distinction is a fine one, based on the premise that "restitution ends where repayment begins". Arguably, in such cases, restitution of money would be possible in the unlikely event that the precise notes or coins lent could be identified. The limitations of equitable restitution are unlikely to be of more than academic interest since the adult now has a preferable option, created by statute, described in the next section.

6.3.6 Statutory Restitution

The statutory rules on restitution by a minor, in Hong Kong, are to be found in the Age of Majority (Related Provisions) Ordinance.[49] Section 4 states:

(1) Where–
  (a) a person ("the applicant") has after the commencement of this Ordinance entered into a contract with another ("the respondent"); and
  (b) the contract is unenforceable against the respondent, or he repudiates it, because he was a minor when the contract was made,
  the court may, if it is just and equitable to do so, and on such terms as it may think fit, require the respondent to transfer to the applicant any property acquired by the respondent under the contract, or any property representing it.
(2) This section shall not prejudice any other remedy available to the applicant.

---

46. [1914] 3 KB 607.
47. R. Goff and G. H. Jones, *The Law of Restitution* (London: Sweet & Maxwell, 4th edn, 1993).
48. Ibid at p 537.
49. Cap 410.

This section reproduces section 3(1) of the (English) Minors' Contracts Act 1987. Although the section preserves existing remedies, including equitable restitution, it is clearly more advantageous to the adult. Under the statutory rules, restitution is at the discretion of the court, as with the equitable principle, *but* there is no need to establish fraud. So, for example, the minor in a *Nash v Inman*[50] situation could be made to return the non-necessary waistcoats he has acquired from the adult under the unenforceable contract, even though no fraud is involved. Further, the minor can be required to transfer property "representing" the property acquired under the contract so that the equitable problem, of identifying the precise property acquired, does not arise under the statutory rules. Where the *Nash v Inman* minor has sold the waistcoats he can, at the court's discretion, be required to transfer the money received.

---

50. Discussed at 6.3.1.1 above.

7

Formality

The general rule, in Hong Kong and England, is that contracts can be made in any form. Despite a common misapprehension on the part of the layman, there is no general requirement that contracts be made in writing (though reducing a contract to writing assists the question of proof in cases of dispute). Contracts may, generally, be made entirely orally or even, in exceptional cases, by conduct.

However, there are many important exceptions to the general rule on formality, some of which are of great significance. First, some agreements are required to be made by deed, notably those stipulated in the Powers of Attorney Ordinance (PAO).[1] Very importantly, in Hong Kong, a legal estate in land can be created, extinguished or disposed of only by deed: section 4(1) of the Conveyancing and Property Ordinance (CPO).[2]

Other types of contracts require particular formalities and these are contained in various statutory provisions. Some contracts must actually be "in writing" if they are to be enforced by one or both of the parties, notably various types of credit agreement.

Most important of all, in Hong Kong, the actual contract for the "sale or other disposition of land" must be evidenced in writing if it is to be enforceable at common law. The requirement of evidence in writing can be satisfied if there is a note or memorandum in writing containing all the essential terms and signed by "the party to be charged".[3] The memorandum need not be in any particular document and can even be formed by joining together two or more documents provided they relate to each other.

---

1. Cap 31.
2. Cap 219.
3. That is, by the person against whom the agreement is to be enforced.

Under the doctrine of part performance, equity may intervene where there has been clear agreement and the parties have acted on this agreement but without sufficient written evidence. Examples of acts of part performance include taking possession of the property by the plaintiff with the consent of the defendant, alterations to the property or, exceptionally, payment of money. The doctrine of part performance continues to apply in Hong Kong, although it has been abolished in England.

The main reasons for requiring a particular form of contract are the need for certainty and the need to protect certain types of parties. The requirement that contracts concerning land have to be evidenced in writing dates back to the ancient Statute of Frauds, 1677, which was intended to protect those entering into important contracts by ensuring that they could not be sued on a contract unless they had signed the necessary written memorandum. However, the requirement of a "memorandum in writing" involves considerable complexity which could be simplified were Hong Kong to follow the English law lead for land transactions and substitute a requirement that the *contract itself* must be written.

Formal requirements may also exist for the rescission or variation of a contract but these will be covered in chapter 14.

7.1 The General Rule

The general rule, in Hong Kong and England, is that contracts can be in any form. They can be made under seal or wholly in writing or evidenced by writing or orally or evidenced by the conduct of the parties or in any combination of these methods. It is important to note that the perception of many laymen that an oral contract is not as valid as a written one is incorrect. The problem that may arise with oral contracts is that it will be more difficult to adduce cogent evidence when dealing with issues that arise from a breach of an oral contract rather than a written one.

There are important exceptions to the general rule and they are contained in legislation covering certain types of contracts. Hong Kong and England differ substantially in these legislative exceptions; this chapter examines mainly the Hong Kong position; focusing on the most important areas such as contracts relating to land, guarantees, bills of exchange and promissory notes.

When considering the question of form, it will be assumed that other elements necessary for the formation of a contract: offer, acceptance, consideration, intention to create legal relations, certainty, capacity (and lack of illegality) are present.

Treitel[4] lists several purposes for the requirement of form. The first is that it promotes certainty as it is usually easy to see if the required form has been used. Second, it may enable a person to have longer to consider his position. Third, by providing a written record of the terms of the contract, it acts to protect a weaker

---

4.   Edwin Peel, *Treitel: The Law of Contract* (London: Sweet & Maxwell, 14th edn, 2015) at pp 205–206.

party. As a general observation, the more valuable the consideration required for a contract the greater the need for these purposes to be met. This is particularly true of contracts relating to land. Formal requirements are also more likely in respect of those contracts which, by their very nature, involve a likely inequality of bargaining power, such as hire-purchase agreements.

7.2 Contracts Required to Be under Seal

Contracts made under seal (deeds) are significant in the law of contract because they, alone, can be valid in the absence of consideration.[5] The most important example of a contract required to be made by deed is a "conveyance" of an interest in land.

7.2.1 Deeds

A deed is a written document that is signed, sealed and delivered.[6] The terms of a deed are called covenants. At common law, it was not necessary to sign and seal a deed; sealing was sufficient. However, signing is required by statute.[7] The process of sealing a document used to be a formal process but is now done by simply attaching red adhesive paper to the document. In practice, many commercial contracts are made under seal, though this is not formally required, in order to avoid the intricacies of the consideration requirement.

7.2.2 Types of Transactions That Require Sealing

The most important type of transaction here is a contract which also operates to convey land. Section 4(1) of the CPO states that:

> A legal estate in land may be created, extinguished or disposed of only by deed.[8]

Section 2 of the CPO defines a legal estate to include leases, easements and mortgages which must, therefore, all be dealt with by deed. Not all leases of land, though, are subject to the requirement for a deed. Section 4(2)(d) exempts leases of three years or less from this requirement.

Another type of transaction which requires a deed is covered by section 2(1) of the PAO which states that:

> An instrument creating a power of attorney shall be signed and sealed by, or by direction and in the presence of, the donor of the power.

---

5. See chapter 4.
6. Although not all sealed documents are deeds, for instance a share certificate.
7. CPO s 19(1) and PAO s 3.
8. CPO s 4(2) contains a number of exceptions which are best covered in a land law text.

Section 4(2) of the PAO also requires that two other persons must be present as witnesses and attest the instrument.

Although the requirement has been abolished in England,[9] Hong Kong still requires that authority to execute a deed must in turn be granted by deed. An exception is made in the case of foreign companies which have been incorporated in states which do not require the document of authorisation to be under seal.[10]

Despite the simpler procedures today for signing and sealing a deed, the formalities are often overlooked. The CPO recognises this and sections 19, 20, 23, and 23A contain presumptions that act as saving provisions in the event that any oversights or lapses occur.

Additional sealing requirements, requiring the use of a company's "common seal" to effect transactions, have been relaxed under the new Companies Ordinance[11] which permits documents signed by one[12] or two directors (or one director and a company secretary)[13] to have the same effect as a deed effected via the company's common seal.[14]

7.2.2.1 The Effect of Non-compliance

Where there is a requirement for a deed the consequence of non-compliance is that the document is void at common law. As between the parties, however, the failure of a document to qualify as a deed may not render it entirely ineffective.

In respect of contracts concerning land, the law will readily construe an abortive attempt to grant the interest in property as an agreement to grant the interest in question. For example, if X purports to grant to Y a lease of land for five years but does so in writing rather than under seal, the transaction will be construed as an agreement by X to grant Y a lease of five years. Y can call on X to execute a deed granting a lease of five years. If necessary, this could be by way of an order for specific performance. Meanwhile, Y would hold in equity under an equitable lease for five years.[15]

A document that does not qualify as a power of attorney under PAO may still be a valid appointment of agency but such an agent would generally not be authorised to execute deeds on behalf of the principal.[16]

---

9. Section 1(1)(c) of the Law of Property (Miscellaneous Provisions) Act 1989.
10. Law Amendment and Reform Consolidation) Ordinance (LARCO) (Cap 23) s 26.
11. Cap 622. In force from 3 March 2014.
12. Where the company has only one director.
13. Where there two or more directors.
14. Section 127(3). For fuller coverage of company law documentary requirements, the reader should consult a specialised company law text.
15. See, for example, *Parker v Taswell* (1858) 2 De G & J 559.
16. See Betty Ho, *Hong Kong Agency Law* (Hong Kong: Butterworths, 1991), p 24.

7.3 Contracts in Writing or Evidenced in Writing

There are numerous types of contract that must be *in* writing or *evidenced in* writing. The distinction is important since the requirement of evidence merely requires that there is a written memorandum of the important terms of the contract "signed by the party to be charged". This memorandum need not have been specifically prepared as such and may consist of several "joined" documents. The requirement of "evidence in writing" originates in the old English Statute of Frauds, 1677, which listed a number of different types of contract. Of these, only guarantees, the rules for which no longer apply in Hong Kong, remain. However, the formal rules for the disposition of land, while reformed in England, remain in force in Hong Kong.

7.3.1 Contracts Required to Be in Writing

Contracts which must be (wholly) in writing include, most importantly, bills of exchange and promissory notes. Very basically a bill of exchange is an order to a third party to pay the amount of the bill, while a promissory note is a promise to pay by the maker of the note. The Bills of Exchange Ordinance (BEO)[17] defines both of these instruments more fully[18] and enacts that not only must they be entirely in writing, they must also satisfy the statutory requirements.

A further (and increasingly important) example of an agreement which must be written is one to submit disputes to arbitration.[19]

7.3.1.1 The Effect of Non-compliance

In the case of bills of exchange, the consequence of non-compliance with the requirement of writing and the "statutory requirements" is that the document becomes "non-negotiable". Thus, a third party cannot be compelled to honour a defective bill of exchange and pay the amount of the bill. The deficient document may, however, be used as evidence of the debt of one party to the other.

In the case of an agreement to submit to arbitration, non-compliance with the formal requirement of writing will render the agreement unenforceable.

7.3.2 Contracts Required to Be Evidenced in Writing

The requirement that a contract be evidenced in writing means that, unlike the need for a contract to be entirely in writing, all that is required is some written evidence of the contract. The main category of agreements required to be "evidenced in writing"

---

17. Cap 19.
18. Section 3(1) defines a bill of exchange and s 89(1) defines a promissory note.
19. Section 19 of the Arbitration Ordinance (Cap 609), adopting Article 7 of the UNCITRAL Model Law.

are contracts for the sale or other disposition of land.[20] They are of great importance in Hong Kong, given the significance of land transactions here, and the law in Hong Kong differs substantially from that in England.

7.3.2.1 Land Contracts

"Land" is not fully defined by CPO although section 2 explains that "land" *includes* "land covered by water"; "any estate, right, interest or easement in or over any land"; "the whole or part of an undivided share in land"; and "things attached to land or permanently fastened to anything attached to land". As this definition is only partial, recourse may still be needed to the common law in determining the meaning of "land". In *Chan Juen v Yu Fook Shung*,[21] it had to be decided whether an oral contract to allow the cultivation of ginger on the respondent's land was a contract for the disposition of land. It was held that the contract was for "goods" not land, since cultivated produce "*fructus industriales*" are goods at common law. As such the oral agreement was enforceable without written formality.

7.3.2.1.1 Sufficient Memorandum in Writing

In Hong Kong, under statute, contracts for the sale and disposition of land must be evidenced in writing if they are to be enforceable at common law.

Section 3(1) of the CPO states:

> Subject to section 6(2), no action shall be brought upon a contract for the sale or other disposition of land unless the agreement upon which such action is brought, or some note or memorandum thereof, is in writing and signed by the party to be charged or by some other person lawfully authorised by him for that purpose.

This requirement largely mirrors the now abolished English rules[22] on the requirement of a memorandum in writing if a contract concerning land is to be enforceable. Although the subsection talks of an interest in land, most disputes, in practice, focus on buildings on land. Given that there is a significant difference between a requirement that the agreement itself must be in writing and the need for a mere memorandum in writing, the heading of section 3—"Land contracts to be in writing"—is misleading and does not reflect its actual content.

---

20. It appears that the English law requirement that "guarantees" must be evidenced in writing was inadvertently abolished in Hong Kong (see Ho, n 16 above, p 87). This view was endorsed by Suffiad J in *Global Bridge Assets Ltd & Others v Sun Hung Kai Securities Ltd* [2009] 3 HKC 445, and although his judgment was overturned on appeal (unrep, CACV 161/2009, 24 February 2010), the Court of Appeal emphasised (at para 18) that no argument had been put to it on the guarantee/evidence in writing issue and that, therefore, it should not be taken to have considered the matter.

21. [1987] 3 HKC 539.

22. Statute of Frauds 1677.

The CPO does not specify what constitutes an effective note or memorandum. These requirements have developed via the common law cases. The main requirements are that the parties, the consideration, the subject matter and any special terms must be clearly identified *and* that the note or memorandum must be signed by "the party to be charged" or his authorised agent.[23] The Court of Final Appeal in *Kwan Siu Man Joshua v Yaacov Ozer*[24] held that the date of completion is an essential term of any contract for the sale and purchase of land in Hong Kong. Thus, in *Centaline Property Agency Ltd v Suen Wai Kwan (Samantha)*[25] the court held unenforceable an agreement where the alleged memorandum contained an amended completion date but no signature on same by the "party to be charged". Judge CB Chan cited with approval the words of Judge Lok, in a previous unreported case,[26] that:

> As the Plaintiff had not initialled the amendment relating to the date for the execution of the formal agreement, it is common ground that there was no binding agreement between the Plaintiff and the Vendor relating to the sale of the property.[27]

The memorandum need not have been prepared as such and can even be formed by joining together two or more documents provided they relate to each other.[28] The memorandum must also be signed by the party *against whom* the contract is to be enforced (the "party to be charged") or by his authorised agent. This means that the memorandum does not need to be signed by both parties but that the party seeking to enforce the agreement must show that the *other party* or his authorised agent[29] has "signed"[30] the memorandum. The requirement of signing arises because of the importance of this type of contract. England has abolished the equivalent of this legislation[31] but most of the leading cases on what constitutes an effective memorandum in writing are English and are applicable to Hong Kong today.

---

23. Emphasised in *Kwok Chor Shan v Empire Properties Development Consultants Ltd* (unrep, DCCJ 14764/2000, 17 July 2003).
24. [1999] 1 HKC 150.
25. [2004] 4 HKC 294.
26. *Advanced Chemicals Ltd v Centaline Property Agency Ltd* (unrep, DCCJ 16630/2000, 31 August 2001).
27. Ibid at para 5. The generally crucial nature of the identification of the completion date was affirmed in *Kwok Chor Shan v Empire Properties Development Consultants Ltd.* cited above.
28. The leading English case on joinder of documents is *Timmins v Moreland Street Property Co Ltd* [1957] Ch 110.
29. Where land is sold by auction, the auctioneer has authority to sign on behalf of both parties.
30. The word "sign" has been liberally construed by the English courts (see, for example, *Leeman v Stocks* [1951] 1 All ER 1043). It is clear that both in England and Hong Kong, courts will now be called upon to recognise "electronic" signatures (see Electronic Transactions Ordinance (Cap 553) s 6(1)).
31. English law now requires the contract itself to be in writing: Law of Property (Miscellaneous Provisions) Act 1989 s 2.

The following Hong Kong case illustrates the factors a court must take into account in determining whether a sufficient memorandum in writing exists (albeit not in a single document).

Chan Yat v Fung Keong Rubber Manufactory Ltd [32]

The parties had negotiated a draft lease. Following a subsequent dispute, the plaintiff sued and the defendants argued that there had never been any contract as there was no adequate memorandum. The plaintiff maintained that there were several documents which constituted such a note or memorandum. It was found, in the Hong Kong High Court, that there was an enforceable oral agreement of which there was a sufficient memorandum in writing. All the necessary terms were found to have been included: the parties, the consideration, the terms etc and that the necessary signature was present. With regard to the description of one of the parties as merely "landlord", the judge found this to be sufficient description as the identity of this party could be ascertained from the relevant register. Although the commencement date had been incorrectly stated, the judge found this to be sufficiently minor to be overlooked.

Having reviewed the precedents, Pickering J said:

> it has long been settled that a plaintiff can rely on two or more documents to prove his case. At one period it was necessary that the one document should specifically and on its face refer to the other . . . but the severity of this attitude has since been relaxed . . . in *Pearce v Gardner* [33] an envelope and letter shown by the evidence to have been enclosed in the envelope, were allowed to form a joint memorandum. The modern position is that whilst oral evidence designed to introduce a second document to which no reference at all was made in the first is still excluded, nonetheless if without any express reference the language or form of the document signed by the defendant indicates another document as relevant to the contract oral evidence will be allowed to identify that second document. [34]

The Statute of Frauds, 1677, was the first piece of English legislation to require documentary evidence for dealings in land. This statute has been incorporated in Hong Kong law and its provisions relating to the grant and transfer of interests in land are now found, in an updated form, in sections 3, 5, 6, and 7 of the CPO. The approach of the courts to the legislation in this area of formality has always been dominated by the fact that it is intended to prevent fraudulent claims. Therefore, if a signed document does not contain all the required details for a sufficient memorandum, the temptation might be to supply these details in a separate document and claim the right to join the documents together to form one, complete memorandum.

---

32. [1967] HKLR 364.
33. [1897] 1 QB 688.
34. [1967] HKLR 364 at 384–385.

To prevent this, the courts have been restrictive in allowing joinder, permitting it only when the signed document relates to the unsigned one.

7.3.2.1.2 Intervention of Equity: The Doctrine of Part Performance

The "memorandum in writing" rules do produce certainty, but they might also produce unfairness. This will often be so when people conduct their affairs in ignorance of these rules. Few people outside (and not all those inside) a lawyer's office understand the detailed requirements of these rules. Defendants may seize on non-compliance with the legislation as a way out of genuine agreements. Equity has, therefore, intervened, where there has been a clear concluded agreement (albeit not evidenced in writing) and the parties have acted on this agreement, by virtue of the doctrine of *part performance*. Under this doctrine, where there have been acts consistent with the oral contract alleged to have been made, and for which the most likely explanation is that the alleged contract has, indeed, been made, the agreement will be "enforced" in equity.[35]

The doctrine of part performance has been abolished in England[36] but continues to apply in Hong Kong. Legislation acknowledging the role of the doctrine of part performance is contained in the CPO. Section 3 is headed "Land contracts to be in writing" but section 3(2) states:

> This section applies to contracts or other dispositions and does not affect the law relating to part performance or sales by the court.

Equity has adopted the doctrine of part performance so that legislation aimed at preventing fraud, such as the Statute of Frauds 1677 and the CPO, should itself not be used as an instrument of fraud. Under the doctrine of part performance, where there is an alleged oral contract concerning land and there have been acts consistent with the alleged contracts, the most obvious explanation for which is that the contract alleged has, in fact, been concluded, equity will enforce the agreement by means of the equitable remedy of specific performance.[37] The remedy is granted where the claimant has acted in reliance on the oral contract and where, in the circumstances, it would be unjust to allow the other party to argue the contract is unenforceable because of the lack of formal written evidence.

The approach to part performance was once very strict, requiring that the acts must be "unequivocally referable" to the alleged contract.[38] This meant that if there were other explanations for the acts, even if unlikely, the requirement of

---

35. Provision exists for an award of damages where there is a sufficient act of part performance but specific performance (compelling performance) is inappropriate; see Law Amendment & Reform (Consolidation) Ordinance (Cap 23) s 13A.
36. By Law of Property (Miscellaneous Provisions) Act 1989 s 2.
37. In Hong Kong damages can be awarded where specific performance is not available, as a result of LARCO s 13A.
38. As stated in *Maddison v Alderson* (1883) 8 App Cas 467.

part performance would not have been met. This strict approach was relaxed in later cases including the definitive decision on part performance delivered by the House of Lords.

Steadman v Steadman[39]

The parties were husband and wife. The wife left the husband and obtained an order for maintenance for herself and her child. Later, the wife wanted an order that the house be sold and the proceeds split; the husband, in arrears of maintenance, wanted a variation of the maintenance order. The parties met outside the court and orally agreed that the wife would sell her half share of the matrimonial home to her husband for £1,500 plus £100 of the maintenance arrears. This agreement was announced to the court. The husband paid the £100 and sent the draft deed of transfer to the wife for her to sign. She refused to sign. The husband brought an action for specific performance of the agreement which was upheld by a majority of four to one (Lord Morris dissenting) in the House of Lords. It was held that, while the transfer of money could not, in itself, be enough, taken together with the other circumstances there were sufficient acts of part performance to satisfy the court.

The judgment is authoritative but the judges in the majority used differing reasoning and the *ratio* is not clear. Lord Reid said that the fact that there is an explanation for the plaintiff's behaviour other than the existence of the contract will not be fatal. It is sufficient if it is the most likely explanation. However, he was not clear about whether the acts must unequivocally refer at least to *some* contract relating to land. This doubt was removed by the later decision in *Re Gonin*[40] which reasserted the requirement that the contract to which the acts refer must be one relating to land. The question of whether or not the payment of money could ever constitute an act of part performance was also raised, with the majority deciding that such payment could be an act of part performance when seen in the context of the surrounding circumstances.

Taking possession of a property by the plaintiff with the consent of the defendant is the most usual act of part performance.[41] Alteration to the property is another common example.[42] However, the Hong Kong courts have emphasised that the acts of part performance must prove the existence of an already *concluded* agreement and not merely the confident expectation that such an agreement would eventually be reached. It was in stressing this principle that the Court of Final Appeal was critical of the Court of Appeal's approach in *The World Food Fair Ltd & Another v*

---

39. [1974] 2 All ER 977. There is some irony in the fact that this area of Hong Kong law is still governed by an English decision overturned, in England, by legislation in 1989.
40. [1979] Ch 16.
41. *Kingswood Estate Co Ltd v Anderson* [1963] 2 QB 169.
42. For instance, *Rawlinson v Ames* [1925] Ch 339.

Hong Kong Island Development Ltd,[43] a case more fully discussed in the context of "certainty".[44] The CFA found that the Court of Appeal had applied "circular" logic in finding part performance[45] in acts which were consistent with the existence of a contract but not conclusive. Ribeiro PJ stated:

> In regarding payment of the deposit and the giving of possession for fitting out works as "performance" which decisively proved the existence of a concluded contract, the Court of Appeal implicitly assumes that there existed a concluded contract of which such acts constituted "performance", which "performance" is then relied on to prove the existence of that very contract.[46]

7.3.2.1.3 The Effect of Non-compliance

Where there is neither a sufficient memorandum in writing nor an adequate act of part performance, the agreement will be unenforceable rather than void. This means that, while no action may be brought on it, the contract is not void *ab initio*. Therefore, if money has already been paid under the unenforceable, but still valid, contract, it cannot be recovered.[47]

7.3.3 Other Contracts

There are a number of other different types of contracts that are subject to specific writing requirements contained in legislation. Some of these are discussed below.

7.3.3.1 Money Lending Contracts

The Money Lenders Ordinance (MLO)[48] covers loans advanced by persons other than banks and other exempted companies licensed under the Banking Ordinance.[49] The MLO is aimed at protecting the public from the unscrupulous practices of "loan sharks". It does this by imposing licensing requirements on all money lenders and placing ceilings on the interest rates they can charge. Section 18 of the MLO is headed "Form of agreement". Section 18(1) requires that within seven days after the making of a money lending agreement, a note or memorandum in writing of the agreement be made in accordance with subsection (2) and signed personally by the borrower and a copy of such note or memorandum be given to the borrower

---

43. Court of Appeal decision [2005] 1 HKC 594. The CFA at (2006) 9 HKCFAR 735 appears to have adopted a rather more restrictive approach than the English judges in *Steadman*.
44. See chapter 3 at 3.8.
45. It was clear to the CFA that there was no sufficient "evidence in writing" so that enforceability required sufficient part performance.
46. Applied in *Lo Lee, Marilyn v Goel Arun Kumar* [2015] HKDC 1429.
47. *Thomas v Brown* (1876) 1 QB 714 at 723.
48. Cap 163.
49. Cap 155. It seems to have been assumed, over-optimistically, that banks would not resort to unscrupulous practices; but see 12.1.4.

at the time of signing. Also a summary of certain provisions of the MLO must be included or attached to such a copy. Section 18(2) lists the required contents of the note or memorandum including, *inter alia*, the names and addresses of the parties, the amount of principal, relevant dates, the form of security for the loan (if any) and the rate of interest charged.

This list of requirements leaves little area for dispute between the parties. However, should a claim be made that an agreement is unenforceable because of non-conformity with MLO, the court has a discretion, under section 18(3), to declare such an agreement enforceable. The subsection states:

> Notwithstanding subsection (1), if the court before which the enforceability of any agreement or security comes in question is satisfied that in all the circumstances it would be inequitable that any such agreement or security which does not comply with this section should be held not to be enforceable, the court may order that such agreement or security is enforceable to such extent, and subject to such modifications or exceptions, as the court considers equitable.

7.3.3.2 Bills of Sale

The Bills of Sale Ordinance (BSO)[50] imposes certain formalities on a bill of sale. Like MLO (above), the BSO aims to protect individual borrowers. Section 2 of the BSO contains a wide definition of a bill of sale. A bill of sale includes any document of assurances of personal chattels, any document authorising the taking possession of certain chattels and any agreement by which a right in equity to any personal chattels, or to any charge or security thereon is conferred. Section 15 is headed "Form of bill of sale" and requires the bill of sale to be made in accordance with the statutory form[51] or else be void. Section 7 requires the bill to be attested and registered.

7.3.3.3 Marine Insurance Policies

The Marine Insurance Ordinance (MIO)[52] applies to all contracts which indemnify the insured against marine losses. Section 22 of the MIO requires such contracts to be in the form of a marine insurance policy that accords with the MIO. Sections 23–26 also stipulate requirements as to the contents of the policy, its signing and how the subject matter must be designated.

---

50. Cap 20.
51. Form 2 of the Schedule to the BSO.
52. Cap 329.

7.3.3.4 Other Statutory Provisions

The contracts discussed above constitute the most important exceptions to the general rule that contracts may be created without any special formal requirements. Mention may also be made of formal requirements under the Apprenticeship Ordinance[53]— dealing with the employment of persons between 14 and 19 years of age—and the Contracts for Employment Outside Hong Kong Ordinance.[54] Both these categories of contract are more appropriately dealt with in works on employment law.

---

53. Cap 47.
54. Cap 78.

8

Contractual Terms

OVERVIEW

Having examined those elements necessary for the formation of a valid contract, we now turn to the contents or "terms" of the contract. Here a distinction must be drawn between those statements made by the parties which are regarded as part of the contract ("terms") and other statements which, even though they may *induce* the making of the contract, are not part of the contract itself ("representations"). This distinction is important, since a breach of a term gives the "innocent" party a right to sue for breach. In the case of "mere" representations, a right of action, if it exists at all, will lie in misrepresentation rather than breach.

Whether the statement is a term or not depends on various factors including the timing and importance of the statement, whether or not such a statement is usual, the relative expertise of the parties and whether or not the parties later produce a written agreement.

Terms may be express or implied. "Express" terms, of course, are those actually stated by the parties (either orally or in writing). The courts can, additionally, "imply" terms into a contract based either on the common law or statute. The courts are reluctant to imply terms into a contract on common law grounds and have produced a number of tests—principally the business efficacy and the officious bystander tests—to decide what the true intentions of the parties are and whether a term should be implied into the contract to give effect to those intentions. Statutory implied terms derive from many sources, the most important of which, from the contract perspective, is the Sale of Goods Ordinance.[1]

Courts are often called on to determine the "meaning" of express terms. Just as an objective test is used to determine whether the parties "intended" agreement *and* to determine whether they "intended" it to be binding, an objective test is used to determine the *meaning* of the contractual agreement. The test, put simply, is what

---

1. Cap 26.

a reasonable man (armed with the parties' background information) would have believed the parties to have intended by their words. In determining such meaning, it remains established law that the courts will not look at pre-contractual negotiations, since the parties' intentions may change before the contract is finally concluded.

Terms are not all of equal importance and may be classified as either "conditions" or "warranties". Breach of a condition entitles the innocent party to choose either to terminate the contract (and sue for damages if appropriate) or continue with the contract and sue for damages only. Breach of the lesser term, a warranty, only entitles the innocent party to sue for damages. The contract continues in existence.

The rigid classification of terms into conditions and warranties and the differences in remedies available to the innocent party, however, may result in injustice. A third category of intermediate or "innominate" term has, therefore, been introduced by the courts. This approach permits the court to determine the innocent party's rights based on the *effect* of a term's breach rather than on the status of the term itself. This affords the courts the flexibility to reach a "just" resolution in the circumstances of the individual case but at the expense of certainty.

A major emphasis of this chapter is the exemption clause. An exemption clause either totally or partially excludes the liability of one of the parties to a contract. As a result of concerns over the rights of consumers in their dealings with parties of greater bargaining power, the courts, and more recently legislation, have acted to restrict the scope of exemption clauses and, thereby, protect the interests of consumers.

If an exemption clause is to operate it must, at common law, be found to be a part of the contract; that is, it must be "incorporated" either in writing or via notice. It must also, of course, clearly cover, the breach from which exemption is sought. If the clause does *not* unambiguously cover the breach, the courts will construe the clause against the party seeking to rely on it. The courts also refuse to allow reliance on exemption clauses where their effect has been misrepresented or where they are contradicted by a clear "overriding" statement of the "exemptor". The rules of "privity" may also be invoked so as to preclude a non-contracting party from taking the benefit of an exemption clause.[2]

Despite the efforts of the courts to reduce the scope of exemption clauses, legislators, in England and Hong Kong, have found that additional restrictions are necessary, particularly in the area of consumer protection. Major legislation, in the form of the Control of Exemption Clauses Ordinance (CECO),[3] was enacted in Hong Kong, based on previous English legislation.[4] CECO largely, though not exclusively, regulates the relationship between business and consumer. It encompasses attempts to restrict liability for breach, misrepresentation and negligence, precluding entirely certain types of exemption and making others subject to a test of reasonableness.

---

2. See chapter 16.
3. Cap 71.
4. The Unfair Contract Terms Act 1977.

8.1 Representations and Terms

Not all statements made in connection with a contract are regarded as terms by the courts. A distinction must be drawn between statements which merely induce the other party to form a contract and statements which form part of the contract itself. The former are representations while the latter are terms. If a term is broken, the innocent party has a right to damages for breach of contract. If a representation proves to be false, the remedies of the innocent party lie in an action for misrepresentation.[5]

There are no clear rules for distinguishing a representation from a term. The courts[6] will try to determine objectively the true intention of the parties[6] based on the facts of each case. In *Oscar Chess v Williams*,[7] Lord Denning stated that the intention of the parties depends on their conduct, words and behaviour rather than on their thoughts. His criterion was whether an "intelligent bystander" would reasonably infer that the parties intended a statement to be contractual. While much will depend on the words and actions of the parties in each individual case, the courts have developed certain guidelines and identified certain factors to help them distinguish a representation from a term.

8.1.1 Timing

A statement is likely to be only a representation if it was made sometime before the formal contract was established. In *Routledge v McKay*,[8] the seller of a motor cycle stated, on 23 October, that it was a 1942 model when it was, in fact, a 1930 model. The buyer referred to the log book as corroboration. On 30 October the same year, the formal contract of sale was concluded. It did not make any reference to the age of the motor cycle. It was held that the earlier statement was not a term of the contract but only a representation. The time gap of seven days was too long for the statement made to be a term. It was also significant that the seller made clear that he had no special knowledge of his own; that he got his information from elsewhere and was just passing it on.

8.1.2 Importance of the Statement

A statement is more likely to be regarded as a term if one of the parties stresses its importance and makes it clear to the other party that it is crucial to a decision whether or not to enter into a contract. In *Bannerman v White*,[9] the parties negotiated the sale and purchase of some hops. The buyer asked if the hops had been cultivated

---

5. See chapter 9.
6. See *Jumbo King Ltd v Faithful Properties Ltd & Others* [1999] HKLRD 757.
7. [1957] 1 WLR 370.
8. [1954] 1 All ER 855.
9. (1861) 10 CB 844.

using sulphur. He said he would not be interested in buying them if they were so cultivated. The seller stated that no sulphur had been used and the contract was formed. It later became apparent that sulphur had been used in the cultivation of the hops. The seller sued for the price but the buyer claimed he was entitled to reject the hops. The court found for the buyer.

Similarly, in *Couchman v Hill*[10] the plaintiff contemplated bidding for a heifer at auction but needed to know if it was "unserved" (not pregnant). The owner gave an oral assurance to that effect. This proved to be incorrect and the cow later gave birth to a calf. Despite the wording of the auction conditions that no undertakings were given as to the condition of lots, the owner's separate assurance was taken to be binding. The owner's undertaking was crucial to the plaintiff making a bid and sufficiently important to amount to a term of the contract rather than a mere representation.

8.1.3 *Where a Warranty Is Normally Given*

A statement is more likely to be a term if the transaction is of a type where such a warranty (in the sense of "assurance") would normally be given. By contrast, if such a warranty is not normally given in that type of transaction then the court is less likely to find that the statement is a term. Another animal case, *Schawel v Reade*,[11] illustrates the point. In *Schawel*, the parties were discussing the possible sale of the defendant's horse for stud purposes. The plaintiff began to inspect the horse but the defendant said: "You need not look for anything: the horse is perfectly sound. If there was anything wrong with the horse I would tell you." The plaintiff then ceased his inspection and, three weeks later, bought the horse which was totally unfit for stud purposes. The House of Lords unanimously held that, in these circumstances, the defendant's statement as to the soundness of the horse was a term of the contract.

Lord Moulton said that an examination of the words and actions of the parties showed that the seller intended to take upon himself the responsibility of the soundness of the horse by making the quoted statement.

The defendant's statement in *Schawel* as to the soundness of the horse did not merely affect the nature of the contract; it affected its very creation. Had the plaintiff known the truth he would not merely have paid less for the horse but not have bought it at all. This can be contrasted with *Routledge v McKay*[12] where the age of the motor cycle probably would have only affected the price.

By contrast, the court more recently found that there was no warranty in *Ecay v Godfrey*.[13] Here, the plaintiff orally agreed to buy the defendant's boat following

---

10. [1947] 1 KB 554.
11. [1913] 2 Ir Rep 81.
12. Discussed at 8.1.1 above.
13. (1974) 80 Lloyd's Rep 286.

a conversation between them in which the defendant suggested that the plaintiff should have a survey completed of the boat. The boat was unsound and the plaintiff claimed damages for breach of contract. It was held that the defendant had given no undertaking as to the condition of the boat and had even suggested a survey. There was, therefore, no term to the effect that the boat was sound.

It should be noted that the word "warranty" is used by the courts in two ways. One means a contractual promise amounting to a term. The other means a lesser term, as opposed to a condition.[14] Here "warranty" is used in the former sense. Indeed, in *Schawel* the soundness of the horse was of the utmost importance and, therefore, a condition.

8.1.4 Where the Maker of the Statement Has Special Expertise

A statement is more likely to be a term if the maker of the statement had significantly more expertise in the relevant area than the other party. Two important contrasting cases involving Lord Denning illustrate well how the courts apply this factor to distinguish a representation from a term. In *Oscar Chess Ltd v Williams*,[15] the defendant sold a car to the plaintiffs, who were car dealers, in part-exchange for a new car. The defendant, honestly relying on a false entry in the car's registration book made before he purchased it, stated that the car was a 1948 model and received £290 discount on the price of the new car. In fact, the car was a 1939 model and the plaintiffs, had they known this, would have given only £175 discount. The plaintiffs, on discovering the truth, sued the defendant for damages, arguing that the statement as to age was either a term of the contract of sale or "collateral" (see below at 8.1.4.2) to it. A majority of the English Court of Appeal rejected the plaintiffs' claim.

Denning LJ agreed with the judge at first instance that both parties assumed that the car was a 1948 model and that this assumption was fundamental to the contract. However, he said that it must have been obvious to both parties that the seller himself had no personal knowledge of the year when the car was made. He also placed great store on the fact that the plaintiffs were experts in this field and that, as they did not check the accuracy of the log book at the time, they should not be allowed to recover against an innocent seller who produced to them all the evidence he had; namely, the registration book.

The opposite result occurred in *Dick Bentley Productions Ltd v Harold Smith (Motors) Ltd*.[16] Here the plaintiff asked the defendants, who were car dealers, to find him a "well-vetted" second-hand car. The defendants found a car which, they said, had done only 26,000 miles with a new engine. The plaintiff agreed to buy the car which, in fact, had done over 100,000 miles. There was no reference to mileage in

---

14. See below at 8.5.
15. [1957] 1 WLR 370.
16. [1965] 1 WLR 623.

the written contract of sale. Nonetheless the English Court of Appeal unanimously upheld the plaintiff's claim for damages for breach of contract on the basis that the defendant's statement as to mileage was a term of the contract. Lord Denning MR said that the defendants were in a position to know or at least find out the history of the car.

The decision in this case is no doubt "equitable". There was clearly a misrepresentation by the defendants which would have fallen within section 2(1) of the Misrepresentation Act 1967, passed soon after. Given the inadequacy of the provision for damages for misrepresentation prior to the statute, it was necessary to "convert" the statement into a term if the plaintiff was to receive damages. However, the explanation by Lord Denning as to why the statement should be viewed as a term is not convincing since it stresses the negligence of the defendants as opposed to the weight attached to the statement by the parties.

Both these English Court of Appeal decisions seem to have similar facts but produce different results. The decisive factor distinguishing them appears to be that in *Oscar Chess* the parties had, more or less, the same amount of expertise in the relevant field, while in *Dick Bentley* the sellers, as car dealers, were in a better position than the buyer to know whether the statement was true or not.

8.1.5 *Where Agreement Later Reduced to Writing*

A statement is less likely to be a term if the parties took the time to record their agreement in writing and did not include that statement in the written document. An example is *Routledge v McKay*, discussed above,[17] where a formal contract was drawn up omitting the oral statement about the age of the motor cycle made seven days beforehand. The court found that this oral statement was not a term of the contract both because of the time gap and also because of the later reduction into writing.

Another important case in this area is *Heilbut Symons & Co v Buckleton*,[18] where the House of Lords dealt with a number of issues including the legal status of oral statements where a later written contract is executed. In *Heilbut*, the defendants were rubber merchants. The plaintiff spoke to the defendant's manager and the following conversation took place:

Plaintiff: "I understand you are bringing out a rubber company?"
Defendant: "Yes."
Plaintiff: "Is it all right?"
Defendant: "We are bringing it out."
Plaintiff: "That is good enough for me. I will take 5,000 shares."

---

17. See 8.1.1.
18. [1913] AC 30.

The next day, in a written contract which made no reference to a "rubber company", the plaintiff bought 5,000 shares from the defendant. The shares depreciated and the plaintiff claimed damages for breach of contract, on the ground that the company was not, technically, a rubber company. The plaintiff's action failed in the House of Lords on the basis that the statement that the company was a rubber company was not a term of the contract.

8.2 Written Contracts: The Parol Evidence Rule

In attempting to incorporate a statement as a contractual term, a party may often be faced with the obstacle of the "parol evidence rule".

A Law Commission (England and Wales) Report has described the parol evidence rule as follows:

> When it is proved or admitted that the parties to a contract intended that all the express terms of their agreement should be recorded in a particular document or documents, evidence will be inadmissible (because irrelevant) if it is tendered only for the purpose of adding to, varying, subtracting from or contradicting the express terms of that contract.[19]

The purposes of the parol evidence rule are to allow parties to rely upon their written contracts and to prevent fraud. This clearly makes much commercial sense in that the parties to a written contract wish to have certainty and finality in their dealings.[20] However, there are so many exceptions to the parol evidence rule that the rule is scarcely of value. Indeed, coverage of the so-called "rule" is avoided in many law texts and contract law syllabuses. McMeel[21] talks of the "demise" of the rule and adds that:

> several generations of law students and lawyers may be unfamiliar with (or only dimly aware of) the parol evidence rule . . . the vast number of identified exceptions to the supposed rule suggests that this must be a case where the exception has swallowed up the rule.

Nonetheless, for the sake of completeness, some of the major exceptions will now be briefly considered.

Parol evidence may be permitted to show that the written contract is not yet in force;[22] that it has already been fully performed; that the contract was procured by fraud or other vitiating element; that it does not reflect the parties' true intention and should be rectified; that a party lacks contractual capacity; that an implied term

---

19. See *Report on the Parol Evidence Rule* (Law Com No 154).
20. See *Value Capital Ltd v Ke Junxiang* [2011] 1 HKLRD 1011.
21. G. McMeel, "Interpretation and Mistake in Contract Law", (2005) LMCLQ 49.
22. See *Pym v Campbell* (1856) 6 E&B 370.

should be added on the basis of a trade or market custom;[23] that there is an "over-riding" parol undertaking; and that the contract was not intended to be entire, such that parol additions are permitted. This last exception is illustrated in *J Evans & Son (Portsmouth) v Andrea Merzario Ltd*.[24] Here, the plaintiffs were importers of machinery who regularly used the defendants to arrange the carriage of their goods. The parties' original agreement specified that machinery must be carried below deck to avoid rust. Later the defendants moved to container carriage and gave the plaintiffs an oral assurance that machinery would continue to be shipped below deck. On a subsequent voyage the defendants mistakenly placed the plaintiffs' machinery on deck whence it was washed overboard. The plaintiffs sued for compensation and the defendants argued that the oral assurance was not intended to be binding and was, in any event, contrary to the express written terms of the contract by which "the Company reserves to itself complete freedom in respect of the means, route and procedure to be followed in the handling and transportation of goods." The court found in favour of the plaintiffs, holding that the contract was intended to be partly in writing and partly oral.

This exception to the parol evidence rule has been said to reduce the "rule" to a tautology. If the agreement is entire, it cannot be amended by parol evidence; but if it is not entire, it can be so amended. Thus, if courts which to amend a written contract they will hold it is not entire; if they wish to accept it as it stands, they will hold it to be entire and unchangeable.

It is also the case that the parol evidence rule is inapplicable where the parties disagree as to the precise meaning of the written contract and where such disagreement reflects genuine ambiguity or uncertainty. The court's task then is to construe the parties' "intention", as far as possible, via objective means. In *Jumbo King Ltd v Faithful Properties Ltd & Others*[25] Lord Hoffman said:

> in serious utterances such as legal documents, in which people may be supposed to have chosen their words with care, one does not readily accept that they have used the wrong words. If the ordinary meaning of the words makes sense in relation to the rest of the document and the factual background, then the court will give effect to that language, even though the consequences may appear hard for one side or the other . . . But the overriding objective in construction is to give effect to what a reasonable person rather than a pedantic lawyer would have understood the parties to mean.[26]

---

23. See *Smith v Wilson* (1832) 3B & Ad 728.
24. [1976] 2 All ER 930.
25. [1999] HKLRD 757.
26. Ibid at 773–774. The *Jumbo King* approach was endorsed in *Distribution Ltd v Aman & Sonne GMBH and Co KG & Others* [2009] 4 HKLRD 633.

A final, significant, exception relates to so-called "collateral" contracts. Evidence may be admitted to show that a collateral ("running side by side") contract was made before or at the time the written contract was made. The consideration for a collateral contract is, invariably, entering into the main contract in return for a "collateral" assurance. In *Couchman v Hill*, discussed above,[27] for example, the plaintiff entered into the main contract to buy the cow *in return for* the assurance that the heifer was "unserved". Evidence may be admissible, therefore, to show that there are, in fact, two contracts; one oral and one written. The courts are prepared to find such a collateral contract if its terms are independent of the written contract and, generally, do not specifically contradict the terms of the written contract. In *Couchman*, the oral assurance given was found to be a collateral contract and the buyer was able to succeed by adducing evidence under this exception to the parol evidence rule.

In *Heilbut Symons & Co v Buckleton*[28] the House of Lords, while acknowledging the existence of collateral contracts, showed a marked reluctance to finding that a collateral contract exists. Lord Moulton said:

> It is evident, both on principle and on authority, that there may be a contract the consideration for which is the making of some other contract. 'If you will make such and such a contract I will give you 100 pounds,' is in every sense of the word a complete legal contract. It is collateral to the main contract, but each has an independent existence, and they do not differ in respect of their possessing to the full the character and status of a contract. But such collateral contracts must from their very nature be rare . . . Such collateral contracts, the sole effect of which is to vary or add to the terms of the principal contract, are therefore viewed with suspicion by the law. They must be proved strictly.[29]

Despite this apparently restrictive approach, collateral warranties have often been found.[30]

Esso Petroleum Co v Mardon[31]

Esso's experienced representative told Mardon that the throughput of petrol at a certain site which Mardon proposed to lease would reach 200,000 gallons a year. In fact, despite Mardon's best efforts, throughput reached only 60,000–70,000 gallons. Eventually he was unable to pay for petrol supplied. Esso sued for possession and

---

27. See 8.1.2 above. See also *Shanklin Pier Ltd v Detel Products Ltd* [1951] 2 All ER 471.
28. [1913] AC 30.
29. Ibid at 47.
30. Hong Kong courts have appeared less reluctant to uphold collateral contracts; see *Bank of China (Hong Kong) v Fung Chin Kan* [2003] 1 HKLRD 181.
31. [1976] 2 All ER 5.

money due. Mardon counter-claimed for breach of warranty in respect of the representation about the throughput of petrol. The English Court of Appeal, led by Lord Denning MR, gave judgment for Mardon saying that the representation by Esso was a collateral warranty.

Lord Denning MR said:

> They knew the facts. They knew the traffic in the town. They knew the throughput of comparable stations. They had much experience and expertise at their disposal. They were in a much better position than Mr Mardon to make a forecast. It seems to me that if such a person makes a forecast—intending that the other should act on it and he does act on it—it can well be interpreted as a warranty that the forecast is sound and reliable in this sense that they made it with reasonable care and skill.[32]

Usually a collateral warranty will only be recognised if it does not contradict the terms of the main contract. Exceptionally, in *City and Westminster Properties (1934) Ltd v Mudd*,[33] a collateral contract was found to exist where a tenant was permitted to reside on property despite the fact that the lease contained a clause that the premises were to be used solely for business purposes. While this decision seems questionable, Treitel[34] states that there is no compelling reason why an oral agreement cannot contradict the written document. If this is so, of course, it adds weight to the view that "the exception has swallowed the rule".

8.3 The "Meaning" of Express Terms

In cases of dispute, courts may be called upon to determine the "meaning" of contractual terms. The courts are said to be "construing" the terms. Such construction (also referred to as "interpretation") is based on the intention of the parties. However, such "intention" is determined, in Hong Kong and England, using an "objective" test. The courts cannot read the minds of the parties but they can attribute intention based on what a "reasonable person", with the background knowledge of the parties, would have meant by the words used. In the Court of Final Appeal case of *Jumbo King v Faithful Properties Ltd*[35] Lord Hoffmann NPJ described contractual construction as:

> [an] attempt to discover what a reasonable person would have understood the parties to mean. And this involves having regard not merely to the individual words they have used, but to the agreement as a whole, the factual and legal background against which it was concluded and the practical objects which it was intended to achieve.

---

32. Ibid at 14.
33. [1958] 2 All ER 733.
34. (See footnote 38) at p 243.
35. [1999] 3 HKLRD 757, (1999) 2 HKCFAR 279.

The *Jumbo King* approach was endorsed by the Hong Kong Court of Appeal (overturning a judgment of the Lands Tribunal) in *Win Glories Ltd v Majorluck Ltd*.[36] The key issue in the case was whether a manager-tenant of a wet market should pay a share of "management fees" like all other tenants in the same building. In deciding that it should not, the court took account of the fact that there was no reference to "management fees" in the appellant's contract (unlike that of the other tenants) *and* that the appellant's lease required the performance of onerous cleaning and other duties, not required of other tenants.

This "background" to which Lord Hoffmann referred might, for example, include the fact that both parties were expert in a particular field where words were used in a specialised way. More generally, it has been said that, "a business sense will be given to business documents".

Lord Hoffmann, again, in the English case of *Investors Compensation Scheme Ltd v West Bromwich Building Society*,[37] said:

> Interpretation is the ascertainment of the meaning which the document would convey to a reasonable person having all the knowledge which would reasonably have been available to the parties in the situation in which they were at the time of the contract.

A minor gloss was put on the above by Lord Clarke in *Rainy Sky SA v Kookmin Bank*[38] where he said that where there are "competing meanings" the more commercially sensible will be chosen. More recently, Lord Neuberger cautioned against applying "common sense" at the expense of the clear words of a contract.[39] This plea for caution is well expressed (endorsing Lord Neuberger's warning) by Leggatt LJ in the *Merthyr (South Wales)* case (see 8.4.2). He said:

> Lord Neuberger (in *Arnold v Britton*) signalled a need for caution in relying on considerations of commercial common sense in interpreting contracts . . . It is salutary to recall that the persons best placed to judge what is a commercially sensible agreement to make are the parties who have chosen to make it, and the courts should be correspondingly wary of rejecting a natural interpretation of contractual language because it appears to produce a commercially unreasonable result.

There is clearly some potential for tension between a "literal" approach to the words used and a focus on "background and purpose". Treitel asks, "what matters most: the words used or the 'background'?".[40] In the *Investors* case, for example, Lord Hoffmann was prepared to "re-write" the contractual terms slightly to bring it into accord with what he saw as the parties' clear contractual purpose. A contrary

---

36. [2019] 5 HKLRD 471.
37. [1998] 1 WLR 896.
38. [2011] UKSC 50.
39. See *Arnold v Britton* [2015] UKSC 36.
40. E. Peel, *Treitel: The Law of Contract* (London: Sweet & Maxwell, 14th edn, 2015) at p 2229.

view is that the contract should be construed/interpreted strictly on the words used, leaving the courts an equitable discretion to "rectify" the contract in cases of obvious mistake.[41] The "plain words/purpose" dichotomy has been expressed in terms of a "textual" rather than a "contextual" approach. However, in *Wood v Capita Insurance Services Ltd*[42] Lord Hodge stated:

> Textualism and contextualism are not conflicting paradigms in a battle for exclusive occupation of the field of contractual interpretation.[43]

Put simply, Lord Hodge's view is that literalism may be more appropriate where words have been used technically by experts in the field, while a more purposive approach, derived from the presumed intention of the parties, may be more appropriate in less technical, more informal contracts, involving parties acting without legal advice.

One traditional rule of construction which has survived "purposive" interpretation is that which precludes all consideration of the parties' pre-contractual negotiations. The rule was established in England in *Prenn v Simmonds*[44] and followed in Hong Kong. More recently, in *Chartbrook Ltd v Persimmon Homes Ltd*[45] the English courts have affirmed that the rule has survived the more purposive approach of *Investors*, and this approach was quickly endorsed in the Hong Kong case of *Urban Renewal Authority v Agrila Ltd & Another*.[46] Here, Le Pichon JA (with whom Rogers VP agreed) cited with approval Lord Hoffmann's statement in *Chartbrook*:

> there is no clearly established case for departing from the exclusionary rule. The rule may well mean . . . that the parties are sometimes held bound by a contract in terms which . . . a reasonable observer would not have taken them to have intended. But . . . this may be justified in the more general interest of economy and predictability in obtaining advice and adjudicating disputes.

More succinctly, in *Fok Chun Yue Benjamin v Fok Chun Wan Ian*,[47] Lam VP stated that the rule in *Prenn v Simmonds* "is still good law".[48]

As indicated above, there remains, in *Prenn/Chartbrook* situations where the pre-contractual negotiations indicate that the concluded contract has not properly reflected the parties' intention, the possibility of equitable intervention via rectification for mistake.

---

41. See chapter 10. This was the view of *Investors* dissenting judge Lord Lloyd who criticised "creative interpretation".
42. [2017] AC 1173.
43. Cited with approval in *Win Glories Ltd v Majorluck Ltd* [2019] 5 HKLRD 471 para 1.1 per Cheung JA.
44. [1971] 3 All ER 237.
45. [2009] UKHL 38.
46. [2010] 1 HKLRD 578.
47. [2015] 2 HKLRD 212.
48. Cf also *Konwall Construction & Engineering Co Ltd v Strong Progress Ltd* [2013] 3 HKLRD 503.

8.4 Implied Terms

An implied term is a term that is not expressed by the parties, either orally or in writing, but is, nonetheless, part of the contract. Traditionally courts have been reluctant to find such terms. This is in keeping with the principle of freedom of contract, which requires that it is for the parties to make the contract and not the courts. However, the courts may, and increasingly do, imply a term into a contract on various grounds. One is that the parties probably had such a term in mind but simply neglected to express it. Here the court can say that it is giving effect to the parties' actual intentions. Another ground is that the parties did not have such a term in mind but would have, "of course" wanted it in the contract had they thought of it. Other types of implied terms have nothing to do with the parties' intentions but are implied by either the common law or by legislation.

8.4.1 Terms Implied by Custom

Custom and usage may be used by the court to add an implied term. The rationale is that the parties did not express all of the terms of the agreement but only those necessary for this particular case; relying on regular trade customs and practices to complete the remainder of the terms. As the courts are reluctant to imply such terms, the person arguing in favour of the inclusion of such a term has to show that the custom is well established in that particular trade, industry or locality. The implied term must be consistent with any express term as it is within the parties' powers to expressly exclude any customary term.

Some nineteenth-century English cases illustrate the operation of the above. In *Hutton v Warren*[49] it was proved by local custom that a tenant, on quitting in accordance with notice given by the landlord, was entitled to a fair allowance for the seeds and labour he had spent on the land. This was only proper, as the landlord could benefit from the results of the tenant's endeavours. Similarly, in *Fleet v Murton*,[50] the defendant was an agent whose principal defaulted. Under the normal principles of agency, the defendant would have assumed no personal liability but in this case the defendant was held liable since his principal's name had not been stated in the contract and, in the business in question—the colonial fruit trade—agents would, by custom, be personally liable in such circumstances.[51] The essential criterion for these trade custom implied terms is that they must be "certain, notorious and reasonable".

---

49. (1836) 1 M&W 466.
50. (1871) LR 7 QB 126.
51. See also *Smith v Wilson* (1832) 3 B & Ad 728 and *British Crane Hire Corp Ltd v Ipswich Plant Hire Ltd* [1975] QB 303.

8.4.2 Terms Implied "in Fact"

The courts, as noted above, are reluctant to imply terms into a contract as this is contrary to the traditional idea of the parties making the contract and not the courts. The courts often rationalise implying terms into a contract on the basis that they are merely "filling in the gaps" in the contract to give effect to the unexpressed intentions of the parties.

The earliest test used by the courts for implied terms was the *business efficacy* test. In applying this test, the court decides whether or not the contract would be unworkable without such a term being implied into the contract. The genesis of this test lies in the old case of *"The Moorcock"*.[52] In this case the parties had a contract for the hiring of a jetty for loading cargo. At low tide the plaintiff's boat ran aground and was damaged. It was clear that the jetty was not safe for the purpose of the contract. There was no express term that the jetty was safe but the English Court of Appeal held that it was an implied term that the jetty should be fit for the basic purpose of the contract. This implied term was necessary to give the contract "business efficacy" and it could be assumed that the parties so intended.

Bowen LJ said:

> In business transactions such as this, what the law desires to effect by implication is to give such business efficacy to the transaction as must have been intended at all events by both parties who are businessmen.[53]

Forty years later MacKinnon LJ devised a related test for implied terms. In *Shirlaw v Southern Foundries (1926) Ltd*[54] he said:

> That which is implied and need not be expressed is something so obvious that it goes without saying; so that, if while the parties were making their bargain an officious bystander were to suggest some express provision for it in their agreement, they would testily suppress him with a common "Oh, of course".[55]

This test has become known as the "officious bystander" test and has been endorsed by the English courts on numerous subsequent occasions.[56] It is, however, a restricted approach, and will always be eschewed where the alleged term is far from obvious.[57]

---

52. (1889) 14 PD 64.
53. Ibid at 68.
54. [1939] 2 KB 206.
55. Ibid at 227.
56. See, for example *Independiente Ltd & Others v Music Trading Online (HK) Ltd* [2007] EWCA Civ 111.
57. See discussion of *Spring v National Amalgamated Stevedores & Dockers Society* below.

It is not clear from the cases whether the "business efficacy" and "officious bystander" these two tests are cumulative or alternative. Some cases treat the tests as being one. In *Reigate v Union Manufacturing Co*[58] Scrutton LJ said:

> A term can only be implied if it is necessary in the business sense to give efficacy to the contract; that is, if it is such a term that it can confidently be said that if at the time the contract was being negotiated someone had said to the parties, 'What will happen in such a case,' they would both have replied, 'Of course, so and so will happen; we did not trouble to say that; it is too clear.'[59]

Other cases have treated the two tests as alternatives. In *Mosvolds Rederi A/S v Food Corporation of India*,[60] Lord Steyn held that an implied term was not needed to give the contract business efficacy *but* should be implied anyway, since the reasonable businessman would say that "of course" the term should be present. In *Yoo Design Services v Ltd v Iliv Realty Pte Ltd*,[61] Carr LJ stated that:

> The business efficacy and the obviousness tests are alternative tests. However, it will be rare (or unusual) for case where one but not the other is satisfied.[62]

In *Liverpool City Council v Irwin*[63] Lord Denning MR tried, unsuccessfully, to expand the scope for implied terms by suggesting that a term could be implied into a contract if it was "fair and reasonable" to say that the contract would be a better one for its inclusion. However, on appeal, this approach was rejected as too broad by the House of Lords, with Lord Cross confirming that a term will be implied only if it was possible to state that the insertion of the term was "necessary". This deference to party autonomy was applied in the case of *Yoo Design Services v Iliv Realty PTE Ltd*[64] where Carr LJ stated:

> The test is one of necessity, not reasonableness. That is a stringent test.[65]

An exhaustive consideration of the requirements for an implied term in fact was conducted by Master Dagnall in *Bank of New York Mellon (International) Ltd v Cine-UK Ltd*.[66] In this case, one of many based on COVID, various tenants argued a "temporary frustration" of contracts, based on an implied term that rent charges should be suspended during COVID. Master Dagnall opined that the contract could work perfectly well without such a term and that such a term failed to pass the

---

58. [1918] 1 KB 592.
59. Ibid at 605.
60. [1986] 2 Lloyd's Rep 68 at 70–71.
61. [2021] EWCA Civ 560.
62. At para 51.
63. [1976] QB 319.
64. Cited above.
65. At para 51.
66. [2021] zewhc 1013.

"officious bystander" test. Once again, it was made clear that mere "reasonableness" is not enough.

The limitations of the officious bystander test are illustrated in *Spring v National Amalgamated Stevedores and Dockers Society*.[67] Here, the defendant trade union had been ordered to dismiss the plaintiff as he had been illegally "poached" from another union contrary to the "Bridlington agreement". The plaintiff sued for wrongful dismissal and succeeded. The defendants had argued that the Bridlington agreement was an implied term of the plaintiff's contract but the court rejected the argument, applying the officious bystander test. If asked about the agreement the officious bystander would not say "of course" but "what's that?"

Finally, it should be noted that a term will not be implied "in fact" into a contract if it would plainly contradict an *express* term. This was made clear in *Lynch v Thorne*,[68] where the defendant built a house with nine-inch brick walls. This was according to an express term to that effect. However, the walls would not keep out the rain and so the house was rendered unfit for human habitation. The English Court of Appeal held that they could not imply a term into the contract that the house be fit for human habitation as this would be inconsistent with the express wording of the contract.

In Hong Kong, the courts have adopted a test that combines both the officious bystander test and the business efficacy test and other conditions. This test was laid down by the Privy Council in *BP Refinery (Westernport) Pty Ltd v President, Councillors & Ratepayers of Shire of Hastings*.[69] These conditions are that the term must:

1. be reasonable and equitable;
2. be necessary to give business efficacy to the contract;
3. be so obvious that it "goes without saying";
4. be capable of clear expression; and
5. not contradict any express term of the contract.[70]

This test has been applied in numerous Hong Kong cases such as *Attorney-General v Melhado Investments Ltd*,[71] *Shun Shing Hing Investment Co Ltd v Attorney-General*,[72] and *On Park Parking Ltd v Secretary of Justice & Others*.[73] The *BP Refinery* approach was (seemingly) briefly challenged by dicta of Lord Hoffmann, also in the Privy Council, in the case of *Attorney-General of Belize v*

---

67. [1956] 1 WLR 585.
68. [1956] 1 All ER 744.
69. [1978] 52 AJLR 20.
70. Ibid at 26.
71. [1983] HKLR 327 at 329.
72. [1983] HKLR 432 at 440.
73. [2004] 3 HKC 476.

Belize Telecom[74] in which he suggested that the five conditions of *BP Refinery* are merely guidelines to assist the court in determining the meaning of the contract. To Lord Hoffmann:

> There is only one question: is that what the instrument, read as a whole against the relevant background, would reasonably be understood to mean?[75]

If, as many assumed, Lord Hoffmann was advocating the abolition of the five conditions in favour of a more general "reasonable man" approach as to what should be implied in a contract, the position has been "clarified" by the United Kingdom Supreme Court in *Marks & Spencer plc v BNP Paribas Securities Services Trust Company (Jersey) Ltd & Another.*[76] Here a unanimous court made clear that the *BP Refinery* approach remains sound. In an implicit criticism of Lord Hoffmann,[77] Supreme Court President Lord Neuberger stated that the five conditions "represent a clear, consistent and principled approach". Lord Neuberger did add some points of clarification; notably that the "business efficacy" and "officious bystander" conditions (conditions 2 and 3) were alternatives (there is no need to satisfy both). Moreover, he re-emphasised that a term would not be implied merely because it would "improve" the contract; a term will be implied only where, without it, the contract would lack commercial or practical coherence. Crucially, Lord Neuberger rejected the notion (attributed to Lord Hoffman, rightly or wrongly) that the issue of implied terms is simply a matter of contractual construction. He said:

> Lord Hoffmann's analysis in *Belize Telecom* could obscure the fact that construing the words used and implying additional words are different processes governed by different rules . . . it is only after the process of construing the express words is complete that the issue of implied terms falls to be considered.[78]

Lord Neuberger praised Lord Hoffmann's outstanding contributions "in so many areas of law". Such a eulogy is invariably followed by the word "however", and this was no exception.

While neither *Belize* nor *Marks & Spencer* (as post-1997 decisions) are binding precedents in Hong Kong, there seems little doubt that, given their previous approach, the Hong Kong courts will follow the *Marks & Spencer* approach.[79] Indeed, in a

---

74. [2009] 1 WLR 1988.
75. Ibid at para 21.
76. [2015] UKSC 72.
77. Lord Neuberger stated, *inter alia*, that "some interpretations" given to Lord Hoffmann's "observations" in *Belize* are "wrong in law" (at para 31).
78. At paras 26 and 28.
79. While *Belize* was referred to by Seagroatt J in *Elco Holland BV v Airwell Air-Conditioning (Asia) Co Ltd* [2015] 5 HKC, it was applied consistently with *BP Refinery* to which the judge also referred.

recent Court of First Instance case, Ng J applied the *BP Refinery* five conditions without question.[80]

A recent illustration of the *BP Refinery* condition 5 is provided in the recent English Court of Appeal decision in *Merthyr (South Wales) Ltd (FKA Blackstone (South Wales) Ltd) v Merthyr Tydfil County Borough Council.*[81] Here the court endorsed the view that the "commercial common sense" approach should not be adopted where it runs clearly contrary to the parties' clearly expressed intentions. Moreover, in rejecting a purported implied term, Leggatt LJ stated, succinctly:

> The reasons why such a provision cannot be implied into the agreement are not only that the result would be irrational and contrary to business common sense. They are also that such a provision is inconsistent with the express terms of the agreement.

8.4.3 Terms Implied "in Law"

The category of terms implied "in law" covers those terms which can be implied into all contracts of a certain type. They are implied because the nature of the contract involved is such that they *should be* present. These terms, unlike those implied in fact, cannot be said to be based on the intention of the parties. Such terms are often implied into, for instance, contracts of employment and tenancy agreements; they have become attached to these classes of contractual relationships over time. Very often the parties may not be aware of these terms but the courts will imply such terms irrespective of the parties' intentions. It could be argued that these implied terms are really imposed obligations that result from policy considerations.

An example of terms being implied by law in the landlord-tenant relationship is *Liverpool City Council v Irwin*[82] where the House of Lords held that there is an implied term that the landlord has an obligation to take *reasonable care* to maintain the common parts of an apartment building, including the stairs and lifts.[83] This implied term could scarcely be said to arise from the "intention" of the parties.

Similarly, the House of Lords, in *Malik v Bank of Credit and Commerce International SA (in liquidation)*,[84] implied a term into a contract between an employer and employee not to conduct a dishonest or corrupt business. In *Malik*, employees were made redundant when the defendant bank collapsed. The bank had been operating fraudulently. The employees argued that they had been damaged, not only because they had lost their jobs but also because they were tainted with the stigma of having worked for a dishonest company. They successfully sued for a

---

80. See *Lo Yuk Sui v Fubon Bank (HK) Ltd* [2016] 1 HKC 462. See also *Kwang Qian Wen Marie v Kwan Kit Yuk* [2016] 1 HKLRD 891.
81. [2019] EWCA Civ 526.
82. [1976] QB 319.
83. However, the House of Lords did not imply an *absolute* obligation by the landlord to maintain these services.
84. [1988] AC 20.

breach of the implied term of "trust and confidence". It was held that this obligation was part of a general obligation of both parties not to engage in conduct likely to undermine the trust and confidence required if the employment relationship was to continue in the manner the employment contract implicitly envisaged.

A recent example in Hong Kong of a court implying terms into an employment contract is provided by the *Andayani* case, which involves several areas of contract law.

Andayani v Chan Oi Ling[85]

The plaintiff was an Indonesian domestic helper employed by the defendant. The plaintiff had orally agreed with an employment agency that she would come and work in Hong Kong for $2,000 per month. This was well below the prescribed minimum wage. She did, however, sign a standard form employment contract which stated that she was to receive the minimum wage of $3,860 per month. After about ten months the plaintiff left the defendant's employ and went to the police fearing for her safety. She subsequently claimed arrears of wages. The Hong Kong Court of First Instance had to determine whether there was a contract of employment, what its terms were regarding wages, whether the contract was illegal and whether the claimant could sue given that she was a willing party to the illegality. Deputy Judge To held the written agreement was void for illegality, fraud and undue influence. However, the *de facto* relationship between the parties created an employment contract. The Deputy Judge then implied into the contract the terms of the standard employment agreement because it was only on those terms that she could enter and stay in Hong Kong. This meant that her lost wages should be assessed at $3,860 per month. While the outcome is a just one, there is no doubt that the implied term had nothing to do with "intention"; indeed, *both* parties intended otherwise, albeit that one had little bargaining power.

The Hong Kong Court of Final Appeal in *Twinkle Step Investment Limited v Smart International Industrial Limited*[86] implied a term into an agreement for the sale and purchase of land with vacant possession that the vendor afford the purchaser an opportunity to inspect the property prior to completion (the formal transfer of title to the purchaser). While the implied term may have arisen automatically via the legal relationship between the parties, it was viewed as giving force to the parties' intentions. Litton PJ said:

> What more natural then, when the vendor had contracted to give vacant possession to the purchaser, that he should afford the purchaser an opportunity to see that he was indeed getting what he had bargained for, prior to handing over his money? . . . the court is not exercising a discretion by imposing terms which appear to the court

---

85. [2001] 1 HKC 252.
86. [1994] 4 HKC 441.

to be fair and reasonable; the court is simply giving true effect to the contract which the parties themselves have made.[87]

More recently, the Court of Final Appeal in *Kensland Realty Limited v Whale View Investment Limited and Another*[88] implied a term for the split payment of the purchase price into contracts for the sale and purchase of land wherever the agreement does not expressly so provide and the land is subject to an existing mortgage or the sale is a sub-sale to be completed before completion of the head sale takes place.

In England, Lord Bridge, in *Scally v Southern Health and Social Services Board*,[89] described the distinction between terms implied in fact and those implied by law terms as follows:

> A clear distinction between the search for an implied term necessary to give business efficacy to a particular contract and the search, based on wider considerations, for a term which the law will imply as a necessary incident of a definable category of contractual relationship.[90]

8.4.4 Terms Implied by Statute

Despite considerable flexibility on the part of the courts, the scope of implied terms, both in Hong Kong and in England, has been extended by legislation. The most important source of statutory implied terms, in the context of Hong Kong contract law, is the Sale of Goods Ordinance (SOGO).[91] SOGO lays down a large number of implied terms to be found in contracts for the sale of goods. Principal amongst these are the provisions of sections 14–17. While an in-depth examination of these sections is more appropriate to a commercial law text, it is useful to have some knowledge of how these provisions work as they are relevant to the later discussion of exemption clauses.[92]

Section 14 of SOGO[93] is headed "Implied undertaking as to title etc". It imposes an implied term that in every sale the seller has the right to sell. This term is a "condition",[94] such that breach would entitle the innocent party to terminate the contract and sue for damages. Liability here, as with all four of the sections 14–17, is "strict", meaning there is no defence if the terms are broken. The only relevance of "innocence" is that if a person innocently believes himself to be the true owner and improves the goods, he may be able to recover the enhanced value from the owner.

---

87. Ibid at 444.
88. [2002] 1 HKC 243.
89. [1992] 1 AC 294.
90. Ibid at 306.
91. Cap 26.
92. See 8.5.
93. Cf Sale of Goods Act 1979 (SGA) s 12.
94. See 8.5 below.

Section 15[95] is entitled "Sale by description". This section imposes an implied condition that, where goods are sold by description, the goods must correspond with that description. This section is not concerned with the quality of goods but merely that they correspond with their description. Although "description" is widely defined, a key factor is that the courts have held, in relation to the English equivalent, that section 15 does not apply unless the buyer *relies on* the description so that the sale is effected *by* the description. In *Harlingdon & Leinster Enterprises Ltd v Hull Fine Art Ltd*,[96] the parties entered into a contract for the sale of a painting described as being the work of Gabriel Munter. Both parties were art dealers. The buyer was an expert in this area of art but the seller was not. The painting turned out to be a forgery. It was held, in an action under the corresponding section of the Sale of Goods Act 1979, that although there was a description of the painting it had not been sold *by* description since the buyer had not relied on the seller.

Section 16[97] is headed "Implied undertakings as to quality or fitness". This section is concerned with the quality of goods sold and imposes two implied terms— both conditions—that goods must be of "merchantable quality"[98] and, where appropriate, that goods must be "reasonably fit" for the buyer's purpose.[99] The section only applies to goods which are sold "in the course of a business". "Business" is defined in section 2(1) as including "a profession and the activities of a public body, a public authority, or a board, commission, committee or other body appointed by the Chief Executive or Government".

The phrase "merchantable quality" is defined in section 2(5), which states:

> Goods of any kind are of merchantable quality within the meaning of this Ordinance if they are
> (a) as fit for the purposes or purposes for which goods of that kind are commonly bought;
> (b) of such standard of appearance and finish;
> (c) as free from defects (including minor defects);
> (d) as safe; and
> (e) as durable,
> as it is reasonable to expect having regard to any description applied to them, the price (if relevant) and all other relevant circumstances; and any reference in this Ordinance to unmerchantable goods shall be construed accordingly.

An important defence under section 16(2) is that the condition of "merchantability" does not apply to those defects which have been "specifically drawn to the buyer's attention before the contract is made." The defence was raised in *Wong Ng*

---

95. Cf SGA s 13.
96. [1990] 1 All ER 737.
97. Cf SGA s 14.
98. Section 16(2).
99. Section 16(3).

Kai Fung Patsy v Yau Lai Chu,[100] where the plaintiff bought a dog from the defendant's pet shop. The dog died shortly afterwards from distemper and the plaintiff sued for breach of the condition of merchantability. The defendant attempted to rely on the "drawn to the buyer's attention" defence since the shop manager had warned of the possibility of latent illness. It was held that this was far too vague for the defence to apply. The defence can only be raised where specific, known defects are communicated to the buyer before sale. The fact that this was not possible in this case, or that the sellers had "done their best", was irrelevant.

In England the term "merchantable" has been replaced by the term "satisfactory", but Hong Kong has yet to so amend SOGO.

It is clear from the above definition of merchantable quality that a breach of section 16(2) (merchantability) is often also a breach of section 16(3) (fitness for purpose) since unmerchantable goods may well be unfit for purpose. However, for a breach of section 16(3) to occur the buyer must make known to the seller, either expressly or implicitly, any special purpose for which the goods are bought.

Section 17 of SOGO is headed "Sale by sample". It provides that where goods are sold by sample, there is an implied condition that the "bulk" must correspond with the sample.

One other important source of statutory implied terms in Hong Kong is the Supply of Services (Implied Terms) Ordinance (SOSITO).[101] This provides that where a supplier acts in the course of a business, there is an implied term that the supplier will carry out services with reasonable care and skill.[102] If no time is fixed in the contract there is an implied term that the service will be provided within a "reasonable time"[103] and if no price is fixed there is an implied term that the customer will pay a "reasonable charge".[104]

8.5 Classification of Terms: Conditions, Warranties, and Innominate Terms

Some terms are more important than others and it is necessary to classify terms since the effect of breach generally depends on the importance of the term broken. It obviously would not be fair for a party to a contract to be able to escape from major obligations under the contract if the other party had committed only a trivial breach. On the other hand, it would only be right for an innocent party to terminate the contract if a major breach by the other party has occurred. This distinction between

---

100. [2005] 4 HKC 42.
101. Cap 457.
102. Section 5.
103. Section 6.
104. Section 7.

terms has been recognised by the courts for a very long time. In the early part of the last century Fletcher Moulton LJ in *Wallis, Son & Wells v Pratt and Haynes*[105] said:

> But from a very early period of our law it has been recognised that such obligations are not all of equal importance. There are some which go directly to the substance of the contract or, in other words, are so essential to its very nature that their non-performance may fairly be considered by the other party as a substantial failure to perform the contract at all. In the other hand, there are other obligations which, though they must be performed, are not so vital that a failure to perform them goes to the substance of the contract.[106]

Traditionally, terms have been divided into conditions and warranties. A condition is a serious term, the beach of which permits the innocent party, if he wishes, to terminate the contract and also seek damages.[107] Alternatively, the innocent party can treat the contract as still continuing and claim damages. A warranty is a lesser term, the breach of which permits the innocent party only to claim damages, not to terminate the contract. The division of terms into conditions and warranties is reflected in section 55 of SOGO[108] which goes into some detail on how the quantum of damages for breach of warranty should be calculated.

The advantage of a rigid distinction between conditions and warranties is that it provides certainty. The innocent party, for example, will know that if the other party has broken a condition there is a right to terminate. If a warranty has been broken there is no such right and, indeed, a wrongful termination is itself a breach. However, this strict classification could result in practical injustice in the case of a breach of a so-called "condition" where the effects of the breach are inconsequential. As a result, the courts have sometimes abandoned what might be termed the "certainty" approach in favour of a more flexible "justice" approach via the introduction of a third type of term, the intermediate or "innominate" term.

8.5.1 *"Conditions" in Practice*

The word "condition"[109] has many meanings and the court may decide in any given case that the parties using the expression have not intended it to carry its narrow, legalistic meaning; namely a term the breach of which will entitle the innocent party to terminate the contract.

---

105. [1910] 2 KB 1003.
106. Ibid at 1012.
107. See chapter 15.
108. Cf Sale of Goods Act 1979 s 53.
109. Even lawyers use the word carelessly since the widely used expression "terms and conditions" is tautologous.

Schuler AG v Wickman Machine Tool Sales Ltd[110]

The respondents were given the sole selling rights for the products of the appellants (a German company) in England. It was described as a "condition" of the contract that the respondents should visit the six leading UK motor manufacturers each week for the four and a half years' duration of the contract. The respondents failed to make some of the visits and the appellants sought to terminate the contract. The respondents claimed that such termination was wrongful since, despite the word "condition", the parties had not intended that a single breach of requirement for some 1,400 visits would entitle the appellants to terminate. By a majority of four to one, Lord Wilberforce dissenting, the House of Lords found for the respondents. They held that the appellants were only entitled to damages.

Lord Reid, for the majority, said:

> No doubt some words used by lawyers do have a rigid inflexible meaning. But we must remember that we are seeking to discover the intention as disclosed by the contract as a whole. Use of the word "condition" is an indication—even a strong indication—of such an intention but it is by no means conclusive.[111]

He went on to say that it would be so unreasonable for such a breach to result in a right to terminate that it made him search for some other possible meaning of the contract.

Lord Wilberforce did not agree. He said:

> My Lords, I am clear in my own mind that [the term] is a condition, but your Lordships take the contrary view. On a matter of construction of a particular document, to develop the reasons for a minority opinion serves no purpose . . . to introduce . . . the ubiquitous reasonable man (I do not know whether he is English or German) is to assume, contrary to the evidence, that both parties to this contract adopted a standard of easygoing tolerance rather than one of aggressive, insistent punctuality and efficiency. This is not an assumption I am prepared to make, nor do I think myself entitled to impose the former standard on the parties if their words indicate, as they plainly do, the latter.[112]

Two key factors influenced the majority in this case. First, the term involved a huge number of visits, failure to make any of which would have entitled cancellation had the court strictly upheld the "condition". Second, the parties were probably not using "condition" in its technical sense since they spoke elsewhere in the contract of "determination" of the contract for "material" breach.

The problem with this approach, as Lord Wilberforce said in his dissenting judgment, is that it produces potential uncertainty. Even though the parties are

---

110. [1974] AC 235, [1973] 2 WLR 683.
111. [1973] 2 WLR 683 at 689.
112. Ibid at 700.

experienced businesses, with access to legal advice and even though they choose to use the word "condition" which has a clear legal meaning, the innocent victim of the breach of such "condition" does not know whether he is entitled to terminate the contract for breach or not. The words used by the parties are no longer definitive since a court is entitled to find that a term described as a "condition" is no such thing. Furthermore, if the innocent party rescinds the contract for breach of a "condition" which the court finds not to be such, that party will himself be liable for wrongful repudiation of the contract.

Just as the word "condition" may be used in different ways so, too, can the word "warranty", which is sometimes used to mean, merely, a promise. Section 13(2) of SOGO makes clear that whether a stipulation in a contract of sale is a condition or not depends in each case on the construction of the contract and that a stipulation may be a condition even though called a warranty in the contract.

Lord Wilberforce's "certainty" approach received implicit support a decade later in *Lombard North Central plc v Butterworth*.[113] Here, the parties made a contract for the hire of a computer. The contract provided that prompt payment of instalments was "of the essence" and that failure to make "due and punctual payment" entitled the plaintiffs to terminate the contract. The plaintiffs cancelled the contract and sued for damages when the defendant was late in paying. The defendant argued that the consequences of the breach were not serious and that, therefore, the plaintiffs themselves had repudiated the contract. The English Court of Appeal unanimously held for the plaintiffs on the basis that, where the parties state that breach of a particular term would amount to repudiation, this should be upheld irrespective of the consequences of the breach.

The combined effect of the *Schuler* and *Lombard* cases is that the use of the word "condition" will not always be conclusive (since the courts may believe that the parties were not using the word in its technical sense) but that the courts will *not* interfere when the parties have unequivocally stated their position as to the effect of breach.

A later English case showing the court's willingness to intervene in extreme cases is *Rice (t/a Garden Guardian) v Great Yarmouth Borough Council*,[114] where a clause in a standard form contract provided that there was a right to terminate the contract for "a breach of any of its obligations under the Contract". The English Court of Appeal refused to uphold the strict literal meaning of the words used since to have done so would have rendered every term in the contract, however minor, a "condition". The court found that this was too broad and contrary to commercial sense. The terms should be judged on their merits and only those of sufficient seriousness should be judged as conditions.

---

113. [1987] QB 527.
114. [2001] 3 LGLR 4.

In mercantile contracts, *time* is usually treated as being of the essence of the contract and, therefore, a condition. This is especially true in respect of the volatile housing market. In *Sun Lee Kyoung Sil v Jia Weili*[115] Recorder Patrick Fung SC stated:

> in Hong Kong, when parties entered into a provisional agreement for the sale and purchase of real property, they usually proceeded on the basis that time was "of the essence" . . . despite the absence of any express provision to that effect in the agreement.[116]

However, it should be noted that section 12(1) of SOGO states:

> Unless a different intention appears from the terms of the contract, stipulations as to time of payment are not deemed to be of the essence of a contract of sale. Any other stipulation as to time being of the essence depends on the terms of the contract.

8.5.2 Intermediate or "Innominate" Terms

The courts have, in some cases, argued that there are terms which cannot be classed as conditions or warranties. In the case of such intermediate or "innominate" terms what is crucial is the *effect* of the breach: if the effect is sufficiently serious there will be a right to terminate the contract and sue for damages; if not, the right will be restricted to a claim for damages. The concept of "intermediate" terms was developed in the *Hong Kong Fir Shipping* case.

Hong Kong Fir Shipping Co Ltd v Kawasaki Kisen Kaisha Ltd[117]

The plaintiffs chartered a ship to the defendants for a period of 24 months from delivery in February 1957. It was a term of the contract that the ship would be "in every way fitted for ordinary cargo service". On delivery there were a number of defects involving the size of the crew and its inability to handle the old engines on board, so that the ship was not seaworthy. The ship suffered long voyage delays because of engine failure and the crew's incompetence. In June 1957 the defendants repudiated the contract on the grounds of the plaintiffs' breach. The plaintiffs, though admittedly in breach, sued for wrongful repudiation. The English Court of Appeal found unanimously for the plaintiffs on the basis that their breaches, though entitling the defendants to claim for damages, were not serious enough to justify repudiation.

All three judges gave substantial judgments. Sellers LJ said:

---

115. [2010] 2 HKLRD 30.
116. Ibid at para 22.
117. [1962] 1 All ER 474.

it was submitted that the delay due to the breach of contract by the owners was sufficient to entitle the charterers as innocent parties, that is, in no way to blame for what had happened, to have regard to their interests under the contract and that it was just in all the circumstances that they should be held free to terminate as they did . . . In my judgment, authority over many decades and reason support the conclusion in this case that there was no breach of a condition which entitled the charterers to accept it as a repudiation and to withdraw from the charter. It was not contended that the maintenance clause is so fundamental a matter as to amount to a condition of the contract. It is a warranty which sounds in damages.[118]

Upjohn LJ added:

Why is this apparently basic and underlying condition of seaworthiness not, in fact, treated as a condition? It is for the simple reason that the seaworthiness clause is breached by the slightest failure to be fitted 'in every way' for service. Thus . . . if a nail is missing from one of the timbers of a wooden vessel, or if proper medical supplies or two anchors are not on board at the time of sailing, the owners are in breach of the seaworthiness stipulation. It is contrary to common sense to suppose that, in such circumstances, the parties contemplated that the charterer should at once be entitled to treat the contract as at an end for such trifling breaches . . .

In my judgment, the remedies open to the innocent party for breach of a stipulation which is not a condition strictly so called, depend entirely on the nature of the breach and its foreseeable consequences.

. . . as the stipulation as to seaworthiness is not a condition in the strict sense, the question to be answered is, did the initial unseaworthiness as found by the learned judge . . . go so much to the root of the contract that the charterers were then and there entitled to treat the charterparty as at an end? The only unseaworthiness alleged, serious though it was, was the insufficiency and incompetence of the crew, but that surely cannot be treated as going to the root of the contract for the parties must have contemplated that, in such an event, the crew could be changed and augmented.[119]

Finally, Diplock LJ commented:

Where an event occurs the occurrence of which neither the parties nor Parliament have expressly stated will discharge one of the parties from further performance of his undertakings, it is for the court to determine whether the event has this effect or not. The test whether an event has this effect or not has been stated in a number of metaphors all of which I think amount to the same thing: does the occurrence of the event deprive the party who has further undertakings still to perform of substantially the whole benefit which it was the intention of the parties as expressed in the contract that he should obtain as consideration for performing those undertakings? . . .

---

118. Ibid at 478.
119. Ibid at 483.

It is . . . by no means surprising that, among, the many hundreds of previous cases about the shipowner's undertaking to deliver a seaworthy ship, there is none where it was found profitable to discuss in the judgments the question whether that undertaking is a 'condition' or a 'warranty'; for the true answer, as I have already indicated, is that it is neither, but one of the large class of contractual undertakings, one breach of which may have the same effect as that ascribed to a breach of 'condition' . . . and a different breach of which may have only the same effect as that ascribed to a breach of 'warranty.[120]

As can be seen from the above the extracts, while the judges found for the owners in deciding that the charterers had no right to repudiate the contract, they reached the conclusion by different means. Seller LJ adopted the traditional condition/warranty classification of terms and concluded, simply, that the term broken was merely a warranty, permitting damages but not termination. Upjohn and Diplock LJJ adopted a more novel approach by suggesting that there may be an intermediate class of terms which are not conditions but the breach of which might justify termination provided that the consequences of the breach are sufficiently serious.

While there was clear support in subsequent cases for this third category of intermediate or "innominate" terms, there was a strong argument that it did not apply to contracts for the sale of goods since legislation relating to the sale of goods specifically defined "conditions" and "warranties", raising the implication that all terms in such contracts must be one or the other. The issue was resolved in *Cehave NV v Bremer Handelsgesellschaft mbh (the Hansa Nord).*[121] In *Hansa Nord*, a dispute arose between the parties over the buyer's right to reject goods which were received not "in good condition" contrary to the terms of the contract. The buyers argued that the intermediate or innominate term approach of *Hong Kong Fir* did not apply to a contract for the sale of goods and that the term broken should be viewed as a condition.

The English Court of Appeal unanimously held that the intermediate term concept *is* applicable to contracts for the sale of goods; that the "good condition" term in this case was intermediate; and that, since the effect of the seller's breach was not serious, the buyer had the right to damages only and *not* to reject the goods. Roskill LJ said it was not easy to see why contracts relating to the sale of goods should be different from the law relating to the performance of other contractual obligations. He noted that sale of goods law was but one branch of the general law of contract, that the same legal principles should apply to the law of contract as a whole and that different legal principles should not apply to different branches of

---

120. Ibid 485–488.
121. [1976] QB 44.

that law.[122] Ormrod LJ was less categoric and said that even if one used the condition/warranty classification, the relevant term was a warranty, giving the same result as Roskill LJ.

More recently, the trend has been away from the old condition/warranty dichotomy towards one involving "conditions" and "intermediate" terms, with warranties recognised only in exceptional cases. Indeed, in *Spar Shipping v Grand China Logistics*,[123] Hamblen LJ went as far as to state:

> The modern approach is that a term is innominate unless a contrary indication is made clear.

8.5.3 The Continuing Importance of Classification of Terms

The *Hansa Nord* case makes it clear that, even in a sale of goods contract, there are terms which cannot be classified as either "conditions" or "warranties" when the contract is made. However, the classification of terms remains important in the interests of certainty. Where terms *can* be classified as conditions (or warranties) as at the time the contract was formed, the consequences of breach, as explained above,[124] are clear. It is *only* where a term must be regarded as intermediate that the *effects* of breach need to be considered. This point was re-emphasised in the following recent Hong Kong case.

Okachi (Hong Kong) Co Ltd v Nominee (Holding) Ltd.[125]

The parties negotiated the sale and purchase of one fully paid up Hong Kong Futures Exchange share which required that the defendants became authorised "dealers". The defendants warranted that they were qualified for membership and dealership and would lodge an application without delay. As a result of the defendants' breach completion did not take place on time. The plaintiffs sought to rescind and the defendants resisted. The right to rescind was upheld in The Court of First Instance.

Deputy Judge Poon held that the defendants were in breach of conditions, entitling the plaintiffs to rescind. He added:

> Mr Aiken (for the defendants) seemed to have suggested that in determining whether a contractual provision is a condition or not, the court should look at the consequences of breach. With respect, this approach must be wrong, a similar argument having been firmly rejected by the House of Lords in *Bunge Corp v Tradax SA* [1981] 1 WLR 711.

---

122. See also 1.1.1.
123. [2016] EWCA Civ 982.
124. See 8.5 above.
125. [2005] 3 HKC 408.

Deputy Judge Poon made clear that it is only after a term has been classified as "intermediate" that the effects of the breach become relevant.

A preference for certainty over flexibility is still frequently expressed by the courts, especially in mercantile cases. In *The Mihalis Angelos*,[126] a charter party dated 25 May 1965 stated that the ship *Mihalis Angelos* was "expected ready to load under this charter about 1 July 1965". It was found as fact that the owners, when the contract was made, did not realistically expect that the vessel could load by that date. Indeed, it was not so ready until over three weeks later. The English Court of Appeal were urged to follow the *Hong Kong Fir* intermediate term approach but decided that the classification of terms into conditions and warranties still had a valuable role to play in certain types of contracts of which a charterparty was one.

The English courts adopted the same "certainty" approach ten years later in the following case.

Bunge Corporation v Tradax Export SA[127]

The parties had a contract to ship materials in three instalments. It was a term of the contract that the buyers, who were to provide the ship, should give 15 days' notice of their readiness to load. They were four days late and the sellers claimed the right to treat the contract as repudiated. The buyers argued that the term was intermediate and that the effect was not sufficiently serious to justify cancellation. The courts, ultimately the House of Lords, held that the term was a condition and that breach justified cancellation of the contract.

Lord Wilberforce said:

> in suitable cases, the courts should not be reluctant, if the intentions of the parties as shown by the contract so indicate, to hold that an obligation has the force of a condition, and . . . they usually do so in the case of time clauses in mercantile contracts. To such cases the 'gravity of the breach' approach of the *Hong Kong Fir* case would be unsuitable.[128]

By way of clear contrast, a term in a "bareboat charter"[129] as to the continuing "class" of a vessel, was held to be "intermediate" only. Key to this finding was that the "class" term was not described as a condition *and* did not involve the issue of "time" (*Ark Shipping Company LLC v Silverburn Shipping (IOM) Ltd*).[130]

---

126. [1970] 3 All ER 125.
127. [1981] 2 All ER 513.
128. Ibid at 542.
129. In which the "charterer" actually takes a lease of the vessel, and is normally expected to provide crew.
130. [2019] EWCA Civ 1161.

8.6 Exemption Clauses

Exclusion clauses aim to exempt the liability of one of the parties to a contract from his legal obligations. Such obligations are normally contractual but the exclusions may extend to tortious liability, most commonly negligence. A limitation clause is a type of exemption clause that does not seek totally to exclude liability but, instead, to limit or restrict it to, for example, a fixed amount of damages.

In terms of "freedom of contract",[131] parties should be permitted to insert whatever exemption clauses they wish into a contract. In practice, however, such clauses are unlikely to be "negotiated" and are more likely to be the result of a dominant party imposing the clauses on the weaker. That being the case, the courts, over a considerable time, have sought to restrict the operation and scope of exemption clauses by a variety of common law devices. Legislation is also playing an increased role in curbing exemption clauses, especially in the area of consumer protection.

No exemption clause may operate unless it is "incorporated" as a term of the contract between the "exemptor" and "exemptee". Even where the clause has been incorporated, however, it may be defeated, or reduced in scope, by the effect of judicial intervention or legislative rules.

8.6.1 Incorporation of Exemption Clauses

When a party, usually the defendant, seeks to rely on an exemption clause, the other party will often argue that the exemption clause is not really part of the contract. The party seeking to rely on the exemption clause must prove that the exemption clause has been incorporated as a contractual term. Incorporation may be via a signed document or by virtue of notice or previous dealings.

8.6.1.1 Incorporation by Signature

The basic rule is that if a party signs a contractual document—unless there is fraud, misrepresentation, or other vitiating factor such as duress or undue influence—he is bound by its terms. These terms may include an exemption clause. This position is unaltered even if the party signs the document without reading it. The rule is essentially an application of the "parol evidence rule".[132]

---

131. See chapter 1.
132. See 8.2. The principle has been applied in Hong Kong. See for example *Ming Shiu Chung & Others v Ming Shiu Sum & Others* [2006] 2 HKLRD 831; *Pathak Ravi Dutt v Sanjeev Maheshwari* [2014] 3 HKLRD 597. But *quaere* the position if the other party *knows* that the document has not been read before signing: *Tilden Rent-a Car Co v Clendenning* (1978) 83 DLR (3d) 400.

L'Estrange v Graucob[133]

The plaintiff, who owned a café, bought a cigarette vending machine on terms contained in a document described as a "Sales Agreement". She signed the agreement without reading it. The machine was defective and the plaintiff sued. Her action was unsuccessful. It was held that the plaintiff was bound by the agreement which she had signed and the defendants were able to rely on a clause "in regrettably small print", which excluded their liability.[134]

8.6.1.2 Incorporation by Notice

If a contractual document containing exemption clauses is not signed, its terms may, nonetheless, be incorporated provided that reasonable notice of such terms has been conveyed to the other party. The party seeking to rely on the exemption clause need not show that he actually brought it to the attention of the other party but only that he took reasonable steps to do so. The question is generally an "objective" one; would a reasonable person assume that the document in question contained exemptions? The principle was famously explained by Mellish LJ in *Parker v South Eastern Railway*.[135] He said:

> The railway company must . . . take mankind as they find them, and if what they do is sufficient to inform people in general that the ticket contains conditions, I think that a particular plaintiff ought not to be in a better position than other persons on account of his exceptional ignorance or stupidity or carelessness.[136]

The objective test was applied in the following case, also concerning a railway ticket.

Thompson v London, Midland and Scottish Railway[137]

The plaintiff's niece bought for the plaintiff an "excursion" ticket. On the back of the ticket were the words: "Issued subject to the conditions and regulations in the company's timetables and notices and other bills." The conditions in the timetable, available at a cost of sixpence, included the term that excursion passengers should have no right of action against the company in respect of any injury, however caused. The plaintiff who was injured on alighting from the train, allegedly by the defendants' negligence, failed in her action for damages in the English Court of Appeal which held unanimously that the exemption clause was part of the plaintiff's contract even though she was illiterate and was unaware of its existence.

---

133. [1934] 2 KB 394.
134. Such a case would probably now be decided differently on statutory grounds; see 8.6.4.
135. (1877) 2 CPD 416.
136. Ibid at 421.
137. [1930] 1 KB 41.

Lord Hanworth MR said:

> two things are plain, first, that any person who takes this ticket is conscious that
> there are some conditions on which it is issued and also, secondly, that it is priced at
> a figure far below the ordinary price charged by the railway company, and from that
> it is a mere sequence of thought that one does not get from the railway company the
> ticket which they do provide at the higher (price). The plaintiff in this case cannot
> read; but, having regard to the authorities, and the condition of education in this
> country, I do not think this avails her in any degree. The ticket was taken for her by
> her agent . . . he had the notice put before him before ever the ticket was taken, that
> there were conditions on the issue of excursion and other reduced-fare tickets.
>
> . . . when that ticket was taken it was taken with the knowledge that the condi-
> tions applied, and that the person who took the ticket was bound by those condi-
> tions. If that be so, the conditions render it impossible for the plaintiff to succeed
> in her action . . . it has not ever been held that the mere circuity which has to be
> followed to find the actual condition prevents the passenger having notice that there
> was a condition.[138]

This is a harsh decision given that the passenger had to make a considerable
search for the terms and at some significant expense (sixpence was a large sum in
those days!). It might be thought that if a company is to make use of a document to
substantially reduce its potential liability to customers, it should be obliged to make
such document freely available.

Having said that the test is usually objective, the question remains as to whether
additional steps need to be taken to bring terms to the notice of persons who makes
known their "exceptional ignorance or stupidity" (to borrow Mellish LJ's phrase).
Would the decision have been different, in *Thompson*, if the passenger had bought
the ticket direct, said to the ticket-seller that she was illiterate and asked if there were
any special terms of which she should be aware? There is English case authority for
the assertion that a notice in English will not bind a party who does not understand
English where this fact is known to the other party: *Geir v Kujawa, Weston and
Warner Bros (Transport) Ltd.*[139]

Essentially the test is invariable; the "exemptor" must do what is reasonable in
all the circumstances to bring the existence of an exemption to the notice of the other
party. Circumstances, however, vary and the Hong Kong situation will not necessarily be the same as the English one. To take an obvious example, Mellish LJ's starting
point, that a party is "entitled to assume" that the other can read and understand the
English language, is often inapplicable to the Hong Kong experience where colonial

---

138. Ibid at 46–47.
139. [1970] 1 Lloyd's Rep 364 at 368; and see *Harvey v Ventilatorenfabrik Oelde Gmbh* (1988) 8 Tr L
     138.

society was never monolingual and where the current aspiration is trilingualism.[140] Even a known ignorance of the language of a contract may be immaterial, however, in appropriate circumstances. In *Chan Woon-hung (t/a Ocean Plastic Factory) v Associated Bankers Insurance Co Ltd*[141] it was held by the Privy Council that the fact that the appellant had in his possession, for a prolonged period, all the contract documents, and could at any time have obtained a translation thereof, negatived any disability from which he suffered by his lack of understanding of English. It might be thought that providing a translation to the other party of significant terms of the contract would solve the notice problem. This is not without danger to the "exemptor" however, since it has been held that translating only *part* of a document implies that other terms are insignificant.[142]

Emphasis on "cultural difference" can be seen in the following case.

Wong Wai-chun v The China Navigation Co Ltd[143]

The plaintiff's husband had been killed while a passenger on board the defendants' ship. The case involved aspects of tort/negligence law (and even an alternative plea that the deceased had committed suicide!) but from the contract perspective the crucial issue was whether the defendants had taken reasonable steps to bring to the deceased's notice exemptions in the company's "terms and conditions" referred to *on the back of* his ticket. The "Full Court" in Hong Kong found unanimously for the plaintiff. Huggins J said:

> there are one or two things I feel compelled to say concerning this not very satisfactory branch of the law . . .
>
> . . . (the law) has, indeed, become completely divorced from reality . . .
>
> . . . Anyone who thinks that in the Far East the majority of persons who enter into these types of contract know that conditions are likely to be imposed and that such conditions will be set out in a ticket is living in a dream world of his own . . .
>
> . . . Nothing on the face of that counterfoil gave any indication that there was a warning on the back of it to the effect that the ticket was subject to conditions. Even applying the principles of *Parker v South Eastern Railway Co*, therefore, it has not been shown that reasonable notice was given.[144]

---

140. In *Oriental Pearl South Africa Project CC v Bank of Taiwan* (unrep, DCCJ 6509/2002, 4 October 2006) the negligent defendant bank was unable to rely on an exclusion clause which they had failed adequately to explain to the plaintiff who, they knew, had difficulty reading English.
141. [1993] 2 HKLR 127.
142. See *H Glynn (Covent Garden) Ltd v Wittleder* [1959] 2 Lloyd's Rep 409 at 420.
143. [1969] HKLR 471.
144. Ibid at 533–536. It may have been of some significance that the deceased was a first-time passenger.

It should be noted that, given the facts as alleged by the plaintiff, the case, like *L'Estrange* and *Thompson*, would now be decided differently on statutory grounds.[145]

The "reasonableness" of the "exemptor's" efforts was also a key consideration in *Chapelton v Barry UDC*.[146] Here, the plaintiff hired two deck chairs from the defendants' employee who gave the plaintiff two tickets in return for the plaintiff's payment of four pence. When the plaintiff was injured as a result of the deck chair collapsing he was able to bring a successful action against the defendants (ultimately in the English Court of Appeal) on the basis of their negligence. The defendants were unable to rely on a clause which stated that: "The council will not be liable for any accident or damage arising from the hire of the chair." The court held that the defendants had not taken sufficient steps to bring this clause to the plaintiff's notice, since the ticket appeared to be no more than a receipt to prove payment.

This case illustrates the fact that what is "reasonable notice" will depend on the facts of each case. Once again it should be noted that the clause above, even if incorporated, would today be made void by legislation, assuming, of course, that the collapse of the chair was as a result of the defendants' negligence.

Another significant English case is *Olley v Marlborough Court Ltd*,[147] where it was held that a notice in a hotel bedroom, which included a clause exempting liability for the loss of guests' luggage, was not incorporated into the contract between the hotel and a guest. The contract had been made in the lobby of the hotel before the guest, the plaintiff, had entered her bedroom and before she had an opportunity to see the notice. This is a sensible decision showing that the requisite notice must be given at or before the time the contract is concluded. A similar finding was made in *Thornton v Shoe Lane Parking Ltd*,[148] a case which also has implications for the law of offer and acceptance.[149] In *Thornton*, the plaintiff wished to park his car in the defendants' parking area. At the entrance was a notice stating: "All cars parked at owner's risk." The plaintiff paid a fee, obtained a ticket and drove in. On the ticket were further terms, which the plaintiff did not read, excluding the defendants' liability for personal injury to customers. The plaintiff was subsequently injured, partly as a result of the defendants' negligence and sued the defendants who attempted to rely on the further exemptions. The English Court of Appeal unanimously found for the plaintiff. It was held that the additional terms were ineffective as they had been brought to the plaintiff's attention too late.

Lord Denning MR said:

---

145. See 8.6.4.
146. [1940] 1 KB 532.
147. [1949] 1 KB 532.
148. [1971] 2 QB 163.
149. See chapter 3.

The customer pays his money and gets a ticket. He cannot refuse it. He cannot get his money back. He may protest to the machine, even swear at it. But it will remain unmoved. He is committed beyond recall. He was committed at the very moment when he put his money into the machine. The contract was concluded at that time. It can be translated into offer and acceptance in this way: the offer is made when the proprietor of the machine holds it out as being ready to receive the money. The acceptance takes place when the customer puts his money into the slot. The terms of the offer are contained in the notice placed on or near the machine stating what is offered for the money. The customer is bound by those terms as long as they are sufficiently brought to his notice before-hand but not otherwise. He is not bound by the terms printed on the ticket if they differ from the notice, because the ticket comes too late.[150]

Sir Gordon Willmer agreed and stressed that in the case of a ticket offered by an automatic machine the process affords the customer no chance to refuse acceptance.[151] No further terms can be added.[152]

Where a contract contains a particularly onerous or harsh clause, extra steps must be taken to bring it to the other party's notice. This principle is not limited to exemption clauses but applies generally to contractual terms. Two English cases highlight this need for extra steps to be taken. First, in *Spurling v Bradshaw*,[153] Lord Denning, in an often-quoted (*obiter*) phrase, said:

Some clauses would need to be printed in red ink on the face of the document with a red hand pointing to it before the notice could be held to be sufficient.[154]

Second, and more recently, the same principle emerged in *Interfoto Pictures Library Ltd v Stiletto Visual Programmes Ltd*.[155] Here, the defendants ordered photographic transparencies from the plaintiffs. It was a term of the contract, as stated on the delivery note, that the transparencies must be returned by a specified date and that a fee of £5 per day plus tax would be levied on late returns. The defendants were several weeks late, having not used the photos and forgotten about them. The plaintiffs sued for almost £4,000 based on the contractual term. The claim was rejected and a much lower sum substituted on the basis that the term was particularly onerous and could only operate if extra steps had been taken to bring it to the notice of the other party. The clause here was not an exemption clause but the same "extra steps" principle would be equally applicable to "unusual or onerous"[156] exemption clauses.

---

150. [1971] 2 QB 163 at 169.
151. See chapter 3.
152. [1971] 2 QB 163 at 173.
153. [1956] 1 WLR 461.
154. Ibid at 466.
155. [1988] 1 All ER 348.
156. There is some academic debate as to whether the special steps rule requires that the terms must be both unusual *and* onerous.

The question arises as to whether the "onerous terms" approach is applicable where the "exemptee" has signed the document containing the exemption clause. The English approach, at common law, was that the exemptee would still be bound, in the absence of fraud or other vitiating factor.[157] This, the *L'Estrange* principle, appears to have been abandoned in England in an extreme case where clearly onerous and unusual terms were included in terms and conditions in "*just over a page of detailed text, in closely spaced small type with no separate clause headings . . . not in any way user-friendly to any reader, let alone a non-legal reader*".[158]

Hong Kong courts had, previously and inconclusively,[159] considered a Canadian precedent, *Tilden Rent-a-Car Co v Clendenning*,[160] which appears to endorse the view that, even in the case of a signed document, an exemption could be defeated where it is "unusual and onerous" and where special steps have not been taken to explain it to the other party.

Two points need to be stressed: the first being that the key factor in *Tilden* appears to have been that the "exemptor" knew that the other party had not read the exemption before signing the document containing it. The second important point is that, in most cases, the *Interfoto* approach has been overtaken by events, since in respect of exemptions, "unusual and onerous" terms would almost certainly be statutorily overturned.[161] In short, the *Interfoto* "special steps" requirement is generally only relevant in Hong Kong outside the area of exemption clauses *unless* the contract is one to which legislation does not apply. In *Mau Wing Industrial Ltd v Ensign Freight Pte Ltd & Another*[162] (a carriage of goods case to which Control of Exemption Clauses Ordinance legislation does not apply)[163] a serious breach was made by the defendants' agent such that the trial judge, Stone J, stated:

> (this construction would) result in a situation whereby the *entirely advertent* misde-livery of the goods . . . was to be subject to a limitation of liability clause . . .
>
> In blunt terms, if the contractual Carrier wished this to be the result, it strikes me that it would have to say so in the bill of lading contract in the most explicit language.[164]

---

157. See 8.6.1.1.
158. Per Stephen Davies HHJ, *Blu-Sky Solutions Ltd v Be Caring Ltd* [2021] EWHC 2619.
159. See Deputy Judge Chan L (*obiter*) in *Wing On Properties and Securities Co Ltd v Wave Front Enterprise (HK) Ltd* [2007] 2 HKC 54.
160. (1978) 83 DLR (3d) 400 and see 8.6.1.1.
161. The Control of Exemption Clauses Ordinance (see 8.6.4 et seq) prohibits some exemption clauses and subjects most others to a "reasonableness" test which harsh and onerous terms would fail. The same would apply in England by virtue of the Unfair Contract Terms Act 1977.
162. [2010] 1 HKC 364.
163. See 8.6.4 et seq.
164. [2010] 1 HKC 364 at paras 61–62.

8.6.1.3 Incorporation by Previous Course of Dealing

It is possible for a court to incorporate terms, including exemption clauses, where there has been a previous course of dealing between the parties.[165] There is some overlap here with the other methods of incorporation in that the document containing the contractual terms, including the exemption clause, will have been incorporated in previous dealings either by signature or by notice. In *Spurling v Bradshaw*,[166] the parties, who had dealt with each other for many years, made a contract under which the plaintiff was to store barrels of the defendant's orange juice. When the defendant later came to collect the barrels they were empty. The defendant refused to pay the storage charges and the plaintiff sued. The defendant counter-claimed for negligence but the plaintiffs successfully relied on a clause exempting them from liability for "loss or damage occasioned by . . . negligence, wrongful act or default." The defendant had not received the document containing this clause until after the contract was concluded but he admitted to receiving a similar document often in the past. The English Court of Appeal unanimously held that the defendant was bound by the exemption clause.

Once again it should be noted that the above situation is now affected by legislation and the relevant exemption clause purporting to exclude liability for negligence would be subject to a test of reasonableness.[167]

It is important to note that the course of dealing must be regular and consistent. In *McCutcheon v David MacBrayne Ltd*,[168] the House of Lords held that an exemption clause had not been incorporated, on the basis of previous dealings, when the plaintiff had sometimes been ask to sign the document and other times had not. There had been, held the court, no "consistent" course of dealing. In the Hong Kong case of *Always Win Ltd v Autofit Ltd*[169] the issue of consistency also arose. The plaintiffs had delivered their car to the defendants for repairs. The repairs were completed but, later that day, the car was stolen from a car park from which, despite security precautions, a number of cars had been stolen. The plaintiffs sued the defendants for damages for a negligent failure to secure the safety of the car. The defendants and the car park management were held jointly liable. The defendants had sought to rely on exemption clauses in the Vehicle Repair Order arguing that, by signing the invoices, the plaintiffs should be deemed to have notice of the exemption clause which was printed on the back of the invoice. Cheung J, in the Hong Kong High Court, held that the clauses had not been brought to the plaintiffs' notice in time and

---

165. Incorporation is also possible in respect of a regular trade practice, where both parties operate in the same trade or profession: *British Crane Hire Corp Ltd v Ipswich Plant Hire Ltd* [1975] QB 303; *Ofir Scheps v Fine Art Logistic Ltd* [2007] EWHC 541.
166. [1956] 1 WLR 461.
167. Unfair Contract Terms Act 1977 s 2(2).
168. [1964] 1 WLR 125.
169. [1995] 2 HKC 48.

were, therefore, inoperative. The key factor, for the judge, was that the invoice was signed on *collection* of the car which was too late. This was despite the fact that the plaintiffs were regular customers and had received invoices before which they had "sometimes" signed.

The *Always Win* decision can be criticised on the basis that the judge's focus seems to have been on the plaintiffs' *knowledge* of the exemption rather than the (objective) effect of the previous dealings and whether or not the defendants had taken sufficient steps to bring the clause to the plaintiffs' notice.

How often must the parties have been dealing for the exemption clause to be incorporated? This is clearly a question of fact in each case. In *Hollier v Rambler Motors (AMC) Ltd*[170] the English Court of Appeal held that three or four transactions over a five-year period was not sufficient to incorporate an exemption clause into a consumer contract. By contrast in *Petrotrade Inc v Texaco Ltd*[171] five transactions over a 13-month period was sufficient.

8.6.2 Interpretation or Construction of Exemption Clauses

Once an exemption clause has become incorporated into a contract the court must interpret or construe its meaning. As with all terms, the courts look to determine the parties' intention adopting an "objective" approach based *prima facie* on a reasonable construction of the words used by the parties.[172] Clearly, if the exemption is to be effective, the clause must actually cover the defendant's breach of contract (or other breach of duty). The basic approach of the courts is that unless the clause clearly and unambiguously protects the "exemptor" it will be construed against him. This approach is generally summarised by the Latin expression *contra proferentem*.

An early example of the *contra proferentem* rule is provided by *Andrews Bros Ltd v Singer & Co Ltd*[173] Here, a contract for the sale of "new Singer cars" contained a clause that "all conditions, warranties and liabilities, *implied* by statute, common law or otherwise" were excluded. One of the cars sold was a used car. As the term "new Singer cars" was an *express* condition of the contract and not an implied one, the exemption clause did not protect the sellers.

Similarly, in *Houghton v Trafalgar Insurance Co Ltd*,[174] the court held that six people in a car built for five did not constitute "overloading" but was instead "over-crowding", thereby allowing a motorist to successfully claim under an insurance policy which excluded claims for overloading.

---

170. [1972] 1 All ER 399.
171. [2000] CLC 1341.
172. See 8.3 above.
173. [1934] All ER 479.
174. [1954] 1 QB 247.

A specific aspect of *contra proferentem* can be seen in the attitude of the courts to clauses seeking to exclude liability for negligence at common law. There is no common law rule that negligence liability cannot be excluded. However, the courts regard it as unlikely that a party to a contract would agree to the other party being exempt from liability for negligence under the contract. As such, very clear words were required for such liability to be exempted. The case of *Hollier v Rambler Motors (AMC) Ltd*[175] illustrates the courts' reluctance to permit the exclusion of negligence liability. In *Hollier*, the plaintiff had agreed that his car could be towed to the defendants' garage for repairs. While there the car was destroyed by fire as a result of the defendants' negligence. The terms of the contract included a clause that "the company is not responsible for damage caused by fire to customers' cars on the premises". The English Court of Appeal held that the defendants could only be liable for such a fire if it was caused by their negligence. However, the court also held that a customer could understand the clause to mean that the defendants would not be liable for a fire caused without their negligence. This created a sufficient degree of ambiguity to prevent the defendants from excluding their liability for negligence.

In the UK Supreme Court case of *Triple Point Technology Inc v PTT Public Co Ltd*,[176] Lord Leggatt described *contra proferentem* as an "*old and outmoded formula*", preferring to allow parties freedom to make their own contract. However, since this would entail accepting that a party is "*unlikely to have given up a valuable contractual right without clear words*", the *practical* distinction is likely to be minimal. In the same case, the court adopted a "common sense" interpretation of the word "negligence" (failure to exercise proper care and skill) as opposed to a strained, narrower meaning of a breach of a duty of care, as required in the law of tort.

It should be noted, however, that the courts have applied the *contra proferentem* rule less vigorously when construing *limitation* as opposed to *exclusion* clauses, covering negligence liability. This is largely based on the presumed intention of the parties, since it is thought more likely that a party would intend to agree to a clause limiting liability for negligence than to a total exclusion. An important case on this point is *Ailsa Craig Fishing Co Ltd v Malvern Fishing Co Ltd and Securicor (Scotland) Ltd*[177] which concerned the sinking of the appellants' boat in Aberdeen Harbour (Scotland). The respondents, Securicor, had been employed to provide security at the harbour. Their contract contained a clause that any liability for loss on their part should be limited to £1,000. The appellants sued and argued that the limitation clause should not protect the respondents as they had totally failed to provide security. The House of Lords held that the respondents were protected by the clause. Lord Wilberforce said:

---

175. [1972] 1 All ER 399.
176. [2021] UKSC 29.
177. [1983] 1 All ER 101.

whether a condition limiting liability is effective or not is a question of construction of that condition in the context of the contract as a whole. If it is to exclude liability for negligence, it must be clearly and unambiguously expressed, and, in such a contract as this, must be construed *contra proferentem*. I do not think there is any doubt so far. But I venture to add one further qualification, or at least clarification: one must not strive to create ambiguities by strained construction, as I think the appellants have striven to do. The relevant words must be given, if possible, their natural, plain meaning. Clauses of limitation are not regarded by the courts with the same hostility as clauses of exclusion.[178]

The Hong Kong courts appear to have taken a less hostile view to the exclusion of negligence liability. In *Nanyang Credit Card Co Ltd v Ying Wei (Hop Hick) Cargo Service*,[179] the defendants were employed to hoist some computer equipment up to the plaintiffs' premises on the fifth floor of a building. The defendants dropped the equipment but denied liability for the damage caused. The defendants sought to rely on terms, which had been drafted without legal assistance, as follows:

Notes:
– Price not included insurance charges.
– Insurance against damage should be covered by Nanyang Credit Card Co Ltd.
– Not damage claim to our company for this hoisting operation.

The Hong Kong Court of Appeal found for the defendants, rejecting the plaintiffs' claim that the wording of the exemption did not cover the particular liability.[180] Nazareth, JA, giving the judgment of the court, said that the plaintiffs' approach was "over-legalistic". The court noted that "negligence" had not been included in the clause. However, Nazareth JA went on to say:

the clause is plainly wide enough in its ordinary meaning to cover negligence on the part of the servants of the *proferens* in this case ie the defendant . . . we reject . . . [the] contention that the exception clause is not clear because it is ungrammatical and not even a sentence . . . Its plain meaning, in our view, is that no damage claim against the defendant is to be made in respect of the hoisting operation.[181]

Similarly, in *Bewise Motors Co Ltd v Hoi Kong Container Services Ltd*,[182] where cars had been stolen from a shipping container, the Court of Final Appeal was asked to construe the following clause which the defendants sought to rely on to exempt liability for negligence:

178. Ibid at 104.
179. [1993] 1 HKC 56.
180. The court adopted and applied a formula laid down by Lord Morton in *Canada Steamship Lines Ltd v R* [1952] 1 Lloyd's Rep 1.
181. [1993] 1 HKC 56 at 61.
182. [1998] 4 HKC 377.

The company shall not be liable for any loss or damage whether direct or consequential or loss of market suffered by a Customer or Merchant due to fire, explosion,
theft unless by employees of the Company, its agents, servants or subcontractors,
riots or civil commotion, strikes, lock outs or labour restraint, inherent vice of any
equipment or container or goods, typhoon, floods, lightning or Act of God, delay
or detention of any vessel, containers or cargoes, act of omission of the Customer
or merchant as a result of compliance by the company with the instructions of the
Customer or Merchant, or for any other loss or damage unless it is conclusively
proved that such loss or damage was due to the proven neglect or default of the
Company or its employees, nor for any loss damage or expense arising from or in
any way connected with the packing, labelling, marks, brands, weights, numbers,
contents, quality or description of any goods however caused.

The court held, by a majority of four to one (Litton PJ dissenting), that the
clause did cover the breach. Nazareth NPJ said:

In concluding it must be acknowledged that the wording of the clause . . . is neither
elegant nor ideal. But its meaning from a careful reading is so clear and compelling
as to leave no room for ambiguity and obscurity. In the absence of these, there is
neither need nor warrant to resort to secondary rules of construction, including the
contra proferentem rule.[183]

Ching PJ commented that the "interpretation of the clause is not without difficulty." He decided there were two possible constructions to be put on the wording
but opted for the one which did not "strain the language".[184]

Much of the above discussion on negligence liability has been rendered
academic by legislation. Section 3 of the Control of Exemption Clauses Ordinance
(CECO),[185] mirroring section 2 of the Unfair Contract Terms Act (UCTA), 1977,
precludes the exclusion of liability for negligence causing death or personal injury
and permits the exclusion of liability for negligence causing "other loss" only where
the exemption is "reasonable". The common law rules on incorporation and *contra
proferentem* remain significant in "negligence causing other loss" cases, however,
since the "reasonableness" of a clause will be irrelevant if the courts decide it has
not been incorporated or has not unambiguously excluded negligence liability.[186]
Moreover, the common law approach will be crucial in situations where CECO does
not apply.[187]

---

183. Ibid at 396.
184. Echoing Lord Wilberforce's words in the *Ailsa Craig* case.
185. See 8.6.4 below.
186. However, see *Vastfame Camera Ltd v Birkart Globistics Ltd et al* [2005] 4 HKC 117 where the court
     applied the *contra proferentem* approach to rule out the application of a limitation clause.
187. In *Max Components Ltd v Cyclo Transportation Co Ltd* [2012] 3 HKLRD 151 Deputy District
     Judge Hui found that CECO (Cap 71) *did* apply but found that, in any event, the defendant (a bailee)
     had not expressly excluded liability for negligence as required. (The defendant had claimed unsuc-
     cessfully that the contract was an "exempted supply contract" under CECO s 16.)

8.6.2.1 Excluding Liability for "Fundamental Breach"

The so-called doctrine of "fundamental breach" once held prominence in English and Hong Kong law but has arguably been disposed of by the House of Lords decision in *Photo Production Ltd v Securicor Transport Ltd*[188] and by legislation discussed below. A brief discussion is warranted here, given the previous significance of the "fundamental breach" doctrine.

Essentially, one line of cases, associated with the English Court of Appeal in general and Lord Denning MR in particular, had expressed the doctrine in terms of a "rule of law" that liability for the most serious (fundamental) breaches, "going to the root of the contract", could not be excluded.[189] A second line of cases, espousing the House of Lords view, held that there was no such rule of law but that everything depended on the "construction" of the contract. Liability for any breach, even a fundamental one, is possible *provided that* this is the intention of the parties, express or implied.[190]

At first sight, the approaches appear very different; in practice they generally produce the same result, since a court will be reluctant to hold that a party really "intended" that the other should be exempt from liability for "extreme" breaches. Indeed, in criticising the "theory" of the Court of Appeal approach, the House of Lords, in *Photo Production* opined that the same result would have been obtained in the cases considered using the "correct" construction approach.

In short, the more serious the breach, the less likely it would be that a clause would be "intended" to protect the party in breach, but no clause would be automatically defeated by a breach, however serious.[191] Moreover, even where an innocent party rescinds a contract on the basis of the other's "repudiatory" breach,[192] this will not automatically invalidate an exemption clause within the contract.

Photo Production Ltd v Securicor Transport Ltd[193]

The plaintiffs, who owned a factory, employed the defendants to protect it by security services, including night patrols. One night an employee of the defendants deliberately started a small fire which went out of control and completely destroyed the factory and stock. The plaintiffs sued but the defendants successfully relied on an exemption clause which stated that the defendants should not be liable for fire

---

188. [1980] AC 827.
189. See, for example, *Karsales (Harrow) Ltd v Wallis* [1956] 1 WLR 936 at 940.
190. See *Suisse Atlantique Societe d' Armement Maritime SA v NV Rotterdamsche Kolen Centrale* [1967] 1 AC 361.
191. A serious breach was held to be covered by an "incorporated, wide, but not onerous" limitation clause in *Orient Technologies Ltd v A Plus Express (HK) Ltd* [2004] 4 HKC 72 where, significantly, the parties were both businesses (the fact was also significant that at issue was a limitation rather than total exclusion of liability).
192. See 8.5 and 14.3.
193. [1980] AC 827.

damage "except in so far as such loss (was) solely attributable to the negligence of . . . employees acting within the course of their employment".

The House of Lords unanimously found for the defendants. They held that the clause on a proper interpretation protected the defendants (the fire had not been started negligently within the course of employment) and that there was no such thing as a doctrine of "fundamental breach" as previously applied by the Court of Appeal. Lord Wilberforce said:

> The doctrine of "fundamental breach" in spite of its imperfections and doubtful parentage has served a useful purpose. There was a large number of problems, productive of injustice, in which it was worse than unsatisfactory to leave exception clauses to operate . . . After the [Unfair Contract Terms] Act, in commercial matters generally, when the parties are not of unequal bargaining power, and when risks are normally borne by insurance, not only is the case for judicial intervention undemonstrated, but there is everything to be said, and this seems to have been Parliament's intention, for leaving the parties free to apportion the risks as they think fit and for respecting their decisions . . . In these circumstances nobody could consider it unreasonable, that as between these two equal parties the risk assumed by Securicor should be a modest one, and that the respondents should carry the substantial risk of damage or destruction.[194]

The courts should, in other words, let the parties make their own contract (at least when they are of equal bargaining power) subject to statutory intervention. Such statutory intervention, much of which did not apply to the *Photo Productions* case, will often now be crucial, since legislation on unfair terms precludes many exemptions absolutely and makes many others subject to a test of reasonableness.[195] Most widely-drawn exemptions, especially where a business is dealing with a consumer, will be regarded as unreasonable. Of course, the fundamental breach approach (or "primary purpose" approach) may still be relevant where exemption clause legislation does not apply. In *Carewins Development (China) Ltd v Hecny Shipping Ltd*[196] the Court of Final Appeal, dealing with a carriage of goods by sea case, declined to uphold an exemption clause in a bill of lading. This was because there was ambiguity in the clause (to be construed *contra proferentem*) and because the clause, on the defendants' construction, would undermine the primary purpose of the contract; something which is permitted but only if the clearest wording is used.[197]

---

194. [1980] AC 827 at 843.
195. Notably CECO and UCTA: see 8.6.4 below.
196. [2009] 3 HKLRD 409.
197. Applied in *Link Folk Ltd v Glorious Motors Ltd* [2011] HKDC 188.

8.6.3 Other Common Law Controls on Exemption Clauses

As with the common law restrictions outlined above, many of the other common law limitations would now be affected by legislation enacted in England and Hong Kong.[198] The common law rules should still be considered, however, not least because in many situations a common law restriction will be absolute while the relevant statutory restriction will depend on a finding of "unreasonableness".

8.6.3.1 Exemption Clauses and Third Parties

The privity of contract doctrine[199] prevents those who are not party to a contract taking benefits under it. As such, a non-party cannot take the benefit of an exemption clause even if it is drafted for his benefit. This was "apparently" the result in *Adler v Dickson*.[200] Here, the plaintiff booked a cruise on the steamship *Himalaya,* with the P & O company. The plaintiff's ticket made it clear that "the company" would not be liable for any injury to passengers. The plaintiff was injured because of the negligent securing of the ship's gangplank and sued. It was held that, although the company was protected by the exemption clause, the ship's captain and boatswain were liable in the tort of negligence. The exemption clause did not protect them since they were not party to the contract containing the exemption. A similar result occurred in *Scruttons Ltd v Midland Silicones Ltd*,[201] eventually decided in the House of Lords. In *Scruttons*, the respondents made a contract under which their drums of chemicals were to be shipped from America to London. Under the contract the liability of "the carrier" was to be limited to US$500. The appellants were stevedores who damaged one of the respondent's drums causing £593 worth of damage.[202] The respondent sought to recover for their full loss; the appellants sought to take protection from the limitation clause. The House of Lords, by a majority of four to one, found that the appellants were not protected by the clause since they were not party to the contract containing the limitation clause and because it was not expressed to be for their benefit. The court found no reason for saying that the word "carrier" meant or included a stevedore.

Crucially, in neither of the previous cases was the exemption clearly expressed to be for the benefit of the third party. Where the clause is carefully worded, however, it may protect an "apparent" third party by stating that the contract was made on its behalf, thus making it a party via the doctrine of agency.

---

198. Notably CECO and UCTA, considered in detail at 8.6.4 below.
199. See chapter 16.
200. [1955] 1 QB 158, [1954] 3 All ER 397.
201. [1962] AC 446, [1962] 1 All ER 1.
202. At the time there were approximately US$4 to the pound.

New Zealand Shipping Co Ltd v AM Satterthwaite & Co Ltd
("The Eurymedon")[203]

A drilling machine was to be carried from England to New Zealand. Under the bill of lading the liability of the carrier was limited. The carriers purported to make the contract with the shippers on their own behalf and that of their servants or agents. The appellants were a firm of stevedores (of which the carriers were a subsidiary) who damaged the machinery and sought to take the protection of the limitations in the bill of lading. On appeal to the Privy Council it was held, by a majority of three to two, that the stevedores were protected by the clause[204] (which purported to protect them) and, the contract having been made on their behalf, they were contracting parties and had provided consideration by unloading the goods for the benefit of the shipper.[205]

While the third party is protected, in *Eurymedon* by ingenuity, such devices are generally no longer required in English (or Hong Kong) law, where the rigours of the privity doctrine have been statutorily eroded such that an intended third party beneficiary may be afforded contractual rights and protection.[206]

8.6.3.2 Misrepresentation

In *Curtis v Chemical Cleaning and Dyeing Co Ltd*[207] the court held that a party cannot rely on an exemption clause which has been misrepresented to the other party. In *Curtis*, the plaintiff took a wedding dress to be cleaned at the defendants' shop. She was asked to sign a document headed "receipt" and she asked the shop assistant the purpose of the document. She was told that the document excluded the defendants' liability for damage to beads and sequins on the dress; in fact, the document excluded liability for *all damage* to the dress. The dress was returned badly stained. The plaintiff sued and her action succeeded in the English Court of Appeal. The defendants were unable to rely on the exemption clause, despite the plaintiff's signature, because they had misrepresented its effect, albeit innocently. This is a rare example of an exemption clause being inoperative even though in a document signed by the "exemptee".

---

203. [1975] AC 154; [1974] 1 All ER 1015.
204. Ironically, given the outcome of the *Adler* case, a clause successfully protecting a "third party" is generally called a "Himalaya clause".
205. See chapter 4 at 4.5.3. Note that under English law the consideration factor would now be irrelevant: Contracts (Rights of Third Parties) Act 1999.
206. The right of contracting parties (generally) to draw up agreements for the benefit of third parties *and for those third parties to enforce such agreements* is dealt with at length in chapter 16.
207. [1951] 1 KB 805.

8.6.3.3 Overriding Undertaking

An exemption clause may be ineffective if it is clearly contradicted by a statement of the exemptor made at the time of, or before, the formation of the contract. Such a result occurred in *Couchman v Hill*, discussed previously.[208]

8.6.4 Legislation on Exemption Clauses

The many judicial devices for limiting the application of exemption clauses went some way towards precluding the worst exemption clauses and providing some consumer protection. The courts, however, were not able to strike down an exemption clause merely because it was unreasonable. Further consumer protection was thought necessary by Parliament in England and followed by the Legislative Council in Hong Kong. The most important and comprehensive piece of legislation in relation to exemption clauses in Hong Kong is the Control of Exemption Clauses Ordinance (CECO) which is largely based on the English Unfair Contract Terms Act 1977 (UCTA). The title of the Hong Kong legislation, enacted in 1989, far more accurately conveys the function of the legislation.[209] It should also be noted that England, partly as a result of its membership of the European Union, enacted the (now abolished) Unfair Terms in Consumer Contracts Regulations, 1999, and the Consumer Rights Act, 2015,[210] which does not apply in Hong Kong. Given such changes, the legislative rules in England and Hong Kong would diverge further.

8.6.4.1 The Control of Exemption Clauses Ordinance (CECO)

In general, CECO is intended to affect the relationship between a business and a customer and to assist the latter given his weaker bargaining power. Parts of CECO, however, do affect the business-business relationship. CECO makes some exemption clauses totally void and renders others subject to a test of reasonableness. CECO does not specifically define "exemption clause" but the legislation is aimed at clauses that attempt either to exclude or restrict liability. This liability will often be contractual but CECO extends to attempts to exempt liability in tort.

8.6.4.1.1 Section 2: Interpretation and Application

Section 2 is a defining section, explaining the meaning of terms found throughout CECO. Most importantly, it defines the meaning to be given to the term "negligence" and to the phrase "business liability". For the purposes of the Ordinance:

---

208. See discussion at 8.1.2 and 8.2.
209. The legislation is not restricted to contract terms, nor is it essential that they be "unfair"!
210. In response to the *Law Commission Report on Unfair Terms in Consumer Contracts* (2005).

"Negligence" means the breach –

(a) of any obligation arising from the express or implied terms of a contract, to take reasonable care or exercise reasonable skill in the performance of the contract;

(b) of any common law duty to take reasonable care or exercise reasonable skill (but not any stricter duty);

(c) of the common duty of care imposed by the Occupiers Liability Ordinance (Cap 314);

There is a clear overlap here with the tort law of negligence. Part (a) may be termed "contractual negligence"; part (b) refers to negligence in the *Donoghue v Stevenson*[211] (tort of negligence) sense; and part (c) covers the common duty of care owed by an occupier to all lawful visitors.

Sections 7 to 12 of CECO only apply (unless otherwise stated) to "business liability" which is defined as liability for breach of obligations or duties arising—

(a) from things done or omitted to be done by a person in the course of a business (whether his own business or another's); or

(b) from the occupation of premises used for business purposes of the occupier.

"Business" includes a profession and the activities of a public body, a public authority, or a board, commission, committee or other body appointed by the Chief Executive or government.

While "business liability" extends to the occupation of premises, therefore, it does not apply to things done on *private* premises, such as a dwelling house not used for business purposes.

CECO applies whether or not the breach of contract was intentional or not and whether the liability arose vicariously or not.[212] Vicarious liability is that liability arising from the wrongful acts of another for whose conduct one is responsible; such as arises in an employer/employee, principal/agent or car owner/car driver relationship.

8.6.4.1.2 Section 7: Exemption of Liability for Negligence

Section 7 states:

(1) A person cannot by reference to any contract term or to a notice given to persons generally or to particular persons exclude or restrict *liability for death or personal injury* resulting from negligence.

(2) In the case of *other loss or damage*, a person cannot so exclude or restrict his liability for negligence except in so far as the term or notice satisfies the requirement of reasonableness.

---

211. [1932] AC 562 and see 8.6.4.1.8 below.
212. CECO s 2(3).

(3) Where a contract term or notice purports to exclude or restrict liability for negligence a person's agreement to or awareness of it is not of itself to be taken as indicating his voluntary acceptance of any risk.[213]

It should be noted, therefore, that section 7(1) of CECO does not depend on reasonableness but section 7(2) does. As such, there are more cases on the latter subsection which provides scope for dispute on the issue of reasonableness. However, it is unfortunately the case that, in Hong Kong, many institutions (notoriously schools) still attempt to rely on clauses excluding liability for death/injury caused by negligence which have no legal validity. In England, there tends to be more awareness of legislative restrictions. However, a classic inoperative exemption is illustrated in the case of *Harrison v Intuitive Business Consultants Ltd (t/a Bear Grylls Survival Race)*,[214] involving the well-known "survivalist", Bear Grylls. The case involved injury to a competitor in a "Bear Grylls Race". The claimant signed a waiver form, the material part of which read:

> A risk of injury and/ or death from the activities involved in the Bear Grylls Survival Race . . . is significant . . . I knowingly and freely assume all such risks, both known and unknown, even if arising from the negligence of the Releases or others and assume full responsibility for my participation.

The trial judge, Freedman J, stated that:

> It is of course, trite law that liability cannot be excluded where personal injury has been caused as a result of negligence . . . see section 2 (1) of the Unfair Contract Terms Act 1977.

Despite the invalidity of the clause, however, the claimant's tort action failed as the court found no evidence that the race organisers had been negligent.

The most difficult problem in relation to section 7 is to determine whether a clause is actually a clause restricting liability or whether it merely makes it clear that a party is not intending to undertake a duty of care at all. This difficulty stems from the lack of a clear definition of "exemption clause".[215] The problem can be illustrated by the following examples:

(1) "X will not be liable to Y for losses caused by X's negligence."
(2) "X undertakes no duty to Y in respect of the gratuitous financial advice which he may give to Y, both parties accepting that X has no special expertise in these matters."

---

213. Emphasis added.
214. [2021] EWHC 2396.
215. See 8.6.4.1 above.

The first is clearly an exemption clause but the second is much less clear and may be seen simply as a clarification by X that he has no special skill in these matters so that section 7 has no application. The dividing line is very narrow as can be seen from two English cases: *Phillips Products Ltd v Hyland*[216] and *Thompson v T Lohan (Plant Hire) Ltd*.[217] In *Phillips*, the plaintiffs hired machinery and a driver from the second defendants. The (first defendant) driver was negligent and caused damage to the plaintiffs' property. The defendants tried to rely on a clause which said that, in relation to the hire, drivers should be regarded as servants of the hirer who should be responsible for all claims arising. It was held that this was still an exemption clause by virtue of section 13 of UCTA (section 5 of CECO) and therefore caught by section 2 of UCTA (section 7 of CECO). This was because, without the clause, the defendants would have been clearly liable to the plaintiff in tort. Slade LJ said:

> it is not relevant to consider whether the *form* of a condition is such that it can aptly be given the label of an "exclusion" or "restriction" clause. There is no mystique about "exclusion" or "restriction" clauses. To decide whether a person "excludes" liability by reference to a contract term, you look at the *effect* of the term.[218]

Thompson was decided differently on superficially similar facts. Here, a driver and machinery were hired. The driver injured a third party, who successfully recovered damages from the owner of the machinery. The owner sought to recover from the hirer on the basis of a "transfer of liability" clause. Here, as the clause was not being used to preclude the rights of the victim, but simply to transfer the burden of compensation between two commercial parties, it was held to fall outside the scope of UCTA.

The distinction between these cases is that in *Phillips* if the clause had been effective it would have meant no one was liable for the negligence. Therefore, in effect, it was an exemption. In *Thompson*, however, the effect of the clause was merely to transfer liability from the driver's regular employer to his temporary one such that the injured party still had a remedy.

The same issue arose in *Smith v Eric Bush*[219] where it was argued that an exclusion clause can negative the existence of a duty of care rather than provide a defence for the negligent breach of a duty of care. In the *Smith* case, the plaintiff was a prospective purchaser of a house. The defendants were surveyors appointed by a building society[220] to make a pre-sale report. The surveyor's valuation report, which was negligently prepared, stated that no major repairs were needed and overlooked

---

216. [1987] 1 WLR 659.
217. [1987] 1 WLR 649.
218. Note 199 above, at 666. Emphasis added.
219. [1989] 2 All ER 515.
220. At the time most house-buying finance in Britain was provided by "Building Societies". The surveyor's report was paid for by the prospective buyer *but* prepared on behalf of the Society! On this basis, surveyors argued they owed no duty of care to prospective buyers but the courts eventually

serious defects. The plaintiff sued in the tort of negligence and the defendants sought to rely on a disclaimer of responsibility to the plaintiff contained in a form signed by the plaintiff. The defendants argued that the disclaimer was not an exemption clause but a disclaimer of responsibility and was, therefore, not subject to the requirement of reasonableness under UCTA. The House of Lords rejected the defendants' arguments and found for the plaintiff, on the basis that the clause, in effect, excluded liability for negligence so that section 2(2) of UCTA (section 7(2) of CECO) applied. The clause was held to fail the required test of reasonableness largely because of the unequal bargaining power of the parties and the fact that the defendants could have insured against such a claim.

8.6.4.1.3 Section 3 and Schedule 2: The "Reasonableness" Test

The word "reasonable" is found throughout CECO and is defined, in section 3, as follows:

(1) In relation to a contract term, the requirement of reasonableness for the purposes of this Ordinance and section 4 of the Misrepresentation Ordinance (Cap 284) is satisfied only if the court or arbitrator determines that the term is a *fair and reasonable one* to be included having regard to the circumstances which were, or ought reasonably to have been, known to or in the contemplation of the parties when the contract was made.

(2) In determining for the purpose of section 11 or 12 whether a contract term satisfies the requirement of reasonableness, the court or arbitrator shall have regard in particular to the matters specified in Schedule 2; but this subsection does not prevent the court or arbitrator from holding, in accordance with any rule of law, that a term which purports to exclude or restrict any relevant liability is not a term of the contract.

(3) In relation to a notice (not being a notice having contractual effect), the requirement of reasonableness under this Ordinance is satisfied only if the court or arbitrator determines that it would be *fair and reasonable* to allow reliance on it, having regard to all the circumstances obtaining when the liability arose or (but for the notice) would have arisen.

(4) In determining (under this Ordinance or the Misrepresentation Ordinance (Cap 284) whether a contract term or notice satisfies the requirement of reasonableness, the court or arbitrator shall have regard in particular (but without prejudice to subsection (2)) to whether (and, if so, to what extent) the *language* in which the term or notice is expressed is a language understood by the person as against whom another person seeks to rely upon the term or notice.[221]

(5) Where by reference to a contract term or notice a person seeks to *restrict liability to a specified sum of money*, and the question arises (under this Ordinance or

---

refuted this argument, at least in relation to serious errors (see *Yianni v Edwin Evans & Sons* [1982] QB 438).

221. This subsection is not in UCTA.

the Misrepresentation Ordinance (Cap 284)) whether the term or notice satisfies the requirement of reasonableness, the court or arbitrator shall have regard in particular (but without prejudice to subsections (2) or (4) to –

(a) the *resources* which he could expect to be available to him for the purpose of meeting the liability should it arise; and

(b) how far it was open to him to cover himself by *insurance*.

(6) It is for the person claiming that a contract term or notice satisfies the requirement of reasonableness *to prove* that it does.[222]

Although the wording of subsections (1) and (3) gives the court a wide discretion in determining the question of reasonableness, it is important to note that the court should focus on the point in time at which the contract was made.[223] The key, once again, is the parties' "agreement".[224]

Section 3(4), relating to language, has no equivalent in the English legislation and reflects Hong Kong's position as an international territory with a multilingual population.

Section 3(5) specifically covers limitation clauses. Reference should also be made to the common law approach to such clauses as stated in the *Ailsa Craig* case.[225]

Section 3(6) emphasises that the burden of proof, in relation to reasonableness, lies with the party seeking to rely on the clause.

Further reference to "reasonableness" is to be found in Schedule 2 of the Ordinance which is headed "Guidelines for Application of the Reasonableness Test". It lays down additional guidelines on reasonableness *in relation to sections 11 and 12*, which concern the sale or other transfer of goods.[226] Schedule 2 states:

the matters to which the court or arbitrator shall have regard in particular for the purposes of sections 11 (3) and 12 (3) are any of the following which appear to be relevant–

(a) the strength of the *bargaining positions of the parties relative to each other*, taking into account (among other things) alternative means by which the customer's requirements could have been met;

(b) whether the customer received an *inducement* to agree to the term, or in accepting it had an opportunity of entering into a similar contract with other persons, but without having to accept a similar term;

(c) whether the customer knew or ought reasonably to have known of the existence and extent of the term (having regard, among other things, to any custom of the trade and any previous course of dealing between the parties);

---

222. Emphasis added.
223. Supported, albeit *obiter*, by Litton NPJ in *Green Park Properties Ltd v Dorku Ltd* [2002] 1 HKC 121.
224. See 3.1.
225. See 8.6.2 above.
226. See 8.6.4.1.6 and 8.6.4.1.7.

(d) where the term excludes or restricts any relevant liability if some condition is not complied with, whether it was reasonable at the time of the contract to expect that compliance with that condition would be practicable;

(e) whether the goods were manufactured, processed or adapted to the special order of the customer.[227]

8.6.4.1.4 Exemption of Liability for Misrepresentation

Subsections 3(1), 3(4) and 3(5) make it clear that any clause that attempts to exclude or restrict liability for misrepresentation will be subject to the reasonableness test previously described.[228] Attempts are sometimes made, in Hong Kong and England, to escape liability for what appears to be misrepresentation by means of an "entire agreement clause" which states that the said agreement is the entire contract and anything said before can have no effect. Where, however, the courts view this as, in *effect*, an exemption of liability for misrepresentation, it will be subject to the usual "reasonableness" requirement.[229]

8.6.4.1.5 Section 8: Exemption of Liability for Breach of Contract

Section 8 states:

(1) This section applies as between contracting parties where one of them *deals as consumer* or on the *other's written terms of business*.

(2) As against that party, the other *cannot* by reference to any contract term –
   (a) when himself in breach of contract, exclude or restrict any liability of his in respect of the breach; or
   (b) claim to be entitled –
      (i) to render a contractual performance substantially different from that which was reasonably expected of him; or
      (ii) in respect of the whole or any part of his contractual obligation, to render no performance at all, except in so far as (in any of the cases mentioned above in this subsection) the contract term satisfies the requirement of *reasonableness*.[230]

While this section is concerned primarily with the business/consumer relationship, it is clear from subsection (1) that business/business relationships are also covered where they are based on the written standard terms of one of the businesses. Section 8 is extremely significant since the exemption of liability for any breach (or substitute performance or non-performance) is ineffective unless it can be proved reasonable. Again the burden of proof in respect of reasonableness is on the party

---

227. Emphasis added.
228. See 8.6.4.1.3.
229. See *Glory Gold Ltd v Star Play Development Ltd* [2008] 2 HKLRD 416; *Lee Fu Wing v Yan Po Ting Paul* [2009] 5 HKLRD 513; *Link Folk Ltd v Glorious Motors Ltd* [2011] HKDC 188. For further discussion, see chapter 9 at 9.5.
230. Emphasis added.

seeking to rely on the exemption clause. In *St Albans City & District Council v International Computers*,[231] the plaintiffs made a contract with the defendants whereby the latter were to provide and install a database of all eligible "poll tax" (local tax) payers. As a result of software deficiencies the amount payable by the plaintiffs, a local authority, to central government was excessive. The plaintiffs sued the defendants for breach of contract and the latter sought to rely on a limitation clause limiting liability to £100,000. It was held that the clause was unreasonable and therefore ineffective.

The defendants were liable under section 3 of UCTA (section 8 of CECO) since, although business to business, the contract was made on the defendants' standard form terms. Therefore, the clause was required to be reasonable under section 11 of UCTA (section 3 of CECO). In deciding that the clause was unreasonable, the court took into account the fact that the defendants were a very large company with resources to pay damages; that the defendants had very large insurance cover; that the defendants were in a stronger bargaining position because they were one of only a small number of possible suppliers; and that finding for the defendants would mean a loss to St Albans ratepayers.[232]

Where the relevant contract is not "standard form" it is crucial to determine that one party "deals as consumer". In defining the term, section 4 states:

(1) A party to a contract "deals as consumer" in relation to another party if –
    (a) he neither makes the contract in the course of a business nor holds himself out as doing so;
    (b) the other party does make the contract in the course of a business; and
    (c) in the case of a contract governed by the law of sale of goods or by section 12, the goods passing under or in pursuance of the contract are of a type ordinarily supplied for private use or consumption.
(2) Notwithstanding subsection (1), on a sale by auction or by competitive tender the buyer is not in any circumstances to be regarded as dealing as a consumer.
(3) It is for the person claiming that a party does not deal as consumer to prove that he does not.

The definition is not without difficulty and the approach of the English courts has been somewhat restrictive. In *R&B Customs Brokers Ltd v United Dominions Trust Ltd*,[233] a director of the plaintiff company bought a car for business and personal use. The car proved to be defective. The English Court of Appeal, in determining that the defendant was liable under section 3 of UCTA (section 8 of CECO) found that a

---

231. [1995] FSR 686.
232. The defendant was also liable under UCTA s 7 (CECO s 12, and see 8.6.4.1.7) because this was a contract under which goods were transferred other than by a contract for sale or hire purchase. Since the transfer was "business to business" the exemption was required to be reasonable under UCTA s 11 and Schedule 2. (The Hong Kong CECO equivalent is s 3 and Schedule 2.)
233. [1988] 1 All ER 847.

contract is only made "in the course of a business" where it is integral to the business or it forms part of a regular course of dealing of that business. The customer was, therefore, "dealing as a consumer".

The decision is controversial in that it gives a very narrow interpretation of "in the course of a business" and, by implication, widens the scope of "dealing as a consumer". A wider interpretation of the same wording was applied, by the Court of Appeal, to the English equivalent of s 16 of SOGO[234] in the later case of *Stevenson v Rogers*.[235] The court justified the different interpretations as being necessary because of the different meanings of the word "business" in the two statutes. The Court of Appeal, rather reluctantly, followed the *R&B Customs Brokers* approach in *Feldarol Foundry plc v Hermes Leasing (London) Ltd*.[236]

8.6.4.1.6 Section 11: Exemption of Seller's Liability

Section 11 states:

(1) Liability for breach of the obligations arising from section 14 of the Sale of Goods Ordinance (Cap 26) (seller's implied undertakings as to title, etc) *cannot* be excluded or restricted by reference to any contract term.

(2) As against a person *dealing as consumer*, liability for breach of the obligations arising from section 15, 16 or 17 of the Sale of Goods Ordinance (Cap 26) (seller's implied undertakings as to conformity of goods with description or sample, or as to their quality or fitness for a particular purpose) *cannot* be excluded or restricted by reference to any contract term.

(3) As against a person dealing otherwise than as consumer, the liability specified in subsection (2) can be excluded or restricted by reference to a contract term, but only in so far as the term satisfies the requirement of *reasonableness*.

(4) The liabilities referred to in this section are not only the business liabilities defined by section 2(2), but include those arising under any contract of sale of goods.[237]

Sections 14–17 of the Sale of Goods Ordinance are discussed above.[238] It is important to note that any contract clause attempting to exclude liability for breach of the condition (as to title) implied under section 14 will be made void. No distinction is drawn between consumer contracts and business to business contracts. Such a distinction is, however, made with regard to sections 15–17. Attempts to exclude the conditions implied by sections 15–17 in business/consumer contracts will be void but, in respect of business to business contracts, will be subject to the reasonableness test defined in section 3 and Schedule 2 of CECO.

---

234. Sale of Goods Act 1979 s 14.
235. [1999] QB 1028.
236. [2004] EWCA Civ 747.
237. Emphasis added.
238. See 8.4.4.

Section 11(4) states that liabilities here are not restricted to "business liabilities". This implies that private sales may be affected. While this is true in respect of the section 14 implied term (as to title) it is unlikely to be significant in respect of section 15–17 implied terms. First, the "absolute prohibition" on exemption only applies as against someone "dealing as consumer" and one can only deal as a consumer when dealing with a business. Moreover, even the "reasonableness" restriction is of only limited significance outside section 14 since, crucially, the section 16 implied conditions as to merchantability and fitness for purpose *only* apply when goods are sold "in the course of a business". Further, given the need for "reliance" on a description[239] (in respect of section 15) and since non-businesses rarely sell "by sample" (to which section 17 relates) in reality private sales will rarely be affected by sections 15–17.

8.6.4.1.7 Section 12: Exemption of Liability in Relation to Other Transfer of Goods

Section 12 is headed "Miscellaneous contracts under which goods pass". It applies similar rules as laid down in section 11 to contracts, not governed by the law of sale of goods, where possession or ownership of goods passes. This section would apply, for example, to a contract for work or materials which is not a contract of sale of "goods". It would also apply to a simple contract of *hire* of goods. Thus, for example, in any contract for the *sale* of goods to a consumer there would be an "unexcludable" implied term that the goods correspond to their description under section 11. In a contract for the *hire* of such goods by a consumer, a similar "unexcludable" implied term would apply by virtue of section 12.

8.6.4.1.8 Section 10: "Guarantees" of Consumer Goods by a "Non-party"

Section 10 relates to goods "ordinarily supplied for private use or consumption" and prohibits the exclusion of liability for loss or damage arising from the defective nature of the goods which has resulted from negligent manufacture. The section does *not* apply as between the parties to a contract by which ownership or possession of the goods passes. In other words, this section is concerned *not* with the contractual relationships covered by sections 11 and 12 but with, generally, the manufacturer/consumer relationship established in the "narrow rule" of *Donoghue v Stevenson*.[240]

8.6.4.1.9 Section 5: Attempts to Avoid the Provisions of CECO

Section 5 states:

(1) To the extent that this Ordinance prevents the exclusion or restriction of any liability it also prevents –

---

239. Ibid.
240. [1932] AC 562. For further reference, see any work on tort dealing with "duty of care".

(a) making the liability of its enforcement subject to restrictive or onerous conditions.

(b) excluding or restricting any *right or remedy* in respect of the liability, or subjecting a person to any prejudice in consequence of his pursuing any such right or remedy;

(c) excluding or restricting rules of evidence or procedure, and (to that extent) sections 7,10,11 and 12 also prevent excluding or restricting liability by reference to terms and notices which exclude or restrict the relevant obligation or duty.

(2) An agreement in writing to submit present or future differences to arbitration is not to be treated under this Ordinance as excluding or restricting any liability.[241]

An example of a restrictive or onerous term would be where an unrealistic time limit is placed on the reporting of any breach of contract.

8.6.4.1.10 Schedule 1: Excluded Contracts

Schedule 1 provides that sections 7, 8, and 9 of CECO do not apply to certain contracts: notably contracts of insurance, contracts for the disposition of land, contracts for the transfer of intellectual property rights, contracts for the formation or dissolution of a company and contracts creating and transferring securities. These exempted areas largely mirror those of UCTA. However, it should be noted that some of the "gaps" in UCTA were filled in UTCCR and its broader successor, the Consumer Rights Act, 2015, such that legislative consumer protection is now more extensive in England than in Hong Kong.[242]

8.6.4.2 Supply of Services (Implied Terms) Ordinance (SOSITO)[243]

This legislation came into operation in Hong Kong on 21 October 1994. It is based largely on Part II of the equivalent English legislation, the Supply of Goods and Services Act, 1982. It provides an additional piece of consumer protection legislation that applies only to contracts for the supply of services. "Services" is not defined in the Ordinance.

However, section 3 (1) states:

In this Ordinance a 'contract for the supply of a service' means, subject to subsection (2), a contract under which a person ("the supplier") agrees to carry out a service.

Section 3(2) states that a contract of service or apprenticeship is not a contract for the supply of a service. However, it goes on to state that a contract is a contract

---

241. Emphasis added.
242. For example, contracts pertaining to land were apparently within the scope of UTCCR: *Khatun & Others v Newham LBC* [2004] EWCA 55.
243. Cap 457.

for the supply of a service whether or not goods are also transferred, or to be transferred, or bailed, or to be bailed.

SOSITO provides that certain terms are implied into every contract for the supply of services: to carry out the service with reasonable care and skill (section 5); to carry out the service within a reasonable time (section 6); and for the consumer to pay a reasonable charge (section 7).

Section 8(1) SOSITO states:

> As against a party to a contract for the supply of a service who deals as consumer, the other party cannot, by reference to any contract term, exclude or restrict any liability of his arising under the contract by virtue of this Ordinance.[244]

"Dealing as a consumer" is covered in section 4 and is similar to the definition found in section 4(1) of CECO.

---

244. There is no equivalent restriction in the Supply of Goods and Services Act 1982.

9

Misrepresentation

OVERVIEW

The vitiating element of misrepresentation is concerned with those statements which are viewed as having played a part in inducing the making of a contract (representations) but which are not regarded as terms of the contract. So, if a term of a contract is broken, the remedy sought will be for breach of contract; if a mere representation proves false, the remedy must lie in misrepresentation. The distinction between representations and terms, as already seen, is not always easy to draw.[1] One difficulty is that older cases sometimes involve courts eager to find a term, given the unavailability of a suitable misrepresentation remedy.[2] With the greatly improved remedies for misrepresentation since the Misrepresentation Ordinance[3] the courts are now unlikely to act so creatively.

The law on misrepresentation is concerned primarily with false, or inaccurate, "statements".[4] The focus is on positive affirmations of fact, and non-disclosure is generally beyond the scope of misrepresentation.[5] Indeed, despite the lack of a statutory definition of misrepresentation, the Misrepresentation Ordinance implies the need for a positive assertion rather than mere non-disclosure.[6]

Since there is no statutory definition, the meaning of "misrepresentation" must be gleaned from the relevant case law. A misrepresentation is "a false statement of fact which induces the representee to make a contract with the representor". This very basic definition requires considerable exposition since the extent to which silence can amount to misrepresentation, the meaning of "statement of fact", and the concept of "inducement" all require considerable elaboration.

---

1. See 8.1.
2. See, for example, *Dick Bentley Productions Ltd v Harold Smith (Motors) Ltd* [1965] 1 WLR 623.
3. Cap 284, modelled on the UK Misrepresentation Act 1967.
4. The word "statement" is interpreted liberally; see 9.1.2.
5. See 9.1.2.1.
6. Since it talks of "a misrepresentation has been made to him by another party".

Once a misrepresentation has been established, the representee (the person induced by the false statement) has two possible remedies: rescission and damages. Rescission was once the only remedy available in the absence of fraud or breach of fiduciary duty. It requires that the parties return to their pre-contractual position. It may be possible for this to be done amicably, with the representor agreeing to the representee's call to cancel the agreement. Far more likely, the representee will need to seek an order for rescission from the courts. Rescission, a largely equitable remedy,[7] involves considerable discretion on the part of the court, since it will always have the power to reject the remedy and substitute damages "in lieu" (instead). Moreover, there are situations in which the court *must* reject rescission since one of the recognised "bars" to the remedy exists. In such circumstances it is doubtful that the court can give damages as an alternative.[8] The availability of rescission is, therefore, considerably restricted. It is also an inadequate remedy when consequential loss has been suffered. Equity does allow the award of an "indemnity" in addition to rescission but this is very restrictive in scope.[9]

Damages, the common law remedy, are far more readily available for misrepresentation since legislation was passed in the 1960s.[10] Prior to the legislation, the common law was very restrictive in that damages were available only in the unlikely event that the representee could prove fraud on the part of the representor.[11] Fraud was defined narrowly and required proof that the representor knew that what he was saying was false or that he was reckless as to whether it was false. The new legislation provided that the representor would be liable to pay damages for misrepresentation *unless* he could prove that his statement was made honestly and reasonably. Thus, for the first time, the *negligent* representor would be liable to pay damages. Moreover, the legislation introduced a presumption of liability; it is not for the representee to prove fraud or negligence, but for the representor to disprove them. Curiously, however, though the legislation is aimed primarily at the negligent representor; it treats him as if he were fraudulent and he must pay the same damages as would the deliberately deceitful representor. This feature of the legislation, the "fiction of fraud", is so strange that many academics refused to accept that the legislation would be so interpreted. Decisions, both in Hong Kong and England, however, leave no doubt that the "fiction of fraud" does exist. The practical consequence is that there will now be little point in the representee bringing an action asserting fraud since he will be better advised merely to bring an action under the Misrepresentation Ordinance which will produce as good a remedy and throw on the representor the obligation of disproving fraud and negligence.

---

7. Though the common law did permit rescission for misrepresentation in the rare situations where fraud could be proved.
8. See 9.3.4.2.
9. See *Whittington v Seale-Hayne* (1900) 82 LT 49.
10. The Hong Kong Misrepresentation Ordinance mirrored the English Misrepresentation Act 1967.
11. Although parallel moves to develop the tort of negligence had begun.

It is possible to exclude liability for misrepresentation but only where the exclusion is reasonable.[12] Strangely, perhaps, statutory limitations on the right to exclude liability for misrepresentation were introduced considerably before similar restrictions in relation to breach of contract.

The UK Misrepresentation Act 1967, though brief, is poorly drafted. It is impossible to understand without knowledge of the pre-existing law and, even then, only with difficulty. Yet, despite the immediate criticisms of the Act it was reproduced almost without amendment by the Hong Kong legislature.[13]

9.1 The Scope of Misrepresentation

"Misrepresentation" is generally defined as a "false statement of fact which induces a representee to make a contract with the representor". This definition, which derives from the common law rather than statute, requires some further elaboration.

9.1.1 False

The word "false" applies to statements which are merely inaccurate. There is no requirement that the maker of the statement be dishonest. The nature of the *remedy* for misrepresentation may vary according to whether the statement was made fraudulently, negligently or innocently but a statement made both honestly and on reasonable grounds may nonetheless amount to misrepresentation.

9.1.2 Statement

The word "statement" indicates that misrepresentation requires some form of words, but actions, such as a nod of the head, which clearly convey a particular meaning may also be regarded as representations. In *Spice Girls Ltd v Aprilia World Service BV*,[14] the participation of a pop music group in the making of an advertising film was held to constitute a representation that the group *presently* intended to stay together for the duration of the advertising contract. Since one of the group had already decided to leave there was held to be a misrepresentation by conduct.

---

12. Misrepresentation Act 1967 s 3; Misrepresentation Ordinance (Cap 284) s 4.
13. In an interesting article, the author points out that most of the contemporary debate on the proposed Misrepresentation Bill concerned the now relatively uncontroversial question of excluding liability, rather than the still disputed "fiction of fraud" (both are discussed post). See Alan Brener, "The Misrepresentation Act 1967: Its Historical Origins and Socio-political Context", UCL Discussion Paper ORCID number 0000-0002-9038-492X.
14. [2000] EMLR 478.

An act of concealment, such as hiding a defect, may be treated as equivalent to a statement that the defect does not exist. Covering dry rot in a house so as to conceal its existence is equivalent to a "statement" that the house is free from dry rot.[15]

9.1.2.1 Silence as Misrepresentation

Since there is no general duty of disclosure, "mere" silence will generally not amount to misrepresentation. In *Bank of China v PR of Fu Kit Keung (deceased)*[16] Chu J stated:

> As a matter of law, mere silence or inaction does not constitute a representation unless the person concerned has a duty to disclose in law or he knowingly withholds a material part of a representation.[17]

In *Fletcher v Krell*,[18] a woman seeking a job as a governess did not disclose, since she had not been asked, that she was divorced. While divorce at the time was very unusual there was held to be no misrepresentation in respect of the applicant's silence on the matter. The principle that there is no "free-standing" duty of disclosure was upheld by the Hong Kong courts in *Aktieselskabet Dansk Skibfinansiering v Wheelock Mardon & Co Ltd and Others*.[19] In the Court of Appeal Godfrey and Liu JJA cited with approval the following words of Bingham LJ in *Interfoto Picture Library Ltd v Stiletto Visual Programme Ltd*:[20]

> In many civil law systems . . . the law of obligations recognises and enforces an overriding principle that in making and carrying out contracts parties should act in good faith. [This includes] 'playing fair', 'coming clean' or 'putting one's cards face up on the table'.

English law has, characteristically, committed itself to no such overriding principle.[21] The *Wheelock* decision was later upheld in the Court of Final Appeal.[22] However, even silence can amount to misrepresentation where it constitutes a failure to correct a previous truth now no longer accurate.

---

15. See *Gordon v Selico Co Ltd* (1986) 278 EG 53.
16. [2009] 5 HKLRD 713.
17. Ibid at para 43.
18. (1873) 42 LJ (QB) 55.
19. [1998] 3 HKC 153.
20. [1989] QB 433.
21. Ibid at 439. Cited at [1998] 3 HKC 153 at 164.
22. [2000] 1 HKC 511.

With v O'Flanagan[23]

The parties discussed the sale of the defendant's medical practice. The defendant, truthfully, stated that the practice was valued at £2,000 a year. By May, when the sale of the practice was concluded, the value had decreased enormously because of the defendant's illness. The defendant did not disclose the change of circumstances. The plaintiff's subsequent claim for rescission was upheld by a unanimous Court of Appeal.

Romer LJ summarised the view of the court. He stated:

> If A with a view to inducing B to enter into a contract makes a representation as to a material fact, then if at a later date and before the contract is actually entered into, owing to a change of circumstances, the representation then made would to the knowledge of A be untrue and B subsequently enters into the contract in ignorance of that change of circumstances and relying upon that representation, A cannot hold B to the bargain. There is ample authority for that statement and, indeed, I doubt myself whether any authority is necessary, it being, it seems to me, so obviously consistent with the plainest principles of equity.[24]

Misrepresentation will also arise where silence follows a literally accurate statement which tells only part of the truth so as to give a misleading picture. In *Curtis v Chemical Cleaning and Dyeing Co*,[25] for example, a statement that an exemption clause applied to beads and sequins was literally true. There was silence as to its more extensive nature, however. As a result, the statement conveyed the impression that the exemption extended *only* to beads and sequins; there was a duty to complete the story and failure to do so amounted to misrepresentation. In *Notts Patent Brick & Tile Co v Butler*,[26] a purchaser of land asked the seller's solicitor whether there were any restrictive covenants affecting the property. The solicitor replied that he was "not aware" of any. The solicitor did not explain that this was because he had not read the relevant documents! The statement was, of course, literally true but conveyed a misleading impression. It was held that there was a misrepresentation though, strictly, there was no false statement, merely silence as to the full explanation.

It will, of course, generally be acceptable for someone who does not know the answer to a question to say so. In the *Notts Patent* case, however, a solicitor acting for a party would be expected to have read the relevant documents.

---

23. [1936] Ch 575.
24. Ibid at 582.
25. [1951] 1 KB 805 and see 5.4.
26. (1866) 16 QBD 77.

9.1.2.2 *Uberrimae Fidei*

There are also cases where the law imposes a duty to make positive disclosure, such that failure to do so is actionable. The main example concerns those contracts (generally involving insurance) which are said to be *uberrimae fidei* (of the utmost good faith). It is well established that a failure to make full disclosure of all relevant information in a proposal for insurance may permit the insurer to cancel the policy.

The United Insurance Company Ltd v Chan Park Sang and Others[27]

The defendant wished to take out a policy of third party insurance with the plaintiffs for his motor car and signed a proposal form. In English, the form required the defendant to state whether he "or any person who to your knowledge will drive [has] been convicted during the past 5 years of any offence in connection with the driving of any Motor Vehicle". The defendant answered "No" although his son, an intended driver, did have such a conviction. The plaintiffs sought to avoid the contract because of the failure to disclose the information. It was held, in the Hong Kong High Court, that the policy could be avoided even though it was agreed by the court that the translation of the above question, into Chinese, was not accurate.

Reece J stated:

> It seems to me perfectly clear that when the proposal form was filled up the person who filled it up had one person and one person only in mind as the person who would normally drive and that was Chan Tung [the son]. There was no mention of the insured as a driver and it would seem that the insured had no intention of driving the vehicle . . .
>
> The duty of disclosure which rests upon the parties to a contract of insurance is to make a complete and accurate disclosure and the parties must disclose material facts which they know or ought to know.
>
> . . . it must be established that the false or undisclosed statement was material and that it induced the insurers to issue the policy.[28]

Although the *Chan Park Sang* case does involve a *positive*, inaccurate answer, Reece J suggests that mere silence on a material point may also invalidate a policy since he refers to "false *or* undisclosed" statements. The English courts have clearly accepted that silence as to "material" information, not requested by the insurance company, may invalidate a policy.

---

27. [1960] HKLR 267.
28. Ibid at 274.

Lambert v Co-Operative Insurance Society Ltd[29]

The plaintiff signed a proposal form for an "all risks" insurance policy to cover jewellery belonging to her and her husband. She was not asked about, and did not mention, her husband's conviction for receiving stolen goods. In the policy it was stated that non-disclosure of a material fact would render it void. On a subsequent renewal in 1972, the plaintiff also failed to mention her husband's further conviction for theft in 1971. The plaintiff later made a claim under the policy for loss or theft of jewellery. The defendants refused to honour the claim because of the previous non-disclosures. The refusal was upheld at trial and on the plaintiff's subsequent appeal to the Court of Appeal.

MacKenna J, at first instance, stated that the insured's duty is to disclose such facts as a reasonable or prudent insurer might have treated as material. He added that:

> Every circumstance is material which would influence the judgment of a prudent insurer in fixing the premium, or determining whether he will take the risk.

MacKenna J, however, lamented the "unsatisfactory state of the law", expressed sympathy for Mrs Lambert and felt that the insurers had a moral, though not a legal, duty to pay the insured.

The approach of the English courts has been criticised as unduly harsh. The English Law Commission[30] recommended that the law on non-disclosure should be reformed, referring particularly to the fact that laymen would often be unaware of the duty to disclose and that they would often be unaware as to which facts were "material". However, the English courts have clarified that, as in *Chan Park Sang*, the misrepresentation (or silence) must not only have been "material", in the sense of being a factor that a reasonable insurer would consider, but must actually have induced the particular insurer to insure on the terms agreed.[31] It may be, going forward, that the English courts will be more favourably disposed than those in Hong Kong towards the insured. Consumer protection legislation, in the form of the Unfair Terms in Consumer Contracts Regulations (UTCCR),[32] has been enacted and, unlike the Unfair Contract Terms Act 1977, enacted as the Control of Exemption Clauses Ordinance in Hong Kong, encompasses insurance contracts. It is unlikely that UTCCR-type legislation will be enacted in Hong Kong so the potential improvement in the insured's position in England will not be applicable here.

While non-disclosure in these *uberrimae fidei* cases is clearly actionable, it is questionable whether it should be regarded as misrepresentation as opposed to a separate area of law in itself. In English law, for example, it now seems clear that

---

29. [1975] 2 Lloyd's Rep 485.
30. Law Commission Working Paper No 73: *Insurance Law—Non-disclosure and breach of warranty.*
31. *Pan Atlantic Co Ltd v Pine Top Insurance Co Ltd* [1994] 3 All ER 581.
32. Now superseded by the Consumer Rights Act, 2015.

while non-disclosure in an insurance context would entitle the insurer to rescind, no action for damages would generally arise.[33] The wording of the Misrepresentation Ordinance also indicates that damages under section 3(1) arise only where "a misrepresentation has been made to him" and do not extend to non-disclosure, so that the "no damages" approach would be adopted by the Hong Kong courts. However, a *fraudulent* non-disclosure would permit the award of damages.[34]

9.1.3 Of Fact (or Opinion?)

Misrepresentation involves statements of "fact". As such, false statements of an *opinion*, genuinely held, cannot constitute misrepresentations. However, where the so-called "opinion" is not actually held by the representor this will constitute a misrepresentation; one cannot escape liability for misrepresentation merely by adding the words, "I think". A person's real opinion (or intention) may be difficult to ascertain but, where it can be proved to have been falsely stated, this is as actionable as any other misrepresentation.

Smith v Land and House Property Corporation[35]

The plaintiffs, who wished to sell a hotel, described it as "let to a most desirable tenant". In fact, the tenant had often been in arrears, as the plaintiffs well knew. On discovering the truth, the defendants, who had agreed to buy the hotel, refused to complete, pleading misrepresentation. The plaintiffs' action for specific performance was rejected by the Court of Appeal.

Bowen LJ stated:

> it is often fallaciously assumed that a statement of opinion cannot involve the statement of a fact. In a case where the facts are equally well known to both parties, what one of them says to the other is frequently nothing but an expression of opinion. The statement of such opinion is in a sense a statement of a fact, about the condition of the man's own mind, but only of an irrelevant fact, for it is of no consequence what the opinion is. But if the facts are not equally known to both sides, then a statement of opinion by the one who knows the facts best involves very often a statement of a material fact, for he impliedly states that he knows facts which justify his opinion. Now a landlord knows the relations between himself and his tenant, other persons either do not know them at all or do not know them equally well.[36]

---

33. *BG plc v Nelson Group Services (Maintenance) Ltd* [2002] EWCA Civ 547. But see exception for fraud cited below. It was first suggested *obiter* that a *dishonest* non-disclosure may permit an award of damages: *Hih Casualty and General Insurance Ltd and Others v Chase Manhattan Bank and Others* [2003] UKHL 6 and this is now confirmed.
34. *Conlon v Simms* [2006] EWHC 401.
35. (1884) 28 Ch D 7.
36. Ibid at 12.

The words of Bowen LJ seem equally applicable to the situation where the representor knows that what he is saying is untrue and the situation where his knowledge is such that he *ought* to know that the opinion he is expressing is incorrect.[37] In contract law, then, the difference is unimportant. In Hong Kong criminal law, however, the obtaining of property, or a pecuniary advantage, by a deception as to one's opinion is a criminal offence, so that the difference between an opinion held to be carelessly formed and one which is expressed dishonestly may be crucial.[38]

Just as an apparent statement of opinion may be determined to be one of fact, so a statement couched as one of fact may be viewed as merely expressing an opinion if the context shows that the representor was in no better position to know the truth than the representee.

Bissett v Wilkinson[39]

The parties discussed the possible sale of a piece of land in New Zealand. The seller asserted it would support 2,000 sheep if worked properly. The buyer knew that the seller had never farmed sheep on most of the land. The land was not capable of supporting the number of sheep indicated and the buyer subsequently refused to complete, alleging misrepresentation. The Privy Council rejected the plea of misrepresentation holding that the assertion, in reality, was a statement of opinion.

Lord Merrivale, speaking for the court, stated:

> when misrepresentation is the alleged ground of relief . . . it is, of course, essential to ascertain whether that which is relied upon is a representation of a specific fact, or a statement of opinion, since an erroneous opinion stated by the party affirming the contract, though it may have been relied upon and have induced the contract on the part of the party who seeks rescission, gives no title to relief unless fraud is established . . . the most material fact to be remembered is that, as both parties were aware, the appellant had not and, so far as appears, no other person had at any time carried on sheep farming upon the unit of land in question.[40]

9.1.3.1 Fact or Intention?

A statement of future *intention* similarly will not give rise to a misrepresentation. This was one reason for the failure of the plaintiff's action in *Yang Dandan v Hong Kong Resort Co Ltd*[41] discussed below.[42] This seems to be the case even if such intention changes but the other party is not informed of such; it is to be expected that people's future intentions may alter.

---

37. Supported in *BG plc v Nelson Group Services (Maintenance) Ltd* [2002] EWCA Civ 547.
38. See the Theft Ordinance (Cap 210) ss 17–18.
39. [1927] AC 177.
40. Ibid at 184.
41. (unrep, CACV 247/2015, 9 August 2016).
42. See 9.1.4.

Wales v Wadham[43]

The plaintiff, a husband who had left his wife, offered her a generous settlement on her frequent assertion that she did not intend to remarry. She accepted after changing her mind but did not mention her plans to marry Mr Wadham. The plaintiff challenged the settlement on the basis that the defendant (his ex-wife) had a duty to inform him of her change of mind. The plaintiff's action was rejected in the Family Division of the English High Court.

Tudor Evans J stated:

> I am satisfied that the wife's views, when expressed, were honestly held and that they were in no way calculated to mislead the husband. The wife had not met Mr Wadham at that time.[44]

The key point is that the wife had truthfully conveyed her intention as it then existed. If it had been shown that Mrs Wales had *already* decided to remarry when she disclaimed such intention, the agreement would have been voidable for misrepresentation. The position, then, appears to be that there is a duty to correct previous statements of *fact*[45] when circumstances change but no corresponding duty in relation to an altered *intention*.[46]

9.1.3.2 Fact or Law

It was previously the case that false statements as to the law would not be actionable.[47] This meant that the distinction between statements of fact and those of law, often a fine one, was of great significance. Curiously, perhaps, the English courts had held that a statement as to *foreign* law could be treated as a statement of fact.[48] By analogy, were the Hong Kong courts to follow this approach, they would find a statement as to PRC law to be a statement of fact.

The English courts have now abandoned the rule that *innocent* false statements as to law cannot be misrepresentations.[49] This has arisen following a previous House of Lords decision to abandon the long-established rule that *mistakes* of law are not operative (the *Kleinwort Benson* amendment).[50] In *Pankhania v Hackney London Borough Council*[51] the court allowed a claim for damages for misrepresentation

---

43. [1977] 1 WLR 199.
44. Ibid at 207.
45. See *With v O'Flanagan* at 9.1.2.1.
46. But see *Traill v Baring* (1864) 4 DJ & S 318 for a contrary view.
47. Though as with statements of opinion, a statement of law *known* to be false would be actionable in deceit.
48. *Andre et Cie v Ets Michel Blanc & Fils* [1979] 2 Lloyd's Rep 427.
49. By analogy with statements of opinion and intention, a *deliberately* false statement of law would already have been actionable.
50. *Kleinwort Benson Ltd v Lincoln City Council* [1999] 2 AC 349 and see chapter 10.
51. [2002] NPC 123.

against National Car Parks who had claimed to be contractual licensees when in fact they were protected business tenants. The court rejected the defendants' argument that any false statements were as to law, finding that, by analogy with *Kleinwort Benson*, this was now irrelevant. While *Pankhania* is not binding on Hong Kong courts, it is likely that the approach will be followed.

9.1.3.3 "Mere Puffs"

A statement will not be regarded as a misrepresentation if it is obviously intended not to be taken seriously and where no reasonable listener would take it seriously. Such statements are described as "mere puffs". An illustration is provided by the ancient case of *Weeks v Tybald*,[52] where a father, seeking a husband for his daughter, "affirmed and published" that he would pay £100 to anyone who married his daughter with his consent. The plaintiff made the marriage and claimed the reward. It was held that his action must fail since the words of the father were not intended to be taken seriously but merely to "excite suitors".[53]

A notable example in Hong Kong relates to estates agents' advertising where it is generally accepted that descriptions should not be taken literally. Attempts to sell new properties on the Pokfulam coast may feature photographs of apartments on the Mediterranean with the justification that what is being indicated is a "concept". Such behaviour is so widespread that it is fair to say that few Hong Kong people would take the images seriously.[54] This view is given judicial support in *Chan Yeuk Yu & Another v Church Body of the Hong Kong Sheng Kung Hui & Another*[55] where Burrell J, dealing with the words "regal surroundings for the select few", stated:

> taken in its context, namely on page 4 of a 27-page glossy and colourful sales brochure, I find it difficult to conclude that it is any more than "mere puff" or "sales pitch".[56]

9.1.4 Inducement

The key aspect of misrepresentation is "inducement", so that a false statement which does not affect the decision to make a contract is not actionable. This will be so if the other party is unaware of the statement, or ignores it, or *knows* that it is false and decides to contract anyway. Provided that the representation is "material" it does not matter whether the representee is "reasonably" induced as long as he can prove

---

52. (1605) Noy 11.
53. See also *Lambert v Lewis* [1982] AC 225 where it was held that the words "foolproof" and "needs no maintenance" should not be taken literally.
54. However, the *South China Morning Post* reported widespread concern over estate agents' ethics in Hong Kong on 20 April 2005.
55. [2001] 1 HKC 621.
56. Ibid at 627.

himself to have been induced.[57] The test, then, is subjective rather than objective. Of course, if a reasonable person would not have been induced by the statement, the court will *presume* that the representee has not been induced *unless* he can prove otherwise. In short, the onus of proof in cases of unreasonable inducement will be on the representee to show he was *in fact* induced. Thus, in *Link Folk Ltd v Glorious Motors Ltd*[58] it was stated by Au-Yeung DDJ:

> Since the representation on mileage was a material representation calculated to induce . . . the plaintiff to enter into the Agreement, it is an inference of law that the plaintiff was induced . . .

The position is excellently summarised in a passage from Goff & Jones,[59] cited with approval by Lam JA in the case of *Master Yield Ltd v Ho Foon Yung Anesis & Others.*[60] The authors state:[61]

> any misrepresentation which induces a person to enter into a contract should be a ground for rescission of that contract. If the representation would have induced a reasonable person to enter into the contract then the court will . . . presume that the representee was so induced and the onus will be on the representor to show [other-wise] . . . If, however, the misrepresentation would not have induced a reasonable person to contract, the onus will be on the representee to show that the misrepresen-tation induced him to act as he did.

In *Yang Dandan v Hong Kong Resort Co Ltd*[62] the Court of Appeal rejected a claim of misrepresentation arising from the plaintiff's asserted reliance on an implied assertion that the flat she purchased from the defendants would have an uninter-rupted view of the sea (because she had purchased an upper floor flat on a "high rise" development overlooking a "low-rise" one). The court found that a reasonable person would not have made the assumptions which the plaintiff alleged; and that, as an intelligent person, she could not realistically have done so.

A somewhat different approach applies where the representation involved is fraudulent since it is said that the presumption that a "material" representation *did* induce the contracting representee is even stronger where the representation is fraudulent.[63] This view was endorsed in the case of *BV Nederlandse Industrie*

---

57. Cf *Museprime Properties Ltd v Adhill Properties Ltd* [1990] 2 EGLR 196.
58. (unrep, DCCJ 552/2010, 15 September 2011).
59. Lord Goff of Chieveley and G. H. Jones, *The Law of Restitution* (London: Sweet & Maxwell, 3rd edn, 1987).
60. [2013] 6 HKC 520.
61. At p 168.
62. (unrep, CACV 247/2015, 9 August 2016).
63. *Chitty on Contracts* quoted with approval in *Haywood v Zurich Insurance Company* [2016] UKSC 48.

Van Eiprodukten v Rembrandt Enterprises Inc.[64] Here, having established that the relevant representation had been made fraudulently, Longmore LJ stated:

> The law as I conceive it to be . . . requires the representee to prove inducement albeit with the assistance of a presumption which will be 'very difficult to rebut'.

A number of cases have equated inducement with reliance in suggesting that the misrepresentation will be actionable only where the representee "believes in" or "relies on" the representor's statement. Of course, this will normally be the explanation for an inducement. However, the UK Supreme Court has indicated that the correct word is "inducement" and that inducement is not synonymous with "reliance". In *Hayward v Zurich Insurance Co plc*[65] the respondents had paid medical insurance monies to the appellant following his dishonest exaggeration of his medical condition. The respondents had doubts as to the veracity of the appellant's statements, but recognised that they might be accepted by a court and paid out accordingly. It was held that they could recover damages for deceit since they had been "induced" by the appellant's representations, though not necessarily believing them.

Lastly, as implied above, a representee does not have to prove that s/he was induced to make the contract "solely" by the representor's statements. It is enough that the statements were part of the inducement. Thus:

> The fact that there were other reasons (besides the representation) for the claimant to have made the contract did not mean that he was not induced by the representation made.[66]

9.1.4.1 Ignorance of the Statement

There would be no inducement, for example, where a false advertisement is made and a contract is later entered into, if it can be proved that the contracting party "victim" had never seen the advertisement.

Horsfall v Thomas[67]

The plaintiff sold a large gun to the defendant which exploded during test firing. The plaintiff had concealed a defect in the gun by inserting a "plug". The defendant refused to honour payment for the gun and the plaintiff sued. The defendant asserted, by way of defence, that the concealment was a misrepresentation, equivalent to a statement that the gun was in reasonable condition. It was held that concealment was capable of amounting to misrepresentation but that, since the defendant had not inspected the gun, he was not *induced* by the concealment.

---

64. [2019] EWCA Civ 596.
65. [2016] UKSC 48.
66. Longmore LJ, *BV Nederlandse* case (n 64 above).
67. (1862) 1 H&C 90.

Bramwell B stated:

the plaintiff never examined the gun, and therefore it is impossible that an attempt to conceal the defect could have had any operation on his mind or conduct. If the plug, which it was said was put in to conceal the defect, had never been there, his position would have been the same.[68]

9.1.4.2 Ignoring the Statement

A misrepresentation will have been ignored where the representee makes a contract based on reliance on independent advice rather than the representor's false statement. In *Attwood v Small*,[69] for example, the parties had discussed the possible sale of the defendant's mine. The defendant made exaggerated claims about the mine's yield. The plaintiff asked his agents to inspect the mine and those agents agreed with the defendant's exaggerated figures. The plaintiff then agreed to buy the mine. His subsequent claim to rescind the contract on the grounds of misrepresentation was rejected by the House of Lords as there had been no inducement. The plaintiff had decided to contract solely on the basis of the independent advice and not the defendant's false statement.

It remains possible, of course, that a representee may be induced partly by the representor's statements and partly by other factors. In such a case, liability for misrepresentation may still be found.[70] It has also been suggested[71] that in an *Attwood* case the representor would not escape liability where his statement is made dishonestly. While a more generous "remoteness" test for the representee in such circumstances can be easily justified,[72] it is difficult to see how the representor's *motive* can affect the issue of whether or not the representee has been induced.

9.1.4.3 Statement Known to Be False

A representee who *knows* that the other party's statement is false but decides to contract anyway will not have been induced. An action for misrepresentation is not, however, precluded merely because the representee should (or could) have known the statement was false but did not take the opportunity to find out.

---

68. The case is distinguishable from *Gordon v Selico Co Ltd* (discussed above at 9.1.2) because in that case there was an inspection, although it revealed nothing because of the concealment.
69. (1838) 6 Cl & Fin 232.
70. See *Edgington v Fitzmaurice* (1885) 29 Ch D 459.
71. See *S Pearson & Son Ltd v Dublin Corporation* [1907] AC 351.
72. See 9.3.3.

Redgrave v Hurd[73]

The plaintiff, a solicitor, advertised for a partner. The defendant was interested. The plaintiff said the practice was worth about £300 per year. The plaintiff produced figures for the last three years indicating the business was worth only £200 per year. The defendant questioned this discrepancy. The plaintiff said there were other transactions making up the difference; he produced papers but the defendant did not read them. The defendant then agreed to the partnership. The unread papers would have shown that the business was worth only £200 per year. On discovering the truth, the defendant refused to complete and the plaintiff sued. The action failed as the Court of Appeal unanimously upheld the defendant's plea of misrepresentation. The defendant's counter-claim for rescission (though not for damages) was upheld.

Jessel MR unequivocally stated:

> If a man is induced to enter into a contract by a false representation it is not a sufficient answer to him to say, "If you had used due diligence you would have found out that the statement was untrue. You had the means afforded you of discovering its falsity, and did not choose to avail yourself of them." Nothing can be plainer, I take it, on the authorities in equity than that the effect of false representation is not got rid of on the ground that the person to whom it was made has been guilty of negligence.[74]

The decision may be supported on the basis that an action was being brought by the representor in equity where the court has a discretion to deny a remedy where to grant it would be unfair. If the courts were to clearly extend the "defence of ignorance" principle to a claimant seeking damages we would be left with the curious position that the prudent investor, such as Attwood, who takes independent advice, is worse off than the representee, like Hurd, who blithely accepts the word of the representor, even when armed with the information which would have alerted him to the truth. It has been suggested that, in England, the representee's action for non-fraudulent misrepresentation would now fail where he failed to take the opportunity to discover the truth in a situation where it is reasonable to expect him to do so.[75] However, the *Redgrave* approach seems to remain good law in Hong Kong.[76] Indeed, in *Ngai Keung v Ming Yiu Heng*[77] To J stated:

> I consider I am bound to follow *Redgrave v Hurd*. I conclude that the fact that the misrepresentee might have discovered the falsity of the misrepresentation is no defence to a claim for rescission.

---

73. (1881) 20 Ch D 1.
74. Ibid at 15.
75. Treitel (at p 417) argues that this is the effect of *Smith v Eric S Bush* [1990] 1 AC 831.
76. See *Welltech Investment Ltd v Easy Fair Industries Ltd* [1996] 4 HKC 711.
77. (unrep, HCA 1584/2010, 16 July 2012).

An "appropriate" use of a *Redgrave*-type approach can be seen in the Hong Kong case of *Wong Ka Lee v EL Fight Sports (HK)*[78] where the defendant's unconscionable and repeated assertions that the plaintiff had to pay for extra martial arts classes as her quota was exhausted, was found to be fraudulent (not least because the mentally unstable plaintiff was in hospital on some of the dates when she was alleged to have had lessons!). Whether the plaintiff could have discovered the truth (as asserted by the defendant) was regarded as irrelevant and rescission was granted.

9.1.5 A Contract with the Representor

A statement can only be a misrepresentation if it induces the representee to make a contract *with the representor*. If the representor suffers loss in some other way as a result of acting on the statement, for example by forming a loss-making contract with a third party, no action can lie in misrepresentation, though an action in the tort of negligence may be possible.[79]

9.2 Rescission for Misrepresentation

Rescission involves returning the contracting parties to their original, pre-contractual position. Since misrepresentation makes a contract "voidable" rather than void, it will remain in force unless and until the representee exercises his right to rescind it. The representee has a choice on discovering the misrepresentation: he may "affirm" and carry on with the contract or he may rescind and cancel. Once the choice has been made the representee may not change his mind; his "election" is final.

9.2.1 Form of Rescission

Rescission requires that the parties return to their pre-contractual position. This state of affairs may be produced amicably by, for example, a mutual return of goods and the price thereof. More commonly, the representee will require an order of rescission from the court. It is nearly always the case that rescission cannot be effected until the representee has made known his intention to rescind to the representor. This will be practically very difficult where the misrepresentation has been made by a fraudulent representor who intends to disappear as soon as possible and who may well not have given his real name. In such a situation, exceptionally, a court has allowed a representee to rescind by taking all reasonable steps short of communicating with the dishonest representor.

---

78. [2021] 2 HKC 644.
79. Via the doctrine which emerged from *Hedley Byrne & Co Ltd v Heller & Partners Ltd* [1964] AC 465, [1963] 3 WLR 101 and subsequent related decisions.

Car and Universal Finance v Caldwell[80]

The defendant sold a car to a rogue who paid with a bad cheque and vanished. The defendant discovered the fraud and, with no hope of finding the rogue, immediately informed the police and the Automobile Association who issued a "stop list" to people in the motor trade. The plaintiffs bought the car in good faith from M Ltd, who were motor dealers. There was a dispute as to title and the Court of Appeal unanimously held for the defendant as his notification was held to be an effective rescission.

Upjohn LJ stated:

> Where one party to a contract has an option unilaterally to rescind or disaffirm it by reason of the fraud or misrepresentation of the other party, he must elect to do so within a reasonable time . . . he must in the ordinary course communicate his intention to rescind to the other party.
>
> If one party, by absconding, deliberately puts it out of the power of the other to communicate his intention to rescind which he knows the other will almost certainly want to do, I do not think he can any longer insist on his right to be made aware of the election to determine the contract. In these circumstances communication is a useless formality. I think that the law must allow the innocent party to exercise his right of rescission otherwise than by communication or repossession. To hold otherwise would be to allow a fraudulent contracting party by his very fraud to prevent the innocent party from exercising his undoubted right.[81]

The decision has been criticised on the basis that it undermines the purpose of section 23 of the English Sale of Goods Act 1979,[82] which states that a sale by a party with a voidable title should confer a good title on an innocent purchaser unless there has already been a rescission. If rescission becomes easier the intention to protect the innocent third party in these situations will be defeated. This would also be out of line with the general trend in "mistaken identity" cases, to support the innocent third party.[83] In practice, the decision will almost certainly be limited to its special facts; the court was doubtless influenced by the fact that M Ltd were motor car dealers and therefore had "notice" of the fraud via the stop-list. Since M Ltd's title was therefore void anyone acquiring from them would obtain a similarly void title.

9.2.2 Bars to Rescission

Since the common law permits rescission only for fraud, the remedy is primarily equitable. While it is available for all categories of misrepresentation—fraudulent,

---

80. [1965] 1 QB 525, [1964] 2 WLR 600, [1964] 1 All ER 290.
81. [1964] 2 WLR 600 at 612–613.
82. Enacted in Hong Kong as Sale of Goods Ordinance (Cap 26) s 25.
83. See discussion of mistaken identity in chapter 10 at 10.5.2 and compare *Newtons of Wembley Ltd v Williams* [1965] 1 QB 560.

negligent and wholly innocent—rescission is subject to certain "bars", that is, situations where the remedy will not be granted.

Following legislative changes,[84] the four remaining bars are: affirmation; undue lapse of time; unavailability of full restitution; and the acquiring of contrary rights by an innocent third party. In addition to these specific bars, there is now a general discretion for a court to award damages "in lieu of" (instead of) rescission, wherever it is dealing with a claim for rescission but feels that damages would be a more appropriate remedy.[85]

9.2.2.1 Affirmation

"Affirmation" refers to the representee's decision to continue with the contract despite his awareness of a right to rescind.[86] The decision to affirm is final and a representee who has chosen to affirm cannot subsequently rescind. In *Long v Lloyd*,[87] the plaintiff bought a lorry from the defendant following alleged misrepresentations by the defendant as to the quality of the vehicle. When defects were first discovered the parties agreed to share the cost of repairs and continue with the contract. Following a subsequent breakdown of the lorry, and without a remedy in damages,[88] the plaintiff sought to rescind the contract. It was held that his previous decision to continue constituted an affirmation which deprived him of the right subsequently to rescind.

9.2.2.2 Lapse of Time

Rescission will also be barred where the representee takes too long to seek the remedy.

Leaf v International Galleries[89]

The plaintiff bought a painting from the defendant which both believed to be by the artist John Constable. Five years later the plaintiff discovered that the painting

---

84. Misrepresentation Ordinance (Cap 284) s 2, following the UK Misrepresentation Act 1967 s 1 which removed two previous bars relating to representations which later became terms and fully performed contracts.

85. Misrepresentation Act 1967 s 2(2); Misrepresentation Ordinance s 3(2).

86. It is not affirmation merely to continue after becoming aware of the misrepresentation. One must also be aware of the right to rescind therefor (see *Peyman v Lanjani* [1984] 3 All ER 703 where the claimant knew of the misrepresentation but, as a foreigner receiving incomplete legal advice, did not know he could therefore rescind).

87. [1958] 2 All ER 402.

88. The statements as to quality had not become terms and, at the time, no damages were available for non-fraudulent misrepresentation.

89. [1950] 2 KB 86, [1950] 1 All ER 693.

was not by John Constable and tried to rescind for misrepresentation. The plaintiff's claim was unanimously rejected by the English Court of Appeal.

Denning LJ expressed the view that the case involved breach of a condition in a sale of goods contract which would have permitted the buyer to reject the goods but for the fact that he had accepted them. The right to reject having been lost for breach of a condition, the buyer had sought to rescind for misrepresentation rather than claim damages. Denning LJ stated:

> five years passed before he intimated any rejection. That, I need hardly say, is much more than a reasonable time. It is far too late for him at the end of five years to reject this picture for breach of any condition. His remedy after that length of time is for damages only, a claim which he has not brought before the court.
>
>   . . . an innocent misrepresentation is much less potent than a breach of condition. A condition is a term of the contract of a most material character, and, if a claim to reject for breach of condition is barred, it seems to me *a fortiori* that a claim to rescission on the ground of innocent misrepresentation is also barred.[90]

Leaf is not a case of affirmation since the plaintiff acted promptly on discovering the misrepresentation. Instead the case illustrates the equitable principle of "laches"; that excessive delay will preclude an equitable remedy. However, the "delay" bar must now be seriously doubted (at least as far as English law is concerned) since the Court of Appeal decision in *Salt v Stratstone Specialist Ltd*[91] suggested it was no longer good law given the implementation of section 1 of the Misrepresentation Act 1967.[92] Since section 1 is replicated in Hong Kong by section 2 of the Misrepresentation Ordinance, it is reasonable to assume that the "delay" bar would no longer be applied in Hong Kong.

9.2.2.3 Restitution Impossible

A further bar to rescission involves the *restitutio in integrum* principle, whereby, since rescission requires a reversion to the status quo prior to the formation of the contract, the remedy is barred where such a reversion is impossible. In practice the courts apply some flexibility and require only that the parties must be able to return, *substantially*, to their pre-contractual position.[93]

---

90. [1950] 1 All ER 693 at 694. It should be noted that, at the time, there was no category of negligent misrepresentation, either at common law or under statute. "Innocent" in this context, therefore, means merely non-fraudulent.
91. [2015] EWCA Civ 745.
92. A further influential factor in *Salt* was that s 35 of the Sale of Goods Act 1893 (on which Denning LJ had relied in his judgment) had been amended by the 1979 SGA.
93. See, for example, *Hulton v Hulton* [1917] 1 KB 813.

9.2.2.4 Rights of Innocent Third Party

The final bar to rescission arises where a return to the pre-contractual position would have an adverse effect on an innocent third party. In such cases rescission is generally barred, though the *Caldwell* case[94] provides a rare exception. Many "innocent third party" cases involve a mistaken identity situation caused by the fraudulent misrepresentation of a "rogue". In *Lewis v Averay*,[95] the plaintiff advertised his car for sale and was induced to part with it, in return for a worthless cheque, by a rogue who falsely claimed to be Richard Green, a then famous actor. The agreement would, of course, have been voidable as against the rogue but he had sold the car on to the innocent defendant. Since an innocent third party had acquired an interest in the car, rescission was no longer possible. As a result, the defendant obtained a good title to the car and the plaintiff's action against him was unanimously rejected by the Court of Appeal.

Voidability for misrepresentation will not, therefore, assist the defrauded party, other than in the highly unlikely scenario that he can contact the "rogue" before the latter has sold on to an innocent third party. Since an action against the fraudulent rogue is practically unlikely, the defrauded party will bear the loss *unless* he can convince the court that the contract with the rogue was not merely voidable but void *ab initio* on the grounds of mistake. The relationship, in this context, between misrepresentation and mistaken identity will be considered in more detail in the next chapter.[96]

9.2.2.5 Damages in Lieu of Rescission

Under s3(2) of the Misrepresentation Ordinance, whenever a party seeks rescission on the grounds of misrepresentation, a court has the discretion to order that the contract must continue in force and to give the claimant damages instead. This "discretionary bar" to rescission will be dealt with below.[97]

9.2.3 Indemnity

In addition to any claim for rescission in equity, a representee may also seek a so-called "indemnity". Historically, equity would not grant damages but would permit indemnity. This indemnity is recoverable whether the misrepresentation is fraudulent, negligent, or wholly innocent. However, the award is far more restrictive than damages in that only sums *automatically* expended as a result of making the contract

---

94. See 9.2.1.
95. [1972] 1 QB 198, [1971] 3 All ER 907, [1971] 3 WLR 603 and see 10.5.2.
96. See chapter 10 at 10.5.2.
97. See 9.3.4.

are recoverable; merely "foreseeable" loss will not be compensated. The limitations of indemnity are well illustrated by the following case.

Whittington v Seale-Hayne[98]

The plaintiffs, who were poultry breeders, were induced to take a lease on premises by the defendant's non-fraudulent misrepresentation that the premises were sanitary. The plaintiffs agreed, in the lease, to fulfil any works required by the local authority. As a result of the premises not being sanitary the plaintiffs suffered various losses including loss of stock, loss of profits and cost of medical treatment for their manager. The plaintiffs claimed rescission, which was granted. They also sought to recover compensation for their losses but were largely unsuccessful.

Farwell J attempted to distinguish the concept of indemnity from that of damages. He stated:

> The defendant admits liability so far as regards anything which was paid under the contract, but not in respect of any damages incurred by reason of the contract; and I think the defendant's view is the correct one.

Farwell J then quoted with approval the following words of Bowen LJ in the Court of Appeal case of *Newbigging v Adam*:[99]

> It seems to me that when you are dealing with innocent misrepresentation that you must understand that proposition that he is to be placed *in statu quo* with this limitation—that he is not to be replaced in exactly the same position in all respects, otherwise he would be entitled to recover damages, but is to be replaced in his position so far as regards the rights and obligations which have been *created* by the contract into which he has been induced to enter.[100]

In practice, this meant that the plaintiff was entitled to the cost of rendering the premises sanitary and paying rent/rates (a legal requirement) but not, for example, compensation for the loss of profit on lost stock since such loss, though foreseeable, was not an inevitable consequence of the contract.[101]

Curiously, in *Link Folk Ltd v Glorious Motors Ltd*,[102] the trial judge Au-Yeung DDJ awarded the plaintiff rescission on the grounds of the defendants' *negligent* misrepresentation but limited the additional monetary award to what he called an

---

98. (1900) 82 LT 49.
99. (1886) 34 Ch D 582.
100. Ibid at 590.
101. There would now be the possibility of a claim for damages under s 2(1) of the Misrepresentation Act 1967, as well as the rescission claim; see 9.3.3.
102. (unrep, DCCJ 552/2010, 15 September 2011).

"indemnity". This despite the fact that negligent misrepresentation permits an action for rescission *and* damages.[103]

9.3 Damages for Misrepresentation

Until legislative and common law change in the 1960s, there was no provision for damages for misrepresentation in the absence of fraud or a "fiduciary" relationship between the parties. As a result, representees seeking damages would often assert that what appeared to be a pre-contractual representation was actually a term. Courts favourably disposed towards the claimant would sometimes accede to the argument that the statement was a term in order to permit the award of damages. This occurred particularly where the statement was crucial to the formation of a contract or where it was made by a party with superior skill or knowledge on which the other relied. A good example from the English courts is provided by the case of *Dick Bentley Productions Ltd v Harold Smith (Motors) Ltd*,[104] where a statement by a dealer as to a car's mileage was regarded as a term because the customer relied upon it, even though the statement was not repeated in the formal contract of sale.

The need to "convert" representations became less pressing with the recognition of a category of negligent misstatements at common law[105] and, more importantly, with the passing, in England, of the Misrepresentation Act 1967, soon followed, in Hong Kong, by the Misrepresentation Ordinance. The introduction, in this legislation, of a presumption of liability and the adoption of a scale of damages based on the tort of deceit meant that remedies for misrepresentation were generally as good as, and sometimes better than, those for breach of contract. While the statutory actions will now generally be used by the claimant, the common law actions will also be considered.

9.3.1 Damages for Deceit

In theory, a representee may still bring an action in the tort of deceit. Here, the representee must show that the representor was deliberately dishonest in making his statement or was at least reckless as to its accuracy. While the damages awarded will include compensation for all direct consequences of entering into the subsequent contract,[106] deceit is very hard to prove and this form of action is now unlikely to be attractive. The difficulty in succeeding in deceit is illustrated by the following landmark case.

---

103. Cf 9.3.3 infra. To add to the confusion, the judge awarded sums which were clearly damages rather than indemnity.
104. [1965] 1 WLR 623, [1965] 2 All ER 65 and see 8.1.4.
105. Via the *Hedley Byrne* line of cases which extended the scope of the tort of negligence in respect of negligent statements.
106. There is no justification for restricting the victim of fraud to compensation only for foreseeable loss.

Derry v Peek[107]

The appellants stated that they had "the right to use steam or mechanical motive power", in their tram operation, believing that the necessary Board of Trade permission would be granted as a matter of course. The respondents bought shares on the strength of this statement. Permission was subsequently denied and the company was wound up. The respondents claimed damages for deceit. The action failed in the House of Lords which held that there was no deceit.

The views of Lord Herschell were shared by his fellow law lords. He said:

> Such an action differs essentially from one brought to obtain rescission of a contract on the ground of misrepresentation of a material fact . . . Where rescission is claimed it is only necessary to prove that there was misrepresentation; then, however honestly it may have been made, however free from blame the person who made it, the contract, having been obtained by misrepresentation, cannot stand. In an action of deceit, on the contrary, it is not enough to establish misrepresentation alone; it is conceded on all hands that something more must be proved to cast liability upon the defendant, though it has been a matter of controversy what additional elements are requisite.
>
> . . . A man who forms his belief carelessly, or is unreasonably credulous, may be blameworthy when he makes a representation on which another is to act, but he is not, in my opinion, fraudulent . . .
>
> To prevent a false statement being fraudulent, there must, I think, always be an honest belief in its truth. And this probably covers the whole ground, for one who knowingly alleges that which is false, has obviously no such honest belief.[108]

The law lords concluded that there was no deliberate dishonesty and therefore no deceit. Given that the representee's action here failed even though the representor had no grounds for his belief, and, indeed, *knew* it to be literally untrue,[109] deceit is clearly difficult to prove. A rare Hong Kong example is provided in *Santani Ltd v Shum Shuk Fong*,[110] where the trial judge, Burrell DJ, came to the conclusion that the defendant had told the plaintiff, to induce her to buy a flat and car park from her well over the market price, that she would have "no problem"[111] with the tenancy of a garden commercially leased from the government, provided that she made no alterations (the defendant denied this unsuccessfully). In fact, the defendant had had several problems involving her erection of illegal structures in the garden. The judge granted damages for "fraudulent misrepresentation" (deceit). The judge further

---

107. (1889) 14 App Cas 337.
108. Ibid at 342.
109. The appellants did not say they "expected" to have the right to use steam power but that they *had* such a right.
110. [2013] 2 HKLRD 131.
111. The defendant's contention that this was a promise as to the future rather than of present fact was rejected.

expressed the view that the defendant could not plead an honest belief in her statement, given that she had denied ever making it!

Where dishonesty *is* proved, however, the defendant will be liable for all consequential losses, foreseeable or not. The courts' hostility to the deceitful representor does not allow for a defence that losses were "unforeseeable". Moreover, the courts may, exceptionally, even permit recovery of damages, in a sale situation, for loss which has been increased by the time of judgment, not restricting the claimant to the "difference in value" at the date of the transaction.

Smith New Court Securities Ltd v Scrimgeour Vickers (Asset Management) Ltd[112]

The plaintiff company bought shares at an inflated 82.25 pence per share as a result of the defendants' fraudulent assertion that there was a rival bidder. The shares were worth about 78 pence each. Before the plaintiffs discovered the fraud, a quite separate major fraud on the company reduced the value of its shares to less than 40 pence per share. There was no doubt of the defendants' liability but the question was whether compensation should be on the basis of the difference between 82.25 and 78 pence (the difference at the time of sale) *or* 82.25 and less than 40 pence (the date at trial). The House of Lords imposed the latter figure, which produced a greatly larger *quantum* of damages.

Lord Browne-Wilkinson stated:

> it is not an inflexible rule that the plaintiff must bring into account the value as at the transaction date of the asset acquired: . . . the plaintiff [is required] to mitigate his loss once he is aware of the fraud. So long as he is not aware of the fraud, no question of a duty to mitigate can arise.[113]

Hostility towards the fraudulent representor can also be seen in the following English case.

4 Eng Ltd v Harper & Simpson[114]

The defendants sold the shares in a company they owned (and managed) to the claimants having fraudulently exaggerated its worth. The company then went into liquidation. The claimants sued for damages and recovered:

1. the purchase price of the company;
2. the costs incurred in acquiring the company (legal costs, stamp duty, etc);
3. the cost of investigating the fraud;

---

112. [1997] AC 254, [1996] 4 All ER 769.
113. [1996] 4 All ER 769 at 777–778.
114. [2008] EWHC 915.

4. the loss of a chance to buy another (profitable) company, T Ltd which it had considered acquiring.

Richards J, applying the same reasoning as in *East v Maurer*,[115] held that there was an 80% chance they would have been successful in acquiring T. He therefore allowed 80% of the notional profitability of acquiring T Ltd by way of damages. Richards J stated:

> It does not previously appear to have been decided that damages for the loss of a chance are recoverable for deceit but . . . if the loss of a chance is damage directly caused by the defendant's deceit, it is as much within the scope of damages for deceit as the hypothetical alternative business established on the balance of probabilities in *East v Maurer*.[116]

The judge estimated profitability based on profits which could have been made while owning T Ltd and the profits from any subsequent sale of the profitable business. The tortious nature of the damages were stressed; the purpose is to put the claimant in the position he would have been but for the misrepresentation.[117] In this case but for the misrepresentation the claimant would have bid for T Ltd (with an 80% chance of success).

9.3.2 Damages in the Tort of Negligence

The second *theoretical* option to obtain misrepresentation damages involves an action in the tort of negligence, asserting that the representor owed a duty to the representee under the principle first established in the case of *Hedley Byrne & Co Ltd v Heller & Partners Ltd*.[118] Although it was previously established, in English law, that such a duty of care may exist even though the parties subsequently enter into a contract,[119] in practice, this form of action was always unlikely to be used since a statutory action, under the Misrepresentation Ordinance, is preferable for the claimant.[120] *Hedley Byrne* actions, which derive from the duty of care of a party giving expert advice in the context of a "special relationship",[121] were likely, in practice, only to be brought where a negligent statement resulted in loss to the claimant *other than* by making a contract with the maker of the statement.[122] Indeed,

---

115. Discussed at 9.3.3 below.
116. [2008] EWHC 915 at 931.
117. See 9.3.3 below.
118. [1964] AC 465.
119. *Esso Petroleum Co Ltd v Mardon* [1976] QB 801, [1976] 2 WLR 583, [1976] 2 All ER 5.
120. See 9.3.3 below.
121. Subsequent (untypical) cases even found the necessary relationship where the careless statement was made other than to the claimant, provided that his potential loss should have been in the representor's contemplation: see *Ross v Caunters* [1979] 3 WLR 605.
122. See, for example, *Smith v Eric S Bush (A Firm)* [1990] 1 AC 83.

the case that established the common law duty (*Esso v Mardon*)[123] owed much to the "policy" consideration that the Misrepresentation Act 1967 could not be invoked as the relevant careless statements preceded the coming into force of the statute.

The English courts have since indicated (arguably *obiter*) that where the representee subsequently makes a contract with the representor any right of action *must* be via the statute rather than the common law.[124] This (post-1997) determination is not binding on Hong Kong courts which may choose to follow the pre-1997 English common law position. In practice, as has been explained,[125] this is relatively insignificant, since the statutory claim is preferable. The possible overlap between an action in "pure" negligence (under *Hedley Byrne*) "statutory presumed negligence" (next) can be attributed to the fact that the legislation was passed to fill a lacuna which had already been partly filled by contemporaneous common law tort developments.[126]

9.3.3 Damages under Section 3(1) of the Misrepresentation Ordinance

This statutory action, which is additional to any claim for rescission, arises via the presumption of liability imposed by section 3(1) of the Misrepresentation Ordinance, which follows section 2(1) of the (English) Misrepresentation Act 1967. This subsection enacts that:

> Where a person has entered into a contract after a misrepresentation has been made to him by another party thereto and as a result thereof he has suffered loss, then, if the person making the misrepresentation would be liable to damages in respect thereof had the misrepresentation been made fraudulently, that person shall be so liable notwithstanding that the misrepresentation was not made fraudulently, unless he proves that he had reasonable grounds to believe and did believe up to the time the contract was made that the facts represented were true.

The unquestioned consequence of this enactment is that where the representee suffers loss as a result of making a contract with the representor following the latter's misrepresentation, the representor will have to pay damages unless he can prove that he genuinely *and reasonably* believed in the truth of his statement up to the time when the contract was made. The loss-suffering representee thus does not have to prove fault on the representor's part; *the representor has to disprove it*. Given this reversal of the normal burden of proof, an action under this subsection will almost always be preferable to an action in common law negligence via the *Hedley Byrne*

---

123. Note 114 above.
124. See *IFE Fund SA v GSI International* [2007] EWCA Civ 811.
125. See Overview above and 9.3.3 below.
126. See Brener, cited at n 13 above.

doctrine.[127] In practice, where there is both reliance on a statement and a contract is made with its maker, the claimant may sometimes sue under both *Hedley Byrne* and the Misrepresentation Act/Ordinance.[128]

It is now clear that both in Hong Kong and England, damages under this subsection are tortious.[129] The purposes of tort damages is to put the claimant, as far as money can do, into his pre-tort position. Thus, the representee, under section 3(1), should be put back to the position he would have been in had the misrepresentation not induced him to make the contract. Contractual damages, on the other hand, seek to put the claimant into the position he should have been had the contract been fulfilled. The significance of a tortious approach is illustrated in the following Hong Kong case.

Polaroid Far East Ltd v Bel Trade Co Ltd and Others[130]

The respondents supplied film to the respondents on the basis of their fraudulent assurance that the film was only to be used in the PRC. The appellants re-exported 96% of the film purchased to more lucrative markets in North America and Europe. The respondents were awarded damages for fraudulent misrepresentation and the appellants appealed against the *quantum* (amount) of damages. A majority of the Hong Kong Court of Appeal upheld the original decision on *quantum*.

Hunter JA, for the majority, stated:

> It is accepted that for fraudulent misrepresentation "the object of damages is to compensate the plaintiff for all the loss he has suffered, so far, again, as money can do it" per Lord Denning MR in *Doyle v Olby Ironmonger Ltd* [1962] 2 QB 158, 167. By reason of this fraud, the plaintiff was induced to part with 600 films at a specially discounted price and with some "free goods" for nothing. Value in such circumstances means "real or actual value . . . or in other words . . . the price which . . . the property would have fetched as between reasonable and honest sellers and purchasers" . . . These goods were obtained in Hong Kong. The dealer's list price there, albeit by reason of the plaintiff's monopoly fixed by the plaintiff, was the price at which "reasonable and honest dealers" bought. It was the only price at which Bel Trade, had it behaved honestly, could have bought. The judge accordingly accepted that it represented the true value of these goods.
>
> [The purpose is] to place them in a position in which they would have been if the deceit had not been perpetrated . . . the fair and proper test to apply is that which we would have applied if the defendant had deprived the plaintiffs of their goods

---

127. For an example of how onerous this can be for the representor, see *Howard Marine & Dredging Co Ltd v Ogden & Sons (Excavations) Ltd* [1978] 2 All ER 1134; discussed at 9.5.

128. For an English case example, see *Thomson v Christie Manson & Woods Ltd & Others* [2005] EWCA Civ 555.

129. *Naughton v O'Callaghan* [1990] 3 All ER 191 (despite some earlier English court *dicta* to the effect that damages would be contractual).

130. [1990] HKLR 447.

by converting them—in other words, the market value and not the cost of replacing them.[131]

It is easy to say that the plaintiff should be returned to the position he would have been in had the misrepresentation not been made but this involves considerable speculation. In the *Polaroid* case the respondents would not have supplied their film to the appellants, but what would they have done instead? It may be that a more satisfactory result would be that the defendant, in a case like this, should be required to account for profits received via fraud. This is counter to the theory of contractual damages, that they should compensate and not punish, but fraudulent misrepresentation (deceit) damages are not contractual. A similar approach to the *Polaroid* one was taken by the English Court of Appeal in the following case.

East v Maurer[132]

The plaintiff had bought a hair salon induced by the defendant's false representations that he would no longer work in his neighbouring salon and intended to move abroad. The plaintiff, despite all her efforts, was unable to trade successfully in the new salon because of the defendant's continued competition and established name. The plaintiff's action in deceit was successful. The trial judge awarded damages based on the profits the plaintiff should have obtained, absent the defendant's competition. That figure was reduced on appeal where it was held that such an approach was contractual rather than tortious. The correct tort approach was to ask what the plaintiff would have done but for the misrepresentations. The most likely, albeit speculative, scenario was that she would have spent the money on another salon. Damages would be assessed on the basis of likely profits on the hypothetical alternative salon.[133]

Given that section 3(1) damages are tortious, there remains the question as to which tort is applicable. The use of the words "so liable" may indicate that damages under the subsection should be calculated on the same basis as for the tort of deceit. This was certainly the view reached by the Hong Kong courts in the following case.

Pepsi-Cola International Ltd v Charles Lee[134]

The plaintiffs had taken a tenancy of a house following a misrepresentation by the defendant's agent that vacant land surrounding the house was included in the tenancy. After the land had been improved by the tenant as a garden, building construction work began on it. The plaintiffs' action for misrepresentation under section 3(1) was successful. The court had to decide on the appropriate standard to apply in

---

131. Ibid at 451.
132. [1991] 2 All ER 733.
133. Similarly, in the *Santini* case (cf 9.3.1 supra), damages were based on the difference between the cost of the flat and car park bought based on misrepresentations and that of a similar flat and car park.
134. [1974] HKLR 13.

awarding damages under the subsection. Damages were awarded based on the difference between what was paid by the plaintiff and what the house was worth without a garden plus the cost of the landscaping done by the plaintiff.

The trial judge, Cons J, stated:

> I am told that there has yet been no reported case which illustrates the standard by which such damages should be calculated, but it seems clear from the language of the section itself that it would be the standard otherwise adopted in actions based upon deceit, that is what the plaintiff has paid, less the value of what he has received, together with damages for any consequential loss which is not too remote.[135]

Cons J, therefore, adopted a literalist approach to support the so-called "fiction of fraud", whereby the careless representor is to be treated in the same way as a fraudulent one. It took some years for the English courts to reach the same conclusion.[136] The "fiction of fraud" approach continued to be criticised by most academic writers who favoured the negligence approach, since the representor liable under section 3(1) has usually been careless rather than fraudulent. However, the views of the academics were ignored by the English courts in the following curious case.

Royscot Trust Ltd v Rogerson and Another[137]

The first defendant, a customer, and the second defendant, a car dealer, misrepresented the sums involved in their hire purchase arrangement so as to give the impression that the customer had paid 20% of the price as deposit. This was necessary in order to induce the plaintiffs, a finance company, to finance the agreement. Since the amount outstanding was not misrepresented it appeared that the plaintiffs would not be prejudiced. However, the first defendant wrongfully sold the car and the honest buyer obtained good title. The plaintiffs sued for damages under section 2(1) of the Misrepresentation Act 1967. Both defendants were held liable for the loss of the car since, whether or not the result would have been foreseeable by the second defendant, it was nonetheless a "direct" consequence of his misrepresentation. The analogy was to be the tort of deceit, rather than negligence, and this permits recovery for all direct consequences of a statement, foreseeable or not.

The Court of Appeal judges in *Royscot* spent considerable time in contradicting the academic criticism of the fiction of fraud. Balcombe LJ, having examined various academic writings, concluded:

> In my judgment the wording of the subsection is clear: the person making the innocent misrepresentation shall be "so liable," ie, liable to damages as if the representation had been made fraudulently.

---

135. Ibid at 19.
136. See *Chesneau v Interholme* (1983) 134 NLJ 341.
137. [1991] 2 QB 297, [1991] 3 All ER 294, [1991] 3 WLR 57.

... With all respect to the various learned authors whose works I have cited above, it seems to me that to suggest that a different measure of damage applies to an action for innocent misrepresentation under the section than that which applies to an action for fraudulent misrepresentation [deceit] at common law is to ignore the plain words of the subsection and is inconsistent with the cases to which I have referred. In my judgment, therefore, the finance company is entitled to recover from the dealer all the losses which it suffered as a result of its entering into the agreements with the dealer and the customer, even if those losses were unforeseeable, provided that they were not otherwise too remote.[138]

In short, the representor is told, "convince us that you were neither fraudulent nor negligent or we will treat you as fraudulent". So attractive is the subsection for claimants that actions for deceit are unlikely to be brought unless the plaintiff wants the satisfaction of branding the representor as fraudulent in court. A further caveat regarding an action in deceit is that the formal pleading is difficult, and the plaintiff needs to give clear evidence of the representor's absence of honest belief.[139]

Nonetheless, academic reservations have not disappeared and, however sound the *Pepsi Cola* and *Royscot* approaches may be from a literal perspective, serious doubts remain as to the ethical case for treating the "presumed negligent" representor under section 3(1) in the same way as the deliberate fraudster.[140] There is some indication that the English courts may be rethinking their position[141] and, should they change their minds, it will be for the Hong Kong courts to decide their own way forward.[142] In the *Scrimgeour Vickers* case, discussed above,[143] the court had the power to overturn *Royscot* but felt the fiction of fraud issue was not before them. In the latter case of *Forest International Gaskets Ltd v Fosters Marketing Ltd*[144] the fiction of fraud was relevant, but the English Court of Appeal felt that the difference in *quantum* of damages between the fraud and negligence approach was not significant enough to justify the expense of an appeal to the House of Lords, though this may have resolved the "fiction" debate. Were the fiction of fraud to be abolished in English law by the UK Supreme Court, this would not necessarily affect Hong Kong, given the solely "persuasive" value of post-1997 English/UK decisions. However, as

---

138. [1991] 3 WLR 57 at 64.
139. See *Chow How Yeen Margaret v Wex Pharmaceuticals Inc* [2018] 3 HKLRD 163.
140. In "Realist" terms, the *Royscot* Court of Appeal may have regarded the case as one of "unpleaded fraud".
141. See Lord Steyn's judgment in *Smith New Court Securities Ltd v Scrimgeour Vickers (Asset Management) Ltd* discussed in 9.3.1. Reservations have also been expressed by Arden LJ in *Spice Girls v Aprilia* (ante) and by Rix J in *Avon Insurance plc v Swire Fraser Ltd* [2000] 1 All ER (Comm) 573.
142. It should be stressed that the "fiction of fraud" was first asserted in the Hong Kong courts (*Pepsi-Cola* case) and that *Royscot* (which follows the *Pepsi-Cola* approach) has been endorsed here: *Long Year Development Ltd v Tse Fuk Man Norman* [1991] 2 HKC 393.
143. Discussed at 9.3.1.
144. [2005] EWCA Civ 700.

noted in chapter 2, Hong Kong courts continue to give significant attention to such decisions, especially those decided at the highest level.

9.3.4 Damages under Section 3(2) of the Misrepresentation Ordinance

Finally, in this context, damages may be awarded, at the discretion of the court, under section 3(2) of the Misrepresentation Ordinance, which follows section 2(2) of the English legislation. Section 3(2) enacts that:

> Where a person has entered into a contract after a misrepresentation has been made to him otherwise than fraudulently, and he would be entitled, by reason of the mis-representation, to rescind the contract, then, if it is claimed, in any proceedings arising from the contract, that the contract ought to be or has been rescinded the court or arbitrator may declare the contract subsisting and award damages in lieu of rescission, if of opinion that it would be equitable to do so, having regard to the nature of the misrepresentation and the loss that would be caused by it if the contract were upheld, as well as to the loss that rescission would cause to the other party.

What is clear is that *whenever* a plaintiff seeks rescission, the subsection gives the court an absolute discretion to award damages, and treat the contract as still subsisting, where appropriate. Damages under this subsection, unlike those under section 3(1), are *instead of* rather than *additional to* rescission. The award of damages under this subsection can be made even though the representor's statement was made honestly and with reasonable grounds; it is the only basis, therefore, on which damages can be awarded for a "wholly innocent" misrepresentation.

Two issues remain unclear; first, how damages are to be calculated under this subsection, and second, whether section 3(2) damages can be awarded in situations where rescission itself would have been "barred".[145]

9.3.4.1 Measure of Damages under the Subsection

On the first issue, some guidance is provided by the following English case.

William Sindall plc v Cambridgeshire County Council[146]

The plaintiffs agreed to purchase land from the defendants for about £5 million. The plaintiffs obtained planning permission to build on the land 18 months later but the property market had collapsed and the site was worth half its previous value. The plaintiffs discovered a sewer which, they claimed, could not easily be re-routed. The defendants had been unaware of it and, of course, had not disclosed it. The

---

145. See 9.2.2.
146. [1994] 3 All ER 932, [1994] 1 WLR 1016.

plaintiffs claimed to rescind for mistake and misrepresentation, which would have allowed them to escape the consequences of a now unfavourable contract. The Court of Appeal held that there was no operative mistake or misrepresentation. However, *obiter*, the court discussed the question of damages in lieu of rescission and how these should be assessed.

Since the case provides rare guidance on the judicial approach to section 3(2) damages, albeit by an English court and albeit *obiter*, the words of Hoffmann LJ should be noted. He said:

> The discretion conferred by s 2(2) is a broad one, to do what is equitable . . . Under s 2(1), the measure of damages is the same as for fraudulent misrepresentation ie all loss caused by the plaintiff having been induced to enter into the contract . . . it is clear that this will not necessarily be the measure of damages under s 2(2).
>
> . . . s 2(3) contemplates that damages under s 2(2) may be less than damages under s 2(1) and should be taken into account when assessing damages under the latter subsection. This only makes sense if the measure of damages may be different.
>
> If one looks at the matter when Sindall purported to rescind, the loss which would be caused if the contract were upheld was relatively small: the £18,000 it would have cost to divert the sewer, the loss of a plot and interest charges on any consequent delay at the rate of £2,000 a day. If one looks at the matter at the date of trial, the loss would have been nil because the sewer had been diverted.
>
> The third matter to be taken into account under s 2(2) is the loss which would be caused to Cambridgeshire by rescission. This is the loss of the bargain at the top of the market . . . having to return about £8 million in purchase price and interest in exchange for land worth less than £2 million.
>
> Having regard to these matters, and in particular the gross disparity between the loss which would be caused to Sindall by the misrepresentation and the loss which would be caused to Cambridgeshire by rescission, I would have exercised my discretion to award damages in lieu of rescission.[147]

The case is significant in providing some insight into the judicial approach to damages under this subsection. Given the clearly *obiter* nature of the views of Hoffman LJ and his fellow judges on the issue, it remains open to later courts in England and Hong Kong to ignore them. Damages "in lieu" were discussed in the Hong Kong case of *Green Park Properties Ltd v Dorku*,[148] where the "broad discretion" referred to by Hoffman LJ in *Sindall* was applied. The *Green Park* case involved a misrepresentation by a vendor as to the precise scope of a property to be transferred. The defendants (belatedly) argued that even if misrepresentation were found, damages in lieu (under section 3(2)) should be applied. The Court of Appeal[149] disagreed, holding that there must be rescission rather than damages, since

---

147. [1994] 1 WLR 1016 at 1036–1038.
148. [2000] 4 HKC 538.
149. The case went to the Court of Final Appeal but the "in lieu" argument was not raised: [2002] 1 HKC 121.

the contract could not be continued and, in any event, since the precise scope of the property was singularly important to the plaintiff.[150]

9.3.4.2 Situation Where Rescission Is Barred

It remains unclear whether discretionary damages may be awarded under section 3(2) where rescission is "barred" and the Hong Kong courts have not addressed the issue. The general assumption has been that damages *cannot* be awarded under the subsection where one of the four bars to rescission exists. The rationale is that section 3(2) damages are to be given to a claimant who would have been entitled to rescind but where the court feels such a remedy would be inappropriate. Here the claimant is given damages "in lieu" (instead). Where rescission is barred, there is nothing to give damages instead of. This assumption was rejected in the High Court case of *Witter (Thomas) Ltd v TBP Industries Ltd*[151] where it was suggested that damages in lieu would be available where the right to rescind had once been available but had since been lost. However, the case is not of the highest authority and its premise was rejected shortly afterwards in the case of *Government of Zanzibar v British Aerospace (Lancaster House) Ltd*,[152] a decision of equal status The views expressed in the *Zanzibar* case are to be preferred and the matter has all but been resolved in English law by the view of the Court of Appeal in *Salt v Stratstone Specialist Ltd*[153] that the *Zanzibar* view is the correct one. Though this view may *technically* be viewed as *obiter*[154] it is certain to be applied in English law and is likely to be adopted by the Hong Kong courts.

9.4 Contributory Negligence

Contributory negligence arises most often, though not exclusively, in relation to claims in the tort of negligence. Its effect is that the plaintiff's damages are reduced according to his own share of responsibility for his loss. It has been indicated, *obiter*, in the English courts, that contributory negligence should apply to a section 2(1) action (the equivalent of a Hong Kong section 3(1) action) on the basis that the action is analogous to one brought in the tort of negligence.[155]

---

150. Damages in lieu were also denied (in broadly similar circumstances) in *Balchita Ltd v Kam Yuk Investment Co Ltd* [1983] 2 HKC 333.
151. [1996] 2 All ER 573.
152. [2000] 1 WLR 2333; followed in *Floods v Shand Construction* [2000] BRL 81 and *Pankhania v London Borough of Hackney* [2002] EWHC 2441. *Witter* is an interesting illustration of the perils of the *Pepper v Hart* doctrine in relation to statutory interpretation, since the decision was influenced by the statement of government minister, Dingle Foot, at 3 am after an all-day sitting of Parliament!
153. [2015] EWCA Civ 745.
154. Since the court found that rescission had *not* been barred.
155. See *Gran Gelato Ltd v Richcliff (Group) Ltd and Others* [1992] 1 All ER 865 per Sir Donald Nicholls VC.

However, the application of contributory negligence to section 3(1) actions is problematic since it is clear that the representee's negligence will not reduce his damages where the representor's fraud is proved via an action for deceit.[156] To apply contributory negligence to a section 3(1) action would run counter to the view of Cons J in the *Pepsi-Cola* case that the representee should be liable under section 3(1) on the same basis as for the tort of deceit.[157] Conversely, if contributory negligence is not to apply, the defendant *proved* negligent at common law, under the *Hedley Byrne* doctrine, would be able to raise contributory negligence, whereas the representor merely *presumed* negligent under section 3(1) would not!

9.5 Exemption of Liability for Misrepresentation

The rules on exemption of liability for misrepresentation are to be found in the Misrepresentation Ordinance. The amended section 4 states that:

> If a contract contains a term which would exclude or restrict—(a) any liability to which a party to a contract may be subject by reason of any misrepresentation made by him before the contract was made; or (b) any remedy available to another party to the contract by reason of such a misrepresentation, that term shall be of no effect except in so far as it satisfies the requirement of reasonableness as stated in section 3(1) of the Control of Exemption Clauses Ordinance (Cap. 71); and it is for the person claiming that the term satisfies that requirement to show that it does.

This section mirrors the English statutory rules, which include an amendment to the original section 3 of the Misrepresentation Act 1967, introduced by section 8 of the Unfair Contract Terms Act 1977.[158] The original rule was that an exclusion would not be permitted by the courts if *reliance on* the clause would be unreasonable. The new rule is that the clause itself (rather than reliance thereon) must be proved reasonable by the "exemptor". The significance of the amendment is that it makes clear that it is for the representor to prove reasonableness and that this reasonableness will be assessed as *at the time when the contract was made*[159] rather than in the light of subsequent developments. The following case is based on the pre-amendment rules.

---

156. *Alliance and Leicester Building Society v Edgestop Ltd* [1994] 2 All ER 38 per Mummery J.
157. A view endorsed by the English Court of Appeal in the *Royscot* case (discussed at length at 9.3.3).
158. While the Unfair Contract Terms Act 1977 was reproduced in Hong Kong by the Control of Exemption Clauses Ordinance (Cap 71) this enactment did not take place until 1989.
159. This point was stressed (albeit *obiter*) by Litton NPJ in *Green Park Properties Ltd v Dorku Ltd* [2002] 1 HKC 121 (CFA).

Cheng Kwok-fai v Mok Yiu-wah, Peter and Another[160]

The parties made an agreement for the sale of a flat. The vendor had misrepresented the size of the flat. On the purchaser's action for rescission, the defendant successfully relied on a term in the contract stating that:

> 20. This agreement sets out the full agreement between the parties. No warranties or representations express or implied are or have been made or given by the vendor or by any person on his behalf relating to the property or to the user thereof or the possibility of any redevelopment thereof and if any warranty or representation express or implied has been made the same is withdrawn or deemed to have been immediately before the parties entered into this agreement unless made in writing and expressed to survive this agreement.

In keeping with normal judicial practice, Godfrey J treated the "entire agreement" clause as a form of exemption.[161] However, he upheld it, stating:

> the clause is of no effect except to the extent that I am prepared to allow reliance on it as being fair and reasonable in all the circumstances of the case: see s.4 of the Misrepresentation Ordinance (Cap. 284).
>
> Should I allow the vendors to rely on Clause 20? In my judgment, I should. I have found they did nothing to mislead the purchaser . . . I see nothing unfair or unreasonable, in all the circumstances of this case, in allowing the vendors to rely on Clause 20.[162]

This case is decided on the basis of the earlier rules on excluding liability for misrepresentation where the question was whether *reliance on* the clause was reasonable. The minor amendment made by the Control of Exclusion Clauses Ordinance, that the clause itself must be proved reasonable, would be unlikely to change the outcome in such a case.

The English Court of Appeal dealt with the exemption of liability for misrepresentation in the following case.

Howard Marine & Dredging Co Ltd v Ogden & Sons (Excavations) Ltd[163]

The representors incorrectly stated the tonnage of a barge relying on incorrect Lloyd's Register figures (although they had access to correct information). The representees agreed that "the charterers' acceptance of handing over the vessel shall be conclusive that they have examined the vessel and found her . . . in every other way satisfactory to them". A majority of the Court of Appeal (Lord Denning MR dissenting) found the representors liable for breach of section 2(1) of the Misrepresentation

---

160. [1990] 2 HKLR 440.
161. See *Glory Gold* case discussed below.
162. Ibid at 451.
163. [1978] QB 574.

Act (reliance on Lloyd's was not enough!) and, further, found that reliance on the exemption clause was unreasonable in the circumstances.

The decision was a harsh one, given that the information relied upon (Lloyd's Register) is generally reliable and the majority view as to reasonableness was not shared by Lord Denning. Subsequent English cases seem to have adopted a less harsh approach towards the "exemptor". In any event, since the determination of reasonableness is largely a factual issue based on the circumstances of the case before the court, Hong Kong courts are entirely free to make their own determination as to the reasonableness (or otherwise) of an exemption clause before them, unfettered by *Howard Marine*.

A "variation" on exemption of liability for misrepresentation is the "entire agreement" clause, essentially utilising the "parol evidence rule".[164] The essence of entire agreement clauses is that the subsequent written contract contains the entire contract such that anything said before or afterwards will have no legal effect. This then raises the question of whether the courts will take note of pre-contractual "inducements" or will accept the view that anything said prior to the "entire agreement" is without effect. The tendency of the (English and) Hong Kong courts is to look at the "substance" rather than the "form" of the clause. If it operates as an exemption of liability for misrepresentation, it will be treated as such and must pass the "reasonableness" test. In *Glory Gold Ltd v Star Play Development Ltd*,[165] the defendant landlord made a false statement to a prospective tenant that there would be no letting to a rival business. On discovering the truth, the tenant sought to rescind the lease. This action was successful despite a clause in the tenancy which stated that:

> This Agreement sets out the full agreement between the parties hereto . . . no other representations, commitments, warranties or understandings, written or verbal, have been made or given relating to the Premises.

The Hong Kong Court of Appeal held that that this clause did not preclude an action for misrepresentation.[166] A similar approach was taken in *Link Folk Ltd v Glorious Motors Ltd*,[167] where a clause stating that "the traveled [*sic*] distance of such Vehicles are [*sic*] for reference only and the Vendor do [*sic*] not give any warranty or [*sic*] at all" was held, in *substance*, to be an exclusion clause which failed to satisfy the reasonableness test. This emphasis on "substance rather than form" echoes the approach seen in chapter 8 in determining whether "I assume no duty to you" is, in substance, an attempt to exclude liability for harm caused by negligence. The English courts have adopted a similar approach to the Hong Kong one, in determining whether an assertion that a representee has placed "no reliance"

---

164. See 8.2 above.
165. [2008] 2 HKLRD 416.
166. See also *Lee Fu Wing v Yan Po Ting Paul* [2009] 5 HKLRD 513.
167. (unrep, DCCJ 552/2010, 15 September 2011).

on the other party's pre-contractual representations is, in fact, an exemption of liability for misrepresentation. Thus, in *First Tower Trustees Ltd v CDS (Superstores International) Ltd*,[168] a lease contained the term:

> The tenant acknowledges that this lease has not been entered into in reliance wholly or partly on any statement or representation made by or on behalf of the tenant.

The English Court of Appeal held that in "substance" this was an attempt to exclude liability for misrepresentation and was, therefore, subject to the reasonableness test of s 3, Misrepresentation Act.

Given the "reasonableness" requirement (and general principles of equity) it seems obvious that one cannot exempt oneself from liability for intentional (fraudulent) misrepresentation. However, it has been suggested in the English courts that exemption of liability for the fraud of one's *agents* might just be possible provided that the clearest words are used[169] (the *Interfoto* approach).[170] However, in practice, there will be a strong presumption against upholding such an exemption which, in any event, would have to be proved reasonable by the "exemptor".

---

168. [2018] EWCA Civ 1396.
169. *HIH Casualty & General Insurance v Chase Manhattan Bank* [2003] UKHL 6.
170. See 8.6.1.2 above.

10

Mistake

OVERVIEW

Mistake is the most perplexing and academically complex of all the areas of contract. Some writers question the very need for its existence; others argue that its scope should be greatly limited.[1] Almost all textbooks now devote less coverage to mistake than was previously the case and many law schools omit mistake from their curriculum: avowedly because it is now less significant; in practice because it is too complicated!

The risk of making a mistake is always present when making a contract. However, the law of mistake is only concerned with the circumstances under which relief will be given to the mistaken party. In other words, the law will only grant relief when there is an "operative" mistake. Most "mistakes", as the term is understood by the layman, are inoperative. The shopper who spends too much on an item may well decide he has made a "mistake"; this will, of course, have no legal effect. To be operative, a mistake must be as to the terms of the contract and must be "reasonable". This "objective" aspect greatly reduces the scope of the doctrine of mistake since, generally, what is important is not whether a party is mistaken, but whether a reasonable person would have made such a mistake. Operative mistakes may take one of three forms: first, where both parties make the same mistake (common); second, where the parties are at cross-purposes (mutual); and third, where only one party is mistaken and the other party knows it (unilateral).[2]

The law of mistake is a complex one as it is extremely difficult to ascertain the *ratio* of many of the cases. Some important cases involve split decisions and the

---

1. See, for example, C. J. Slade, "The Myth of Mistake in the English Law of Contract", (1954) 70 LQR 386.
2. This adopts the classification used by Cheshire, Fifoot and Furmston: M. Furmston, *Cheshire, Fifoot & Furmston's Law of Contract* (Oxford/New York: Oxford University Press, 17th edn, 2016), p 282.

issue of mistake often overlaps with other areas of law such as offer and acceptance, misrepresentation and frustration.

The consequences of an operative mistake at law are that the contract is made void *ab initio* (from the beginning). This "all or nothing" approach can be harsh on an innocent third party who has obtained rights in the subject matter of the contract, as these rights can be overridden. In the past, therefore, equity intervened to provide a fairer result as between the various parties involved. The equitable approach is more flexible in that a mistake is more likely to be recognised and, if so, makes the contact "voidable"; that is, it may be set aside at the discretion of the court and made subject to such terms as the court thinks just. However, the role of equity in mistake has been controversial as it has been very difficult, if not impossible, to distinguish the test for an operative mistake at law from the test used by the courts for an operative mistake in equity. The very existence of "mistake in equity" is now questionable.

Two areas of mistake relate to documents. First, a document may be "rectified" if it does not accurately reflect the true intention so the parties. They may have written down an incorrect price or mistakenly entered other terms. Alternatively, one party may have made a mistake over the terms of the document and the other party may have deliberately taken advantage of this. An order for rectification will result in the amendment of the document to accord with the parties' true intention. The second area concerns the application of *non est factum* (it is not my deed). The application of this narrow principle serves to nullify the signature of someone who has radically misunderstood its significance. Both rectification and *non est factum* represent exceptions to the parol evidence rule[3] and the rule established in cases such as *L'Estrange v Graucob*[4] that one is bound by any document one signs; as such, the courts will only apply them in exceptional circumstances.

The role of the doctrine of mistake has been exhaustively re-examined by the higher courts in two English cases. First, in *Great Peace Shipping Limited v Tsavliris (International) Limited*,[5] the English Court of Appeal narrowed the application of equity in the area of common mistake. Second, the House of Lords in *Shogun Finance Limited v Hudson*[6] reaffirmed the strong presumption in cases of unilateral mistake that, in face-to-face situations, the contract is intended to be with the person with whom the offeror is face-to-face and not with some other person with whom he may have mistakenly thought he was dealing. Both cases have, therefore, resulted in restrictions being placed on the role of the doctrine of mistake. This role has been questioned repeatedly in the past, with some persuasive arguments for the proposition that there is no room in contract law for such a doctrine, overlapping as it does with other areas of contract law that do a much better job of achieving

---

3. See 8.2.
4. See 8.6.1.1.
5. [2002] EWCA Civ 1407.
6. [2003] 3 WLR 1371.

fairness between parties to a contract while at the same time preserving business certainty. However, there are still some areas of law where the only cause of action for a plaintiff is in mistake. This leaves the question of the apportionment of losses when an operative mistake is established. The present law on mistake often results in unfair treatment of an innocent third party and the only way to amend this position may be to enact legislation similar to that for the associated areas of frustration and misrepresentation.

10.1 Is a Doctrine of Mistake Necessary?

Serious doubts have been raised as to the need for a doctrine of mistake. In cases of "common" mistake, where both parties share the same mistaken belief, the law rarely recognises a mistake as operative unless it concerns the very existence of the subject matter (*res extincta*) or the acquisition of an interest in something the "acquirer" already owns (*res sua*). In both these cases it could be argued that there is an implied term that the subject matter still exists or does not already belong to the acquirer. Indeed, the implied term solution was preferred in the influential Australian High Court case of *McRae v Commonwealth Disposals Commission*.[7] It may be seen as significant that the "parent" case for common mistake is one where the expression "mistake" is nowhere to be found in the judgments![8]

There have been few cases where a "mutual" mistake (where the parties are at cross-purposes) has been held operative. The reason for this is that if B accepts A's offer based on a misunderstanding, this will normally be because B has carelessly misunderstood the offer, in which case B will suffer the consequences *or* because A has framed his offer ambiguously (in which case either A will bear the loss or the court will find the agreement insufficiently certain to amount to a contract). Where an operative mutual mistake *is* present, the case could equally well be determined on the basis of offer and acceptance principles.

"Unilateral" mistakes are operative only where one contracting party is aware of the other's mistake. As such, they generally involve fraud on the part of the non-mistaken party. The solution is, normally, to find that such agreement is voidable on the grounds of misrepresentation rather than void for mistake. Again, of course, "mistake", as such, is redundant. Those cases which have determined that the contract is void for unilateral mistake have invariably been the subject of criticism, not least on the basis that they have produced injustice to an innocent third party.

It should also be noted that the mere fact that "something serious" was unknown to the parties at the date of contracting will *not* invoke the doctrine of mistake where it is clear that one of the parties clearly assumed the risk that the "something serious" may eventuate. For example, in the *Mcrae* case, dealt with below, the Australian

---

7. (1950) 84 CLR 37.
8. See *Couturier* case at 10.3 below.

High Court decided that there was no operative mistake because the defendants had clearly assumed the risk of the wrecked ship's non-existence.[9]

Despite the above, there are sufficient leading cases based on a finding of mistake to conclude that, whether or not mistake *should* stand alone as a separate doctrine, in practice it does so. Before embarking on an analysis of the law of mistake, however, it should be noted that the issue of mistake only becomes relevant if the contract itself does not readily identify and allocate to the parties responsibility for mistakes. This has been recognised in a number of cases such as *William Sindall plc v Cambridgeshire CC*.[10] If, for example, a contract makes clear that a "buyer" is purchasing the "risk" of a cargo still being in existence, the courts will of course so interpret the agreement. The doctrine of mistake, therefore, is more likely to operate where the parties are relatively unsophisticated[11] and have not put much thought or expertise into the drafting of the contract and allocated the risks, including those of mistaken assumptions, accordingly.[12] There have been calls to rationalise the effect of mistake cases by the allocation of risk, either by the parties themselves in the contract terms or else by the courts. Such an approach would substitute "the construction of the contract" for a doctrine of mistake.[13]

10.2 Types of Mistake

It is useful when discussing the application of the doctrine of mistake to classify the different types of mistake. The best-known categorisation of mistakes is that of Cheshire, Fifoot and Furmston[14] which classifies mistakes as *common*, *mutual* and *unilateral*. Common mistake arises when the parties are in agreement, but that agreement assumes some fact to be true when it is not. Mutual mistake arises when the parties are at cross purposes, each misunderstanding the other. Unilateral mistake

---

9. See discussion of *Mcrae* at 10.3 below and see *Standard Chartered Bank v Banque Marocaine du Commerce Exterieure* [2006] EWHC 413.
10. [1994] 3 All ER 932, in which Hoffmann LJ quoted Steyn J in *Associated Japanese Bank (International) Ltd. v Credit du Nord SA* [1988] 3 All ER 902: "Logically, before one can turn to the rules as to mistake, whether at common law or equity, one must first determine whether the contract itself, by express or implied condition precedent or otherwise, provides who bears the risk of the relevant mistake." The "implied term" rather than "mistake" approach was also adopted in *Graves v Graves* [2007] EWCA Civ 660.
11. That expertise is a key consideration is illustrated by *George Wimpey UK Ltd v VI Components Ltd* [2005] EWCA Civ 77 where the defendants were "entitled to assume" that the claimants, "one of the country's largest construction and development enterprises" should be aware of a drafting mistake in the contract.
12. A comparison can be made with frustration (see below) which occurs after the contract has been entered into. It is easier to allocate risks already known to the parties when entering into the contract than to foresee future events and, therefore, make provision for the effects of such events in the contract.
13. Betty Ho, *Hong Kong Contract Law* (Hong Kong: Butterworths, 2nd edn, 1991), p 207 and see *Tiken* case discussed at 10.6.1 below.
14. Note 2 above.

occurs where only one party is mistaken, and is operative only where the other party is aware of the other's mistake.

In *Bell v Lever Bros*[15] Lord Atkin said: "If mistake operates at all, it operates so as to negative, or in some cases to nullify consent." Treitel[16] explains this to mean that mistake "negatives" consent where it prevents the parties from reaching agreement and it "nullifies" consent where the parties have reached agreement but one based on a fundamental mistaken assumption. Unilateral and mutual mistakes are instances where the mistake *negatives* consent; the parties never reach agreement. Common mistakes fall into the latter category of mistakes which *nullify* consent; there is true agreement but it is based on a common false assumption. One example would be a contract to paint the portrait of a third person who, unknown to the contracting parties, has already died.

10.2.1 *Effect of an Operative Mistake*

In all the above cases the mistake, if it operates at common law, will render the agreement void. Such voidness is described as *ab initio* (from the very beginning). Mistake, therefore, is the only one of the "vitiating elements" which can render a contract void as opposed to merely "voidable". There are, with mistake at common law, no "bars to rescission" as there are in misrepresentation[17] and this may have serious consequences for an innocent third party who may have acquired the property in question from the victim of the mistake. Equity, at least until recently, has had a wider scope[18] but an effect which is less drastic, rendering the agreement merely "voidable" rather than void *ab initio* and permitting the court to impose conditions on the party seeking rescission.

10.3 Common Mistake

Common mistake occurs when both parties are in agreement—there is *consensus ad idem*—but the agreement is based on a fact[19] which is not true. Whether or not a mistake is recognised as being operative depends on how serious it is. The common law only recognises the most fundamental mistakes as rendering a contract void. Equity adopts a more flexible approach in that it more readily recognises an operative mistake which will render a contract voidable rather than void and then imposes terms on the party seeking to rescind the contract. However, the role of equity in

---

15. [1932] AC 161.
16. Op cit at p 346.
17. See 9.2.2.
18. The equitable remedies of rescission, refusal of specific performance and rectification may be available.
19. The mistake may also be one "of law": *Kleinwort Benson Ltd v Malaysian Mining Corp Bhd* [1989] 1 All ER 785, extended in *Brennan v Bolt Burdon* [2004] EWCA Civ 1017 (see n 43).

mistake may be much narrower than before as a result of the *Great Peace Shipping* case, discussed below.

It is clear that a common mistake must be "fundamental" if it is to be operative. One such scenario occurs where the subject matter of the contract no longer exists at the time when the contract is made: the so-called "*res extincta*"[20] cases. The following is the best-known English example.

Couturier v Hastie[21]

The respondent shipped a cargo of corn and employed the appellant to sell it. The appellant "sold" the cargo to Callender but it had already been sold by the master of the ship as it was rotting. Callender repudiated the sale as there was no subject matter. The appellant was a "del credere" agent which meant he guaranteed payment if the buyer defaulted. The respondent sued the appellant for the price arguing that Callender was liable to pay, since he had bought a "risk" rather than a cargo, and that, therefore, the appellant was liable for Callender's default. The dispute went all the way to the House of Lords which decided that Callender was not liable to pay and that, therefore, the appellant was not liable.

A guarantee is a promise to answer for someone else's fault. In *Couturier* there was no primary debt and so the guarantor also escaped liability. Callender was not obliged to pay as the agreement was for the sale of a specific cargo and liability depended on the continued existence of the cargo. The problem with this case is that the *ratio* is difficult to determine. Some regard the agreement as void because of the common mistake as to the subject matter of the contract. However, many writers point out that the word "mistake" was not used in any of the judgments in the case and it could be explained on other grounds such as a decision as to which party assumed the risk of non-existence or lack of consideration.[22] The proposition that a mistake as to the existence of the subject matter makes a contract void is supported, in the sale of goods context, by legislation in Hong Kong and England. Section 8 of the Sale of Goods Ordinance (SOGO)[23] states that:

> Where there is a contract for the sale of specific goods, and the goods, without the knowledge of the seller, have perished at the time when the contract is made, the contract is void.

---

20. Latin for "the thing has ceased to exist". Similar considerations also apply to "*res sua*" cases, such as *Cooper v Phibbs* (1867) LR 2 HL 149, where the subject matter of a contract already belongs to the intended purchaser.
21. (1856) 5 HL Cas 673.
22. See 10.3.2 below.
23. Cap 26. Identical wording is found in the Sale of Goods Act 1979 s 6.

This proposition is not exactly synonymous with the "common mistake" approach since all that matters, under section 8, is that "the seller" is unaware that the goods have perished.[24]

Nearly one hundred years later, *Couturier* was considered in the Australian case of *McRae v Commonwealth Disposals Commission*.[25] The decision in *McRae* is not binding on English or Hong Kong courts but it does provide an interesting comparison with *Couturier*. In *McRae*, the defendants advertised for tenders for a wrecked oil tanker said to be lying off "Jourmand reef" and to contain oil. The plaintiff's tender was accepted. The plaintiff then expended a considerable amount of money searching for the wreck. It was later found that Jourmand reef did not exist and there was no wreck in the area designated. The plaintiff successfully claimed damages in the Australian High Court.[26] Damages were based on the principle that there was breach of an implied term that the boat existed and were computed on a "reliance loss" basis.[27]

The court believed that *Couturier* does *not* hold that mistakes as to the existence of the subject matter automatically make agreements void. They argued that everything depends on the *construction*[28] of the contract. If both parties contract on the assumption that an object exists the agreement can be void if the assumption proves false; but, if one party relies on the other's indication as to the existence and that other party is in a position to know the truth, the party with knowledge will bear the risk of non-existence. There was no express provision in the contract allocating the risk on non-existence of the wreck but the Commission must have known that any tenderer would rely *implicitly* on their assertion of the existence of a tanker.

The advantage of the "implied term" approach, as opposed to the "void for mistake" approach is that the former allows for damages to be paid as compensation for breach of contract rather than for the simple return of money paid. Simply returning the money paid would not have been fair for the plaintiffs who had expended considerable sums in trying to locate the wreck.

The Australian High Court accepted that the then equivalent of section 6 of the Sale of Goods Act 1979[29] supported the voidness argument but distinguished it from the *McRae* scenario on the ground that the statutory rule applies to goods which have "perished" rather than those that have never existed.

---

24. In practice, the buyer will also be unaware; it is difficult to envisage a situation in which a buyer would enter into a contract knowing the subject matter is no more.
25. (1950) 84 CLR 377.
26. The court of final appeal in Australia.
27. See 15.1.4.3.
28. The words "interpretation" and "construction" tend to be used interchangeably. Technically, "interpretation" is of the words actually used while "construction" is a determination of meaning which can include "implied" terms
29. Section 6 of the Sale of Goods Act 1893.

In England and Hong Kong, *Bell v Lever Brothers Ltd*[30] is generally regarded as being the leading case in the area of common mistake. This authority is, however, extremely problematic, not least because Lever Bros succeeded at first instance, won unanimously in the Court of Appeal and only lost (3:2) in the House of Lords. Even then only two of the law lords—Lords Atkin and Thankerton—analysed this as a case where the issue was whether or not an operative common mistake existed.

Bell v Lever Brothers Ltd[31]

An employee, Bell, was paid compensation on the early termination of his contract with Lever Brothers, the respondents. Levers would have been able to dismiss Bell without compensation, because of certain breaches of his contract of employment, of which they were then unaware. At the time of the compensation payment, Bell had forgotten the breaches so the mistake was a common one. Levers later argued that the contracts for compensation were void for mistake. The House of Lords, while recognising the possibility of a contract being void where there was a fundamental mistake as to the subject matter of the contract, nevertheless held that on the facts the contracts were not void.

The test established by the majority was expressed by Lord Thankerton who said that the common mistake must "relate to something which both parties must necessarily have accepted in their minds as an essential element of the subject matter." However, Levers had paid £50,000 to the defendant—which must have been a huge sum in 1929—when they could have dismissed him without paying any compensation. Why was the mistake not fundamental? The answer to this question is not entirely clear. McKendrick[32] suggests that a partial answer is that the court did not want to lay down a principle which would enable parties to escape from what was merely a bad bargain. More interestingly he suggests that on closer analysis of the facts the mistake may not have been as significant as it appears at first sight. It seems that the employers were very anxious to carry through the reorganisation of the company and to secure their employees' consents to the termination of their service agreements. This anxiety and urgency suggested to the majority of their Lordships that the claimants might have entered into the same agreement, even if they had known of Bell's breaches of duty. The existence of such a doubt was fatal to Lever's claim as they had the burden of proving an operative mistake.

---

30. [1932] AC 161.

31. Ibid.

32. E. McKendrick, *Contract Law: Text, Cases & Materials* (Oxford: Oxford University Press, 2017), p 292.

What is clear from the judgments is that for a common mistake to render a contract void, the mistake must be "fundamental".[33] Indeed, the examples to which the court referred were primarily *res extincta* (existence of subject matter) mistakes.

Whatever the interpretation of the test formulated by Lord Thankerton above, it is clear that a claimant seeking to prove his case is faced with a major hurdle in successfully establishing an operative common mistake following the decision in *Bell*.

The *existence* of the subject matter was obviously fundamental in *Couturier* and also in *Galloway v Galloway*,[34] where a separation deed between a man and a woman, who mistakenly thought they were married to each other, was held to be void. Similarly, in *Griffith v Brymer*,[35] a contract for the hire of a room to watch a coronation procession which had already been cancelled was held to be void. More recently, in *Associated Japanese Bank (International) v Credit du Nord*,[36] a guarantee relating to non-existent machinery was also held to be void. In this case, Steyn J discussed *Bell* and held that a mistake could make a contract void provided that it rendered the contract "essentially and radically" different from the one the parties thought they were making. This is in keeping with the view that common mistakes should be operative only in the most extreme cases, since the circumstances were viewed as analogous to *res extincta*. In the *Credit du Nord* case, a rogue represented to the plaintiffs that he owned industrial machines. The plaintiffs reasonably believed that the machines existed and entered into a sale and leaseback transaction with the rogue. The defendants guaranteed the rogue's obligations under the leaseback transaction. The rogue defaulted and it was discovered that the machines never existed. The question before the court was whether the guarantee of obligations under a lease for non-existent machines was essentially different from a guarantee of obligations under a lease for machines. The court held that it was and the guarantee was void for mistake. The mistake was clearly fundamental although, technically, the guarantee could still have been effected. An analogous case arose in *Apvovedo NV v Terry Collins*[37] where it was held that a promise to repay £1 million if documents were not obtained on time from an agent could be void for common mistake since the agent was a "rogue" who had no authority to act for the supposed principals.

In light of the above it appears that *quality* as opposed to *existence* (or *quasi*-existence) mistakes will rarely, if ever, render a contract void for common mistake. Lord Atkin in *Bell*, however, did not totally reject the idea that a mistake as to quality could ever be an operative mistake. He said:

---

33. In *Kyle Bay Ltd (t/a Astons Nightclub) v Underwriters* [2006] EWHC 607, the English court rejected mistake where the subject matter of a contract was not "essentially and radically different" from what the claimant believed it to be.
34. (1914) 30 TLR 531.
35. (1903) 19 TLR 434.
36. [1988] 3 All ER 902.
37. [2008] EWHC 775.

Mistake as to the quality of the thing contracted for raises more difficult questions. In such a case a mistake will not affect assent unless it is the mistake of both parties, and is as to the existence of some quality which makes the thing without the quality essentially different from the thing as it was believed to be.[38]

In practice, however, the courts have proved extremely reluctant to uphold a common mistake as to quality. This reluctance was confirmed in the misrepresentation case of *Leaf v International Galleries*,[39] in the English Court of Appeal. Lord Denning MR considered the applicability of mistake in the circumstances of a common mistake by the parties as to the subject matter (a painting) of the contract. Both parties erroneously believed the painting in question to be by the famous artist, Constable. This was a mistake which was arguably essential or "fundamental". Nonetheless, the mistake did not render the contract void since it was as to the quality rather than the existence of the subject matter.

10.3.1 The Role of Equity in Common Mistake

In the *Great Peace Shipping* case, the power to rescind a contract in equity, derived from *Solle v Butcher*,[40] was firmly rejected by the English Court of Appeal.

Great Peace Shipping Ltd v Tsavliris (International) Ltd[41]

The parties were mistaken about the location of the merchant vessel the *Great Peace* in relation to the evacuation of the crew of another vessel. Both parties thought that the *Great Peace* was "in close proximity" but that turned out to be erroneous. In other words, there was a common mistake. The court found that the mistake was not operative because even though the distance that the *Great Peace* was away from the stricken vessel was large it was not so far away as to be incapable of providing the required service under the contract. The Court of Appeal concluded that the agreement could not be void for mistake and, far more significantly, that in the absence of voidness, voidability in equity was not permissible since it was inconsistent with the House of Lords decision in *Bell*.

Before the decision in *Great Peace Shipping*, the Court of Appeal decision in *Solle v Butcher* had been followed in England for over 50 years. This was despite the fact that the *ratio* of *Solle* is difficult to discern (all three Court of Appeal judges had adopted different approaches in coming to their decisions) and hard to reconcile with the decision in *Bell*.

---

38. [1932] AC 161 at 218.
39. [1950] 1 All ER 693. For facts see 9.2.2.2.
40. [1949] 2 All ER 1107.
41. [2002] EWCA Civ 1407.

Solle v Butcher[42]

The parties, a landlord and tenant, had entered into a lease agreement under the mistaken assumption that the flat was free from rent control after the premises had undergone extensive alterations. As a result, the tenant had paid more than he was legally required to do and subsequently sought to recover the over-payment. The Court of Appeal found the agreement to be voidable rather than void and gave the tenant the option of rescinding the lease or continuing on the basis of the payment of his existing rent. Bucknill LJ said that the operative mistake made was that the alteration work on the flat had made it a different flat. He said this was a common mistake of fact. Lord Denning MR said that the mistake made was that the flat was not tied down to a controlled rent, whereas in fact it was. Jennings LJ, who gave a dissenting judgment, said that the mistake made was a mistake of law and was, therefore, not operative.[43]

Lord Denning noted the drastic effects of finding a contract void at law. He stated his version of the ratio in *Bell* as follows:

> The correct interpretation of that case, to my mind, is that, once a contract has been made, that is to say, once the parties, whatever their inmost states of mind, have to all outward appearances agreed with sufficient certainty in the same terms on the same subject matter, then the contract is good unless and until it is set aside for failure of some condition on which the existence of the contract depends, or for fraud, or on some equitable ground.[44]

On the last ground he noted that a court of equity would often relieve a party from the consequences of his own mistake, so long as it could do so "without injustice to third parties".

He then went on to say that this power to set aside the contract could be exercised whenever the court was of the opinion that it was unconscientious for the other party to avail himself of the legal advantage which he had obtained. He added that if a contract was not void for mistake at common law it could still be rescinded and set aside in equity if the mistake was "fundamental".

The difficulty with the exposition of this equitable doctrine is that it appears to draw a distinction between the "essentially different" requirement for common law voidness and the "fundamentally different" requirement for equitable voidability. This problem was addressed by Lord Phillips MR in *Great Peace Shipping*. In his

---

42. [1949] 2 All ER 1107.
43. The distinction between a mistake of fact and a mistake of law has now been removed by the House of Lords in *Kleinwort Benson Ltd v Lincoln City Council* [1998] 4 All ER 513 where restitution was permitted for a mistake of law. See also *Brennan v Bolt Burdon* [2004] EWCA Civ 1017 and *Halpern v Halpern* [2006] EWHC 603. The principle that money paid under a mistake of fact *or law* may be recovered has been accepted by the Hong Kong courts (even where the payer may have been careless): *Dex (Asia) Ltd v DBS Bank (HK) Ltd* [2009] 5 HKLRD 160.
44. [1949] 2 All ER 1107 at 1119.

leading judgment he listed and discussed a number of cases which had followed *Solle*.[45] He remarked:

> yet none of them defines the test of mistake that gives rise to the equitable jurisdiction to rescind in a manner which distinguishes this from the test of mistake that renders a contract void at law, as defined in *Bell v Lever Brothers*.[46]

Lord Phillips MR said that the combined effect of *Bell* and *Solle* was that the intervention of equity took place only in circumstances where the common law would have, anyway, ruled the contract void for mistake. He agreed with the judge at first instance[47] that the doctrine of common mistake leaves no room for the intervention of equity.[48] In words very similar to those in the paragraph above the judge had concluded that it was:

> not possible to differentiate between the test of mistake identified in *Bell v Lever Brothers* and that advanced by Lord Denning as giving rise to the equitable jurisdiction to rescind.[49]

While deciding that there was no equitable jurisdiction to rescind on the ground of common mistake a contract that was valid at common law, the court did recognise that there was a need for a codified doctrine of common mistake which allows for an appropriate element of discretion in determining the terms of any court order relieving the parties of their bargain. Lord Phillips said:

> Just as the Law Reform (Frustrated Contracts) Act 1943 was needed to temper the effect of the common law doctrine of frustration, so there is scope for legislation to give greater flexibility to our law of mistake than the common law allows.[50]

As *Great Peace Shipping* is only a Court of Appeal decision it cannot, technically, overrule *Solle v Butcher*, another Court of Appeal case.[51] So, if a similar case should come before a future Court of Appeal, it would be free to choose between

---

45. Such as *Rose (Frederick E) (London) Ltd v Pim Junior (William H) 7 Co Ltd* [1953] 2 QB 450; *Grist v Bailey* [1967] 1 Ch 532; *Magee v Pennine Insurance Co Ltd* [1969] 2 QB 507; *Laurence v Lexcourt Holdings* [1978] 1 WLR 1128.
46. *Great Peace* at para 153.
47. Toulson J.
48. Toulson J had described the decision by Lord Denning in *Solle* as one which sought to "outflank" *Bell v Lever Brothers*.
49. Cited at *Great Peace* (CA) at para 97.
50. Ibid at para 161; Hong Kong enacted similar frustration provisions in Law Amendment and Reform (Consolidation) Ordinance (Cap 23) (LARCO) ss 16–18.
51. Following *Young v Bristol Aeroplane Co. Ltd.* [1944] KB 718.

these two cases.[52] Realistically, this is unlikely and subsequent judgments have treated *Great Peace* as definitive.[53]

The decision in *Great Peace Shipping* has been welcomed by some on the basis that it brings clarity to the law of mistake. Its central premise is that mistake either renders a contract void or is inoperative; there is no halfway house. Courts need no longer endure the difficult task of determining if a case is a suitable subject for equitable intervention and, if so, how such intervention will operate. *Great Peace Shipping* has, however, been subject to trenchant criticism by McMeel.[54] McMeel's twofold criticism is that the court had *no authority*, in precedent terms, to depart from *Solle* in *Great Peace Shipping*, and that *Solle v Butcher* was largely beneficial. As to the first point, he writes:

> as a matter of the doctrine of precedent *Solle* should have been seen as binding in the High Court and the Court of Appeal. To undo 50 years of consistent, if sporadic, common law development should be a matter for Parliament or the House of Lords.[55]

As to the *desirability* of overturning *Solle*, McMeel describes the case as "comparatively benign" and adds:

> its preference for voidability and flexibility ensured no ill-effects for innocent third parties. It was in the view of many academics and practitioners mostly harmless as a judicial flexible friend for extreme cases.[56]

McMeel adds that Lord Phillips MR's rejection of judge-made discretion sits oddly with his subsequent call for legislation to provide the very flexibility which *Great Peace Shipping* seeks to curb!

The impact of *Great Peace Shipping* on the doctrine of mistake in Hong Kong has still to develop but such jurisprudence as exists suggests support for its premise that only the most serious common mistakes could render a contract void. Such was the view expressed in *Tony Investments Ltd v Fung Sun Kwan*.[57] The authority is not a strong one, however, given the court's finding that there was no true common mistake at all since one party was clear as to the relevant terms and the other had made, at most, an (unjustified) assumption. Moreover, the case says little about the "demise" of equitable mistake. It remains possible that the (English) Supreme Court may disagree with the Court of Appeal and restore the flexibility afforded by equity. Even if the Supreme Court does not so intervene, it is important to note, given

---

52. Hong Kong courts (post-1997) have total freedom to ignore English Court of Appeal decisions. They should treat them with the "utmost respect" (per Li CJ in *A Solicitor v Law Society of Hong Kong* [2008] 2 HKC 1) but where the previous cases conflict this is of only academic significance.
53. See, for example, *Dany Lions Ltd v Bristol Cars* [2013] EWHC 2997 (mistake "important" but not "fundamental" so inoperative).
54. Gerard McMeel, "Interpretation and Mistake in Contract Law", (2006) LMCLQ 49.
55. Ibid at p 65.
56. Ibid.
57. [2006] 1 HKLRD 835 and see 10.4 below.

the controversy outlined above, that Hong Kong courts are completely at liberty to ignore *Great Peace Shipping* (and any other post-1997 English precedents).[58] The indications, however, are that the narrower application of the doctrine of common mistake adopted in England will be followed by the courts in Hong Kong. Despite the potential for expansion of the doctrine in equity following the decision in *Solle*, there have been few attempts at such expansion in Hong Kong. The defence of mistake *was* raised, unsuccessfully, in *Jan Albert (HK) Ltd v Shu Kong Garment Factory Ltd*[59] where the parties were mistaken as to the proper classification of garments which were to be shipped from China to Germany. At first instance Deputy Judge Cruden found that there was an operative common mistake. However, this finding was overturned by the Hong Kong Court of Appeal, which found that the mistake did not affect the goods radically at all. The higher court also overturned a finding of the first instance court that there was a frustration. It did so based on the allocation of risk under the terms of the contract and the parties' knowledge and acceptance of such risk. Neither in *Jan Albert* nor in subsequent cases has equitable mistake been seriously broached by Hong Kong litigants or the courts. Post-*Great Peace* the possibility of the equitable "middle path" being explored in Hong Kong is even more remote.

10.3.2 Common Mistake: Just a Total Failure of Consideration?

If one is to conclude that the only role for the doctrine of common mistake is in cases of non-existence of subject matter (unknown to the parties) at the time the contract was made, an argument can be made that such a doctrine is unnecessary since such cases are examples of a complete failure of consideration. If the subject matter of the contract does not exist, then the party who has the obligation to provide such subject matter cannot perform his part of the contract.

Indeed in several nineteenth-century English cases[60] money paid out by a party under circumstances which today would ground a common mistake was recovered on the basis of total failure of consideration. Chitty[61] explains that there were three possible conceptual routes which were employed in considering whether a fundamental mistake had prevented the formation of a valid contract: total failure of consideration; that the contract was subject to an express or implied condition that the facts were as the parties believed them to be; and that there was a separate doctrine of mistake. The second route of the implied term arose out of the analogy with frustration,[62] but the notion of frustration based on an implied term has now

---

58. See *A Solicitor v Law Society of Hong Kong* [2008] 2 HKC 1.
59. (unrep, HCA 4434/1986, 4 November 1988); on appeal (unrep, CACV 160/1988, 14 September 1989).
60. See cases cited in *Chitty on Contracts* (London: Sweet & Maxwell, 29th edn, 2004), 5-017.
61. Ibid at 5-016.
62. See 14.4.

been discarded by the courts.[63] One is left with the other two routes. Chitty makes the argument that:

> the fact that a mistake has led to there being a total failure of consideration cannot lead straight to the conclusion that the contract is void, since it might be that the seller is liable for non-performance. In other words, total failure of consideration is not an independent ground on which a contract may be held void.[64]

The correct conclusion appears to be that there is a separate doctrine of common mistake. This is supported by Lord Atkin in *Bell* and the English Court of Appeal in *Great Peace Shipping*. While they appear to differ over the origin of the doctrine— the former reflecting the Roman law notion of mistake,[65] the latter based on parallels to frustration and construction of the contract—they proceed on the basis that there is a separate doctrine of mistake, albeit one of limited application.

10.4 Mutual Mistake

A mutual[66] mistake occurs where both parties are mistaken but do not make the same mistake. The parties are at cross-purposes and never reach agreement. The terminology is not universally applied and, for example, the court in *Bell* described the common mistake obtaining in that case as "mutual". Mutual mistake, where it operates, is said to "negative" consent since the party are never truly *ad idem*.

In practice, it is in the area of so-called "mutual mistake" that the doctrine of mistake is at its most "mythical", not least because the doctrine only applies to mistakes made "reasonably". In *Tamplin v James*,[67] the defendant was the highest bidder for a public house and adjoining premises. He believed, erroneously, that a field was included but it was, in fact, held under a separate lease. Having discovered his error, the defendant sought to resist the award of an order for specific performance to the plaintiff. The plaintiff's action was, nonetheless, successful since, viewed objectively, the defendant had agreed to buy the property without the field.[68] The view that a mistaken "assumption" is inoperative has been endorsed by the Hong Kong courts.[69]

Of course, if the mistake had been made by the seller (for example, mistakenly agreeing to include the field) the latter would have borne the loss. The key

---

63. Ibid.
64. Chitty (n 58 above) at 5-017.
65. Ibid at 5-020.
66. For further discussion of the distinction between "mutual" and "common", see Cheshire, Fifoot and Furmston (n 2 above) at p 297.
67. (1880) 15 Ch D 215.
68. On the same basis, an unreasonable mistake was disregarded in *Brennan v Bolt, Burdon* [2004] EWCA Civ 1017.
69. See *Patel's Wall Street Exchange Ltd v SK International* [2005] 2 HKLRD 551; *Tony Investments Ltd v Fung Sun Kwan Bernard* [2006] 1 HKLRD 835.

consideration is the *construction* of the contract. Only rarely will a court find that both parties have been "reasonably" mistaken.

Raffles v Wichelhaus[70]

The parties agreed on the sale of a cargo of cotton arriving "Ex Peerless from Bombay". There were two ships with the name *Peerless* sailing from Bombay, one in October the other in December. The plaintiff intended to sell the later cargo but the defendant intended to buy the earlier cargo and refused to accept and pay for the later one. The plaintiff's action for breach of contract failed in the Court of Exchequer.

No clear reasons were given for the decision and so it is very difficult to ascertain the *ratio* of the case. However, the court must be presumed to have accepted the argument from counsel for the defendant that there was nothing on the face of the contract to show that any particular ship called the *Peerless* was meant; but the moment it appeared that two ships called the *Peerless* were about to sail from Bombay there was latent ambiguity, and parol evidence[71] could be given to show that the defendant meant one *Peerless* and the plaintiff another; that being so, there was no *consensus ad idem* and therefore no binding contract.[72]

There are a two ways of looking at this decision: either that the agreement was void for mutual mistake, or that there was a contract for the sale of the earlier cargo so that the defendant did not have to pay for the later cargo. If the agreement is void for mutual mistake it is an unusual example of a situation where each party misunderstands the other but neither is at fault. There is an unfortunate coincidence whereby two ships of the same name left the same port but on different dates. One could equally say that, as there was no *consensus ad idem*, this could be viewed as an offer and acceptance issue.[73] Indeed, it is difficult to envisage a situation where the parties can reasonably misunderstand one another unless the agreement is insufficiently certain.[74]

As made clear in the *Tamplin* case, discussed above, the courts take an objective approach and will ask not what the parties intended but what a reasonable third party would think they intended. In other words, can any ambiguity be resolved? In *Raffles* it appears that the ambiguity could not be resolved as it was impossible to give a clear answer as to which ship was intended. By contrast, in *Smith v Hughes*[75] the

---

70. (1864) 2 H&C 906.

71. See 8.2.

72. *Raffles* was distinguished in *NBTY Europe Ltd v Nutricia International BV* where there was held to be no clear ambiguity in the relevant agreement.

73. For instance, McKendrick (n 30 above) treats this case as an offer and acceptance issue only. Ho (n 12 above) considers it to be a case of operative "unilateral mistake" but her classification of mistake is not reconcilable with that in this book since she uses "mutual" for our common mistake and opines that "unilateral mistake" may be experienced by both parties.

74. See 3.8.

75. (1871) LR 6 QB 597.

adoption of an objective test by the court led to the conclusion that there was a valid contract and no operative mistake.

Smith v Hughes[76]

The plaintiff was a farmer and the defendant a trainer of racehorses. The defendant purchased from the plaintiff a quantity of oats which he believed were old oats. They were, in fact, new oats and therefore unsuitable for the buyer's proposed use. When he discovered his mistake the defendant refused to accept the oats and the plaintiff sued for the price. The key question was whether the expression "old oats" had been used in negotiations (a "terms of the contract" issue) and, if not, whether the seller had taken advantage of the buyer's known mistake (unilateral mistake). The court applied the objective test and said there was no ambiguity about the contract. The plaintiff had agreed to sell and the defendant had agreed to buy a quantity of "oats" rather than "old oats". The defendant's mistake, as with the *Tamplin* case, was his own fault and not a reason for finding an operative mistake.

10.5 Unilateral Mistake

A unilateral mistake occurs when only one of the parties is mistaken. However, if such a mistake is to be operative, it must be known to the other party. In practice, such cases normally involve fraud on the part of the non-mistaken party; he is aware of the other party's mistake since he has helped to cause it. If a unilateral mistake operates, it is because it negatives consent. The parties never reach a true agreement.

10.5.1 Operative Unilateral Mistake: Mistake about Terms Known to Other Party

Operative unilateral mistake occurs where one contracting party is under a mistake as to the terms of the contract *and* that mistake is known to the other party.[77] Such an event occurred in *Hartog v Colin and Shields*,[78] where an offer was accepted to sell skins. The defendant sellers mistakenly quoted the selling price as 10d per pound instead of 10d per piece. When they discovered their mistake, the defendants refused to deliver the skins. The claimants brought an action for the defendants' non-delivery of skins. It was held that they were not entitled to succeed because the negotiations had proceeded on the basis that the skins were to be sold at a price per piece and that, as there were three pieces to the pound, the claimants must be taken to have known the mistake made by the defendants in the formulation of their offer.

---

76. Ibid.
77. The "known to the other party" requirement was confirmed, in Hong Kong, in *Long Ford Garment Ltd v JAS Forwarding (Hong Kong) Ltd* [2005] 4 HKC 136 per Rogers VP.
78. [1939] 3 All ER 566.

More recently, Rajah JC, sitting in the High Court of Singapore, was faced with a similar case involving a sale over the internet.

Chwee Kin Keong and Others v Digilandmall.com Pte Ltd[79]

A laser printer was advertised at the wrong price of $66. The actual price was $3,854. When they discovered the mistake the defendants refused to meet the many orders placed by the plaintiffs who sued for non-delivery. The plaintiffs argued that they, themselves, were unaware of the mistake made. However, the court found that the circumstances under which the orders had been placed and the quantities sought to be purchased wholly undermined the contention that the plaintiffs had lacked knowledge or belief in the existence of the mistake.

Rajah JC stated:

> The stark gaping difference between the price posting and the market price of the laser printer would have made it obvious to any objective person that something was terribly amiss . . . There was no doubt that the plaintiffs had acted with haste in the dead of night in placing as many orders as each of them had felt their financial resources credibly permitted them to do so. They had clearly been anxious to place their orders before the defendant took steps to correct the error.[80]

He went on to find that the contract was void from the outset. Although, initially, a low level decision[81] and one that is not binding in Hong Kong, this is, nonetheless, an interesting application of contractual principles involving mistake to the recent phenomenon of e-commerce and online transactions. The court found that the "snapping up" of the laser printers imputed knowledge of the mistake and that was sufficient to ground an operative unilateral mistake.

10.5.2 Operative Unilateral Mistake: The Rogue Cases

The majority of situations in which the question of unilateral mistake has arisen have been cases of mistaken identity. In the area of unilateral mistake one long-standing difficulty has been reconciling the differing decisions, on similar facts, of *Lewis v Averay*[82] and *Ingram v Little*.[83] In the earlier case, *Ingram*, the English Court of Appeal held, by a majority (Lord Devlin dissenting), that the mistake was operative.

---

79. [2004] 2 SLR 594.
80. At para 143.
81. It was confirmed on appeal: [2005] 1 SLR 502.
82. [1971] 3 All ER 907.
83. [1961] 1 QB 31.

Ingram v Little[84]

A rogue, introducing himself as Hutchinson, offered to buy a car from the plaintiffs. He was taken for a run in the car in the course of which he talked about his family and said they were in Cornwall but that his home was in Caterham. Later, the rogue offered a sum to Elsie Ingram for the car which she was prepared to accept. The sisters had advertised the car for sale by cash only. They refused to accept a cheque from him. He then said he was a P. G. Hutchinson with business interests in Guildford and living at Stanstead House, Stanstead Road, Caterham. Hilda Ingram then checked in the telephone directory that there was such a person as P. G. Hutchinson, living at that address. The plaintiffs then let the rogue have the car in exchange for the cheque. The rogue sold on the car to the defendant who bought it in good faith. The plaintiffs subsequently sued the defendant for the return of the car or damages and their action succeeded. The court said that the identity of the person with whom the Ingrams were dealing was fundamental and that the contract was void for mistake. As such, the rogue could not pass on good title to the unfortunate defendant who had to bear the loss.

Lord Devlin delivered a significant dissenting judgment. He started with the presumption that a person intends to contract with the person with whom he is face-to-face and to whom he is addressing his words. It was then up to the plaintiff, here the Ingram sisters, to rebut this presumption. He noted that they had initially required cash as payment and that checking a telephone directory to see if such a name existed did not prove that the culprit was the person whose name appeared in the directory. His conclusion was that it was not identity which was crucial to the sisters but the creditworthiness of the person in front of them. They would have sold to anyone who could pay them. Such a mistake as to creditworthiness might render the agreement with the rogue "voidable",[85] such that it could have been rescinded by notice to the rogue, but could not make the contract void *ab initio* so as to invalidate the rights of an innocent third party. They had, therefore, failed to rebut the presumption and their claim should fail.

Lewis v Averay[86]

A rogue pretended to be Richard Greene, the (then) well-known actor famous for portraying Robin Hood in a long running television series. The rogue signed a cheque in the name of "R. A. Green" in order to purchase a car. Lewis asked if he had anything to prove he was Richard Greene and the man produced an admission pass to Pinewood Studios, bearing an official stamp, the name of "Richard A Green" and a photograph of the man. The man was not Richard Greene and the cheque

---

84. Ibid.
85. Perhaps for mistake; certainly for misrepresentation.
86. [1971] 3 All ER 907.

was dishonoured. The rogue then sold the car to a *bona fide* purchaser, Averay. The English Court of Appeal held that the mistake was not operative so as to make the contract with the rogue void and that Averay had, therefore, acquired good title to the car. The rogue had obtained title to the car, albeit one which was "voidable", and the plaintiff could not rescind the contract with the rogue since an innocent third party had acquired an interest.[87]

Lord Denning MR agreed with the presumption proposed by Lord Devlin in *Ingram* and then said:

> There is a contract made with the very person there, who is present in person. It is liable no doubt to be avoided for fraud, but it is still a good contract under which title will pass unless and until it is avoided.[88]

Lewis and *Ingram* are very difficult to reconcile as the essential facts are indistinguishable. Most writers[89] agree that *Lewis* appears to be the correct decision and point out that it is far more consistent with the approach of other courts dealing with mistaken identity in "face-to-face with the rogue" situations. The precedent position remained unclear, however, until the House of Lords considered the position in *Shogun Finance Ltd v Hudson*.[90]

In *Shogun Finance*, the House of Lords affirmed the principle that, in face-to-face cases, there is a strong presumption that the contract is intended to be with the person the offeror is face-to-face with, as in *Lewis* and a number of other cases.[91] The result is that the chances of establishing an operative mistake on similar facts to these cases is extremely remote and *Ingram*, which has long been doubted, may now be viewed as "deceased". The *Shogun* case is not, however, without its difficulties, dealing as it does with what the House of Lords viewed as a non-"face-to-face" situation.

Shogun Finance Ltd v Hudson[92]

A rogue went into a car showroom and showed an interest in purchasing on hire-purchase a Mitsubishi Shogun car. He posed as a Mr Patel and used Mr Patel's driving licence—which he had improperly obtained—and address to evidence his false identity. This information was passed on by fax to Shogun Finance. They checked Mr Patel's credit rating and then instructed the car dealer, by phone, to pass possession of the car to the rogue. A written contract of hire-purchase was entered into by Shogun Finance naming Mr Patel as the hire-purchaser and the rogue signed it,

---

87. See 9.2.2.
88. [1971] 3 All ER 907 at 911.
89. Such as McKendrick (n 30 above) at p 72.
90. [2003] UKHL 62, [2004] 1 AC 919.
91. For example, *Phillips v Brooks* [1919] 2 KB 243.
92. [2003] UKHL 62, [2004] 1 AC 919.

forging Mr Patel's signature. The rogue then sold the car to Hudson and disappeared with the proceeds of sale. Shogun brought a claim against Hudson in the tort of conversion. The case turned on whether Mr Hudson had acquired good title to the car from the rogue. Legislation, in the form of the Hire Purchase Act 1964, gives good title to one who buys a car from a hire purchase "debtor" who has acquired it on hire purchase terms. The question was whether the rogue had so "acquired" it; whether in hire purchase terms, he was "the debtor".

At trial the judge held that there was no valid contract between the rogue and Shogun Finance and so found for Shogun Finance. Mr Hudson appealed to the Court of Appeal, which upheld, by a majority, the judge's decision. The House of Lords dismissed the appeal by a bare majority made up of Lords Hobhouse, Phillips and Walker. Lords Millett and Nicholls dissented. The House found there was no valid contract between Shogun Finance and the rogue. The contract was made, ostensibly, between Shogun Finance and Mr Patel. This was a nullity as it had been made without Mr Patel's authority. The presumption of voidability did not apply as this was not a face-to-face case.[93]

Although the law lords' views endorsing the voidability presumption in face-to-face cases are necessarily *obiter* there is little doubt they will be followed in England. However, the majority of the law lords in *Shogun* left unchallenged, and indeed reinforced, the principle established in *Cundy v Lindsay*[94] that an agreement made "at arm's length" with a rogue is likely to be declared "void".

Cundy v Lindsay[95]

The plaintiffs received an order for handkerchiefs from a rogue called Blenkarn of 37 Wood Street. Blenkarn signed his name so that it looked like "Blenkiron & Co", a reputable firm operating at 123 Wood Street. The plaintiffs despatched the goods on credit to "Blenkiron & Co" but to Blenkarn's address. Blenkarn took the goods, failed to pay for them and sold them on to others, including the defendants. The plaintiffs sued the defendants in the tort of "conversion", asserting that title in the goods remained with the plaintiffs. This plea was upheld, ultimately in the House of Lords. The plaintiffs' action was successful at the expense of the innocent defendants. The rationale was that the plaintiffs had made no contract with Blenkarn since they wished to deal with another entity, Blenkiron & Co.

As a House of Lords case, *Cundy* could be overturned only by legislation or by later decision of the House of Lords. The majority in *Shogun* approved *Cundy*

---

93. The rogue had been face-to-face with the car dealer but *not* with the other contracting party (the finance company).
94. (1878) 3 App Cas 459.
95. Ibid.

and accepted the difference between face-to-face and arm's length transactions. The *Shogun* case does have elements of the face-to-face situation. Much was concluded face-to-face with the car dealer as an agent for some purposes of Shogun Finance. However, the majority of the law lords treated the case as *not* face-to-face and said the written document specified the parties and must prevail. Two problems arise from this approach. The first is that the distinction between face-to-face and arm's length will sometimes be blurred and the second is that important issues of "policy" have been ignored.

As regards "the distinction", Lord Walker in *Shogun* suggested that contracts made over the telephone should be treated as face-to-face contracts. Videophones, mentioned in this case, would presumable also be treated as face-to-face situations. Lord Millett also made reference to modern technology and noted that in the emerging era of e-shopping over the internet "identity theft" impersonations are on the increase.[96] With the growth in the use of the internet and other modern means of electronic—especially visual—communication, the argument that the number of rogue cases might be on the increase, both in Hong Kong and elsewhere, appears compelling. Rogues, moreover, are likely to use more sophisticated methods of identity theft than mere impersonation. The availability of photo identity cards, fingerprint and iris identification may, however, stem the flow of such cases.

10.5.3 Policy Issues: Who Should Bear the Loss in Rogue Cases?

In the *Ingram* case, Devlin LJ suggested that where, as is usually the case with mistaken identity, the action is between two innocent parties, some sharing of loss should be adopted. This might have been possible in England via the doctrine of contributory negligence. Thus, the defrauded person would bring his action against the innocent purchaser in "conversion", win the action but have his damages reduced to the extent that his carelessness permitted the fraud to be perpetrated. Legislation, however, has precluded this possibility in England.[97] As such the courts are required to make "all or nothing" decisions.

Lord Nicholls in his dissenting judgment in *Shogun* said:

> the loss is more appropriately borne by the person who takes the risks inherent in the parting with his goods without receiving payment.[98]

---

96. For a discussion on the role of criminal law in this area, see D. G. Greenwood, "Is Mistake Dead in Contract Law?", (2004) 34 HKLJ 495 at 504.
97. See Torts (Interference with Goods) Act 1977 s 11(1).
98. *Shogun v Hudson* [2003] UKHL 62, [2004] 1 AC 919 at para 35.

He noted that this approach is consistent with approaches adopted elsewhere in the common law world, especially in the United States in their Uniform Commercial Code.[99]

The approach also conforms to the underlying "policy" considerations in cases like *Lewis v Averay*. Why then does it not apply to arm's length cases? The House of Lords in *Cundy* (and the majority in *Shogun)* emphasised narrow, legalistic concerns with insufficient emphasis, it is submitted, on policy considerations. With respect, it is suggested that Lord Nicholls' dissenting view in *Shogun*, that there should be no distinction between face-to-face and arm's length, is to be preferred. The real decision for the courts in these cases is as to which of two innocent parties should bear the loss. In *Cundy* the House of Lords found in favour of a party who had sent goods to the wrong address, at the expense of a purchaser in good faith. In *Shogun*, the majority favoured a finance company at the expense of an innocent party in clear contravention of the legislative intent of the Hire Purchase Act 1964, that finance companies should bear the loss of improper sale by the hirer and protect themselves via insurance.

In short, in the absence of an opportunity to share loss, the courts should find in favour of the innocent third party, at least where there is no hint of his collusion in the original fraud. With the advent of sophisticated identity cards and other, more scientific, means of identification, there is rarely an excuse for the defrauded party not to discover the truth; where he takes inadequate steps to do so, he should bear the loss.

10.5.4 Mistaken Identity in Hong Kong

It may be that much of the above has little significance to Hong Kong. Leaving aside that much of what was said in *Shogun* is *obiter* and that the case is not binding in Hong Kong, factual circumstances are very different here. Hong Kong people use credit cards or cash and the likelihood of a *Lewis* or *Ingram* scenario is very small. Stolen driver's licences, as in *Shogun*, are also unlikely to feature, as more sophisticated identification methods would be employed.[100] Hong Kong has introduced sophisticated smart cards (soon to be upgraded). Across the boundary, in mainland China, more than a billion new "second generation" plastic identity cards with embedded microchips have been issued since 2013 to replace the paper documents

---

99. For example, Article 3-404 states with regard to negotiable instruments: "If an impostor, by use of the mails or otherwise, induces the issuer of an instrument to issue the instrument to the impostor, or to a person acting in concert with the impostor, by impersonating the payee of the instrument or a person authorized to act for the payee, an indorsement of the instrument by any person in the name of the payee is effective as the indorsement of the payee in favor of a person who, in good faith, pays the instrument or takes it for value or for collection."

100. *Shogun Finance* was cited in *Shanghai Tongji Science & Technology Industrial Co Ltd v Casil Clearing Ltd* [2004] 2 HKLRD 548, but not in relation to the law of mistake *per se*.

previously carried by adult Chinese citizens. Proposals for similar high-tech identity cards have proved controversial in countries such as Australia, the United States and Britain[101] where the carrying of such cards is not ingrained nearly as deeply as it is in Hong Kong and China.[102] Moreover, despite increased terrorist attacks and the greater need for security, resistance to the introduction of compulsory identity cards has remained strong. In short, even if identity theft does occur in Hong Kong it is likely to be different in *form* (if not in *substance*) than in England.

10.6 Rectification of Written Documents

The court has a discretionary power in equity to rectify a document—order its wording to be changed—if, as a result of a mistake, it fails properly to record the terms of an agreement. The power to rectify is available where the mistake made is in the *recording* of the document and not in its formation. Thus, in theory, courts do not rectify contracts; they rectify the *instrument* wrongly recording the contract. Rectification is normally granted only for a *common* mistake, where the parties have simply failed properly to record their agreement. However, as we shall see, a court may exceptionally grant rectification for *unilateral* mistake, where it is clear that one party is mistaken *and* that the other party has taken advantage of this. In this latter situation, of course, there is an element of misfeasance involved.

The courts have developed various rules concerning the exercise of this equitable power and the requirements for rectification for common mistake are clearly summarised in the following case.

Joscelyne v Nissen[103]

A father and daughter negotiated the transfer of a business and premises whereby it was understood that the father would continue to live in the premises while the daughter paid his utility bills. A later formal contract omitted provision for such payments. Rectification was ordered, in the English High Court, even though the agreement between the parties, before the execution of the formal contract, had no contractual force.

The requirements established in the *Joscelyne* case are that:

1. there must be an antecedent agreement (though not necessarily of contractual force);
2. this agreement must remain unchanged until the time of the formal written contract;

---

101. Britain's former Conservative/Liberal Democrat coalition government scrapped the identity card scheme which the previous Labour government intended to introduce. While issues of principle were involved, a key error was the decision to charge a high fee for the ID "privilege".
102. *The Standard* newspaper, 4 May 2004, page A10.
103. [1970] 2 QB 86.

3. the formal written contract must have failed to reflect the antecedent agreement.[104]

A clear principle is that there can be no rectification if there is no literal disparity between the language of the original agreement and the written contract. The courts are not to intervene just because parties have later "changed their minds": *Rose (Frederick E) (London) Ltd v Pim Junior (William H) & Co Ltd.*[105]

Rectification is normally only granted where the written contract fails to record the intention of *both parties* (that is, there is a common mistake). A slight variation arose in the English case of *Hawksford Trustees Jersey Ltd v Stella Global UK Ltd.*[106] Here, the claimant's *negotiator* (without authority) and the defendant were under a common mistake. Although the negotiator was not, legally, a contracting party his intention was the determining factor in the decision whether or not to grant rectification.

A court may also, exceptionally, grant rectification for a unilateral mistake, but only in very narrow circumstances as established in *Roberts & Co Ltd v Leicestershire CC*[107] These circumstances exist where one party, X, knew of, or wilfully shut his eyes to, the mistake of the other party, Y; and/or where X was guilty of fraud or other unconscionable conduct. The courts have had a lot of difficulty with this area of law as the boundary line between legitimate negotiation and unfair dealing can often be difficult to draw. The courts will generally be reluctant to intervene and rewrite a contract but English cases have seen the courts follow the *Roberts* approach.[108] The key issue is that the courts will presume that "the contract is the contract" and will be reluctant to rectify without compelling evidence of operative mistake being provided by the party seeking rectification. In the Court of Final Appeal case of *Kowloon Development Finance Ltd v Pendex Industries Ltd*[109] (see discussion below). Lord Hoffmann NPJ repeated the view he had expressed in the *Chartbrook* case (below) that rectification for *common* mistake involves an "objective" determination of what both parties must actually have agreed (while rectification for *unilateral* mistake is concerned with "the subjective states of mind of the parties", as in the *Roberts* case).

---

104. These criteria were endorsed, with only minor extension, in *WG Mitchell (Gleneagles) & Another v Jemstock One Ltd* [2006] EWHC 3644 (Ch) and *Swainland Builders Ltd Freehold Properties Ltd* [2002] 2 EGLR 71.
105. [1953] 2 QB 450 (court refused to insert "feveroles" after "horsebeans" in a written contract as the original accurately recorded a previous oral agreement).
106. [2012] EWCA Civ 55.
107. [1961] Ch 555.
108. See, for instance, *Hurst Stores and Interiors v ML Europe Property* [2004] EWCA Civ 490; *QRS Sciences v BTG International* [2005] EWHC 670.
109. (2013) 16 HKCFAR 336.

This objective test approach had previously been adopted by the English Court of Appeal in *Daventry DC v Daventry Housing Ltd*.[110]

For *English* law, doubt has been cast upon Lord Hoffmann's subjective/objective dichotomy in *FSHC Group Holdings Ltd v Glas Trust Corporation Ltd*.[111] Here, the Court of Appeal indicated that while an objective approach should be applied in respect of alleged common mistake in a formal, concluded *contract* (as in the *Rose v Pim* case) where the rectification claimant is seeking to show that an "antecedent agreement", falling short of being a concluded contract, has not been properly reflected in the later written document, the parties' "subjective" intention must be considered. Leggatt LJ (for the court) stated:

> there is in our view no anomaly in applying an objective test where rectification is based on a prior concluded contract and a subjective test where it Is based on a common continuing intention. Different principles are in play . . . we are unable to accept that the objective test of rectification for common mistake articulated in Lord Hoffmann's *obiter* remarks in the *Chartbrook* case correctly states the law.

Given the House of Lords status of Lord Hoffmann's view, the *precedent* status of Leggatt LJ's statement is clearly problematic, albeit justified by downgrading the Hoffmann view to *obiter* status. Professor McKendrick[112] has opined that *FSHC* will not be the last word on the subject for English law. *A fortiori* for Hong Kong, of course, where the *Pendex* case remains binding, and where, in particular, the views of Lord Hoffmann NPJ tend to be treated with reverence.

In the case of rectification, as with other areas of mistake, the overlap with "agreement" is significant and judges inserting words into a contract may determine that this is a matter of "construction" rather than rectification.[113] However, in England, the House of Lords, in the *Chartbrook* case,[114] has affirmed the principle that in *construing* a contract, no recourse may, generally, be had to the parties' pre-contractual negotiations. These negotiations *are* relevant, of course, to rectification. Since *Chartbrook* merely affirms a pre-1997 common law principle established in *Prenn v Simmonds*,[115] it is likely to be followed in Hong Kong. An important difference in *effect* between rectification and "construction" of a contract is that the latter

---

110. [2011] EWCA Civ 1153. However, it has been criticised both judicially and academically. See particularly Leggatt J in *Tartsinis v Navona Management* [2015] EWHC 57 at para 92. (Leggatt J admitted that he had no power to change a rule established by a higher court.)

111. [2020] 2 WLR 429. The lack of a common "subjective" intention was later accepted as a bar to rectification in *Ralph v Ralph* [2021] EWCA Civ 1106 (CA).

112. Ewan McKendrick, *Contract Law: Text, Cases and Materials* (Oxford: Oxford University Press, 10th edn, 2022).

113. See, for example, *"The Starsin"* [2004] 1 AC 715 in the House of Lords and, in Hong Kong, *Re Kansa General International Insurance Co Ltd* [2007] 1 HKLRD 897 ("and" construed as "or").

114. *Chartbrook Ltd v Persimmon Homes Ltd* [2009] UKHL 38.

115. [1971] 3 All ER 237.

may have implications for innocent third parties, while the existence of such third parties will preclude rectification.

10.6.1 Rectification in Hong Kong

In Hong Kong, most reported cases on mistake are in connection with applications to rectify agreements relating to the sale and purchase of land. Such applications seek to take advantage of the long established rule of equity discussed above which gives effect to the intentions of the parties as expressed orally before entering into the written contract. The courts will rectify the written agreement to carry out the parties' common intention. Rectification will not be granted, though, if it has no practical purpose or if the parties had simply overlooked the matter.[116] The burden is on the party seeking rectification and the courts require convincing proof before granting such an order.

The conservative attitude of the courts was shown by the Hong Kong Court of Appeal in *Citilite Properties Ltd v Innovative Development Company Ltd*[117] where the court noted that it must be cautious in granting rectification. This was consistent with the approach of the same court in *Cheuk Tze Kwok v Leung Yin King and Another*.[118] Here Penlington JA referred to the "parol evidence rule"[119] which does not allow extrinsic evidence to be admitted to prove oral agreements which alter the terms of written contract. He acknowledged that there are various exceptions to this rule but emphasised that these were:

> however exceptions and there is a danger, especially in the light of the highly volatile property market of the floodgates being opened to the challenge of written contracts, as Barnett J said below, if each case is not examined with care to see if it does fit within the exception claimed.[120]

The reluctance of the Hong Kong courts to permit rectification (for common or unilateral mistake) was again illustrated in the case of *Yu Kam Por v New Central Ltd*[121] where the (plaintiff) seller of land made the unilateral mistake of believing that he was selling only a part of his land when in fact he was selling the whole. The court rejected the plaintiff's assertion that the buyer "must have known" that the seller did not intend to sell all the land at such a low price. The court's view was that the seller

---

116. See the examples quoted in *Chitty on Contracts* (29th edn), 5-049ff.
117. [1998] 4 HKC 62.
118. [1993] 2 HKLR 169.
119. See 8.2.
120. [1993] 2 HKLR 169 at 175.
121. [2005] 1 HKC 77.

must prove the buyer's bad faith; he must show that the buyer actually knew of the mistake rather than merely "strongly suspected" it if there is to be rectification.[122]

As with the English law approach, rectification for mistake in Hong Kong is closely aligned to "agreement" issues and the question of "construction". Indeed, in some cases, determination of the construction issue may render rectification immaterial. The following case provides a good example.

Tiken Ltd & Paul Y ITC Construction Holdings Ltd v BIL International Ltd[123]

The parties made an agreement concerning the defendants' guarantee to indemnify the plaintiffs against losses on certain existing and potential business ventures. Having suffered significant losses on one venture, the plaintiffs sought recompense from the defendants. The latter resisted on the basis of an asserted oral agreement to settle the matter for $4 million or, alternatively, that this particular venture was not included in the list of "guaranteed" ones. The plaintiffs argued that this venture *was* included "in the list" but even if it was not it should have been and the guarantee contract should be rectified accordingly. They further contended that no binding settlement had been concluded.

As to the settlement point, the trial judge, Stone J, determined that no oral contract had been concluded. He was sustained in this view, no doubt, by the premise that an agreement of this magnitude ($4 million) would, if *concluded*, have been reduced to writing.[124] As a matter of *construction*, Stone J decided that the venture *was* within the terms of the guarantee contract and this, effectively, settled the case. Stone J stated:

> As earlier observed, if the construction element of this case was resolved (as it now has been) in favour of the plaintiffs, the issue of rectification no longer remains a 'live' issue. However, should the conclusion the court has reached on the construction argument be in error, I turn briefly to consider the question of rectification, which represented the other string to the plaintiffs' liability bow.[125]

Stone J then expressed the view (*obiter*) that, were it necessary to decide the point, rectification would have been awarded since there was clearly the necessary "common intention" that this venture should have been included within the guarantee contract.

That the rules on rectification, either for common or unilateral mistake, are similar in England and Hong Kong is illustrated by the Court of Final Appeal

---

122. Similarly, in *Million Way Ltd v To Shing Wo* (unrep, HCA 436/2007, 25 May 2010). it was held that the unilaterally mistaken party must prove the "fraud" of the other.
123. [2005] 4 HKLRD 622.
124. See 7.1 above.
125. [2005] 4 HKLRD 622 at 634.

decision in *Kowloon Development Finance Ltd v Pendex Industries Ltd & Others*[126] in which Lord Hoffmann NPJ distinguished rectification for common mistake (which he described as "mutual") and rectification for unilateral mistake. Lord Hoffmann, delivering the court's unanimous judgment, said:

> [F]irst I should say something about the legal requirements of mutual [*sic*] and unilateral mistake in an action for rectification. They sound like two varieties of mistake about the same thing, made in one case by both parties and in the other by only one of them. But they are actually the expression of quite different principles. They deal with different kinds of mistakes. In the case of mutual or common mistake—the adjectives in this context are interchangeable—the mistake is about whether a written document correctly reflects what the parties had, on an objective assessment, agreed it should contain . . .
>
> Rectification for unilateral mistake, on the other hand is very much concerned with the subjective states of mind of the parties. If the contract contains a provision which one party knows that the other party thinks is not there, or knows that the other party is mistaken about its meaning, the court may, as a matter of discretion, either refuse to allow him to enforce the contract as it would ordinarily be construed . . . or go further and rectify the written agreement to give effect to what the mistaken party thought had been agreed.[127]

Lord Hoffmann went on to explain that civil law systems have a broader principle that parties should "negotiate in good faith" which would be applicable to the unilateral mistake situations. As we saw in chapter 3,[128] English (and Hong Kong) law does not recognise a general duty to negotiate in good faith.

10.7 *Non Est Factum*

Non est factum (meum) is an area of mistake relating solely to the mistaken signing of documents. This Latin expression means "it is not my deed". *Non est factum* is a plea by someone who has signed a document that he should not be bound by the signature since what he has signed is not what he thought he was signing. The *non est factum* doctrine was primarily intended to protect the illiterate though it has successfully been pleaded by others. As recognition of the *non est factum* doctrine marks a departure from the usual principle that one is bound by a document which one has signed,[129] the doctrine is kept within very narrow confines. Indeed, it has become so difficult to succeed under this doctrine that there have been suggestions that it is now obsolete.

---

126. [2013] 6 HKC 443.
127. In the event, the CFA upheld the lower courts' order of rectification for common mistake though Lord Hoffmann held the two types of mistake *not* to be mutually exclusive and opined that rectification for unilateral mistake could alternatively have been granted.
128. See 3.8.5.
129. See 8.6.1.1.

Saunders v Anglia Building Society[130]

The original plaintiff, Mrs Gallie, was 78 years old and wanted to help her nephew, Parkin, to raise money on the security of her house, provided she could live in it rent free until her death. Parkin did not want to become the owner in case his wife's claim to maintenance was affected. He devised a plan with Lee. They prepared a document of sale from Gallie to Lee for £3,000. Mrs Gallie was told it was a gift to Parkin. She signed it but did not read it because her glasses were broken. Lee did not pay any of the £3,000 to Gallie, or to Parkin. He raised £2,000 by mortgaging the property with the respondents, a building society, but did not pay over any of that money either. The plaintiff pleaded *non est factum* to escape the consequences of her signature. The plea was rejected by the House of Lords since Mrs Gallie's mistake was viewed as being insufficiently serious.

Lord Reid laid down the (restrictive) requirements for a plea of *non est factum* to succeed. He said:

> Originally this extension [*non est factum*] appears to have been made in favour of those who were unable to read owing to blindness or illiteracy and who therefore had to trust someone to tell them what they were signing. I think that it must also apply in favour of those who are permanently or temporarily unable through no fault of their own to have without explanation any real understanding of the purport of a particular document, whether that be from defective education, illness or innate incapacity . . .
>
> The plea cannot be available to anyone who was content to sign without taking the proper trouble to try to find out at least the general effect of the document . . . It is for the person who seeks the remedy to show that he should have it.[131]
>
> Finally, there is the question to what extent or in what way must there be a difference between that which in fact he signed and that which he believed he was signing . . . In particular I do not think that the modern division between the character and the contents of a document is at all satisfactory; . . .
>
> There must I think be a radical difference between what he signed and what he thought he was signing—or one could use the words 'fundamental' or 'serious' or 'very substantial'.[132]

The House of Lords, here, lays down three requirements for a successful plea of *non est factum*: the signer's permanent or temporary *disability*; a *radical difference* between what is signed and what the signer thinks he has signed; and proof that the signer has *not been careless*. These requirements make it very unlikely the plea

---

130. [1970] 3 All ER 961; also referred to as *Gallie v Lee* (Mrs Gallie had died by the time the case reached the House of Lords!).
131. The onus of proof, then, is on the party asserting *non est factum*. This was confirmed, for Hong Kong, in *Security Pacific Credit (Hong Kong) Ltd v Wong Kwong Shing & Another* [1983] HKCFI 126.
132. Note 126 above, at 963.

will succeed. A person should normally be aware of the nature of what he is signing unless he is suffering from a disability; if he is suffering from a disability, such that he does not understand what he is signing, it would normally be careless to sign without having the document explained to him.

The case makes one clear change to the law in that it is no longer necessary for the signer to show that what he has signed is different in "character" from what he thought he was signing; the test is whether it is "radically different". For example, a guarantee of an overdraft up to $10,000 may well be radically different from a guarantee up to $100,000 yet it is not different in character.

In Hong Kong the defence of *non est factum* was raised by the defendant in *Sun Hung Kai Credit Ltd v Szeto Yuk-Mei and Others*.[133] Here, a dispute arose between the parties to a guarantee. The defendant had guaranteed the liabilities of the hirer of a bus. The defendant pleaded *non est factum* on the basis that he did not understand the contents of the document, believing it to be a document required for the transfer of ownership of the bus. District Court Judge Downey applied the *Saunders* test and ruled that the defence should fail as the defendant was extremely careless in putting his signature on a blank document.[134]

Hong Kong presents problems with language different from most other common law jurisdictions. If a document is in a language that is not understood by the signer, then such a disability will usually not give rise to the defence of *non est factum* as the other party could reasonably expect that the party with the language disability could obtain a translation: *Chan Woon-hung v Associated Bankers Insurance Co Ltd*.[135]

A bizarre first instance decision is provided by *Kincheng Banking Corporation v Kao Yu Kuei*[136] where the trial judge upheld the plea of *non est factum* from a Mandarin speaker who claimed not to understand what he was signing because the document was explained to him in Cantonese! On appeal the Court of Appeal reversed the decision because the "translator" had been given no reason to believe the signer did not understand Cantonese; because the signer had, broadly, understood what he was signing (even if not the precise effect); and because, in any event, he had been careless in signing a document which (as he claimed) had not been properly explained to him. In short (even accepting the lack of Cantonese as satisfying the "disability" requirement), two of the three requirements established in *Saunders* were lacking![137]

---

133. [1986] HKDCLR 1.
134. See also *United Dominions Trust Ltd v Western* [1976] 1 QB 513 where an English court reached the same decision on similar facts.
135. [1993] 2 HKLR 127.
136. [1986] HKC 212.
137. *Non est factum* was pleaded on equally weak grounds in *Wing Hang Bank Ltd v Liu Kam Ying* [2002] 2 HKC 57.

A similarly weak attempt to invoke *non est factum* is evident in *Bank of China (Hong Kong) Ltd v PR of Fu Kit Keung (deceased)*[138] where trial judge Chu J stated:

> Any misunderstanding or lack of understanding on her part of the effect of the two guarantees was the result of her failure to gain a clear idea of the documents before she signed them. As she had signed the two guarantees negligently and carelessly, she is precluded from relying on *non est factum* as a defence.[139]

That claimants (or their legal advisers!) frequently advance weak *non est factum* claims is further illustrated by *Wing Hang Credit Ltd v Hui Chun Kit Benjamin & Another*[140] where it was held that the second defendant, Mrs Wu, had signed "broadly knowing" what the terms were, and had been careless (even taking her age into consideration) in signing. Given these findings, Deputy High Court Judge Lam felt no need to determine whether the third bar to *non est factum* (radical difference) was present.

10.8 Proposals for Reform

It has been suggested that, in England, legislative reform is required to resolve problems in the area of mistake, at least in relation to unilateral "mistaken identity" cases. It is pointed out that legislation has intervened in the related areas of misrepresentation and frustration.

In the area of misrepresentation, legislation has improved the lot of the representee induced to make a contract by a *careless* representor. Damages are now available in such situations.[141] There is some irony, perhaps, in the fact that the victim of a *fraudulent* misrepresentation, in the mistaken identity cases,[142] will generally be without a remedy, since damages are irrelevant in the case of a non-traceable rogue and the right to rescind is barred where an innocent third party has acquired rights.

There is, therefore, a strong argument for amending the law of mistake by introducing legislation to give the courts some flexibility in apportioning losses between innocent parties.

An analogy may be drawn with frustration. Frustration[143] occurs when, without default of either party a contractual obligation has become incapable of being performed because of circumstances in which performance is called for would render it a thing radically different from that which was undertaken by the contract.[144] The distinction between a common mistake and a situation giving rise to frustration of

---

138. [2009] 5 HKLRD 713.
139. Ibid at para 75.
140. (unrep, HCMP 732/2009, 3 November 2011).
141. Misrepresentation Act 1967 s 2(1); Misrepresentation Ordinance s 3(1); and see chapter 9.
142. See 10.5.2.
143. See 14.4.
144. Per Lord Radcliffe, *Davis Contractors Ltd v Fareham UDC* [1956] AC 696.

a contract is essentially one of timing. A common mistake is one which exists at the time of making the contract while frustration occurs after the contract has been entered into. This distinction is well illustrated by the following case.

Amalgamated Investment & Property Co Ltd v John Walker & Sons Ltd[145]

The defendants sold property to the claimants for a sum of £1.7 million. The property was advertised as being suitable for occupation or redevelopment and the defendants knew that the claimants wished to redevelop the property. The claimants, before contract, asked the defendants whether the property was designated as a building of special historic or architectural interest. The defendants replied that it was not but, unknown to both parties, it had been so listed on 22 August 1973. The parties signed the contract on 25 September 1973. The next day Secretary of State wrote to the defendants informing them that the building had been listed and that the listing would be effective the next day. The effect of the listing was to reduce the value of the property to about £200,000. The claimants argued the contract should be set aside on the grounds of mistake or alternatively that the contract was frustrated by the listing of the building.

The English Court of Appeal held that the building did not become a listed one until the listing was signed by the Secretary of State on 27 September 1973 after the contract was made and there could be no operative mistake before that event. The appropriate ground was, therefore, frustration. On the facts, frustration could not be established. The court held that the claimants knew of the risk that the building could be listed and had taken a commercial risk.

If a claimant can prove that the contract has been frustrated the contract will be brought to an immediate end. Legislation[146] then permits the courts a considerable discretion as to whether full, or only partial, recovery of money paid before frustration will be permitted. Such flexibility is not available to a court considering a plea of mistake.

Since there is currently no provision for apportioning loss in mistake cases in England, and since the courts have produced an unsatisfactory dichotomy between face-to-face and arm's length contracts in cases of mistaken identity, it has been suggested that legislative change is required. In fact, much could be achieved by the simple legislative removal of section 11(1) of the Torts (Interference with Goods) Act 1977,[147] such that courts could adopt apportionment via the doctrine of contributory negligence.

As regards Hong Kong, there seems little need for legislative change. Common mistake is of theoretical rather than practical significance (except in the area of

---

145. [1977] 1 WLR 164, [1976] 3 All ER 509.
146. Law Reform (Frustrated Contracts) Act 1943; Law Amendment and Reform (Consolidation) Ordinance (Cap 23); and see 14.4.5.
147. See 10.5.3 above.

documents where rectification already suffices) and mutual mistake is a category which will rarely, if ever, be operative. Even unilateral mistake, in the form of the "rogue" cases, appears to have little relevance to Hong Kong and rectification for unilateral mistake poses no insurmountable difficulties.

In short, whatever may be the requirements in England, Hong Kong's need for legislative change in the area of mistake is doubtful. Indeed, there is a strong case to be made that Hong Kong has no need for a doctrine of mistake at all outside, perhaps, the area of documentary mistake. Certainly, while mistake is sometimes *pleaded* in Hong Kong (often half-heartedly!), it is rare for a plea of mistake to be successful here.

11

Duress and Undue Influence

OVERVIEW

Duress is illegitimate pressure put on a person to enter into a contract. It is a vitiating element recognised at common law. It can be divided into duress of the person, duress of goods and economic duress. The law has had no problem with setting aside contracts in the first category. The last category is relatively recent and has, to a large extent, overtaken duress of goods. Economic duress occurs where some unfair and unlawful economic pressure is placed on a party to a contract. While it may sometimes be difficult to distinguish between duress and legitimate, hard bargaining, the key elements of economic duress are "illegitimate pressure" and lack of a practical alternative.

Operative duress renders a contract voidable. The contract will not terminate automatically but continue in existence until the innocent party exercises his option to rescind the contract. However, the exercise of this power of rescission is, as is the case with misrepresentation,[1] subject to certain bars in respect of undue delay (lapse of time), affirmation of the contract by the innocent party, and the acquisition of an interest by an innocent third party.

The equitable counterpart of duress is the doctrine of undue influence. The term "undue influence", while not statutorily defined, relates to those situations where the courts are prepared to intervene on behalf of a weaker party because pressure has been used, of a more subtle nature than previously recognised by the doctrine of duress, to persuade a party to enter into a contract. This pressure arises because of the nature of the relationship between the parties which places one party in a dominant position over the other. As the concept of duress has broadened, the original rationale for undue influence has become less significant and there are now cases in which duress and undue influence are pleaded as alternatives and where the court could decide on either basis.

---

1. See chapter 9.

Undue influence may be divided into two categories: actual undue influence and presumed undue influence. In the former category the complainant has the burden of proving undue influence; once proved, however, the agreement is automatically rendered voidable. There is no requirement here that the influenced party show the agreement to be disadvantageous to him.[2]

In the latter category, "presumed" undue influence, the relationship between the parties is such that one party has put "trust and confidence" in the other (dominant) party. When this relationship of trust and confidence has been established, and the agreement entered into "calls for explanation", the transaction will be voidable *unless* the dominant party can prove that no undue influence was in fact exercised. In other words, the courts "presume" the exercise of undue influence in these cases but the presumption can be, in legal terminology, "rebutted". The dominant party will normally rebut the presumption by showing that the weaker party relied primarily on independent legal or financial advice in making the agreement in dispute.

The relationships giving rise to the presumption of undue influence are generally further subdivided into two groups. The first group arises from a "special relationship" between the parties, such as that between a trustee and a beneficiary, a guardian and a ward, a parent and a child. In these cases, there is an irrebuttable presumption that a position of influence *exists* (but not that it has been *exercised* unduly). In other words, the dominant party cannot deny the existence of such a position of influence. The second group is based not on a special relationship but on proof that, *in the circumstances*, one party was in a position to exert influence over the other because that other had put himself entirely into the hands of the "influencer". So, for example, there is no special relationship between husband and wife *but* it may be possible for one of them (usually the wife) to convince the court that she has put her legal matters entirely into the hands of her husband such that the existence of a position of undue influence can be presumed.

It must be emphasised that, contrary to the views expressed in some older precedents, the existence of a position of presumed undue influence will not, by itself make a contract voidable (unless the dominant party proves the agreement was made by the weaker party's own free will). It must *also* be shown that there is something about the agreement which "calls for an explanation" (this more recent expression has now replaced the old rule that the agreement must be "manifestly disadvantageous" to the weaker party). So, for example, while there might be a special relationship between parent and child, the courts will not intervene merely because a child has bought a parent a small Christmas present; it is not unusual so does not call for an explanation.

The effect of undue influence on a third party has been the subject of much recent debate and major judicial decisions in England and Hong Kong. Traditionally,

---

2.   *CIBC Mortgages Plc v Pitt* [1993] 4 All ER 433.

a third party would be unaffected by the undue influence of another unless that other was acting as agent for the third party in exerting the influence or, at least, the third party had knowledge of the undue influence. So, by analogy with most "mistaken identity" cases,[3] where property is obtained from A by the undue influence of B and then disposed of to C prior to rescission, the right to rescind will be lost unless B was acting on C's behalf or C bought the property in bad faith.

The "traditional" limitations have been amended considerably in respect of those transactions where the "influencer" persuades the "influenced" to deal directly with a third party, usually a bank, lender or similar institution. Here, where the transaction is such that it "calls for an explanation" and is "non-commercial", the bank, or similar, should be "put on inquiry" as to the possibility that the agreement made was affected by undue influence (or misrepresentation). This does not mean that such agreements can automatically be set aside as against the third party but it does mean that the third party is required by law to take certain steps to advise the possibly-influenced party of the implications of the transaction for him (or usually her). The leading decision in this area, and indeed on undue influence as a whole, is the House of Lords case of *Royal Bank of Scotland Plc v Etridge (No 2)*.[4]

Etridge also reviewed the steps that a third party, usually a bank, should take to discharge its obligations in such cases and avoid liability. The steps that the third party should take are of a practical nature but essentially require that the innocent party be given the opportunity to have independent legal advice before entering into the contract.

Hong Kong courts have applied the findings in *Etridge* in subsequent cases. Lord Scott, who sat in the House of Lords in *Etridge*, also sat as a non-permanent judge in the Court of Final Appeal case of *Li Sau Ying v Bank of China (HK) Ltd*,[5] the most important Hong Kong case to date on undue influence involving a third party. The Hong Kong Law Society has also issued guidelines on solicitors' duties in relation to security transactions with a potentially unduly influenced party in the light of *Etridge* and subsequent local decisions.[6]

Undue influence, like misrepresentation and duress, renders the contract voidable. This means it can be rescinded by the influenced party provided that none of the recognised "bars" to rescission exist, such as undue delay or the acquisition of an interest by an innocent third party. However, since undue influence is a product of equity, "a court of conscience", the court may allow the "influencer" to retain some of the benefits of the contract where it appears just to do so.

---

3. See 10.5.2.
4. [2002] 1 AC 773.
5. [2005] 1 HKLRD 106.
6. "Guidelines on solicitors' duties in relation to security transactions with potentially unduly influenced party" (issued 19 March 2003).

11.1 Duress

Duress is a common law doctrine which renders voidable[7] a contract entered into as a result of improper pressure. The pressure must have been a significant cause of the "coerced" party making the impugned contract. Traditionally, this pressure had to take the form of the use or threat of physical force against the coerced party's "person" or, occasionally, his property. Since threats to employees were also within the doctrine, it can be assumed that threats to family would also have constituted physical duress.

The doctrine of duress has considerably expanded in the past 40 years and now includes threats to the coerced party's economic interests. With the development of the doctrine of "economic duress", there are now potential overlaps with the equitable doctrine of undue influence.

11.1.1 Physical Duress

"Physical" duress, or duress of the person, is unusual but is illustrated by the following case.

Barton v Armstrong[8]

Barton was the managing director of a company which made an agreement to pay $140,000 (Australian) to Armstrong, the chairman, and to buy Armstrong's shares in the company. Armstrong had threatened to have Barton killed if he did not make the arrangements. Barton claimed to have the agreement set aside for duress. By a majority of three to two the Privy Council found for Barton. This was despite the fact that Barton may still have entered into the agreement for business reasons. The court made it clear that duress would be operative even if the plaintiff had other reasons for executing the agreement and that the burden of proof lay on the defendant to prove that the death threat had no effect at all on Barton's decision to sign the document. Lord Cross (for the majority) stated:

> if A threatens B with death if he does not execute some document and B, who takes A's threats seriously, executes the document it can be only in the most unusual circumstances that there can be any doubt whether the threats operated to induce him to execute the document. . . . If Barton had to establish that he would not have made the agreement but for Armstrong's threats then their Lordships would not dissent from the view that he had not made out his case. But no such onus lay on him. On the contrary it was for Armstrong to establish, if he could, that the threats which he was making and the unlawful pressure which he was exerting for the purpose of

---

7. While there were previous judicial statements that duress made an agreement "void", *voidability* is now clearly accepted (see *Mir v Mir* [2013] 4 HKC 213 and discussion of *The Atlantic Baron* below).
8. [1975] 2 All ER 465.

inducing Barton to sign the agreement . . . contributed nothing to Barton's decision to sign.[9]

So, in the case of actual, physical duress, there is no need for the "pressured" party to prove that the duress caused the coerced party to make the contract; it is for the "coercer" to prove that the force had no effect on the weaker party. When threats to the life of the other party have been made it will obviously be very difficult to convince a court that they have had no effect at all. In the case of other (non-physical) types of duress, as discussed below, it appears enough to prove that the duress was at least a *partial* cause of the coerced party's subsequent agreement to contract.[10]

11.1.2 Duress of Goods

The narrow limits of physical duress were relaxed by the extension of the duress doctrine to situations where the coerced party's property was threatened. Thus, in *The Siboen and the Sibotre*,[11] Kerr J said that a plea of coercion would also be upheld where a party had been forced to make a contract by the threat that, otherwise, his house would be burned down or a valuable painting slashed.[12] There is no doubt that threats of this nature would now be recognised, provided that they "coerced the will" of the other party. However, there is little need to examine the scope of duress of goods given the far more general expansion of the duress concept via the doctrine of "economic" duress.

11.1.3 Economic Duress

The recognition, in cases such as *The Siboen and the Sibotre*, that the doctrine of duress had been too narrowly confined may be seen as paving the way for a far wider concept of "economic" duress. Indeed, Stone writes:

> The first recognition of economic duress is probably to be found in the *obiter* statements of Kerr J in *The Siboen and the Sibotre*.[13]

However, some writers have identified the origin of economic duress in Lord Denning MR's judgment in *D&C Builders and Rees*[14] in which he held that a demand by a creditor's wife that the debtor accept a reduced figure for an outstanding debt on a "take it or leave it" basis had amounted to holding the creditor to ransom such that there was no true accord. He said:

---

9.   Ibid at 474.
10. It must be a "significant cause": *The Evia Luck* [1986] 2 Lloyd's Rep 165 per Goff J.
11. [1976] 1 Lloyd's Rep 293.
12. Ibid at 335.
13. R. Stone, *Contract Law (Lecture Notes)* (Oxford: Routledge Cavendish, 2006), p 166.
14. [1965] 3 All ER 837.

The creditor was in need of money to meet his own commitments and she knew it
. . . she was putting undue pressure on the creditor. She was making a threat to break
the contract (by paying nothing) and she was doing it so as to compel the creditor
to do what he was unwilling to do . . . No person can insist on a settlement procured
by intimidation.[15]

It appears, however, that while the actual decision in *D&C Builders* is uncontroversial, involving, as it does, established principles for the part-payment of debt,[16]
Lord Denning's "explanation" for the decision is based on his support for the recognition of a broad principle of "inequality of bargaining power", a principle expressly
rejected by the Privy Council in *Pao On v Lau Yiu Long*.[17]

In *The Siboen and the Sibotre*, the parties effected a renegotiation of two charters
under the threat that the charterers would otherwise go out of business. The charterers subsequently pleaded duress but the plea was rejected on the basis that they were
affected not by duress but by "ordinary commercial pressures". Kerr J expressed the
view that where the pressure involved "crossed the line" separating ordinary hard
bargaining from improper pressure, the agreement would become voidable.

Kerr J's views on the possibility of economic duress invalidating a contract are
clearly *obiter* but there is no doubt that they have been approved and followed in
subsequent cases, including the following.

North Ocean Shipping v Hyundai (The Atlantic Baron)[18]

The plaintiffs, shipowners, agreed to have the defendants build a ship for them for
$30 million (US) payable in five instalments. After the first payment the US dollar
was devalued. The defendants then asked for an additional 10% on the four remaining payments. The plaintiffs initially refused but then reluctantly agreed in order to
avoid losing a lucrative charter. They paid the surplus "without prejudice". The ship
was delivered. Eight months after delivery, the plaintiffs claimed back the overpay-
ment. Mocatta J in the English High Court found that there was economic duress
exerted on the plaintiffs. However, the action failed because, while duress makes a
contract voidable, the owners had lost the right to rescind because of lapse of time
in taking action.

Economic duress as a ground for redress has also been recognised by the Privy
Council.

---

15. Ibid at 841.
16. See 4.6.
17. [1979] 3 All ER 65 discussed below.
18. [1978] 3 All ER 1170.

Pao On v Lau Yiu Long[19]

The plaintiffs owned all the shares in a private company Tsuen Wan Shing On Estate Company Limited ("Shing On"). The defendants were major shareholders in a public company Fu Chip Investment Company Limited ("Fu Chip") which wanted to acquire a Shing On holding. Instead of a sale the parties agreed on an exchange of shares. The plaintiffs had the right to sell the shares but promised to keep 60 per cent for one year so as not to depress their value. In return the defendants promised to buy the shares back at $2.50 each so that the plaintiffs would not suffer loss. The plaintiffs then realised that if the share price rose, the defendants would get the benefit of a cheap purchase so they then refused to complete the transfer of the building unless the agreed sale-back was replaced by a simple indemnity against loss. The defendants agreed as they were concerned at a possible loss of public confidence. They did not think that the share price would decline but it did. They refused to pay on the indemnity but their plea of economic duress was rejected by the Privy Council since there was no "coercion of the will". Lord Scarman stated:

> Duress, whatever form it takes, is a coercion of the will so as to vitiate consent . . .
> In determining whether there was coercion of the will such as there was no true consent, it is material to inquire whether the person alleged to have been coerced did or did not protest; whether, at the time he was allegedly coerced into making the contract, he did or did not have an alternative course open to him such as an adequate legal remedy; whether he was independently advised; and whether after entering the contract he took steps to avoid it. All these matters are . . . relevant in determining whether he acted voluntarily or not.
>
> In their Lordships view, there is nothing contrary to the principle in recognising economic duress as a factor which may render a contract voidable, provided always that the basis of such recognition is that it must amount to a coercion of will, which vitiates consent. It must be shown that the payment made or the contract entered into was not a voluntary act.[20]

Since the plea of duress was unsuccessful in both *Atlantic Baron* and *Pao On*, the views of the judges in these cases, that economic duress should be recognised, are strictly *obiter*. However, the doctrine has been firmly accepted by the House of Lords.

Universe Tankships Inc of Monrovia v International Transport Workers Federation (The Universe Sentinel)[21]

The plaintiffs were "persuaded" by the defendant trade union to pay money to the union's welfare fund without which the defendants would have instructed their

---

19. [1979] 3 All ER 65.
20. Ibid at 78.
21. [1982] 2 All ER 67.

members not to allow the plaintiffs' ship to leave port. The plaintiffs sought to rescind on the basis of economic duress but the defendants argued that they were pursuing a legitimate trade dispute. The House of Lords rejected the defence and held that the agreement was voidable and the payment could be recovered. Lord Diplock stated:

> it is conceded that the financial consequences to the shipowners of the Universe Sentinel continuing to be rendered off hire under her time charter to Texaco, while the blacking continued, were so catastrophic as to amount to a coercion of the ship-owners' will which vitiated their consent to those agreements and to the payments made by them to the ITF . . . That economic duress may constitute a ground for such redress was recognised, albeit obiter, by the Privy Council in *Pao On v Lau Yiu Long* . . . The rationale is that his apparent consent was induced by pressure exercised on him by that other party which the law does not regard as legitimate, with the consequence that the consent is treated in law as revocable unless approbated either expressly or by implication after the illegitimate pressure has ceased to operate on his mind.[22]

The two **key elements** of economic duress, therefore, are *illegitimate pressure* and *coercion of the will*. Both elements were present in *Atlas Express Ltd v Kafko (Importers and Distributors) Ltd*.[23] Here, the plaintiffs, a large carrier, agreed that they would carry the defendants' cartons for £1.10 per carton. The plaintiffs believed there would be 400 cartons per shipment. In fact, there were only 200 cartons on the first load and the plaintiffs refused to continue unless the defendants guaranteed £440 per subsequent shipment. The defendants were a small firm which could not find an alternative carrier. They reluctantly agreed rather than disappoint their customers. The defendants later refused to pay the extra amount and the plaintiffs sued. The court found for the defendants on the basis that there was operative economic duress.

The key factors in this case were that the plaintiffs had made "illegitimate" threats to break the original contract and that the defendants had no practical alternative but to agree. The court also held that there was no consideration for the revised agreement but, given the decision in *Williams v Roffey*, shortly afterwards, that finding must now be viewed as questionable.[24]

The principles of economic duress have been considered and applied in the Hong Kong courts. In *Tung Wing Steel Co Ltd v George Wimpey International Limited*,[25] the plaintiffs had been supplying the defendants with steel rods. In September 1982 they refused to sell any more rods except at a higher price. The defendants faced the consequences of "penalty" clauses if they missed a deadline on another contract with the MTRC. The defendants, therefore, entered into a contract for the supply

---

22. Ibid at 75.
23. [1989] 1 All ER 641.
24. See 4.5.2 and 11.1.3.3 below.
25. (unrep, HCA 3285/1984, 28 June 1985).

of the rods at a higher price but then withheld payment. The plaintiffs sued for the price but the defendants relied on a number of defences including economic duress. Rhind J found that there was no economic duress exerted by the plaintiffs on the defendants. He noted that the plaintiffs were wholly within their rights to refuse to sell any more rods as the only arrangement between the parties was in the nature of a standing offer and there had never been any agreement to supply all of the defendants' requirements for the MTRC contract. In short, there was hard bargaining but no "illegitimate pressure".[26]

In contrast, operative economic duress *was* found in the following case.

Estinah v Golden Hand Indonesian Employment Agency[27]

The claimant[28] was an Indonesian domestic helper who lodged a claim in the Small Claims Tribunal against the defendant agency for the sum of $9,633 representing the difference between the amount the claimant had paid to the agency to assist her to obtain a job for her in Hong Kong and the amount that the defendant could charge legally.[29] The defendants had made clear that, without the additional payments, they would not process the papers necessary for the claimant to continue in employment in Hong Kong. The claimant's action succeeded; while there had been no physical threats to the claimant, it was clear that both elements of economic duress: "illegitimate pressure" and "coercion of the will" were present.

Kwan J held:

> For there to be economic duress, the pressure applied does not have to be in the manner of an express threat or coercion. Pressure for this purpose could take many forms. If the victim is left with no practical choice but to submit because of the course of action of the other party, this would suffice.[30]

11.1.3.1 Coercion of the Will

The requirement that there must be "coercion of the will", first introduced in *Pao On*, highlights the (sometimes difficult) distinction which courts must draw between hard but acceptable bargaining, which the courts approve, and improper pressure. The often fine distinction between the two concepts is highlighted by two contemporaneous but contrasting English cases: *DSND Subsea Ltd v Petroleum Geoservices*

---

26. See also *Liu Chong Hing Bank Limited v Ocean Importers & Exporters Company Limited and Others* (unrep, HCA 18412/1998, 8 June 2001); *ING Bank NV v Tsui Tsin Tong* (unrep, CACV 354/1999, 28 March 2000).
27. [2001] 4 HKC 607.
28. Note that in the Small Claims Tribunal the party initiating an action is called a "claimant", in contrast to a party who starts an action in the District Court or High Court, who is still called a "plaintiff".
29. Under Employment Ordinance (Cap 57) s 57.
30. *Estinah* at 614.

ASA[31] and *Carillon Construction Ltd v Felix (UK) Ltd*[32] In the *DSND* case, a project was behind schedule and the main contractor and the subcontractor were in dispute. The employer threatened to sue for liquidated damages. The main contractor then entered into an agreement, on terms unfavourable to the main contractor, with the subcontractor so that the subcontractor would resume work. The main contractor then terminated the agreement with the subcontractor, alleging that the agreement was entered into under economic duress. Mr Justice Dyson found that there was no economic duress; the pressure placed on the main contractor amounted to reasonable behaviour by the subcontractor acting in good faith in a very difficult position. The behaviour of the subcontractor was part of the "rough and tumble of normal commercial bargaining".[33] The judge noted that the victim took no steps to see whether there was any practical alternative, had been on amicable terms with the subcontractor and, crucially, had failed to produce any evidence, in the form of documents, supporting a claim that the agreement had been entered into under duress. In the contrasting *Carillon* case, a project was (again) behind schedule, with the employer threatening to sue for damages. The main contractor and subcontractor were also in dispute, with the subcontractor refusing to make necessary deliveries until a final account was agreed. The main contractor reluctantly did agree to this account and the subcontractor resumed deliveries. The main contractor then terminated the agreement and sued the subcontractor alleging that the final account was agreed under duress. The judge agreed that there was operative economic duress. Here the plaintiffs could show that they had little alternative but to "agree" the final account. They had explored using alternative suppliers and discussed their legal options with in-house counsel. These alternative options were considered to be too time-consuming. The plaintiffs had kept written records of meetings with the defendants and had made clear that the agreement was entered into under protest.

In reaching his decision, Dyson J drew heavily on factors first enunciated in *Pao On*: the existence of any protest by the victim, lack of a practical alternative, the availability of independent legal advice and the need to take swift steps to have the agreement overturned. The criterion of "lack of a practical alternative" was endorsed by Lord Burrows in the *Times Travel* case, discussed below and in *Morley Estates v The Royal Bank of Scotland plc*[34] where, in rejecting a plea of intimidation and economic duress, the Court of Appeal held:

---

31. [2000] BLR 530.
32. (2000) 74 Con LR 144.
33. Cited with approval by Lam J in *Zebra Industries (Orogenesis Nova) Ltd v Wah Tong Paper Products Group Ltd* [2016] 1 HKC 213.
34. [2021] EWCA Civ 338.

a critical ingredient of any case of intimidation or economic duress is missing from Mr Morley's case. With hindsight, Mr Morley may feel a sense of grievance. But he entered into the agreement with the bank of his own free will.[35]

11.1.3.2 Illegitimate Pressure

The requirement that the pressure by the "coercer" must be "illegitimate" can present difficulty. In cases where there is a threat to act illegally, as in *Atlas v Kafco*, the requirement is obviously fulfilled. Where, however, the threat is to do a legal act which, nonetheless "pressures" the other party, the law is not entirely clear. The general proposition is that there is no economic duress in threatening a lawful act.

R v Her Majesty's Attorney-General for England and Wales (the Bravo Two Zero Case)[36]

The appellant, R, was a former member of the elite Special Air Service (SAS) Regiment. He was a member of patrol B20 (hence the name of the case) which was dropped by helicopter behind enemy lines in the Gulf War to find "Scud" missiles and cut communication cables. The patrol was detected and hunted down by Iraqi forces. Three of the eight members died attempting to escape. One succeeded in getting across the Syrian border and the other four (including the appellant, R) were captured, tortured and interrogated. After the end of the war they were released and returned to England. Some of the survivors published accounts of the affair. The books sold very well and films were made based on these books. The ethos of the regiment before then had been for its members to preserve total secrecy. The publications caused great concern among the surviving members of the patrol who had not gone into print, and the regiment generally, because of the break with tradition and alleged errors in the publications.

As a result, it was decided to require all members of the SAS to sign confidentiality agreements to "prevent unauthorised disclosure". Failure to sign this agreement would result in a member being penalised by being returned to unit. This meant going back to the regiment from which they had joined the SAS. This was normally imposed as a penalty for some disciplinary offence or on the grounds of professional unsuitability for the SAS. It involved exclusion from the social life of the regiment and loss of its higher rates of pay. R signed the agreement.

Shortly afterwards R changed his mind and decided to apply for premature voluntary release. He went home to New Zealand. He then decided to put his own version of the Bravo Two Zero patrol story before the public and entered into a contract with a New Zealand publisher. As a result, the Attorney-General, on behalf of the Crown, commenced proceedings in the High Court of New Zealand, claiming

---

35. Per Males LJ ibid at para 58.
36. [2003] UKPC 22.

an injunction to restrain publication, damages and an account of profits. R pleaded duress in his defence. R's defence was successful in the New Zealand High Court but rejected on appeal. R then made a further appeal to the Privy Council which found that the "threat" was lawful and rejected the defence of duress.

Lord Hoffmann referred to Lord Scarman's statement in *The Universe Sentinel*[37] that there were two elements to economic duress. The first was pressure amounting to compulsion of the will of the victim and the second was that this pressure was illegitimate. He accepted that the alternative of being returned to unit, regarded in the SAS as being a public humiliation, was a compulsion of his will. It left R with no practical alternative. However, as to the legitimacy of the pressure, Lord Hoffman said:

> Although return to unit was not ordinarily used except on the grounds of delin-quency or unsuitability and was perceived by members of the SAS as a severe penalty, there is no doubt, that the Crown was entitled at its discretion to transfer any member of the SAS to another unit.[38]

He also held that the Ministry of Defence had a legitimate concern about the increasing number of unauthorised disclosures by former SAS personnel which could undermine the effectiveness of the force.

The question of whether a threat to do a *lawful* act can ever ground a claim for economic duress has been discussed in several cases, including the next, without any firm conclusion.

CTN Cash & Carry Ltd v Gallagher Ltd[39]

The plaintiffs bought cigarettes from the defendants for resale. The defendants were not legally obliged to sell to the plaintiffs and each sale was a separate contract. The defendants had arranged credit facilities for the plaintiffs but could withdraw these facilities at any time. An order for cigarettes worth £17,000 was placed by the plaintiffs in November 1986. The defendants mistakenly sent this consignment to the wrong warehouse. Before the defendants could rectify their error, the consignment was stolen. The defendants believed, incorrectly, that the goods were at the plaintiffs' risk and demanded payment of the price. The plaintiffs refused to pay. The defend-ants then made it clear that they would not in future grant credit facilities unless the price was paid. The plaintiffs paid the price. Their later action to recover the price on the ground of economic duress failed, ultimately in the English Court of Appeal.

Steyn LJ delivered the leading judgment. He noted that the dispute arose out of arm's length commercial dealings between two trading companies. The defendants were in a monopoly position but that did not by itself convert a legitimate threat into

---

37. [1982] 2 All ER 67.
38. *R v A-G* at para 17.
39. [1994] 4 All ER 714.

duress. The defendants were legally entitled to refuse to grant credit facilities to the plaintiffs. Could such a refusal amount to economic duress? Steyn LJ described this as "lawful act duress". He said:

> We are being asked to extend the categories of duress of which the law will take cognisance. That is not necessarily objectionable, but it seems to me that an extension capable of covering the present case, involving 'lawful act duress' in a commercial context in pursuit of a bona fide claim, would be a radical one with far-reaching implications. It would introduce a substantial and undesirable element of uncertainty in the commercial bargaining process.[40]

He then concluded:

> Outside the field of protected relationships, and in a purely commercial context, it might be a relatively rare case in which 'lawful act duress' can be established. And it might be particularly difficult to establish duress if the defendant bona fide considered that his demand was valid. In this complex and changing branch of the law I deliberately refrain from saying 'never'. But as the law stands, I am satisfied that the defendants' conduct in this case did not amount to duress.[41]

A simple finding that the defendants were not liable because they had neither done, nor threatened to do, anything illegal would have produced a clear legal principle. Unfortunately, the decision is not so clear cut, Steyn LJ indicating that duress via a lawful act *may*, exceptionally, be possible, where the coercer is not "*bona fide*". This reference to "*bona fide*", or "good faith", adds an unnecessary element of uncertainty into the law. The possibility of "lawful act duress" was also recognised, in the *Bravo Two Zero* case,[42] by Lord Hoffmann who said:

> Generally speaking, the threat of any form of unlawful action will be regarded as illegitimate. On the other hand, the fact that the threat is lawful does not necessarily make the pressure legitimate.[43]

Lord Hoffman quoted Lord Atkin in *Thorne v Motor Trade Association*[44] that the ordinary blackmailer normally threatens to do what he has a perfect right to do, namely, communicate some compromising conduct to a person whose knowledge is likely to affect the person threatened. What he has to justify is not the threat, but the demand for money.

Support for "lawful act duress" is to be found in the Hong Kong Court of First Instance case of *Tam Lup Wai Franky v Vong Shi Ming Nicolas*,[45] where Carlson DJ

40. Ibid at 719.
41. Ibid.
42. [2003] UKPC 22.
43. Ibid at para 16.
44. [1937] 3 All ER 157.
45. [2002] 4 HKC 135.

found that a 12-hour meeting coupled with a (lawful) threat to expose the alleged fraud of the defendant and his wife amounted to operative duress. The Deputy Judge relied on the criminal case of *Lynch v DPP for Northern Ireland*,[46] which laid down the principle, applicable to both civil and criminal cases, that duress does not overbear the will of the innocent party, nor destroy it but, instead, "deflects" it. The innocent party knows what he is doing but he does so unwillingly. With respect, the *Tam Lup Wai* authority is not a strong one, not least because its facts sit squarely with those of *Williams v Bayley*,[47] an established undue influence case. To base the decision in *Tam Lup Wai* on an uncertain doctrine of "lawful act duress", instead of the established principle of undue influence[48] (not even discussed in the case report!), seems curious to say the least. However, stronger support is provided in *Esquire (Electronics) Ltd v The Hong Kong and Shanghai Banking Corporation Ltd*,[49] where Waung J, in the Court of First Instance, cited with approval the words of Lord Scarman in *The Universe Sentinel*,[50] that:

> Duress can, of course exist even if the threat is one of lawful action . . . what one has to justify is not the threat but the demand.[51]

Waung J explained this more succinctly for laymen by adding:

> Translated into common parlance, it is the character of "the stick" that is required to be closely examined, and not the character of "the carrot".[52]

Although Waung J's judgment was the subject of significant criticism by Hong Kong's Court of Appeal,[53] the views quoted above were not themselves expressly disavowed.[54] By way of contrast, however, an implicit denial of lawful act duress is to be found in *Wing Hang Bank Ltd v Crystal Jet International Ltd*[55] where Deputy Judge Saunders refused to find duress where the alleged "pressure" consisted of "a threat to enforce . . . legal rights by instituting civil proceedings". Deputy Judge Saunders found that since such a threat was "perfectly lawful" there could be no

---

46. [1975] AC 653.
47. (1866) LR 1 HL 200.
48. Discussed below at 11.2.
49. [2005] 3 HKLRD 358.
50. [1982] 2 All ER 67.
51. *Esquire* (at first instance) at para 115.
52. Ibid at para 133.
53. At [2007] 3 HKLRD 439.
54. Most of the deficiencies in *Esquire* at first instance stemmed from delay: delay in bringing the issues to court "which could not be laid at the trial judge's door" and delay from hearing to delivery of judgment (which could). As to the latter, the CA became convinced that the trial judge had "forgotten" important interventions which he had made at trial and which he appeared to contradict in his judgment. It is a matter of some note that the judgment delivered in 2005 concerned a dispute centred on transactions made in 1987!
55. [2002] 3 HKC 279.

defence of duress. Such a view was also expressed *obiter* by Stock JA in the *Esquire* case appeal to the Court of Appeal.[56]

In conclusion, we may agree with the *obiter* view of Fok J in *Profit Step Development Ltd & Another v Sun Rising Development (Agriculture) Ltd & Another*[57] that the issue of lawful act duress has yet to be *academically* resolved,[58] while noting that, to date, neither the Hong Kong nor English courts have set aside a contract (solely) for duress via a lawful act. This view, at least as far as English law is concerned, must now be read in light of the following case, resolved ultimately in the UK Supreme Court.

Pakistan International Airline Corporation v Times Travel (UK) Ltd[59]

Times Travel (TT) had contemplated joining a combined action against PIAC to demand commission payments which it considered were owed by the airline. PIAC threatened to reduce ticket allocation to TT unless it agreed to a waiver of the action. Although PIAC was contractually entitled to cut the allocation, it was a serious potential blow to TT which reluctantly agreed to the waiver. The question before the highest UK court was whether a "lawful act duress" is recognised and, if so, whether such applied on the facts of the case.

The Supreme Court Justices were unanimous in upholding the view of the English Court of Appeal[60] that "lawful act duress" exists and *may*, in exceptional cases, be grounds for rescission of a contract. The sort of exceptional circumstances needed were, notably, those involving a sort of "blackmail", where the dominant party is prepared to give up its legal right to inform the police of the commission of a crime in return for payment or similar.[61] A second example, favoured by the majority, occurs where one party "manoeuvres" the other into a position where it feels compelled to give up a legal right. Lord Burrows resisted this seemingly vague criterion, asking why it was not applicable in the instant case, and favouring a requirement of a "bad faith demand".

The court was also unanimous in holding that the exceptional circumstances necessary to constitute lawful act duress were not present in the case. PIAC had made a demand, *"motivated by commercial self-interest"* which, said Lord Burrows is *"in general, justified"*.[62]

There was one area in which there was some disagreement amongst the Justices. Lord Hodge, representing the majority, stated:

56. [2007] 3 HKLRD 439.
57. (unrep, HCA 1649/2008, 30 November 2010).
58. Ibid at para 109.
59. [2021] UKSC 40.
60. [2019] EWCA Civ 828.
61. As in *Williams v Bayley*, discussed below (11.2.1) in the context of "actual" undue influence; and consistent with Lord Hoffmann's views in *Bravo 2 Zero* (above).
62. [2021] UKSC 40 at para 136.

In any development of the doctrine of lawful act duress it will also be important to bear in mind not only that analogous remedies already exist in equity, such as the doctrines of undue influence and unconscionable bargains, but also the absence in English law of any overriding doctrine of good faith contracting or any doctrine of imbalance of bargaining power.

Lord Burrows would, in contrast, have gone further and applied the doctrine on clear evidence that PIAC had no genuine belief in its defence to TT's proposed commission claim, coupled with unjustified economic pressure on TT to give up its claim.

11.1.3.3 Economic Duress and Consideration

The applicability of the relatively recent doctrine of economic duress has been cited as the means to resolve the traditional approach to consideration in "duty" situations with the more modern "practical benefit" approach, founded in the case of *Williams v Roffey*.[63] Since the issue is dealt with in depth in chapter 4,[64] it suffices, here, to say that there is an "apparent" conflict between the traditional view, established in *Stilk v Myrick*, and the *Roffey* decision, which, though claiming to support *Stilk*, is difficult to reconcile with it. The *Roffey* approach is that there is no reason, in principle, not to enforce a promise to give extra reward for one who merely agrees to do his existing duty, as long as there is no evidence of economic duress. Clearly, in *Roffey*, it would be easy to envisage an only slightly different scenario in which the carpenter refused to continue unless extra payment was promised. This scenario would be more akin to *Atlas v Kafco*[65] and would be regarded as economic duress. The dividing line between a freely made promise of additional reward to gain a practical benefit and a promise made "under duress" will often be a narrow one.

11.2 Undue Influence

Undue influence is a doctrine of equity that applies to more subtle forms of pressure than that formerly required to constitute duress at common law. The nature and effect of undue influence is stated by Treitel as follows:

> A transaction can be set aside in equity if, because it has been procured by undue influence by one party (A) on the other party (B), it cannot fairly be treated as the expression of B's free will.[66]

---

63. [1990] 1 All ER 512.
64. See 4.5.
65. *Atlas Express Ltd v Kafco (Importers & Distributors) Ltd* [1989] 1 All ER 641 discussed at 11.1.3.
66. Edwin Peel, *Treitel: The Law of Contract* (London: Sweet & Maxwell, 14th edn) at p 505.

Given the development of duress, especially in relation to "economic" duress, the two concepts of duress and undue influence will increasingly overlap.

Undue influence may be "actual" or "presumed". The "victim" of actual undue influence is required to prove the existence of, and exercise of, undue influence. Where he does so the agreement will be voidable automatically. The existence of "presumed undue influence" is easier to establish but will not automatically render an agreement voidable.

11.2.1 Actual Undue Influence

Treitel[67] states that actual undue influence occurs where, an agreement has been obtained by certain kinds of improper pressure which were "thought not to amount to duress at common law because no element of violence to the person was involved." The leading case is *Williams v Bayley*.[68] Here, a father was pressured into giving a mortgage of his property to cover the debts of his son. The father was threatened that the son would otherwise be prosecuted for a crime which could involve transportation for life to Australia. The father later claimed to cancel the agreement. This was upheld by the House of Lords which found evidence of actual undue influence.

It is for the "influenced" party to prove actual undue influence, as the father did in *Williams*. Once actual undue influence is established, however, the agreement becomes automatically voidable. The view previously expressed,[69] that the agreement must be "manifestly disadvantageous" to the influenced party, has been specifically overruled by the House of Lords.[70]

The requirements of actual undue influence were set out by Slade LJ in *BCCI v Aboody*.[71] These requirements are that: the other party had the capacity to influence the complainant; the influence was exercised; its exercise was undue; and its exercise brought about the transaction. In *Aboody*, a husband bullied his wife into signing an agreement which used the matrimonial home as security for the husband's debts. The wife's undue influence claim failed in the English Court of Appeal because, although the court found evidence of actual undue influence, the transaction was held not to be to the wife's "manifest disadvantage".

Since the requirement of "manifest disadvantage" no longer exists,[72] the decision in *Aboody* is now discredited.

---

67. Op cit at p 507.
68. (1866) LR 1 HL 200.
69. In *BCCI v Aboody* [1989] 1 QB 923.
70. In *CIBC Mortgages v Pitt* [1993] 4 All ER 433.
71. Note 63 above.
72. Since *CIBC*, discussed immediately below.

CIBC Mortgages v Pitt[73]

A wife was induced by her husband to remortgage the matrimonial home, of which she was joint owner, as security for a loan by CIBC. The husband said he wanted the money to buy shares but the couple told CIBC the money was for the joint purchase of a holiday home. In a subsequent action for possession of the house on grounds of non-payment of the mortgage, the wife pleaded undue influence. It was held by the House of Lords that there was *actual*, as opposed to presumed, undue influence. As such, the agreement was voidable *as against her husband* without proof of it being disadvantageous to her. Actual undue influence is analogous to fraud and renders an agreement automatically voidable. There is no need to prove "manifest disadvantage" (or its successor "an agreement that calls for an explanation"). Moreover, it has since been confirmed (by analogy with fraud and physical duress)[74] that it is no defence for the "influencer" to claim that the other party may have made the agreement anyway.[75] However, when third parties are involved, as here, they would be affected by the undue influence only if the influencer had acted as their agent or if they had actual or constructive notice of the influence. Since neither factor applied here, the wife's defence against CIBC failed.

While the criteria for determining the responsibility of the (third party) bank are now subject to the revised rules established in the landmark *Etridge* case,[76] the explanation, in *Pitt*, of the effect of actual undue influence, as between the influencing and influenced parties, remains unquestioned.

In Hong Kong a plea of actual undue influence was considered, *obiter*, by the Court of Appeal in the following case.

Diners Club International (Hong Kong) Ltd v Ng Chi Sing and Ng Yan Kiang[77]

A dispute between the parties centred on two guarantees which the second defendant signed, in Macau, in favour of the plaintiffs. The guarantees were held to be ineffective since they related only to the use of credit cards after the date of the signing and not to the past debts on which the plaintiffs based their action. The court went on to consider the second defendant's plea that he had been the victim of undue influence. Fuad JA thought it was right to address this issue in case he was wrong in the conclusion he had reached about the ambit of the guarantees. The evidence showed that the second defendant was taken by surprise by three men who had confronted him determined to get him to sign the guarantees. The second defendant was aged 60 at the time and hard of hearing. He was given no opportunity to consult his son nor

---

73. [1993] 4 All ER 433.
74. See *Barton v Armstrong* discussed at 11.1.1.
75. See *UCB Corporate Services Ltd v Williams* [2002] EWCA Civ 555.
76. [2002] 1 AC 773 and see 11.2.3.
77. (unrep, CACV 143/1985, 11 April 1986).

seek legal advice. He did not fully understand the significance of what he was being asked to do. His visitors deliberately aroused anxiety in him by suggesting that his son might be reported to the Commercial Crimes Bureau with possible disastrous consequences for the son.

Counsel for the plaintiffs conceded that there had been undue influence exerted on the second defendant but argued that the contract was not void but merely voidable and that the inaction of the second defendant until he was sued two months later amounted to affirmation of the contract. The court rejected this "affirmation" argument.

The facts of this case show a parallel with those of *Williams v Bayley*.[78] In the circumstances, there was little dispute that actual undue influence had been present and the plaintiffs' contention that a delay of only two months should prevent the defendant from claiming the assistance of equity was extremely optimistic.

It will be observed from the above cases, and the *Tam Lup Wai* case,[79] that cases of actual undue influence may overlap with common law duress. Lord Nicholls noted this in *Etridge*[80] when he said:

> Equity identified broadly two forms of unacceptable conduct. The first comprises overt acts of improper pressure or coercion such as unlawful threats. Today there is much overlap with the principle of duress as this principle has subsequently developed.[81]

An example of such a possible overlap can be seen in *Drew v Daniel*,[82] where a "forceful and insensitive" nephew emotionally bullied his aunt into resigning as trustee of a family trust. A plea of actual undue influence was upheld in the circumstances.

11.2.2 Presumed Undue Influence

Presumed undue influence arises where there is a relationship between the parties in which one of the parties (the weaker party) reposes "trust and confidence" in the other (the dominant party). The expression "presumed undue influence" is confusing since it might suggest that courts presume that undue influence has been *exercised* in such circumstances unless the dominant party can show otherwise. Indeed, such a view was expressed in earlier cases. However, in the landmark case of *Etridge* it was made clear that all that is "presumed" in these cases is that the dominant party is in *a position to* exercise undue influence. The courts do not presume that the influence

---

78. (1866) LR 1 HL 200.
79. [2002] 4 HKC 135.
80. [2002] 1 AC 773.
81. Ibid at para 8.
82. [2005] EWCA Civ 507.

has been unduly *exercised* unless the agreement in question is one that "calls for an explanation".[83]

The relationship of trust and confidence is "irrebuttably presumed" (that is, there can be no argument by the dominant party) where the parties' relationship is "special". In all other cases, the relationship of trust and confidence must be proved by the party seeking to have the agreement set aside.

11.2.2.1 Special Relationships

Special relationships arise in a variety of situations specifically recognised by the law. These include the relationship between parent/child, guardian/ward, trustee/beneficiary, doctor/patient, solicitor/client and religious adviser/disciple. Such relationships were described in the House of Lords case of *Barclays Bank v O'Brien*[84] as "class 2A" relationships, adopting terminology previously introduced by the Court of Appeal in *BCCI v Aboody*.[85]

Whenever such a special relationship exists the courts automatically and "irrebuttably" presume that a position to exercise undue influence exists. This, alone, does not make any agreement entered into by the weaker party voidable since it must also be shown that the agreement in question "calls for an explanation". The courts, in other words, do not presume from a special relationship that undue influence has been "exercised".

Lord Nicholls, in *Etridge*, explained the "special relationship" as follows:

> The law has adopted a *sternly protective attitude* towards certain types of relationship in which one party acquires influence over another who is vulnerable and dependent and where, moreover, substantial gifts by the influenced or vulnerable person are not normally to be expected. Examples of relationships within this special class are parent and child, guardian and ward, trustee and beneficiary, solicitor and client, and medical adviser and patient. In these cases the law presumes, irrebuttably, that one party had influence over the other. The complainant need not prove he actually reposed trust and confidence in the other party. It is sufficient for him to prove the existence of the type of relationship.[86]

A famous early case on special relationships is *Allcard v Skinner*.[87] Here, the plaintiff was introduced by her spiritual adviser, Nihill, to the defendant who ran the order of the Sisters of the Poor. Three years later the plaintiff joined the Sisters and gave property worth £7,000 to the order. All but £1,671 were spent on the order. The plaintiff left the Sisters in 1879 and, in 1885, claimed back the £1,671 on the grounds

---

83. See 11.2.2.3 below.
84. [1993] 4 All ER 417, [1994] 1 AC 180.
85. [1989] 1 QB 923.
86. [2002] 1 AC 773 at para 18.
87. (1837) 36 Ch D 145.

of undue influence. The English Court of Appeal upheld the view that a presumption of undue influence did exist and had not been rebutted. Unfortunately for the plaintiff her action failed as she had taken such a long time to pursue her equitable remedy.

Were *Allcard* to be decided today the court would have to decide not only that a special relationship existed but also that the agreement to transfer property "called for an explanation". On the facts, however, such a requirement is likely to have been discharged.

11.2.2.2 Other Relationships of Trust and Confidence

In relationships which fall outside the recognised "special relationship" category, a presumption of influence will only arise if there is evidence that the relationship is one where one party (the weaker party) has reposed (placed) trust and confidence in the other. These are the relationships classified in *Barclays Bank v O'Brien*[88] as "class 2B". In these class 2B cases the weaker party may show that a relationship of trust and confidence exists by producing clear evidence of this. For example, although there is no "special relationship" in a banker/client situation,[89] a client may convince the court that a class 2B relationship existed where he has put himself entirely into the hands of the bank and left his financial affairs entirely to them. This was said to be the situation in the following Hong Kong case.

Esquire Electronics Ltd v The Hong Kong and Shanghai Bank[90]

The plaintiffs bought a very expensive property at far too high a price, encouraged by the defendants' employees. The plaintiffs' financial position became hazardous and they were "persuaded" to sell the property by improper threats as to the alternatives. The representatives of the defendant bank, Hong Kong's largest and extremely powerful, were found to have acted reprehensibly in putting unfair pressure on the plaintiffs' "big boss" to sell. The bank was held liable, at first instance, in duress and undue influence. A presumption as to a position of undue influence was raised because, after two restructurings, the plaintiffs became, in the view of the first instance trial judge, "so dependent on the bank that it was wholly vulnerable to all adverse actions taken by the bank, its carer'".[91]

While the principle that a client putting himself entirely in the hands of a bank may produce a "confidential" relationship remains sound, the Hong Kong Court of Appeal upheld an appeal by the bank against the trial judge's findings of fact in the *Esquire* case and subjected the trial judge's findings to significant criticism.

---

88. [1993] 4 All ER 417 and previously in *BCCI v Aboody* [1989] 1 QB 923.
89. See *Chekiang First Bank v Fong Siu Kin* [1997] 2 HKC 302.
90. [2005] 3 HKLRD 358; on appeal [2007] 3 HKLRD 439.
91. A similar relationship was found in *Lloyd's Bank Ltd v Bundy* [1974] 3 WLR 501, [1974] 3 All ER 757.

Similarly, although the husband/wife relationship is not "special", a wife may show a 2B relationship on proof that she left her financial affairs entirely in the hands of her husband.[92] In these cases, where the weaker party has to prove the trust and confidence relationship, it is of course open to the other party to produce evidence disputing the relationship and showing that the "weaker" party was actually a "free agent". The threshold for a "confidential relationship" appears high. In *Bank of China (HK) Ltd v Wong Kam Ho*,[93] for example, Lam J said that:

> I am not satisfied that there was anything more than the usual trusting relationship between husband and wife and the usual confidence a housewife placed in these matters on her husband who is better versed in business.[94]

Once again, as with the "special relationships", once the situation of trust and confidence has been proved, the courts will accept that the dominant party is in a *position to exert* undue influence. If the agreement in dispute (the impugned agreement) is to be voidable, however, there must *also* be evidence that there was something suspicious about the agreement which "called for an explanation".

The status of the class 2B category is now in some doubt post-*Etridge*. Lord Nicholls, who delivered the leading judgment, implicitly accepted the category, though he did not use the same terminology. Lords Scott and Hobhouse, however, expressed some doubts about the usefulness of the class 2B category. Treitel suggests that these reservations should be restricted to husband/wife or similar relationships and that, elsewhere, the category remains useful.[95] This book retains the category since it was not expressly rejected in *Etridge* and has been clearly approved post-*Etridge* in the Hong Kong courts. Indeed, in the leading Court of Final Appeal case of *Li Sau Ying v Bank of China*,[96] Lord Scott, who appeared as a non-permanent judge, was happy to use the class 2B category.

11.2.2.3 Proof of Undue Influence

Once the weaker party has shown a relationship of trust and confidence, either through a "special" relationship" or via positive proof, there remains the problem of showing that the agreement was one in which "an explanation is called for". This requirement is a novel one, emanating from *Royal Bank of Scotland v Etridge*,[97] and described as follows by Lord Nicholls:

---

92. For example, *Barclays Bank v Coleman* [2000] 3 WLR 405 (one of the eight *Etridge* appeals).
93. [2014] 1 HKLRD 41.
94. Ibid at para 53.
95. And see *Malik v Sheikh* [2018] EWHC 973 (Ch).
96. [2005] 1 HKLRD 106.
97. [2002] 1 AC 773.

It is a necessary limitation . . . It would be absurd for the law to presume that every gift by a child to a parent, or every transaction between a client and his solicitor or between a patient and his doctor, was brought about by undue influence unless the contrary is affirmatively proved. Such a presumption would be too far- reaching. The law would be out of touch with everyday life if the presumption were to apply to every Christmas or birthday gift by a child to a parent, or to an agreement whereby a client or patient agrees to be responsible for the reasonable fees of his legal or medical adviser . . . So something more is needed before the law reverses the burden of proof, something which *calls for an explanation*. When that something more is present, the greater the disadvantage to the vulnerable person, the more cogent must be the explanation before the presumption will be regarded as rebutted.[98]

Prior to this case there were decisions which implied that once the "presumption" was shown, the agreement would be automatically voidable in the absence of proof by the dominant party that the weaker party had acted of his (or her) own free will. Later it was stated that the weaker party must also show that the agreement was "manifestly disadvantageous".[99] The current position is laid down by *Etridge*,[100] now the leading case on undue influence in England. Given that *Etridge* is a post-1997 decision it is not strictly binding on Hong Kong courts. It is clear, however, that the case is being followed by the Hong Kong judges. The House of Lords, in *Etridge*, fully examined the law on undue influence, especially the effect which undue influence has on the position of a (non-influencing) third party.[101] Given the significance of *Etridge*, previous precedents should be read in the light of it and, where they appear to conflict, should be treated with caution.

Royal Bank of Scotland plc v Etridge (No 2)[102]

Eight appeals came before the House of Lords. Each arose out of a transaction in which a wife charged her interest in her home in favour of a bank as security for her husband's indebtedness or the indebtedness of a company through which he carried on business. The wife later asserted that she had signed the charge under the undue influence of her husband. Seven of the appeals were concerned with the applicable principles in such circumstances. In each case the bank sought to enforce the charge signed by the wife. The bank claimed an order for possession of the matrimonial home. The wife raised a defence that the bank was on notice that her concurrence in the transaction had been procured by her husband's undue influence. The eighth appeal concerned a claim by a wife for damages from a solicitor who advised her

---

98. *Etridge* at para 24.
99. *Barclays Bank v O'Brien* (n 77 above).
100. Discussed at length below.
101. See 11.2.3 below.
102. [2002] 1 AC 773.

before she entered into a guarantee obligation. In the circumstances of the individual cases the court found in favour of some of the claimants and against others.

The leading judgment is that of Lord Nicholls who stated:

> Whether a transaction was brought about by the exercise of undue influence is a question of fact. Here, as elsewhere the general principle is that he who asserts a wrong has been committed must prove it. The burden of proving an allegation of undue influence rests upon the person who claims to have been wronged. This is the general rule. The evidence required to discharge the burden of proof depends on the nature of the alleged undue influence, the personality of the parties, their relationship, the extent to which the transaction cannot be readily accounted for by the ordinary motives of ordinary persons in that relationship, and all the circumstances of the case.
>
> Proof that the complainant placed trust and confidence in the other party in relation to the management of the complainant's financial affairs, coupled with a transaction that calls for explanation, will normally be sufficient, failing satisfactory evidence to the contrary, to discharge the burden of proof.[103]

In short, once the claimant has shown a relationship of trust and confidence (irrebuttably presumed in the case of "special relationships")[104] and that the agreement is such that *"an explanation is called for"*, this will "normally" be enough for a "presumption" that undue influence has been *exercised*. The agreement will then be voidable *unless* the dominant party can prove that no undue influence was exercised in fact and the allegedly "weaker" party acted of his (or her) own free will.

The courts in Hong Kong have largely followed the decision in *Etridge*, notably in the following case.

Bank of China (Hong Kong) Ltd v Wong King Sing & Others[105]

A brother acted as surety for an elder brother. He then sought to have the agreement set aside on the grounds of undue influence. The judge, Geoffrey Ma SC (as he then was), extensively reviewed the undue influence precedents, including *Etridge*, and even went so far as to ask the parties to make further submissions based on this then very recent case. The judge decided that there was no undue influence in this case. As such there was no need to determine the issue of whether the plaintiff bank should have been put "on inquiry".[106]

Despite the misgivings of Lords Hobhouse and Scott in *Etridge*, Ma SC made use of the "2A and 2B" categories of presumed undue influence, enunciated in *Barclays Bank v O'Brien/BCCI v Aboody*. Clearly there was no "special" 2A relationship here, since siblings are not included in that category. Nor did Ma SC believe

---

103. Paras 13–14.
104. See 11.2.2.1 above.
105. [2002] 1 HKLRD 358, [2002] 1 HKC 83.
106. See 11.2.3 below.

there was any indication of a relationship in which trust and confidence had been reposed (2B). In case he should be deemed wrong, however, Ma SC went on to make clear that even if a presumption of undue influence were to apply, there was clear evidence in the case that no undue influence had in fact been exercised. He noted that the younger brother was a graduate of the Chinese University of Hong Kong in sales and marketing and understood what he was signing. He was knowledgeable in commercial matters and had good commercial sense. The judge stated that:

> A person may be educated, confident and able, but still be unduly influenced by his or her spouse. There are many instances one can recall in real life where very able men or women implicitly trust their spouse in financial matters so much so that abuses can sometimes occur. The present case, however, is not such an instance.[107]

Ma SC's conclusion was that the younger brother was "very much his own man".[108]

Probably the most important application of *Etridge* in Hong Kong is the Court of Final Appeal's decision in another case involving the Bank of China: *Li Sau Ying v Bank of China (Hong Kong) Ltd*.[109] Lord Scott of Foscote NPJ, who gave the leading judgment in this case, was one of the judges in the House of Lords in *Etridge*.

Li Sau Ying v Bank of China (Hong Kong) Ltd[110]

The appellant granted a mortgage over a flat she owned to a bank as security for the indebtedness to the bank of a company in which she had no interest. The company was controlled by a Mr Ip and the appellant had granted the mortgage at the suggestion of a friend of hers, a Mr Li, who was an associate of Mr Ip. The appellant claimed to be entitled to rescind the mortgage contract on the ground that she had been procured to enter into it by misrepresentations made by Mr Li or by the undue influence of Mr Li over her. The bank, it was alleged, had actual or constructive notice of these improprieties.

The judge at first instance, Deputy Judge Bunting, held that there was undue influence exerted on the appellant. He found she had trust and confidence in Mr Li and because the mortgage, and her role as surety, did not appear to be a normal commercial transaction, a presumption of undue influence arose and had not been rebutted. He found the bank had notice of this undue influence and that the bank had failed to do enough to bring home to the appellant the risks she was running in entering into the mortgage agreement. The appellant was, therefore, entitled to compensation from the bank.

---

107. [2002] 1 HKC 83 at 103.
108. Ibid at 105.
109. [2005] 1 HKLRD 106.
110. Ibid.

The bank appealed to the Hong Kong Court of Appeal which unanimously allowed the appeal. The higher court found that there was no presumption of undue influence and the claim of undue influence should fail. They said that even if there was undue influence there was nothing that should have put the bank on inquiry and so there was no case for attributing constructive notice of that undue influence to the bank.

The appellant appealed, *inter alia*, on these findings to the Court of Final Appeal which unanimously rejected the appeal on the basis that there had been no undue influence exercised and no failure by the bank to perform its duties.

Lord Scott noted that the relationship between the appellant and Mr Li was one of friends but was not sexual in nature. He criticised the lower courts for over-complicating the undue influence issue and said:

> The strong message from *Etridge* . . . is that, particularly in Class 2B cases, concentration on a so-called presumption of undue influence is likely to detract from the real issue, namely, whether the evidence justifies a conclusion that the impugned transaction was procured by undue influence.[111]

Lord Scott found on the facts that the appellant had reposed a high degree of trust and confidence in Mr Li but that there was no disadvantage to her in the transaction and the use of the influence was not undue. He added:

> The concentration in the courts below on whether there was trust and confidence reposed by the appellant in Mr Li sufficient to give rise to a Class 2B presumption of undue influence has, in my opinion, served to distract attention from the real issue, namely, whether in advising, or persuading, the appellant to enter into . . . mortgage . . . Mr Li was unconscionably abusing the trust and confidence she had in him.[112]

A similar approach was taken by the Hong Kong Court of Appeal in *Bank of China (Hong Kong) Ltd v China Hong Kong Textile Co Ltd*,[113] where the court rejected a plea of undue influence by a mother who had mortgaged her property to finance her sons' business debts. The court felt that there was no "call for an explanation" since, in Hong Kong at least, it would be customary for a mother to financially assist her children *and* because there was no evidence of impropriety on the part of the sons in requesting their mother's help.

11.2.2.4 Rebutting the Presumption

Once it has been shown that the parties were in a relationship in which trust and confidence has been reposed by one in the other and that the agreement in dispute (the impugned agreement) "calls for an explanation", the "burden of proof" shifts to

---

111. Ibid at para 30.
112. Ibid at para 33.
113. [2011] 4 HKLRD 457.

the dominant party. If the agreement is not to be declared voidable he must produce evidence that undue influence was not, in fact, exercised; that the other party acted of his own free will. In legal terminology the dominant party has to "rebut the presumption" of undue influence.

The normal way in which the presumption will be rebutted is by proof that the weaker party obtained independent legal advice. In *Etridge*, Lord Nicholls said:

> Proof that the complainant received advice from a third party before entering into the impugned transaction is one of the matters a court takes into account when weighing all the evidence. The weight, or importance, to be attached to such advice depends on all the circumstances. In the normal course, advice from a solicitor or other outside adviser can be expected to bring home to a complainant a proper understanding of what he or she is about to do. But a person may understand fully the implications of a proposed transaction, for instance, a substantial gift, and yet still be acting under the undue influence of another. Proof of outside advice does not, of itself, necessarily show that the subsequent completion of the transaction was free from the e free from the exercise of undue influence. Whether it will be proper to infer that outside advice had an emancipating effect, so that the transaction was not brought about by the exercise of the undue influence, is a question of fact to be decided having regard to all the evidence in the case.[114]

Independent advice, in other words, is a strong indication that the weaker party has acted of his own free will but it is not conclusive. Conversely, although unusually, it may be possible for a court to find that the weaker party acted of his own free will even though independent legal advice was absent. In *R v The Attorney-General* (The *Bravo Two Zero* case),[115] dealt with above in the context of duress,[116] the Privy Council was prepared to accept that there was a relationship in which the claimant reposed trust and confidence in his superior officer. However, on the facts of the case, a majority of the court concluded that no undue influence had been exercised in fact. The claimant was found to have acted of his own free will out of a desire to stay with the SAS even though no independent legal advice was given to him and even though such advice had been prohibited.[117] Lord Hoffman expressed the view of the majority as to the significance of independent legal advice. He said:

> The absence of independent legal advice may or may not be a relevant matter according to the circumstances. It is not necessarily an unfair exploitation of a relationship for one party to enter into a transaction with the other without ensuring that he has obtained independent legal advice. On the other hand, the transaction may be such as to give rise to the inference of undue influence even if the induced party was

---

114. *Etridge* at para 20.
115. [2003] UKPC 22.
116. See 11.1 above.
117. Lord Scott dissented in this case because of the lack of independent legal advice.

advised by an independent lawyer and understood the legal implications of what he was doing.[118]

He went on to find that even if there was a presumption of influence arising out of the relationship between R and his superior officers, no undue influence had been exercised in the circumstances. Anyone serving in the SAS could reasonably be required to sign such an agreement, R had understood the implications of signing, and the contract was in simple terms. A similar approach was taken by the Privy Council in *National Commercial Bank (Jamaica) v Hew*,[119] the facts of which are bizarre. In *Hew*, the respondent, Hew, had a close relationship with Cobham, the branch manager of the appellant bank. Hew told Cobham he had always wanted to borrow £1 million! Cobham said there must be a stated purpose so the loan was made to develop a plot of Hew's land. The interest rate on the loan was very high, Hew could not keep up repayments and, after the debt rose dramatically, the bank sought repayment from Hew's estate (Hew having died). The Privy Council, reversing the decision of the Jamaican Court of Appeal, found the bank liable in neither negligence nor undue influence.

In respect of undue influence, it was accepted that the very close relationship between the banker and client raised a presumption of a position of undue influence. Clearly, too, the agreement was one that "called for an explanation", given that it was commercially unwise for Mr Hew to act as he did. However, even in the absence of independent advice, this was a case where the necessary "explanation" was present; Hew had wanted the arrangement and the bank had offered him the same terms it would to any other customer.

11.2.3 Undue Influence and Third Parties

So far we have concentrated on the relationship between the "influencer" and the "influenced", the conclusion being that where A unduly influences B, the agreement is voidable *as against A*. The position is more complicated, however, where a third party is involved. In the first type of case, A exercises undue influence to persuade B to make a contract with him (A). He may then, for example, pass on property so obtained to a third party, C. The legal position here is that C will get good title in the goods unless he was a party to the influence or aware of it.

In the second type of case, A persuades B, by undue influence, to make a contract with C (usually for A's benefit). It is this area, crucial to the *Etridge* case and where the law has developed dramatically in recent times, on which we now primarily focus.

---

118. *Bravo Two Zero* at para 30.
119. [2003] UKPC 51.

11.2.3.1 Where the "Influencer" Is a Party to the (Impugned) Contract

In the "normal" case where A exerts influence over (contracting party) B, this will not affect a third party, C, unless C is a party to the influence or has knowledge, actual or constructive, of it. So, for example, if A, having exerted such influence, obtains property from B for an unrealistically low figure, B will lose his right to rescind against A after C has bought the property in good faith. In this respect, C is in a similar position to the innocent party who acquires in good faith from the "rogue" in a "face-to-face" mistaken identity case.[120]

11.2.3.2 Where the "Influencer" Is NOT a Party to the Impugned Contract

It is in this area that the law on undue influence has developed most dramatically via several significant cases culminating in *Etridge* itself. A typical scenario would involve a husband persuading his wife to guarantee his personal or business debts with a bank, often by using her share of the matrimonial home as a surety. Problems would then arise where the husband defaulted on his debts and the third party sought to enforce the guarantee.

The traditional view was that in these cases the bank, or similar, would not be affected by any undue influence (or misrepresentation) which the husband exercised over his wife unless the husband was acting as the bank's agent or the bank had knowledge of the undue influence. Agency was found in the case of *Avon Finance Co Ltd v Bridger*.[121]

Here, the plaintiffs lent money to the defendant's son and, in return, required the son to persuade his parents to sign a document giving the plaintiffs a legal charge on their home as security for the son's debts. The son told his parents they were signing forms for a building society mortgage. The son later fell into debt and the plaintiffs claimed the house. The action failed as the English Court of Appeal held that the plaintiffs were liable for the misrepresentation of the son as he was acting as their agent. Although the case was decided, ultimately, on the basis of misrepresentation, the requirement that liability depends on the existence of agency is equally applicable to undue influence.

A finding of agency in these situations is rare. In *Bank of China (HK) Ltd v Tsang Sheung Bun*[122] in the Hong Kong Court of Appeal Kwan JA stated:

---

120. See 10.5.2.
121. [1985] 2 All ER 281.
122. [2013] 5 HKLRD 62.

The mere fact that a debtor is required by his bank to obtain security for facilities and the debtor then approaches the surety does not mean that the debtor is acting as the agent for the bank.[123]

The limitations of the previous rules became increasingly apparent especially as increased numbers of married women came before the courts who had been unduly influenced by their husbands to make contracts (generally involving the wife's share of the matrimonial home) with "innocent" banks or other financial institutions. The problem has been exacerbated by the substantial growth in home ownership in England over the last 50 years and the large increase in the number of homes owned jointly by husbands and wives. The courts are aware that such couples should be free to use their homes as a means of raising money. Such funds could be used to finance the business of the husband or wife or for any of a number of other purposes. It is important then for a bank, or other lending institution, to be confident that the signature of each of the joint owners of the family home on a guarantee will be binding, otherwise banks will be reluctant to lend money on the security of jointly owned property.[124]

The task of the law in this area is, therefore, to balance the need to protect the weaker joint owner of property party against the stronger and the need for the bank to have reasonable confidence in the strength of its own security.

The first case in which the courts attempted, as a matter of policy, to strike a better balance and improve the lot of the "influenced wife" was the *O'Brien* case.

Barclays Bank v O'Brien[125]

Mr O'Brien's company had a large overdraft with the plaintiff bank. The plaintiffs wanted him to guarantee payment and to use his home as security. The house was owned jointly by Mr O'Brien and his wife. O'Brien persuaded his wife to agree to a charge on the house by falsely telling her it was only for £60,000 and only for three weeks. Both O'Briens signed the charge without reading the documents. The plaintiffs knew that Mrs O'Brien had not taken independent legal advice. When the company failed to pay the overdraft the plaintiffs tried to take possession of the house. Mrs O'Brien pleaded undue influence and misrepresentation by her husband. Although the decision in her favour was made largely on the basis of misrepresentation, the House of Lords laid down principles also applicable to undue influence.

The House of Lords decided that a better balance must be struck between protecting the interests of wives (or co-habitees) and preserving the commercial freedom of financial institutions. The court laid down guidelines as to when a bank,

---

123. Ibid at para 41.
124. While joint ownership may be less common in Hong Kong, marital breakdown is an increasing phenomenon. Moreover, spiralling property prices make the "home as security" issue one of fundamental concern.
125. [1993] 4 All ER 417, [1994] 1 AC 180.

or other lender, should be "put on inquiry" as to the possibility of misrepresentation and undue influence and the extent of the bank's duty once put on inquiry. These guidelines, though refined in *Etridge*, were hailed in that case as a necessary attempt to improve matters.

11.2.3.2.1 When the "Bank" Should Be "Put on Inquiry"

The court, in *O'Brien*, decided that the third party should be "put on inquiry" wherever the transaction in question was one not apparently for the benefit of the influenced party.

In such cases, the court ruled, the third party must take steps to ensure that the agreement is properly obtained by, for example, holding a private meeting, explaining the extent of the wife's liability and advising independent legal advice. Lord Browne-Wilkinson, in *O'Brien*, spoke in terms of a bank having "constructive notice" of the possibility of wrongdoing where a non-beneficial contract was agreed by the wife. The concept of constructive notice suggests that a bank would be treated as if it had actual knowledge of any wrongdoing by the husband if it had been "put on notice" or ought to have known about such wrongdoing.

The emphasis on the agreement being non-beneficial to the wife explained why in *CIBC Mortgages Plc v Pitt*[126] the House of Lords noted that a bank is *not* put on enquiry where money is advanced to a husband and wife jointly for an "apparently" beneficial purpose (the joint purchase of a holiday home). Here there is no apparent disadvantage to either husband or wife. To have expected a lending institution to be put on inquiry in such seemingly innocuous circumstances would be going too far.

O'Brien represented a considerable advance in protection for the influenced party and the so-called "wife's special equity" in *O'Brien* was praised as "sorely needed" and a "practical solution" to a difficult problem in *Etridge*, where protection for the influenced party was further extended. The major development in the law, as regards third parties, in *Etridge* is the extension of the situations in which a bank or other lender will be put "on inquiry" and the more detailed explanation of the steps which a bank must take to discharge its responsibilities once put on inquiry. The expression "put on inquiry" was preserved, in *Etridge*, even though it was regarded as not strictly accurate. Lord Nicholls stated, quite simply, that a bank should be put on inquiry whenever a wife stands surety for her husband's debts, either personal or business. For the sake of clarity, Lord Nicholls also emphasised that the courts would expect the bank to be put similarly on inquiry where the relationship involved was analogous (for example, co-habiting "partners", heterosexual or homosexual) and the lending institution was aware of the relationship. Lord Nicholls, therefore, does not place any restriction on the type of relationship where the bank may be put on enquiry except to limit it to where the relationship between the surety and the debtor

---

126. [1993] 4 All ER 433.

is "non-commercial". The couple need not even be cohabiting: *Massey v Midland Bank plc*;[127] nor have any sexual relationship. For the sake of simplicity, we may talk in terms of "the husband" and "the wife" though this should be taken to include the other analogous, non-commercial relationships. Where such "non-commercial" relationships exist *and* the transaction "calls for an explanation",[128] the bank should be put on inquiry.

The *Etridge* requirement, then, is not that the transaction appears "non-beneficial" but that it must "call for an explanation". In theory an agreement could still call for an explanation (and become voidable if none is provided) even where the agreement in question is beneficial to the complainant. This echoes the view expressed in *CIBC v Pitt*[129] that in cases of "actual" undue influence "manifest disadvantage" is not required. In practice, however, the tests are unlikely to differ markedly. The non-beneficial nature of an agreement is the most obvious reason that it would call for an explanation and, unless the agreement is disadvantageous, there are unlikely to be complaints. As Lord Nicholls said, in *Etridge*:

> In CIBC Mortgages PLC v Pitt your Lordships' House decided that in cases of undue influence disadvantage is not a necessary ingredient of the cause of action. It is not essential that the transaction should be disadvantageous to the pressurised or influenced person, either in financial terms or in any other way. However, in the nature of things, questions of undue influence will not usually arise, and the exercise of undue influence is unlikely to occur, where the transaction is innocuous. The issue is likely to arise only when, in some respect, the transaction was disadvantageous either from the outset or as matters turned out.[130]

This approach differs little from Lord Browne-Wilkinson's, in *Pitt*, that:

> disadvantage had to be shown, not as a constituent element of the cause of action for undue influence, but in order to raise a presumption of undue influence.[131]

These words were cited with approval in the Hong Kong High Court in *Esquire (Electronics) Ltd v The Hong Kong and Shanghai Bank*[132] and (unlike much of the judgment!) were not disavowed on appeal to the Court of Appeal.

The tests may, however, produce different results in exceptional cases. The *Hew* case,[133] for example, provided clear evidence of a "disadvantageous" transaction for

---

127. [1995] 1 All ER 929.
128. The very large number of unsuccessful claims that a bank should have been "put on inquiry" in Hong Kong suggests that claimants (and their legal advisers) have overlooked the "calls for an explanation" requirement.
129. [1993] 4 All ER 433.
130. *Etridge* case at para 12.
131. [1993] 4 All ER 433 at 439.
132. Discussed at 11.1.3.2 and 11.2.2.2. The first instance decision in *Esquire* was reversed on appeal but on grounds unrelated to the criteria for establishing the presumption.
133. [2003] UKPC 51.

which there was a reasonable explanation. Had the Privy Council focused on "disadvantage" rather than "explanation" they would have been more likely to find the agreement voidable.

An unusual (but unsuccessful) attempt to argue that a lender should have been put on inquiry was made by one Madam Yu in *Lei Shing Hong Credit Ltd v San Tong Lee Co Ltd & Others*,[134] much of the argument in which revolved around assertions of breach of money-lending regulations.[135] Madam Yu argued that her mental state had been badly impaired by a frightening burglary at her home, about which the lender was aware from newspaper accounts, and as a result of which the lender was able to exert undue influence. The court rejected her claims. Trial judge, Lam J, stated:

> there is no evidence that her mental faculties were relevantly impaired . . . The burden is on San Tong and Madam Yu to prove that Madam Yu's understanding of the documents was materially impaired by her mental condition. In my opinion they have failed to discharge that burden.
>
> Further, . . . there is no basis to show that the plaintiff knew or ought to have been aware of any abnormality in Madam Yu's mental condition.

11.2.3.2.2 The Steps a Bank Should Take When "Put on Inquiry"

In *Etridge*, Lord Nicholls identified the steps a bank should take when it has been put "on inquiry". He noted that while *O'Brien* had laid down guidelines in this area, he was not satisfied that these steps were sufficient to ensure that the legal advice so given was truly independent. However, he pointed out that it would not be required for the bank itself to investigate whether undue influence or other wrongdoing had been exercised on the wife. Such a requirement would lead to an intrusive, inconclusive and expensive exercise that would be a disproportionate response to the need to protect the wife. In this respect the statement that a bank is "put on inquiry" is slightly misleading. Lord Nicholls added:

> The furthest a bank can be expected to go is to take reasonable steps to satisfy itself that the wife has had brought home to her, in a meaningful way, the practical implications of the proposed transaction. This does not wholly eliminate the risk of undue influence or misrepresentation.[136]

What are the steps that a bank, when put on enquiry, must now take to avoid being fixed with constructive notice of any wrongdoing by the husband on the wife? These can be summarised as follows:

---

134. [2021] 2 HKC 572.
135. Discussed in chapter 13.
136. *Etridge* at para 54.

1. The bank should take reasonable steps to ensure that the wife has explained to her the practical effect of the transaction. A personal meeting with the wife is not required.

2. The bank should communicate directly with the wife, informing her, that for its own protection, it will require written confirmation from a solicitor acting for her, to the effect that the solicitor has fully explained to her the nature of the documents and the practical implications they will have for her. She should be asked to nominate a solicitor to act for her. In order to avoid unnecessary cost, this could be the same as the solicitor acting for her husband.

3. The bank, if it is unwilling itself to explain the husband's financial affairs, must provide the wife's solicitor with the financial information he needs for this purpose.

4. If the bank has reason to be suspicious about the transaction, the bank must inform the wife's solicitor of the facts giving rise to this suspicion.

5. The bank, in every case, should obtain a written confirmation from the wife's solicitor that the above steps have been complied with.

The bank would not be liable to the wife for any negligent advice given to her by her solicitor unless the bank knew, or ought to have known, that the proper advice had not been given. This might arise where, for example, the bank knew that the solicitor advising the wife was only a trainee or had no experience in this field or the advice given did not meet the requirements set out above. The solicitor's duty is to give proper advice including, of course, to point out to a wife that a transaction is not in her best interests. However, the ultimate decision on whether to proceed is hers.

Following the decision in *Etridge*, the Law Society of Hong Kong issued guidelines on solicitors' duties in relation to security transactions with potential victims of undue influence.[137] The purpose of the guidelines was, *inter alia*, to remind members that they should carefully consider their position when conducting such transactions in order to prevent exposure to claims and an adverse impact on the Professional Indemnity Scheme. The guidelines mirror the requirements set out in *Etridge*. They seem to place a greater burden on solicitors but are steps that a prudent law firm should take in any event. Failure to comply with the *Etridge* and post-*Etridge* guidelines led to the Hong Kong Court of Appeal granting rescission of contract for banking services in *Wing Hang Bank Ltd v Kwok Lai Sim & Another*.[138] The bank had tried to enforce a charge against the defendant sisters who, it was found, had been victims of misrepresentation by their brother. Since the bank had taken insufficient steps to protect the sisters and had "constructive notice" of the brother's

---

137. Entitled "Guidelines on solicitors' duties in relation to security transactions with potentially unduly influenced party", issued 19 March 2003.
138. [2009] 4 HKC 71.

misrepresentation, the action on the charge failed and the sisters' counter-claim for rescission was upheld.

Finally, it should be pointed out that even if a solicitor fails to follow the guide-lines, the transaction between the bank or lending institution and the complainant will only be voidable if there is indeed some misrepresentation, undue influence or other wrongdoing exerted on the complainant by the husband or other third party.

11.2.4 Remedies for Undue Influence

Since undue influence renders a contract voidable, at the option of the influenced party, the most obvious remedy is one of rescission, to put the parties back into their pre-contractual position. Similar "bars" to rescission apply to undue influence as to misrepresentation.[139] Thus a contract cannot be rescinded if the influenced party "affirms" the contract or takes too long to seek his remedy. Moreover, the acquisition of rights by an innocent party in property obtained by undue influence will also bar the remedy, as will the impossibility of returning the parties substantially to their pre-contractual position.

"Affirmation" involves a party deciding to continue with a transaction after discovering his right to rescind. An example is provided by *First National Bank v Walker*,[140] where a wife agreed to a joint charge on the matrimonial home, which clearly "called for an explanation" and would have been voidable against the husband (and ultimately the lending bank) but for her subsequent affirmation.

The lapse of time "bar" is illustrated by *Allcard v Skinner*,[141] where the agreement was held to be voidable on the grounds of undue influence *but for* the fact that the religious disciple took several years after becoming free of her religious adviser's influence before bringing her action.

The question of third party rights has been dealt with above. To summarise, however, in the normal course of things, the third party will be affected by undue influence only where he is a party to it or knew of its existence; otherwise he will acquire good title in any relevant property acquired before rescission. In other cases, those deriving from *O'Brien* and *Etridge*, special factors will apply and the third party will have additional responsibilities.[142]

Rescission requires that the parties be returned to their pre-contractual position. As such, it will be barred where such a return to the *status quo* is not possible. It is not permitted to rescind the offending part of the contract and continue with the rest. In *TSB Bank plc v Camfield*,[143] a wife thought she was guaranteeing only

---

139. See chapter 9.
140. [2001] 1 FLR 505.
141. (1837) 36 Ch D 145. See also *Samuel v Wadlow (aka Seal)* [2007] EWCA Civ 155.
142. See 11.2.3.2.2 above
143. [1995] 1 All ER 951.

her husband's future debts when, in fact, she was guaranteeing both future and past debts. The English Court of Appeal held that where rescission is ordered, the entire transaction must be set aside. It rejected the argument that the charge be set aside only in respect of the past debts and to enforce it in respect of the future debt of £15,000 which was the maximum liability the wife thought she was incurring. To have restricted rescission in this way would be rewriting the contract.

As with misrepresentation,[144] the courts allow some flexibility in respect of "substantial restitution" to the pre-contractual position and the influenced party may be allowed to rescind in spite of the fact that he cannot make *precise* restitution, so long as equity can achieve a result that is "practically just".[145]

Moreover, since rescission for undue influence is an equitable remedy and equity is "a court of conscience", the court may "impose terms" on the party granted rescission in order to do justice to both parties.

Cheese v Thomas[146]

The plaintiff and defendant, his great nephew, jointly paid for a house which was purchased in the defendant's sole name. The price was £83,000 of which the plaintiff paid £43,000. The plaintiff discovered that the defendant was not making mortgage repayments on the £40,000 he had borrowed. The plaintiff sought rescission for undue influence, by which time the value of the property had declined by £27,500. The English Court of Appeal granted rescission but on the basis that each party bore a share of the loss.

If the plaintiff in this case had received back all his £43,000 he would have escaped the effect of the housing price fall (on which both parties had taken the risk) while the defendant would have borne all the loss. As Sir Donald Nicholls V-C stated:

> If the transaction was to be set aside, the next step was the restoration of the parties to their original positions. Achieving that would mean sale of the house and repayment of what each had paid over. Unhappily, although £83,000 had been spent on the house, only £55,400 had come from the sale.
>
> The question therefore arose: on whom should the loss fall? The plaintiff contended that he was entitled to look to the defendant personally to make good all of the shortfall . . .
>
> It was well established that a court of equity would set aside a transaction even when it could not restore the parties precisely to the state they had been in before the contract . . .

144. See chapter 9.
145. Treitel (op cit) at p 518. Substantial restitution is also required for the common law doctrine of duress: *Halpern v Halpern* [2006] EWHC 603.
146. [1994] 1 All ER 35.

In the instant case justice required that each party should be returned as near to his original position as was possible. Each should get back a proportionate share of the net proceeds of the house, before deducting the amount paid to the building society.

. . . the plaintiff was seeking the assistance of a court of equity and he who seeks equity must do equity.[147]

The "practical justice" aspect was also alluded to in the *Hew* case,[148] where it was held that even if the Privy Council had allowed the contract to be rescinded on the grounds of undue influence, Hew had been lent money which he (or his estate) would have had to return or be unjustly enriched. Moreover, interest would have been payable at a rate fixed by the court; the only difference would have been that the rate of interest fixed by the court would have been less than that fixed by the bank. A similar approach was adopted in the following case.

O'Sullivan v Management Agency and Music Ltd[149]

The plaintiff, while a struggling young pop singer, made a contract for the defendants to act as his management. He later sought to have the agreement set aside on the basis of, *inter alia*, undue influence. It was held that the relationship was "fiduciary", a relationship of trust, giving rise to a presumption of a position of undue influence. The agreement was, overall, not in the plaintiff's best interests and had been obtained from a position of superior bargaining strength. The English Court of Appeal permitted rescission even though complete restitution was not possible. The court, however, allowed the defendants to retain an allowance for skill and labour which had contributed to the plaintiff's success but, "not as much as the defendants might have obtained if the contracts had been properly negotiated between fully advised parties".

Achieving a just solution may even require an award that looks more like damages than rescission.

Mahoney v Purnell[150]

Mahoney had been persuaded to sell his 50 per cent shareholding in a business to his son-in-law, who owned the other 50 per cent, for £200,000. Payment was to be made over a ten-year period. Although the company's solicitor had explained the proposed terms, he had stated that he could not advise Mahoney on the commercial reasonableness of the proposal because he was acting for the company. However, Mahoney was not explicitly advised to obtain independent legal advice. One year after this agreement was made the son-in-law sold the business for over £3 million. Mahoney

---

147. See also 15.2.
148. [2003] UKPC 51 and see 11.2.2.4.
149. [1985] 3 All ER 351.
150. [1996] 3 All ER 61.

sought rescission of the agreement and equitable relief of a money judgment on the basis of undue influence. However, the company went into liquidation at a time when Mahoney was still owed £80,000. The issue in the case related to the remedy for the undue influence since the parties could not be restored to their former positions. It was held that the court had power to award compensation in equity where, as here, there was a relationship based on trust which was fiduciary in nature and this fiduciary relationship had been abused. Accordingly, May J made an award whereby the son-in-law was to compensate Mahoney in an amount equal to the value at the date of the agreement of what he had surrendered with credit being given for what he had received. This was calculated at approximately £202,000.

The court emphasised that this remedy, which looked very like "damages", would only be applicable where undue influence is exercised in a "fiduciary" relationship; a special relationship of trust and confidence.

12

Unconscionability

Overview

The vitiating elements of duress and undue influence are sometimes viewed as two aspects of a more general element of "unconscionability". However, it is necessary to treat unconscionability separately, especially in Hong Kong, since legislation has intervened, in the form of the Unconscionable Contracts Ordinance (UCO)[1] and because, outside the scope of the legislation, there remain instances where neither duress nor undue influence would apply but where the Hong Kong courts have found a contract to be tainted by unconscionability. What also distinguishes unconscionability from other vitiating elements such as mistake, misrepresentation and undue influence is the need for some malfeasance on the part of the defendant. Such malfeasance *may* be present in the case of these other elements but it is not a *requirement*. Unconscionability, on the other hand, requires both a "disability" and knowledge thereof on the part of the defendant.

In this area the law of Hong Kong differs explicitly from English law. In English law, recognition of unconscionability is limited to a few specific cases such as unconscionable agreements made in anticipation of an inheritance and unconscionable dealings with "poor and ignorant" persons. There is no general recognition of a broad category of unconscionability. However, on occasion, notably in *Lloyd's Bank Ltd v Bundy*,[2] previous Master of the Rolls Lord Denning suggested that, as a general principle, contracts could be set aside on the basis of "inequality of bargaining power". This approach has not been generally accepted by the judiciary and the view has more often been expressed that such an approach would lead to uncertainty and that if there is to be change it should be via legislation. At present no English legislation has been introduced relating *directly* to unconscionability.

---

1. Cap 458.
2. [1975] QB 326, [1974] 3 WLR 501, [1974] 3 All ER 757.

New legislative rules dealing *indirectly* with unconscionability were, however, enacted in England in the form of the Unfair Terms in Consumer Contracts Regulations (UTCCR), 1994.[3] These Regulations were a response to a European Community Council Directive and were directed at "unfair" terms in contracts for the sale or supply of goods or services where one party deals as a consumer and where the term is not "individually negotiated". "Unfairness" and "unconscionability" are, of course, not synonymous. However, since the Regulations defined the unfairness of a term as being "contrary to the requirement of good faith" and causing "a significant imbalance in the parties' rights and obligations", there was clearly a close connection between unfairness under the Regulations and Lord Denning's concept of unconscionability. The Regulations did not permit the amendment of unfair terms; the terms were merely "not binding" on the consumer.

In Hong Kong, on the other hand, the UCO permits courts to rewrite contracts. The Ordinance, passed in October 1994, and in force one year later, is modelled on Australian legislation, and gives courts wide powers on finding that a contract is unconscionable. However, the Ordinance is, importantly, restricted to contracts involving the sale of goods or supply of services[4] where one party deals as a consumer. At this stage it is too early to tell how far the Hong Kong courts will go in using the powers, clearly spelled out in the Ordinance, to amend contracts.

Because of the limitations on statutory unconscionability in Hong Kong, the common law rules remain important and it is now clear that cases may be determined on the basis of unconscionability which are outside the scope of the legislation.

12.1 Statutory Unconscionability in Hong Kong

The UCO, based largely on Australian legislation, received assent on 20 October 1994. It reflects a trend in Hong Kong away from a non-interventionist approach towards increasing interference in the market and statutory consumer protection. Nonetheless, it is unlikely to be of great significance given that it is limited in scope and, at the same time, overlaps with existing common law and statutory rules

12.1.1 Background to the Legislation

The enactment of the Ordinance followed a Report by the Law Reform Commission of Hong Kong (LRC)[5] which considered legislation in various common law jurisdictions and recommended that:

---

3. Amended by UTCCR 1999 and now replaced by the Consumer Rights Act 2015; see 8.6.
4. Because the terms of reference of the Law Reform Commission of Hong Kong, on whose recommendations the Ordinance was based, were so restricted.
5. Report on Sale of Goods and Supply of Services (Topic 21).

a provision such as section 52A of the Australian Trade Practices Act (dealing with unconscionable contracts) be adopted in sale of goods and supply of services in Hong Kong.[6]

The LRC was obviously convinced of the need for increased statutory control in respect of "unconscionable" contracts for the sale of goods or supply of services, in spite of the paucity of evidence of serious deficiencies, but recommended that legislation should "apply only to extreme cases, which would be very rare".[7]

12.1.2 The Substance and Scope of the Ordinance

The UCO, which applies to all contracts made after its commencement, is brief and limited in scope. It does not apply to all unconscionable contracts but only those involving the sale of goods or supply of services. Further, it only applies where one of the parties "deals as consumer", as defined by the Ordinance.[8]

Four of the eight sections of the Ordinance deal with preliminary matters,[9] two with "miscellaneous" points[10] and another largely with matters that may be considered in determining the question of "unconscionability".[11]

The crux of the Ordinance is section 5, which determines the powers of a court which finds a contract to be unconscionable. On such a finding a court may:[12]

(a) refuse to enforce the contract;
(b) enforce the remainder without the unconscionable part;
(c) limit the application of, or revise or alter, any unconscionable part so as to avoid any unconscionable result.

The Ordinance adds that the onus is on the party alleging unconscionability to prove it.[13]

While powers (a) and (b) are unexceptional, power (c) is very wide-ranging. In cases of exorbitant pricing, for example, it would presumably allow the court, instead of simply not enforcing the contract under power (a), to "alter" the price amount so as to "avoid any unconscionable result". Such overt rewriting of the parties' contract has generally been eschewed in common law systems. It remains unclear how the words "revise" and "alter" differ in this context.

---

6. Ibid at para 7.7.5.
7. Ibid at para 7.1.2.
8. Section 3(1).
9. Sections 1–4.
10. Sections 7 and 8.
11. Section 6.
12. Section 5(1).
13. Section 5(2).

The Ordinance does not provide a complete definition of "unconscionability", though it lists factors to which the court may have regard "among other things".[14] The factors listed include the relative strength of the parties' bargaining position; the requirement that the consumer comply with unnecessary conditions; the consumer's understanding of contractual documents; the presence of undue influence, pressure or unfair tactics; and the availability of cheaper alternatives. The court is entitled to consider other factors and until there is a body of decided cases it is impossible to predict how broadly the word "unconscionability" will be interpreted.

12.1.3 Significance of the Ordinance

The legislation is unlikely to be of great practical significance given its limited scope and since, in most cases where it is relevant, other legislative and common law rules are applicable. Most of the examples cited in the LRC Report which appear to have convinced members of the need for legislation could be resolved under existing rules on, for example, unfair terms, undue influence, misrepresentation and mistake. Moreover, in most such situations the existing remedies would normally be adequate and easier to obtain given the difficulty of proving unconscionability and the intention to restrict it to "rare and extreme" cases.

If it was felt that Hong Kong really requires increasing statutory intervention in the market, the opportunity should have been taken to draft *general* unfairness/ unconscionability legislation. For example, a major gap in the (English) Unfair Contract Terms Act (UCTA) relates to dispositions of land. Neither the Control of Exemption Clauses Ordinance (CECO),[15] Hong Kong's equivalent to UCTA, nor the new UCO, address this deficiency and there is little doubt that if its terms of reference had allowed the LRC to look into terms regularly inserted into, for example, tenancy agreements, they would have found many more examples of real unconscionability and genuine consumer concern. By way of comparison, the (English) Unfair Terms in Consumer Contracts Regulations (UTCCR),[16] despite apparent wording to the contrary, *was* held to extend to land-related issues.[17]

One *potential* advantage of UCO lies in the *flexibility* of remedies, since courts may disallow *part of* the impugned contract only and may even rewrite the contract if appropriate. While there is yet to be an example of a *rewritten* contract, partial unenforceability can be seen in *Shum Kit Ching v Caesar Beauty Centre Ltd*[18] (also decided on the basis of non-enforceable "penalties")[19] where an onerous "Clause 19" was held unenforceable, while the rest of the contract was allowed to stand.

---

14. Under s 6.
15. Cap 71.
16. Now replaced by the Consumer Rights Act 2015.
17. *Khatun & Others v Newham LBC* [2004] EWCA 55.
18. [2003] 3 HKLRD 422.
19. Cf chapter 15 at 15.1.4.6.

An attempt to restrict the scope of the Ordinance even further was made by trial judge Bharwaney J in *Chang Pui Yin & Others v Bank of Singapore Ltd.*[20] The judge held that while two of the three criteria for "dealing as a consumer" (not dealing in the course of business, while the defendant *does* deal in the course of business), the third (services of a type ordinarily provided for private use) was lacking because the service was a private bank account available only to the rich![21] Fortunately, this "rather surprising conclusion"[22] was declared wrong on appeal.[23] Hong Kong's Court of Appeal found for the claimants on the basis that, although the defendants relied on standard terms in a private banking arrangement which did extend to the factual scenario, the banking agreement was one relating to the provision of services and, in the circumstances, unconscionable. The customers, here, were unsophisticated in financial matters and the bank had taken advantage of them by selling high risk financial products (causing large losses) despite a request for a low-risk product.

The welcome intervention of the Court of Appeal notwithstanding, the Ordinance is likely to remain of limited jurisprudential significance, given the restrictions already discussed. In a 2014 article,[24] Professor Lee Mason criticised the limited scope and application of statutory unconscionability. He wrote:

> In light of the clear deficiencies in Hong Kong's consumer protection regime with regard to unfair terms in standard form consumer contracts, there is an urgent need for reform.[25]

Mason attributes such deficiencies to the narrow interpretation of "unconscionability" by the Hong Kong courts, to the restricted scope of the legislation, and to the lack of a specific enforcement body which acts as a deterrent to consumers who would need to risk their own financial resources in proceeding with any unconscionability claim.

12.1.4 The Operation of the Ordinance

In the first significant case decided under the UCO, the court was called upon to consider moneylending practices in the case of *Hang Seng Credit Card Ltd & Others v Tsang Nga Lee & Others.*[26] Here the Court of First Instance held that contractual clauses in various credit card agreements requiring customers to pay costs at the highest (indemnity) rate, in the event of the plaintiff companies having to take action

---

20. [2016] 5 HKC 329 (dealt with below).
21. The judge *did* find for the claimants on different grounds (rejected on appeal!).
22. Per Lam VP in the Court of Appeal (n 22 below).
23. [2017] 4 HKLRD 458.
24. Lee Mason, "Inadequacy and Ineffectuality: Hong Kong's Consumer Protection Regime against Unfair Terms in Standard Form Contracts" (2014) 44 HKLJ 83.
25. Ibid at 91.
26. [2000] 3 HKC 269.

to recover payment, was unconscionable. Thus, since the contract was held to be one involving the provision of services, the Ordinance was applicable and the indemnity costs provision was unenforceable.

Certain factors were crucial to the decision in this case. The first was that the court seems to have been as much influenced by the circumstances of the plaintiffs' loans as by the requirements regarding costs in the event of default. In fact, the plaintiffs were found to be lending at a rate sometimes as high as 59% per annum! Such a rate, if offered by a moneylender, would have been legally prohibited under section 25 of the Money Lenders Ordinance.[27] The plaintiffs, a credit card company, a bank and a finance company respectively, were exempt from the Money Lenders Ordinance[28] but the Court was clearly influenced by this "extortionate" interest rate in making its decision to reject the indemnity rate of interest in respect of a defaulter's costs.

In respect of the costs provision itself the court made plain that costs are a matter for the court's discretion and that "the contractual provision cannot override the discretion of the court".[29] More particularly, the court was moved to exercise its discretion against the plaintiffs because various criteria existed which pointed to unconscionability. In particular, the parties were in an unequal bargaining position; the defendants had no real choice of alternatives and the costs provision in the credit card agreements was drafted far too widely.

Most of these findings by the court are uncontentious but more questionable is the court's attitude to the burden of proof. It was accepted that it is for the party claiming that an agreement is unconscionable to so prove. In this case, therefore, such burden fell on the defendant defaulters. The court determined, however, that:

> It does not mean, however, that when a defendant fails to appear, the issue cannot be raised. It does not preclude the court in a proper case from looking at all available circumstances in order to decide whether the cost provision is unconscionable. This is particularly so when the matters to be considered by the court under the UCO can be decided on circumstances not necessarily specific to individual consumers or defendants but apply generally and on matters not in dispute.[30]

So, curiously perhaps, the non-attending defendants were held to have discharged the burden of proof upon them despite being absent from court and unrepresented. The necessary elements of unconscionability were discovered by the court itself, aided by an *amicus curiae*.[31]

---

27. Cap 163.
28. It had been assumed that while customers might need protection from unscrupulous moneylenders, no such protection was needed from more "respectable" lenders.
29. Per Yam J at 273I.
30. Per Yam J at 274F.
31. Audrey Eu SC.

The Ordinance was discussed for the first time by the Court of Appeal in *Chang Pui Yin & Others v Bank of Singapore Ltd.*[32] The case involved the giving of negligent advice by the defendants to the plaintiffs: a "simple couple who led uncomplicated lives". The plaintiffs had inherited money and had sought the defendants' advice as to how to invest it. They had been sold financial products by the defendants' agent, Mrs Li, who, crucially, "had never informed the Plaintiffs that in recommending products to them, she was merely acting as a salesperson with no particular expertise".[33] The products had produced significant losses for the plaintiffs who successfully sued in the Court of First Instance. Liability was based on breach of contractual duties. The trial judge had found that the Ordinance was inapplicable.[34] In rejecting the defendants' appeal, the Court of Appeal added the ground of unconscionability, stating: "We hold that the judge erred in his conclusion that UCO was not applicable to private banking services."[35]

The court rejected the defendants claim that they were protected by exemption clauses since such clauses were required to satisfy the "reasonableness" test under section 3 of the Control of Exemption Clauses Ordinance[36] and:

> Given our conclusion that on unconscionability . . . we have little difficulty in concluding that the Bank fails to satisfy us that the clauses are fair and reasonable ones.[37]

There are noteworthy comments in the Court of Appeal judgment. The first is the emphasis on the "non-exhaustive" nature of the list of factors to be taken into account under section 6.[38] The court, indeed, looked at relevant Australian jurisprudence[39] on the basis that "additional factors recognised in Australia, could also be relevant in the examination of the unconscionability of the contract in the Hong Kong UCO context".[40]

Moreover, the court emphasised that some impropriety was necessary for unconscionability (unlike, for example, mistake or misrepresentation). However, this need not be "at a high level".[41] The impropriety present in the case was a failure by the bank to comply with its regulatory duties, which deprived "the Plaintiffs of the opportunity to make informed decisions".[42]

---

32. [2017] 4 HKLRD 458.
33. Ibid at para 76.
34. See 12.1.3 above.
35. Per Lam VP who delivered the judgment of the court.
36. Cap 71.
37. Para 113.
38. See 12.1.2 above.
39. See, especially, *Commercial Bank of Australia v Amadio* (1983) 151 CLR 447.
40. Para 64.
41. See para 67.
42. Para 79.

12.2 Unconscionability at Common Law

Given the limitations on the scope of the Hong Kong legislation, in particular the restriction to sale and supply of services, it is clear that the common law unconscionability rules will continue to be of some significance in Hong Kong. These rules, however, are so vague and the jurisprudence so scarce that a precise definition of unconscionability is difficult to formulate. The issue is further complicated by the fact that cases seemingly determined on the basis of unconscionability are often capable of alternative explanation.

Non-statutory unconscionability has its origins in equity where it has been a rather limited doctrine. Most of the leading precedents are of some antiquity and recourse to such unconscionability by the courts today, either in Hong Kong or England, is rare. While the term "unconscionable" seems to be well accepted, a precise definition is elusive.

Mozley and Whiteley[43] define "unconscionable bargain" thus:

A bargain so one-sided and inequitable in its terms as to raise a presumption of fraud and oppression.

Two of the key elements described, one-sidedness and inequity, add little to lay notions of unfairness and the consumer required by a business to pay an excessive price would claim to be the victim of a "one-sided" and "inequitable" bargain. Such "unfairness", however, is rarely a cause of action per se.

The key additional element is the need for a presumption of "fraud and [sic] oppression" to be raised. It is doubtful, however, that fraud, at least in the common law sense, is actually a requirement for unconscionability. In (Earl of) Aylesford v Morris[44] for example, Lord Selborne states the requirement of "a presumption of fraud" but adds:

fraud does not here mean deceit or circumvention; it means an unconscientious use of the power arising out of these circumstances and conditions; and when the relative position of the parties is such as prima facie to raise this presumption, the transaction cannot stand unless the person claiming the benefit of it is able to repel the presumption by contrary evidence, proving it to have been in point of fact fair, just and reasonable.[45]

This clearly differs from fraud as generally recognised at common law, which requires an absence of honest belief.[46] The Lord Selborne definition requires merely a dominant position coupled with an abuse thereof. It is probably safe to add a further requirement that the result of the abuse must be unfairness. Certainly, de facto, the

---

43. J. E. Penner, *Mozley & Whiteley's Law Dictionary* (London: Butterworths, 12th edn, 2001).
44. (1873) LR 8 Ch App 484.
45. Ibid at 490–491.
46. See *Derry v Peek* (1889) LR 14 App Cas 337 and 9.3.1.

cases in which relief have been granted have involved an unfair outcome for the weaker party. Moreover, the most analogous doctrine, that of "presumed undue influence", provided (until recently) for relief only where the outcome is "manifestly disadvantageous" for the influenced party.[47]

The emphasis here, then, is on inequality of bargaining power rather than actual fraud. This emphasis on "domination" by one party of the other in the leading cases led Lord Denning MR to link unconscionability with the analogous undue influence and to propound a general doctrine of "inequality of bargaining power" under which equity could always grant relief where one party has taken unfair advantage of his dominant position. Both Treitel[48] and Anson[49] place the "Denning doctrine" within the area of unconscionability. As such it appears to offer scope for the increased application of unconscionability. In practice, however, the Denning view has added little. The few cases in which he attempted to apply the doctrine were disparate and its limits were poorly defined. Most importantly, in every case in which Lord Denning sought to apply the doctrine, alternative, more conservative *rationes* can be discerned. In *D&C Builders v Rees*,[50] for example, the court had merely to determine that a party acting inequitably should be denied equitable intervention on his behalf and then to apply established principles of consideration. In *Lloyd's Bank Ltd v Bundy*,[51] too, Denning's fellow judges applied established principles of undue influence as opposed to the more vague notion of "unequal bargaining" on which he founded his decision.

The "Denning" cases are thus sufficiently ambiguous to be ignored in Hong Kong where, traditionally, there has been a greater acceptance of the legitimacy of unequal bargaining. Certainly the "inequality as unconscionability" doctrine found little support in the case of *OTB International Credit Card Ltd v Au Sai Chak, Michael*[52] where the Hong Kong Court of Appeal doubted whether there was any need to pronounce on inequality/unconscionability given the paucity of relevant authority.

Ho,[53] in an important earlier text on Hong Kong contract law, states simply that:

> Hong Kong courts would probably reject any such doctrine of inequality of bargaining power.[54]

---

47. See *National Westminster Bank plc v Morgan* [1985] AC 686, [1985] 2 WLR 588 and chapter 11. The accepted requirement, post-*Etridge*, is that the transaction must "call for an explanation".
48. Op cit.
49. Sir J Beatson & A Burrows, *Anson's Law of Contract* (Oxford: Oxford University Press, 30th edn, 2016).
50. [1966] 2 QB 617, [1966] 2 WLR 288.
51. [1975] QB 326, [1974] 3 WLR 501.
52. [1980] HKLR 296.
53. Betty Ho, *Hong Kong Contract Law* (Hong Kong: Butterworths, 2nd edn, 1994).
54. Ibid at p 141.

Given the weakness of the *OTB International* case precedent, this statement is perhaps over-emphatic. What can clearly be stated, however, is that there is no Hong Kong authority in support of Lord Denning's extended doctrine of unequal bargaining. The clearest statement of the requirements for common law unconscionability in a Hong Kong case is to be found in *Standard Chartered Bank v Shem Yin Fung*[55] where it was stated that a successful plea of unconscionability required:

1. The complainant's "disabling circumstances";
2. Unconscionable conduct by the other party; (resulting in an)
3. Oppressive bargain.

The trial judge, Deputy High Court Judge Poon emphasised that:

> the court in addressing the issue of unconscionability is not concerned with the quality of the weaker party's consent but with the other party's conduct.[56]

Common law unconscionability will then, it appears, be sparingly applied by the Hong Kong courts and applied only to those cases where there is a clear abuse of a dominant position giving rise to manifest unfairness. In *Lo Wo and Others v Cheung Chan Ka Joseph and Another*,[57] the Hong Kong Court of Appeal unanimously upheld a decision of Waung J which was based on a finding of common law unconscionability. In *Lo Wo*, the plaintiffs were elderly sisters living in a remote part of mainland China. The second defendants were Hong Kong property developers who wished to acquire property, a half share in which had been inherited by the plaintiffs. The developer's representatives had persuaded the plaintiffs to assign their half share to the developer for $870,000 not mentioning that they had acquired the other half share for $2.4 million. Another representative of the developer had also been chosen as the plaintiffs' attorney. One year later, when the developer sought to pay the balance of the purchase money, the plaintiffs, now cognisant of the undervaluation of their share, refused to accept the balance and sought to have the contract set aside on the basis of unconscionability. Their claim was upheld at first instance and on appeal.

UCO was not relevant to the case since the scenario involved neither a sale of goods nor a supply of services.[58] Both courts agreed, however, that the actions of the defendants amounted to unconscionability in the established common law (non-statutory) sense and the initial trial judge's decision to order rescission of the contract was upheld. The two key factors were the developer's failure to make known the price paid for the other half share and the failure to advise that the plaintiffs take independent legal advice. Given the superior knowledge and expertise of the

---

55. (unrep, HCMP 3289/1998 & 3289A/1998, 13 May 2002).
56. At para 150.
57. [2001] 3 HKC 70.
58. See 12.1.2 above.

defendants and the clear fact that they had taken advantage of this to the other party's detriment it could clearly be said that this contract fell within the definition of:

> A bargain so one-sided and inequitable in its terms as to raise a presumption of fraud and oppression.[59]

A similar finding was also made in *Daiwa Bank Ltd v Foco Woollen Yarns Co Ltd*[60] where unconscionability was found in respect of an agreement made by a "poor and ignorant" defendant who had made an agreement "vastly to her disadvantage and vastly to the plaintiff's advantage".[61]

What emerges from the few cases in Hong Kong involving a finding of unconscionability is that all could have been (or were) found also to involve other vitiating factors. The *Daiwa Bank* case was found to involve both misrepresentation and undue influence. Deputy Judge Muttrie added:

> The 2nd defendant also argues that in any event the transaction cannot be allowed to stand on the ground of unconscionability . . . counsel places strong reliance on various dicta, particularly those of Lord Millett, in Credit Lyonnais Bank Nederland v Burch [1996] EWCA Civ 1292 . . . In fact the decision in that case did not rest on unconscionable bargain but rather on an extension of the principles in O'Brien (undue influence).[62]

In the *Bachicha* case[63] a constructively dismissed domestic helper "agreed to" and signed a "compromise" on the basis of legally incorrect advice from a labour relations officer lacking full knowledge of the factual background. The agreement was found to be unconscionable and the employer to have notice of the incorrect advice. Again the case could have been decided on the basis of the plaintiff's unilateral mistake which "must have been known to the defendant".[64]

The Australian unconscionability case of *Commercial Bank of Australia Ltd v Amadio*,[65] cited with approval by Ribeiro PJ in *Ming Shiu Chung & Others v Ming Shiu Sum & Others*[66] is a further example of a case which could have been decided on more traditional grounds, its crucial facts of a child's misrepresentation to his parents known to the defendant being factually similar to the English case of *Avon Finance v Bridger*,[67] decided on the basis of misrepresentation. Nonetheless, in *Tong Kwok Cheong v Tong Wai Lin*[68] the trial judge, Mayo DJ, accepted that the principles

---

59. See also *Bachicha (Evelyn Semana) v Poon Shiu Man Henry* [2000] 3 HKC 452 discussed at 15.1.4.5.
60. [2002] 3 HKC 258.
61. The agreement was also found to have been secured via undue influence.
62. At para 68.
63. Note 59 above.
64. Per Ribeiro JA at para 24; and cf chapter 10.
65. (1983) 151 CLR 447.
66. (2006) 9 HKCFAR 334.
67. [1985] 2 All ER 281.
68. (unrep, HCA 1939/2007, 5 November 2012).

for unconscionability laid down by Mason J (as he then was) in the *Commercial Bank of Australia* case were to be applied. The key principle is that the frailty of the claimant or the adverse nature of the agreement are not enough. What is required is that the defendant has taken "unconscientious advantage" of the plaintiff's circumstances.[69] This is in accord with views expressed by the Judicial Committee of the Privy Council in *Boustani v Pigott*.[70]

In short, most cases involving common law unconscionability could be determined on other grounds. Even the possible exception, *Lo Wo*, might be seen as an example of actual undue influence.[71]

---

69. Mayo DJ's views were accepted in the subsequent appeal ([2014] 1 HKLRD 339).
70. [1993] UKPC 17.
71. See chapter 11.

13

Illegal Contracts

OVERVIEW

The courts will generally not permit the enforcement of a contract which is illegal. A contract is illegal if its creation or performance is prohibited at common law, by public policy or via legislation.

Although writers sometimes disagree about classification,[1] it is generally agreed that the category of illegal contracts includes those contracts described as illegal by statute, such as gaming or wagering contracts, and those illegal at common law on the grounds of public policy, such as contracts to commit crimes or torts, contracts to promote sexual immorality, contracts to oust the jurisdiction of the courts, and contracts in restraint of trade. Of the long list of contracts illegal by statute, common law or public policy, the most significant, in the Hong Kong context, are those concerning gambling contracts, illegal loans, "small house" frauds, and restraint of trade. In this chapter we will list the major types of illegal contract but focus in depth only on these particular areas.

While it is often a simple task to determine if a contract is illegal under statute, "public policy" is an elusive concept, since it is not defined by statute and depends on the views of judges as to what is publicly acceptable. Naturally, over time, as public attitudes change, "public policy" will change accordingly. One category of contract illegal under common law is that involving the promotion of "sexual immorality". It is, of course, the case, that views on sexual immorality may vary considerably, even in a single jurisdiction, over time.

In determining the effects of illegality the courts have to take into account two competing propositions. The first is that if a party has taken the benefit of a contract,

---

1. "Illegal contracts come in so many different shapes and sizes that it is difficult to find an appropriate classification for all the cases . . . No two commentators appear to adopt the same classification": E. McKendrick, *Contract Law: Text, Cases & Materials* (Oxford: Oxford University Press, 2017), p 338.

even an illegal one, he should recompense the other party, otherwise he will be unjustly enriched. The second is that no party should be allowed to base an action on his own improper or illegal conduct: the so-called *ex turpi causa* principle. In general, the courts endorse the second proposition and prevent a party who has acted illegally from suing under the contract, even though this results in an "unfair" benefit to the other party. The prime consideration of the courts is that illegal contracts should be discouraged by preventing their enforcement. The principle is enshrined in the Latin maxim *in pari delicto melior est conditio defendentis* (*in pari delicto*) which means that where both parties are equally at fault the court should favour the defendant. The motivation is not protection of the defendant but the indirect benefit to the public which results from the discouragement of illegal practices. There are, however, exceptional cases where the courts assist a plaintiff who has knowingly made an illegal contract.

Judges, in deciding the outcome of illegality cases, often draw a distinction between contracts which are illegal as *formed* and those illegal as *performed*. Thus, for example, a contract to jointly rob a bank and then divide the proceeds is obviously illegal as formed. On the other hand, a contract under which A agrees to ship B's goods is not, on the face of it, illegal but may be performed illegally if A decides to overload the ship contrary to law.

Generally, when contracts are illegal as formed, the courts refuse to allow enforcement by either party. However, they may allow limited enforcement of an illegally formed contract via the "severance" of the part that is illegal.

When, however, the contract is illegally performed, the courts tend to permit enforcement by an "innocent" party (ie one who has not performed illegally) but not by the guilty.

On rare occasions, even the guilty party may be allowed to enforce the contract if his action can be asserted without reference to the illegality of the contract.[2] This, the *Tinsley v Milligan* approach, was previously accepted at the highest level in both the UK and Hong Kong jurisdictions. The UK Supreme Court has now abandoned *Tinsley* in favour of a multi-factorial approach. This approach, established in *Patel v Mirza*,[3] raises important precedent issues for Hong Kong which will be considered in depth.

At common law, many types of gambling were lawful. Most, however, are unlawful in Hong Kong on the grounds of public policy or under statute. The Gambling Ordinance[4] makes most forms of gambling unlawful with only limited exceptions. Gambling includes gaming, bookmaking and "wagering" (betting).

Contracts in restraint of trade, a very important phenomenon in Hong Kong, are in some ways distinct from other illegal contracts in that the restraint is only

---

2. See, for example, *Bowmakers Ltd v Barnet Instruments Ltd* [1945] KB 65, [1944] 2 All ER 579.
3. [2017] AC 467.
4. Cap 148.

"presumed" to be void. If it can be shown to be reasonable in the interests of the parties and the public, it will be upheld. Moreover, it is only the restraint which is void and it may be possible to enforce the rest of the contract without the restraint via the severance doctrine.

13.1 Types of Illegal Contracts

The list of illegal contracts is extensive and only the more significant types will be listed. With the exception of gambling contracts and contracts in restraint of trade, the forms of illegal contract will be listed with little further discussion.

13.1.1 Contracts to Commit Crimes or Civil Wrongs

A contract to commit a crime is illegal. In *Everet v Williams*,[5] two men made an agreement to rob a stagecoach and split the proceeds. When one party refused the other his share, the latter sued. Not surprisingly, especially given the seriousness of the crime involved, the court rejected the claim. Contracts to commit a tort are also illegal as is a contract to indemnify a party for unlawful acts. It is uncertain whether a contract to break a contract is illegal, though it will normally involve the tort of inducing breach of contract. The most common type of illegal contract in Hong Kong involves abuse of the so-called "small house" policy, a relic of colonial government by virtue of which:

> an adult male indigenous villager[6] in the New Territories (being a descendant in the male line from a resident in 1898 of a recognised village) is entitled, once in his lifetime, to build a small house, up to 700 square feet in area and 3-storey[7] high, in his village for himself on a piece of land owned by him or assigned to him by the Government at a concessionary rate.[8]

Abuses take various forms but usually involve prior agreements with commercial developers and a subsequent false statement by the villager to the Lands Department that he[9] has the sole interest in the land involved.

13.1.2 Contracts Prejudicial to the Administration of Justice

A contract to give false testimony in return for money is, of course, illegal.[10] Similarly, a contract to "oust the jurisdiction of the courts" is illegal. Thus, parties

---

5. 1725, cited at [1899] 1 QB 826.
6. There is no requirement of New Territories (or even Hong Kong) residency!
7. In fact, the limit is two storeys (three floors).
8. Per Lam J, *Chan Yau v Chan Calvin & Another* [2014] 5 HKLRD 304 (at para 2).
9. It *is* always "he".
10. For example, *R v Andrews* [1973] 1 QB 422.

may not form an agreement and specify enforcement of it without permitting at least the "supervisory" jurisdiction of the courts.[11] A statutory exception exists in that "arbitration clauses", whereby parties agree to resolve disputes through arbitration rather than through the courts, are valid.[12]

13.1.3 Contracts Which Promote Corruption in Public Office

Contracts relating to corruption are governed by both common law and statutory rules in Hong Kong. The leading common law case is that of *Parkinson v College of Ambulance Ltd*,[13] decided in the English High Court. In *Parkinson*, the secretary of the defendant charity promised to help secure the plaintiff a knighthood in return for the plaintiff's donation to the charity. The plaintiff paid £3,000 to the charity but no honour of any kind was forthcoming. His action for the return of his donation failed on the basis that the agreement was illegal and he knew it.

The *Parkinson* principle is endorsed by statute in England[14] and is within the scope of legislation in Hong Kong.[15] It is apparently lawful in England, however, to reward those who have made political donations or acted "generously" in the past, where such past generosity was not expressed to be "conditional".[16] The Hong Kong rules, as enshrined in the Prevention of Bribery Ordinance, are considerably more restrictive.

13.1.4 Contracts Prejudicial to the Family

In the area of contracts prejudicial to the family, changing legal and societal views on morality are involved, such that older precedents have to be treated with caution. Nonetheless the common law principle that contracts prejudicial to the family are illegal is lent support by the International Covenant on Civil and Political Rights (ICCPR) to which Hong Kong is a signatory. Article 23(1) of the ICCPR states:

> The family is the natural and fundamental group unit of society and is entitled to protection by society and the State.

It is presumably still good law that "marriage brokerage", by which a person promises to arrange a marriage for a fee, is illegal.[17] In other areas, legal and societal views may be changing. In England, "civil partnerships", whereby couples of the

---

11. Parties to an agreement may, of course, say that an agreement is not binding at all but merely a social arrangement; see chapter 5.
12. Arbitration Ordinance (Cap 609).
13. [1925] 2 KB 1.
14. See Honours (Prevention of Abuses) Act 1925.
15. See the Prevention of Bribery Ordinance (Cap 201).
16. Tony Blair's Labour government was a particularly "grateful" one in this regard.
17. See *Hermann v Charlesworth* [1905] 2 KB 123.

same sex may formalise their relationship, are now recognised, despite their apparent conflict with the traditional notion of family and older common law precedents.[18] Hong Kong's approach to notions of the "family" are more conservative than those in England in many respects[19] and there is considerable tension between the views of those who oppose same-sex unions and those who support them on grounds of anti-discrimination. It is inevitable that society's view of "the family", just like that of "morality" generally, will continue to change and the law will, eventually, reflect such change.[20]

13.1.5 Contracts Contrary to Sexual Morality

In respect of contracts involving sexual immorality, again, it should be noted that societal (and judicial) attitudes change and that older precedents must be treated with caution. The well-known English case of *Pearce v Brooks*[21] involved a finding that a contract to provide a carriage to be used for prostitution was illegal on the grounds of sexual immorality. In the Hong Kong case of *Ki Hing Lau v The Shun Loong Lee Firm*[22] it was held that a contract to deliver shark's fin soup to a brothel was illegal, since its purpose was to render the brothel a more attractive place to visit.[23] In the more recent Hong Kong case of *Chuang Yue Chien Eugene v Ho Yau Kwong Kevin*,[24] however, Ma J concluded that:

> The court may . . . expect evidence of what does and what does not constitute modern day morality . . . The cases . . . such as *Pearce v Brooks* . . . were decided in a bygone age where different standards of morality may well have prevailed.[25]

At common law, just as a promise to reward past, as opposed to present, cohabitation is lawful,[26] a promise to pay for past sexual services is lawful while a promise to pay for such services in the future is not.[27] Of course, the past services will normally be subject to the past consideration principle[28] but, if the agreement is under seal, consideration need not be shown.[29]

---

18. See *Franco v Bolton* (1797) 3 Ves 368 (contract to cohabit without marrying).
19. Of course, traditionally, China has been far more tolerant of polygamous unions.
20. Divorce is now increasingly common in Hong Kong (and mainland China).
21. (1866) LR 1 Exch 213.
22. [1910] 5 HKLR 83.
23. A contract to provide accommodation to a known prostitute is lawful unless the accommodation is known to be used for "business purposes": *Appleton v Campbell* (1826) 2 C & P 347.
24. [2002] 4 HKC 245.
25. At 261.
26. *Annadale v Harris* (1727) 2 P Wms 432.
27. *Franco v Bolton* (above).
28. See 4.2.
29. *Annadale v Harris* (above).

13.2 Gambling Contracts

Gambling is an activity which arouses considerable controversy in Hong Kong. Most types of gambling are illegal with exceptions for horse racing (betting via the Hong Kong Jockey Club) and licensed mahjong parlours. Legal betting on horse racing, though in slight decline, still produces a huge income which, since the Jockey Club is a charity, is spent on a variety of good works. There is, therefore, a curious ambivalence towards gambling which is seen, at one and the same time, to produce considerable charitable funding while resulting in much misery for those losing gamblers who incur debts that they are unable to repay. Any proposal to increase the scope of legal gambling is invariably met by fierce opposition from religious and other opponents who focus on the human cost. The success of such opposition has, in fact, provided the bedrock on which the entire economy in Macau is now based.[30]

The rules on gambling in Hong Kong are primarily statutory and the most important piece of legislation is the Gambling Ordinance.[31] This prohibits all gambling unless specifically authorised.[32] The term "gambling" includes gaming, "wagering" (betting), and bookmaking.

13.2.1 Gaming

Gaming typically involves casino-type games where there is a "bank". The key requirement for such gaming to be legal (ignoring the licensing/authorisation issue) is that the chances of the game must be equally favourable to all the players.[33] Roulette, for example, is illegal in Hong Kong because only the "house" has the bank and because the odds paid to winners do not reflect true odds. Thus, for example, on a 36 number roulette wheel with single zero, the house pays out 35 to one on a winning number when the "correct" odds are 36 to one.[34] Under the Gambling Ordinance all unauthorised gaming is illegal as are loans made for the purpose of gaming.

13.2.2 Wagering (Betting)

Wagering is illegal at common law. The main definition is to be found, strangely, in a case generally associated with agreement and consideration: *Carlill v Carbolic Smoke Ball Co.*[35] The defendants in *Carlill* argued that their promised reward was not enforceable since it was, *inter alia*, based on a wager that Mrs Carlill would or would

---

30. Just as the refusal to legalise gambling in California has been the foundation for Nevada's gambling-based economy.
31. Cap 148.
32. Ibid, s 3.
33. Ibid, s 2.
34. *A fortiori* in the case of the Nevada "double zero" wheel.
35. [1892] 2 QB 485 and see 3.3, 3.5 and 4.1.

not catch influenza. The argument was rejected and, in attempting to define "wager" the court emphasised the key ingredient that the parties must hold opposite views, such that one will win and the other shall lose. In *Carlill*, of course, both parties were "on the same side" in that both intended that Mrs Carlill would not catch influenza. Since unauthorised betting is rendered illegal by the Gambling Ordinance, and since wagering is synonymous with betting, the illegality of this activity is now statutory. It has been held by the Hong Kong courts that transactions in the Hang Seng Futures market are not wagers or bets but legitimate, authorised and controlled transactions.[36]

13.2.3 Bookmaking

Bookmaking is defined as, "the soliciting, receiving or negotiating of a bet by way of trade or business whether personally or by letter, telephone, telegram or by other means."[37] Bookmaking, which is usually associated with betting on horse racing, is illegal[38] unless permitted under the Betting Duty Ordinance.[39]

13.2.4 Other Common Illegal Contracts in Hong Kong

It is perhaps a sign of Hong Kong's straitened, post-COVID situation that, from 2020, claims of illegality involving moneylending eclipsed abuses of the "small-house policy" as the most numerous illegal contract claims.

Moneylending rates by official banks are largely unpoliced, but maximum repayment rates are fixed for all licensed moneylenders. Those without assets do not qualify for bank loans so, when in financial trouble, they are compelled to use frequently unscrupulous moneylenders.[40]

"Small house" frauds generally involve the "indigenous" New Territories villager (with the right to buy land at a discount for the purpose of building a small house for his own use) making a pre-purchase arrangement with a property developer to transfer the property post-acquisition.[41]

---

36. *Richardson Greenshields of Canada (Pacific) Ltd v Keung Chak Kiu & Hong Kong Futures Exchange Ltd* [1989] 1 HKLR 476.
37. Gambling Ordinance s 2.
38. Ibid, ss 7–8.
39. Cap 108, s 3(7), (8).
40. See, for example, *Gain Wealth Global Credit & Investment Ltd v Chan Suk Fong* [2020] HKCA 737 which involved, initially, a loan of almost HK$2 million at over 60% p.a. (!) followed by a further deception which involved pledging the borrower's Housing Authority property as security.
41. See the *Best Sheen* case et al. discussed at 13.3.1.1 below.

13.3 The Effects of Illegality

The effects of illegality are extremely difficult to summarise. Although a number of general propositions may be made, almost all are subject to exception. The courts are concerned with competing principles. Thus, it may appear wrong that one who has profited from an illegal contract should retain the benefit without recompensing the other. On the other hand, the "public conscience" may dictate that the other party should not be able to seek a remedy where he has been a party to the illegality. As a result, the courts sometimes draw a distinction between the rights of an "innocent" party and those of a party aware of the illegality. The general proposition, however, is that, in cases of illegality on both sides, the courts favour the position of the defendant, the *in pari delicto* principle, since it is felt that, ultimately, the public is protected to some degree by the discouragement of illegality.

Courts will also draw a distinction between those contracts illegally "formed" and those illegally "performed". In the case of an illegally formed contract it may be impossible for even an innocent party to enforce it. Illegally performed contracts, on the other hand, can generally be enforced by an innocent party, and even, on occasion, by a guilty one.[42]

The courts will also take into account the severity of the illegality. The refusal to allow enforcement of an illegal contract is not based on a desire to protect the "profiting" party, but on the public good in preventing a claim based on illegality, thereby discouraging such illegality. It naturally follows that, since the public conscience would be less concerned about minor illegality, enforcement in such cases is more likely to be permitted.

A distinction may also be drawn between statutory illegality, which may be of a technical nature and may involve a party or parties ignorant of the relevant law, and contracts contrary to public policy, which are likely to involve more obviously reprehensible conduct. For obvious reasons, the courts may be more favourably disposed towards a claimant in the former case.

"Severance" of the illegal part of a contract is possible in the case of those contracts illegal on the grounds of public policy, such that what remains may be enforced. However, severance is primarily of concern in the area of restraint of trade.

13.3.1 Contracts Illegally Formed

The general proposition is that where a contract is illegally formed it cannot be enforced by either party, whatever his state of mind. Any action on the contract would require the disclosure of an illegal act and would therefore be defeated by the

---

42. The distinction between illegal formation and performance/execution, although subject to exceptions, is retained by the author as a useful general proposition.

ex turpi causa (non oritur actio) doctrine.[43] The position, then, is that the loss lies where it falls. So, if one party transfers money to another under an illegal contract and that other defaults, no action may be brought to recover the money. On the basis of *ex turpi causa* this seems sound and produces a just result if a "knowing" party is unable to enforce against an innocent one. Such was the case in *Vakante v Addey & Stanhope School*.[44] Here the claimant was a Croatian who had applied for asylum in Britain. As such it was illegal for him to work. He nonetheless obtained a job as a trainee teacher with the defendants. He subsequently sued them for unfair dismissal on the basis of racial discrimination. His action failed in the English Court of Appeal which found that his action was "so bound up" with his illegal conduct as to preclude his claim.

The position may be less satisfactory where both parties are aware of the illegality; since this involves one party pleading in his defence an illegal contract to which he was a willing partner. This defence has been viewed as "very dishonest"[45] but is generally successful. This is usually the case even where the illegality is unknown to the claimant who has acted in good faith. In *Re Mahmooud and Ispahani*,[46] the plaintiff agreed to sell linseed oil to the defendant who refused to take delivery. Under statute the sale or purchase of linseed oil was illegal without a licence. The plaintiff had a licence and believed the defendant's false statement that he, too, had a licence. Since the contract was illegal (because of the defendant's lack of a licence) the plaintiff's action for non-acceptance failed, even though he had acted honestly and the defendant had not.

The same principle of non-recovery has already been seen in the *Parkinson* case, above, where the plaintiff was unable to recover the money he paid to obtain a knighthood (illegally) even though the defendants were also aware of the illegality which they were then able to set up in their defence. A Hong Kong example is provided in *Yim Wai-tsang v Lee Yuk-har*.[47] Here, the plaintiff, the head of a Chinese money loan association, sued a member who owed $1,000. The money loan association was not registered under the Societies Ordinance[48] and it was held that the money was irrecoverable since the association was an unlawful society.

An extremely unusual illustration of the same principle was seen in the case of *Johnson, Stokes & Master (JSM) v Trevor Ernest Boucher*[49] in the Hong Kong Court of First Instance. In the *JSM* case the plaintiffs were a firm of solicitors who had practised for many years in Hong Kong with more than 20 partners. On their action for payment for legal services the defendant pleaded that: "The plaintiff is an illegal

---

43. See Overview above for explanation.
44. [2004] 4 All ER 1056.
45. Sir William Grant MR in *Thomson v Thomson* (1802) 7 Ves 470.
46. [1921] 2 KB 716.
47. [1973] HKLR 1.
48. Cap 151.
49. [1989] 1 HKLR 219.

organisation and by reason thereof no sum is recoverable from the defendant". The substance of the defence was that the plaintiffs had, illegally, not registered under the rules of the Societies Ordinance. Although that legislation had been amended, retro-spectively, to exclude solicitors' firms, the reform was not to affect litigation already commenced. The Court held that the plaintiffs were, indeed, an illegal organisation under the previous law and could not recover payment from the defendant.[50]

The general proposition, then, is that where both parties are party to an illegally formed contract, the court will prevent any action on the contract and find for the defendant (the *in pari delicto* principle). The purpose is the indirect protection of the public rather than the direct protection of a defendant who benefits from an illegal contract to which he was a willing partner. Nonetheless the latter benefit is the unde-sired effect of the courts' approach. Such was the case in *Prosperous Nursing Centre Ltd v Cheung Yuk Ying*. Here, the parties made an agreement whereby a non-regis-tered party would (illegally) be permitted to run a nursing home. A subsequent claim for a refund of deposit was rejected since the claimant was aware of the illegality and was *in pari delicto*. The other (illegal) party, of course, benefited from the decision.

13.3.1.1 Where Illegality Need Not Be Pleaded

As with so many of the "rules" on illegality, however, exceptions have been made. The most important is that a claim may be made by a party to an illegal contract if the claim can be made without reference to the illegal contract. The most famous case is that of *Tinsley v Milligan*,[51] the decision in which was characterised by con-siderable judicial disagreement.

Tinsley v Milligan

The parties were a lesbian couple who had jointly purchased a house. They regis-tered the property in the name of Tinsley as the sole owner so that Milligan could continue to make benefit claims. This was illegal since, had Milligan's "asset" been disclosed, she would have been denied the benefits. The house was used commer-cially and was the couple's main source of income. Milligan subsequently disclosed her illegal conduct to the authorities and no prosecution was brought against her. The parties subsequently split up and Tinsley moved out. She then claimed for posses-sion of the house as the sole owner. Milligan counter-claimed to ensure a sale of the house and an equal division of the proceeds. Milligan's action was finally successful in the House of Lords.

---

50. It is gratifying to note that while the plaintiff solicitors were unaware of their illegal status, it had been identified by a legal academic: see M Olesnicky, "Are Large Law Firms Legal?", (1987) 17 HKLJ 188.
51. [1993] 3 All ER 65.

The decision is understandable, given Milligan's previous confession and the obviously dishonourable conduct of Tinsley. The rationale, however, is a difficult one. It is significant that this case occupied considerable space in the subsequent English Law Commission's exhaustive consideration of illegal contracts and trusts and it appears to have been a major catalyst for a call for change and clarification of the law.[52] Tinsley argued, with some justification, that Milligan had been a willing participant in the initial illegality. She also argued that Milligan's claim for a "constructive trust" to be declared, as a claim in equity, should be barred since Milligan had not come with "clean hands".[53] The House of Lords could have based its decision on Tinsley's greater impropriety or on the offence to the "public conscience" which might have been caused by punishing Milligan excessively in rejecting her claim. However, neither of these routes was followed. Indeed, all members of the House of Lords rejected the extension of the principle of "public conscience" to cover cases where the public would be said to disapprove of punishing excessively a party to an illegal contract. This was seen by the court as synonymous with conferring total discretion to the judges. Instead, the majority (the House was divided 3:2 in the case) based their decision on the fact that Milligan's claim could be pleaded without reference to the illegal contract; the so-called *Bowmakers* principle.[54] As a contributor of half the purchase price of the house, Milligan was entitled to a resulting trust which did not depend on the illegality, and the fact that the illegal agreement was pleaded or disclosed during the trial did not, in itself, bar the action.

The *Tinsley* case has been the subject of considerable criticism. The "reliance" rule was rejected, in favour of a greater degree of *flexibility* in the UK (9 member) Supreme Court case of *Patel v Mirza*.[55] The case involved a criminal conspiracy[56] whereby the plaintiff was to pay £620,000 to the defendant in return for advance information (to be leaked unlawfully by the defendant's contacts at RBS Bank) of government policy which would enable the plaintiff to benefit financially. In fact, the government announcement was never made, so advance notice became impossible. The plaintiff sought to recover his money but the defendant argued that restitution of same (on the basis of unjust enrichment) could only be sought by pleading the plaintiff's involvement in the illegal scheme. The situation was distinguishable from that in *Tribe v Tribe* (discussed below) where the claimant had deliberately *withdrawn* from the illegal transaction before performance. In *Patel*, the illegal purpose was unfulfilled *not* because of "conscientious" withdrawal but because performance had become impossible. The general view of the Court was that recovery of the money paid should be permitted unless it would "undermine the integrity of the justice

---

52. Indeed, in his dissenting judgment, Lord Goff specifically advocated "a full inquiry into the matter by the Law Commission".
53. See 4.6.
54. See *Bowmakers Ltd v Barnet Instruments Ltd* [1945] KB 65.
55. [2016] UKSC 42.
56. See para 12.

system".[57] In criticising *Tinsley*, the Supreme Court (though not speaking with one voice) determined that:

> it should no longer be followed. Unless a statute provides otherwise ... property can pass under a transaction which is illegal as a contract.[58]

Moreover:

> the anticipated inside information was not forthcoming and the contract effectively lapsed. I see no good reason on these simple facts for not applying the (restitutionary) Rule and accordingly I consider that Mr Patel is entitled to the return of the £620,000.[59]

Nonetheless, despite the *Patel* Supreme Court majority rejection of *Tinsley*, in favour of a "range of factors" approach,[60] it should be remembered that post-1997 English (or UK) decisions are not binding in Hong Kong and that *Tinsley* was applied in the Hong Kong Court of First Instance in the *Best Sheen* case (below) (which in turn has been followed on numerous occasions, *including the Court of Final Appeal*).[61] The Hong Kong Court of Appeal has, curiously, supported following *Patel in Monat Investment Ltd v All Persons in Occupation* [2023] HKCA 479, but the case is the subject of an appeal to the Court of Final Appeal.

Best Sheen Development Ltd v Official Receiver and Trustee[62]

The plaintiff, a developer, entered into an illegal contract with a New Territories villager. The purpose was that the villager should obtain permission, on behalf of the plaintiff, to build under the New Territories "small house" scheme. In order to obtain the permission, the villager purported to be the legal and beneficial owner. The plaintiff had purchased the land for $250,000 but immediately assigned it to the villager who, in theory, was to pay for it. The court held that in fact this was an illegal "development scheme" and the villager had no interest in the property. On the villager's bankruptcy, the plaintiff successfully sought a declaration that it was the sole beneficial owner. Applying the *Tinsley* approach, the court found that the plaintiff could assert its interest without pleading its illegality. The transfer to the

---

57. Per Lord Toulson at para 121.
58. Ibid at para 110.
59. Per Lord Neuberger at para 163.
60. In particular, the "underlying purpose" of the rule infringed, "public policy" and "proportionality".
61. For example, *HKSAR v Lau Kam Ying* (2013) 16 HKCFAR 595; *Tang Teng & Others v Cheung Tin Wah & Another* [2014] 2 HKLRD 1032; *Law Pak Fun & Another v Tai Lee Fat International Ltd & Others* [2015] 4 HKLRD 339; *Ryder Industries Ltd v Chan Shui Woo* (2015) 18 HKCFAR 544. More recently, in *Zhang Junxian v UBS AG & Ors* [2020] 3 HKLRD 568, Master Gary Lam in Chambers posited following *Tinsley* in contract cases but *Patel* in tort, while admitting that this is somewhat unsatisfactory.
62. [2001] 3 HKC 79.

villager had been a voluntary one and the relationship between the parties did not raise a presumption of gift.[63] Yuen J stated:

> the 'development scheme' was a contract . . . which had as its object the deliberate commission of the tort of misrepresentation on the Government as landlord, the misrepresentation being that Lai (the villager) owned the land. A contract to commit a civil wrong is illegal under common law . . .
>
> However, I am satisfied that a declaration that the plaintiff is the beneficial owner of the land does not amount to enforcement of the illegal contract.[64]

The illegality of such "development schemes", to take advantage of the special "small house" concession available to indigenous New Territories residents, was confirmed in *Chung Mui Teck & Others v Hang Tak Buddhist Hall Association and Another*[65] where the court was asked to prevent a developer completing a fictitious arrangement with local villagers, whereby the latter would claim the right to acquire a plot cheaply which would then be used by the defendants for a building development. The court agreed that the arrangement was illegal since its performance would require the villagers to make false declarations. The court issued injunctions to prevent the planned development. Illegal "small house" scams continue to proliferate[66] as the small house policy, intended as a temporary measure by the colonial government, is zealously defended by the Heung Yee Kuk, which represents the interests of the so-called "indigenous" inhabitants of the New Territories (who are not legally required to reside there!).[67] An indication of the widespread nature of "small house policy" abuse can be seen from the opening sentence of Recorder H. Wong in *Best Star Holdings Ltd v Lam Chun Hing & Others*:[68]

> This is yet another action that concerns the development of "small houses" in the New Territories.

A clear illustration of the widespread nature of the abuse can be seen from the following extract from Recorder Stewart Wong's judgment in *Li Ting Kit Tso & Others v Cheung Tin Wah & Another*:[69]

---

63. Unlike in the *Cheerbond* case discussed below at 13.3.3.
64. Ibid at 87. In *Yick Fung Holdings Ltd v Sandwood Ltd* [2009] 4 HKC 43, the Hong Kong Court of Appeal, citing *Tinsley*, ignored illegality which emerged "as part of the background".
65. [2001] 2 HKLRD 471.
66. See also *Tiu Sum Fat & Others v Shun Sing Development Ltd & Another* [2010] 1 HKC 258; *Lau Ting Tai v Chung Chun Kwong & Others* [2010] 3 HKC 352; *Chan Yau v Chan Calvin & Another* [2014] 5 HKLRD 304.
67. The "Kuk" was regarded as "loyal to the motherland" and, as a reward, Article 40 of the Basic Law guarantees the protection of the "traditional" rights and interests of the "indigenous inhabitants" of the New Territories. This has resulted in the despoliation of much of the New Territories by the proliferation of "small houses" sold or let by indigenous villagers (usually living overseas).
68. (unrep, HCA 409/2008 & 409A/2008, 26 April 2012).
69. [2017] 1 HKLRD 722.

> Mr Yan, counsel for the plaintiff, accepts . . . that in the performance of
> the agreements, it would be inevitable or likely that false representations
> would be made by indigenous villagers, in whose names the application
> to build small houses . . . would be made, to the Lands Department and
> thus they were illegal.[70]

13.3.1.2 Where Plaintiff Is Part of Class Protected by Law

A party to an illegal contract may also be permitted to enforce it where he is held to
be within a class of persons which the statute is intended to protect from the exploitation of others. Employees, for example, may agree to operate dangerously as a way
of obtaining or maintaining employment, fearing that refusal might jeopardise their
position. In *Gray v Southouse*,[71] the courts permitted a tenant to recover an illegal
premium which he had paid knowing it to be unlawful. The court made clear that the
rule against the payment of such premiums was made precisely to protect tenants
from exploitative behaviour by landlords.[72] The *Gray v Southouse* approach was specifically endorsed in the Hong Kong case of *Hong Chi Mui v Tong Ching Company*,[73]
also involving the recovery of an illegal premium. The point is further illustrated in
the Court of First Instance case of *(Peter) Chan Ting-Lai v Same Fair Co Ltd*[74] where
the plaintiff had paid $50,000 to the defendant as a deposit for engaging the latter
as a commodity dealer. The plaintiff subsequently brought an action to recover the
money on the basis that the contract was illegal, since the defendants had employed
unregistered dealers. The plaintiff's action was successful even though he was a
party to the illegal contract.

The decision was based on the fact that the parties were not equally at fault,
that is, not *in pari delicto*, but this was based not on the plaintiff's ignorance of
the illegality but on the fact that the relevant legislative rules, sections 26(2) and
section 28 of the Commodities Trading Ordinance,[75] were viewed as being intended
to protect customers, such as the plaintiff, from the dangers of dealing with unregistered dealers. Judge Eric Li stated:

> I specifically find . . . the contract for brokerage service between the parties was
> illegal . . . the object of Sections 26(2) and 28 . . . was clearly to protect that class of
> the public who resort to dealers and their representatives for trading in commodities

---

70. Ibid at para 8. Despite the multiple abuses and sexually discriminatory nature of the policy, it has
    been recognised as a "lawful traditional" right by the HKCFA, to be protected under Article 40 Basic
    Law.
71. [1949] 2 All ER 1019.
72. See also *Kiriri Cotton Co Ltd v Dewani* [1960] AC 192, [1960] 1 All ER 177.
73. [1964] HKLR 146.
74. (unrep, DCCJ 5210/1984, 20 June 1984).
75. Cap 250.

. . . As a person under the protection of Cap 250, I find that the Plaintiff was not in pari delictum at least not to the extent as [*sic*] the defendant was.[76]

13.3.1.3 The "Oppressed" Plaintiff

The courts may also allow a party who has "willingly" entered into an illegal contract as a result of pressure by the other to sue on it. In *Atkinson v Denby*,[77] a debtor paid an illegal £50 premium without which a creditor refused to make a composition agreement (an agreement whereby creditors each agree to accept part-payment of a debtor's debts). The debtor subsequently sued to recover the premium and his action succeeded. Although he knew the premium payment to have been illegal, he was pressured by the creditor to make it, such that they were not equally to blame (that is, not *in pari delicto*).

A very clear Hong Kong example is provided by *Andayani v Chan Oi Ling*,[78] dealt with more fully elsewhere.[79] In *Andayani*, the court found in favour of an Indonesian domestic helper who had knowingly agreed to a contract under which she was paid less than the legal minimum, since without such agreement she would not have secured employment.

13.3.1.4 The "Morally Superior" Claimant

Although the House of Lords judges, in *Tinsley*, expressed opposition to the idea of comparing the relative iniquity of the parties, there are still cases in which the moral superiority of the claimant is taken into consideration. In *Mohamed v Alaga & Co*,[80] the court decided that a contract between an interpreter and a firm of solicitors for the (illegal) payment of a share of legal aid fees was entered into innocently by the claimant, who was therefore allowed reasonable remuneration on a *quantum meruit*[81] basis, the *delictum* of the parties not being equal. Conversely, in *Awwad v Geraghty*,[82] where a similar agreement was entered into by a solicitor who should, at least, have been aware of the illegality, no compensation was permitted. It is true to say that the rules as to when the "innocence" of the claimant will support his claim are very unclear. It might also be considered that of the three factors which the *Patel* Supreme Court advocated applying, "proportionality" might well encompass the relative morality of the claimant.

---

76. At paras 2-12. Given that *in pari* encompasses equality of guilt, the last words of Li J's statement are redundant.
77. (1862) 7 H&N 934.
78. [2001] 1 HKC 252.
79. See 8.3.3.
80. [2000] 1 WLR 1815, [1999] 3 All ER 699.
81. See, for example, 14.2.
82. [2000] 3 WLR 1041, [2001] QB 570.

13.3.1.5 Illegal Act Too "Remote"

A contract may be enforced despite an illegal connection, where that connection is so tenuous or remote that it is thought improper to allow it to be used to avoid liability under the contract. The position was considered in the following English case.

21st Century Logistic Solutions v Madysen[83]

A crook named Darren King set up in business calling himself "21st Century Logistics" in order to effect a Value Added Tax (VAT) fraud. He delivered computer processing units (CPUs) to the defendants for a price which included VAT. The defendants genuinely agreed to pay the necessary VAT to King but he intended all along that he would not pay the required VAT and would "vanish" before payment was due. The defendants discovered King's illegal intent after taking delivery of the goods for which they refused to pay, pleading King's illegality. The dilemma for the court was that "21st Century" (King) had undoubtedly formed the contract with an illegal intent but the defendants (who had been "innocent" at the time of the contract) had acquired goods which they admitted were of suitable quality. To allow the defendants to keep the goods without payment would have given them an unmerited benefit. The court ruled that the defendants must pay for the goods, since the criminal purpose (VAT avoidance) was "remote" from the contract of sale and had not, in any event, been fulfilled.

The decision of the court, though expressed in terms of "remoteness" of the illegal purpose, could have been based on the *Tinsley* principle that it was possible for the plaintiffs to seek payment without pleading their illegality. There was a sale of goods, which had been properly delivered in suitable condition, such that the agreed price should have been paid. Equally, although there was no true "remorse", the plaintiffs had been unable to fulfil their illegal purpose.[84] From a "policy" point of view it was no doubt significant that "21st Century" were in liquidation, such that payment from the defendants would go not to the criminal, King, but to his creditors.

13.3.1.6 The Passing of Property

A further complication is that, even though a contract is illegally formed, there are situations, as indicated in the *Tinsley* case, in which property can pass once the contract has been "executed". This controversial proposition is supported by the English Court of Appeal[85] and The Privy Council.[86]

The English Law Commission has indicated that this approach has caused confusion, not least in determining at what point the property passes. Of course where

---

83. [2004] EWHC 231.
84. See 13.3.3 below.
85. See *Belvoir Finance Co Ltd v Stapleton* [1971] 1 QB 210, [1970] 3 All ER 664.
86. See *Singh v Ali* [1960] AC 167, [1960] 1 All ER 269.

only the two parties to the illegality are concerned, the passing of property is imma-terial. Quite simply, neither party can enforce the illegal contract since this would require pleading the illegality and the loss would lie, as previously stated, where it falls. Only where a third party is involved does it become crucial to determine whether such a party has acquired an interest.

13.3.2 Contracts Illegally Performed

Where a contract is perfectly legal when formed but is *performed* illegally by one of the parties, the general rule is that the "innocent" party can enforce it but the guilty cannot. An action by the guilty party would, of course, be precluded by the *ex turpi causa* doctrine. The principles are well illustrated in *Marles v Philip Trant & Sons Ltd (No 2)*,[87] where the defendants made an agreement to buy "spring wheat" from a supplier. The supplier delivered winter wheat in breach of contract (the first contract). The defendants innocently sold on the wheat to the plaintiff. The second contract was legal as formed but illegal as performed since the defendants wrong-fully failed to comply with a statutory requirement to supply an invoice with the goods. The plaintiff, as an innocent buyer, was held entitled to damages from the defendants for delivery of the wrong wheat. The illegality of performance did not preclude his action since he was not involved in the illegal performance. It was also possible for the defendants to bring an action for breach of contract against their supplier since the first contract was not illegal, either as formed or performed.

This decision may be contrasted with that in *Ashmore, Benson, Pease & Co Ltd v AV Dawson Ltd*,[88] where the claimant was clearly aware of the illegal perfor-mance. In the *Ashmore* case the parties made a lawful agreement for the transport of a large piece of the plaintiffs' machinery by the defendants. The plaintiffs' transport manager watched the machinery being loaded on to the defendants' vehicle, which was not permitted to carry such a heavy load. The vehicle later overturned and the plaintiffs made a claim for compensation for negligence. On appeal the action failed since the court held that the plaintiffs' employee must have been aware of the illegal performance.

It can be seen once again that the underlying principle here is *in pari delicto*; the aim is not the protection of the defendant, who has himself acted illegally, but the general public who are thought to benefit by the prevention of actions by a willing partner in an illegal transaction. However, on rare occasions, where the claimant has been technically guilty of illegality but has acted in good faith, the courts may allow him to bring an action.

---

87. [1954] 1 QB 29, [1953] 1 All ER 651.
88. [1973] 2 All ER 856, [1973] 1 WLR 828.

Strongman (1945) Ltd v Sincock[89]

The plaintiffs, who were builders, contracted to modernise houses belonging to the defendant, an architect. It was illegal to carry out the work without a licence and the defendant, having promised to obtain the necessary licences, obtained only some of them. The defendant then refused to pay for the unlicensed work, pleading the illegal performance (in which he had been the main protagonist). The Court of Appeal upheld the plaintiffs' claim for payment on the basis of a collateral contract; that they would enter the contract to do the work in return for the defendant's promise to obtain the necessary licences. The court stressed, however, that such a finding was exceptional and owed much to a clear finding that it is the task of the architect in such cases to ensure the necessary licensing.

It might be thought that this case hints at an approach of finding in favour of the party whose conduct is less reprehensible. Indeed, the *in pari delicto* principle would favour such a view since the parties "while both *in delicto* are not in fact *in pari delicto*, that is they are not *equally* at fault."[90] However, this approach, while offering support for the eventual majority finding in the *Tinsley* case, was specifically rejected by the House of Lords in that case. The "moral" superiority of the claimant is, however, still capable of influencing the court.[91]

It is also the case that illegal performance which is not at "the core" of the contract may not preclude recovery. In *St John Shipping Corporation v Joseph Rank Ltd*,[92] the plaintiffs carried goods for the defendants by ship. The latter refused to pay the freight charges as the plaintiffs had overloaded the ship, contrary to statute. The statute made clear that such overloading was unlawful and imposed financial penalties. It was held, however, that the overloading was not central to the contract of carriage but, as Devlin J stated, merely incidental.

The case is, at first sight, difficult to reconcile with *Ashmore, Benson*. The distinction is said to be based on "public policy" and it has been suggested that such policy opposes the non-enforcement of contracts unless there are serious reasons to do so. Alternatively, the explanation may be that in *Ashmore, Benson* the relevant legislation envisaged that non-compliance would invalidate a contract, whereas in *St John* it intended only a financial penalty. The issue was central to the following Hong Kong case.

Yip Alice v Wong Shun (No 2)[93]

The plaintiffs were squatters on government land whose family had been in occupation for many years and operated a restaurant on the land. They employed the

---

89. [1955] 2 QB 525, [1955] 3 All ER 90.
90. R. Stone, *Contract Law (Lecture Notes Series)* (Oxford: Routledge Cavendish, 2006), p 196.
91. See 13.3.1.4 above.
92. [1957] 1 QB 267.
93. [2003] 2 HKC 528.

defendant to manage the restaurant in return for the promise of a monthly sum. In a subsequent claim for arrears of payment the defendant set up the plaintiffs' illegal occupation of the land in his defence. The plaintiffs' action for arrears and to recover possession of the land was upheld by the Hong Kong Court of Appeal. The court held that the occupation of government land probably did not become illegal until a notice was served and not complied with. Even if the occupation was illegal there was no indication that the relevant statutory rule should affect the civil rights of the parties whose dealings involved the occupation of the land. The court cited with approval the statement that public policy "may at times be better served by refusing to nullify a bargain save on serious and sufficient grounds."[94]

13.3.3 Contract Not Yet Performed

The principle that an illegal contract is void and permits no recovery of property passed under the illegal contract is subject to an exception where the claimant can show he withdrew from the contract before it was fully performed. This was previously said to be based on "repentance" by the claimant but it appears that this "moral" element is now no longer required and withdrawal before performance is all that is required.

Tribe v Tribe[95]

The plaintiff, in order to keep assets away from his (landlord) creditors, transferred shares to his son in a fictitious sale, the payment for which was never made. Ultimately the landlords needed to make no call on the assets and the father sought his shares back. The son refused and argued the father would have to plead the illegal transaction to further his action. The court permitted the father's claim since he had sought to cancel the illegal transfer before any illegal purpose was effected.

The case makes clear that "repentance" is required only in the sense of regretting the illegal transaction rather than actually "repenting" in the spiritual sense. A similar view was taken by the Hong Kong court in the *Best Sheen* case,[96] where Yuen J stated that, as an alternative justification for allowing the developer to recover the land, the building licence had not yet been executed by the government and no houses had been built on the land, such that the developer was withdrawing before the illegal purpose of the contract had been fulfilled. The "withdrawal before completion" situation is well illustrated in the following Hong Kong case.

---

94. *Vita Food Products v Unus Shipping Co Ltd* [1939] AC 277 at 293 per Lord Wright.
95. [1996] Ch 107.
96. See 13.3.1 above.

Cheerbond Development Ltd v Tung Kwok Yu[97]

A property had been bought in the name of "Madam Yan" for the purpose of defrauding potential business creditors of the "true" owner, Mr Tung. Madam Yan later tried to sell the property which the defendant, Mr Tung, refused to vacate. The Court of Appeal found there to be a "presumption of advancement" (essentially a presumption of gift) which, said the court, could only be rebutted by showing the illegal purpose had never been fulfilled. Since the defendant's business had prospered and no creditors had, in practice, been defrauded,[98] the court was prepared to accept the rebuttal and recognise the defendant's rights in the property. Just as in *Tinsley* it was held that such rights existed independently of the illegality.[99]

13.3.4 Severance

While severance is most often found in respect of contracts in restraint of trade,[100] it is applicable to other illegal contracts. The principle is that it may be possible to take out, or "sever", the illegal part of a contract and permit enforcement of the rest of the contract. The severance may apply to illegal *consideration* or illegal *promises*. Given the considerations of "public conscience" and the need to discourage illegal contracts, severance outside the area of restraint of trade is likely to be rare. In *Napier v National Business Agency*,[101] an employment contract between the plaintiff employee and the defendant employers was formed illegally. The contract stated that the plaintiff was to receive £13 per week in salary and £6 a week in expenses. In fact, his expenses never exceeded £1 per week. The purpose of the agreement was to reduce the plaintiff's tax liability and thereby defraud the Inland Revenue. This attempted deceit came to light when the plaintiff sought payment in lieu of notice on his dismissal. Although the plaintiff claimed only £13 per week, the judge discovered the fraud and denied him any compensation. This refusal was upheld by the Court of Appeal. A plea to sever the £13 figure from the £6 figure was rejected, since the whole agreement was tainted by the deliberate illegality of the arrangement.

While the conclusion may seem harsh on the plaintiff, especially since he had previously made a "confession" to the Inland Revenue authorities, the need to uphold the public conscience and deter criminality was the main consideration. Denning LJ emphasised the point in stating:

---

97. [2010] 2 HKLRD 546.
98. Once again, no requirement of repentance was felt to be needed.
99. See also *Wong Kwok Leung Baldwin & Others v International Trading Co Ltd* [2010] 2 HKLRD 334.
100. See 13.4 below.
101. [1951] 2 All ER 264.

He cannot recover either the part described as expenses or even the part described as salary . . . It will have a very salutary effect if it stops people putting in fictitious figures for expenses.[102]

The case clearly did not involve both legal and illegal consideration since, as the court found, the whole arrangement was tainted by illegality. There are cases, however, where it has been held possible to sever legal from illegal consideration. The situation arose in *Frank W Clifford Ltd v Garth*.[103] Here, the defendant engaged the plaintiff to convert premises to a coffee bar and restaurant and to do the necessary repair work. Given that the work was likely to be extensive the defendant agreed to pay on a "cost plus" basis. Existing legislation required a licence for such work if the value was over £1,000 and no licence was obtained. The cost of the work exceeded £1,000 and when the plaintiffs claimed the balance of £1,324 owed, the defendant refused to pay anything more, pleading illegality as a defence. The Court of Appeal severed the legal consideration from the illegal and allowed the claim up to the legal limit of £1,000. The work was legal until the limit was reached but not thereafter. Denning LJ, however, was of the opinion that, had the contract been an "entire" one, for a consideration of more than £1,000, the whole contract would have been void for illegality.

Cases of illegal *promises*, as opposed to consideration, usually arise out of excessive restraints of trade, such that severance is used to reduce the promise to reasonable levels in terms of duration, geographical area or scope. Since this aspect of severance is found overwhelmingly in the area of restraint of trade, it will be dealt with, below, in that context.[104]

13.3.5 The Need for Reform

As the above should have indicated, the law on illegality is confused. Almost every proposition is subject to exception. So, where a contract is illegally formed, generally neither party can enforce it *unless this can be done without reference to the illegal contract*. Where a contract is illegally performed, the "guilty" party cannot enforce it *unless* the illegal performance is "incidental" to the contract. Where both parties form an illegal contract neither can sue, irrespective of his state of mind, *except* where the court decides that the claimant's innocence means the parties are not *in pari delicto*. It may be possible to "sever" offending, illegal, parts of a contact but *not* where this would change the overall nature of the contract.

The list of apparent contradictions is a large one and has prompted a call for reform of the law in England. Lord Goff's call, in *Tinsley*, for Law Commission consideration of the issue has been heeded and an extensive Report has been published.

102. Ibid at 266.
103. [1956] 1 WLR 570.
104. See 13.4.

This report makes various recommendations based on a fundamental tenet that the courts should have a discretion but that such discretion should be "structured". The key considerations of the court should be:

1. the seriousness of the illegality;
2. the knowledge and intention of the plaintiff;
3. the deterrent effect of non-enforcement;
4. whether refusal of enforcement will further the purpose of the original prohibition;
5. whether denying relief is "proportionate".

Given that all of the above have already influenced courts, to a greater or lesser extent, in the cases described above, it is unclear how the Law Commission's recommendations will improve matters or increase certainty. Even the rejection of the "public conscience" test, endorsing the House of Lords approach to *Tinsley*, is less significant than first appears since, in practice, taking into account "the knowledge and intention of the plaintiff" and whether denying relief is "proportionate" are really only aspects of the supposedly rejected "public conscience" test.

Of course, any legal reform in England to this area of law, based on the Law Commission recommendations, will have no direct effect on Hong Kong law. Moreover, the Law Commission's Report does not encompass restraint of trade, the most significant aspect of illegal contracts in Hong Kong.

13.4 Contracts in Restraint of Trade

Contracts in restraint of trade are agreements restricting a person wholly or partially in the carrying on of his trade, business or profession. The most commonly found types of restraint are: restraints in contracts of employment; exclusive services contracts; restraints on the seller of a business; and so-called "solus" agreements. These contracts differ from other contracts in this chapter since, although "presumed" to be void, they are valid if proved to be reasonable. Indeed, the lengthy English Law Commission Report on Illegal Transactions omitted restraint of trade from its considerations. Moreover, when a restraint is found to be unlawful, it is only the restraint clause, rather than the contract itself, which is void.

13.4.1 The Basis of the Doctrine of Restraint of Trade

Although restraints of trade were once presumed to be valid unless they could be shown to be unreasonable, the "modern" doctrine is that a court will presume a restraint to be void unless it can be shown to be reasonable. The onus of proof, then, is upon the party seeking to enforce the restraint. It must be shown that the restraint is reasonable in the interests of the parties involved *and* in the interests of the public.

The leading authority on the meaning and effect of restraint of trade remains that of *Nordenfelt v Maxim Nordenfelt*,[105] which involved an attempt by the buyers of a worldwide armament business to prevent the famous seller setting up in competition with them. The House of Lords upheld the restraint on the basis that it was reasonable. Delivering the main judgment, Lord Macnaghten stated:

> Mr Nordenfelt sold his business to a limited company which was formed for the purpose of purchasing it. At the same time and as part of the same transaction he entered into a restrictive covenant with the purchasers intended to protect the business in their hands . . .
>
> The true view at the present time, I think, is this. The public have an interest in every person's carrying on his trade freely; so has the individual. All interference with individual liberty of action in trading, and all restraints of trade of themselves, if there is nothing more, are contrary to public policy, and, therefore, void. That is the general rule. But there are exceptions. Restraints of trade and interference with individual liberty of action may be justified by the special circumstances of a particular case. It is a sufficient justification, and indeed it is the only justification, if the restriction is reasonable—reasonable, that is, in reference to the interests of the parties concerned and reasonable in reference to the interests of the public.[106]

Two aspects of the restraint doctrine are highlighted by the recent case of *Dwyer (UK Franchising) Ltd v Fredbar Ltd & Another*,[107] involving the franchising of a plumbing and drain-cleaning operation. The first is to emphasise that the onus of proof lies with the "restrainer" to prove the reasonableness of the restraint. The second is that "equality of bargaining power" is very much a factor for the court to consider in determining the reasonableness of a restraint. Thus, as here, a restraint found unreasonable because of the inexperience (and therefore weak bargaining position) of the franchisee, may well have been found reasonable in the case of an experienced franchisee, even though dealing with the same standard form franchise contract.

13.4.2 Restraints on Employees

The general proposition here is that employers are entitled to restrict the activities of *current* employees. It is clearly unobjectionable for employees to demand the exclusive services of their employees during the contract of employment. This is in keeping with various implied terms in the contract of employment such as that the employee will serve the interests of the employer, obey all reasonable orders, not compete with his employer etc. The employer may, of course, permit a measure of outside practice but if he insists on exclusive services this will normally be upheld

---

105. [1894] AC 535.
106. Ibid at 565.
107. [2022] EWCA Civ 889.

against a serving employee. However, since the employer will generally seek to enforce a restraint via an injunction, the courts will seek to ensure that the effect is not to compel the employee to continue working unwillingly for his employer or "starve". If the granting of an injunction would give the employee no reasonable alternative to working on, it will be tantamount to specific performance of a personal service contract and the remedy will be refused accordingly.[108]

In the case of *past* employees, the first principle is that if their contract has come to an end as a result of serious breach by the employer justifying termination by the employee, any restraint in the employee's contract of employment will be rendered ineffective.

Where the contract comes to an end other than via the employer's breach, restraints will be *prima facie* void but will be permitted if they protect a "legitimate interest" and are in the interests of the parties and the public.

13.4.2.1 Legitimate Interest

The sort of interest which it is permissible to protect are those involving trade secrets and the possible "poaching" of previous customers by the employee while still employed. Many Hong Kong cases involve hairdressers and it is easy to appreciate the opportunity which exists for an employee contemplating setting up his own business to encourage clients to move with him when he leaves his current employment. This is particularly likely in an area such as hairdressing where a certain amount of stylist/ customer loyalty is built up and even encouraged. It is also especially relevant to Hong Kong which has a relatively small geographical area and good transport infra-structure, such that it is relatively easy for customers to "migrate" to a new salon.

An employer is not entitled to restrict the mere use of a former employee's skills, even if those skills were developed during the contract of employment and even if they are to be used contrary to the former employer's interests. A football club, for example, cannot prevent an employee, on leaving the club, using his skills on behalf of a new club, even where these are used in playing against his former team. Obviously, too, it is not legitimate to restrict the activities of past employees merely as a punishment for disloyalty or as a way of "encouraging" other employees to remain in post. The following is a leading Hong Kong case on "legitimate interest".

GSL Engineering Ltd v Yau Hon Yin Sammon & Others[109]

The plaintiffs were seeking to prevent the first defendant using, to their trade detri-ment, information regarding customers, pricing policy, etc, which he had obtained prior to leaving their employment and which, they argued, he should, on principle, be prevented from using. The Hong Kong High Court refused to uphold the plaintiffs'

---

108. See 15.2.
109. [1990] 2 HKC 360.

arguments that the information acquired was a trade secret, but affirmed an injunction against the defendant based on his alleged misconduct while in office.

In delivering the judgment of the court, Godfrey J relied heavily on the principles laid down in the English Court of Appeal case of *Faccenda Chicken v Fowler*.[110] He concluded:

> the plaintiff's evidence comes nowhere near establishing that the knowledge of the plaintiff's business of which the defendants are intending to make use is information which has that sufficient character of confidentiality necessary to support the plaintiff's case.[111]

There was no express covenant relating to confidential information in the *GSL Engineering* case but this would not have been fatal to the plaintiffs' case were the judge to have found the defendant to have made use of a trade secret or, perhaps, confidential information since there are implied terms in any contract of employment governing the employee's obligations in this respect. The *Faccenda* case makes clear that trade secrets may not be divulged by the employee even after leaving his employer's business. While this may well be covered by a specific restrictive covenant, it would operate irrespective of this, since the misuse of trade secrets is a breach of an employee's implied obligations. The use of highly confidential information is subject to the same limitations though, as stated in the *Faccenda* case, this restriction does not apply to the sort of information which is only confidential during the currency of the employment contract. The distinction between trade secrets and confidential information was discussed, by the English Court of Appeal, in *Lansing Linde Ltd v Kerr*[112] where Staughton LJ asked:

> what are trade secrets and how do they differ (if at all) from confidential information? . . . trade secret in this context . . . can thus include not only secret formulae for the manufacture of products but also, in an appropriate case, the names of customers and the goods which they buy.[113]

In *PCCW-HKT & Another v Aitken & Another*,[114] the Hong Kong plaintiffs had allowed the first defendant to join the second defendant without waiting all of the three months stipulated in his contract. However, things later became less amicable and the plaintiffs sought injunctions to prevent the disclosure of confidential information (uncontested) *and* to severely restrict the type of work which the first defendant could engage in. This the plaintiffs sought to justify on the basis that rules are more restrictive for *solicitors* who change employment.[115] The Court of Final Appeal

---

110. [1987] Ch 117.
111. [1990] 2 HKC 360 at 365.
112. [1991] 1 All ER 418.
113. Ibid at 425–426.
114. [2009] 2 HKC 342.
115. Citing *(HRH Prince Jeffri) Bolkiar v KPMG* [1999] 2 AC 222.

refused the latter injunction, doubting that solicitors are in a different position and stressing that, in any event, the first defendant, although qualified as a solicitor, was not admitted in Hong Kong and was not acting for the plaintiffs as in-house counsel.[116]

13.4.2.2 Reasonableness in the Interests of the Parties

It might at first appear that a restraint on a previous employee which he now seeks to evade would never be in the interests of that employee; why else would he seek to evade it? It must be remembered that the reasonableness factor must be judged as at the time the contract of employment was made and that, implicitly, the "consideration" given to the employee takes account of subsequent restraints.

Above all, however, the restraints must be no wider than is reasonable, both in geographical and temporal terms. The courts will also consider the scope of the restraint, in terms of what activities are precluded. The wider a restraint is, in terms of time, scope or area,[117] the more likely it is to be declared unreasonable. A classic example is provided in *Attwood v Lamont*[118] where the English Court of Appeal refused to uphold a restraint by which:

(the employee) . . . will not at any time thereafter . . . carry on or be in any way directly or indirectly concerned in any of the following trades or businesses, that is to say, the trade or business of a tailor, dressmaker, general draper, milliner, hatter, haberdasher, gentlemen's, ladies' or children's outfitter at any place, within a radius of 10 miles of the employers' place of business at Regent House, Kidderminster, aforesaid.

In underlining the unreasonableness of the restraint, Younger LJ described it as:

nothing more than an agreement not to trade in opposition with the employers in any part of their business. It will be broken if the appellant not only carries on but is directly or indirectly concerned in any of the specified businesses; and the period of restriction is to cover the whole life of the appellant, although the employment was itself an employment only for a month certain.[119]

Similarly, an excessive restraint was rejected in the Hong Kong case of *Ho Wing Cheong and Others v Graham Margot and Another*.[120] In the *Ho Wing Cheong* case the defendant had worked for the plaintiffs. On leaving their employ at the end of

---

116. Bokhary PJ added the significant point that Hong Kong's Basic Law guarantees "freedom of choice of occupation".
117. A five-mile competition restraint on an ex-employee estate agent was rejected in *Tim Russ & Co v Robertson & Others* (before Judge Mann, Chancery Division, 5 April 2011) though an injunction was granted in respect of "customer solicitation".
118. [1920] 3 KB 571.
119. Ibid at 577.
120. [1991] 1 HKLR 245.

his probation period he had set up in competition contrary to a restraint clause to which he had previously agreed. He had contacted customers to inform them of his new position and had encouraged them to do business with his new venture. By way of defence the defendant argued that the restraint was unreasonable and, therefore, void. His plea was upheld in the Hong Kong High Court.

Godfrey J, having concluded that the defendant was clearly in breach of restrictive covenants in his contract of employment, went on:

> But is the covenant enforceable? . . .
>
> . . . where an employee is placed in a position in which he has that type and degree of contact with the employer's customers which means that, after the employee leaves, the customers may leave with the employee, the law will uphold against the employee any restrictions which go no further than is reasonably necessary to prevent that happening.
>
> . . . however, the plaintiffs have failed to satisfy me that a period as long as 3 years was needed for the protection of their legitimate interests. It appeared from the evidence of Kwek Leng Hai that the major reason for the imposition of this length of restriction was to tie Mr. Margot to the plaintiffs for a period over which they could amortise the cost of bringing him from England to Hong Kong and setting him up here: in effect to get value for money from Mr. Margot. But this could and should have been done by getting him to sign a contract for a three-year term. It was illegitimate, in my judgement, to try and do so by the imposition of a 3-year restriction on the termination of his employment, which was determinable, after the end of the probationary period of 6 months, on 3 months' notice.[121]

There was no doubt in this case that the employee was acting contrary to the covenants in his employment contract. The key issue was whether the restraint was reasonable. The judge felt it was not, largely because it was one-sided; it tied the defendant to the restriction for three years but left the employer free to dispose of the employee within nine months.

A typical Hong Kong scenario is provided by the case of *Susan Buchanan v Janesville Ltd*[122] where the respondents were the proprietors of La Coupe Salon, a high class hairdressing salon in Central. The appellant had entered into a two-year contract with the respondents, terminable on two months' notice, clause 7 of which stated:

> At the termination of employment the Employee agrees not to work in the colony of Hong Kong as a hairdresser or in any capacity connected with hairdressing in competition with La Coupe Salon for a period of one year.

The appellant left the employment of La Coupe Salon and went to work at an establishment called "Le Salon" in Tsim Sha Tsui. Given the appellant's skill

---

121. Ibid at 253.
122. [1981] HKLR 700.

and popularity as a hairdresser and stylist, the respondents sought an injunction to enforce clause 7, fearing that their business would suffer from her competition.

In rejecting the application for an injunction, Barker JA accepted the principle that restraints are *prima facie* void. They would be upheld only if reasonable in the interests of the parties and the public. The latter point had no bearing on the case but, as between the parties, the restraint was seen to be unreasonably wide in geographical terms since it extended to the whole territory of Hong Kong. This was greater than necessary to protect the respondents' legitimate interests. Of course, in appropriate cases, even a wide geographical restraint could be justified. In the *Nordenfelt* case the court upheld a worldwide restraint since the business involved was worldwide in nature.

A restraint was upheld in another Hong Kong "hairdressing" case, where the geographical restraint was narrower (and the employees' conduct more reprehensible!).

Rever (AMA) Salon Ltd v Kung Wai For Danny (No 2)[123]

The employing salon imposed restraints on their employees in respect of post-employment competition (within one mile of the plaintiffs' salon) and in respect of "poaching" the plaintiffs' customers. Deputy Judge Gill upheld the restraints in the Court of First Instance as reasonable as regards the parties and the public interest. He also found that there was a "well-laid plan" for employees to leave *en masse* and found the poaching employees to be in breach of their implied duty of fidelity to their employer and, in the case of the "ringleaders", found them to be guilty of inducing breach of contract.

Given Hong Kong's limited area and the close relationship which lawyers often have with their clients, it is not surprising that post-employment restraints on solicitors are also a major source of restraint of trade litigation. The Hong Kong case of *Robin Bridge v Deacons (a firm) (Hong Kong)*,[124] was ultimately appealed to the Privy Council and remains a leading case on restraint of trade.

Bridge v Deacons

A partnership agreement provided that for five years after leaving a solicitors' partnership in Hong Kong, the appellant would not engage with previous clients of the firm anywhere in Hong Kong. The agreement was held, by the Privy Council, to be valid as in the interests of the parties, since all the partners benefitted from the restriction on competition, and to be in the public interest.

The wording of the restrictive covenant was as follows:

> Except on dissolution, no partner ceasing to be a partner for any reason whatsoever
> shall for a period of five years thereafter act as a solicitor, notary, trade mark or

---

123. [2003] 2 HKC 268.
124. [1984] UKPC 11.

patent agent or in any similar capacity in the Colony of Hong Kong whether as principal, clerk or assistant for any person, firm or company who was at the time of his ceasing to be a partner or had during the period of three years prior thereto been a client of the partnership provided however that this clause shall not apply to a partner acting in any such capacity in the course of employment with government or any public body or with any company or organisation which is not itself engaged in professional practice in any of the above fields.

In delivering the leading judgment in the Privy Council, Lord Fraser, in upholding the restraint, dealt with reasonableness in respect of both the parties and the public. As to the former, he said:

> As regards the five-year period of restriction, and the application of the restriction to persons who had been clients within three years before the particular partner retired
> . . . The inclusion of persons who have been clients within the previous three years appears to be perfectly reasonable, having regard to the intermittent nature of a solicitor's employment for a particular client.
> . . . The adequacy of the consideration and the reasonableness of the contract as between the parties must be judged in 1974 (when the contract was formed).
> . . . Their Lordships accordingly find no reason to consider that the restriction was unreasonable between the parties by reason of the consideration paid to the appellant having been inadequate.[125]

The reasonableness criteria were considered in depth in the case of *Kao Lee & Yip v Edwards*.[126] The case involved a restraint in a solicitor's contract of employment with the plaintiff solicitors' firm. The employee challenged the restraint as an unreasonable restraint of trade. The Hong Kong Court of Appeal, in rejecting the restraint, made clear that a balance must be held between the freedom of the contracting parties and the public interest in preserving freedom to trade. In the leading judgment, Litton JA stressed that it was insufficient that the agreement, when made, was fair to the parties; the public interest has also to be considered. This, he pointed out, is a complex consideration since:

> While the community is rightly interested in people being free to contract and being held to their bargains, it is equally interested in trade being free.[127]

The reason for overturning the restraint, however, was that it was not shown to be reasonable by the plaintiffs. They may have had a legitimate interest to protect, in terms of "goodwill or client connections", but the worldwide restraint imposed was far too wide given that the parties had been involved only in English and Hong Kong practice.

---

125. [1984] 2 WLR 837 at 844–845.
126. [1993] 1 HKC 314.
127. Ibid at 316.

13.4.3 Indirect Restraints

The restraint on an employee usually takes the form of an explicit covenant not to compete. However, the same result can be obtained by, for example, the employer promising to pay a pension which the employee will forfeit if he subsequently competes. The courts have held that such an agreement is also subject to the rules on restraint of trade.[128] Similarly, adopting a "substance rather than form" approach, the courts have held that an agreement between potential *employers* not to engage each other's past employees, is also an agreement in restraint of trade.[129]

13.4.4 Exclusive Services Contracts

Generally the courts will not intervene with respect to a restraint on an existing employee or contractor preventing him working for others, since it is generally acceptable to insist on an employee's exclusive services.[130] In extreme cases, however, where it is clear that the agreement is very one-sided and favours a party in a dominant bargaining position, a restraint will be overturned[131] even where it relates to a still-existing contract or engagement. This is particularly likely where the contract is a long-term one.

Exclusive service agreements are particularly common in the sporting or entertainment fields. They are theoretically distinct from restraints on "employees" since there need be no contract of employment; the "restrained" party merely promises that if he does offer his services it will be solely to the "restrainer". Since the effect of such restraints is similar to that on employees, however, the same reasonableness principles apply.

Schroeder (A) Music Publishing Co Ltd v Macaulay[132]

The respondent, at the time an unknown songwriter, aged 21, made a contract with the appellants to provide the exclusive use of his services for five years. The appellants were to have the world copyright on all his songs in return for a fixed percentage on royalties. The agreement could be terminated by the appellants, by one month's notice, but not by the respondent. Rights under the contract could be assigned by the appellants but not by the respondent. Most importantly, the appellants did not promise to publish any songs, without which the respondent would receive no royalty payments. The respondent sought a declaration that the contract

---

128. *Bull v Pitney-Bowes Ltd* [1967] 1 WLR 27.
129. *Kores Manufacturing Co Ltd v Kolok Manufacturing Co Ltd* [1959] Ch 108.
130. This point seems to have been overlooked by counsel for the defendants in the *Hummingbird Music* case discussed below.
131. Or at least an injunction will be refused.
132. [1974] 1 WLR 1308, [1974] 3 All ER 616. See also *Panayiotou v Sony Music* [1994] EMLR 229 (involving the late George Michael).

was an unlawful restraint, contrary to public policy. His action succeeded, ultimately in the House of Lords.

Lord Reid stressed the one-sided nature of the agreement. He suggested that the court's decision might have been otherwise if the songwriter had had the option of recovering his copyright in the event of the publisher's refusal to publish. Lord Diplock emphasised the inequality of bargaining power and said:

> The terms of this kind of standard form contract have not been the subject of nego-tiation between the parties to it, or approved by any organisation representing the interests of the weaker party. They have been dictated by that party whose bargain-ing power . . . enables him to say: ". . . Take it or leave it."[133]

An "exclusive" management" agreement was upheld in the Hong Kong case of *Hummingbird Music Ltd v Acconci & Acconci*[134] where the court distinguished contracts which limit trade and those which encourage it. The *Acconci* contract was regarded as more like a "joint venture" with each party initially enthusiastic, with the "restrainer" expending considerable sums to further the defendants' singing careers, and with the "restrained" parties signing only after taking legal advice.

In these "exclusive service" cases, any unreasonably wide restraint may nonethe-less be part of an overall package whereby the "victim" obtains significant benefits. This was recognised in the English case of *Proactive Sports Management Ltd v Rooney*[135] where Judge Hegarty QC found an eight-year exclusive "image rights" agreement with the star footballer Wayne Rooney an unreasonable (and therefore unenforceable) restraint of trade. The judge, nonetheless, allowed the plaintiff a sig-nificant sum on a "*quantum meruit*" basis for the value of the management work he had done for Rooney prior to the ending of their professional relationship.

13.4.5 Restraints on the Seller of a Business

It is clear that, when a person buys a business, it may well be worth far more to him if the previous proprietor promises not to set up locally in competition, thereby luring back his previous customers. The courts recognise this and will generally uphold a covenant by the seller not to compete. It is recognised that the parties will have nego-tiated on an equal footing and there is little likelihood that one has dictated terms to the other, unlike the position with restraints on employees which might be imposed by a dominant employer.

Nonetheless, the doctrine of restraint of trade still applies to restraints on the business-seller since they limit competition, and the restraint must be shown to be reasonable if it is to be upheld. Thus, the restraint must protect a genuine interest of

---

133. [1974] 3 All ER 616 at 624.
134. [2010] 5 HKLRD 587.
135. [2010] EWHC 1807 (QB).

the buyer of the business: the area of the restraint must not prevent the seller moving to a new geographical area where he did not previously trade and the restraint must not keep the seller out of an area of business in which he was previously not engaged.[136] The factors to be considered in determining the reasonableness of a restraint on the seller of a business are illustrated by the case of *Nordenfelt v Maxim Nordenfelt Guns and Ammunition Company Ltd*[137] where a worldwide restraint on the seller of a business was, unusually, upheld, on the basis that the buyer had paid a considerable sum for a business that was worldwide in nature.

13.4.6 *"Solus" Agreements*

"Solus" means "only". Thus a solus agreement is one by which a party agrees to sell the products of only one supplier. For example, in return for financial assistance from an oil company in developing a petrol station, a petrol seller may promise to sell only the oil company's products. Solus agreements in England have, traditionally, been coupled with mortgages for a fixed period which cannot be redeemed early. It has been held in England that solus agreements are subject to the restraint of trade doctrine but that they will usually be upheld as reasonable in the interests of the parties and the public, as long as they are not too lengthy in duration. The situation is analogous to agreements for exclusive services. Since there is little legislation or litigation on this area it will be dealt with briefly though the common law principles involved are equally applicable to Hong Kong. Basically, the English courts have taken the view that the type of mortgage/solus agreement outlined above is reasonable as between the parties, provided that the term is not excessively lengthy, since they increase the seller's business opportunities. Moreover, they make petrol supply more assured for the seller in an industry which deals with a notoriously fluctuating product. From the public's point of view, too, the agreements tend to ensure the viability of a greater number of retail outlets than would otherwise be the case. The leading case remains *Esso Petroleum v Harper's Garage (Stourport) Ltd.*[138] Here, the respondents had two garages and entered into solus agreements with the appellants in respect of both. The respondents promised: to take all their petrol from the appellants; to keep open at all reasonable times; not to sell the garages unless the purchaser made a similar agreement; and not to redeem the mortgages early. One mortgage was for four-and-a-half years, the other for 21 years. In a subsequent dispute, the House of Lords accepted that the restraint of trade doctrine applied to solus agreements and upheld the shorter restraint as reasonable but rejected the longer one as unreasonable.

The House of Lords, whose leading judgment was delivered by Lord Reid, agreed that the case involved agreements within the restraint of trade doctrine which,

---

136. See *British Reinforced Concrete Engineering Co Ltd v Schelff* [1921] 2 Ch 563.
137. [1894] AC 535.
138. [1968] AC 269, 1967 1 All ER 699.

therefore, had to be proved reasonable. The court took into account a report from the English Monopolies Commission which had been generally supportive of solus agreements in the petrol trade. The five-year restraint was held to be reasonable in protecting Esso's legitimate expectations but:

> A tie for 21 years stretches far beyond any period for which developments are reasonably foreseeable.[139]

In one instance, however, the doctrine of restraint of trade would not previously apply to solus agreements at all. This was where the agreement was not, for example, by a site owner who wished to develop his site via petrol company finance, but by a person who needed the assistance of a petrol company to buy or lease a site. Here, it was felt, the solus arrangement does not restrict trade at all; in fact it *increases* competition by allowing into the petrol-selling business someone who would otherwise be unable to join it.[140] It has been suggested that the *Harper's* case excluded such types of solus agreement from the restraint of trade doctrine because "*it was apparently feared that to say otherwise might cause unnecessary interference in the law of real property relating to restrictive covenants*".[141] However, it seems preferable to adopt Lord Reid's view that:

> A person buying or leasing land had no previous right to be there at all, let alone to trade there, and when he takes possession of that land subject to a negative restrictive covenant he gives up no right or freedom which he previously had.[142]

This restriction on the restraint of trade doctrine (Lord Reid's "pre-existing freedom test") no longer applies in the UK since the case of *Peninsular Securities Ltd v Dunnes Stores (Bangor) Ltd (Northern Ireland)*.[143] Here, the Supreme Court examined at length the practice elsewhere in the common law world and the numerous criticisms of the previous distinction between giving up a right previously enjoyed and the acceptance of restraint to "get into the market". Quite simple, as Lord Carnwath stated:

> we should finally discard the much-criticised "pre-existing freedom test".[144]

The Supreme Court favoured Lord Wilberforce's alternative approach in *Esso*, the so-called "trading society test", which would allow, exceptionally, restraints

---

139. [1967] 1 All ER at 711.
140. See, on this point, *Cleveland Petroleum Co Ltd v Dartstone Ltd* [1969] 1 WLR 116; not followed in *Alec Lobb (Garages) Ltd v Total Oil (Great Britain) Ltd* [1985] 1 WLR 173, where a sale and lease-back was recognised as a device to circumvent the restraint of trade doctrine, but the restraint was upheld anyway as reasonable.
141. See T. A. Downes, *Textbook on Contract* (London: Blackstone Press, 5th edn, 1997), p 204.
142. [1967] 1 All ER 699 at 707.
143. [2020] UKSC 36.
144. At para 59.

which *"had passed into the accepted and normal currency of commercial or contractual or conveyancing relations"*.[145]

As with all post-1997 overseas decisions, Hong Kong is free to make up its own mind, mindful, of course, of the additional implications for the Competition Ordinance.[146] In reality, there has been little Hong Kong jurisprudence on solus and similar agreements.[147]

13.4.7 The Public Interest

It has been suggested that no agreement in the parties' interests will be against the public interest.[148] This is because individual agreements are unlikely to have a major impact on the overall position in a particular market or profession. It is, in practice, unusual to find a restraint found reasonable between the parties to be disallowed on the grounds of public interest. In *Bridge v Deacons*,[149] for example, in upholding the solicitor's restraint, Lord Fraser said:

> On the question of reasonableness in the public interest, their Lordships are of the opinion that there is a clear public interest in facilitating the assumption by established solicitors' firms of younger men as partners. It benefits clients by tending to secure continuity in the practice. It also tends to encourage the entry of younger men in to the profession . . . the continuing partners in the respondent firm would only feel able to take on new capital partners if they knew that in doing so they would not run the risk that the new partners would acquire a connection with the clients of the respondent and then depart with that part of the respondent's goodwill.[150]

The interest of the Hong Kong public in not losing a skilled practitioner in a then undermanned profession was not paramount in a situation where the agreement was fair to the parties. Conversely, in the *Kao Lee & Yip* case,[151] Litton JA seemed to put greater emphasis on the public interest but based his rejection of the restraint on the unreasonable nature of the restraint in respect of the parties. The seminal *Nordenfelt* case involved the upholding of a very wide restraint based on its fairness to a very well remunerated party; there was found to be no overwhelming public interest objection.

---

145. Those interested in judicial precedent may note that the Supreme Court consciously made use of its sparingly applied power (in existence since 1966) to depart from previous decisions made at the highest level.
146. Cap 619.
147. It is perhaps also worthy of note that Hong Kong Court of Final Appeal non-permanent overseas judge, Lord Sumption, was a strong dissenter in *Patel v Mirza*!
148. See judgment of Lord Diplock in *Shroeder Music Publishing Co Ltd v Macaulay* [1974] 3 All ER 616.
149. Cited above at footnote 119.
150. [1984] 2 WLR 837 at 845.
151. [1993] 1 HKC 314.

There is, then, a very high correlation, in the view of the courts, between fairness as between the parties and fairness in respect of the public interest. There are, however, occasional examples of the courts overturning a restraint on the grounds of public interest even though the restraint was a reasonable one to impose as between the parties. In *Bull v Pitney-Bowes Ltd*[152] an indirect restraint on a retired former employee, which excluded pension rights for an employee who subsequently competed, was held void primarily on the basis of the public interest. Thesiger J said:

> It may be very much in the public interest that the services of experienced salesmen skilled in a particular technique should be available to promote sales from this country overseas in competition with other sellers from elsewhere.[153]

It is not the individual's expertise which is at issue here but the general principle that the availability of skilled employees is a benefit to the public.[154] Such a principle was endorsed by the Hong Kong Court of First Instance in *Natuzzi SPA v De Coro*[155] where the court rejected an 18-month restraint on a former employee as too long despite the "adequate" consideration given to the employee. Lam J felt it was not in the public interest to keep a skilled worker out of the workforce for so long.

13.4.8 Cartels and Price-Fixing

Cartels are agreements between "competitors" on issues such as limitation of supply, price-fixing and non-competition generally. Clearly the parties themselves see the agreements as beneficial in that they reduce opportunities for competitors and ensure that the market is divided up between the parties to the cartel. Nevertheless, the common law, too, recognised these agreements as valid and in the interests of both the parties and the public.[156] However, the fact that the public are likely to suffer as a result of these market restrictions has led to a number of pieces of legislation against cartels in England. Such legislation has never been properly implemented in Hong Kong,[157] even though in the case of transport, power supply, construction, supermarkets etc there are clear signs of market "rigging" which make a mockery of Hong Kong's much-flaunted "free" economy.

Price-fixing is a similar phenomenon and has been abolished in England via numerous pieces of legislation. Curiously, the issue of public interest has often been raised, unsuccessfully, by those wishing to preserve the fixing of minimum resale prices. It was argued that the abolition of manufacturers' minimum resale prices

---

152. [1967] 1 WLR 273; see also 13.4.3 above.
153. Ibid at 277.
154. "[T]he public interest (in relation to services) lies in their general availability and not in their being rendered by a particular individual." Treitel (op cit) at p 578.
155. [2007] 3 HKC 74.
156. See *Attorney-General of Australia v Adelaide Steamship Co* [1913] AC 781.
157. The Competition Ordinance (Cap 619) appears toothless.

would drive out small village and town retailers who would be unable to compete with large, often "out-of-town" supermarkets. The argument was rejected, and small retailers are now all but extinct in England. Similarly, it was argued that price-fixing for books was in the public interest by preserving small, independent booksellers from the predation of large retailers, often selling a few populist titles as a sideline. Again the argument was rejected and the independent bookseller is now all but extinct in England. Hong Kong does not have similar legislation on price-fixing, except where the fledgling Competition Ordinance (Cap 619) is invoked. Small businesses are equally dominated by large ones, however, by virtue of the high rental costs of business property.

13.4.9 Severance

While severance is not limited to restraints of trade, it is in this context that it most often appears. Where a restraint is found to be unreasonable and therefore void, it is only the restraint itself which is affected. Thus, it may be possible simply to remove the whole restraint and enforce the rest of the contract without it. Alternatively, where a restraint is only partially unreasonable, it may be possible to remove, or "sever", the unreasonable part and enforce the rest. The courts are constrained, in relation to severance, by two requirements: it must be possible to remove the offending part without affecting the overall nature of the restraint; and it must be possible to remove it without amending the grammar of the contract, the so-called "blue pencil" test. The blue pencil test means that the offending, illegal, words can simply be deleted rather than the contract be redrafted.[158] It is generally said that the contract must still make grammatical sense without the severed words though this is not always strictly applied. The "overall nature" approach means that severance is not permitted where, even though possible in "blue pencil" terms, it would render the contract a different one from that initially formed. Suppose, for example, that a post-employment restraint covers a huge geographical area and restricts a whole range of activities in which the employee was not previously engaged. It might be possible to delete the offending, excessive restraints but to do so would be to enforce a different contract from that first formulated. The effect would be that employers could always "try their luck", imposing wide restraints by which gullible employees might feel bound. In the case of the less compliant ex-employee, prepared to go to court, the employer could simply admit the excessive nature of the restraint and sever the offending excesses. The courts should instead, it is felt, encourage proper drafting in the first place. For this reason, there are cases of very wide restraints which have been "blue pencilled" and others which have been declared void as an

---

158. In *(Robert WH) Wang & Co v Bridge* [2002] 4 HKC 435, the Court of First Instance was prepared to sever, if necessary, a restraint covering clients "and intermediaries" so as to exclude the latter.

entire, unseverable, excessive restraint.[159] This dilemma explains the judicial reluctance to "sever", though there is some indication that this reluctance is declining. Severance was permitted in the following English Court of Appeal case.

Scorer v Seymour-Johns[160]

The plaintiff was an estate agent who appointed the defendant as a clerk in his new Kingsbridge office. Clause 8 of the defendant's employment contract stated that after the termination of his employment the defendant would not, for three years: "undertake or carry on either alone or in partnership or be employed or interested directly or indirectly in any capacity whatsoever in the business of an auctioneer, surveyor or estate agent . . . within a 5-mile radius of (the) Kingsbridge or Dartmouth office."

The defendant left and set up as an estate agent near Kingsbridge. The plaintiff successfully claimed an injunction. It was held that the restraint was generally reasonable and the unreasonably wide reference to the Dartmouth office could be removed by "severance".

In supporting the original trial judge's decision to sever, Sellers LJ made clear that the restraint could not operate as it stood, since the reference to the new office, in which the defendant had never previously worked, was clearly unreasonable; there was no legitimate need to prevent the former employee "poaching" previous customers with whom he had never dealt. However, given the overall reasonableness of the restraint, he was prepared to sever the offending reference since this could be done without changing the words or the overall meaning of the original agreement. Similarly, in *Tillman v Egon Zehnder Ltd*,[161] the UK Supreme Court upheld an otherwise reasonable six-month restraint on a previous employee after excising the single word "interest", which the past employee argued had rendered the restraint unreasonable. The exclusion was possible within the blue pencil test and without affecting the overall sense of the restraint.

Conversely, Younger LJ had made clear in the *Attwood* case,[162] in which severance was refused, that the court was there concerned with an improper attempt by an employer to enforce one *single*, hugely excessive, restraint clause. He said:

> The doctrine of severance has not, I think, gone further than to make it permissible in a case where the covenant is not really a single covenant but is in effect a combination of several distinct covenants. In that case and where the severance can be carried out without the addition or alteration of a word, it is permissible. But in that case only.[163]

---

159. Contrast *Goldsoll v Goldman* [1915] 1 Ch 292 (severance) with *Attwood v Lamont* [1920] 3 KB 571 (no severance).
160. [1966] 3 All ER 347.
161. [2019] UKSC 32.
162. [1920] 3 KB 571.
163. Ibid at 578.

Were the courts to allow severance in *Attwood*-type cases there would be no incentive for employers to draw up restraints as narrowly as possible, since even the most excessive restraints would permit the fall-back position of severance and would, effectively, give courts the task of rewriting employment contracts. Such rewriting was emphatically rejected by Litton JA in the *Kao Lee & Yip* case,[164] where he asked:

> if the wide covenants were to be construed in this way, so that they would always be cut down to the extent necessary to protect the employer's legitimate interests, as found by the court, what incentive would there be for employers to draft their covenants restrictively? And how is the employee, faced with a covenant in wide terms, to know that the courts would ultimately trim the covenant down?[165]

---

164. [1993] 1 HKC 314.
165. Ibid at 325.

14

Termination of Contracts

Overview

A contract may be terminated in one of four different ways: by agreement; by performance; via breach; and by the operation of law, principally through frustration.

Termination by *agreement* is usually a simple process as the parties are free, if they so wish, to end the contract. Consideration[1] may, however, be a problem in relation to termination by agreement. When both parties still have outstanding obligations and agree to terminate, no consideration problem arises since each confers a benefit on the other; namely, the avoidance of further obligation. However, there is a consideration problem where X, having completely discharged his obligations under the contract, agrees to release Y from his (Y's) outstanding obligations. There is "accord" (agreement) but no "satisfaction" (consideration). The rule is that there must be both accord *and* satisfaction. The rule that an agreement to accept part payment of a debt in full satisfaction is not binding (the rule in *Pinnel's* case),[2] is an illustration of the accord and satisfaction rule.

The general rule regarding termination by *performance* is that a party's contractual obligation is not discharged until performance is complete; before performance is completed there is no right to payment under the contract: *Cutter v Powell*.[3] There are, however, some notable exceptions to this rule. First, one party may accept partial performance by the other. In this case, provided that the acceptance is freely given, there will be a requirement to pay for the accepted performance. This will not be the full contract price but a reasonable amount for what has been done, a *quantum meruit*. Second, reasonable payment may be awarded where the reason for non-completion is that the other party has prevented full performance. Third, a *quantum meruit* may also be possible if the court decides to treat a contract as "divisible"

---

1. See chapter 4.
2. [1602] 5 Co Rep 117a.
3. [1795] 6 TR 320.

rather than entire. The courts, though, are somewhat reluctant to divide a contract[4] unless such is clearly seen to be intended by, for example, provision for "staged payments". Finally, the doctrine of "substantial performance" may be applied by the courts. Substantial performance occurs where a contract is almost completely performed, except for minor defects or omissions. Here there is a right to the contract price although the other party will be entitled to make deductions for the cost of remedying the defects or omissions.

Breach of contract may result in the termination of a contract but only if the breach involved is a serious one and the innocent party chooses, or "elects", to exercise his right to cancel, or "rescind", on the grounds of serious breach. Breach of a condition will automatically permit the innocent party to make an election. Breach of an "innominate" term may also entitle the innocent party to such an election but only if the consequences of breach are serious enough. Breach of a mere warranty only entitles the innocent party to claim damages, but does not give him the choice of terminating the contract.[5]

A contract may be terminated by *frustration* where "the further fulfilment of the contract is brought to an abrupt stop by some irresistible and extraneous cause for which neither party is responsible."[6] Although frustration is not statutorily defined it is clear, from the cases, that the doctrine only applies to the most extreme events (making performance effectively impossible) occurring *after* the contract is formed, for which neither party is responsible and which the parties neither provided for in the contract nor foresaw. Typical frustrating events include subsequent destruction of the subject matter of the contract, subsequent illegality of the contract and the subsequent destruction of the fundamental purpose of the contract. Frustration may provide the basis of a claim for compensation, or be pleaded simply as a defence against an action for breach by the other party to the contract. In either case the plea is more likely to succeed if made by a consumer than by a commercial party.

The *consequences* of frustration (though not its definition) are governed by legislation. The most important provisions are in section 16 of the Law Amendment and Reform (Consolidation) Ordinance (LARCO),[7] which is essentially based on the corresponding English legislation.[8] The legislation permits the courts considerable discretion in determining how loss should be apportioned in the event of frustration.

---

4. Treitel (op cit) argues that it is "obligations" rather than contracts themselves which may be divisible (see discussion at 14.2.1.2 below).
5. See 8.5 for further discussion of classification of terms.
6. M. Furmston, *Cheshire, Fifoot & Furmston's Law of Contract* (Oxford/New York: Oxford University Press, 17th edn, 2015), p 712
7. Cap 23.
8. Law Reform (Frustrated Contracts) Act 1943.

14.1 Termination by Agreement

If both parties decide they wish to bring their contract to an end, they are free to do so. There are usually few difficulties with this but problems can arise in relation to consideration. Where each party still has obligations to perform—that is the agreement is still "executory" on both sides—there is no consideration problem. Each party gives up his right to insist on further performance and releases the other party from the requirement of further performance. Where, however, only one party has executed his side of the contract but promises to release the other from his remaining obligations, the rule is that something of value must be given for the release. There must be "accord and satisfaction".

The law on accord and satisfaction is based on early English authority[9] and summarised in Chitty[10] as follows:

> Definition: Accord and satisfaction is the purchase of a release from an obligation whether arising under contract or tort by means of any valuable consideration, not being the actual performance of the obligation itself. The accord is the agreement by which the obligation is discharged. The satisfaction is the consideration which makes the agreement operative.[11]

The above definition was applied in Hong Kong in *Edward Long & Co Ltd v Polytex Cotton Goods Traders Ltd*.[12] More recently the Hong Kong Court of Appeal applied the same definition, in *Kin Wah JF Construction & Engineering Co Ltd v L&M Foundation Specialist Ltd*,[13] in deciding whether to uphold a settlement agreement whereby the plaintiff would accept a sum of $179,169.90 in "full and final settlement" of a debt of $826,847.20, with the express condition that payment would be made within ten working days. While the performance of this early payment may have been considered good consideration for the release from the balance of the debt, the fact that the payment was not made on time meant that the plaintiff was no longer bound by the agreement and could still claim the full amount of $826,847.20.

The rule in *Pinnel's* case,[14] that an agreement to accept part payment of a debt in full satisfaction of the debt is not binding, is a specific application of the accord and satisfaction rule. This very old rule was applied by the House of Lords in the

---

9. *Morris v Baron & Co* [1918] AC 1 at 35 and *British Russian Gazette & Trade Outlook Ltd v Associated Newspapers Ltd* [1933] 2 KB 616 at 643–645, 652, 654–655.
10. H. G. Beale (ed), *Chitty on Contracts* (London: Sweet & Maxwell, 32nd edn, 2015).
11. Ibid at vol 1 para 22-012.
12. (unrep, HCA 2260/1984, 17 October 1986).
13. (unrep, CACV 28/2005, 28 July 2005).
14. [1602] 5 Co Rep 117a.

nineteenth century in *Foakes v Beer*[15] and has more recently been affirmed by the English Court of Appeal in *Re Selectmove*[16] and *Ferguson v Davies*.[17]

Ferguson v Davies

A "swap" agreement was entered into between the plaintiff and the defendant whereby the plaintiff agreed to provide the defendant with specialised tapes, records and discs. The parties agreed that the defendant would provide records, in return, to the value of £600 by a certain date, failing which he would pay to the plaintiff the cash value of the individual items to a total of £1,700. The defendant did not comply with the time limit and the plaintiff sued for breach of contract limiting his claim to £486.50. The defendant admitted £150 of the claim but otherwise disputed it. He wrote to the plaintiff enclosing a cheque for £150 as full payment. The plaintiff cashed the cheque but informed the defendant that he was continuing with the action until he received full payment of his claim, which had been increased to £1,745.79.

The judge at first instance dismissed the plaintiff's claim saying that the cashing of the cheque had compromised his claim by a binding accord and satisfaction. The claimant then appealed successfully to the English Court of Appeal. The higher court held that acceptance of the lesser sum did not constitute accord and satisfaction so as to compromise the action unless the plaintiff received some additional benefit by way of consideration. The plaintiff was entitled to understand that the payment of the £150 was to the effect that that amount was admittedly due and had been paid but that the balance was still in dispute. Acceptance of the cheque did not give rise to an agreement that he would forego the balance of his claim and therefore there had been no binding accord and satisfaction.

14.2 Termination by Performance

The great majority of contracts are terminated, or discharged, by performance. These do not give rise to any litigation and do not appear in any law textbook. Generally, performance will be in accordance with the terms specified in the contract. In a minority of cases, though, performance is not precise or exact and disputes arise. In the case of such disputes, the decision for the court is often whether there has been full performance or, instead, whether there is an issue of breach,[18] on the basis that performance has not been precise, exact or complete.

The general rule, then, is that termination of the contract only takes place when performance is complete; that is, when each of the parties has performed his obligations under the contract. Until a party has completed performance he is entitled to

---

15. (1884) 9 App Cas 605.
16. [1995] 2 All ER 531.
17. [1997] 1 All ER 315.
18. See 14.3.

nothing. This "entire performance" approach is illustrated in the old case of *Cutter v Powell*.[19] Here no recovery of payment was allowed to the estate of a deceased sailor who had been promised wages on completion of a voyage but had died before completion.[20] The rule also operated in *Vigers v Cook*[21] to deprive a funeral undertaker of any of the contract price when he failed to deliver a coffin to a church to enable the conduct of a funeral service in a proper manner. He had delivered the coffin to the church but had failed to make it possible for the coffin to be taken into the church.

As can be seen from the above two cases, the entire performance approach can result in hardship or injustice to one party and unjust enrichment to the other. In *Cutter*, for example, Powell obtained the services of Cutter for seven weeks free of charge.[22] This harshness is, however, mitigated by a number of exceptions.

14.2.1 Exceptions to the Entire Performance Rule

The potential for injustice occasioned by the entire performance "rule" is mitigated by a number of exceptions which permit the party performing partially or defectively to obtain at least some benefit in appropriate cases and to reduce the scope for unjust enrichment.

14.2.1.1 Acceptance of Part Performance

Where partial performance is *freely* accepted by the other party, the latter is obliged to pay a reasonable price for the benefit received on a *"quantum meruit"*[23] basis. There will not be true acceptance of partial performance when a party has no alternative but to "accept" the part-performance as in the following case.

Sumpter v Hedges[24]

Building work, for the defendant, had been about 50% completed by the plaintiff and then abandoned. The court held that the plaintiff was not entitled to payment for the work he had done as the defendant had no real alternative to "accepting" the work. The defendant had to complete the building himself as it was useless in its half-completed state. The plaintiff, however, was entitled to a reasonable sum for materials left behind and used by the defendant in completing the building. A promise to pay such a reasonable sum could be inferred from the defendant's decision to use the materials. The outcome was that there was no issue of unjust enrichment.

---

19. [1795] 6 TR 320.
20. The case would probably now be considered one of frustration; see 14.4 below.
21. [1919] 2 KB 475.
22. It appears, however, that he was to be paid considerably more than the normal wage rate in return for the condition that payment was to be only on completion.
23. Latin for "as much as he has earned".
24. [1898] 1 QB 673.

A statutory example of the above exception is found in section 32 of the Sale of Goods Ordinance (SOGO).[25] This is headed "Delivery of wrong quantity" and states:

(1) Where the seller delivers to the buyer a quantity of goods less than he contracted to sell, the buyer may reject them, but if the buyer accepts the goods so delivered, he must pay for them at the contract rate.

(2) Where the seller delivers to the buyer a quantity of goods larger than he contracted to sell, the buyer may accept the goods included in the contract and reject the rest, or he may reject the whole. If the buyer accepts the whole of the goods so delivered he must pay for them at the contract rate.

(3) Where the seller delivers to the buyer the goods he contracted to sell mixed with goods of a different description not included in the contract the buyer may accept the goods which are in accordance with the contract and reject the rest, or he may reject the whole.

(4) The provisions of this section are subject to any usage of trade, special agreement, or course of dealing between the parties.

14.2.1.2 Divisible or "Severable" Contracts/Obligations

If a court is able to find that a contract is divisible, that is, it can be divided into separate, recognisable units, payment will be permitted for those parts that have already been completed even though there has not been completion of the entire contract. In *Roberts v Havelock*,[26] the plaintiff was a shipwright who contracted to put the defendant's ship into "thorough repair". He chose not to complete the work but was held to be entitled to payment for the work completed. The contract was treated as severable. The justification for this approach is that the defendant would otherwise be unjustly enriched.[27]

A court will wish to ensure reasonable remuneration for services if possible, but where payment is clearly expressed as being dependent on complete performance, severability is not possible. Whether a "contract" is entire or severable depends on the intentions of the parties.

Treitel[28] argues that it is not the contract itself which is severable or entire but "obligations".[29] Severable obligations, once discharged, should be paid for. Entire obligations must be "entirely" discharged unless one of the exceptions applies (for example, that partial performance has been freely accepted). The sailor's obligation (to complete the voyage) in *Cutter* was entire and there was no "acceptance" of partial performance. A simple illustration is provided by the case of *Kyocera*

---

25. Cap 26.
26. [1832] 3 B&D 404.
27. See also *Ritchie v Atkinson* [1808] 10 East 295.
28. As with so many seminal texts, Treitel is no longer written by Treitel! (The author of this still brilliant text is now Edwin Peel.)
29. See E. Peel, *Treitel: The Law of Contract* (14th edn) at pp 919–920.

Corporation v W Haking Enterprises & Another,[30] which involved a contract for the sale and purchase of optical lenses. The buyer argued that the contract was divisible and that it should be liable, if at all, only for shipments accepted, with a right to terminate before later deliveries. The judge, Recorder Houghton SC disagreed, stating:

> the contract was for a stated total quantity to the value of US$283,800, and was placed as one order not as four orders as could easily have been done . . . I conclude that on its true construction, the . . . contract was an entire contract . . . for the supply and delivery of 110,000 lenses.

14.2.1.3 Prevention of Performance by the Other Party

If a party performs part of the work he is obliged to do under the contract but is then prevented, by the fault of the other party, from completing his obligations, he will be able to sue for breach of contract regardless of whether the obligations were entire or severable. Alternatively, given the inability to complete performance, remuneration may be, again, on a *quantum meruit* basis. In *Planché v Colburn*,[31] the plaintiff had agreed to write a book in a series of articles in the defendant's publication. He was to receive £100 on completion. He collected material and wrote part of the book but the defendant abandoned the series. The plaintiff was held entitled to £52.50 on a *quantum meruit* basis.[32]

14.2.1.4 Substantial Performance

If a party has substantially performed, that is, has completed his obligations subject only to minor defects or omissions, he is entitled to the contract price minus any deduction for the defects or omissions. In *Hoenig v Isaacs*,[33] the defendant employed the plaintiff to decorate his (the defendant's) flat for a total price of £750 "net cash as the work proceeds and balance on completion". When the plaintiff had completed, the defendant refused to pay the outstanding balance of £350 as there were defects in the work. The total cost of remedying the defects was £55. The English Court of Appeal held that the plaintiff was entitled to the balance on the basis that he had substantially performed, subject to a deduction for the cost of remedying the defects.

---

30. [2019] HKCFI 2753. The case was appealed, but on other grounds.
31. [1831] 8 Bing 14.
32. The case is not without difficulty. The *quantum meruit* claim (as opposed to an action for breach) is generally regarded as "restitutionary". Yet restitution is based on the prevention of "unjust enrichment" and the defendant appears not to have been enriched (unjustly or otherwise). Moreover, the precise nature of the author's obligation is unclear: Cheshire, Fifoot and Furmston (n 6 above) argue that he could have continued the work and claimed the full contract price (see 14.3.2.3 below).
33. [1952] 2 All ER 176.

By contrast, the court held there was no substantial performance in another English Court of Appeal case, *Bolton v Mahadeva*.[34] Here, the plaintiff had agreed to install a central heating system for a total cost of £560 on completion but had refused to put right defects which cost £174 to remedy. Clearly there was no "substantial" performance given the relatively high costs of remedying the defects. Moreover, as payment was to be on completion, the obligation to complete the work was entire rather than severable. As such, the plaintiff was entitled to nothing.

The criticism of this case centres on the fact that the defendant, of course, was able to obtain a central heating system worth £560 for only £174. Certainly he was enriched but, given the plaintiff's rejection of the opportunity to remedy the defects, it is hard to see why such enrichment is "unjust".

The question of whether or not there has been substantial performance depends on the facts of each case and the courts will attempt to use "substantial" in its normally accepted meaning; a matter of degree.[35] There can be no "substantial" performance of an "entire" obligation so, for example, substantial performance could not apply to the uncompleted work in *Bolton* nor to the uncompleted voyage in *Cutter*.

14.2.2 Tender of Performance

The expression "tender of performance" means an offer to perform, including being in a state of readiness to perform. So, if X, one party to a contract, cannot perform without the concurrence of Y, the other party, an offer to perform by X and a rejection of that offer by Y entitles X to a discharge from further liability. The rule then is that a tender of performance is equivalent to performance itself and will be a valid defence against any claim for breach of contract. A good illustration of the rule is the old English case of *Startup v Macdonald*.[36] Here, the plaintiff agreed to sell a large quantity of oil to the defendant and deliver the consignment "within the last fourteen days of March". Payment was due at the end of March. Delivery was tendered at around 8.30 pm on the last day of March and the defendant refused to accept delivery or pay for the oil because of the lateness of the hour. The court held that the tender of the oil was equivalent to actual performance and the plaintiff was entitled to recover damages for non-acceptance.

The effect of a tender depends on the nature of the subject matter of the contract. If there is production of goods of the right description, quality and quantity, then rejection of the offer entirely discharges the offeror from further liability and, as in *Startup*, he can recover damages for breach of contract. However, if the tender consists of the exact amount of money that is contractually due, no further tender need be given, but the obligation to pay the debt remains. If action is taken for breach

---

34. [1972] 2 All ER 1322.
35. See *Young v Thames Properties Ltd* [1999] EWCA Civ 629.
36. (1843) 6 Man & G 593.

of contract, the required sum can be paid into court.[37] Special rules apply for the offering of payment by "legal tender".[38] Payment by cheque or other negotiable instrument, once accepted, constitutes discharge, conditional on clearance. Payment by credit card or equivalent constitutes immediate and absolute discharge as such cards are treated as money.

14.3 Termination via Breach

A breach of contract always entitles the innocent party to claim damages but never automatically brings a contract to an end. This will be determined by whether the term broken is a condition, warranty or an innominate term.[39] If a breach is sufficiently serious, the innocent party has a right to cancel, or terminate, the contract and refuse performance but he need not exercise that right. The innocent party has a choice, or "election". He can choose either to carry on with the contract—"affirm" it, or be relieved from further performance—"terminate" it. If the innocent party accepts the repudiatory breach, his decision is irrevocable. The contract is terminated and cannot be re-created. If, however, the choice is to affirm the contract, the position is less clear cut. This will depend on whether the repudiation is a one-off event or a continuing breach.[40]

The common expression "termination by breach" is, therefore, misleading in that it is not the breach which discharges the contract but the acceptance of the breach by the innocent party and the exercise of his right to terminate.

Failure to perform in accordance with the terms of the contract is a breach unless there is some lawful excuse (the most important such excuse is frustration).[41] Breach may be "actual" or "anticipatory". Actual breach occurs where there is a failure to perform properly, or at all, on the date fixed for performance. Anticipatory breach occurs where, before the required time of performance, one party clearly intimates by words or conduct that he will not perform the contract or otherwise disables himself from performing the contract. Whether it be actual or anticipatory, only a serious breach entitles the other party to terminate and in both cases the contract will only come to an end if the innocent party exercises his right to terminate. As a matter of terminology various expressions have been used to describe the innocent party's decision to terminate. He is sometimes said to be treating the contract as discharged or to "rescind" the contract. The difficulty with the latter expression is that it can be confused with the representee's right to rescind for misrepresentation which is something different.[42]

---

37. Rules of the High Court (Cap 4A) Ord 22.
38. See the Legal Tender Notes Issue Ordinance (Cap 65) and the Coinage Ordinance (Cap 454).
39. See 8.5 for classification of terms.
40. See 14.3.2.2 below.
41. See 14.4 below.
42. See chapter 9.

If the innocent party elects to treat the contract as discharged, he must make his decision known to the party in default. There is no formal procedure for doing so. Whether the innocent party has clearly accepted the other party's breach is a matter of fact; everything depends on the circumstances of the individual case and the mere refusal to carry on may, or may not, be enough.

Vitol SA v Norelf Ltd (the "Santa Clara")[43]

The plaintiffs sent a telex attempting to cancel a contract which the court held amounted to an anticipatory repudiation. The defendants then took no further steps to perform and it was held, on appeal to the House of Lords, that this was capable of amounting to acceptance of repudiation. Everything depends on the facts of the case. The mere inaction of the defendants could amount to unequivocal notification. Here an arbitrator had found, as a fact, that repudiation had been accepted. The House of Lords held that, unless this was clearly wrong, his finding should be upheld. There was no need for a particular form of acceptance of repudiation but the language or conduct used had to be "clear and unequivocal". Lord Steyn said:

> a failure to perform may sometimes be given a colour by special circumstances and may only be explicable by a reasonable person in the position of the repudiating party as an election to accept the repudiation.[44]

Moreover, held the court, as long as the innocent party's acceptance of the repudiation came to the attention of the repudiating party it need not be notified personally or through an agent.

In the Hong Kong case of *Chao Keh Lung v Don Xia*[45] a similar result was reached at first instance whereby, in relation to "inaction", Deputy High Court Judge Carlson said:

> the proper analysis of the evidence and the surrounding circumstances is that the failure to pay the 4th instalment can only be explicable as an unequivocal acceptance of the defendant's renunciation.[46]

This decision was overturned on appeal where the Court of Appeal disagreed that the non-payment was unequivocal. Ma JA said:

> where a repudiatory breach takes place, in order to terminate the contract, the so-called innocent party must clearly and unequivocally accept the repudiation. If he

---

43. [1996] AC 800.
44. Ibid at para 812D. Cited with approval in *Kar Ho v Axis* [2000] HKCA 373 and *Chao Keh Lung* (below).
45. (unrep, HCA 9289/2000, 8 August 2002).
46. Ibid at para 32.

does not do so, he will run the risk of being in breach himself were he not to perform his side of the bargain.[47]

14.3.1 Actual Breach

Actual breach is failure to perform properly, or at all, on the date fixed for performance. The consequences of breach depend on whether the term broken is determined to be a condition, a warranty or an innominate term.[48]

14.3.1.1 Breach of Condition

Breach of a serious term, a "condition", gives the innocent party the right to terminate the contract. However, the use of the word "condition" by the parties is not conclusive and the courts will look behind the actual "label" used to find the intention of the parties and, thereby, ascertain the status of the term concerned. They may, in short, decide that a term labelled "condition" is *not* a condition in the narrow, legal sense. This was the result of *Schuler AG v Wickman Machine Tools Sales*,[49] discussed in chapter 8.[50]

The parties may, instead of using the inconclusive word "condition", say, for example, "breach of this term will allow the party not in breach to terminate the contract". Such emphatic words will be accepted by the courts as showing a clear intention by the contracting parties to permit termination in the event of breach. The expression "of the essence" is often attached to a term and usually relates to the time for performance. Where "time is of the essence", any breach, however minor, will permit termination. This was dramatically illustrated in *Union Eagle Ltd v Golden Achievement Ltd*[51] where the plaintiff agreed to buy a flat from the defendant and paid 10% of the purchase price as deposit. The contract clearly stated the time for the payment of the balance. It made clear that time was of the essence and the deposit would be forfeited for lateness. The plaintiff was 10 minutes late in completing and the defendant forfeited the deposit. The plaintiff claimed that the short delay should be overlooked and equity should intervene and grant specific performance. This claim was rejected by the Hong Kong courts and, on appeal, by the Privy Council.

A similar result occurred in *Lombard North Central v Butterworth*,[52] where the defendant leased a computer from the plaintiff. The contract stated that time was "of the essence" for the payment of instalments and that failure to pay on time would entitle the plaintiff to terminate the agreement. The defendant made several late

---

47. [2004] 2 HKLRD 11, [2003] 4 HKC 660.
48. See 8.4.
49. [1973] 2 All ER 39.
50. See 8.5.1.
51. [1997] 1 HKC 173, [1997] 2 All ER 215 (PC).
52. [1987] 1 All ER 267.

payments and the plaintiff terminated and sought damages for breach. The defendant argued that the effects of the breach here were not serious but the English Court of Appeal stated that the payment clauses here were clearly conditions, in the strict sense, and clearly gave the plaintiff the right to terminate for breach. Unlike the *Schuler* case it was not possible to argue that the parties had not intended to make the terms "conditions" in the technical sense.

Where the contract expressly states that a breach of a term entitles the innocent party to terminate, it would be only in highly exceptional circumstances that the court would deny such an effect, though this *did* occur in the unusual circumstances of *Rice v Great Yarmouth Borough Council.*[53]

A Hong Kong variation on the "time of the essence" theme is provided by *Health Link Investment Ltd v Pacific Hawk,*[54] where the parties had agreed on the sale of a property in Hong Kong. Under the terms of the sale and purchase agreement (the "Agreement") the purchaser was to pay a deposit of 20% of the purchase price "simultaneously" with the signing of the Agreement. The date for the signing of the Agreement was extended and the Hong Kong Court of Appeal held that this extension implied that the obligation to pay the deposit was also extended. Therefore, the failure by the purchaser to pay the deposit on the original due date did not amount to repudiation of the contract.

Historically, at common law, time was always of the essence unless the contract expressly stated otherwise. Equity took the opposite view; time was not of the essence unless the parties specifically made it so. This is now the accepted position in England.[55] In Hong Kong section 11 of LARCO adopts equity's approach and the time of performance is *not* of the essence unless otherwise stipulated by the parties. In normal circumstances, then, performance must be within a "reasonable" time.[56] There are three situations, however, where the "not of the essence" rule will not apply.

First, as indicated above, if the parties have *expressly* provided that time is of the essence, the courts will so hold.[57] Wording such as "at the latest" or "not later than" will be taken to mean that it is of the essence that performance must be before the next day. This was upheld in the English case of *Harold Wood Brick Co v Ferris*[58] and followed in Hong Kong in *Chong Kai Tai & Another v Lee Gee Kee & Another.*[59]

---

53. Dealt with in chapter 8 at 8.5.1.
54. [1995] 1 HKC 249.
55. See, for example, *Valilas v Januzaj* [2014] EWCA Civ 436, where all three judges agreed that the claimant's obligation to make a prompt monthly payments was "innominate".
56. See *Postlethwaite v Freeland* (1880) App Cas 599 at 608; *Hick v Raymond & Reid* [1893] AC 22 at 28.
57. For example, *Union Eagle* case discussed at 14.3.1.1 above.
58. [1935] 2 KB 198.
59. [1997] 1 HKC 359.

Second, where time was not initially of the essence, one of the parties may make it so by issuing a notice expressly to that effect.[60] This is subject to the proviso that the notice must afford a reasonable opportunity for the other party to perform his obligations.[61] In *Creatiles* (see footnote below) persistent refusal to accede to legitimate demands for payment of required monies was held to be a "repudiatory" breach. Another common repudiatory breach in Hong Kong is a refusal to answer (properly or at all) requisitions as to title.[62]

In practice, the nature of the subject matter of the contract or the surrounding circumstances of the contract may show that the parties intended time to be of the essence. If so, the court will construe the contract accordingly. In the Hong Kong context, this is particularly applicable in respect of contracts for the sale and purchase of land.[63]

Further examples of "repudiatory" breach concern the likely repetition of ongoing significant breaches[64] and the exercise of "illegitimate commercial pressure".[65] Both situations entitle the innocent party to refuse further performance and/or claim damages.

14.3.1.2 Breach of Warranty

Breach of a lesser term, a "warranty", does not give the other party the right to terminate but merely the right to seek damages. As indicated above, the use of the term "condition" by the parties is not conclusive. Similarly, the courts may determine that a term is a condition even though described by the parties as a warranty. The more likely scenario, however, as noted in chapter 8, is that a "non-condition" term will be regarded as innominate.

14.3.1.3 Breach of an Innominate or Intermediate Term

Where a term cannot be classified as either a condition or a warranty everything depends on the *effect* of the breach. If the effect is serious the innocent party has a right to terminate; if not, the innocent party has a right only to seek damages. The genesis of the innominate term is the *Hong Kong Fir* case, discussed in detail in chapter 8.[66]

---

60. See *Creatiles Building Materials Co Ltd v To's Universe Construction Co Ltd* [2003] 2 HKLRD 309.
61. *Behzadi v Shaftesbury Hotels Ltd* [1991] 2 All ER 477.
62. See *Homyip Investments Ltd v Chu Kang Ming Trade Development Co Ltd* [1995] 2 HKC 458.
63. See *Sun Lee Kyoung Sil v Jia Weili* [2010] 2 HKLRD 30 discussed at 8.5.1.
64. *Chin Luk Properties Ltd v Casil Clearing Ltd* [2007] 1 HKC 231 (dealt with in chapter 15 at 15.1.1).
65. See *ATAL Technologies Ltd v Stratech Systems Ltd* [2012] 3 HKLRD 281.
66. See 8.5.2.

The advantage of the "intermediate" approach is that it gives the courts more flexibility; contracts cannot be brought to an end in relatively trivial circumstances. However, it has been criticised as reducing commercial certainty.[67]

14.3.2 Anticipatory Breach

It is possible to be in breach even *before* the date fixed for performance if one improperly repudiates the contract. For example, a party to a contract, A, may call the other party, B, in advance and tell him he is unable or unwilling to deliver by the required date. This would amount to "express" repudiation. Alternatively, A may deliver the relevant consignment to C before the required delivery date, thereby making delivery to B impossible. This would constitute "implied", repudiation.

It is not always easy to decide whether a party has repudiated a contract in advance. In the words of Lord Selborne:

> You must look at the actual circumstances of the case in order to see whether the one party to the contract is relieved from its future performance by the conduct of the other; you must examine what that conduct is so as to see whether it amounts to a renunciation, to an absolute refusal to perform the contract . . . and whether the other party may accept it as a reason for not performing his part.[68]

If, for example, a party wishes to perform his obligations but mistakenly believes he has the right to terminate because of the other's repudiation, his refusal of further performance may not itself be a repudiation.

Woodar Investment Development Ltd v Wimpey Construction (UK) Ltd[69]

The parties made a contract to sell 14 acres of land for development under which the defendants/respondents had the right to cancel if, before completion, a local authority "shall have commenced" compulsory acquisition. Both parties knew that the government minister had begun such proceedings concerning two acres of the land in question. When land prices fell the respondents tried to cancel in the belief that they were entitled to do so. The plaintiffs/appellants claimed this was a wrongful repudiation. The House of Lords held that there was no right to cancel because the right did not apply to compulsory purchases begun *before* the contract was made. However, it also held that the respondents had not improperly repudiated since they wished to honour their obligations and thought (wrongly) that they were legally allowed to cancel. They had done so in good faith. Lord Wilberforce, for the majority, stated:

> It would be a regrettable development of the law of contract to hold that a party who bona fide relies upon an express stipulation in a contract in order to rescind or

---

67. See *Bunge v Tradax* [1981] 2 All ER 513 and discussion at 8.4.
68. *Mersey Steel & Iron Co v Naylor Benzon & Co* (1884) 9 App Cas 434 at 441.
69. [1980] 1 WLR 277.

terminate a contract should, by that fact alone, be treated as having repudiated his contractual obligations if he turns out to be mistaken as to his rights. Repudiation is a drastic conclusion which should only be held to arise in clear cases of a refusal, in a matter going to the root of the contract, to perform contractual obligations.[70]

Lords Salmon and Russell dissented. Lord Salmon argued that the respondents "honest belief in a bad point of law" should not assist them. This argument seems strong, particularly when the House of Lords in *Federal Commerce and Navigation Co Ltd v Molena Alpha Inc*[71] had, only a year earlier, come to the conclusion (on seemingly similar facts) that a belief in a bad point of law would not assist a claimant. However, Cheshire, Fifoot and Furmston[72] state that the two cases can be distinguished in that in *Woodar v Wimpey* there was no need for the appellants to take immediate action and they could, for instance, have taken out a construction summons to test the correctness of their view of the contract's meaning. By contrast, in *Federal Commerce*, although the breach was probably anticipatory, the gap between repudiation and the performance date was fairly short and the pressure on the other party correspondingly great enough to amount to a repudiatory breach.

Moreover, if a party asserts rights under a contract mistakenly but in good faith, this may not amount to repudiation. In *Vaswani v Italian Motors (Sales & Services) Ltd*[73] the defendants agreed to sell a new car to the plaintiff. The defendants asserted their right to the list price for the new car at the time of delivery. In fact, they were entitled only to the lower price at the time of the contract. The plaintiff argued that this excessive demand amounted to repudiation justifying him in making no further payments. It was held that the mistaken claim did not amount to repudiation and the contract should have remained in force. The plaintiff buyer's refusal to make further payments was thus itself a wrongful repudiation.

Neither *Woodar* nor *Vaswani* is entirely satisfactory if viewed from the perspective of the "non-mistaken" party. In *Woodar*, the non-mistaken party had the option of continuing, with the fear that the other party's "repudiation" would be upheld or, as happened, accepting the other party's mistaken "repudiation" only to find that the courts have not treated it as such because of the other party's error of law; an error not traditionally recognised at common law. Equally, in *Vaswani*, the plaintiff had the option of "paying up" the larger sum, when not obliged to do so, or refusing to pay the additional amounts and risk being sued for non-payment. The potential then arises for the "tables to be turned" on the non-mistaken party, who now finds himself a potential "wrongfully repudiating" defendant. This was the position in *Tse Ping Shun v Lai Ho Man Shan*,[74] where the apparently innocent party's refusal of

---

70. Ibid at 283.
71. [1979] 1 All ER 307.
72. Note 6 above, at p 673.
73. [1996] 1 WLR 270.
74. [2010] 4 HKC 191.

further performance because of the other's failure to discharge all responsibilities *before completion* was itself a repudiatory breach, given the court's finding that such discharge could be made *after* receipt of payment. Such a reversal of roles may also arise where an apparent breach is created by one party's insistence on impossible conditions. Thus, in *Kensland Realty Ltd v Whale View Investment Ltd*,[75] the time of completion of payment under a sale and purchase agreement (normally an obvious condition) became unduly onerous when the purchaser was required to make multiple "split" payments to different payees within an unreasonably short time period (with a request for extension refused). In the circumstances, the Court of Final Appeal rejected the seller's claim for forfeiture of deposit and granted specific performance to the buyer.

14.3.2.1 Acceptance of Anticipatory Breach

An important feature of anticipatory breach is that the innocent party need not wait until the due date of performance by the other party but may accept the breach and seek a remedy forthwith.

Hochster v De La Tour[76]

The defendant agreed, in April 1852, to employ the plaintiff for three months from 1 June 1852. In May 1852, the defendant wrote saying that he had changed his mind and would no longer require the plaintiff's services. The plaintiff began proceedings for breach of contract at the end of May 1852. The defendant's argument that the plaintiff would have to wait until the performance date was rejected.

In the above scenario the innocent party is said to "accept the (repudiatory) breach". He does not have to prove that he would have been ready or able to perform at the contract date. This is illustrated by the case of *Frost v Knight*.[77] Here, the defendant promised to marry the plaintiff on the death of the defendant's father. While the defendant's father was still alive the defendant changed his mind and broke off the engagement. The plaintiff sued for breach of promise of marriage (a right which has since been abolished) while the defendant's father was still alive. Her right to do so was upheld by the court even though, of course, one of the parties may have died before the father, thus rendering performance impossible. *Frost* also extends the rule in *Hochster* to cases where the date of performance is not fixed but is contingent on the occurrence of a future event, here the death of the defendant's father.

---

75. (2001) 4 HKCFAR 381.
76. (1853) 2 E&B 678.
77. [1872] LR 7 Ex 111.

Since the party "accepting" a repudiatory breach is not normally required to prove his ability to perform on the due date for performance,[78] liability may depend on "who cracks first". If X has ordered goods from Y to be paid for "cash on delivery" and is then having extreme difficulty in raising the necessary money, he may be relieved from his obligation, and have the right to sue, if Y makes clear, *before* X communicates his difficulty, that he (Y) will be unable to deliver on time.

Of course, as noted above,[79] anticipatory breach gives the innocent party the right to terminate only if the anticipatory breach is sufficiently serious.

The Afovos[80]

Under a charter party, the charterers were required to pay punctually and regularly. If they were late the owners would have the right to withdraw the ship. There was also a clause to prevent default on a technicality which stated that where the charterers were late the owner would give them 48 hours to rectify the position. When it appeared that the charterers would be late with a payment the owners served a notice which was sent before the end of the last day for payment. The charterers argued this was premature. They also asserted that the owners could not say they (the charterers) were in anticipatory breach since the single late payment was not serious enough to confer the right to terminate. The House of Lords upheld the charterers' case and held that the owners' repudiation was unjustified given the non-fundamental nature of the charterers' breach.

An anticipatory breach *was* held to be "repudiatory" in *A-Mayson Development Co Ltd v Betterfit Ltd*,[81] in the Hong Kong High Court. In *A-Mayson*, a vendor failed satisfactorily to answer the purchaser's requisitions on title. This was held to be sufficiently serious to entitle the purchaser to refuse to complete and to do so before the date fixed for completion. The requisition arose because the occupation permit had allowed only five shops on the premises when eight shops had actually been erected there. Godfrey J held that it had become obvious that the vendor could do nothing to get over this discrepancy in the time available.

14.3.2.2 Anticipatory Breach: The Right of Election

As already noted, serious, or "repudiatory", breach alone does not terminate the contract. The law requires the innocent party to elect either to accept the breach and terminate the contract or reject the breach and "affirm" the contract. Once a decision is made to accept the breach this decision is irrevocable and the contract is terminated. The alternative is to reject or ignore the breach, treat the contract as still

---

78. Unless the claim is for specific performance.
79. See 14.3.
80. [1983] 1 All ER 449.
81. [1992] 2 HKC 533.

being in force and wait for the performance date in hope of the other party performing after all. If the innocent party does ignore the breach and continue, the contract is treated in all respects as if it is still in effect and the innocent party is still required to perform his own obligations under the contract.

Fercometal SARL v Mediterranean Shipping Co SA, The Simona[82]

The parties made a charterparty contract for carriage of goods on the appellants' ship by the respondents. The respondents were entitled to cancel the contract if the appellants' ship was not ready to load by 9 July 1982. On 2 July 1982 the respondents made an anticipatory breach by chartering another ship to carry the cargo. The appellants could have accepted this breach but ignored it and announced they would start loading on 8 July 1982. In fact, the ship was not ready to load on 8 July which constituted a breach by the appellants. The respondents then cancelled for the appellants' breach and the appellants appealed finally to the House of Lords. This appeal was rejected. The appellants had ignored the respondents' earlier breach and, therefore, the contract remained in existence. This meant that the appellants had to continue with their obligations to load. They could not do nothing and wait to see what the other side did next. The election is therefore absolute: accept the anticipatory breach or ignore it. The former terminates the contract; the latter does not. There is no middle way of ignoring the breach but not continuing with one's own obligations. The court indicated that further performance by the appellants would only have been excused if the respondent had clearly told them that performance was no longer required.

However, while a decision to accept a repudiatory breach and terminate a contract is irrevocable, a decision to ignore the breach and carry on with the contract may, where the breach continues, be revoked.

Wong Wui v Yin Shiu Hee, Peter[83]

The plaintiff purchaser and the defendant vendor entered into a sale and purchase agreement in respect of a flat in Kwai Chung, Hong Kong. The agreement contained a clause entitling the purchaser to inspect the property once before completion. Subsequently, in breach of the agreement, the vendor demanded payment of a further sum of $50,000 when the purchaser asked for an inspection. Completion did not take place and the purchaser took action for specific performance or damages in lieu of specific performance. At first instance Deputy Judge Muttrie held that the vendor was in repudiatory breach of the agreement and awarded damages to the purchaser. He ruled that the purchaser's election to affirm the agreement by claiming specific performance was revocable and, accordingly, the purchaser was entitled to claim

---

82. [1988] 2 All ER 742.
83. [2001] 2 HKC 466.

damages in lieu of specific performance. The vendor's appeal to the Hong Kong Court of Appeal was dismissed.

Keith JA stated:

> The principle in relation to revocability of a decision to affirm a contract . . . was that if the repudiating party persisted in his refusal to perform, the innocent party might later treat the contract as being at an end on account of the continuing repudiation reflected in the other party's behaviour after the affirmation.
>
> The purchaser's affirmation of the agreement was revocable, and the purchaser was entitled to accept the vendor's repudiation of the agreement prior to being permitted to inspect the flat. The vendor's failure to permit the purchaser to inspect the flat after receiving the purchaser's solicitor letter was a continuing repudiation of the agreement. Once there was a claim for specific performance, it was for the vendor to remedy the breach by offering the inspection that had been sought all along.[84]

Keith JA relied heavily on the following passage from *Safehaven Investments Inc v Springbok Ltd*[85] which summarises the position very clearly:

> If the 'innocent' party to a repudiated contract elects to bring it to an end, there is no difficulty in treating his decision as irrevocable. The contract is destroyed and cannot be re-created. If, however, the innocent party's decision to affirm the contract, the position is less clear cut. In *Johnson v Agnew*,[86] the House of Lords had to consider this question in a case in which the innocent party had obtained a decree of specific performance from the court. The House approached the matter on the footing that the legal significance of the decree was that obtaining it was an affirmation, albeit a particularly emphatic one. Yet they declined to treat the innocent party's decision to affirm as irrevocable so as to prevent him from bringing the contract to an end when the repudiating party persisted in his failure to perform.

Given that the party accepting an anticipatory breach does not have to show his own ability to perform on time, there are obvious benefits in accepting an anticipatory breach and suing immediately, particularly if the "innocent" party would have had difficulty in performing himself.[87]

Immediately taking action for breach also avoids the potential dangers in waiting since something may happen before the performance date. There may be a change of law or frustrating event which means that the other party will no longer be in breach and innocent party's right to sue will be lost. This drastic result occurred in the following case.

---

84. Ibid at 466–467.
85. (1996) 71 P & CR 59 at 68.
86. [1979] 1 All ER 883.
87. See 14.3.2.1 above.

Avery v Bowden[88]

The defendants chartered the plaintiffs' ship and agreed to load a cargo at Odessa within 45 days. Before the 45 days had elapsed, the defendants told the plaintiffs that no cargo would be ready in time. The plaintiffs ignored this anticipatory breach and remained in port treating the contract as still in force in the hope that a cargo would be found. Before the final deadline, war broke out which made it illegal to load at Odessa. The contract was, therefore, frustrated and the plaintiffs no longer had an action for breach. Had they accepted the anticipatory breach and sailed away they could have claimed damages immediately.

While the advent of a frustrating event following rejection of an anticipatory breach might seem a "freak" circumstance, a similar issue arose, in factually very different circumstances, in *Billy Graham Evangelistic Association v Scottish Event Campus Ltd*.[89] Here, an Evangelic Meeting agreed by the parties to be held at the "Defender's" venue in Glasgow, Scotland, was cancelled by the Defenders, under pressure from the local council because (asserted the council) of the professed homophobic and Islamaphobic views of the nominated speaker, Franklin Graham. This was treated by the "Pursuer" as an anticipatory breach. However, the Pursuer rejected the breach and was determined to hold the event. Before the date for performance, however, the advent of COVID "frustrated" the contract as stipulated in the parties' force majeure clause (see 14.4.4.1 below).

However, while subsequent events will not affect the "right" to claim damages for an *accepted* anticipatory breach they may, if likely at the time of breach or made known by the date of trial, affect the "quantum" of damages. This was the approach of the English House of Lords in the "*Golden Victory*" case[90] in which the possibility of the Iraq War existed at the time of breach but had actually occurred by the time of trial. This approach was adopted in the Hong Kong Court of Appeal case of *Hong Jing Co Ltd v Zhuhai Kwok Yuen Investment Co Ltd*[91] where it was stated that the court would "take into account what had actually happened"[92] in considering the plaintiffs' claim for damages for "loss of a chance".[93]

14.3.2.3 Affirmation and the "Duty" to Mitigate Loss

If the innocent party ignores the breach and treats the contract as still in force, the so-called "duty to mitigate loss"[94] may be avoided, as in the curious case below.

---

88. (1855) 5 E&B 714.
89. [2021] SC GLW 9.
90. See *Golden Strait Corporation v Nippon Kubishika Kaisha (The Golden Victory)* [2007] UKHL 12 discussed in chapter 15 at 15.1.5.
91. [2013] 1 HKLRD 441.
92. Per Cheung JA at para 90.
93. See chapter 15 at 15.1.4.5.
94. See chapter 15.

White & Carter (Councils) Ltd v McGregor[95]

The parties made a contract that for three years the plaintiffs/appellants would prepare litter bins with advertising for the defendants/respondents and would distribute these bins to local authorities. On the same day, and before any preparation had begun, the defendants attempted to cancel the contract. The plaintiffs refused to accept the repudiation. They prepared and distributed the advertising for three years, and then claimed the full contract price. Their action succeeded in the House of Lords by a three-to-two majority. The majority view was that, provided the plaintiff has a "legitimate interest", he may, in cases of anticipatory breach, refuse to accept the breach and continue with the contract. While he does so, the issue of mitigation does not arise and the full contract price is recoverable. The minority view was that damages should be recoverable only in so far as they take into account the plaintiff's failure to mitigate.

This case represents an extreme application of the theory that, in cases of anticipatory breach which the innocent party refuses to accept, the contract is treated as still existing and there is no requirement to "mitigate" loss (to reduce losses to a minimum). It may have been significant that this was a case not of a claim for damages for breach, but of an action for an entire agreed sum. However, the Hong Kong Court of Appeal, in *Diamond Jubilee Investment Ltd v Chan Yiu Chung Sidney*,[96] has made clear the "general rule" as to the plaintiff's "election" in cases of anticipatory breach. Ma CJHC (as he then was) stated:

> In the absence of contractual provisions to the contrary, the general rule is that there is no duty on an innocent party to accept a repudiatory breach, either within a reasonable time or at all.[97]

This harsh general rule may not, it appears, be applied where it would be "wholly unreasonable". Lord Reid, one of the majority judges in *White & Carter*, added two important qualifications. First, it should be noted that in practice it is unusual for a party to be able to ignore an anticipatory breach and continue without the assent and co-operation of the other party. Where this is lacking there is no alternative but to accept the breach. Second, the innocent party should only be allowed to continue where he has a "legitimate interest" in doing so. Treitel[98] says that "legitimate interest" means that the innocent party must have reasonable grounds for keeping the contract open, bearing in mind also the interests of the party in breach.

The effect of the decision in *White & Carter*, though perhaps logical, is open to criticism and has been reduced in scope by some later decisions which have focused on Lord Reid's qualifications. As to the first qualification, where "assistance" is

---

95. [1961] 3 All ER 1178.
96. [2010] 1 HKLRD 638.
97. Ibid at para 19.
98. Op cit at p 1226.

needed, it was held in *Hounslow LBC v Twickenham Garden Developments Ltd*,[99] by Megarry J at first instance, that where the innocent party can only carry on with the help of the party in breach, the latter can merely refuse to assist so that the innocent party has to sue for damages as at the time of breach.

With regard to Lord Reid's second qualification, the courts have supported the idea that the innocent party should only be permitted to carry on with the contract where he has a "legitimate interest" in continuing.[100]

Clea Shipping Corporation v Bulk Oil International (The Alaskan Trader) (No 2)[101]

The owners of a ship chartered it to charterers for two years. After almost one year it was clear the ship needed major repair, which would take several months. The charterers then said they did not want the ship (this was regarded as a breach). The owners went ahead with expensive repairs and after several months stated that the ship was again ready. The charterers ignored this as they regarded the charter as at an end. The owners kept the ship ready with a crew until the two-year period expired. The dispute was whether the charterers were entitled to recover payments for the months after they had tried to cancel (subject to the owners' right to damages for wrongful repudiation) or whether the owners could ignore the charterers' breach and continue. It was held that the charterers could recover payments, since the owners had acted unreasonably in rejecting the anticipatory breach and had no legitimate grounds for continuing with the contract. They should have accepted the breach and claimed damages. More recently, in *MSC Mediterranean Shipping Company SA v Cottonex Anstalt*,[102] the English Court of Appeal found that a claimant had no legitimate interest in continuing with a shipping contract and claiming continuing "demurrage".[103] In any event, however, the court felt that the whole purpose of the contract had already been defeated, such that continuation was effectively impossible as in the *Hounslow* case.[104]

Conversely, in *Reichman v Beveridge*,[105] a landlord who ignored an anticipatory breach was held to have a legitimate interest in continuing with the contract, since the relevant English rules on recovery of rent arrears damages would have produced an inadequate remedy.

---

99. [1971] Ch 233.
100. Though the onus of proof is on the party asserting "no legitimate interest" to prove that it would be "wholly unreasonable" to continue: *Ocean Marine Navigation Ltd v Koch Carbon Inc* [2003] EWHC 1936 (Comm).
101. [1984] 1 All ER 129.
102. [2016] EWCA Civ 78.
103. Damages for delay.
104. See above.
105. [2006] EWCA Civ 1659.

Contract Law in Hong Kong

The "legitimate interest" principle was applied in the Hong Kong case of *Fuji Xerox (Hong Kong) Ltd v Vigers Hong Kong Ltd*.[106] Here the defendants committed an anticipatory breach of a contract whereby the plaintiffs would supply and maintain fax machines for the defendants over a lengthy period. The plaintiffs refused to accept the anticipatory breach and take back the machines. The court accepted that the refusal was legitimate since (now the machines were no longer new) there was little likelihood of leasing or selling them elsewhere.[107]

14.4 Termination by Frustration

A contract will be brought to an end by frustration when:

> its performance depends on the existence of a particular thing or state of things, (and) the failure or destruction of that thing or state of things, without default of either side, liberates both parties.[108]

While the *consequences* of frustration are now dealt with by statute, its definition remains a common law one, to be gleaned from the decided cases. What emerges from the cases is that, if frustration is to be successfully pleaded, three requirements must be met:

1. an event must have occurred *after* the contract has been made (but before the date for performance) which makes performance "impossible"; and
2. the event was neither provided for in the contract nor foreseen by the parties; and
3. the event was not the result of the "fault" of either party.

14.4.1 The Development of Frustration

Frustration is a relatively recent development in the common law. Traditionally, courts adopted the principle of "sanctity" of contract; once a party has undertaken contractual duties he must fulfil them or face legal consequences. This principle was established in the very old ancient case of *Paradine v Jane*.[109] Here, the defendant, who was sued for rent due on land, claimed, as a defence, that he had been denied use of the land by an enemy army. The court held this to be no excuse and that he should have made provision for such an event in the contract. The only recognised excuse for non-performance would be that such performance is illegal.

---

106. (unrep, HCA 3735/2003, 9 August 2006); upheld on appeal (unrep, CACV 311/2006, 30 March 2007).
107. And see *Funfair Co Ltd v Wong Lui Wing* [2007] 3 HKLRD 609.
108. *Denny Mott & Dickson v Fraser & Co* [1944] 1 All ER 678 per Lord Macmillan.
109. (1647) 82 ER 897 (KB) and see 1.2.4.

The harshness of the sanctity approach was first mitigated some 200 years after the *Paradine* case.

Taylor v Caldwell[110]

The parties made a contract whereby the defendants agreed to let the plaintiffs have the use of a music hall for concerts on various specified dates. Before the date for the first concert, the hall was destroyed by fire. The plaintiffs sued for breach but the defendants successfully pleaded frustration in their defence.

Blackburn J, delivering the judgment of the English High Court, based his judgment on an "implied condition" that the subject matter of the contract would remain in existence.

As an exception to the long-established sanctity principle, the doctrine of frustration continued to be used sparingly. Indeed, to this day, courts are reluctant to find frustration, especially in respect of commercial contracts, and do so only in the most extreme cases. The courts have insisted that the "supervening event" must destroy a fundamental assumption on which the contract is based and that frustration should not become an escape route for a party for whom the contract has simply become a bad bargain.

The initial rationale for frustration was, as in *Taylor*, the concept of the "implied term"; if the parties' basic implicit assumptions have been undermined by the "event" the contract is frustrated.[111] This approach has the attraction that it purports to uphold the parties' intentions rather than undermine them. It produces, however, a somewhat contradictory result, given that frustration is said to depend on the "event" being "unforeseen". Since implied terms have, traditionally, been based on the parties' "presumed intention", the *Taylor* approach attributes an intention to the parties in respect of an event they have not foreseen! The unsatisfactory nature of the implied terms approach has led courts to substitute, in later cases, what could be termed a "changed obligation" test. This test is summarised in the leading House of Lords case of *Davis Contractors Ltd v Fareham Urban District Council*,[112] where Lord Radcliffe said:

> frustration occurs whenever the law recognises that without default of either party a contractual obligation has become incapable of being performed because the circumstances in which performance is called for would render it a thing radically different from that which was undertaken by the contract.[113]

---

110. (1863) 3 B&S 826.
111. The "implied term" approach was adopted in a Hong Kong case analogous to *Taylor*: *The Wai Lee Firm v Ku Chung Ming* (1911) 6 HKLR 146. Here, a contract to repair a building was frustrated by the collapse of adjoining property, such that the continuation of repair work would have been illegal.
112. [1956] AC 696.
113. Ibid at 728–729.

Lord Radcliffe clearly disapproved of the "implied term" approach and the artificial attribution of the parties "intention" to an event they had probably never considered. Moreover, even on the basis of a "presumed" intention, it will not always be clear that the parties are in accord. *Henry* may well have thought his contract of hire depended on a procession taking place; *Krell*'s view was, more likely, "that's a chance you take".[114] Nevertheless, the implied term approach has not been entirely abandoned. Lord Wilberforce, for example, in *National Carriers v Panalpina (Northern) Ltd*,[115] was rather reluctant to choose between the two tests suggesting that they had now merged into one.

14.4.2 Frustration and Mistake

Since frustration requires a "serious event" it is compared, by some writers, with the doctrine of common mistake[116] which, too, will only operate in extreme cases. The crucial difference between the two doctrines is that the "event" has already occurred *before* the contract is made in mistake cases (albeit unknown to the parties) whereas frustration deals with events occurring *after* the contract is formed. An illustration of the "timing" factor is provided by *Amalgamated Investment & Property Co Ltd v John Walker & Sons Ltd*[117] described in detail in 10.8.

In this case, involving a planned development rendered impossible by "listing" as a historic site, the plaintiffs pleaded both mistake and frustration. They argued a common mistake in that neither party was aware, at the time of contracting, that discussions had been held with a view to "listing" the building (intended for commercial development by the plaintiffs) as a historic site. Alternatively, they argued frustration by the listing itself (which precluded development and drastically reduced the commercial value of the building). The court held that there was neither an operative mistake nor a frustration since neither the plans for listing nor the listing itself were serious enough. Only the most extreme mistakes render a contract void and only the most extreme events can frustrate a contract. The (commercial) buyers had got what they paid for; it was simply of inferior quality.

While similar "seriousness" requirements may be applied by the courts in considering mistake and frustration, it should be pointed out that the *effects* of the two doctrines are very different. Frustration rules allow the courts a considerable discretion in apportioning loss, while mistake is an "all or nothing", "void or valid" doctrine, especially now that the ability of equity to set agreements aside on terms has been curtailed.[118]

---

114. See 14.4.3 below.
115. [1981] 1 All ER 161.
116. See chapter 10.
117. [1977] 1 WLR 164, [1976] 3 All ER 509.
118. See chapter 10.

14.4.3 *The Seriousness of the Event*

The essence of frustration is that the "event" renders performance impossible in its essential respects. While the first significant case, *Taylor v Caldwell*,[119] deals with the physical destruction of the subject matter, frustration may also occur where the whole "underlying basis" of the contract has been defeated by the frustrating event.

Krell v Henry[120]

The parties had agreed on a contract for the hire of a room which was to overlook the coronation procession of King Edward VII. After the contract was made the procession was cancelled because of the king's illness. The defendant, having already paid a deposit, refused to pay the balance of the hire price. The plaintiff's action for the recovery of the balance failed in the English Court of Appeal where it was held that the contract was frustrated because the whole underlying objective had been destroyed.

The case represents a gradual development of the frustration doctrine, since frustration is seen to be possible even without the total destruction of the subject matter. There was still, clearly, a room to occupy but it no longer provided a view of the coronation procession. Nonetheless, the frustrating event was fundamental, since there was no doubt that the "purpose" of the hire was to obtain a "room with a view".

By contrast, in *Herne Bay Steam Boat Co v Hutton*,[121] the plaintiffs contracted to let the defendant use their ship for the purposes of viewing the royal naval review and for a day's cruise around the fleet. The review was cancelled because of the king's illness but the contract was held not to be frustrated as the cruise around the fleet was still possible so that the contract was not entirely undermined.

The obvious difference between the two cases is that in *Krell* the contract had a single major objective which had been defeated by the frustrating event, whereas in *Hutton* there were two objectives, one of which was still capable of being fulfilled. It has also been argued that the crucial difference between the cases is that in *Hutton* the contract involved a businessman taking a commercial risk while in *Krell* the contract was non-commercial.[122]

The view that the courts are more restrictive in their approach to frustration when the contract is commercial in nature is borne out by later cases including the following (which reached the House of Lords).

---

119. (1863) 3 B&S 826.
120. [1903] 2 KB 740. There were a number of "coronation" cases involving similar facts.
121. [1903] 2 KB 683.
122. See, for instance, R. Brownsword, "Henry's Lost Spectacle and Hutton's Lost Speculation", (1985) 129 SJ 860.

Davis Contractors Ltd v Fareham UDC[123]

The appellants agreed to build 78 houses for the respondents at a total cost of £92,425. The work was intended to take eight months. Because of an unexpected shortage of labour and materials the work took 22 months and the appellants incurred extra expenses of £17,651. They pleaded frustration so that they could claim more than the agreed price. The House of Lords held that the contract was not frustrated. Although the contract had become more difficult and expensive this did not amount to frustration, which only occurs where a supervening event goes to the very root of the contract.[124]

English courts have continued to emphasise the *exceptional* nature of frustration.[125] In *Edwinton v Tsavliris (The Sea Angel)*,[126] Rix LJ stated:

> the test of radically different is important: it tells us that the doctrine is not lightly to be invoked; that mere incidence of expense or delay or onerousness is not sufficient; and that there has to be as it were a break in identity between the contract as provided for and contemplated and its performance in the new circumstances.

A very clear example is provided in the following English Court of Appeal case.

CTI Group Inc v Transclear SA[127]

The parties made an agreement whereby the defendants were to sell cement to the claimants. The claimants wanted to buy from the defendants because they (the buyers) were the victim of a "cartel" (rigged market) organised by Cemex. The defendants made an agreement for supply with an Indonesian company which was then pressured to stop supplying by Cemex. The defendants then made an agreement with Taiwanese suppliers with the same result! Eventually the defendants felt unable to deliver the cement and the claimants sued for breach, claiming the difference between the (Transclear) contract price and what they had to pay to buy from a Russian supplier. The defendants pleaded frustration. This was upheld by the appointed arbitrator but the decision was reversed on appeal to the High Court (Commercial). The rejection of frustration was upheld by the Court of Appeal. That court relied heavily on the *Davis v Fareham* approach. The delivery had become more difficult and the defendants' suppliers had let them down *but* this was not enough to amount to frustration. The contract had become more onerous but not impossible to perform. The outcome may, perhaps, have been different if the defendants had made a binding contract for supply from one of the suppliers before making the contract with the claimants and had made clear that performance depended on

---

123. [1956] AC 696.
124. See also *Amalgamated Properties* case discussed at 14.4.2 above.
125. Law students tend to uphold a plea of frustration far more readily than the courts!
126. [2007] EWCA Civ 547.
127. [2008] EWCA Civ 856.

this specific supply. In general, therefore, the legal position is that a seller is assumed to take the risk that his supplier will let him down.

In *Salam Air SAOC v Latam Airlines Group SA*,[128] in which a plea of frustration of aircraft leasing contracts adversely affected by COVID was rejected, Foxton J again stressed the exceptional nature of the doctrine, stating:

> Mr Page accepts that it is necessary for SalamAir to establish a sufficiently arguable case of "frustration of purpose", a doctrine which has seldom been applied since it first emerged in the Coronation cases at the start of the last century.[129]

Foxton J accepted the "radically different" test and quoted, with approval, the view of Rix LJ (in *The Sea Angel*, noted above) that the "radically different" test is "a doctrine of justice".[130]

The requirement that the frustrating event must be fundamental is equally applicable in relation to "personal service" contracts. The death of a contracting party would, of course, frustrate such a contract, and *Cutter v Powell*[131] would clearly be decided differently today. In the case of illness much will depend on its seriousness and the duration of the contract. In *Condor v Barron Knights Ltd*,[132] a drummer in a pop group became ill. The group was contracted to perform seven nights in a week and the illness meant the drummer could play only four nights a week. It was held that the contract was frustrated as it was impracticable to hire a replacement drummer for the remaining three nights a week as this would mean a doubling of rehearsals. One might envisage, in modern Hong Kong, a situation in which a short-term personal service contract could be frustrated by the "compulsory lockdown" of the party charged with performance.

If the law is changed *after* a contract is made such that performance of the contract is made illegal, the contract will be discharged by frustration. Examples include *Denny, Mott & Dickson v James Fraser*[133] (where a contract to supply timber was frustrated because dealings in timber were prohibited by wartime controls) and *Avery v Bowden*, discussed above.[134]

The issue of whether *delay* can amount to frustration turns on the facts of each case. In keeping with the restrictive application of frustration, delay will only frustrate a contract if it is extreme and goes to the root of the contract. In *Jackson v Union Marine Insurance Co Ltd*[135] a delay of eight months caused by a ship running

---

128. [2020] EWHC 2414 (Comm).
129. At para 49.
130. Ibid at para 46.
131. See 14.2.
132. [1966] 1 WLR 87.
133. [1944] AC 265.
134. See 14.3.2.2.
135. (1874) LR 10 CP 125.

aground was held to frustrate a contract as the ship was not available for the particular voyage for which it was chartered.

Where a charter of a ship is expressed to run for a given length of time the courts have to weigh up the length of time the ship is unavailable against the total length of time of the charter. In *Pioneer Shipping Ltd v BTP Tioxide Ltd (the "Nema")*[136] the number of voyages possible during a nine-month period was halved because of a strike. The contract was found to be frustrated because the extremely limited performance possible was not comparable with that envisaged by the contract.

In the Hong Kong case of *Wong Lai-Ying & Others v Chinachem Investment Co Ltd*[137] the Privy Council held a contract to be frustrated by a long delay. In *Wong Lai-Ying*, the parties had made a contract under which the respondents agreed to sell to each of the appellants a flat in buildings to be constructed on land owned by the respondents. During construction there was a major landslide, causing destruction of the work already done and precluding any work for some time.[138] The flats were completed two and a half years late and the respondents pleaded frustration. The appellants sued for a declaration that there was no frustration and for specific performance of the contract. Their action failed, the court upholding the plea of frustration and rejecting the argument that the contract had provided for such an event.[139] A lengthy delay (56 months) in completing a land transaction (caused by the "contumelious" delay of the District Lands Officer (DLO)) also resulted in frustration in *Cheung Kit Lai & Another v Rich Prosper & Another*.[140] Mindful that both parties were innocent and one must suffer because of the non-feasance of the DLO, Judge To castigated the DLO and "invited" them to take prompt action to remedy, as far as possible, the loss suffered by plaintiffs resulting from their inability to enforce the agreement through no fault of their own.[141]

14.4.4 *Non-applicability of the Doctrine*

Even though a serious event has occurred which profoundly affects the contract, the doctrine of frustration will not apply where the event has been provided for in the contract; where the event is foreseen or, perhaps, "foreseeable"; and where the "frustration" is "self-induced". Moreover, frustration will rarely, if ever, apply to a lease.

---

136. [1981] 2 All ER 1030.
137. [1979] HKLR 1.
138. This "University Heights" landslip was of epic proportions and 67 people were killed.
139. See 14.4.4.1 below.
140. (unrep, HCA 972/2011, 10 April 2014).
141. With Hong Kong's volatile housing market, late or non-completion may cause a loss of millions, as in this case.

14.4.4.1 Event Provided For (Allocation of Risk)

If the parties have, in the contract, made clear provision for the occurrence of an event, that event cannot constitute frustration. This exemplifies the principle that frustration takes account of "allocation of risk". Where, for example, the contract makes clear that party A has promised to pay irrespective of subsequent developments ("come hell or high water"), his liability to perform will remain despite later events making his job harder or more expensive. Thus, if, in *Krell v Henry*, the parties had contracted that the hirer must pay for the room "whether or not the procession takes place", the cancellation of the procession could not have amounted to frustration.

Prudent businessmen anticipate the occurrence of unusual, adverse events and provide for them in their contracts. The best known express provision clauses are known as *"force majeure"*[142] clauses, an extremely common feature of commercial contracts. The following is a typical example:

> If the Agreement cannot be performed for any reason beyond the control of either party to the Agreement as a result of war, labour disputes, natural disasters or Acts of God then such non-performance by either party shall be conclusively deemed not to be in breach of the Agreement.

A commercial variation of *force majeure* is the "hardship" clause. This clause defines what "hardship" is and lays down a procedure to be followed should such a hardship occur. A further variation is the "intervener" clause which is similar to the hardship clause but which gives a third party authority to resolve a dispute which may arise between the parties.

The above clauses provide a degree of certainty. They also allow the parties to limit or expand those events which constitute *force majeure* and to make provision for the consequences of a *force majeure* or "hardship" event.

The argument that "the event" had been provided for was raised in the "University Heights landslip" case (above). The vendors were, of course, unable to provide the promised housing on time and pleaded frustration. The purchasers alleged breach on the part of the vendors, relying on a clause in the contract which said:

> should any unforeseen circumstances beyond the Vendor's control arise whereby the Vendor becomes unable to sell . . . the Vendor shall be at liberty to rescind this Agreement forthwith . . . and neither party hereto shall have any claim against the other.

It was held that this clause did not operate to preclude a plea of frustration in the case of an "event" of such uncontemplated magnitude. Frustration *was*, however, precluded in *Jan Albert (HK) Ltd v Shu Kong Garment Factory Ltd*[143] dealt with

---

142. French for "irresistible force".
143. [1989] 2 HKC 156.

previously in the chapter on mistake.[144] The Hong Kong Court of Appeal felt that the alleged frustrating event had been very clearly provided for in the contract.[145]

Huge potential for claims of frustration (and application of "force majeure" clauses) has arisen with the advent of COVID,[146] coupled with, in Hong Kong, the 2019 social unrest. *Billy Graham Evangelistic Association v Scottish Event Campus Ltd*[147] is a Scottish case in which a force majeure clause was held to cover the COVID "event". The relevant clause in the contract covered:

> Any act outside the reasonable control of either party including . . . chemical, bio-logical . . . contamination; the acts of any public authority or imposition of any embargo, sanction or similar action . . . and other difficulties including failures of suppliers.[148]

The Hong Kong courts have been similarly reluctant to uphold a plea of frustra-tion: on either COVID or "social unrest" basis (*a fortiori* where the asserted frustra-tion involves a lease).[149]

14.4.4.2 Events Foreseen or Foreseeable

If the "event" has been foreseen as likely to occur by the parties, it cannot constitute frustration. If only one of the parties has foreseen the likelihood of the event, that party will be precluded from pleading frustration. Clearly, in such cases the "foresee-ing" party should make provision for the event in the contract or protect himself by insurance. By way of example, in *Walton Harvey Ltd v Walker & Homfrays Ltd*,[150] the defendants made a contract to allow the plaintiffs the right to display advertising on the defendants' hotel for seven years. Within that period the hotel was "com-pulsorily acquired", making full performance impossible. This was treated by the English Court of Appeal as a case of breach rather than frustration. The defendants (though not the plaintiffs) knew of the risk of compulsory acquisition and could have provided for the risk.

The position is less clear if the event is merely "foreseeable" and there are con-tradictory *dicta*. In *"The Eugenia"*, for example, Lord Denning MR stated (*obiter*):

> It has often been said that the doctrine of frustration only applies where the new situation is 'unforeseen' or 'unexpected' or 'uncontemplated' as if that were an

---

144. See 10.3.1.
145. Indeed, it is somewhat surprising that the plea of frustration was upheld at first instance.
146. Commonly known worldwide as the "Wuhan Virus" after its place of origin.
147. [2021] SC GLW 9.
148. At para D11 (Defender's submissions). The *Transclear* defendants should have had such a clause!
149. See 14.4.4.4 below.
150. [1931] 1 Ch 274.

essential feature. But it is not so. The only thing that is essential is that the parties should have made no provision for it in the contract.[151]

By way of contrast, in *Krell v Henry*, Vaughan Williams LJ said:

> In each case one must ask . . . Was the event the performance of the contract of such a character that it cannot reasonably be said to have been in the contemplation of the parties at the date of the contract?[152]

The better opinion seems to be that if an event is "foreseeable" in the sense of being *likely* to occur (rather than being merely possible),[153] it cannot amount to frustration. Treitel, for example, makes the point that it was clearly foreseeable as "possible" that (the "hard-living", 60-year-old) Edward VII would be ill on the day appointed for his coronation. This did not prevent the cancellation of the procession from being recognised as a frustrating event.[154] Further, it seems clear that non-completion of the voyage must have been foreseeable as a possibility to the defendant in *Cutter v Powell* given that extravagant wages were promised "on completion". It is generally assumed, however, that the case would now be viewed as one of frustration.

14.4.4.3 Self-induced Frustration

The application of frustration is limited by the fact that it will not apply where the event is the result of the fault of either party. This doctrine, known as "self-induced frustration", flows naturally from Lord Radcliffe's requirement, in the *Davis v Fareham* case,[155] that the event must occur "without the default of either party". The two leading cases on self-induced frustration are the *Maritime Fish* and *Super Servant Two* cases.

Maritime National Fish Ltd v Ocean Trawlers Ltd[156]

The appellants chartered from the respondent a trawler which could only operate with a net called an "otter trawl". These could only be used with a licence. The appellants, who also had four boats of their own, applied for five licences. They were given only three licences but could select as to which of the boats they assigned a licence. The appellants chose to give licences to three of their own boats and then claimed that the contract with the respondents was frustrated. It was held by the Privy Council, on appeal from the Supreme Court of Nova Scotia, Canada, that

---

151. [1964] 2 QB 226 at 229. Similar sentiments were expressed by Goddard J, as he then was, in *Tatem v Gamboa* [1939] 1 KB 132.
152. [1903] 2 KB 740 at 744.
153. *Chitty*, the leading practitioner text, supports this view.
154. See 14.4.2 above.
155. [1956] AC 696 at 728–729 quoted at 14.4.1 above.
156. [1935] AC 524.

there was no frustration, since it was the deliberate act of the appellants which had deprived the boat of a licence.

This decision seems acceptable in that the appellants could have given one of the licences to the respondents' boat and laid up one of their own boats instead. They made a deliberate decision to deprive the respondents' boat of a licence and break a contract. The question arises, however, as to the attitude of the courts were the appellants, with only three licences, to have been hiring all five boats. Clearly they could not have applied licences to all the hired boats and the fulfilment of three contracts would inevitably have left the other two "defective". In such circumstances, it has been argued that the two "defective" contracts should be viewed as frustrated.[157] This view does not, however, appear to have been shared by the courts.

J Lauritzen AS v Wijsmuller BV (The "Super Servant Two")[158]

The defendants contracted to carry the plaintiffs' oil rig (The "Dan King") from Japan to the Netherlands by "transportation unit". They had two such units, *Super Servant One* and *Super Servant Two*. They were permitted to use either vessel under the contract. *Super Servant Two*, which the defendants had earmarked to carry the rig, sank after the contract was made but some months before the date of delivery, so it could not be used. *Super Servant One* had, by now, been promised for use in contracts with other parties. The defendants' plea that the contract with the plaintiffs was frustrated was rejected by the English Court of Appeal on the basis that it was self-induced.

Since the defendants clearly could not perform both contracts it seems harsh to treat the non-performed one as a case of breach rather than frustration. Treitel,[159] not surprisingly, finds the apparent judicial view that the "frustration" was "self-induced" (and therefore inoperative) unconvincing, since the deliberate choice of the defendants had merely been to break one contract *instead of another*. The decision seems to have been based on the principle, at common law,[160] that frustration must occur, if it occurs at all, *immediately* the "event" occurs.[161] Since the sinking of *Super Servant Two* could not immediately be a frustration, as the defendants could still have chosen to perform it, it could not be a frustration at all. The decision in *Super Servant Two* shows, once again, how difficult it is to sustain a plea of frustration. While both *Maritime Fish* and *Super Servant Two* deal with deliberate actions of the defendant, doubt remains as to whether *negligence* will defeat a plea of frustration. To take an example: there would have been no frustration in *Taylor* if the owner had deliberately burned down the music hall; but would frustration have applied if

---

157. Treitel (op cit) at p 1082.
158. [1990] 1 Lloyd's Rep 1.
159. Op cit at p 1082.
160. But not in "many Continental systems": see Cheshire, Fifoot and Furmston (n 6 above) at p 728.
161. See 14.4.5 below.

the owner's employees had "carelessly" started the fire?[162] Some insight into this question was provided by Lord Russell in *Joseph Constantine Steamship Line Ltd v Imperial Smelting Corp Ltd*.[163] He said:

> The possible varieties (of fault) are infinite, and can range from the criminality of the scuttler who opens the sea-cocks and sinks his ship, to the thoughtlessness of the prima donna who sits in a draught and loses her voice. I wish to guard against the supposition that every destruction of corpus for which a contractor can be said, to some extent or in some sense, to be responsible, necessarily involves that the resultant frustration is self-induced within the meaning of the phrase.[164]

The position of a negligently caused "frustration" therefore remains uncertain. The difficulty is exacerbated by the fact that the burden of proof falls on the person alleging self-induced frustration. This burden can be difficult to discharge as shown in the *Joseph Constantine* case itself where the respondents chartered the appellants' steamship to proceed to Port Pirie, Australia to load a cargo. While at anchor an explosion occurred on the ship which resulted in a delay that frustrated the commercial object of the contract. The respondents claimed damages. The appellants pleaded frustration while the respondents argued that any "frustration" was self-induced, the result of the appellants' negligence. The arbitrator at first instance had found that there was no satisfactory explanation as to how the explosion had occurred. The House of Lords, overturning the Court of Appeal, held that the onus was on the respondents to prove that the appellants were negligent in order to establish self-induced frustration, not for the appellant to prove they were not negligent. As the cause of the explosion could not be established the respondents could not discharge this burden. There was, therefore, no "self-induced frustration"; the contract was held to be frustrated and the respondents' action failed.

It can be seen that in this case, and many others, the burden of proving that the party pleading frustration has been "at fault" is difficult to discharge; a shipowner might well know why his boat has sunk, but it will be very difficult for the other party to establish the facts.

Without recourse to a "doctrine" of self-induced frustration, it seems sensible to suggest that where an allegedly "frustrating" event can be proved to be the result of the negligence of the party pleading frustration, the plea should fail since, applying Lord Radcliffe's definition, the event will not have arisen "without default of either party".[165] This appears to have been the view of the judges in *Super Servant Two*.

---

162. It appears to have been the case that the defendants' employees left a fire unattended.
163. [1941] 2 All ER 165.
164. Ibid at 175.
165. In *Davis v Fareham* discussed at 14.4.1 and 14.4.3 above.

14.4.4.4 Leases

Whether or not a lease of land can be frustrated has long been a controversial issue.[166] Those arguing that a lease cannot be frustrated have pointed to the fact that a lease constitutes a legal estate which will remain, irrespective of the fate of the land itself. However, the House of Lords in *National Carriers v Panalpina (Northern) Ltd*[167] expressly stated that, given the proper circumstances, they could see no reason why a lease could not be frustrated. Such circumstances may be where, for example, land was entirely swallowed up by the sea or a permanent building ban was placed on the land. In the *National Carriers* case, the parties agreed a lease of a warehouse for ten years. The only means of access to the warehouse was an access road which was closed by a temporary order for one year. This interruption, in the view of the court, was not significantly serious to constitute a frustration.

Since the court decided that no frustration existed in the case, its views as to the "theoretical possibility" of a lease being frustrated are necessarily *obiter*. Indeed, irrespective of the theoretical possibility, in practice a lease has never been held to have been frustrated, either in England or (Hong Kong). Two recent English cases have endorsed the (theoretical) "not never, but hardly ever" approach to frustration of a lease. In *Canary Wharf Ltd v European Medicines Agency*,[168] the Agency pleaded that their lease of the claimants' premises was frustrated by Brexit. They pleaded that the common purpose of the contract had been frustrated and that continuation of the lease post-Brexit would be illegal, since they would be required to relocate. Both arguments were rejected by Marcus Smith J, so that once again a plea of lease frustration had failed. Smith J stated:

> both parties approached the Lease from their own commercial standpoint and the Lease represents the outcome not of a common purpose but of rival negotiations driven by different objectives.

In *London Trocadero (2015) LLP v Picturehouse Cinemas Ltd & Others*,[169] the defendants argued, in defence of their refusal to pay rent to their landlords under a 35-year lease of property to be used for cinema production and related activities, that the lease had been frustrated by COVID restrictions which prevented the public showing of films. Once again, the court (Deputy Judge Vos) refused to find frustration of a lease.

Frustration was pleaded, unsuccessfully, as a defence to a claim for accrued rent in the following Hong Kong District Court case.

---

166. See, for example, *Cricklewood Property & Investment v Leighton's Investment Trust* [1945] AC 221 where the House of Lords was split on this question.
167. [1981] 1 All ER 161.
168. [2019] EWHC 335.
169. [2021] EWHC 2591 (Ch).

Li Ching Wing v Xuan Yi Xiong[170]

An outbreak of the disease "SARS"[171] resulted in the issuing of an Isolation Order, which forced the defendant tenant to move out of his flat for 10 days. After the Order was lifted, 15 months remained on the lease. The defendant relied on the Order as a ground to frustrate the lease. Judge Lok, citing the decision in the *National Carriers* case, held that, while a plea of frustration could apply to a lease in extreme circumstances, there was no frustration in this case as the time which the defendant was excluded from the flat because of the Order was insignificant when compared with the two-year term of the lease. The judge said:

> The outbreak of SARS may arguably be an unforeseeable event, however, such supervening event did not, in my judgment, significantly change the nature of the outstanding contractual rights of obligations from what the parties could reasonably have contemplated at the time of the execution of the Tenancy Agreement. Hence, the defence of frustration cannot possibly succeed in the present case.[172]

More recently, Hong Kong courts have held, in a number of cases involving the Swatch Group, that commercial leases were not frustrated (nor was abatement of rent permitted) merely because Swatch was less able to trade profitably because of COVID and the "social unrest" of 2019–2020. In one of these cases, *Vember Lord Ltd v The Swatch Group (Hong Kong) Ltd*,[173] Le Pichon DHC endorsed the view of English legal academic, Professor Treitel that:

> in cases of partial impossibility, the contract is either frustrated or remains in force. There is no such concept as partial or temporary frustration on account of partial or temporary impossibility.[174]

The conclusion to be drawn from the above cases is that the chances of succeeding in having a lease frustrated[175] are very slim indeed and, if the doctrine is to apply at all, it is more likely to be applicable where the "event" undermines a lease of short duration for a specific purpose, such as the use of a holiday home.

---

170. [2004] 1 HKC 353.
171. Severe Acute Respiratory Syndrome.
172. [2004] 1 HKC 353 at 358.
173. [2022] HKCFI 279. And see *Silvercord Ltd v The Swatch Group (Hong Kong) Ltd* [2022] HKCFI 362; *The One Property Ltd v The Swatch Group (Hong Kong) Ltd* [2022] HKCFI 1693; *Sunbroad Holdings Ltd v A80 Paris HK Ltd & Another* [2022] HKCFI 2251; *The Center (76) Ltd v Victory Serviced Office (HK) Ltd* [2020] HKCFI 2881.
174. At para 86.
175. The Hong Kong courts have also doubted whether an agreement for "sale and purchase" of land can be frustrated: *East Epoch International Ltd v Wong Poon Ting* [2010] 3 HKLRD 495 (though the case was actually concerned with a lesser plea of "temporary impossibility").

14.4.5 *The Effects of Frustration*

The effect of frustration is to bring the contract to an end automatically, from the date of the frustrating event, irrespective of the wishes of the parties. A suggestion that a contract of tenancy might be "temporarily frustrated" by the COVID outbreak (thereby "suspending" the tenant's obligation to pay rent) was rejected in *Bank of New York Mellon (International) Ltd v Cine-UK Ltd*.[176]

The "automatic" discharge effected by frustration distinguishes this method of termination of contract from that of discharge by breach, where the innocent party can elect to affirm or terminate the contract. The House of Lords made this distinction clear in *Hirji Mulji v Cheong Yue SS Co*,[177] holding that "election"[178] was not possible once a frustrating event had occurred. A more recent confirmation of this point occurred in *GF Sharp & Co Ltd v McMillan*,[179] where a company retained the services of a worker even after he had suffered an injury which prevented him working. They did this so he could qualify for increased pension benefits. The Employment Appeal Tribunal held that the sustaining of the injury had frustrated the employment contract with immediate effect.

14.4.5.1 The Common Law Position

Frustration does not make a contract void *ab initio*, but only as to the future. At common law, therefore, quite logically, the effect of frustration was to terminate the contract only in respect of *future* obligations; the parties were not discharged from performing contractual obligations that were already due at the date of frustration. The common law rule that "the loss lies where it falls" is illustrated by another "coronation case": *Chandler v Webster*.[180] In *Chandler*, the defendant agreed to let to the plaintiff a room to view the coronation procession on 26 June 1902 for £141, payable immediately. The procession later became impossible because of the king's illness. The plaintiff had paid £100 on account and the balance remained unpaid. The plaintiff sued to recover the £100 paid, pleading a total failure of consideration. The defendant counterclaimed for the balance of £41. The English Court of Appeal dismissed the plaintiff's claim and upheld the counterclaim. The defendant's right to payment of the whole sum had accrued before the procession became impossible and the effect of frustration was not to wipe out the contract altogether but only to release the parties from further performance.

---

176. Discussed in chapter 8 at 8.4.2.
177. [1926] AC 497.
178. See 14.3.
179. [1998] IRLR 632.
180. [1904] 1 KB 493.

Chandler was later overruled by the House of Lords in *Fibrosa Spolka Akcyjna v Fairburn, Lawson, Combe, Barbour Ltd*[181] which provided for the "quasi-contractual" repayment of money paid before frustration where there had been a *total* failure of consideration. The common law position remained unsatisfactory, however, in respect of frustration following the provision of partial consideration. As a result, shortly after *Fibrosa*, England enacted the Law Reform (Frustrated Contracts) Act 1943, which seeks to remedy the defects in the common law. The corresponding provisions are found in Hong Kong in sections 16–18 of the Law Amendment and Reform (Consolidation) Ordinance (LARCO).[182]

14.4.5.2 Legislation: The Law Amendment and Reform (Consolidation) Ordinance (LARCO)

The legislation in Hong Kong (and England) does not define "frustration". It seeks, however, to improve the legal position where a contract has been brought to an end by frustration. The *effects* of frustration are dealt with by two subsections of LARCO, section 16(2) and (3).

14.4.5.2.1 Section 16(2) of LARCO

Section 16 of LARCO is headed "Adjustment of rights and liabilities of parties to frustrated contracts." Section 16(2) states:

> All sums paid or payable to any party in pursuance of the contract before the time when the parties were so discharged (in this section and section 17 referred to as the time of discharge) shall, in the case of sums so paid, be recoverable from him as money received by him for the use of the party by whom the sums were paid, and, in the case of sums so payable, cease to be so payable:
>
> Provided that, if the party to whom the sums were so paid or payable incurred expenses before the time of discharge in, or for the purpose of, the performance of the contract, the court may, if it considers it just to do so having regard to all the circumstances of the case, allow him to retain or, as the case may be, recover the whole or any part of the sums so paid or payable, not being an amount in excess of the expenses so incurred.

This subsection deals with the situation where money has been paid, or is owing, prior to the frustrating event. Such a scenario would occur where a contract requires the payment of a deposit or "prepayment". The starting point here is that any money paid can be recovered and any money owing, or "payable", is no longer payable. The court, however, does have a very wide discretion to permit the party to whom money has been paid or is payable, to retain, or recover, all or part of the sums

---

181. [1942] 2 All ER 122.
182. Cap 23.

paid, or payable, to reimburse him for *monetary expense* incurred, in relation to the contract, before the frustrating event. The award is discretionary but the wording of the subsection makes it clear that the court may not award more than the amount of expenses already incurred *nor* more than the sums paid or payable, whichever is the lower. So, where no sums are paid or payable prior to the frustrating event, the court would have no power to make an award under this subsection even where monetary expenditure has been incurred.

A useful illustration of the working of this subsection is found in the case of *Gamerco SA v ICM/Fair Warning (Agency) Ltd*,[183] based on the equivalent English legislative rule.[184] In *Gamerco*, the plaintiffs, Spanish pop concert promoters, agreed to promote a rock concert involving the defendant group ("Guns N' Roses") at a stadium in Madrid on 4 July 1992. On 1 July 1992, following a safety report from engineers, the authorities banned all use of the stadium and the permit issued to the plaintiffs to hold the concert was revoked. No alternative venue could be found and the concert was cancelled. Garland J found that the contract was frustrated. The issue, then, was how to apply the provisions of the legislation.[185] The plaintiffs had paid $412,000 on account and had contracted to pay a further $362,500. Both parties had incurred expenses, the plaintiffs about $450,000 and the defendants about $50,000. The judge held that the legislation gave the courts a very wide discretion as to the defendants' expenses. In the circumstances it was established that neither party derived any benefit from the expenses they had incurred or had conferred any benefit on the other party. The judge ordered the defendants to repay the $412,000 that had been paid in advance and made no deduction from this sum in respect of the defendants' expenses.

14.4.5.2.2 Section 16(3) of LARCO

Section 16(3) of LARCO states:

> Where any party to the contract has, by reason of anything done by any other party thereto in, or for the purpose of, the performance of the contract, obtained a valuable benefit (other than a payment of money to which subsection (2) applies) before the time of discharge, there shall be recoverable from him by the said other party such sum (if any), not exceeding the value of the said benefit to the party obtaining it, as the court considers just, having regard to all the circumstances of the case and, in particular–
>
> > (a) the amount of any expenses incurred before the time of discharge by the benefited party in, or for the purpose of, the performance of the contract, including any sums paid or payable by him to any other party in pursuance

---

183. [1995] 1 WLR 1226.
184. Law Reform (Frustrated Contracts) Act 1943 s 1(2).
185. Ibid.

of the contract and retained or recoverable by that party under subsection (2); and

(b) the effect, in relation to the said benefit, of the circumstances giving rise to the frustration of the contract.

The subsection deals with cases where, prior to frustration, one party has conferred a "valuable benefit" on the other. Once again, the court has a discretion to allow what it regards as a "just sum". The just sum cannot exceed the value of the benefit conferred and, in assessing the sum, the court must take into account all the circumstances of the case including the *effect* of the frustrating event.

The only important illustration of the workings of the subsection is the English case of *BP Exploration Co (Libya) Ltd v Hunt (No 2)*,[186] dealing with the equivalent English legislation.[187] This case is very complex and went all the way to the House of Lords but the key judgment concerning the application of the legislation is that of the trial judge, Robert Goff J (as he then was).

BP Exploration Co (Libya) Ltd v Hunt (No 2)

Hunt was given an oil concession by the Libyan government in 1957. He needed to start drilling for oil within three years but lacked capital. In 1960 he made an agreement with BP under which the latter were to pay for all the costs of the exploration, development, and operation of the concession and to make payments in oil and cash to Hunt, in return for which Hunt would give them a half share in the concession. If oil was found, BP were to be repaid for their expenditure out of Hunt's half share. In short, if oil was not found, BP would lose heavily, if it was found they would do very well. A large oil field was discovered. It came on stream in 1967. In 1971 the Libyan government nationalised BP's share of the concession and, in 1973, Hunt's share. BP claimed that the contract was frustrated and most of their claim was for a "just sum" under the English equivalent of section 16(3) of LARCO.[188]

Goff J dealt in detail with the method of determining the just sum. The judge adopted a three-stage approach to assessment under the subsection. First, he "identified" the benefit to Hunt, stressing that what was important was not the extent of BP's labours but the fruits of those labours to Hunt. These were seen to be the development of the concession and the oil received before nationalisation. Second, Goff J "valued" that benefit, at about $85 million, representing the amount received from the concession plus compensation paid by Libya, divided into half to recognise BP's share. This value marked the *maximum* awardable as a just sum. Finally, Goff J awarded a just sum, of about $35 million; representing $10 million paid to Hunt, plus $87 million spent on exploration, minus $62 million recovered in oil before

---

186. [1982] 1 All ER 925.
187. Law Reform (Frustrated Contracts) Act 1943 s 1(3).
188. Ibid.

nationalisation. Since the sum thought to be just was less than the amount of the valuable benefit, it could be awarded in full.

Since Goff J's lengthy judgment was upheld, with minor amendment, in two subsequent appeals, it must be seen as having the seal of approval of the appellate courts although, since the wording of the legislation gives the judge a great deal of discretion, a computation will only be overturned if it is clearly wrong.

Goff J makes clear that the focus must be on payment for a benefit obtained, to prevent unjust enrichment. There should be no payment to a party merely because he has "laboured hard". If, despite all BP's efforts, no oil had been found, no just sum could have been awarded.

Goff J expressed the view, *obiter*, that when the effect of the frustrating event is to destroy any "valuable benefit" previously conferred,[189] the just sum must be valued at zero taking into account the effect of the frustrating event. This approach has been criticised[190] on the basis that the court should focus on the point in time immediately *before* the frustrating event.[191] If, at that time, there has been a benefit conferred, a just sum can be awarded. Of course, the *amount* of that just sum will be reduced since the court has to take account of the effects of the frustrating event but the court is not compelled to reduce the sum to zero. Given that Goff J's comments on this issue are *obiter*, it is open to courts in England and Hong Kong to ignore them and award a just sum even in cases where the frustrating event has destroyed the valuable benefit.

14.4.5.2.3 Insurance Payments

Section 16(5) of LARCO states that in assessing any sum which ought to be recovered or retained under the other provisions of section 16, the court shall give no credit for any insurance proceeds receivable by a party unless there is "an obligation to insure imposed by an express term of the frustrated contract or by or under any enactment".

14.4.5.2.4 Exceptions

Section 17 of LARCO provides for a number of exceptions to the above rules. Section 17(4) allows for the severance of parts of a contract "wholly performed before the time of discharge" and the treatment of a severed part as a separate contract which had not been frustrated. In such a case section 16 would apply only to the remainder of the contract. Section 17(5) states that sections 16–18 do not apply to certain charterparties, contracts of insurance (except as provided by section 16(5)) and any

---

189. As occurred in *Appleby v Myers* (1867) LR 2 CP 651.
190. See Treitel (op cit) at p 1091.
191. Because s 16(3) (and its English equivalent) refers to a valuable benefit obtained "*before* the time of discharge".

contract "for the sale of specific goods, which have perished before the risk has passed to the buyer or which is frustrated by reason that the goods have perished."

This last exclusion, though of minor practical importance, has been criticised as being both "capricious" and unnecessary by Treitel.[192] The second branch of the exclusion is unnecessary because there could be no frustration if the risk in the goods had already passed.[193] The restriction of the subsection's scope to "specific" goods is based, no doubt, on the idea that if the contract is for non-specific goods, which have been destroyed, the seller will still have the obligation to substitute other goods of the same quality. If he fails to do so, he will be liable in breach. However, the existence of separate frustration rules depending on whether goods are specific or non-specific could produce "capricious distinctions".[194]

14.4.5.2.5 Settlements

Section 18 of LARCO states that nothing in sections 16 and 17 "shall affect any settlement or agreement between the parties subsequent to the date of discharge whereby the rights and liabilities of the contracting parties fell to be determined otherwise than in accordance with the said sections".

In other words, post-frustration, the parties are free to make their own agreement as to how loss should be apportioned as an alternative to the statutory rules. This reflects the reluctance of the courts to intervene in bargaining between the parties even where there is frustration.

---

192. (Op cit) at p 1096.
193. That is, the contract would already have been fully performed.
194. Treitel (op cit) at p 1096.

15

Remedies for Breach of Contract

Overview

The most important remedy for breach is the common law remedy of damages. Damages are available "as of right" which means that, wherever there is a breach, the innocent party is automatically entitled to damages. There is no need to prove loss, but without loss, damages will be merely "nominal".

In order to establish the right to "substantial" (as opposed to nominal) damages, the plaintiff must show that the defendant's breach actually "caused" his loss, and, more significantly, that the loss suffered is not too unlikely, or "remote", a consequence of the breach. Causation is rarely a problem in contract cases, particularly since it is established that, where the defendant's breach is *one* of the causes of the plaintiff's loss, he can be liable to the plaintiff.

"Remoteness" is more often encountered as a problem in contract. The rule of remoteness, deriving from the decision in *Hadley v Baxendale*,[1] as refined by later decisions, is that the defendant is liable for the "natural and probable" consequences of his breach; a more restrictive test than that in the tort of negligence where the defendant is liable for all the "reasonably foreseeable" consequences of his negligence. A variation on *Hadley* suggested by Lord Hoffmann[2] in *"The Achilleas"*[3] has found little support in England but has found favour in Hong Kong.[4]

The purpose of contract damages is always to *compensate*. Thus, the court focuses on the loss to the plaintiff and not the gain to the defendant. The "measure" of damages in contract is usually assessed on the basis of "loss of bargain"; putting the plaintiff in the position he would have been if the other party had fulfilled his obligations. On occasion, the alternative measure of "reliance loss" is applied, based

---

1. (1854) 9 Exch 34.
2. The "assumption of responsibility" test.
3. [2009] AC 61.
4. See 15.1.2 below.

on the expense incurred by the plaintiff in reliance on the defendant completing his side of the bargain. In measuring damages, the courts are assisted by a number of specific rules such as the "market rule", in sale of goods contracts, and the rules on mitigation and liquidated damages. As to the latter, significant developments have occurred in English law. It remains to be seen whether Hong Kong law will mirror the changes.

Equitable remedies are available only at the discretion of the court. Although this discretion is absolute, a number of recognised factors influence its exercise. First, since equity developed, historically, to remedy the defects in the common law, equitable remedies are available only where the common law remedy of damages is inadequate. Second, since equity developed as a "court of conscience", an equitable remedy will only be granted where it is "just and equitable" in all the circumstances. In deciding whether it is "just and equitable" to intervene on a party's behalf, equity will take into account the so-called "maxims" of equity: such as that "he who comes to equity must come with clean hands" and "he who seeks equity must do equity".

The major equitable remedies in contract are specific performance and injunction. Specific performance is an order that a party must fulfil his contractual obligations rather than simply pay damages for breach. Specific performance will only be awarded where monetary compensation is inadequate such as in contracts for the sale of land and contracts for the transfer of something unique. Specific performance will not be awarded for a personal service contract and is unlikely to be awarded where enforcement would require constant supervision by the court. Further, under the principle of "mutuality" specific performance will not be awarded to a party to a contract, if it could not be awarded against him as, for example, in the case of a minor.[5]

Injunctions, unlike specific performance, are not an exclusively contractual remedy. In contract, injunctions are used to enforce *negative* undertakings, express or implied. Where a negative undertaking has already been broken a mandatory injunction will be required to undo the improper breach; where the plaintiff merely fears that the undertaking is *about to be* broken, a prohibitive injunction will be sought to prevent the threatened breach taking place.

In the case of equitable remedies, the ultimate sanction, in the event of a failure by the defendant to comply, is the imposition of punishment for contempt.

While it may be thought that the distinction between common law and equity is largely obsolete, given that all courts may award both common law and equitable remedies, the distinctive nature of equity remains important given that equitable remedies continue to be available only at the discretion of the court, and that courts exercising an equitable jurisdiction continue to grant remedies so as to produce a "just and equitable" result.

---

5. See 6.3.1.

It should also be remembered that the "common law" to which Hong Kong adheres, and which will remain in force (at least) until the year 2047, includes the principles of equity.[6]

15.1 Damages

Damages are the major common law remedy for breach of contract. The general principle in contract is that although a contractual agreement is said to be "enforceable", the party in breach is rarely compelled to honour his side of the bargain. Instead, the law requires that the innocent party be compensated. The courts, in assessing damages, focus on the innocent party's loss and not the defendant's profit. There are occasions, admittedly rare, where the defendant makes great profit from a breach which causes the plaintiff no loss. In such cases the plaintiff's damages will be nominal; there is no provision in contract for exemplary or "punitive" damages.[7] The major areas of concern in relation to damages are: first, to establish that the defendant's breach "caused" the plaintiff's loss; second to determine that such loss is not too "remote", and third, to determine how the amount, or "quantum", of damages is to be calculated.

15.1.1 Causation of Damage

The question here is whether the defendant's admitted breach of contract has actually caused the plaintiff's loss. Unlike the position in tort, causation rarely arises as a difficult problem in contract. Nonetheless the principle remains that a defendant is only liable for loss which is caused by his breach.[8] Most of the potential difficulties are solved by the fact that, if a plaintiff suffers loss partly as a result of the defendant's breach and partly as a result of other factors, the defendant can be held liable.[9]

A problem previously existed in the form of the House of Lords decision in the controversial *Liesbosch Dredger* case,[10] which decided that a defendant should not be liable for loss to the plaintiff arising from the latter's "impecuniousness" (lack of money). The House of Lords, in this case, found that impecuniousness was an independent cause.[11] In theory, this principle was also applicable to contract. In practice, since the decision was generally unpopular, courts in contractual cases tended to ignore it. To have applied the principle to contract would have meant that the plaintiff who could not afford to minimise the loss caused by the defendant's breach

---

6. See chapter 2.
7. Though, via a "restitutionary" approach, the defendant may be required to return his ill-gotten gains.
8. See *Malik v BCCI* at 15.1.3.2 below.
9. *De La Bere v Pearson* [1908] 1 KB 280.
10. *Liesbosch Dredger v SS Edison (The Liesbosch)* [1933] AC 449.
11. Despite the fact that one is normally expected to take the victim as one finds him, physically and financially.

would not be compensated for the additional loss resulting. This runs counter to the contractual principle that the plaintiff is only expected to take "reasonable" steps to minimise his loss. In practice, courts in contract cases have allowed the plaintiff to recover compensation for all his loss provided that he has acted reasonably. The matter is now almost certainly resolved by virtue of the fact that *Liesbosch* has been overruled in England by the House of Lords decision in *Lagden v O'Connor*.[12] While the *Lagden* case is not technically binding in Hong Kong,[13] it will almost certainly be followed given the unpopularity of its predecessor.

Causation was crucial, unusually, in the Hong Kong case of *Chin Luk Properties Ltd v Casil Cleaning Ltd*.[14] In this case the defendant was found to be in breach of a contract to provide the plaintiff with the full amount of a loan known to be for the purpose of financing a development. The court allowed the plaintiff only nominal damages on the basis that the subsequent failure to launch the development was the result *not* of the lack of the loan but of the Asian financial crisis.[15]

Slightly more recently, in *Less & Carter v Hussain*,[16] an English court also found against plaintiffs on a non-causation basis. Here, the defendant had given negligent medical advice to Ms Less, downplaying the risks of pregnancy, given Mrs Less's medical condition (including fibroids). Ms Less became pregnant and, after a nightmare pregnancy, gave birth to a still-born child. Ms Less and her partner brought actions in both tort and contract, given the clear breach by the defendant of both contractual and tortious duties and the immense grief suffered by both. The action failed, however, on the trial judge's causation finding of fact, namely that given the strong desire of the couple to have a child together, Ms Less would have still opted to become pregnant even if given proper advice.

15.1.2 Remoteness of Damage

Remoteness is much more important in contract than causation and problems are more likely to arise in this area. The question here is whether the defendant in breach is liable for particular consequences of his breach or whether they are too unlikely or "remote". The case of *Hadley v Baxendale*, though refined by subsequent decisions, remains the leading authority.

---

12. [2004] 1 All ER 277.
13. See chapter 2.
14. [2007] 1 HKC 231.
15. See also *Wiseman v Virgin Atlantic* discussed below. (Customer wrongly denied boarding in Nigeria; subsequently robbed there. Robbery not "caused" by defendants' breach).
16. [2012] EWHC 3513 (QB).

Hadley v Baxendale[17]

The plaintiffs, the owners of a flour mill, employed the defendants to carry a broken driving shaft to be repaired. The defendants, in breach of contract, delayed for five days and while the machine was missing the plaintiffs' factory totally ceased production. Untypically, the plaintiffs had no reserve shaft since the broken one was sent as a pattern for a new one as well as to be repaired. The plaintiffs' claim for compensation for the total shutdown failed as this was held to be "too remote" a consequence of the defendants' breach.

The principle enunciated by Baron Alderson remains the starting point for determining the issue of remoteness. He said:

> Where two parties have made a contract which one of them has broken, the damages which the other party ought to receive in respect of such breach of contract should such as may fairly and reasonably be considered either arising naturally, ie, according to the usual course of things, from such breach of contract itself, or such as may reasonably be supposed to have been in the contemplation of both parties, at the time they made the contract, as the probable result of the breach of it. Now, if the special circumstances under which the contract was actually made were communicated by the plaintiffs to the defendants, and thus known to both parties, the damages resulting from the breach of such a contract, which they would reasonably contemplate, would be the amount of injury which would ordinarily follow from a breach of contract under these special circumstances so known and communicated But, on the other hand, if these special circumstances were wholly unknown to the party breaking the contract, he, at the most, could only be supposed to have had in his contemplation the amount of injury which would arise generally, and in the great multitude of cases not affected by any special circumstances, from such a breach of contract.[18]

The basic principle, then, is that a defendant is liable for the natural and probable consequences of his breach. This principle is sometimes expressed as two rules, the first involving "objectively" likely consequences and the second "subjectively" likely ones (deriving from the defendant's actual knowledge). Alternatively, it has been said there is one rule with two branches or limbs. In reality the principle can be expressed succinctly as follows:

> Given the state of his knowledge, the defendant will be liable to compensate the plaintiff for those consequences of his (the defendant's) breach which he should have foreseen as likely to arise from the breach.

A more recent analysis of the remoteness rule, by the English House of Lords, is to be found in the rather curious case of *Jackson & Another v Royal Bank of*

---

17. (1854) 9 Exch 341.
18. Ibid at 354.

Scotland plc.[19] In *Jackson*, the defendant bank, as a result of a breach of confidentiality owed to the claimants, who were importers, inadvertently disclosed to a third party, dealing with the claimants, the considerable extent of the claimants' mark-up price on goods supplied to the third party. The third party angrily ceased trading with the claimants who sued the defendants for the resulting loss. The defendants ultimately acknowledged their breach but claimed that the trial judge's allowance of damages for a lost four-year period was excessive in that such loss was too remote. The Court of Appeal upheld the defendants' appeal but the House of Lords reinstated the trial judge's decision.

Although the leading judgment of Lord Hope refers throughout to the two rules of *Hadley's* case, Lord Walker preferred to speak of the two "limbs" of the one rule. He states:

> The common ground of the two limbs is what the contract-breaker knew or must be taken to have known, so as to bring the loss within the reasonable contemplation of the parties.[20]

It was once thought that the remoteness rule in contract was synonymous with that applicable to the tort of negligence; namely that the defendant would be liable for the "reasonably foreseeable" consequences of his breach. Such a view derived from statements of Asquith LJ in the case of *Victoria Laundry (Windsor) Ltd v Newman Industries Ltd.*[21] The case itself is worthy of note. The factual scenario was that the plaintiffs ordered a new boiler from the defendants. The defendants, in clear breach of contract, delivered five months late. The plaintiffs claimed damages on the basis of:

(a) loss of £16 per week of likely increased profits during the five-month period;

(b) loss of £262 per week resulting from the loss of a highly lucrative government contract which the plaintiffs intended to fulfil with the new boiler.

The plaintiffs' action succeeded, in the Court of Appeal, only in relation to the first, lesser, amount which was within the scope of the first branch of *Hadley*. Obviously the purpose of the new boiler was to increase capacity such that loss of increased business was a clearly probable consequence of the boiler's late arrival.

The action failed in respect of the larger sum since:

(a) the loss of the lucrative government contract was not a "natural" consequence of the breach; and

(b) the defendant had not been informed of the existence of the lucrative contract.

---

19. [2005] UKHL 3.
20. Ibid at para 33.
21. [1949] 2 KB 528, [1949] 1 All ER 997.

The court decided, then, that the larger sum of loss was too remote.[22] Asquith LJ stated:

> In cases of breach of contract the aggrieved party is only entitled to recover such part of the loss actually resulting as was at the time of the contract reasonably foreseeable as liable to result from the breach . . .
>
> Nor . . . need it be proved that upon a given state of knowledge the defendant could, as a reasonable man, foresee that a breach must necessarily result in that loss. It is enough if he could foresee it was likely so to result.[23]

Despite the confusion produced by Asquith LJ's use of the word "foreseeable", it has since been confirmed that the contract test is narrower than the remoteness test for the tort of negligence.

Koufos v C Czarnikow Ltd, The Heron II[24]

The respondents had chartered the appellant's ship to carry a cargo of sugar to Basrah where it was to be sold promptly on arrival. The ship deviated and arrived nine days late by which time the price for sugar had declined considerably. The appellant did not know of the charterers' intention to sell promptly but did know there was a sugar market in Basrah. The respondents claim for damages for the reduced price of the sugar on arrival was upheld by the House of Lords as a natural consequence of the appellant's breach.

The House of Lords considered at some length the test for remoteness in contract and the question of whether it is the same as that for the tort of negligence. The most important judgment is that of Lord Reid who said:

> The modern rule in tort is quite different and it imposes a much wider liability. The defendant will be liable for any type of damage which is reasonably foreseeable as liable to happen even in the most unusual case, unless the risk is so small that a reasonable man would in the whole circumstances feel justified in neglecting it; and there is good reason for the difference. In contract, if one party wishes to protect himself against a risk which to the other party would appear unusual, he can direct the other party's attention to it before the contract is made, and I need not stop to consider in what circumstances the other party will then be held to have accepted responsibility in that event. In tort, however, there is no opportunity for the injured party to protect himself in that way, and the tortfeasor cannot reasonable complain if he has to pay for some very unusual but nevertheless foreseeable damage which results from his wrong-doing. I have no doubt that today a tortfeasor would be held liable for a type of damage as unlikely as was the stoppage of Hadley's Mill for lack of a crank shaft: to any one with the knowledge the carrier had that may have seemed unlikely, but the chance of it happening would have been seen to be far from

---

22. But see discussion of *Wroth v Tyler* at 15.1.5 below.
23. [1949] 1 ALL ER at 1002.
24. [1969] 1 AC 350, [1967] 3 All ER 686, [1967] 3 WLR 1491.

negligible. But it does not at all follow that *Hadley v Baxendale* would today be differently decided.[25]

Broadly, then, one can say that a defendant in negligence is liable for all the "foreseeable" consequences of his negligence whereas a contract defendant is only liable for the "probable" consequences of his breach. There are good reasons for this distinction, given that the plaintiff in contract makes an agreement with the defendant in which he is able to spell out the consequences of breach; if he fails to do so the defendant should not be liable for non-probable consequences. Nonetheless, given that the plaintiff increasingly has a choice as to whether to sue the careless contract-breaker in contract or tort, the distinction sometimes appears inappropriate.

Lord Denning MR had in mind the increasing overlap between contract and tort when he suggested that the remoteness test for contract and tort should be the same where the plaintiff has suffered *physical*, as opposed to merely *financial*, loss. Lord Denning expounded this view in *Parsons H (Livestock) Ltd v Uttley, Ingham & Co Ltd*.[26] Here, the defendants sold to the plaintiffs a "hopper" for storing pig food. The hopper was improperly ventilated, contrary to the clear terms of the contract, and, as a result, pig food became mouldy. Many of the plaintiffs' pigs became ill as a result of eating the mouldy food. The illness suffered, E. coli, was regarded by the courts as an unusual one. The Court of Appeal unanimously upheld the plaintiffs' claim for damages for loss of stock and profit despite the defendants' argument that the rare illness was too remote a consequence of their breach.

Although the court found unanimously for the plaintiffs, only Lord Denning MR found it necessary to invoke the concept of a different test for remoteness depending on the type of loss suffered by the plaintiffs. He said:

> It seems to me that in the law of contract, too, a similar distinction is emerging. It is between loss of profit consequent on a breach of contract and physical damage consequent on it.
>
> ... In the second class of case, the physical injury or expense case, the defaulting party is liable for any loss or expense which he ought reasonably to have foreseen at the time of the breach as a possible consequence, even if it was only a *slight* possibility. You must assume that he was aware of his breach, and then you must ask: ought he reasonably to have foreseen, at the time of the breach, that something of this kind might happen in consequence of it? This is the test which has been applied in cases of tort, ever since *The Wagon Mound* cases. But there is a long line of cases which support a like test in cases of contract.
>
> ... The present case falls within the class of case where the breach of contract causes physical damage. The test of remoteness in such cases is similar to that in

25. [1967] 3 WLR 1491 at 1502–1503.
26. [1978] QB 791, [1977] 3 WLR 990, [1978] 1 All ER 525.

tort. The contractor is liable for all such loss or expense as could reasonably have been foreseen, at the time of the breach, as a possible consequence of it.[27]

There is merit in Lord Denning's argument given that a plaintiff suffering physical loss from a negligent breach will often have a choice whether to sue in contract or in tort. It seems anomalous that different remoteness rules may operate depending on the form of the plaintiff's action. The problem with the economic/physical distinction is that it was not endorsed by Lord Denning's fellow Court of Appeal judges; has received little subsequent judicial support; and was not recognised in the earlier House of Lords case of *The Heron II*[28] which remains the leading authority on the question of remoteness in contract.

The court's approach to the plaintiffs' loss in the *Parsons* case may be described as "broad brush" in that they did not ask whether E. coli specifically was a probable consequence of the breach but whether some pig-related illness was. That question having been decided in the affirmative, the precise *form* of the illness did not matter. Such an approach has long been prevalent in relation to the tort of negligence[29] and appears sensible. A similar approach, in contract, was adopted in *Wroth v Tyler*,[30] where it was held that, as long as the *type* of damage is foreseeable, the defendant will be liable for its full "extent", however great.[31] This is difficult to reconcile with the *Victoria Laundry* decision; if, in the latter case, some loss of increased business was probable, why should the defendant not have been liable for the whole?

The English courts have, more recently, effected a subtle but significant variation on the *Hadley/Heron II* remoteness principles in the following case, finally determined in the House of Lords.

Transfield Shipping Inc v Mercator Shipping Inc (The Achilleas)[32]

The appellants (the original defendants) had chartered a ship (The *Achilleas*) from the respondent owners and had, in clear breach of contract, returned it late. The issue before the original arbitrators and the later courts was whether the charterers should be liable for the "not unlikely" loss of a lucrative second charter which the owners had lost through non-availability of the ship, or whether *as was the invariable custom in the shipping trade*, they should be liable only for the difference between the market rate and the contract rate for the nine days for which the owners had been deprived of the use of their ship.

Arbitrators, by a majority, found for the owners, on the basis that the loss of the new charter was a "not unlikely" consequence of the late delivery. This represented

---

27. [1977] 3 WLR 990 at 997–999.
28. [1969] 1 AC 350, [1967] 3 All ER 686.
29. See for example *Bradford v Robinsons Rentals* [1967] 1 WLR 337.
30. [1973] 2 WLR 405.
31. Ibid per Megarry J at 431.
32. [2009] AC 61.

a simple application of general principles of remoteness as enunciated in *Hadley* and *Heron II*, principles which had previously not been applied in this particular shipping context. The view of the arbitrators was endorsed in the English High Court and Court of Appeal. However, at final appeal, the House of Lords found for the charterers, holding that they should be liable to pay damages only for the much lower "nine days' difference" loss.

In reaching his decision, Lord Hoffmann adopted an "assumption of responsibility" test described by Baroness Hale[33] as follows:

> one must ask, not only whether the parties must be taken to have had this type of loss within their contemplation when the contract was made, but also whether they must be taken to have had *liability for* this type of loss within their contemplation then. In other words, is the charterer to be taken to have undertaken legal responsibility for this type of loss?[34]

The case is an interesting example of the occasional tension between legal principle and "custom of the trade". It has, indeed, been argued that if courts divorce themselves from trade practice the will "lose business" to more pragmatic alternative dispute resolution. It is perhaps ironic that, in *Transfield*, the majority arbitrators favoured legal principle while the highest law court favoured trade practice.

It is questionable whether Lord Hoffmann's approach represents the majority House of Lords view, with other law lords upholding the appeal on more conservative grounds.[35] Certainly, subsequent English cases have indicated that *Transfield* should be limited to its special circumstances.[36]

Following the rejection of "assumption" of responsibility by the Singapore courts,[37] it can also be seen that Lord Hoffmann's formulation was treated somewhat dismissively by the Privy Council in the following case:

Attorney-General of the Virgin Islands v Global Water Associates Ltd[38]

Global Water (GW), the appellants had two interconnected contracts with the Government of the British Virgin Islands (BVI). GW were to "design and build" a

---

33. Baroness Hale was unconvinced by the Hoffmann argument (which she believed had the potential to cause uncertainty) and confessed that her initial disposition was to find for the owners.
34. *Transfield* at para 92.
35. Lord Hope shared Lord Hoffmann's view. The Hong Kong Court of Final Appeal accepted (despite academic views to the contrary) that Lord Walker also supported the "assumption of responsibility" test. Curiously, while numerous comments were made by the CFA as to the view of Lord Walker, he himself, despite being present as an NPJ, merely concurred!
36. See *Sylvia Shipping Co Ltd v Progress Bulk Carriers Ltd* [2010] EWHC 542; *Grimes v Gubbins* 2013 EWCA Civ 37. Moreover, the Hoffmann test has been rejected (in favour of the less uncertain *Hadley* test) in Singapore: *MFM Restaurants v Fish & Co Restaurants* [2010] SGCA 36.
37. See n 35 above.
38. [2020] UKPC 18.

water reclamation plant and, thereafter, to manage[39] the plant. The BVI promised to provide a suitable site, which they failed to do. The breach was clear but arbitrators and the BVI Court of Appeal felt that loss resulting from failure of the management contract was too remote. While surprised that the two contracts had not initially have been conjoined, the Privy Council nonetheless found the loss of management "not unlikely" and clearly recoverable. Significantly, the Privy Council's focus was on three traditional cases: *Hadley, Victoria Laundry*, and *Heron II*. Lord Hodge, for the Court, expressed a preference for "serious possibility" rather than "probability" for the remoteness test in contract. He went on:

> The Board is not concerned in this appeal with the recoverability of damages caused by unusual volatility in the market . . . addressed in (*"The Achilleas"*) in which Lord Hoffmann and Lord Hope . . . sought to bring into play the concept of assumption of responsibility. . . . it is clear that the losses resulting from an inability to earn profits from the MOMA were within the reasonable contemplation of the parties to the DBA when they made that contract. First, the contracts were entered into between the same parties on the same day and they both related to the same Plant on the same site, giving rise to special knowledge under the second limb of the rule in *Hadley v Baxendale*.

It is somewhat ironic, therefore, given its lukewarm reception elsewhere, that Lord Hoffmann's view has been enthusiastically adopted by Hong Kong's Court of Final Appeal (CFA) in *De Monsa Investments Ltd v Richly Bright International Ltd*.[40] The case involved the assessment of damages for breach of a "chain" sale and purchase agreement. All five members of the CFA adopted Lord Hoffmann's "assumption of responsibility" test, concluding that:

> it could not fairly be said that De Monsa had undertaken responsibility for the chain default.[41]

15.1.3 *Injury to Feelings and Reputation*

As a general principle, there may be no recovery of damages for injury to feelings, or loss of reputation. This may be viewed as a particular aspect of remoteness but is more generally considered to be a "policy" restriction on the amount of damages to be awarded. As a matter of policy the courts have said that, in general, damages for distress and disappointment are not available though there are a number of exceptions to the general rule. Similarly, there has been a reluctance to allow recovery for mere injury to the plaintiff's reputation though, where it can be proved that such injury has resulted in financial loss to the plaintiff, such loss is recoverable.

---

39. The design contract was described as DBA and the management one as MOMA.
40. (2015) 18 HKCFAR 232.
41. Per Tang PJ at para 134.

15.1.3.1 Distress and Disappointment

As a general rule, damages are not recoverable for distress and disappointment caused by the defendant's breach of contract. This is so however likely distress and disappointment are to result from the defendant's breach. The general rule was established by the House of Lords in the following case.

Addis v Gramophone Co Ltd[42]

The plaintiff was wrongly dismissed by the defendants and sued. The House of Lords upheld his claim for loss of salary and commission but held he was not entitled to compensation for loss of reputation or mental distress. The court made clear that, in contract cases at least, there should be no compensation for emotional as opposed to financial loss. Lord Atkinson stated:

> In many other cases of breach of contract there may be circumstances of malice, fraud, defamation, or violence, which would sustain an action of tort as an alternative remedy to an action for breach of contract. If one should select the former mode of redress, he may, no doubt, recover exemplary damages, or what is sometimes styled vindictive damages; but if he should choose to seek redress in the form of an action for breach of contract, he lets in all the consequences of that form of action: *Thorpe v Thorpe*. One of these consequences is, I think, this: that he is to be paid adequate compensation in money for the loss of that which he would have received had his contract been kept, and no more.[43]

In such cases the issue is not how much compensation to award for emotional loss but that the loss is not to be compensated at all. The principle of restricting compensation in this way appears unsatisfactory in cases where the mental element (enjoyment etc) is a major feature of the contract. Exceptions to the general rule were first introduced, then, in the so-called "holiday cases". Typically, a holiday provider would supply a substandard product, much to the frustration and disappointment of the customer. Merely to compensate the plaintiff on the basis of "difference in value"[44] would not adequately compensate for the fact that the plaintiff may have looked forward to, and saved up for, this holiday for many months; expected a pleasurable rather than a frustrating experience; and be unable to take another holiday for a considerable time.

Jarvis v Swans Tours Ltd[45]

The defendants provided a substandard skiing holiday for the plaintiff. The defendants had promised a "house-party" atmosphere with lively entertainment and very

---

42. [1909] AC 488.
43. Ibid at 504.
44. See 15.1.4.2 below.
45. [1973] QB 233, [1972] 3 WLR 954, [1973] 1 All ER 71.

convenient ski-hire facilities. In fact, the plaintiff was the only guest in his second week and full-length skis were generally unavailable. The Court of Appeal held that the plaintiff was entitled to damages for disappointment in addition to those for difference in value.

The court took the view that compensation for the purely financial loss resulting from the breach would be inadequate in such cases. Lord Denning MR said:

> In a proper case damages for mental distress can be recovered in contract, just as damages for shock can be recovered in tort. One such case is a contract for a holiday, or any other contract to provide entertainment and enjoyment. If the contracting party breaks his contract, damages can be given for the disappointment, the distress, the upset and frustration caused by the breach. I know that it is difficult to assess in terms of money, but it is no more difficult than the assessment which the courts have to make every day in personal injury cases for loss of amenities. Take the present case Mr Jarvis has only a fortnight's holiday in the year. He books it far ahead, and looks forward to it all that time. He ought to be compensated for the loss of it.[46]

The case has been followed in various "holiday cases"[47] and in even more deserving "once in a lifetime" situations. So, for example, disappointment damages have been awarded against a photographer in breach of a contract to provide wedding photographs;[48] a car hire company which failed to provide promised transport to a wedding ceremony;[49] a solicitors' firm which promised to prevent a client's harassment by a former boyfriend but actually made things worse;[50] and, even more seriously, a solicitors' firm whose negligence facilitated the removal from the jurisdiction, by her husband, of the plaintiff's children.[51] The Hong Kong courts have adopted a similarly "flexible" approach to damages for distress.

Ronald Claud Hardwick & Another v Spence Robinson[52]

The plaintiffs employed the defendants to design their house near the sea and to supervise construction. The system designed was inadequate and, as a result, the plaintiffs suffered serious damage by flooding. The plaintiffs' action for damages, to include compensation for mental distress, was upheld in the Hong Kong High Court.

---

46. [1972] 3 WLR 954 at 957–958.
47. Prior to this case, holiday companies in England had been notorious for making extravagant claims in their brochures. On the rare occasions that customers sued they received only relatively small awards based on the difference in value between what had been promised and what had been delivered. The *Jarvis* case, and others which followed, permitted distress and disappointment damages to be awarded, often in excess of the contract price. The result was a considerable reduction in the amount of excessive brochure claims.
48. *Diesen v Samson* (1971) SLT (Sh Ct) 49.
49. *Cole v Rana* [1993] 5 CL 114.
50. *Heywood v Wellers (A Firm)* [1976] QB 446, [1976] 2 WLR 101, [1976] 1 All ER 300.
51. *Hamilton Jones v David & Snape* [2004] 1 All ER 657.
52. [1975] HKLR 425.

The trial judge, Cons J, decided that the case was within the scope of the exceptions newly recognised in the English courts. He said:

> I was asked to include in the damages something to compensate for the mental distress of the plaintiffs, i.e. the shock occasioned at the time of the floodings, particularly that of the 2nd May, and for the fear and natural apprehension at having to live for some time in a house liable to be flooded in heavy rain. The claim is based on the recent case of *Jarvis v Swan Tours Ltd*. There damages for disappointment were awarded when the actual conditions found on a packaged holiday house party in Switzerland bore little or no relation to the glowing promises of the brochure. It is clear from the judgment given that what might be termed the mental element may be a relevant consideration in future assessment of damages . . . I have not found this an easy matter to decide but have eventually come to the conclusion that the circumstances do justify an award under this head. It was not a purely commercial contract, like for example a contract to design a block of flats. It was a contract with a very personal flavour. Therein I think is the distinction upon which those cases are based.[53]

It should be emphasised that all the above examples given are exceptions to a general rule that damages for distress and disappointment are not to be awarded. That there is no general availability for such damages merely because distress or disappointment are a "natural and probable" consequence of the defendant's breach has been stressed by the courts. In *Bliss v SE Thames RHA*,[54] a case involving the unfair dismissal of a surgeon, the Court of Appeal rejected the trial judge's contention that damages for distress could be awarded merely because they were a probable consequence of the employer's breach. Dillon LJ stated:

> The general rule laid down by the House of Lords in *Addis v Gramophone Co. Ltd.* [1909] A.C. 488 is that where damages fall to be assessed for breach of contract rather than in tort it is not permissible to award general damages for frustration, mental distress, injured feelings or annoyance occasioned by the breach . . .
>
> There are exceptions now recognised where the contract which has been broken was itself a contract to provide peace of mind or freedom from distress: see *Jarvis v Swans Tours Ltd.* [1973] QB 233 and *Heywood v Wellers* [1976] QB 446. Those decisions do not, however, cover the present case.[55]

It is doubtful whether the *Ronald Claud Hardwick* case would fall within the above exceptions. However, it would fall within the other recognised exception; namely that where a breach results in physical injury or discomfort, damages can be

---

53. Ibid at 435.
54. [1985] IRLR 308, 1987 ICR 700.
55. [1985] IRLR 308 at 316. Reinforced by *Hayes v Dodd* [1990] 2 All ER 815.

recovered for the distress *caused by* such physical loss.[56] This is one interpretation of the following case.

Farley v Skinner[57]

The claimant wanted to buy a quiet house in the country. He specifically asked the defendant, a surveyor who inspected the property for him, whether it was likely to be affected by aircraft noise. The defendant negligently answered that it was unlikely that aircraft noise would be a significant problem. In fact, as the defendant should have known, the house was on a major flight path. The claimant bought the property and spent a great deal on modernisation. After moving in he discovered the serious noise problem but decided not to sell. He sought damages for difference in value *and* disappointment. He was held entitled to both.

The House of Lords, overruling the Court of Appeal, upheld the trial judge's view that damages for disappointment were appropriate in this case; even though peace of mind was not the sole purpose of the contract and despite the fact that the surveyor had not "guaranteed" it. The award of damages for non-pecuniary loss here can be viewed as being based on disappointment in respect of a contract to provide peace of mind or compensation for distress resulting from physical inconvenience caused by the defendant's breach.

Lord Steyn, in the *Farley* case, expressed the view that non-pecuniary awards should be restrained and that courts should not encourage a "society bent on litigation". Such "policy" considerations are implicit in *Wiseman v Virgin Atlantic Airways Ltd*[58] where the claimant was refused boarding and falsely accused of criminality (very publicly!) by the defendants. The English court refused to allow damages for distress in a situation that was viewed as not within the *Bliss* exception.[59] Nevertheless, in the "once in a lifetime" cases, such as ruined weddings, disappointment damages can be substantial and may well exceed the contract price payable by the claimant.

15.1.3.2 Damages for Loss of Reputation

The basic principle, established in *Addis v Gramophone Co Ltd*,[60] is that damages are not available merely for injury to reputation. However, where the injury to reputation

---

56. See, for example, *Perry v Sidney Phillips & Son* [1982] 1 WLR 1287, [1982] 1 All ER 1005. Distinguished in *Watts & Another v Morrow* [1991] 1 WLR 1421 where there was no preceding physical loss caused by D's breach.
57. [2001] 4 All ER 801.
58. [2006] EWHC 1566.
59. Presumably, had he been about to board to a holiday destination he would have been entitled to distress damages for his ruined holiday!
60. [1909] AC 488 and see above 15.1.3.1.

leads directly to financial loss, damages can be awarded for such loss.[61] The *Addis* principle was doubted in *Johnson v Unysis Ltd*[62] and "distinguished" in the "stigma damages" cases, discussed below.

Malik v BCCI SA (in liquidation)[63]

The two appellants were long-standing employees of the infamous BCCI bank, which had collapsed with enormous debts as a result of massive fraud perpetrated by its senior officers. The liquidators then made redundant the appellants who had great difficulty in obtaining alternative employment given the "stigma" of association with such a notorious bank. The appellants sued for compensation for the loss they argued had resulted from their diminished reputation. The Court of Appeal rejected their claims stating that, on the basis of *Addis*, no compensation was available for loss of reputation or for the resulting loss of re-employment opportunities. The House of Lords overturned this decision and upheld the appellant's appeal. It was stated that in appropriate cases damages could be awarded for loss of reputation and for resulting financial loss. *Addis* was distinguished since that was a case of wrongful dismissal whereas *Malik* involved a breach by the employer of an implied obligation of trust and confidence.[64] It was implicit that the employers would not conduct a dishonest business and, having failed to do so, they should compensate employees for the consequences

The court stressed that the decision was unlikely to produce large numbers of new cases since there would always be the problem of proving that stigma actually resulted from the defendant employer's breach *and* in proving that any resulting stigma was the cause of a subsequent diminution in job opportunities.[65]

15.1.4 Measure of Damages

Given that loss caused by the defendant's breach is not too remote and is, therefore, compensable, the next question is how the plaintiff's damages are to be assessed. The *almost* universal principle in contract is that damages are to *compensate*. The conduct of the defendant, however greedy or immoral, is irrelevant since it is loss to the plaintiff not gain to the defendant which has to be considered. For this reason, if the plaintiff has suffered no loss as a result of the defendant's breach, only "nominal" damages can be awarded.

---

61. See *Aerial Advertising v Batchelors Peas Ltd (Manchester)* [1938] 2 All ER 788; *GKN Centrax Gears Ltd v Matbro Ltd* [1976] 2 Lloyd's Rep 555.
62. [2001] UKHL 13.
63. *Malik v BCCI SA (in liquidation)/Mahmud v BCCI SA (in liquidation)* [1998] AC 20. See also *BCCI v Ali (No 2)* [2002] EWCA Civ 82.
64. Damages for breach of such an implied obligation were awarded by the Hong Kong Court of Appeal in the *Bachicha* case, discussed below at 15.1.4.5.
65. Ultimately these factors precluded the recovery of damages by the *Malik* appellants.

15.1.4.1 Nominal Damages . . . or "Negotiating Damages"?

The rule that a claimant who has suffered no loss is restricted to nominal damages is almost absolute though it has been challenged in two exceptional English cases. The first case is *Wrotham Park Estate Co Ltd v Parkside Homes Ltd*.[66] Here, the defendants, in breach of a restrictive covenant in their contract with the plaintiffs, built excessive homes on a plot. The plaintiffs, who suffered no loss as a result, sought a mandatory injunction[67] compelling the demolition of the houses. For obvious socio-economic reasons the courts refused an order which would destroy valuable homes. Instead, damages were awarded in lieu of injunction (so-called equitable damages). While the defendants had benefitted greatly from their breach, the plaintiffs had suffered no loss. However, the court found a way to award substantial damages by awarding an amount equivalent to the notional amount which the plaintiffs would have charged for relaxing the restrictive covenant had they been asked to do so.

While the outcome in *Wrotham* appears reasonable it is clearly artificial and, in fact, an example of compelling some "restitution" of ill-gotten gains. In very similar circumstances, in *Surrey County Council v Bredero Homes*,[68] the court refused to award substantial damages to a plaintiff local authority which had suffered no loss as a result of the defendants' overbuilding. The point of distinction was that, since the *Bredero* plaintiffs did not first seek a mandatory injunction (a local authority could scarcely seek the destruction of homes) any damages would have to be "common law" rather than equitable ones. The distinction seems hard to justify and *Bredero* has been criticised both by academics and in the second "exceptional" case, *Her Majesty's Attorney-General v Blake*.[69] In *Blake*'s case, the defendant had been employed as a member of the British Secret Intelligence Service for 17 years. During that time, he became a "double agent" working for the Soviet Union. The information he gave to the Soviet Union did great damage to British interests. He was convicted of spying in 1961 and sentenced to a lengthy term of imprisonment but escaped to Moscow five years later. In 1990 a book was published which told his story. By this time none of the information in the book was confidential or damaging. On behalf of the British "Crown", the claimant sought restitutionary damages to ensure that the defendant did not profit from his treachery. The claim was successful.

This was, of course, a very extreme test of the "compensation only" principle, since Blake was seeking to profit from actions that were not merely a serious breach of contract and a breach of his employee's "fiduciary" duty but also seriously criminal. It is hardly surprising that the House of Lords felt that in such a case the defendant should be made to give up or "disgorge" any profits obtained by reference to his criminal exploits. The case, however, should not be seen as more than a rare

---

66. [1974] 2 All ER 321, [1974] 1 WLR 798.
67. See 15.2.2 below.
68. [1993] 3 All ER 705.
69. [2000] 4 All ER 385.

exception to the principle that damages for breach of contract are to be compensatory rather than punitive.

In three subsequent decisions, *Experience Hendrix LLC v PPX Enterprises Inc*,[70] *WWF-World Wide Fund for Nature v World Wrestling Federation Entertainment Inc*,[71] and *Morris-Garner & Another v One Step (Support) Ltd*,[72] the English Court of Appeal has preferred the *Wrotham* approach to that in the *Bredero* case. The effect of these subsequent cases is that damages may be awarded at *common law* for breaches of a negative covenant on the basis of compensation assessed in terms of what the claimant would, notionally, have charged for relaxation of the restriction. In both the *Hendrix* and *WWF* cases injunctions had been granted to prevent further breaches but in the *WWF* case, Chadwick LJ (*obiter*) felt that compensation should not be dependent on whether or not an injunction had been sought.[73] *Bredero*, therefore, should be regarded as a "disapproved" decision in England. It appears that the *Wrotham/Hendrix/WWF* approach is to be applied in Hong Kong. Indeed, the approach seems to have been extended in *Choy Nga Wai Nancy v Gentle Smart Ltd & Another*.[74] Here, the defendants were in breach of a sale and purchase agreement, for $2.78 million, with the plaintiff who sought damages. Prior to the action the property had been sold at auction as the defendants had a secured debt. The auction price was $3.3 million. The court allowed, as part of the plaintiff's damages, half of the additional sale price as a "disgorging" of profits. This was despite the court's finding that, had the plaintiff sought specific performance promptly, the auction would have been avoided. The decision seems a significant extension of the *Wrotham* approach which was, nominally at least, based on the plaintiff's loss (the loss of the potential charge for relaxing the restriction) while, in *Choy Nga*, the focus seems to have been profit to the defendant.

The UK Supreme Court made very large inroads into the "*Wrotham*" approach in the following case, in which Lord Reed described *Wrotham* as being of "*little more than historical interest.*"

Morris-Garner & Another v One Step (Support) Ltd[75]

The parties entered into an agreement under which the defendant (Morris-Garner) sold its share of a joint business to the claimant (One Step) and, as is common in such situations, covenanted not to compete. In breach of the covenant, the defendant

---

70. [2003] EWCA Civ 323.
71. [2007] EWCA Civ 286.
72. [2016] EWCA Civ 180 where the principle seems to have been abandoned that *Wrotham* damages are available only where no direct economic loss can be shown. The Court of Appeal has now been overruled on this point! [2018] UKSC 20.
73. That view was endorsed in the UK Privy Council in *Pell Frischmann v Bow Valley Iran Ltd* [2009] UKPC 45.
74. [2009] 4 HKLRD 633.
75. [2018] UKSC 20.

did, in fact, compete and the claimant sought damages for breach. The trial judge, upheld by the Court of Appeal, allowed the claimant to choose whether to seek "normal" loss of bargain damages or "*Wrotham*" ones.

The Supreme Court upheld the view that the defendant was in breach and the claimant should be awarded damages. However, having surveyed all the relevant cases, it confirmed that:

1. "*Wrotham Park*" damages should now be termed "negotiating damages";[76]
2. Such damages are *not* an alternative to loss of bargain damages . . . and the latter should *normally* be awarded (irrespective of calculation difficulties);
3. The claimant has *no choice* as to the type of damages to be awarded, it is entirely a matter for the court;[77]
4. Negotiating damages should only be awarded in *exceptional* cases (such as breach of confidence, intellectual property infringements and breach of restrictive covenants over land[78] . . . all categories which, in fact, had already been the subject of successful *Wrotham* claims);
5. Negotiating damages are compensatory . . . they compensate for wrongful denial of negotiating rights;
6. It is irrelevant that the claimant would never, in fact, have negotiated (as in *Wrotham* itself, where the claimants were determined to maintain a low plot ratio).

In conclusion, the UK Supreme Court determined that normal compensatory damages should be awarded by the trial judge and remitted the case back to him for calculation of damages.

What remains unclear post–*Morris-Garner* are the circumstances in which the negotiating damages principle may be engaged. Lord Reed gave examples, but these appear not to have been intended as an exhaustive list.[79]

Where does this leave Hong Kong, given the previous endorsement of *Wrotham* and "plaintiff's choice", and given the non-binding status of *Morris-Garner*? It is not possible entirely to reconcile *Morris-Garner* with the earlier Nancy Choy case. There, Mak DDJ had said:

---

76. A term previously coined by Neuberger LJ (as he then was) in *Lunn Poly Ltd v Liverpool & Lancashire Properties Ltd* [2006] EWCA Civ 430.
77. This abolition of the claimant's choice challenges, it has been argued, the previous "claimant's election" in relation to "reliance" loss. This would, indeed, be a "sidewind" of epic proportions; see Jonathan Chew, "Wrotham Out: Negotiating Damages after *One Step v Morris-Garner*" (2018) *Conveyancing & Property Lawyer: Case Comment.*
78. And see *Alexander Devine Children's Cancer Trust v Housing Solutions Ltd.* [2020] UKSC 45.
79. See *Priyanka Shipping Ltd v Glory Bulk Carriers PTE Ltd* [2019] EWHC 2804 (Comm), a case involving a failed attempt to invoke negotiating damages where the buyer of a ship, agreed to be for "scrap", decided, instead, to "trade" (sail) the vessel.

> *Wrotham Park* damages are not restricted to cases which concern breaches of a restrictive covenant or infringement of property rights, and are generally available for breach of a contractual obligation . . .
>
>   Though there is apparently no precedent in Hong Kong for *Wrotham Park* damages to be awarded and assessed by way of a percentage disgorgement of the contract breaker's benefits, I find such an approach a natural and logical development of a principle already embraced by the Hong Kong Courts.[80]

Of course, Mak DDJ had not had the benefit of considering the UK Supreme Court's view in *Morris-Garner* and, to date, no other Hong Kong court has done so.[81]

15.1.4.2 Loss of Bargain

In assessing damages courts normally make an award intended to put the plaintiff in the position he would have been if the contract had been fulfilled. Contract damages thus look forward, in contrast to tort damages. To use the simple example illustrated by the *Victoria Laundry*[82] case: had the contract been fulfilled and the plaintiffs received the new boiler on time, they would have received an extra five months' increased production; the loss of such production should therefore be recoverable.[83] The normal measure of damages, then, is "loss of bargain". This, in itself, may be considered in two different ways; "difference in value" or "cost of cure". "Difference in value" is calculated by determining what the plaintiff should have received, discovering what he actually received, and assessing the monetary difference between the two. "Cost of cure" is calculated by determining what the plaintiff should have received, identifying any differences or deficiencies in what he actually received, and assessing the cost of remedying the differences or deficiencies. In some cases, the two approaches may yield very different amounts of damages. An illustration is provided in the following, much-discussed case.

Ruxley Electronics and Construction Ltd v Forsyth[84]

The plaintiffs contracted to build a swimming pool for the defendant with a depth of seven feet six inches (for diving). In fact, they built one which was only six feet deep, though deep enough for safe diving. In the subsequent dispute over payment, the Court of Appeal held that the defendant was entitled to the "cost of cure" (over £20,000), but the House of Lords, reinstating the trial judge's finding, preferred the much lower figure produced by the "difference in value" approach.

---

80. At paras 37 and 41.
81. *Morris-Garner* was considered by Master Benny Lo in *Million Add Development Ltd v Nok Wah Logistic (Hong Kong) Co Ltd* [2018] 1 HKLRD 636 . . . but only up to the Court of Appeal decision.
82. [1949] 2 KB 528, [1949] 1 All ER 997; and see 15.1.2 above.
83. Though not, it was held, the loss of an exceptionally lucrative contract.
84. [1995] 3 All ER 268.

The dispute in this case was not about whether there had been a breach but as to the amount or "quantum" of damages. From the customer's point of view, it can be said that he wanted a deeper pool, made clear what he wanted and should be entitled to such a pool or the compensation allowing him to obtain one. From the defendants' point of view, the argument is that building a deeper pool involves major reconstruction and excessive cost.

If the claimant is only to receive "difference" in value damages, his compensation will be minimal since, objectively, a shallower pool is hardly less valuable than a deeper one. The court may not, of course award greater damages merely because the defendant has ignored instructions; the basis should be compensation not punishment. However, despite the fact that the court imposed the lower "difference in value" (in fact, zero in the court's view) approach, it did add an extra sum for "loss of amenity" which is, essentially, a form of disappointment damages in respect of a contract which was intended to bring enjoyment to the claimant. Lord Jauncey stated:

> if a building was constructed so defectively that it was of no use for its designed purpose the owner might have little difficulty in establishing that his loss was the necessary cost of reconstructing.[85]
>
> ... However, where the contractual objective had been achieved to a substantial extent the position might be very different.
>
> ... The trial judge had found that it would be unreasonable to incur the cost of demolishing the existing pool and building a new and deeper one. In so doing he implicitly recognised that the householder's loss did not extend to the cost of reinstatement. He was entirely justified in reaching that conclusion.[86]

The trial judge's view on reasonableness seems to have been coloured by the assumption that, were the claimant to receive cost of cure damages, he would retain this and not reconstruct the pool. However, by the time the case reached the Court of Appeal, the claimant was prepared to give an undertaking that reconstruction would take place. This was not enough to sway the House of Lords where Lord Lloyd asked:

> Does Mr Forsyth's undertaking to spend any damages which he may receive on rebuilding the pool make any difference? Clearly not. He cannot be allowed to create a loss which does not exist in order to punish the defendants for their breach of contract. The basic rule of damages ... is that they are compensatory not punitive.[87]

---

85. *A fortiori* where promised construction is not effected at all: *Radford v De Froberville* [1977] 1 WLR 1262.
86. [1995] 3 All ER 268 at 275.
87. Ibid at 288. Yet the question of whether or not the claimant would affect the cure *was* held relevant in *Birse Construction Ltd v Eastern Telegraph Co Ltd* [2004] EWHC 2512.

It seems, therefore, that the court was concerned with excessive loss to the builder rather than improper gain to the customer.

The *Ruxley* decision has been the subject of much debate. Critics argue that it is a charter for service providers prepared to cut corners and provide an inferior service. A customer may stipulate pink tiles, but if blue tiles are easier to source, they may be used instead. Provided they are not seen as reducing the value of the service objectively the customer's preference may be ignored almost with impunity since no "difference in value" occurs. It has been pointed out that, unlike businesses, individual consumers may specify goods or services of a particular nature even though, in pure monetary terms, the specific requirement is of no greater value than the supplier's substitute; Mr Forsyth specified a seven-foot-six-inch depth because, as Ruxley's knew, *that is what, as a consumer*, he wanted. In this context, some writers talk of the "consumer surplus" and this expression was used by Lord Mustill in *Ruxley*. The consumer surplus was compensated in *Ruxley* by the award of "loss of amenity" damages but it is questionable whether such damages could be awarded in respect of a contract to provide something less "pleasurable" than a swimming pool.[88] This is implicit in Lord Lloyd's statement that,

> (the trial judge) . . . took the view that the contract was one "for the provision of a pleasurable amenity". In the event, Mr Forsyth's pleasure was not so great as it would have been if the swimming pool had been 7 ft 6 in deep . . . That was a view which the judge was entitled to take.[89]

15.1.4.3 Reliance Loss

An alternative method of assessing damages, much less often used than "loss of bargain", is "reliance" loss. Here the objective of the damages award is to return to the plaintiff those sums expended on the basis that the defendant would fulfil his side of the bargain. The following is the leading English authority.

Anglia Television Ltd v Reed[90]

The defendant was contracted to star in a televised play for the plaintiffs but, in breach, pulled out too late for the plaintiffs to find a replacement. In the Court of Appeal, the plaintiffs succeeded, on the defendant's admitted breach, in obtaining an award based on "reliance" loss.

The defendant did not dispute his liability, nor the recovery of reliance loss. However, his team argued that expenditure incurred *before* Mr Reed agreed to

---

88. See 15.1.3.1.
89. [1995] 3 All ER 268 at 289. Contrast *Birse Construction Ltd v Eastern Telegraph Co Ltd* [2004] EWHC 2512.
90. [1972] 1 QB 60, [1971] 3 ALL ER 690, [1971] 3 WLR 528.

perform could not be recovered since it was not the result of reliance on him. The court disagreed. Lord Denning MR said:

> (Mr Reed) did not dispute his liability, but a question arose as to the damages. Anglia Television do not claim their profit. They cannot say what their profit would have been on this contract if Mr Reed had come here and performed it. So, instead of claim for loss or profits, they claim for the wasted expenditure . . . Anglia Television say that all the money was wasted because Mr Reed did not perform his contract.
>
> Mr Reed's advisers take a point of law. They submit that Anglia Television cannot recover for expenditure incurred *before* the contract was concluded with Mr Reed. They can only recover the expenditure *after* the contract was concluded . . .
>
> . . . If the plaintiff claims the wasted expenditure, he is not limited to the expenditure incurred *after* the contract was concluded. He can claim also the expenditure incurred *before* the contract, provided that it was such as would reasonably be in the contemplation of the parties as likely to be wasted if the contract was broken. Applying that principle here, it is plain that, when Mr Reed entered into this contract, he must have known perfectly well that much expenditure had already been incurred on director's fees and the like. He must have contemplated—or, at any rate, it is reasonably to be imputed to him—that if he broke his contract, all that expenditure would be wasted, whether or not it was incurred before or after the contract.[91]

Reliance loss assessment may be claimed by the plaintiff in preference to loss of bargain assessment. Essentially, if the innocent party has made a good bargain which the other has broken, the claim should be based on loss of bargain. Alternatively, if the innocent party has made what may have been a bad bargain and the other has (foolishly) broken it, a claim for reliance loss is preferable. A plaintiff's discretion as to the choice of assessment is almost total.[92] However, if the defendant can show clearly (and the onus of proof is on him) that the bargain was a bad one for the claimant, the claimant will be restricted to loss of bargain damages which will, of course, be nominal.

Reliance loss may also be more appropriate in cases where the loss of bargain approach would involve impossible speculation. In such cases the court itself may insist on a reliance approach. In the curious case of *McRae v Commonwealth Disposals Commission*,[93] the Australian High Court refused loss of bargain damages which would have involved speculation as to how much oil should have been aboard a tanker which was found never to have existed! The court instead allowed recovery of money spent looking for the tanker, in reliance on an implied term as to its existence.

The reliance approach may have relevance to the issue of privity (see chapter 16) in respect of the promisee's rights where the promisor fails to fulfil a reciprocal

---

91. [1971] 3 WLR 528 at 530–531.
92. *CCC Films (London) Ltd. v Impact Quadrant Films Ltd* [1985] QB 16, [1984] 3 All ER 298.
93. (1951) 84 CLR 377 and see 10.3.

promise to pay money to a third party. Suppose that X promises to give T $10,000 if Y will do the same. Y pays the money and X reneges. The third party cannot sue of course at common law. This remains the case in Hong Kong for contracts made before the coming into force of the Contract (Rights of Third Parties Ordinance;[94] although legislation has now made significant inroads into the privity principle. The promisee may, of course, sue since he is party to the contract and has provided consideration. It is generally assumed, however, that he may recover only nominal damages since he has suffered no loss from the promisor's default; the loss is T's. However, on a reliance basis it is possible to argue that Y should be able to recover what he has paid out in reliance on X's contractual promise.

15.1.4.4 Restitutionary Damages

The purpose of restitutionary awards is to compel the defendant to give back what he has received. Restitution is intended to prevent "unjust enrichment". In contract, the general principle is that restitution is available only where there has been a total failure of consideration. Thus, a buyer who has paid for goods will be entitled to a return of the price where no goods have been delivered. Treitel writes:

> A claim for restitution is not strictly one for "damages" since its purpose is not to compensate the claimant for a loss, but to deprive the defendant of a benefit.[95]

In practice, the restoration of what the defendant has received will also, generally, compensate the claimant at the same time. The *focus* of restitution, however, is gain to the defendant rather than loss to the claimant. In exceptional cases, such as *Blake*,[96] where the claimant suffered no loss from the defendant's breach, a restitutionary award produced a very different result from a compensatory one.

15.1.4.5 Speculative Damages

Although damages are generally intended to compensate the claimant, a precise calculation of loss is sometimes impossible. This is particularly the case where the defendant's breach has caused the plaintiff to lose a "chance" which may, or may not, have come to fruition. In *Chaplin v Hicks*,[97] the defendants organised a beauty contest to choose 12 winners who were to be employed by the defendants. The 12 were to be selected at audition from 50 women selected by readers of certain newspapers. All the women had previously paid money to the defendants to enter the competition. The plaintiff was one of the 50 selected and the defendants promised to

---

94. See chapter 16.
95. Treitel (op cit) at p 1127.
96. See 15.1.4.1.
97. [1911] 2 KB 786.

invite her to audition but failed to do so in time. She sued for loss of a "chance" and her action succeeded. The defendants did not deny liability but argued they should pay only nominal damages since any loss to the plaintiff was merely speculative. The Court of Appeal held that, although it could not be said that she would have won, her *chance* to do so was lost and the court must put a value on it.

At first sight this approach seems to contradict the principle that the defendant is only liable for the *probable* consequences of his breach; the plaintiff in *Chaplin* only had a 24% chance of winning. However, the court's view was that the chance itself is something of value and it, of course, had definitely been lost as a result of the defendant's breach. Once this is established the court must speculate as to the value of the chance; the fact that some guesswork is involved does not preclude the court from attempting to make a valuation. The alternative, of awarding only nominal damages, would mean that a defendant in a *Chaplin* scenario would be able to renege on all 50 invitations and be liable to pay only nominal damages in every case.

The *Chaplin v Hicks* approach to speculative damages was applied in Hong Kong in the case of *Bachicha v Poon Shiu Man Henry*.[98] Here, the plaintiff was a domestic helper constructively dismissed by her employer in a manner constituting a breach of the "implied duty of trust". The fact that the plaintiff had been dismissed *and* that her employer had falsely accused her of walking out on her job, made the plaintiff's chances of finding alternative employment very slim under Hong Kong's "14-day rule".[99] The Court of Appeal awarded damages based on the plaintiff's "loss of a chance to secure earnings".

15.1.4.6 Liquidated Damages

The court will avoid the task of calculating the claimant's loss in cases where there is a "liquidated damages clause" in the contract concerned. A liquidated damages clause is a term in a contract which stipulates the amount which will be paid by the party in breach. The benefit of such a clause is that, in cases of dispute, a court need only determine the issue of liability and need not address the issue of "quantum". Moreover, since many disputes involve arguments over quantum rather than liability, the practical effect of liquidated damages clauses is that many cases do not go to court which otherwise would do. As such, the courts encourage such clauses. The approach of the courts is that, as long as the clause is seen as a genuine attempt to pre-estimate the likely loss to be occasioned by a breach, it will be upheld. The innocent party in such cases is entitled to the amount fixed by the contract; no more

---

98. [2000] 3 HKC 452.
99. Dismissed (or out-of-contract) domestic helpers are repatriated if unable to find alternative employment within 14 days of termination. In practice, a dismissed helper accused of abandoning her post would have little chance of finding a new employer.

and no less. A straightforward illustration of the liquidated damages principle is to be found in the following case.

Luen Yick Co v Tang Man Kee Machinery Workshop[100]

The parties made a contract for the sale and purchase of a machine and, in breach of contract, the defendants delivered late. The contract provided for the payment of $150 per day as compensation for delay. The plaintiffs' claim for a further $12,490 compensation was rejected in the Hong Kong High Court.

After dealing with the simple issue of the return of the plaintiffs' deposit and part payment, Reece J added:

> there still remains for consideration the amount of $10,350 claimed as liquidated damages and the (further) claim for $12,490 . . . I allow damages at the rate of $150 per day from the 6th February to the 16th April, 1958, amounting to $10,350 as liquidated damages . . .
> . . . I am of the opinion that the plaintiffs are not entitled to recover these two sums totalling $12,490 beyond the amount of the liquidated damages allowed. I take the view that when the parties to the contract fixed the sum of $150 a day as compensation for every day of delay beyond the agreed date they meant that the *only* damages to be incurred were $150 per day.[101]

There are situations, however, where the court takes the view that a clause is not intended as a genuine pre-estimate of loss but seeks to *punish* the party in breach or to frighten him into complying with the requirements of the contract. Since the fundamental principle of contractual damages is compensation, punitive clauses, described as "penalties", are not countenanced. Where a clause is viewed as a penalty rather than liquidated damages, it will be ignored and the innocent party will have his damages assessed according to the normal principles. The distinction between liquidated damages and penalties is, therefore, a crucial one. The most important guidelines on the distinction are to be found in *Dunlop Pneumatic Tyre Co Ltd v New Garage & Motor Co Ltd*.[102] The facts were that the appellants sold their products to the respondents subject to certain restrictions including the requirement that the latter did not resell under a stated price. If they did, they were to pay "liquidated damages". In a subsequent dispute, arising from a resale under the stipulated price, the House of Lords considered the definition of "liquidated damages".

While the facts of the cases are straightforward, the guidelines issued by the House of Lords are of great significance. Lord Dunedin said:

100. [1958] HKLR 405.
101. Ibid at 418.
102. [1915] AC 79.

to assist this task of construction various tests have been suggested, which if applicable to the case under consideration may prove helpful, or even conclusive. Such are:

(a) it will be held to be a penalty if the sum stipulated for is extravagant and unconscionable in amount in comparison with the greatest loss that could conceivably be proved to have followed from the breach.[103]

(b) It will be held to be a penalty if the breach consists only in not paying a sum of money, and the sum stipulated is a sum greater than the sum which ought to have been paid . . .

(c) There is a presumption (but no more) that it is penalty when a single lump sum is made payable by way of compensation, on the occurrence of one or more or all of several events, some of which may occasion serious and others but trifling damage[104] . . .

(d) It is no obstacle to the sum stipulated being a genuine pre-estimate of damage, that the consequences of the breach are such as to make precise pre-estimation almost an impossibility On the contrary, that is just the situation when it is probable that pre-estimated damage was the true bargain between the parties.[105]

The influence of this case can be seen in the *Luen Yick* case, considered above, where Reece J, in upholding a liquidated damages clause, emphasised that:

There was no suggestion by the defendant that the sum was extravagant or unconscionable.

The use of the terms "penalty" or "liquidated damages" in the parties' contract is not conclusive. Indeed, in the case of building contracts, it is common to use the term "penalty clause" non-technically, when what is really intended is a sum of liquidated damages. In the consideration case of *Williams v Roffey Brothers & Nicholls (Contractors)*,[106] for example, it was never argued that the main contractor's "penalty" for late completion could be avoided; it was recognised on all sides that the clause was actually one of liquidated damages. While not conclusive, however, the term "liquidated damages" in a contract may be viewed as persuasive. Such a view is supported by the (following) leading Hong Kong case.

Philips Hong Kong Ltd v The Attorney-General of Hong Kong[107]

The plaintiffs were one of a number of contractors engaged by the Hong Kong government to fulfil a large project in the New Territories. The contractors promised

---

103. For a clear illustration, see *Volkswagen Financial Services v Ramage* (unrep, Cambridge County Court, 9 May 2007). Of course, the sum fixed in the contract may be clearly *lower* than the innocent party's likely loss. In such a case the rules on "limitation clauses" may be applicable (see chapter 8 at 8.6).
104. For an excellent example, see *CMC Group PLC v Zhang* [2006] EWCA Civ 408.
105. [1915] AC 79 at 86.
106. [1991] 1 QB 1 and see 4.5.
107. [1993] 1 HKLR 269.

that they would comply with flow charts so that their work was completed in time to allow other contractors to continue with their work. In the event of failure to complete tasks by "Key Dates" contractors were obliged to pay liquidated damages to the government at a daily rate. The plaintiffs asked the Hong Kong courts, and ultimately the Privy Council, to declare that clauses in their contracts were penalties rather than liquidated damages since the amounts payable might exceed the actual loss to the Hong Kong government caused by the plaintiffs' breach. The Privy Council rejected the plaintiffs' arguments.

In delivering the leading judgment, Lord Woolf stated:

> In seeking to establish that the sum described in the Philips contract as liquidated damages was in fact a penalty, Philips has to surmount the strong inference to the contrary resulting from its agreement to make the payments as liquidated damages and the fact that it is not suggesting in these proceedings that the sum claimed is excessive in relation to the actual loss suffered by the Government.
>
> . . . the Government in its evidence provides an explanation as to how the liquidated damages were calculated . . . This was a perfectly sensible approach in a situation such as this where it would be obvious that substantial loss would be suffered in the event of delay but what that loss would be was virtually impossible to calculate precisely in advance.[108]

A similar view was expressed in the Hong Kong Court of First Instance in *Re Mandarin Container & Others*.[109] Here, Waung J cited the *Philips Hong Kong* case with approval and expressed the view that the modern approach is that courts should be slow to find a clause agreed by the parties to be a penalty, at least with regard to *commercial* contracts agreed by parties in an equal bargaining position. Such a view has been strongly endorsed in the later English case of *Murray v Leisureplay PLC*.[110] In *Murray*, the claimant had been improperly dismissed by the defendants. He claimed, as liquidated damages, one year's gross salary and other benefits as stipulated in his contract of employment. The year's salary was to be paid unless one year's notice was given (only seven-and-a-half weeks' notice was given in fact). The defendants argued that the clause was a penalty as it did not take into account the claimant's "duty to mitigate"[111] his loss and the likelihood of his finding alternative employment. Though the defence was upheld at first instance it was rejected on appeal to the Court of Appeal, which found the clause to be (enforceable) liquidated damages. The parties had made a genuine attempt to pre-estimate loss which was not "extravagant and unconscionable" (albeit generous to the claimant).

---

108. Ibid at 283.
109. [2004] 3 HKLRD 554.
110. [2005] EWCA Civ 963. Cited with approval by the Hong Kong Court of Appeal: *Ip Ming Kin v Wong Siu Lan* (unrep, CACV 201/2012, 28 May 2013).
111. See 15.1.4.8 below.

The court supported the *Philips Hong Kong* approach that the fact that the claimant *might* end up overcompensated did not prevent the clause being liquidated damages. The clause must be judged as at the time the contract was made and the court took account of the fact that the claimant agreed to considerable restraints of trade in the contract in return for the generous liquidated damages clause. Crucially, this was a "business arrangement" and "both parties knew what they were doing". This robust "contractual freedom" approach has found favour in subsequent Hong Kong cases including *Brio Electronic Commerce Ltd v Tradelink Electronic Commerce Ltd*,[112] where the Court of Appeal agreed with the view that the *Dunlop* tests are too rigid, made clear that the onus of proving a penalty is on the party asserting such, and upheld the judge's view that a major consideration was that this "was a commercial agreement entered into by parties who were very familiar with the trade." Given the enormous importance attached to real property transactions in Hong Kong, and given the volatility of the property market, it is not surprising that Hong Kong has developed its own custom and practice in respect of "deposits" (paid before contract). These are to be regarded as a reasonable "earnest" (and subject to forfeit) provided they are not over 10%.[113] Similarly, an amount to be paid in the event of breach may be stipulated as "liquidated damages". Over that amount (10%) it is *presumed* to be a "penalty" in the absence of evidence to the contrary. In *Polyset Ltd v Pahandat Ltd*[114] the Court of Appeal upheld the forfeit of a 35% deposit given the volatility of the market at the time and the lengthy "settlement period" (prices actually fell 30% during the period!). The Court of Final Appeal, found the 35% figure too high, however, and treated it as a penalty.[115] Deposits (as "earnests") may be forfeit even absent a breach by the prospective buyer. Where the "vendor" does successfully institute proceedings for the "buyer's" breach, the amount of any deposit forfeited will be set off against the amount of the contractual damages award.

The penalty/liquidated damages dichotomy was considered in a consumer context in *Shum Kit Ching v Caesar Beauty Centre Ltd*[116] where the plaintiff had joined the defendant health club and paid for a two month membership. She was subsequently "encouraged" to extend the period to nine months and then to apply for a "gold card", both at considerably greater cost. She paid by means of three separate credit cards and the terms of the contract, written very small, were not explained to her. When she tried to cancel the contract next day the defendants tried to rely on a clause which stated that, in the event of cancellation, no monies would be refunded. In the Court of First Instance the judge, Recorder Chan SC, held the clause to be

---

112. [2016] 2 HKLRD 1449.
113. *Sun Wai Kiu and Another v Wong Mei Yin* [1997] 1 HKC 288.
114. [2000] 4 HKC 203.
115. [2002] 3 HKLRD 319.
116. [2003] 3 HKLRD 422.

both unconscionable[117] and a penalty. It was found that the clause was not a genuine attempt to pre-estimate loss but was intended to punish.

English law has developed significantly with the decision in the (conjoined) cases of *Cavendish Square Holdings BV v Talal El Makdessi/Parking Eye Ltd v Beavis.*[118] The joinder of these two cases is surprising given their differing nature. *El Makdessi* is a business-to-business case (where the parties are expected to be more self-reliant), while *Beavis* is a clearly business to consumer case where a finding of penalty is supposedly more likely. Even more emphatically, the UK Supreme Court made clear that a penalty could only arise in respect of "secondary" obligations and held that the "penalty rule" could not possibly apply in *El Makdessi* which involved only "primary" ones. For this reason, the focus here will be only on *Beavis*. The case was relatively straightforward. Beavis had used a parking area intended only for the use of customers of a nearby shopping centre. The rules displayed on entry stated that customers could park free for two hours *but* would be subject to a hefty £85 charge for *any* parking stay thereafter. The parking area was managed by Parking Eye (rather than the shopping centre). Mr Beavis returned to his car almost one hour late and incurred the £85 charge which he challenged as excessive and thus a penalty.[119] The Supreme Court upheld the validity of the charge.[120] While invited to abolish the "penalty rule",[121] it declined *but* determined that the true test was whether:

> the impugned provision is a secondary obligation which imposes a detriment on the contract-breaker out of all proportion to any legitimate interest of the innocent party in the enforcement of the primary obligation.[122]

Given that the legitimate interest might contain a punitive element, this marks a change in the law as previously understood. Indeed, the Supreme Court suggested that the Hong Kong CFA's decision in *Polyset* requiring liquidated damages to be "a genuine pre-estimate of loss" was too restrictive. Given the "status" of *Polyset* in Hong Kong, it is questionable whether *Beavis* will be followed here.[123]

Of course, as the Supreme Court implied via their requirement of a "secondary" obligation, all that was necessary in *Beavis* was a statement that "the parking charge is £85; this will be waived for customers returning within two hours". In such a scenario, the "penalty rule" would be inapplicable.

---

117. See chapter 12.
118. [2015] UKSC 67.
119. Since the issue was one of importance, he was supported by the Consumers' Association.
120. In addition to finding that the charge was not a penalty the Court also held that it did not contravene the now repealed Unfair Terms in Consumer Contracts Regulations 1999.
121. "Penalties" are generally upheld in the civil law world on the basis of "freedom of contract".
122. Per Lords Neuberger and Sumption at para 32.
123. There is some *obiter* support in *Tictas System Administration v Explorer Travel* [2016] HKEC 2773, where Tracy Chan DJ, having found a clause to be non-penal in traditional terms, added that there was a "legitimate interest" in enforcing it.

15.1.4.7 The Market Rule in Sale of Goods Contracts

The market rule is primarily statute-based and derives from sections 52 and 53 of the Sale of Goods Ordinance.[124] Section 52 states:

(1) Where the buyer wrongfully neglects or refuses to accept and pay for the goods, the seller may maintain an action against him for damages for non-acceptance.

(2) The measure of damages is the estimated loss directly and naturally resulting, in the ordinary course of events, from the buyer's breach of contract.

(3) Where there is an available market for the goods in question the measure of damages is prima facie to be ascertained by the difference between the contract price and the market or current price at the time or times when the goods ought to have been accepted or (if no time was fixed for acceptance) at the time of the refusal to accept.

Section 53 applies similar principles to the situation where it is the seller who defaults.

So, in a simple scenario, if X and Y have agreed on a contract for the sale of goods and the buyer, Y, refuses to accept or pay for the goods, X (the seller) will be entitled to damages. The "quantum" of damages will be the difference between the agreed contract price and the market price. Where X can sell these goods at the same or higher price on the open market, his damages will be nominal. The same principle applies where the seller defaults and the buyer can obtain the same goods on the open market. The rule will not apply, however, where there is no available market in which to sell, or buy, the goods.[125]

15.1.4.8 Mitigation of Loss

Mitigation involves the attempt by the innocent party to keep the losses caused by the party in breach to a minimum. The rule of mitigation is that, although the claimant is sometimes said to have a "duty to mitigate", there is, strictly, no *duty* to mitigate, in the sense that failure to do so is actionable by the other side. However, no compensation will be awarded for loss which arises as a result of a failure by the innocent party to mitigate.[126] In *Brace v Calder*,[127] the plaintiff was technically dismissed when the partnership for which he worked was dissolved. Continued employment was offered to him on the same terms but the plaintiff preferred to claim damages for wrongful dismissal. His claim for *substantial* damages was rejected and he received

---

124. Cap 26.
125. See *Thompson (WL) Ltd v Robinson (Gunmakers) Ltd* [1955] Ch 177. The market rule also does not apply to second-hand cars where no two are the same: *Lazenby Garages Ltd v Wright* [1976] 1 WLR 459.
126. See *Thai Airways International Public Co Ltd v KI Holdings Co Ltd* [2015] EWHC 1250 (Comm) at para 33.
127. [1895] 2 QB 253.

only nominal damages since a reasonable person would have accepted the continued employment.

In *Brace* the issue was clear cut: the plaintiff was refused substantial damages because he had failed to take reasonable steps to "mitigate" his loss, or keep it to a minimum. In other cases, as where an employee is offered re-employment on worse terms, or having been previously dismissed in a humiliating fashion, the issue of reasonable mitigation will not be so clear. While there are many illustrations of the mitigation principles, there is always one key consideration: whether the innocent party has acted reasonably. A claimant, for example, is not expected to take steps which are unduly difficult, or expensive, or which would involve a loss to his personal or business reputation.[128] Provided he has acted reasonably, indeed, the claimant may even be able to recover damages for increased loss caused, unforeseeably, by his reasonable actions.[129] A Hong Kong example of the "reasonableness" consideration in respect of mitigation is provided by *Broad Money Development Ltd v Industrial Engineers Ltd*.[130] Here, the Court of Appeal held that where a purchaser had defaulted on a property purchase contract, it was perfectly reasonable for the vendor to sell elsewhere at a reduced price, rather than wait in the hope that the original "purchaser" would subsequently complete at the previously agreed price. This was especially true at a time of falling property prices. The court, therefore, awarded as damages the full difference between the originally agreed price and the reduced resale price. In *Leung Wan Kee Shipyard Ltd v Dragon Pearl Nightclub Restaurant Ltd & Another*,[131] it was held that, where mitigation required the resale of ship, it was "reasonable" to wait until the plaintiff had read an independent valuation before selling. Moreover, where "adaptation" was necessary to make the ship saleable, the plaintiff should make such adaptation and should receive the cost thereof in damages.

Since everything turns on what is reasonable in the circumstances of each individual case, fine distinctions may arise. In *First Shanghai Enterprises Ltd v Dahlia Properties Ltd (No 2)*,[132] the Court of Appeal confirmed a breach of a contract to buy land and remitted the task of assessing damages to the Court of First Instance. That court held that the vendors' refusal, in a falling property market, to accept lower offers was unreasonable and a failure to mitigate. Master de Souza held that the vendors were "nursing the property in the vain hope of seeing a reversal of market conditions" and the damages awarded reflected this unreasonable failure to mitigate.

The claimant's so-called "duty" to mitigate arises *after* a breach by the other party. As such, it cannot, in principle, arise *before* a breach has occurred. This logical

128. See, for example, *James Finlay & Co Ltd v NV Kwik Hoo Tung Handel Maatschappij* [1928] All ER 110.
129. See, for example, *Hoffberger v Ascot Bloodstock Group* (1976) The Times, 29 January 1976.
130. [2000] 2 HKC 825. See also *Wayfoong Credit Ltd v Cheung Wai Wah Samuel* [1990] 1 HKC 367.
131. [2016] 1 HKLRD 657.
132. [2003] 2 HKC 297.

principle can produce unfortunate consequences in cases of "anticipatory" breach where the innocent party ignores the breach.[133]

White and Carter (Councils) Ltd v McGregor[134]

The respondent made a contract with the appellants whereby the latter would prepare and distribute advertising, via litter bins, for the respondent for a period of three years. *On the same day*, and before any preparation had begun, the respondent attempted to cancel the contract. The appellants refused to accept the repudiation, prepared and distributed the advertising for three years, and then claimed the full "agreed sum" contract price. Their action succeeded in the House of Lords by a three to two majority. The majority view was that, provided the innocent party has a "legitimate interest" he may, in cases of "anticipatory" breach, refuse to accept the breach and continue with the contract. While he does so the issue of mitigation does not arise and the full contract price is recoverable. The minority view was that the damages awarded should reflect the innocent party's failure to mitigate.

Lord Reid, speaking for the majority stated:

> If one party to a contract repudiates it in the sense of making it clear to the other party that he refuses or will refuse to carry out his part of the contract, the other party, the innocent party, has an option. He may accept that repudiation and sue for damages for breach of contract, whether or not the time for performance has come; or he may if he chooses disregard or refuse to accept it and then the contract remains in full effect.[135]

The layman would probably agree with the minority view that the innocent party's proper course of action in such cases would be to attempt to seek alternative advertisers and to claim damages only for any reduced income, or increased costs, resulting. The case is certainly an extreme example of the innocent party's "election" in cases of anticipatory breach. The right to elect, however, is not absolute. Lord Reid stressed that the innocent party must have "a legitimate interest, financial or otherwise, in performing the contract rather than claiming damages", and this requirement has enabled courts in subsequent cases to distinguish the *White and Carter* case where the innocent party's continuation is "wholly unreasonable".[136] Further, as Lord Reid pointed out, ignoring the breach is not possible where continuation requires the co-operation of the other party which is not forthcoming.[137] It may also be significant that *White and Carter* was a case of an action for an agreed sum

---

133. See 14.3.
134. [1962] AC 413, [1962] 2 WLR 17, [1961] 3 All ER 1178 and see 14.3.2.3.
135. [1962] 2 WLR 17 at 20.
136. For example, *Clea Shipping Corporation v Bulk Oil International Ltd (The Alaskan Trader)* [1984] 1 All ER 129 (per Lloyd J).
137. See *Hounslow London Borough Council v Twickenham Garden Developments Ltd* [1971] Ch 233.

(debt) rather than a claim for damages for breach.[138] In *Leung Wan Kee Shipyard Ltd v Dragon Pearl Night Club Restaurant Ltd & Another*,[139] Recorder Stewart Wong SC stated:

> this argument infringes the principle that rules of mitigation do not apply to claims in debt, a proposition which the 1st defendant accepts.[140]

15.1.4.9 Contributory Negligence

The question of whether contributory negligence is applicable to damages in contract has exercised both the Hong Kong and English courts. Although the situation is covered by statutory rules, these cannot be properly understood without knowledge of the pre-legislative position.

Formerly, in the case of negligence and other torts, contributory negligence was an absolute defence. This meant that if the plaintiff had been "injured" by the defendant's tortious act but had contributed to the likelihood of the loss occurring, *or* to the extent of the loss, by his own carelessness, the defendant would escape all liability. This was, theoretically, the case even if the plaintiff's contributory negligence was a minor factor. The unsatisfactory nature of this rule, and its attendant harshness to the plaintiff, led courts to overlook minor carelessness on the part of the plaintiff. Those reading certain pre-legislation cases will note that courts have found the plaintiff to have been in no way careless in circumstances which, to the layman, have obviously involved some contributory negligence on the plaintiff's part. The explanation is that, were the court to have found otherwise, the deserving plaintiff would have been denied any compensation.

The unsatisfactory nature of the law was improved by legislation. In England the relevant Act was the Law Reform (Contributory Negligence) Act 1945. This Act permitted the courts to award damages to the careless plaintiff, *subject to* the power to deduct from those damages to the extent that the plaintiff had contributed to his own misfortune. Thus, the plaintiff driver, injured by the defendant's careless driving, would be awarded damages but have these reduced where, for example, his injuries were increased by his failure to wear a seat belt. It is crucial to bear in mind that the Act is not intended to extend the defences available to a defendant but only to permit an action to a plaintiff, albeit subject to reduced damages, where none existed before.

The relevant Hong Kong legislative rule, section 21 of the Law Amendment and Reform (Consolidation) Ordinance (LARCO),[141] was modelled on the English Act. In both cases, an issue before the courts has been whether, and if so to what extent,

---

138. This is certainly the view of Treitel (op cit at p 1221.
139. [2016] 1 HKLRD 657.
140. At para 42.
141. Cap 23.

contributory negligence extends to actions for breach of contract. Although the wording of the two pieces of legislation is similar, the two jurisdictions have reached opposite conclusions. The English approach, deriving from the Court of Appeal case of *F. Vesta v Butcher*,[142] is that contributory negligence is applicable to actions involving negligent breach which could have been sued upon in contract or tort, but *not* to actions purely contractual in nature. A Hong Kong court, in *International Trading Co Ltd v Lai Kam Man & Others*,[143] held that contributory negligence is not applicable to an action brought by the plaintiff for breach of contract. The Hong Kong judgment, by Tang J in the Court of First Instance, is based on a sound application of "purposive" principles. Since, Tang J argued, the purpose of the legislation was to extend, rather than limit, the plaintiff's rights, and since contributory negligence was never a defence to an action at common law, there is no justification for reducing the careless plaintiff's damages in cases founded on breach of contract. While this decision has much to commend it, it did have "tactical" implications for legal advisers in cases of negligent breach, since the plaintiff would have his damages reduced if he chose to sue in tort but *not* if he opted to sue for breach. The *International Trading* case provides an unusual example of a judge facing competing common law precedents and opting to follow the non-English (Australian) one.[144] Unfortunately, a subsequent case in the Hong Kong Court of Appeal led to the abandonment of Tang J's sensible approach, in favour of the English and (now reformed) Australian one: *PT Asuransi Tugu Pratama Indonesia TBK v Citibank NA*.[145] The Court of Appeal's view has now been endorsed by the Court of Final Appeal.[146]

15.1.5 Time of Assessment of Damages

Of course damages are always assessed by a court at the time of trial. By "time of assessment" we mean the relevant point in time at which loss is to be assessed and compensation calculated. The general principle is that loss is to be calculated as at the time of breach. This principle is implicit in the "market" rule for sale of goods as stipulated in sections 52 and 53 of the Sale of Goods Ordinance (SOGO).[147] There are, however, some exceptions to the "time of breach" principle. For example, where, without default, the innocent party is unaware of the breach, damages should be assessed as at the time when he should "reasonably" have discovered the breach.

Further, when it is not feasible for the innocent party to act on his knowledge of the breach, damages will be assessed from the time when he should, reasonably,

---

142. [1989] AC 852.
143. [2004] 2 HKLRD 937.
144. Tang J was heavily influenced by the Australian decision of *Astley v Austrust Ltd* (1999) 197 CLR 1, (1999) 161 ALR 155.
145. [2022] HKCA 510.
146. [2023] HKCFA 3.
147. See 15.1.4.7 above.

have so acted. In *Wroth v Tyler*,[148] the defendant reneged on a contract to sell his house to the plaintiffs at a time of rapidly rising house prices. The plaintiffs (as the defendant knew) could not afford to buy another house in the circumstances and had to wait until a court judgment in their favour. In refusing specific performance to the plaintiffs, the court gave damages "in lieu" (instead) based on the value of the property not at the time of breach but at the time of judgment.

In cases of "anticipatory breach" where the innocent party "rejects the breach" and waits until performance date rather than suing immediately, damages will be assessed as at the date of performance rather than the date of the (rejected) anticipatory breach.[149] Where the innocent party "accepts the breach" and sues immediately, damages should, logically, be assessed on the basis of loss *at that time*. A majority of the House of Lords, however, adopted a different approach in *Golden Strait Corporation v Nippon Yusen Kubishka Kaisha*[150] where they took into account, in determining damages, events which occurred after the breach was accepted but before trial.[151]

15.2 Equitable Remedies

Historically, equitable remedies are those which were awarded by the courts of equity; notably the Court of Chancery in England. Such remedies originated because of the inflexibility of the (originally Royal) common law courts. Common law would only permit a remedy where a suitable writ was available for an action to commence; where there was no writ there was no remedy. Equity, founded on the principle of "conscience", was based on the principle that there should be no wrong without a remedy. The purpose of equity, and its separate court structure, was to "fill in the gaps" in the common law rather than to be an entire system in itself. Equity developed its own remedies, notably specific performance and injunction, which were "discretionary" in nature. The exercise of discretion was guided by the "maxims" of equity, such as "he who comes to equity must come with clean hands" and "he who seeks equity must do equity". Damages were not, initially, available in the courts of

---

148. [1974] Ch 30.
149. See 14.3.2.
150. [2007] UKHL 12.
151. The "event" was the outbreak of the Iraq war. At the time of the "accepted" anticipatory breach, the war was only a possibility. By the time the case reached the House of Lords via the courts and a lengthy arbitration, the war had occurred. The majority law lords felt they could not ignore what they knew to have happened. Significantly, the three majority law lords were subjected to a "vigorous dissent" from the most eminent of judges, Lord Bingham (the first judge in history to have held the three positions of Master of the Rolls, Lord Chief Justice, and leading law lord). *Golden Victory* was distinguished in *Classic Maritime Inc v Limbungan Makmur SDN BHD & Another* [2019] EWCA Civ 1102, a case involving actual rather than anticipatory breach, and where the court found a non-excludable "absolute" duty to perform.

equity, though, in the nineteenth century, they became available "in lieu of" other equitable remedies in suitable cases.

The separated court system was abolished by legislation in the form of the Judicature Acts 1873–1875. The main provisions of the legislation were that the two court structures would be "fused"; that all courts could give both common law and equitable remedies; and that, in cases of conflict between common law and equitable rules, the rule of equity would prevail.

However, while equity no longer exists as a separate system, an important legacy remains, deriving from its original purpose, scope and functions. Indeed, the preservation of equity as a source of law in Hong Kong, post-1997, is specifically stipulated in the Basic Law.[152]

Since equity developed as a system to supplement the common law rather than replace it,

> It is only where the legal remedy is inadequate or defective that it becomes necessary for courts of equity to interfere.[153]

Equity, then, "follows the law"; supplementing rather than supplanting. In *New Bright Industrial Co v Golden Bright Manufacturer Ltd*[154] Li DJ stated:

> The doctrine of estoppel is an equitable doctrine. Equity follows the law. Given the choice to throw my weight on either the side of the law or that of equity, I would stand by the side of the law.[155]

Yet, were that premise *entirely* true, there would be no need for a rule that in cases of conflict, equity prevails. Thus:

> Equity should not always follow the law. Otherwise it would be difficult to see how it could become distinct jurisprudence.[156]

Certainly the ideal of equity as merely "supplemental" is put under the greatest stress by decisions such as *Collier v Wright*, discussed in chapter 4.[157] The approach of the Court of Appeal in that case, particularly Arden LJ, is perhaps better described as:

> judges and commentators seizing upon the fertile principles of equity to justify some modern departure from classical precedents.[158]

---

152. Article 8. See further discussion of equity and its relationship with common law in chapter 2.
153. *Flint v Brandon* (1808) 3 Ves 159 per Grant MR.
154. (unrep, HCA 15804/98, 6 May 1999).
155. Ibid at para 25.
156. L. Ma and M. Lower, *Principles of Equity & Trusts Law in Hong Kong* (Hong Kong: LexisNexis, 2009) at p 5.
157. At 4.7.3.5.
158. H. Collins, *The Law of Contract* (Weidenfeld & Nicholson, London 1986) at p 17.

Moreover, the remedies recognised as equitable are still available only at the *discretion* of the court; that discretion is still determined by the fact that equity is "a court of conscience". In the case, for example, of a contract voidable for undue influence, which was first recognised in equity, a party allowed to rescind may be required to allow the influencing party to retain part of his profits where the influenced party has received benefits.[159] This approach seeks to do justice to both sides.

The "maxims" of equity are still recognised. So, under the "clean hands" principle, equity will not assist a party who has acted improperly *in respect of the contract*[160] (albeit legally).[161] Under the principle that "he who seeks equity must do equity", a party seeking an equitable remedy must be prepared to comply with the requirements of the court.[162] Again, the court will be seeking an outcome which is fair to both parties.

15.2.1 Specific Performance

Specific performance is the major equitable remedy for breach of contract. It is an order compelling a party in breach to fulfil his contractual obligations. Failure to comply with an order for specific performance may be treated as a contempt of court. Moreover, where the defendant has refused to comply (and continues his refusal), the plaintiff may ask the Court to withdraw the order, bring the contract to an end, and permit the plaintiff to claim (equitable) damages.[163] As an equitable remedy, specific performance is available only at the discretion of the court. Since equity is traditionally a "court of conscience",

> the dominant principle has always been that equity will only grant specific performance if, under all the circumstances, it is just and equitable to do so.[164]

Further, since equity, historically, was intended to fill in the gaps left by the common law, the general principle is that specific performance is only granted where the common law remedy of damages is inadequate. As a result, it is nearly always the case that contracts for the sale of goods are not specifically enforced in practice since goods are rarely unique and damages are, therefore, an adequate remedy. This is despite the fact that legislation clearly provides for the possibility of specific

---

159. See *Cheese v Thomas* [1994] 1 WLR 129 discussed at 11.2.4.
160. See *Sang Lee Investment Co Ltd v Wing Kwai Investment Co Ltd & Another* [1983] HKLR 197, [1983] 1 HKC 68 (Privy Council on appeal from Hong Kong).
161. For example, *D&C Builders v Rees* [1966] 2 QB 617, [1966] 2 WLR 288, [1965] 3 All ER 837 discussed at 4.6 and 4.7.3.3.
162. See *Baskcomb v Beckwith* (1869) LR 8 Equ 100 and *Cheese v Thomas* [1994] 1 All ER 35 discussed at 11.2.4.
163. *Stark Moly Ltd v Lam Fung* [2015] 3 HKC 59 (applying *Johnson v Agnew*, discussed in chapter 14 at 14.3.2.2).
164. *Stickney v Keble* [1915] AC 386 per Lord Parker.

performance in such cases. Section 54 of the Sale of Goods Ordinance[165] provides that:

> In any action for breach of contract to deliver specific or ascertained goods, the court may, if it thinks fit, on the application of the plaintiff, by its judgment direct that the contract shall be performed specifically, without giving the defendant the option of retaining the goods on payment of damages. The judgment may be unconditional, or on such terms and conditions as to damages, payment of the price, and otherwise, as to the court may seem just. The application by the plaintiff may be made at any time before judgment.

The wording of this section of the Hong Kong legislation is almost identical to that of section 52 of the (English) Sale of Goods Act 1979. Despite the discretion given by the section, courts have granted specific performance only where the goods have been seen as "unique". This uniqueness may be an obvious physical one such as that possessed by a ship unavailable elsewhere[166] or it may be a "commercial uniqueness" as in the following case.

Sky Petroleum Ltd v VIP Petroleum Ltd[167]

The plaintiffs successfully sought an injunction to prevent the defendants cancelling their contract to supply petrol. There was evidence that no other supplier was available. The two issues for the court were whether such an injunction would be equivalent to specific performance, since it would in effect compel performance, and, if so, whether such a remedy was justified. It was determined, in the English High Court, that the injunction would be granted.

Despite the fact that the case involved delivery of non-specific goods, Goulding J determined that the facts were exceptional enough to uphold the plaintiffs' claim. He said:

> Now I come to the most serious hurdle in the way of the plaintiff company which is the well-known doctrine that the court refuses specific performance of a contract to sell and purchase chattels not specific or ascertained . . . it is . . . quite plain that I am for the time being specifically enforcing the contract if I grant an injunction. (However) Here the defendants appear for practical purposes to be the plaintiffs' sole means of keeping their business going, and I am prepared so far to depart from the general rule as to try to preserve the position under the contract until a later date. I therefore propose to grant an injunction.[168]

Although specific performance of a contract for the sale of goods is exceptional, *land* is, conversely, regarded as unique, such that contracts for the sale of land are

---

165. Cap 26.
166. See *Behnke v Bede Shipping Co Ltd* [1927] 1 KB 649.
167. [1974] 1 WLR 576, [1974] 1 All ER 954.
168. [1974] 1 WLR 576 at 578–579.

specifically enforced. This exception for land has been so long recognised that it is now unquestioned, even though there are situations in which uniqueness is illusory. It is not, then, doubted that specific performance is available to both the buyer of land, where the seller defaults, *and* the seller, when the buyer defaults.[169] In the latter case, however, the seller has lost only money, which lacks uniqueness.

Were specific performance not available to the seller of land as well as the buyer, it would offend against another requirement of specific performance, that of "mutuality". The mutuality principle requires that specific performance can only be awarded to a party if it could also, potentially, be awarded against him. For this reason, for example, specific performance is not available to a minor since it cannot be awarded against him.[170]

One of the most important limitations on the award of specific performance is that it is not awarded to enforce a contract for personal services. Indeed:

> The courts have never dreamt of enforcing agreements strictly personal in their nature.[171]

This can be seen particularly in the Hong Kong approach to employment law whereby the reluctant employee is never required to honour his contract to work for his employer. Conversely, the employer is never forced to re-employ an employee wrongly dismissed.[172] In both cases the court will restrict itself to the award of damages.

The prohibition on awarding specific performance of a personal service contract has relevance to the study of injunctions,[173] since the courts will refuse an injunction where it would have the same effect as an order of specific performance.

A further restriction on the remedy of specific performance relates to contracts the performance of which would require constant supervision. This would, of course, be true of most personal service contracts, so the two restrictions are related. The "constant supervision" difficulty is applied generally as a reason for refusing specific performance though there is some evidence that the courts are relaxing this limitation. In *Posner v Scott-Lewis*,[174] the defendant had promised to employ a resident porter to do various tasks but had failed to do so. The plaintiff, a tenant, sought specific performance of the promise to engage the porter. He faced the problem that, traditionally, courts have been reluctant to enforce contracts requiring constant

---

169. Provided that the claimant is ready willing and able to complete on the date fixed by the court: *Lau Suk Ching Peggy v Ma Hing Lam & Others* [2010] 4 HKC 193 (CFA). See also *Lai Ke Bin v Capital Project Development Ltd* [2009] 2 HKLRD 49 (purchaser able to pay on contract date, but not at trial, refused specific performance but given damages in lieu).

170. See also 6.3.

171. Per Jessell MR, *Rigby v Connol* (1880) 14 Ch D 482.

172. Though where such dismissal constitutes "unlawful discrimination" (as defined by s10 of the Race Discrimination Ordinance [Cap 602]) s70(4) of the Ordinance allows a court to order reinstatement.

173. See 15.2.2 below.

174. [1987] Ch 25.

supervision. Nonetheless, the remedy was granted on the basis that the appointment itself did not require constant supervision.

The court was able to distinguish the earlier case of *Ryan v Mutual Tontine Westminster Chambers Association*[175] where, because of the specific nature of the porter's stipulated duties, constant supervision by the court may have been necessary to ensure compliance with the order for specific performance. It is important to distinguish the obligation to appoint a porter, which did not need constant supervision and was therefore specifically enforceable, from the obligations of the porter himself. If the porter had refused to perform properly the only remedy against him would have been damages.

The narrow "distinguishing" of the *Ryan* case in *Posner* indicates that the courts may be moving away from strict adherence to the prohibition on specific performance in "continuing supervision" cases. Indeed, in *CH Giles Co v Morris*,[176] Megarry J stated:

> One day, perhaps the courts will look again at the so-called rule that contracts for personal services or involving the continuous performance of services will not be specifically enforced. Performance . . . is normally secured by the realisation of the person enjoined that he is liable to be punished for contempt if evidence of his disobedience to the order is put before the court.[177]

The issue of constant supervision was also to the fore with regard to the refusal of specific performance in *Co-operative Insurance Society Ltd v Argyll Stores (Holdings) Ltd*[178] though a further consideration was that specific performance would have entailed excessive cost to the defendant. Lord Hoffman stated:

> The judges who have said that the need for constant supervision was an objection to such orders were no doubt well aware that supervision would in practice take the form of rulings by the court . . . It is the possibility of the court having to give an indefinite series of such rulings in order to ensure the execution of the order which has been regarded as undesirable . . .
>
> . . . the purpose of the law of contract is not to punish wrongdoing but to satisfy the expectations of the party entitled to performance. A remedy which enables him to secure, in money terms, more than the performance due to him is unjust . . . it cannot be in the public interest for the courts to require someone to carry on a business at a loss if there is any plausible alternative by which the other party can be given compensation.[179]

---

175. [1893] 1 Ch 116.
176. [1972] 1 WLR 307, [1972] 1 All ER 960.
177. [1972] 1 WLR 307 at 318.
178. [1997] 3 All ER 297.
179. Ibid at 302–305.

15.2.2 *Injunctions*

Injunctions, like specific performance, are equitable remedies and, as such, are available only at the discretion of the court. Unlike specific performance, however, injunctions are not merely contractual and are found as often in tort.

Contractual injunctions are applicable only where there is a negative promise, that is, a promise not to do something. Where the plaintiff fears that the defendant is about to break a negative promise he will seek an injunction to prevent the breach: a "prohibitive" injunction. Where the plaintiff complains that the defendant has already acted in breach of a negative undertaking, he will seek an injunction to undo the action in breach: a mandatory injunction.

The distinction between specific performance, prohibitive and mandatory injunctions may be seen in the following scenarios:

1. B has promised A that he will build a wall but has failed to do so. A seeks specific performance to enforce the positive promise;
2. B has promised A *not* to build a wall but is now threatening to do so. A seeks a prohibitive injunction to prevent the threatened breach of a negative promise;
3. B has promised A *not* to build a wall but has done so. A seeks a mandatory injunction to compel B to undo the breach (that is, to remove the offending wall).

An injunction may be issued to prevent the breach of an *express* negative promise, for example "I will not buy electricity from any other seller" or an *implied* one, for example "I will buy electricity only from you".[180] The courts will not, however, grant an injunction in relation to a personal service contract, where this would have the effect of compelling an employee to continue working for his employer, since this would be equivalent to specific performance.[181] In the same way an employer will rarely be restrained by injunction from dismissing an employee whom he no longer wishes to employ since, again, this would be equivalent to specific performance of a personal service contract. The issue arose in *Warner Bros Pictures Inc v Nelson*,[182] where the court adopted a restrictive approach to the question of whether injunction is equivalent to specific performance. In the *Warner Bros* case, the defendant, the film actress Bette Davis, had contracted to give her exclusive services as a film and stage actress to the plaintiffs for one year. She then sought to work for another studio within the period and the plaintiffs claimed an injunction to prevent her doing so. The defendant's argument that this was equivalent to specific performance of

---

180. See *Metropolitan Electric Supply Co v Ginder* [1901] 2 Ch 799.
181. See 15.2.1 above.
182. [1937] 1 KB 209, [1936] 3 All ER 160.

a personal service contract and should, therefore, be refused, was rejected in the English High Court.

The court focused on the fact that the injunction was restricted to Ms Davis's work as an actress and her *theoretical* freedom to engage in other activities on the granting of the plaintiffs' injunction. Branson J said:

> It is conceded that our Courts will not enforce a positive covenant of personal service; and specific performance of the positive covenants by the defendant to serve the plaintiffs is not asked in the present case . . .
>
> The defendant is stated to be a person of intelligence, capacity and means, and no evidence was adduced to show that, if enjoined from doing the specified acts otherwise than for the plaintiffs, she will not be able to employ herself both usefully and remuneratively in other spheres of activity, though not as remuneratively as in her special line. She will not be driven, although she may be tempted, to perform the contract, and the fact that she may be so tempted is no objection to the grant of an injunction.[183]

The approach of Branson J may be regarded as somewhat unrealistic since, in practice, it was unlikely that a leading actress would embark on another career. A more realistic approach was adopted in *Page One Records Ltd v Britton & Other*.[184] Here, the defendants, a pop group known as "The Troggs" had a contract for the plaintiffs to be their exclusive management in the pop music business. The defendants wished later to use new management and the plaintiffs sought an injunction to prevent this. The injunction was refused by the English High Court on the basis that an injunction would amount to specific performance.

In refusing the injunction, the trial judge, Stamp J, determined that the group needed management to succeed and were incapable of managing themselves. Thus, in reality, an injunction preventing them from using new management would be tantamount to specific performance of the original management contract.

A similarly realistic view was taken in the case of *Warren v Mendy*,[185] in which the English Court of Appeal refused an injunction to stop the defendant inducing Nigel Benn, the boxer, to break his contract with the plaintiff and join the defendant, on the grounds that this would have the effect of compelling the boxer to perform his contract if he was to maintain his skill and talent. The court was satisfied that the boxer had "lost all confidence" in the plaintiff.

Both *Page One* and *Mendy* were distinguished in the Hong Kong case of *Beacon College Ltd v Yiu Man Hau & Others*.[186] Here, the plaintiff was a private school offering tutorial lessons to secondary school pupils. The defendants were teachers who resigned from the school and sought similar work elsewhere. The plaintiffs

---

183. [1936] 3 All ER 160 at 167.
184. [1968] 1 WLR 157, [1967] 3 All ER 822.
185. [1989] 3 All ER 103.
186. [2001] 3 HKLRD 558, [2001] 4 HKC 433.

successfully sought interim injunctions to enforce negative covenants in the employees' employment contracts restraining them from working for any rival private
tutorial institution anywhere else in Hong Kong. The restraints were upheld as reasonable[187] and the teachers' argument that the injunctions were equivalent to specific
performance were rejected. The trial judge, Chu J, held that while the teachers may
prefer to go back to the plaintiffs (and would be welcome) they were free to work as
teachers in the Government school sector.

Uniquely, an injunction *was* granted, though it amounted to specific performance, in the peculiar circumstances of *Hill v CA Parsons Ltd*[188] where the plaintiff
was an employee of the defendants close to retirement age. The defendants entered
into a "closed shop" agreement with a trade union under which they could employ
only union members. The plaintiff refused to join a union so the defendants reluctantly dismissed him, and others, though there were no grounds for so doing. The
plaintiff successfully obtained an injunction in the Court of Appeal to prevent the
improper dismissal.

In cases where an employer is reluctant to keep on an employee, the normal
remedy for improper dismissal is damages. In *Hill*, the Court of Appeal no doubt
took note of the fact that the employers had only reluctantly dismissed the non-union
employees and were not reluctant to take them back once required to do so by the
courts.

15.3 Limitation of Actions

The right to claim damages for breach of contract normally expires six years after
the breach of contract occurs[189] (twelve years in the case of a contract made under
seal). Wherever a debt is subsequently acknowledged in writing, the limitation
period starts to run again from the date of the acknowledgement.

A shorter period (of three years) applies in those rare situations where a breach
of contract causes personal injury,[190] though even here there is considerable scope for
courts to extend the period.[191]

The major exception to the rule that the limitation period starts to run from the
breach occurs in cases of fraud or mistake. Here the limitation period starts to run
from the time when the fraud or mistake was, or should have been, discovered.[192]

---

187. Despite being territory-wide, as such was the plaintiff's catchment area. See also 13.4.
188. [1972] 1 Ch 305, [1971] 3 WLR 995, [1971] 3 All ER 1345.
189. Section 4(1) of the Limitation Ordinance (Cap 347).
190. Ibid s 27.
191. Ibid s 31.
192. Ibid s 26(1).

Since misrepresentation, unlike breach of contract, is not actionable until loss has occurred, the limitation period for misrepresentation does not begin to run until loss has resulted from the misrepresentation.[193]

In cases of equitable claims, such as an action for specific performance or injunction, there is no specific limitation period. However, in practice, the systems are not that different since equity precludes enforcement after "undue delay". The undue delay approach is known as the equitable doctrine of "laches" and can be seen at work in the decision to bar rescission for misrepresentation in *Leaf v International Galleries*[194] and for undue influence in *Allcard v Skinner*.[195] Laches will operate only where allowing a delayed action would produce unfairness to the claimant. Thus, in *Wing Ming Garment Factory Ltd v The Incorporated Owners of Wing Ming Industrial Centre*,[196] Lam J stated (*obiter*):

> It is true that there has been a very substantial delay from 1994 before the IO sought to make the present claim . . . There is, however, little that had happened during this period of delay which would, in my view, have made it inequitable to grant the relief sought, if such relief should otherwise have been granted.[197]

Finally, it should be noted that limitation "extinguishes the remedy not the right". What this means is that, for example, a debt will remain perfectly legal even after the limitation period for enforcement has expired; all that is precluded is the creditor's right to sue. Thus, if a debtor repays a statute-barred debt, he will be unable to recover his repayment merely because he was not legally obliged to make it.

---

193. Ibid s 4(1).
194. See 9.2.2.2 but quaere whether the decision remains good law.
195. See 11.2.2.1 and 11.2.4.
196. [2014] 4 HKLRD 52.
197. At para 340.

16

Privity of Contract

OVERVIEW

The doctrine of privity of contract states that "no one . . . may be entitled to or bound by the terms of a contract to which he is not an original party."[1] There are two separate aspects of the doctrine: that third parties cannot acquire rights under a contract *even if the contracting parties so intend*; and that third parties cannot have obligations imposed upon them by a contract. The doctrine is a creation of the common law. As with many common law rules, its rigidity has clashed with the needs and theories of different areas of law such as land law.

The doctrine has been a central, if controversial, part of English and Hong Kong contract law for a considerable period. A fundamental rationale for the doctrine is that contract is said to be based on "agreement" and third parties are generally not part of ("privy to") the contractual agreement. A further reason for the doctrine is that third parties should not be able to sue for breach of contract in the absence of consideration.[2] Another is that, as contract is based on the concept of consent, a third party, who has not given any consent, should not be able to obtain any contractual rights. A third rationale is that if a third party were able to enforce a contractual promise, the promisor could be sued by both the promisee and the third party. A fourth justification is that it would be unfair for a third party to be able to sue on a contract but not be sued.[3] Finally, it is said, the doctrine preserves the contracting parties' right to rescind or vary the contract which would be more difficult were a non-party to have contractual rights.

However, there are strong arguments against the doctrine. These are aimed largely at the first aspect of the doctrine; that is, a third party cannot acquire and

---

1. M. Furmston, *Cheshire, Fifoot & Furmston's Law of Contract* (Oxford/New York: Oxford University Press, 17th edn, 2015) at p 556.
2. See chapter 4.
3. But such one-sided liability is inherent in all "unilateral" contracts: see, for example, *Carlill* case and 3.3.4 above.

enforce rights or benefits under a contract. The second aspect of the doctrine, that a third party cannot be made liable under a contract, is generally regarded as just and sensible. The strongest of the arguments against the first aspect of the doctrine is that it frustrates the intentions of the parties to a contract which is made expressly for the benefit of a third party. A second reason is that the doctrine is complex, uncertain and artificial. This is reflected in the courts having recourse to such devices as agency and the trust to allow a third party to obtain a benefit under a contract. Also legislation has made partial inroads into the doctrine. This has caused the law of contract to become complex and artificial. The very fact that the courts and the legislature have felt it necessary to take such steps indicates that the doctrine causes injustice in some instances. Thirdly, the doctrine means that a third party who has suffered loss of an intended benefit under the contract cannot sue, while the party to the contract, who has suffered no loss, can sue (though probably only for nominal damages).[4] Finally, injustice will result if a third party has relied on the promise and acted to his detriment and cannot sue on the contract.

The reasons given above have resulted in legislation being enacted in England, elsewhere[5] in the common law world and, finally, in Hong Kong. The Law Reform Commission of Hong Kong produced a Report calling for significant reform as long ago as 2005, but only 11 years later was resulting legislation finally in force. The common law rules on privity remain significant, however, since the legislation specifically does *not* affect common law restrictions on the privity doctrine. Moreover, the new legislation permits parties to a contract to exclude the operation of the new legislation; in which circumstance, of course, the common law rules will be crucial.

16.1 The Doctrine of Privity of Contract

The common law doctrine of privity of contract establishes that only the parties to a contract can sue and be sued on it: it can neither confer rights nor impose liabilities on others.[6] The doctrine has existed in English law since the middle of the nineteenth century when it was firmly established in *Tweddle v Atkinson*.[7] The doctrine was later reaffirmed by the House of Lords in *Dunlop Pneumatic Tyre Co Ltd v Selfridge & Co Ltd*.[8]

The second aspect of the doctrine—that contractual liabilities should not be imposed on third parties—has not provoked controversy. It is the first aspect which has proved to be controversial. Even if the parties clearly intended by contract to

---

4. See discussion of *Jackson* and *Woodar* at 16.2.4 below.
5. Such as Australia (in the states of Northern Territory, Queensland, and Western Australia), New Zealand, and Singapore.
6. See, for example, E. Martin, *A Concise Dictionary of Law* (Oxford: Oxford University Press, 5th edn, 1990).
7. (1861) 1 B&S 393.
8. [1915] AC 847.

confer a right on a third party, English and Hong Kong law stated that they could not do so. It is this part of the doctrine which has been addressed and reformed by the English legislation.

The rule that a person could not sue on a contract which was made for his benefit but to which he was not a party was capable of creating hardship. It clashed with the requirements of land law, especially in the area of leases where the tenant transfers some of his interests in the property to a third party. Various methods were used to evade the strictures of the doctrine in relation to third party benefits and it is the attempts to circumvent the doctrine with which this chapter is principally concerned.

16.2 Third Party Benefits

The basic proposition, that those who are not party to a contract cannot acquire rights under it, is closely connected to the rules on consideration. It is usually the case that, where a party is precluded from suing on a contract since he is not party to it, he could equally be precluded on the basis that consideration had not "moved from" the promisee.

The privity rule, in relation to benefits, has been consistently criticised since it frequently thwarts the intention of the contracting parties themselves. For this reason the doctrine has been considerably revised in England via legislation.[9] Such legislation has not been enacted in Hong Kong, though it is under consideration, and the doctrine of privity remains part of Hong Kong law, though it is subject to numerous legislative and common law exceptions.

The doctrine was first established in *Tweddle v Atkinson*.[10] Here, an agreement was made between William Guy and the father of the plaintiff in which the parties promised to pay a sum of money to the plaintiff in consideration of the intended marriage between the plaintiff and the daughter of William Guy. Guy failed to pay and the plaintiff sued his executors. The court dismissed the plaintiff's action. The decision was based on the rule that consideration must move from the promisee. The judge, Wightman J, rejected the argument that the third party was in such a close relationship with the party to the contract that he should be considered a party in his own right.

The decision in *Tweddle* was reaffirmed by the House of Lords in *Dunlop v Selfridge*[11] in which greater emphasis was placed on the privity, rather than the consideration, aspect.

---

9. Contracts (Rights of Third Parties) Act 1999.
10. (1861) 1 B&S 393.
11. [1915] AC 847.

Dunlop Pneumatic Tyre Co Ltd v Selfridge & Co Ltd

The plaintiffs sold tyres to a company called Dew & Co (Dew). Under the contract Dew promised not to re-sell the tyres under a certain price and to exact a similar promise from those to whom they sold the tyres. Dew sold to Selfridge who agreed to the restriction and to pay a sum of money to the plaintiffs for every tyre sold below the list price. However, contrary to their promise, Selfridge re-sold below the list price. The plaintiffs sued Selfridge for breach of contract but their action failed. The House of Lords unanimously held that there was no privity of contract between them.

Viscount Haldane LC, in his judgment, made the following, oft-quoted statement:

> My Lords, in the law of England certain principles are fundamental. One is that only a person who is a party to a contract can sue on it. Our law knows nothing of a jus quaesitum tertio (a right sought by a third party) arising by way of contract . . . A second principle is that if a person with whom a contract not under seal has been made is to be able to enforce it consideration must have been given by him.[12]

It can be seen that while the "no third party benefits" rule and the "consideration must move from the promisee" rule are closely connected, Viscount Haldane treated them as distinct principles.

Hong Kong has followed the English approach to privity and the denial of benefits to third parties. In *B&B Construction Ltd v Sun Alliance & London Insurance*,[13] in the Hong Kong Court of Appeal, Godfrey VP stated:

> Even assuming, in favour of the contractor, that the policy was intended to enure for the benefit of the contractor as well as . . . the sub-contractor, the contractor's claim would fall foul of the well-settled (although much criticised) rule that, on the face of it, a contract between two parties for the benefit of a third party is not enforceable by the third party, who is, as it is sometimes put, 'a stranger to the consideration' . . .
>
> . . . here, in Hong Kong, the law remains as magisterially stated by Viscount Haldane LC in Dunlop Pneumatic Tyre Company Ltd v Selfridge & Co Ltd.[14]

A particular aspect of the "no benefits" rule concerns exemption clauses, dealt with in chapter 8.[15] The principle is that a person cannot take the benefit of an exemption clause in a contract to which he was not a party. This is the case even if the contracting parties intend such third party to be protected. In the *"Eurymedon"*,[16] however, the strictness of the privity approach was lessened by the parties purporting to make an apparent third party "privy" to the contract and expressly protected by its

---

12. Ibid at 853.
13. [2000] 2 HKC 295.
14. Ibid at 300–301.
15. See 8.6.3.1.
16. [1975] AC 154.

wording. The Privy Council upheld the protection, finding that the "stranger" was, indeed, a contracting party and had provided the necessary consideration.[17] The successful "Himalaya clause" procedure (where the third party agent is protected from a tort action) was supported in the Privy Council (from Hong Kong) case of *The Makhutai*,[18] where that court expressed the hope *obiter* that a statutory exemption from the privity rules be eventually enacted in respect of this type of shipping/sub-contracting situation. Of course, as noted later,[19] more extensive reforms have been enacted in England and Hong Kong.

Hong Kong examples of privity in action are provided by *Morison, Son & Jones (Hong Kong) Ltd v Yiu Wing Construction Co Ltd*,[20] in which a sub-contractor was denied a right of action against the employer of the main contractor; and *Otis Elevator Co (Hong Kong) Ltd v Wide Project Engineering & Construction Co Ltd*,[21] in which a main contractor was denied the benefit of protection under an insurance policy made by a sub-contractor and the insurance company.

16.2.1 Attempts to Evade the Doctrine

Both *Tweddle* and *Dunlop* firmly establish that third parties cannot take benefits under a contract even where it is intended to benefit them. This aspect is controversial and has attracted the attention of the legislature in various countries. Attempts have been made to confer benefits on third parties, both at common law and under statute, for two main reasons: first because to deny the third party benefit may defeat the intention of the contracting parties; and second, because it may be desired that a debt due to a third party from one of the contracting parties should be discharged by the other party to the contract. So, in the second case, if A owes money to C he may contract with B, whereby B agrees, for good consideration, to discharge this debt. The question that then arises is whether C can sue B for a failure to keep his promise? The judges in the ancient case of *Crow v Rogers*[22] said no. The result may not be unjust as C keeps his original remedy against A. However, it is certainly inconvenient as it increases the incidence of litigation. If A is sued by C, A may, in turn, sue B.

---

17. Reform enacted in England and proposed for Hong Kong would make the contracting party / consideration issue irrelevant (see 16.5 below).
18. [1996] 2 HKC 1.
19. See 16.5 below.
20. [1989] 1 HKC 11.
21. (unrep, HCA 15214/1983, 6 May 1985).
22. (1724) 1 Str 592.

16.2.2 Contracts Relating to Land

A significant exception to the privity doctrine can be seen in the area of land law. Courts have been prepared to recognise that contracts concerning land are often intended to run with the land and affect subsequent owners or tenants rather than being merely personal agreements between the original parties.

Smith and Snipes Hall Farm Ltd v River Douglas Catchment Board[23]

The defendants, by a deed made in 1938, agreed with eleven owners of land adjoining a certain stream to improve its banks and to "maintain for all time the work when completed". The landowners agreed to pay a proportion of the cost. In 1940 one of the original eleven landowners conveyed her land to Smith, the first plaintiff, and in 1944 Smith leased it to Snipes Hall Farm Ltd., the second plaintiff. In 1946, owing to the defendants' negligence, the banks burst and the land was flooded. Neither plaintiff was a party to the original contract but, nonetheless, sued to enforce the covenant on the basis that it was intended to run with the land and benefit successors of the original covenantees. The plaintiffs' action succeeded in the English Court of Appeal.

While the Court of Appeal was unanimous, Denning LJ went much further than his fellow judges in making clear his dislike of the privity doctrine. He said:

> [the defendants say] that there is no privity of contract between them and the board, and that it is a fundamental principle that no one can sue upon a contract to which he is not a party. That argument can be met either by admitting the principle and saying that it does not apply to this case, or by disputing the principle itself. I make so bold as to dispute it. The principle is not nearly so fundamental as it is sometimes supposed to be. It did not become rooted in our law until the year 1861 (*Tweddle v Atkinson*), and reached its full growth in 1915 (*Dunlop v Selfridge*). It has never been able entirely to supplant another principle whose roots go much deeper. I mean the principle that a man makes a deliberate promise which is intended to be binding, that is to say, under seal or for good consideration, must keep his promise; and that the court will hold him to it, not only at the suit of the party who gave the consideration, but also at the suit of one who was not a party to the contract, provided that it was made for his benefit and that he has a sufficient interest to entitle him to enforce it, subject always, of course, to any defences that may be open on the merits . . .
>
> . . . s 78 of the Law of Property Act 1925 . . . provides that a covenant relating to any land of the covenantee shall be deemed to be made with the covenantee and his successors in title, "and the persons deriving title under him or them" and shall have effect as if such successors, "and other persons" were expressed.
>
> The covenant of the catchment board in this case clearly relates to the land of the covenantees. It was a covenant to do work on the land for the benefit of the land. By the statute, therefore, it is to be deemed to be made, not only with the original

---

23. [1949] 2 All ER 179.

owner, but also with the purchasers of the land and their tenants as if they were expressed. . . . The result is that the plaintiffs come within the principle whereby a person interested can sue on a contract expressly made for his benefit.[24]

The result in this case is not surprising given the statutory exception in the form of section 78 of the Law of Property Act, 1925. What is notable is Denning LJ's clear dislike for the privity of doctrine (in relation to the passing of benefits) generally. While his comments on the doctrine are only *obiter* and represented a minority view at the time they were expressed, they have now been largely vindicated by the intervention of the English legislature.

Lord Denning repeated his criticisms of the doctrine in *Beswick v Beswick*,[25] in the English Court of Appeal. However, his views were emphatically rejected by the House of Lords in the same case.

Beswick v Beswick

The defendant, John Beswick, entered into an agreement with his uncle, Peter Beswick, by which John was assigned Peter's coal-merchant business and promised to pay from the company a £5 per week annuity to Peter's widow after his death. Peter died in November 1963; John made only one payment. The plaintiff, Peter's widow, sued for specific performance[26] of the annuity. She sued as administratrix of her husband's estate and in her own capacity under section 56 of the Law of Property Act, 1925. Section 56(1) states:

A person may take an immediate or other interest in land or other property, or the benefit of any condition, right of entry, covenant or agreement over or respecting land or other property, although he may not be named as a party to the conveyance or other instrument.

The personal application, though successful in Lord Denning's Court of Appeal, failed in the House of Lords. However, the action as administratrix was successful. Their Lordships admitted that if section 56(1) was to be literally interpreted its language was wide enough to support the conclusions of the Court of Appeal that the widow could win in her personal capacity. The agreement concerned "other property" as defined in the Act, and was arguably an "other instrument". But the law lords were reluctant to endorse the broad approach since to do so would mean the legislature, in a statute concerning land law, had accidentally revolutionised the law of contract. They found support for their view in the interpretation section of the Law of Property Act.[27] Although this permits a wide interpretation of the word "property", it requires that definitions should apply "unless the context otherwise

---

24. Ibid at 188.
25. [1967] 2 All ER 1197.
26. See 15.2.
27. Section 205.

requires" which, in the view of the House of Lords it clearly did here. The *ratio* of the House of Lords in Beswick, therefore, is that section 56 is limited to actions concerning land and is, probably, restricted to conveyances under seal.

Therefore, the House of Lords has rejected any attempt to use section 56(1) to enable third parties to sue in contract. The matter is of historical interest since it exemplifies attempts to circumvent privity. However, the broad interpretation of section 56 has never been an issue in Hong Kong as the equivalent provision, section 26 of the Conveyancing and Property Ordinance[28] omits the words "or other property" and is clearly limited to agreements concerning land.

16.2.3 Insurance Contracts

In Hong Kong a statutory exception to the doctrine of privity can be found in the Married Persons Status Ordinance.[29] This enactment follows a similar statutory rule in England. Where a person has taken out a life assurance policy on behalf of a spouse or child, the legislation permits such spouse or child to claim *personally* on the death of the deceased policy-maker, even though, of course, the named beneficiary was not party to the assurance agreement. The legislative rule prevents the intended beneficiary from losing out if the insured's estate has insufficient funds to meet all liabilities. If the beneficiaries were only to be paid from the insured's estate, on the basis that the beneficiary was not a party to the life assurance contract, there would be a danger that others would have a prior claim on the funds. Moreover, a direct claim can be handled more quickly than could one depending on recourse to the deceased's estate.

16.2.4 Action by Promisee on Third Party's Behalf

Privity establishes that if A and B make a contract for the benefit of C, C cannot enforce this contract as he is not a party to it. However, the contracting parties do have a right to sue when the contractual promise to benefit another is broken. The question remaining is what remedies are available. If the contracting party seeks damages, he would probably be awarded only *nominal* damages[30] if he suffers no loss himself. This was affirmed by the House of Lords in *Woodar Investment Development Ltd v Wimpey Construction (UK) Ltd.*[31]

The better result for the third party is for the contracting party to sue for specific performance.[32] This would enable the contracting party to compel the other party

---

28. Cap 219.
29. Cap 182.
30. See 15.1.
31. [1980] 1 All ER 571.
32. See 15.2.

to confer the intended benefit on the non-party and, therefore, achieve the intention of the contract. However, this solution, which was applied in *Beswick*,[33] is subject to the discretion of the court, since specific performance is an equitable remedy.[34] Moreover, if the contracting party refuses to act, there appears to be little that the third party can do to obtain his intended benefit. The issue was considered in the following case.

Jackson v Horizon Holidays Ltd[35]

The plaintiff made a contract with the defendants for a holiday in Sri Lanka for himself, his wife and children. The holiday failed to meet requirements in a number of respects. The defendants admitted breach. The plaintiff claimed damages for the reduced value of the holiday and for the disappointment of himself and his family. The claim was upheld by a unanimous English Court of Appeal.

Lord Denning MR supported the concept of the contracting party recovering *substantial*[36] damages for the loss of others. He said:

> In this case it was a husband making a contract for the benefit of himself, his wife and children . . . What is the position when such a contract is broken? At present the law says that the only one who can sue is the one who made the contract. None of the rest of the party can sue, even though the contract was made for their benefit. But when that one does sue, what damages can he recover? Is he limited to his own loss? Or can he recover for the others? . . . I think he can.[37]

He then went on to cite a principle stated by Lush LJ in *Lloyd's v Harper*[38] which holds that where a contract is made with A for the benefit of B, A can sue on the contract for the benefit of B, and recover all that B could have recovered if the contract had been made with B. This is problematical as it was generally assumed that this only applies where A is a trustee of B. In *Jackson*, the father was not a trustee for the other members of his family. However, Lord Denning was not swayed by this. He added:

> It has been suggested that Lush LJ was thinking of a contract in which A was trustee for B. But I do not think so. He was a common lawyer speaking of the common law. His words were quoted with considerable approval by Lord Pearce in *Beswick v Beswick*. I have myself often quoted them. I think they should be accepted as correct, at any rate as long as the law forbids the third persons themselves to sue for damages. It is the only way in which a just result can be achieved . . . If he can recover for the expense, he should also be able to recover for the discomfort,

---

33. See 16.2.2.
34. See 15.2.
35. [1975] 3 All ER 92.
36. See chapter 15, Overview.
37. [1975] 3 All ER 92 at 95.
38. (1880) 16 Ch D 290.

vexation and upset which the whole party have suffered by reason of the breach of contract, recompensing them accordingly out of what he recovers.[39]

It should be noted that the court had the opportunity to treat the wife as a contracting party by virtue of the doctrine of agency, but did not do so.

The award of damages for distress caused by a ruined holiday is not controversial, having been established in earlier cases.[40] What is contentious is the allowance of *substantial* damages for the distress of others. The majority of the House of Lords in *Beswick* had expressed the view that the promisee should be restricted to nominal damages for loss suffered by a non-party. This view has since been re-established.

Woodar Investment Development Ltd v Wimpey Construction (UK) Ltd[41]

Wimpey claimed a right to rescind a contract and buy land from the appellants, Woodar, under the terms of their contract. Woodar argued that this was an unjustified rescission amounting to a wrongful repudiation of the contract[42] for which they (Woodar) were entitled to damages. The House of Lords held that the rescission claim by Wimpey was made in good faith, although not permitted by the contract, and that Wimpey's honest mistake as to their contractual right to rescind should not be regarded as a wrongful repudiation. The House of Lords then considered, *obiter*, the amount of damages that would have been payable had there been a wrongful repudiation, given that £150,000 of the purchase money payable by Wimpey was to go, not to Woodar, but to a third party, Transworld Trade Ltd. The court held that substantial damages were not applicable in a case like this.

In rejecting Lord Denning's "substantial damages" approach, Lord Wilberforce said:

> I cannot agree with the basis on which Lord Denning MR put his decision in (*Jackson's*) case. The extract on which he relied from the judgment of Lush LJ in *Lloyds v Harper* was part of a passage in which Lush LJ was stating as an 'established rule of law' that an agent . . . may sue on a contract made by him on behalf of the principal . . . if the contract gives him such a right, and is no authority for the proposition required in Jackson's case, still less for the proposition, required here, that, if Woodar made a contract for a sum of money to be paid to Transworld, Woodar can, without showing that it has itself suffered loss or that Woodar was agent or trustee for Transworld, sue for damages for non-payment of that sum. That

---

39. *Jackson* (n 37 above) at 95–96.
40. See 15.1.3.1.
41. [1980] 1 All ER 571.
42. See 14.3.

would certainly not be an established rule of law, nor was it quoted as such authority by Lord Pearce in *Beswick v Beswick*.[43]

The *Woodar Investment* case clarifies the position regarding the recovery of damages for the loss of others without expressly overruling the *Jackson* decision. Lord Denning's words in *Jackson* were "explained" and the sum awarded justified by classifying the suffering of the family as being part of the losses of the father, the contractual party. It could then be argued that his losses included being forced to spend on his family members to ease their suffering. The decision does not affect the right of the contracting party, as confirmed in *Beswick*, to seek specific performance for the benefit of the third party. The *Woodar Investment* approach has not subsequently been questioned by the Hong Kong courts and, as a pre-1997 House of Lords view, presumably represents the current law in Hong Kong subject to judicial or legislative amendment.

However, brief mention should be made of the limited exception, known as "transferred loss", recognised (though rarely found applicable) in several English cases of, of course, persuasive import for Hong Kong. This exception would arise where a key feature of an agreement between A and B would be that B confers a benefit on C. Where C, on B's breach, is unable or unwilling to claim for this loss, a court *may* exceptionally allow A to do so, where it is clear that A has a definite interest in C receiving the benefit.[44] The "transferred loss" principle was explained by Lord Browne-Wilkinson, in *Alfred MaAlpine Construction Ltd v Panatown Ltd*,[45] as follows:

> The essential feature of . . . [this] ground is that the contracting party A, although not suffering the physical or pecuniary damage sustained by the third party C, has suffered his own damage being the loss of his performance interest, ie the failure to provide C with the benefit that B had contracted for C to receive.[46]

It should, in conclusion, be pointed out that, as Lord Sumption has pointed out, this "transferred loss" principle is *"an exception to a fundamental principle of the law of obligations and not an alternative to that principle."*[47]

In short, even were Hong Kong courts to endorse the "transferred loss" principle, the exception would be rarely invoked.

---

43. [1980] 1 All ER 571 at 576–577. It is of some (merely) historical interest that Lord Denning MR's discredited "substantial damages" approach was followed by Judge Caird in the Hong Kong District Court case of *Lee Yu Cheung v Accelspeed Co Ltd* (unrep, DCCJ 827/1982, 1 September 1982).
44. Thereby avoiding "a legal black hole".
45. [2001] 1 AC 518.
46. See also *Swynson v Lowick Rose LLP* [2017] UKSC 32; *The Albazero* [1977] AC 774.
47. *Swynson v Lowick Rose LLP* [2017] UKSC 32 at para 14. See also *BV Nederlandse Industrie Van Eiprodukten v Rembrandt Enterprises Inc* [2019] EWCA Civ 596.

16.2.5 *Agency and Assignment*

Agency and assignment constitute well-recognised "apparent" exceptions to the doctrine of privity. They are large topics in themselves and generally dealt with in "Commercial law" courses. However, a brief overview will be assayed.

The typical agency scenario may be illustrated thus:

P .... A 3

P, the "principal", engages A (its agent) to contract on P's behalf with 3, an "apparent" third party. In *fact*, where a genuine agency exists, A "drops out" and the privity of contract is between P and 3 (there is, of course, a separate employment contract between P and A). It will often "appear" that P is conferring rights/imposing obligations on a third party (3) but, legally, this is not so, since A was acting "on behalf of" P. The agency argument was attempted by the plaintiffs in *Dunlop v Selfridge* (above) to circumvent the privity problem. However, the UK House of Lords rejected the argument, asserting that when Dews sold tyres to Selfridge, they were doing so in their own capacity and *not* as agents of Dunlop.

"Assignment" may also operate as an "apparent" exception to the privity rules. Thus, many contractual and other rights may be assigned. It is not uncommon, for example, for a creditor to assign its rights under a debt to others, obviously for less than the full amount of the debt. The creditor may thereby obtain, for example, 60% of a debt, which would otherwise be troublesome to enforce in court. The "assignee" (often in Hong Kong, a debt collection agency) thus acquires the right to enforce the debt. Since the debtor will not have previously encountered the assignee, it will "appear" that a third party has acquired rights under the original contract, though legally this is not the case. Since contracting parties may well be prepared to undertake obligations to a familiar, long-standing partner, but *not* "a stranger", a "no assignment" clause may be inserted in the original contract, which courts are willing to uphold on the basis of "party autonomy".[48]

16.3 Third Party Burdens

The second aspect of the doctrine of privity is that an agreement between A and B cannot impose obligations or burdens on a third party. This branch of the privity rule is far less controversial than that relating to benefits, discussed above.[49] The proposition that A and B cannot, by their contract, impose obligations on C is an eminently fair and logical one and derives from the concept that contractual duties derive from

---

48. See 1.2.1 and *Linden Gardens Trust Ltd v Lenesta Sludge Disposals Ltd* [1994] 1 AC 85.
49. But see *Au Kai To Karel v End User Technology Ltd & Others* [2019] 1 HKLRD 943, for a rejection by the Hong Kong Court of Appeal of a trial judge's attempts to impose joint contractual liability on a defendant *not* asserted in pleadings to be a contracting party!

agreement.[50] The main exception comes in the area of land law. While a full discussion of this area of law is more appropriately dealt with in a text on land law, it is instructive to investigate in outline how the doctrine of privity of contract is affected by the rules of land law. Here, as was the case with benefits, it has been accepted that the burden of covenants entered into between the owners of different pieces of land concerning the use of land will often be intended to run with the land to successors in title of the original parties rather than being merely personal between the original parties to the agreement. Since the landmark case of *Tulk v Moxhay*[51] in 1848, the courts have developed rules which must be satisfied before equity will regard the burden of a covenant as passing under the doctrine. The requirements are that:

1. the covenant must be negative or restrictive;[52]
2. at the date of the covenant, the covenantee must have owned land benefitted by the covenant;
3. the original parties must have intended the burden to run with the land so as to bind successors in title; and
4. successors in title to the covenantor will be bound by the covenant provided they have notice of it.

The first requirement is a result of the law, first laid down in *Austerberry v Oldham Corporation*[53] and more recently affirmed by the House of Lords in *Rhone v Stephens*[54] that the burden of a positive covenant does not run with the land either at law or in equity. In *Rhone*, the court refused to overturn the *Austerberry* decision even though several Law Commission Reports[55] had called for its removal. The House of Lords (in *Rhone*) based its argument mainly on the doctrine of privity of contract. Lord Templeman stated:

> For over 100 years it has been clear and accepted law that equity will enforce negative covenants against freehold land but has no power to enforce positive covenants against successors in title of the land. To enforce a positive covenant would be to enforce a personal obligation against a person who has not covenanted. To enforce negative covenants is only to treat the land as subject to a restriction.[56]

---

50. See chapter 3.
51. (1848) 2 Ph 774.
52. In England a covenant between owners of freehold land can be either positive or negative. A positive covenant requires expenditure on the part of the covenantee: *Haywood v Brunswick PBBS* (1881) 8 QBD 403. In Hong Kong, the equivalent of a freehold covenant is a land covenant.
53. (1885) 29 Ch D 750.
54. [1994] 2 All ER 65.
55. Such as "The Transfer of Land: Appurtenant Rights" (Law Commission working paper no 36, 5 July 1971).
56. [1994] 2 All ER 65 at 71.

The second requirement was added by *London County Council v Allen*,[57] though implicit in *Tulk*. The third requirement is underpinned by appropriate statutory provisions[58] and the last requirement is now met by satisfying statutory requirements relating to constructive notice via registration, such that "notice" need no longer be subjective.

There have been isolated attempts to extend the restrictive covenant exception outside the area of real property. *Swiss Bank Corporation v Lloyd's Bank Ltd*[59] represents some authority for the principle that promises of a nature similar to restrictive covenants can be imposed on a non-contracting party outside the area of land law.

Swiss Bank Corporation v Lloyd's Bank Ltd

The plaintiffs lent money to the company IFT to enable them to buy FIBI securities. It was a condition (ie, restriction) of the loan that it must be spent on acquiring FIBI securities and that repayment of the loan, including interest, should be made from the sale of these securities. Without the necessary exchange control consent, IFT granted a charge over the securities to the defendants who were unaware of the terms of the original contract. The plaintiffs claimed an injunction to prevent the defendants exercising their rights contrary to IFT's original contractual obligations. It was held that in the absence of actual knowledge of the contractual obligation in favour of the plaintiffs, the defendants could not be restrained by injunction; "constructive" notice was not enough.

Browne-Wilkinson J summarised the existing precedents and stated:

> in my judgment the authorities establish the following propositions. (1) The principle stated by Knight Bruce LJ in *De Mattos v Gibson*, 4 De G & J 276, is good law and represents the counterpart in equity of the tort of knowing interference with contractual rights. (2) A person proposing to deal with property in such a way as to cause a breach of a contract affecting that property will be restrained by injunction from so doing if when he acquired that property he had actual knowledge of that contract. (3) A plaintiff is entitled to such an injunction even if he has no proprietary interest in the property: his right to have his contract performed is a sufficient interest. (4) There is no case in which such an injunction has been granted against a defendant who acquired the property with only constructive, as opposes to actual, notice of the contract. In my judgment constructive notice is not sufficient, since actual knowledge of the contract is a requisite element in the tort.[60]

This case is a good example of the willingness of the courts to try to circumvent the doctrine of privity of contract by drawing parallels with equity and tort law.

---

57. [1914] 3 KB 642.
58. In Hong Kong, s 40 of the Conveyancing and Property Ordinance (Cap 21). Cf s 79 of the Law of Property Act 1925 in England.
59. [1979] 2 All ER 853.
60. Ibid at 874.

However, it is not a strong authority as Browne-Wilkinson J's views on the issue were clearly *obiter*. Moreover, the judge admitted to difficulty in ascertaining the precise *ratio* of *De Mattos* and the related Privy Council decision in *Lord Strathcona Steamship Co v Dominion Coal Co Ltd*.[61] The decision in the *Swiss Bank* case was reversed but on different grounds.[62] At best, the *Swiss Bank* approach should be seen as of limited scope; and the need for the third party to have actual, as opposed to constructive notice of the contract at the time of purchase renders it far narrower than the land law rules on restrictive covenants. Moreover, the fact that the only remedy available is an injunction restraining the third party from acting inconsistently with the contract severely blunts any assault on the doctrine of privity of contract. An order for specific performance requiring the purchaser to carry out the terms of the contract cannot be obtained.

16.4 The Relationship with Consideration

It is a controversial question whether the rule that consideration must move from the promisee[63] and the doctrine of privity of contract are distinct or simply different approaches to the same thing. They usually lead to the same result. However, academic writers, such as Treitel,[64] assert that the two rules appear to be distinct. Treitel says that this can be illustrated by restating the latter rule to be that consideration must move from the party seeking to enforce the promise. He gives the example of a father who promises his daughter to pay a sum of money to any man who might marry her. A man who married his daughter in reliance on such promise might provide consideration—entering the marriage—but could not enforce the promise as it was not made to him. However, as argued in chapter 4 of this book, the separate principles argument may be based on a misconception and there are other writers such as Brian Coote[65] who argue that these rules are really one and the same. If the rule that consideration must move from the promisee requires both that the party seeking to enforce a promise must show consideration and that the promise was made to him, it appears synonymous with privity. However, despite the ongoing debate, the Law Reform Commission of Hong Kong has accepted the position of the English Law Commission that the two rules should be treated separately. Moreover, judgments in several cases indicate that the courts have treated the two principles as distinct. Viscount Haldane MR's judgment in the *Dunlop* case has already been mentioned. The Privy Council has underlined this view by denying an action, on the

---

61. [1926] AC 108.
62. [1982] AC 584.
63. See 4.3.
64. Op cit at p 699.
65. Referred to in B. Ho, *Hong Kong Contract Law* (Hong Kong: Butterworths, 2nd edn, 1994) at p 312.

basis of privity restrictions, even though the jurisdiction in question did not require that consideration must move from the promisee.[66]

16.5 Legislative Reform

In order to address some of the arguments against the first aspect of the doctrine of privity of contract, namely, that a third party cannot acquire and enforce rights or benefits under a contract, England enacted the Contracts (Rights of Third Parties) Act 1999.

In June 2004, the Law Reform Commission of Hong Kong established a Law Reform Sub-committee[67] which issued a consultation paper ("The Paper"). The Paper posed three questions:

1. whether the anomalies of the doctrine of privity of contract are serious enough to warrant its reform;
2. if so, whether ad hoc reforms, either by the courts on their own initiative or by legislation, are adequate in the Hong Kong context, or whether an issue of this magnitude calls for comprehensive legislative reform; and
3. if comprehensive legislative reform is called for, what the main elements of the proposed legislative scheme should be.

The majority of the Sub-committee favoured reform of the general rule but not its complete abolition.[68] This view was endorsed in a Report published by the Law Reform Commission in October 2005. The underlying principle of the proposed reform was to respect the contracting parties' freedom of contract and, where appropriate, to give effect to their intention to benefit third parties. If the parties prefer, they should be able to make it clear in their contract that the proposed legislation is not to apply to their contract. The major recommendations of the Report have been incorporated into the (eventually enacted!) new legislation, in force from 1 January 2016: the Contracts (Rights of Third Parties) Ordinance.

The legislation will now be dealt with in more detail. Of course, since enactment is recent, Hong Kong jurisprudence is lacking. However, since the wording of the legislation is very similar to the English Contracts (Rights of Third Parties) Act 1999, English cases on privity are likely to be followed in Hong Kong.

---

66. See *Kepong Prospecting Ltd v Schmidt* [1968] AC 810.
67. Chaired by Benjamin Yu SC.
68. Recommendation 1 of the Paper and the subsequent Report.

16.5.1 Definition of "Third Party" and Enforcement of Benefits Thereby

The legislation provides that in certain circumstances a "third party" may enforce a term of a contract but does not elaborate on the meaning of "third party", except to say that a "third party" is "a person who is not a party to the contract".

The circumstances in which a third party may enforce terms are stated in section 4 of the Ordinance. These are where the contract *expressly* provides that the third party may do so or "purports to confer a benefit on the third party".[69] Crucially,

The third party must be expressly identified in the contract by name, as a member of a class or as answering a particular description.[70]

"Identification" of the third party is likely to be the most contentious area in Hong Kong, as it has proved in England.

Of limited effect is the stipulation that the third party need not be in existence at the time the contract was made. *Importantly*, however, the Ordinance makes clear that the third party need not have provided consideration. Many academics would argue this is axiomatic; since, while a person who has not given consideration may be party to an "agreement", s/he cannot, by virtue of the function of consideration, be party to a "contract." The Ordinance does, indeed, make clear that a third party is *not* a party to the contract. What the Ordinance does, therefore, is call into question the rule that "consideration must move from the promisee". In so far as many (including the author) take this to mean that a contract cannot be enforced by a person not providing consideration, the "from the promisee" rule no longer applies. Consideration is still required, but it no longer needs to be supplied by the "promisee".

Section 4 (section 1 in the UK legislation) is clearly the crux of the legislation and will have significant practical effects. To take just one example, in cases like *"The Eurymedon"*, discussed above, it will no longer be essential to assert that the distant stevedore is a contracting party, providing consideration. It will be enough, under the proposed reforms, that the wording of the contract makes clear that the party was intended to be protected by the exemption clause.

What remains to be seen is how flexible the Hong Kong courts will be in determining when the claimant has been sufficiently "identified" as a "member of a class" or "answering a particular description". In *Laemthong International Lines Co Ltd v Abdullah Mohammed Fahem & Co*,[71] the English Court of Appeal had to decide whether, under the 1999 Act, an indemnity clause was intended to benefit the claimants (owners of a ship) *and* whether the contract provide for the owners to enforce the indemnity. The Court held that the owners *had* shown that the clause

---

69. Section 4(1).
70. Section 4(2).
71. [2005] EWCA Civ 519.

was intended to benefit them. That determined, the onus of proof shifted to the defendants to show that the contract did *not* provide for the owners to enforce the indemnity. This would be a difficult task since, *prima facie*, a contract intended to benefit a third party would, implicitly, permit such party to sue. This was indeed held to be the case in *Laemthong*, despite the ingenious arguments to the contrary by the defendants. The persuasive authority of *Laemthong* is likely (it is submitted) to be followed in Hong Kong. The issue of "intention to benefit a third party" and the proper identification of same were considered *inter alia* in the complex case of *Chudley & Others v Clydesdale Bank plc*,[72] decided in the English Commercial Court of the Queen's Bench Division. The claimants in this case had lost money on investment following advice from an employee of the defendants which, if not dishonest as alleged, was extremely negligent. The court had to decide whether the defendants had a contract with a company, Arck, involved with property transactions in the Cape Verde Islands, and, if so, whether such contract was intended to affect the third party claimants. The court, applying an "objective" test, held that there *was* an agreement with Arck (as the claimants asserted). It was clear that the claimants had not been "expressly identified" (by name) in the relevant agreement; nor were they aware, at the time of the contract, of their intended "beneficiary" status. However, the trial judge, Hancock J stated:

> the question is whether the reference to a client account serves not only to identify the fact that clients are intended to benefit from the contract, but also serves to expressly identify *such* clients as the category of parties intended to so benefit. In my judgment it does.[73]

The judgment here, while finding against the claimants on a different ground, clearly adopts a generous interpretation as to the requirements of third party identi-fication which was upheld by the Court of Appeal (the Court of Appeal went further and found for the claimants). The decision is not without its detractors,[74] and would not necessarily be followed in Hong Kong.

A less controversial approach to the section 4/section 1 requirement is to be found *obiter* in *Less & Carter v Hussain*, discussed in chapter 15.[75] In addition to finding against the plaintiffs on "non-causation" grounds, the trial judge, Judge Cotter QC, held that, in any event, the second plaintiff's claim for distress caused by the defendant's breach of contract was unsustainable as he was not a party to said contract and:

---

72. [2017] EWHC (Comm) 2177.
73. Such non-express identification, via "construction of the contract as a whole", has been criticised. See Mindy Chen-Wishart, *Contract Law* (Oxford and New York: Oxford University Press, 7th edn), pp 176–177.
74. See n 68 above.
75. See chapter 15 at 15.1.1 and n 16.

it also seems to me that it is a necessary element of the claim as advanced that the existence or identity of the partner said to have been intended to benefit from the contract must have been identified or identifiable from the information provided at the time of either entering into or performing the contract. . . . Accordingly I would not have awarded damages for mental stress to Mr Carter.

16.5.2 Remedies of a Third Party

Under section 5 of the Ordinance, an eligible third party's rights with regard to enforcement of a contractual term should be equivalent to those available to a contracting party. This includes, for example, the availability of equitable remedies. To take a simple example, if A and B enter into a contract under which A agrees to pay a sum of money to C and both parties fully intend that C should take the benefit of A's promise, the previous law meant that, if A defaulted, C could not sue A. However, under the new legislation, C *can* now sue. Similarly in the case of a purchase of a "family holiday", as in *Jackson v Horizon Holidays*,[76] it is no longer necessary to determine whether the buyer of the holiday was acting as agent for the whole family or whether, in the case of defects, he could sue for others' disappointment or merely his own. It is enough that, under the reformed law, the holiday was intended to benefit all family members.

16.5.3 Other Changes

The Ordinance also introduces changes in relation to rescission and variation of contracts,[77] and the implications thereof for a "qualifying" third party. There is, of course, a need to strike a balance between the right of the contracting parties to change the contract and the possibly conflicting interests of the third party who may suffer loss as a result of such a change.

Moreover, and more importantly, the Ordinance makes clear that, in *defending* an action by the third party, a contracting party may raise any defence that would have been available as against the other contracting party.[78] A simple example would arise where the contracting party sued by the third party actually had a right of "set-off" against the other contracting party and may avail himself of this "defence" against the third party. Conversely, where the *third party is being sued* and wishes to take advantage of an exclusion or limitation clause in the contract, this will not be permitted where the clause would have been unavailable to a contracting party[79] because of,

---

76. See 16.2.4 above.
77. Sections 6 and 7.
78. Section 8.
79. Section 9.

for example, of a conflict with the requirements of the Control of Exemption Clauses Ordinance.[80]

The Ordinance makes clear that the fact that a third party may have rights does not in any way undermine the rights of the contracting party.[81] There are, however, rules to prevent a contracting party being "doubly liable".[82] In similar vein, the third party is to be subject to any arbitration or exclusive jurisdiction clause agreed by the contracting parties.[83]

16.5.4 Are the Common Law Exceptions Still Important?

It might be thought that given the liberalising effect of the legislation on third party rights, the old exceptions to the privity rules would no longer be significant. This is incorrect for three reasons. First the Ordinance does not apply in respect of bills of exchange or promissory notes; deeds of mutual covenant; covenants relating to land; employment contracts; nor, generally, to contracts for the carriage of goods by sea or air.[84] In such cases, of course, the common law rules may well be important.

Second, as the Ordinance makes clear, it is "supplemental" in so far as it extends third party rights but does *not* remove any rights or exceptions already established at common law.[85]

Third, the Ordinance only applies *unless* the contract states otherwise; in other words parties can exclude the operation of the Ordinance.[86] Again, in such cases, common law rules may be applicable.

Finally, of course, the Ordinance does not apply to contracts entered into *before* 1 January 2016[87] though, as before the common law rules may be applicable.

In short we now have, in Hong Kong, legislation of *potential* significance, but much will depend on the attitude of the courts and the approach of contracting parties, especially those in business.

---

80. Cap 71 and see 8.6.4.1.
81. Section 10.
82. Section 11.
83. Sections 12 and 13.
84. Section 3.
85. Section 5(4).
86. Section 4(3).
87. Section 3(1).

Appendix 1

Glossary of Terms

The following provides simple definitions of terms that may be encountered in the text and may be difficult, unfamiliar, or used differently from the norm in a legal context.

Burden (or "onus") of proof   The responsibility for proving something. The general rule is that the burden of proof lies with the plaintiff. However, there are many specific exceptions. Where, for example, the reasonableness of an exemption clause is an issue under the Control of Exemption Clauses Ordinance the onus is on the "exemptor" to prove that the clause is reasonable.

Collateral   Running side by side. Thus, a collateral contract is one that is additional to, and runs alongside, the main contract. The device of the collateral contract may be used to evade the privity doctrine (*see* **Privity of Contract**) in carriage of goods situations such that when X agrees to carry Y's goods subject to a limitation clause, there may be an implied "collateral" agreement that Y will confer the same restrictions on liability to C (an apparent third party). Conversely, an exemption clause in a main contract may be defeated by a separate, overriding "collateral" promise to a party without which he would not have agreed to enter into the main contract.

Common law   Common law can be defined in several ways, often by way of contrast. Common law "systems" (originating from the English common law) may be contrasted with the civil law systems which exist in some countries (often based on written codes). More important, in the context of this book, are comparisons with legislation and with equity. When contrasted with legislation, the common law means case law based on precedents established by the courts over the years and, in this context, includes equity. When contrasted with equity, common law is confined to the case law historically developed in the common law courts as opposed to the courts of equity. (*See* **Equity**.)

Condition   There are two relevant meanings of condition in the legal context. Condition may be used in the contract law context just as the layman would use it to signify a "dependent on" qualification. Thus, "this acceptance is conditional on approval of the goods by a qualified analyst".

A second meaning of condition is "serious term". Breach of such a condition entitles the innocent party to terminate the contract and/or claim damages. (*See* **Warranty**.)

Consideration   What is given by a party in return for the other's act or promise ("the price of the other party's promise"). No agreement, unless it is under seal, can be enforced unless the party seeking to enforce the agreement can show consideration. This usually takes the form of showing that something of value has been given to the other party or that some "detriment" has been incurred by the party seeking to enforce the agreement.

Damages   Financial compensation. Damages, the most common remedy for breach of contract, are awarded "as of right" (automatically) to the innocent party whenever the other is in breach. No loss need be shown but, in the absence of loss, damages will be only "nominal". The term "damages" should not be confused with "damage" (loss).

Estoppel   Prevention. There are many different types of estoppel found in different areas of the law. All have the effect of legally preventing a course of action. In the law of evidence, for example, a person who has stated certain facts to be true may be prevented or "estopped" from later denying the truth of the statement. In the area of contract, the doctrine of "promissory estoppel" arises, whereby a party who has made a promise to give up certain legal rights, intending that the promise should be binding, may be prevented or "estopped" from later enforcing these rights where the other party has acted on the promise and it would be unfair to allow the promise to be broken.

Equity   A system of case law, separate from common law, based on principles of fairness and flexibility, historically developed only in the English Court of Chancery. Equity is now administered, in all modern courts within common law jurisdictions, alongside common law. Equitable remedies, such as injunctions, are discretionary and more flexible in nature than the common law remedy of damages (financial compensation). Where there is a conflict between common law and equity, then equity takes precedence.

Executed   Completed. In contract, the term is used particularly in relation to consideration. Consideration which is "executed" is that which has already been completed. So, in a sale contract, a buyer's consideration is executed when the price has been paid.

Executory   Promised though not yet completed. So, in the context of consideration, there is "executory" consideration when there is a promise to give a benefit to the other party or incur a detriment to oneself. In a sale contract, for example, the buyer provides executory consideration by making a promise to pay. Executory consideration is recognised by the courts in the same way as executed consideration.

Mitigate (loss)   Make less severe. It is sometimes said that the innocent party has a "duty" to mitigate loss caused by the other's breach. There is no such duty in fact. However, the innocent party should take all reasonable steps to keep his loss to a minimum since, where he does not do so, no compensation (damages) will be awarded for loss caused by the failure to mitigate.

Non est factum (meum)   It is not my deed. The doctrine of *non est factum* applies where a party has signed a document without understanding its true significance. The doctrine, originally introduced to protect the illiterate, is rarely applied today, not least because carelessness on the part of the signer will preclude *non est factum*.

Nudum pactum Naked bargain. An agreement which lacks consideration. (*See* **Consideration**.) Thus, a promise to keep an offer open is a *nudum pactum* and not enforceable unless something of value is given in return for the promise.

Per se By itself (without more). So, for example, breach of contract is actionable *per se*. There is no need to prove loss. (However, without loss, damages will only be nominal.)

Prima facie At first sight (but subject to further evidence or argument). So, for example, restraints of trade in a contract are *prima facie* void but may be upheld if they can be proved to be reasonable in the interests of the parties and the public.

Privity (of contract) Relationship between the parties to the contract. Only such parties can sue or be sued under the contract. The privity doctrine has been largely abandoned in England but remains, subject to exceptions, in Hong Kong. Reform has, however, been recommended by the Law Reform Commission of Hong Kong.

Promisee Party to whom a promise has been made (by the "promisor"). The rule that "consideration must move from the promisee" requires that consideration must be provided by the party seeking to enforce a promise made to him.

Quantum Amount. Quantum of damages refers to the amount of compensation a successful claimant will recover. The two main issues in any contractual dispute are "liability" (is the defendant in breach?) and quantum (the amount that must be paid in damages to the plaintiff).

Remoteness Loss which is too unlikely is said to be too "remote". Different remoteness rules apply in different contexts. In the tort of negligence, loss is recoverable if it is a "reasonably foreseeable" consequence of a party's negligence; all other loss is too remote. In the case of breach of contract, the party in breach is only liable for the "natural and probable" consequences of his breach. In the case of liability in the tort of deceit for fraudulent misrepresentation, and in actions under s 3(1) of the Misrepresentation Ordinance, a party is liable for all the direct consequences of his misrepresentation, whether or not those consequences were foreseeable.

Representation A statement of fact by one party (the representor) which, while not a term of the contract, induces the other party (the representee) at least in part, to make a contract with the representor. Where it transpires that a representation is false, an action may be brought for misrepresentation.

Rescission (verb to rescind) Cancellation of a contract. This may arise in the case of a contract which is voidable on the grounds of misrepresentation, mistake, duress or undue influence. Rescission may be effected without the intervention of the court if the parties are willing. For example, a buyer may offer to return what he has bought because of a seller's misrepresentation and ask the seller to return the purchase money. In many cases, however, a court order of rescission will be required. The court will require that the parties be returned to their pre-contractual position. Where this is not possible rescission cannot be granted. Since rescission is an equitable remedy, the courts have a discretion whether or not to grant it. (*See* **Voidable**.)

The word "rescission" is also used in a slightly different context when describing the decision of a party not in breach to cancel a contract and refuse further performance because of the other party's serious breach.

Restitutio in integrum   Restoration of contractual parties, by rescission, to the position they were in before the contract was made. (Only available where the parties can be restored to their original position.)

Standard of proof   The extent to which a matter must be proved. The standard of proof in civil cases is "on the balance of probabilities" (ie more likely than not) as opposed to the criminal standard of proof where the prosecution must prove its case "beyond all reasonable doubt". Standard of proof must be considered in conjunction with burden of proof. Thus, a plaintiff would have to prove that the defendant was in breach of contract, that the breach caused the alleged loss and that such loss was not too "remote". All these elements would have to be proved on the balance of probabilities.

Unilateral   One-sided (usually in the context of unilateral contract). A unilateral contract is one in which an offeror makes a binding offer to "reward" the performance of an act but there is no duty on any offeree to perform such act. An offer to pay $1,000 to anyone who swims across Hong Kong harbour in January will give rise to an obligation to pay anyone who does so; however, no one is obliged to perform, or even attempt, the act. Unilateral contracts often involve offers to the whole world but it is quite possible to have a unilateral contract involving a promise made to only one person.

Void   Having no legal effect. A contract that is void is regarded as being no contract at all. It is said to be void, *ab initio* (from the beginning). When a contract is declared void all money paid and all property transferred must be returned. However, since there is no contract, there can be no contractual remedies. It is unusual for a contract to be declared void but this can arise, for example, in cases of very serious mistake or in the case of an illegal contract.

Voidable   Capable of being set aside. A voidable contract is not void from the beginning and will remain in force until the party entitled to set the contract aside chooses to do so. A party is entitled to ask the court to set aside a contract on the grounds of the other's misrepresentation, duress or undue influence. Since the party will be seeking rescission, an equitable remedy, the court will have a discretion whether or not to set the agreement aside. The court may impose certain conditions on the granting of rescission which the claimant must fulfil. There are also situations in which rescission will never be granted (ie it is "barred"). So, for example, where an innocent third party has acquired an interest in property which would be affected by an order of rescission, such rescission will be refused.

Warranty   Less important term (*see* **Condition**). The breach of a warranty never entitles the innocent party to terminate the contract, only to claim damages.

A secondary meaning of warranty is "promise" as in "the seller warrants that the goods are free from defect".

Appendix 2

Important Contract Legislation: English and Hong Kong Equivalents

English Legislation	Hong Kong Equivalent
Contracts (Rights of Third Parties) Act 1999	*Contracts (Rights of Third Parties) Ordinance (Cap 623)*
s 1	s 4
Unfair Contract Clauses Terms Act 1977	*Control of Exemption Ordinance (Cap 71)*
s 1	s 2
s 2	s 7
s 3	s 8
s 4	s 9
s 5	s 10
s 6	s 11
s 7	s 12
s 9	s 13
s 10	s 14
s 11	s 3
s 12	s 4
s 13	s 5
Schedule 1	Schedule 1
Schedule 2	Schedule 2
Misrepresentation Act 1967	*Misrepresentation Ordinance (Cap 284)*
s 1	s 2
s 2(1)	s 3(1)
s 2(2)	s 3(2)
s 3	s 4

English Legislation	Hong Kong Equivalent
Law Reform (Frustrated Contracts) Act 1843	*Law Amendment and Reform (Consolidation) Ordinance (Cap 23)*
s 1(2)	s 16(2)
s 1(3)	s 16(3)
Sale of Goods Act 1979	*Sale of Goods Ordinance (Cap 26)*
s 3	s 4
s 6	s 8
s 8	s 10
s 9	s 11
s 12	s 14
s 13	s 15
s 14(2)	s 16(2)
s 14(3)	s 16(3)
s 15	s 17
s 22	s 24
s 23	s 25
s 50	s 52
s 51	s 53
s 52	s 54
s 57	s 60
Married Women's Property Act 1882	*Married Persons Status Ordinance (Cap 182)*
s 11	s 13
Family Law Reform Act 1969	*Age of Majority (Related Provisions) Ordinance (Cap 410)*
s 1	s 2
Minor's Contracts Act 1987	*Age of Majority (Related Provisions) Ordinance*
s 3(1)	s 4(1)(b)

Please note that these sections are equivalents and therefore the wording may vary when comparing an equivalent section of an English Act with a Hong Kong Ordinance.

Appendix 3

Limitation Periods: English and Hong Kong Equivalents

	English Legislation	**Hong Kong Legislation**
	Limitation Act 1980	*Limitation Ordinance (Cap 347)*
Simple contract (from date of breach)	[6 years] s 5	[6 years] s 4(1)(a)
Mistake (from date of "discoverability")	[normally 6 years] s 32(1)(c)	[normally 6 years] s 26(1)(c)
Fraud (from date of "discoverability")	[normally 6 years] s 32(1)(a)	[normally 6 years] s 26(1)(a)
Personal Injuries caused by negligence, nuisance or breach of duty, whether the duty arises contractually or not (from date of injury)	[3 years] s 11	[3 years] s 27
Discretion to extend period for the above	s 33	s 31
Misrepresentation (from the date of loss)	[normally 6 years] s 2	[normally 6 years] s 4(1)(a)

Note

The expiry of a limitation period does not extinguish liability; it merely precludes enforcement. Thus, if, for example, a debtor pays money on a statute-barred debt, the money is irrecoverable.

Bibliography

Books

Atiyah, PS (1985) *The Rise and Fall of Freedom of Contract* (Oxford) Clarendon Press.

Atiyah, PS (1990) *Essays on Contract* (Oxford) Clarendon Press.

Beale, HG [ed.] (20201) *Chitty on Contracts* (London) Sweet & Maxwell 34th edn.

Beale, HG, Bishop, WD & Furmston, MP (2008) *Contract Cases and Materials* (Oxford) Oxford University Press 5th edn.

Beatson, J, Burrows, A, & Cartwright, J (2020) *Anson's Law of Contract* (Oxford/New York) Oxford University Press 31st edn.

Brownsword, R (2021) *Smith & Thomas: A Casebook on Contract* (London) Sweet & Maxwell 14th edn.

Campbell, D [ed.] (2001) *The Relational Theory of Contract: Selected Works of Ian MacNeil* (London) Sweet & Maxwell.

Chen, A (2018) *An Introduction to the Legal System of the PRC* (Hong Kong) LexisNexis 5th edn.

Chen-Wishart, M (2022) *Contract Law* (Oxford) Oxford University Press 7th edn.

Chui Pedley, C (1988) *Law of Contract in Hong Kong* (Hong Kong) China & Hong Kong Law Studies.

Collins, H (2003) *The Law of Contract* (London) LexisNexis Butterworth 4th edn.

Devlin, P (1979) *The Judge* (Oxford) Oxford University Press.

Downes, TA (1997) *Textbook on Contract* (London) Blackstone Press, 5th edn.

Fisher, MJ (2019) *Text, Cases & Commentary on the Hong Kong Legal System* (Hong Kong) Hong Kong University Press.

Friedmann, M and Friedmann, R (1980) *Free to Choose: A Personal Statement* (Orlando, Austin, New York, San Diego, Toronto, London) Harcourt Inc.

Furmston, M (2017) *Cheshire, Fifoot & Furmston's Law of Contract* (Oxford/New York) Oxford University Press 17th edn.

Genn, Dame H (2008) *Judging Civil Justice* [Hamlyn Lectures] (Cambridge/New York) Cambridge University Press.

Goff, R & Jones, GH (2007) *The Law of Restitution* (London) Sweet & Maxwell 7th edn.

Griffith, JAG (1977) *The Politics of the Judiciary* (Glasgow) Fontana.

Hall, S (2019) *Law of Contract in Hong Kong, Cases and Commentary* (Hong Kong) LexisNexis 6th edn.

Ho, B (1991) *Hong Kong Agency Law* (Hong Kong) Butterworths.

Ho, B (1994) *Hong Kong Contract Law* (Hong Kong) Butterworths 2nd edn.

Hurst, S (2001) *Keating on Building Contracts* (London) Sweet & Maxwell.

Lo, S & Qu, C (2018) *Law of Companies in Hong Kong* (Hong Kong) Sweet & Maxwell 3rd edn.

Lord, RA (2007) *A Treatise on the Law of Contract by Samuel Williston* (Rochester, N.Y.) Lawyers Cooperative Publishing 4th edn.

Ma L, Lower M, & Sham J (2019) *Principles of Equity & Trusts Law in Hong Kong* (Hong Kong) LexisNexis 3rd edn.

Macneil, I (2001) *The Relational Theory of Contract: Selected Works* [Campbell, D ed] (London) Sweet & Maxwell.

Martin, E [ed.] (1990) *A Concise Dictionary of Law* (Oxford) Oxford University Press.

McKendrick, E (2021) *Contract Law: Text, Cases & Materials* (Oxford) Oxford University Press 14th edn.

Merkin R and Saintier S (2021) *Poole's Casebook on Contract* (Oxford) Oxford University Press 15th edn.

Merkin, R and Saintier S (2021) *Poole's Textbook on Contract* (Oxford) Oxford University Press 15th edn.

O'Sullivan, J (2022) *O'Sullivan & Hilliard's The Law of Contract* (Oxford) Oxford University Press 10th edn.

Paterson, A (1982) *The Law Lords* (London) Macmillan.

Peel, E (2020) *Treitel: The Law of Contract* (London) Sweet & Maxwell 15th edn.

Penner, JE (2001) *Mozley & Whiteley's Law Dictionary* (London) Butterworths.

Pollock, F (1876) *Principles of Contract* (London) Stevens.

Radcliffe, Lord (1968) *Not in Feather Beds* (London) Hamish Hamilton.

Schur, EM (1968) *Law and Society* (New York) Random House.

Stone, R & Devenney, J (2022) *The Modern Law of Contract* (London/New York) Routledge 14th edn.

Stott, V (2020) *Hong Kong Company Law* (Hong Kong) Pearson 15th edn.

Upex, R (2008) *Davies on Contract* (London) Sweet & Maxwell 10th edn.

Weber, M (1954) *On Law in Economy and Society* (Cambridge, Mass.) Harvard University Press.

Wesley-Smith, P (1998) *An Introduction to the Hong Kong Legal System* (Hong Kong) Oxford University Press 2nd edn.

Winfield, PH (1950) *Pollock's Principles of Contract* (London) Stevens & Sons 13th edn.

Young, SNM & Ghai, Y [eds.] (2103) *Hong Kong's Court of Final Appeal* (Cambridge) Cambridge University Press.

Articles

Adams, J & Brownsword, R (1990) Contract, Consideration and the Critical Path *Modern Law Review* Vol. 5: 536.

Atiyah, PS (1986) The Hannah Blumenthal & Classical Contract Law *Law Quarterly Review* Vol. 102: 363.

Austen-Baker, R (2008) A Strange Sort of Survival for Pinnel's Case: Collier v P & MJ Wright (Holdings) Ltd. *Modern Law Review* Vol. 71 (4): 611.

Brenner, A (2020) The Misrepresentation Act, 1967: Its Historical Origins and Socio-Political Context *UCL Discussion Paper* ORCID number 0000-0002-9038-492X

Brownsword, R (1985) Henry's Lost Spectacle & Hutton's Lost Speculation: A Classic Riddle Solved? *Solicitors' Journal* Vol. 129: 860.

Chen-Wishart, M (2013) In Defence of Consideration *2013 Oxford Commonwealth Law Journal* 209.

Chu, J (2018) Wrotham Out: Negotiating Damages after One Step v Morris-Garner *Conveyancing & Property Lawyer: Case Comment.*

Davis, AG (1937) Promise to Perform an Existing Duty *6 Camb LJ* 203.

Freeman, M (1996) Contracting in the Haven: Balfour v Balfour Revisited in *Exploring the Boundaries of Contract*, Halson R ed. (Aldershot) Dartmouth.

Godinho, J & Cardinal, P (2013) *Macau's Court of Final Appeal* in Young & Ghai *Hong Kong's Court of Final Appeal* (supra).

Greenwood, DG (2004) Is Mistake Dead in Contract Law? *Hong Kong Law Journal* Vol. 34: 495.

Hudson, AH (1954) The Myth of Mistake in the English Law of Contract Law *Quarterly Review* Vol. 70: 386.

Hudson, AH (1968) Gibbons v Proctor Revisited *Law Quarterly Review* Vol. 84: 503.

Mason, L (2014) Inadequacy & Ineffectuality: Hong Kong's Consumer Protection Regime against Unfair Terms in Consumer Contracts *2014 Hong Kong Law Journal* 83.

McMeel, G (2005) Interpretation and Mistake in Contract Law: "The Fox Knows Many Things . . ." *Lloyd's Maritime & Commercial Law Quarterly* Vol. 21: 49.

Olesnicky, M (1987) Are Large Law Firms Legal? *Hong Kong Law Journal* Vol. 17: 188.

Reiter, B (1981) The Control of Contract Power *Oxford Journal of Legal Studies* Vol. I: 347.

Slade, CJ (1954) The Myth of Mistake in the English Law of Contract *1954 70 LQR* 386.

Index